Principles in Xiangji Operation

Chinese Economic Ethnology

Tingshuo Yang

Translated by Gary Situ

Reviewed by Rui Huang-fu, Hongfei Liu

Paths International Ltd

This book is the final report for *The Analysis of Non-economic Factors Affecting the Social Development in the Ethnic Minority Regions in Guizhou*. This research was one of the eighth Five-Year-Plan's NSSFC (National Social Science Foundation of China) projects and passed the state inspection in March, 1995.

To deceased Professor Yingliang Jiang, my respectable mentor.

Tingshuo Yang

Nov. 11, 1995

Preface

Zuyi Feng

I was attracted by the research topic submitted by the Ethnic Minority Research Institute of Guizhou Minzu University as one of its NSSFC (National Social Science Foundation of China) projects in 1992. Mr. Tingshuo Yang, who took over the lead role in this project in 1993, presented an elaborately structured research methodology to my satisfaction. Unsurprisingly, the research project titled *The Analysis of Non-economic Factors Affecting the Social Development in the Ethnic Minority Regions in Guizhou* was easily approved by the competent authority at the central government level. In 1994, to prepare for the state inspection, Mr. Yang condensed the results from his fieldwork and research conducted in nearly two years into a printout of well over 400,000 Chinese characters under the title of *Principles in Xiangji Operation*. Members of the reviewing committee who spoke highly of the book suggested that the findings in the research be introduced to the public and be put into practice. The author then handed over the reviewed materials thoroughly scrutinized and repeatedly revised by him to the publisher, symbolizing an event to be applauded by the author himself as well as the social science circle in Guizhou.

A few points characterize the book *Principles in Xiangji Operation* that came out of the results from the research.

First, it is a book of extremely practical pertinence

Currently, the issue of economic development in under-developed countries has beset the politicians and economists alike in the world. Similarly, the greater progress brought about by the reform and open policy in China has widened the gap between its coastal and central & western region, raising concerns across the country. The *Outlines of the Ninth Five-year Plan and the Long-term Goals for the Year 2010 for the Economic and Social Development in the People's Republic of China* passed in the recent fourth meeting of the eighth plenary session of the NPC lists the task "to gradually narrow the gap in regional development" as a strategic mission to implement, a hope embraced by all the people in China. To reveal the real reasons that cause the under-developed regions in the world and the Midwest in China to lag behind economically, and find out how to drive the harmonious social and economic development and narrow the gap between the developed and under-developed regions are problems of both theoretical and practical nature, which cannot be solved properly without tremendous efforts and hard work. People may have realized that a pure economic discussion does not suffice a comprehensive and correct theoretical foundation in search of the reasons for lacking progress in economic development, nor will it offer reliable and effective solutions to a faster economic development. The central and western region in China, for instance, is characterized by exceptionally varied landforms and the inhabitants of quite a number of ethnic minority groups. Such natural and social environments have given rise to unique cultural and social backgrounds that unquestionably shape the local economic development. Thus, we must expand our minds and bring non-economic factors, in addition to economic factors, into view. In contrast, approaches that only rely on economic input will, without a doubt, produce unproductive results against our wish. For many years in the past, we have learned enough lessons from the "blood transfusion" type of poverty relief efforts made in many places.

This book has tackled the above questions straightforwardly and given answers to all of them: what are the non-economic factors affecting the economic development in the ethnic groups in Midwestern China; how have they evolved in the history; evaluation of these factors on their specific effect on the economic development in this region; how to screen those non-economic factors that are facilitative to the economic development; and how to avoid or overcome the negative effects, and so on. I am not doubtful that any government officials or ordinary people who care about the economic development in Guizhou or the Midwest in China are capable of finding things to their interest. Although the book focuses on Guizhou for the sake of analysis, it has created a value well beyond that territory due to the characteristics demonstrated by Guizhou itself and the fact that this book constantly benchmarks the entire Midwestern region in China as well as the places of similar nature in the world. It is a powerful work that is universally conducive to all under-developed regions.

Second, the book is structured from a relatively high theoretical perspective with some originality in theory.

The author has established the creative theory on the *Xiangji Operation* by making constant theoretical enhancement and extraction. Why does the author coin the term *Xiang* to define the systems formed by the inherent traits of each ethnic group? It is because: any society regulated by the traditional culture of each ethnic group has its own inherent characteristics, which become overt in different forms such as folklore, language, ethics and morals, social education etc. Meanwhile, each ethnic group lives in a natural environment that has been processed and transformed by the people of the ethnic group, which expresses themselves in a varied way. All these social and natural characteristics regulated by each ethnic group are combined together under the term of *Xiang*. This is agreeable with the Chinese traditional philosophy and corresponds to the definition in the natural science (modern physics). Such a coinage is fully plausible to me. Some experts once argued that X*iangji (cross-Xiang) Relationship* should be replaced by a more plain and easier-to-understand *Zuji (cross-ethnic groups) Relationship.* It is my opinion that *Xiangji Relationship* demonstrates a much stronger ability in theoretical generalization than *Zuji Relationship.* In fact, people from the same ethnic group who are exposed to different natural environment or subject to varying degrees of interaction with neighboring ethnic groups may find themselves immersed in cultures that are different to a certain degree. As a result, more than one *Xiang* may exist in a single ethnic group, making *Xiangji Relationship* irreplaceable by *Zuji Relationship.*

The author has summarized the composition of *Xiang* (sub-system) in the following way: 1. The social custom and culture unique to the ethnic group. 2. The natural environment where the ethnic group lives, which is the result of processing and transformation by the people from the group by virtue of its culture. 3. The country to which the ethnic group belongs and its laws, policies and administrative system. Such an abstraction, while highlighting the certain degree of unchangeability displayed by *Xiang* of each ethnic group in its evolutionary history, does not underestimate the possibility of national policies promulgated on the precondition of a full understanding of the actuality of the ethnic group in changing or driving the social development of the ethnic group. It lays a theoretical foundation for the success of the research. With a thorough understanding of the connotative meaning of this term, one has no difficulty in realizing that the *Principles in Xiangji Operation* discussed in this book are applicable in all the situations and places where developments in a heterogeneous culture take place, making the book a source of universal guidance.

In addition, by sublating the irrelevant and incorporating the useful parts of the leading theories in cultural anthropology, economics and other fields from the West, the author has further enriched and substantiated the *Xiangji* theory, and has therefore enhanced its power in theoretical generalization.

Third, the book is written with a practical purpose in the author's mind, which employs a methodology of generalizing theories from practices and then using these theories in solving more problems in reality in the process of developing the economy of ethnic regions.

The book could not have been completed without the tremendous amount of fieldwork conducted by the author in the ethnic minority regions in Guizhou. Anyone who has finished reading the book agrees that the author has examined the rich and vivid life from the perspective of both a cultural anthropologist and an economist. Everything ranging from customary habits, education, natural environment to economic development in the ethnic minority regions became the objects of his observation and scrutinization. Nothing that has an impact on the local economic development has escaped his attention. Both a dispassionate researcher and, to a larger extent, a participant in the development of the surveyed regions, the author often finds himself ecstatic if he sees a government policy in harmony with the specific *Xiang* in the region and therefore facilitative to the local development, or otherwise feels regretful if the policies lose touch with the local conditions and thus hinder the local development. It is so apparent that the author has endeavored to find a fitting place for the modern economy to take root and grow in the regions of ethnic groups that the readers feel greeted by the thickly rustic and unaffected breeze from the countryside as they open the book and read along. In almost every chapter, you are touched by stories that have already happened or are going to happen right beside you, and you cannot help but think and search for solutions.

Although the two chapters *On Policies* and *On Solutions* specifically talk about *countermeasures,* yet they are different from other books on polices and solutions in that these polices and solutions are proposed by the author under a theoretical guidance and are therefore a reflection of the author's deep thinking at a higher level. Here is an example.

In the chapter with the caption of *On Solutions,* the author brings about the issue of by what principles solutions should be devised. Should they be devised from the perspective of the ethnic Han in the developed regions or of the ethnic minorities in the under-developed regions? Should we trust materials, man power, technology or national policies? Are we developing these regions on behalf of the ethnic groups or should we mobilize the internal power of the local people? These come down to the questions that we often label as either *giving blood* or *creating blood.* In this regard, the author has provided sufficient evidences from both within and outside the country in support of the conclusion that the ethnic minority regions are able to develop their own economy under the condition of market economy. The author firmly holds that wholeness and disequilibrium must be allowed to co-exist and, to exchange at equal values must be supplemented by self-driven optimization, and that the overall economic development in ethnic minority regions in Guizhou must start with a disequilibrium development. Meanwhile, on the basis of exchange at equal values, the economy of ethnic minorities must optimize itself so that it can seize the market opportunities under the protection of a superior socialist system to meet the challenge and achieve a healthy growth. These analyses made from a strategic angle are of profound significance to us all.

I am fortunate enough to read the book before others have the chance to do so. Generally speaking, the author has selected an issue of common interest, structured his research and analyses based on abundant materials and a novel theoretical framework, which has also provided the theoretical basis for making policy proposals and solutions. For these reasons, it is indeed a good book that I highly recommend. What also deserves our attention is the author himself, Mr. Yang Tingshuo, who is a middle-aged scholar with solid theoretical background and proven analytical ability. We have no doubt that the great transformation China has been undergoing currently will pave the way for the author and his prospect is bright. He reminds me of what Engels once said when he talked about Renaissance: “It was the greatest progressive revolution that mankind has so far experienced, a time which called for giants and produced giants - giants in power of thought, passion, and character, in universality and learning.” Despite some possible inaccuracies in its theoretical framework, the book has depicted a writer who is keen to show us his creativity and enormous enthusiasm that echoes the great era of ours. As great times call for “giants”, we wish to see more theorists and experts who will live up to the expectation of the time and its people, and devote themselves to the research of both theoretical and practical issues in China's commitment in reform and opening to the outside world.

April, 1996

Table of Contents

Chapter One Introduction

The development of ethnic minority regions in Guizhou has a long history, which was predominantly driven by the central government in ancient times and private participation in the development did not happen until a much later time. Whoever led the development faced the same question, i.e., the development activities were carried out in a quite different natural environment by applying the Han culture in different cultural settings. In such an environment, pure economic measures are hard to be adopted in similar economic activities. In the situations where similar economic measures are adopted, they tend to produce much less benefit than the central areas of the Han culture. These facts have prompted special theoretical problems that are related to differences in both the natural environment and culture. Such problems cannot be solved exclusively by either economic or cultural anthropological measures, but rather by economic anthropology - an interdisciplinary subject between cultural anthropology and economics.

I The Issue: History and Current Status

China has a vast territory with completely different natural environments in different regions. Economic activities will not produce the desired results unless they are carried out in the ways that fit local conditions. China is also a country consisting of many ethnic groups, each immersed in a unique culture that regulates a different life style. Any attempt to economically develop a heterogeneous ethnic region will be hindered by an over-investment, reduced benefit, lower stability and other difficulties, which are attributable to economic factors as well as differences in social and cultural background. In other words, the success of an economic development in a different ethnic region is not only dependent on economic factors but also non-economic restraints. To ensure that the ethnic minority regions quickly catch up with the more socially developed regions in the country and to make the development efforts more effective, we must find rational and operable solutions to these issues. This is at the center of the missions this book is commissioned to accomplish.

Guizhou is a habitat for quite a number of ethnic minority groups with a natural environment divergent from that in Central China. The development work in Guizhou has been less satisfactory and it remains as one of the poorest provinces in China. Guizhou has witnessed quite a few massive development campaigns in its history, and has been abandoned repeatedly afterwards. It is nonetheless exceptional and similar patterns are seen in other places like Guangxi, Yunnan, Ningxia, Gansu, northern Shaanxi and southern Mongolia, making it a topic of national significance to conduct research on non-economic restraints in the development of ethnic minority regions. Without a deeper understanding of these restraints, we may end up repeating the mistakes of our ancestors and hurting the chance of modernizing places like Guizhou. In worst case scenario, they may encumber China's economic take-off. In a broader sense, this issue has global implications. The independence of developing countries and the establishment of nation states after World War II have not elevated the status of these nations relative to other developed countries. The great economic progress they have made has not narrowed, but rather widened their distance from the developed world. Although they have spent huge amount of money investing in advanced technologies from developed countries and tried all they could to attract foreign capital, none of these measures has truly transformed these nations to be prosperous and powerful. People have tried but failed to explain such perplexing and troublesome facts from the perspective of economics, politics, natural conditions, historical traditions or the so-called "national character." Now, we have gradually waken up to realize that the key to a prosperous future for the developing nations lies in the systematic research of non-economic restraints.

What are the non-economic restraints then? In essence, human being's economic activities are comprehensive social activities, whose unobstructed operation requires support from the social background. On the other hand, economic activities are a process of exchange of materials and energies between man and nature, and unquestionably, every economic activity is reliant on the natural and ecological system that it is exposed to. Objective natural conditions play a key role in determining the success or failure of the economic activities. Subsequently, for any economic activity conducted in a highly homogeneous society in a given natural environment, we may look directly at the economic viability of each component of the economic activity without worrying about non-economic social and natural restraints. Such is a mission traditionally accomplished by economists. However, such an exclusively economic theoretical discussion will be much less pertinent if the same economic activity is carried out in a society regulated by a different culture, specifically between different ethnic groups, and in a completely different natural background. Situations like this demand a look into both economic problems as well as an understanding of all the non-economic restraints before the right solutions are found. We believe that non-economic restraints are a collection of individual sub-systems, as the result of economic activities across multiple ethnic groups and/or regions may be determined by numerous factors that are interdependent on and restrict each other to form an invisible but innately rational network.

To better understand such a network of restraining factors, we must first comprehend the components and the relationship between them, as well as how closely related each one of the components is to economic activities. A lot of natural and social factors are so impactful that they may cause economic activities across multiple ethnic groups to succeed or fail. Generally, the following factors should be brought to our attention. In terms of natural environment, the spacial distance between the two ethnic groups involved, difference in the resource composition and in ecological background, the depth of resource utilization by different ethnic groups, and any objective reality corresponding to such level of resource utilization, etc. The cultures and traditions of each ethnic group may consist of existing social customs, rituals and habits, value propensity toward science and technology, conditions in social and school education, or even religions, ethics and morals. Besides, the policies and laws enforced by the country where the concerned ethnic people live, as well as the level of control by its administrative authorities over economic activities all have significant impact on the result of economic activities across ethnic groups. Each of these non-economic factors restricts while at the same time depends on each other and jointly exert impact to a different degree on the economic development activities across ethnic groups. For instance, all the living environments inhabited by different ethnic groups have, without exception, been processed and transformed to a certain extent by the inhabiting or other related ethnic groups, and are therefore not purely natural and objective environments. In this sense, no economic activities across ethnic groups are carried out in a perfectly natural and unintervened environment but rather in a modified and transformed natural setting. Meanwhile, the customs and social habits of the ethnic group, value propensity toward science and technology, social and school education etc., are never independent from, but rather, interact, restrict and depend on each other. In many ethnic regions, for instance, schools are run by churches, social organizations, individuals or the state. Another example is the customs and habits practiced by an ethic group, which may be part of its tradition, result shaped by its religion, ethics or morals, living conditions, and reflect the stage of scientific and technological development that this ethnic group is in.

In summary, instead of impacting economic activities across ethnic groups independently, these non-economic restraints work as part of an invisible but innately rational network to affect these activities.

From the perspective of studying cross-ethnic group economic activities, these non-economic factors are roughly classified into the following respects. Natural and ecological environments tend to increase the amount of investment in cross-ethnic group economic activities. The spacial distance between two ethnic groups usually restricts the efficiency of the economic activities. The cultural differences between two ethnic groups complicate the operation of the activities even more and often limit the profit-generating ability. The laws and policies governing ethnic regions directly determine the duration of these activities.

The cultural differences between the relevant ethnic groups will be discussed in Chapter Three, Four and Five - *Culture (I, II, III)*. The natural and ecological environments, spacial distance between two interacting ethnic groups as well as their impacts on economic activities will be the topic of Chapter Six - *Background.* How the state laws and policies affect cross-ethnic group economic activities is covered in Chapter Seven - *Capacity* and Chapter Eight - *Policy*. Nonetheless, the existence of non-economic restraints in economic activities across ethnic groups is undeniable, yet they have long been neglected by previous researchers apparently for the following three reasons:

1. Modern economic activities are often driven by individuals or organizations with financial capabilities. As they focus solely on gaining profits in as short a period of time as possible, they usually don't think beyond short terms and limited goals. Even when non-economic restraints have derailed their operation, they don't look into causes other than economic or operational nature. They rarely notice the existence of non-economic

restraints that usually play a long-term and general role. Economics doctrines, in a dogmatic fashion, tend to be universally applied to explain what they are not capable of explaining.

2. In ancient times, economic activities across ethnic minority regions were often sponsored by the state whose primary goal was not to fetch economic gains but to fulfill political and military purposes or simply to meet the needs of the ruling individuals. Failure of these activities would often end up in the political or military accountability, or blaming the militaristic and war-craving rulers, with no mentioning of the real reasons that caused the economic activities to fail. Such has been a repeated pattern in the Chinese history research, which has unsurprisingly concealed the undeniable existence of non-economic restraints.

3. The research in the culture of different ethnic groups has long been a task of cultural anthropologists. In the infancy of this discipline, researchers tended to focus on uncovering and understanding the cultural characteristics of the ethnic group being studied and gave little thought to how heterogeneous ethnic groups might mingle economically. It was not until the early 20th century when Karl Polanyi founded economic anthropology that people started to shift their attention to this important issue. Nevertheless, neither the depth nor the popularity of economic anthropology is satisfactory until today. Non-economic restraints are hardly talked about when people plan economic activities across different ethnic groups.

It is our belief that the existence of non-economic restraints is objectively undeniable and must be highly emphasized by researchers and practitioners alike. If neglected, these restraints will cause economic activities to fail, or even worse, to give rise to other perils. Despite our development of the ethnic minorities in the border regions that has lasted thousands of years, they remain as one of most destitute places in China. To make things worse, on top of a level of economic development that lags far behind the advanced regions, we are seeing a deteriorating ecological environment in these regions that may soon pose a threat to the developed regions traditionally domiciled by Han nationality. Without any doubt, we can not modernize the ethnic regions in China's borderland and uplift their level of development to that in the economically advanced regions simply by taking political or economic measures. Instead, only by bringing the non-economic restraints into consideration and putting the research results in this field into practice can we reverse the blindness and enhance the efficiency in our efforts in developing the ethnic regions.

In the past forty years since the founding of the People's Republic of China, the government has enacted laws that establishes an equal status to all ethnic groups, granted a series of economic preferential treatments to ethnic minority people, invested heavily in these regions, and continuously sent a huge number of talents from developed regions to offer all forms of help in the hope to develop the ethnic minority economy rapidly. Unfortunately, after all these years, we have to admit that all the efforts we have made in the past have not bridged but instead enlarged the gap in the level of economic development between the developed regions and the ethnic minority regions. The Southwest and Northwest of China that lagged behind the rest of the country at the time of the founding of the country are still among the poorest places right now. Neither political nor economic analyses provide sound explanation as to why the regions endowed with such favorable political and economic conditions have been growing surprisingly slowly. The answer apparently lies in the fact that we have not studied and understood the non-economic restraints thoroughly.

Non-economic restraints should be emphasized in both China and the world. With the end of an international arena controlled by the two superpowers, the world has moved toward multi-polarization. All sovereign states have shifted their focus to developing national economies, exploring overseas markets and acquiring foreign resources and technologies, resulting in closer and more frequent economic activities across different nationalities. For the same reason, relationship between countries is not a purely economic one, nor can it be dealt with exclusively by political measures. The issues that are facing the world now, such as a protracted and hard-to-solve economic stalemate between the South and the North, the aborted multilateral trade agreements, the mounting debt for the third world countries, economic recessions in the developed world, are closely related to non-economic restraints. We will not be able to reach an equilibrium in economic development among different countries, which are likely to cause conflicts or chaos in the world, if we continue the current pattern of neglecting the non-economic restraints. A retrospective look at the state of the world during two world wars will make such a hidden danger and its intensity more transparent and overt to us.

Situations were similar before the two world wars where disequilibrium in economic development among countries resulted in economic alliances formed by countries aimed at furthering their own economic interests. Economic alliances were transformed into military allies that eventually clashed against each other which led to world wars. After World War II, although former colonies and semi-colonies won national independence consecutively, their economies have stayed backward for quite a long period subject to economic pressure from the developed countries. To protect themselves, these countries have chosen to form groups of either economic or military nature, while the developed countries have done the same thing. This symbolizes that the world is moving toward a direction of multi-polarization, which, instead of making it more stable, forewarns a riskier world exposed to conflicts of greater intensity and larger scale. To uproot the risks, a mere resort to economic or political measures without looking into non-economic restraints is not a solution. For this reason, the conclusions of this book are, to some extent, universal and applicable in other parts of the world even though they are drawn from the information collected in Guizhou. In other words, the findings documented by this book can be expanded from similar regions in China to the management of international relationship, offering a new perspective or paradigm especially for China in dealing with national relationship with other countries so that it will be equipped with the ability to think and act in a more visionary and insightful way.

What substantial changes have happened in Guizhou after more than two thousand years of economic development? This is an intriguing and significantly important as well as hard-to-answer question. Human economic activities conducted in different times have different components and focus on different priorities, making it hard to consolidate economic data collected in different times. As a result, to compare economic statistics collected in one region from different times in a vertical timeline without referencing other regions will undoubtedly end up in an upward straight line. Such a way of analysis does not reflect the real difference in economic activities due to lack of benchmarks and thus cannot help us uncover the essential facts hidden in a changing economy. To reveal the essence reflected in the differences in Guizhou between its past and current economy, we must find a measurement that can be utilized throughout the entire history and ensure that such a measurement can reflect the essence in all times. Such a measurement does exist but has been overlooked in the past. The following indexes, in our opinion, have the desired value. First, the percentage of economic activities in the ethnic regions in Guizhou over the total economic activities in China. Second, the level of self-sufficiency for the administrative organizational system in ethnic regions in Guizhou. Lastly, the level of economic dependency of ethnic regions in Guizhou on the developed Han regions in China.

Economic activities in different times differ dramatically in the structure of products, ways of investment or combination of labor. Even for the same region, it is extremely hard to find a single product produced or consumed throughout its history, or a uniform pricing standard in calculating the investment made in the production, let alone the mode of combining laborers to complete a certain task. As a matter of fact, there are no items with the same value that can be measured to calculate the difference between ancient and modern economy. The essence cannot be found from the measurement results of any single item. By contrast, as the percentage of the aggregated economic activities in ethnic minority regions in Guizhou over the total GDP of the entire China does not depend on a single index but is a result of comparing comprehensive economic capacities in different times, it is an objective and accurate reflection of how Guizhou does economically relative to the entire China. Subsequently, an examination of the change in such a percentage objectively reveals the change in the Guizhou's weight in overall economic activities in China.

From the mid-Western Han Dynasty（206 B.C.--A.D. 8）, the central government has begun to install administrative agencies of varying sizes in Guizhou, with an aim to control the ethnic minority regions. These administrative organs were given different names in different times. During the two Han Dynasties（206 B.C. – A.D. 220）and the Northern and Southern Dynasties, they were named "Bianjun" (remote prefecture), usually given no authority in levying taxes or intervening in the economic activities in these regions. The Longzhong Plan (the name given to a strategic plan given by the third century Chinese tactician and administrator Zhuge Liang)[①] was an indication of such a situation, where the economic activities carried out by the ethnic groups in Guizhou barely had any substantial impact on China.

① (Jin) Shou Chen, (Liu Song) Songzhi Pei, annotation, *The History of the Three Kindoms • Kindom of Shu • Biography of Zhuge Liang V* (Beijing: Zhonghua Book Company, April 1975，6th reprint), 920-921.

Understandably, these places were viewed at the moment by ethnic Hans as "barren land occupied by useless people."[①]

The central governments in Sui (581-618), Tang (618-907) and Song Dynasties (960-1279) all set up "*Jimi* prefectures and counties" (a system established by the central government that allowed minority groups in the border regions to run their internal affairs on behalf of the central government so as to maintain the subjugating/subjugated relationship between them) in Guizhou, which, according to the people at the moment, followed the principle of "granting entry to those who came and letting go of those who left". The central governments never declined entry to the tribes whose chief expressed the willingness to stay connected with, submitted himself to the rule of, and pay tribute to the imperial court. These submissive tribes often received abundant rewards and were offered official positions. They were rarely punished, however, if someday these tribes discontinued paying tributes to the imperial court or even established ties with other regimes as long as such moves did not pose threat to the central government. The economic importance of these prefectures and counties to the entire country was understandably negligible. It was recorded in the *History of the Song Dynasty* that the "Wuxingfan" (five tribal families)[②]who ruled ethnic Buyi in central Guizhou were so devastated that they submitted themselves to the Song Dynasty and paid tributes each year merely in the hope of receiving generous imperial grants from the Song central government at the expense of a limited quantity of local specialties. It is apparent that the economic activities carried out in Guizhou at the time did not make any substantial contribution to the central government. On the contrary, it cost the central government tremendous amount of money to pacify and appease them so that they would not turn against the government and cause unrest in the border regions, which could result in a much larger expense in military operations. Under such circumstances, the percentage of the economic activities in these ethnic regions over total national production was close to zero.

The Yuan Government (1271-1368) stationed armies in Guizhou and started emigrating ethnic Han people to live in these regions. It marked the beginning of levying of taxes and the corvee system, and the establishment of

① *The History of the Former Han Dynasty • Collected Biographies of Southwestern Barbarians*

② *Twenty-five Histories* vol. 8, *History of the Song Dynasty (II) • Biography of Southern Barbarians,* 1986 ed. (Shanghai: Chinese Classics Publishing House, Shanghai Bookstore, July 1990 7th reprint), 67-85.

direction economic interaction between these regions and the rest of the country. Products made in the ethnic minority regions in Guizhou started to enter the market of central China in bulk via private channels, making Guizhou part of the national economy. Regardless, it remained one of the poorest regions in the country. In the Ming Dynasty（1368-1643）, Guizhou Province was officially established and became the most impoverished one among the thirteen administrative provinces. In the Qing Dynasty（1644-1911）, the number of administrative provinces was increased to 18, but Guizhou stayed at the bottom economically. Many regions in the Northwest and Southwest of China did not belong to any province, but were named "Fanbu" (places inhabited by ethnic groups other than Han) as a whole and "the place under the rule of generals". The economic activities in these regions hardly had any direct impact on the overall national economy, just similar to the situation in Guizhou of the Tang and Song dynasties. In summary, the economic activities in ethnic minority regions in Guizhou were among the lowest ranking regions in the Qing Dynasty.

Guizhou has witnessed a rapid economic growth after the founding of the People's Republic of China, but it is still outpaced by its counterparts in the developed regions in the Southeast of China. As a result, the ranking of Guizhou in terms of the economic performance has not changed substantially and remains in the bottom three, only slightly higher than Tibet and Gansu in a good year and significantly lower than the neighboring Hunan, Sichuan and Yunnan. In short, despite the development that has lasted over two thousand years in Guizhou, its economic status has not changed substantially, which is most clearly indicated by the percentage of its economic activities over a total national economy. In sharp contrast, Zhejiang and Jiangsu provinces that were located far from the national economic center in ancient time have transformed themselves into one of the wealthiest provinces in China. As another example, Guanzhong of Shaanxi Province that used to be the most affluent place in the two Han dynasties has been marginalized economically. It is probably no exaggeration to say that Guizhou may well have remained among the poorest provinces in China.

Remote and *Jimi* Prefectures and Counties were structured administratively in a totally different way from other parts of China. The officials stationed in remote counties were not paid from the local revenue but by the central government. The officials in *Jimi* Prefectures and Counties were appointed from the local ethnic minority groups who only received an official title but not any salary from the central government. Any representative appointed by the government to the *Jimi* Prefectures and Counties was fully covered by the country in salary and other administrative expenses without having to take a penny locally. A provincial administrative system that was similar to other places in China started to appear in Guizhou in Ming Dynasty, but a majority of official positions at the prefecture and county levels were filled by local hereditary headmen (*tu si*). It was not until the Qing Dynasty did Guizhou begin to have a similar administrative structure at the Fu and County Levels to other places in China, but local hereditary headmen and other local heads (*tu mu*) were kept for most of the positions below county levels. Local hereditary headmen paid all their administrative expenses with the money they raised and never had a direct relationship with the central government. The administrative officials appointed by the central government, on the other hand, largely relied on the central government for their salaries, supplies and other administrative expenses. At the time when Guizhou Province was first set up in the Ming Dynasty, unexceptionally all the salaries and expenses incurred by the officials delegated from the central government were paid by their native places, and were later gradually picked up by the neighboring provinces. In the meantime, sporadic taxes were collected within Guizhou to offset some of the fiscal expenditures, but they were so insignificant that supports from other provinces accounted for more than half of the fiscal expenditures until the fall of the Ming Dynasty.[①] In other words, Guizhou Province was established merely for political and military purposes and was never meant to make it self-sufficient.

In the early Qing Dynasty, all the garrisons (*wei suo*) of the Ming Dynasty were abolished and replaced by counties, marking the end of ruling military servicemen and civilians separately (*jun min fen zhi*). However, it did not improve the financial situations in these places. After Emperor Yongzheng（1723-1735）took the measures to replace all local hereditary headmen with the officials sent by the central government (*gai tu wei liu*), he adopted the proposal made by E'ertai and put Zunyi Fu that used to be part of Sichuan Province under Guizhou in an effort to alleviate the fiscal deficit that

① Jizhong Shi et al. eds., *Veritable Records of the Ming Dynasty • A Compilation of Materials about Guizhou* (Guizhou People's Publishing House, 1983), 388.

had long plagued Guizhou. The fiscal revenue from Zunyi Fu accounted for more than half of that in entire Guizhou at the time of transition, even so, Guizhou could not make its ends meet. The situation had not changed significantly by the end of the Qing Dynasty.

The 20th century has witnessed the successive four periods that Guizhou underwent: the Qing Dynasty (1636-1912), the era of Republic of China under the rule of local warlords（1912-1927）, the era of Republic of China under the national government（1927-1949）and the People's Republic of China（since 1949- ）. Despite the different administrative systems during the first three periods, Guizhou could not have survived without subsidies from central China. Only after the founding of PRC, it was possible for us to make a comparison between Guizhou and other parts of China on a comprehensive basis. Generally, the investments in infrastructure, industry and agriculture in Guizhou are mostly made by the central government with minimal funds locally raised in Guizhou. Administrative expenditures at every level in Guizhou rely heavily on fiscal appropriation of funds from the central government. In impoverished counties such as Leishan and Wangmo, tax revenue collected locally barely accounts for half of the county administrative expenditure, and the remainder must be supplied by the country. Given the fact that nearly half of counties in Guizhou Province fall below the poverty line and almost all of them are in need of government administrative subsidy, the size of the total subsidy is humongous. According to government statistics, in 1991, the fiscal revenue in Guizhou was 875,900 thousand Yuan while its total fiscal expenditure amounted to 1,340.01 million Yuan,[①] indicating that the fiscal deficit has not materially improved from its history. This is another undeniable fact in Guizhou's economic condition.

Prior to the establishment of Guizhou Province, ethnic minority groups in Guizhou who largely kept a self-sufficient life style, hardly had any direct economic interaction with ethnic Hans in other parts of China. No stable trade activities existed with the exception of occasional inflow of products made in ethnic Han regions. With the massive emigration of ethnic Hans into Guizhou after it was made a province, a huge quantity of foods, salt, fabric etc., began to be shipped into the ethnic minority regions. Continuous and steady flow of products from the Han regions to minority regions in Guizhou appeared with the military posts or Han emigrants as middlemen, which

① *China's Ethnic Statistical Yearbook* (China Statistics Press, January 1993), 206 transformed Guizhou's closed and self-sufficient economy to gradually depend on product supplies from the central regions in China. In the Ming and Qing dynasties, the majority of products shipped into Guizhou were salt and fabric. At the beginning of the 20th century, modern industry started to appear in Guizhou and the economic interaction between ethnic minorities in Guizhou and ethnic Hans in central China became intensified. However, the values of incoming and outgoing materials in Guizhou Province have always demonstrated an apparent scissors difference: the higher value of incoming materials vs. the lower value of outgoing ones with product influx becoming increasingly wider in category and larger in quantity. Industrial products such as machinery, chemical raw materials and mental materials have begun to flood Guizhou since the middle of the 20th century. In recent years, Guizhou's dependence on other provinces has extended to grains, ending its long history of grain self-supply. By contrast, logs, coals, minerals and similar primary goods have remained on the top of its export. Undeniably, Guizhou has not reversed the unfavorable trend of its outgoing products out-valued by the incoming products, and the gap is still growing. A survey conducted in 1985 showed that all enterprises and individuals in Guizhou Province held a total cash in Renminbi of 1.659 billion Yuan and the cash flow out of the province equaled 1.554 billion Yuan, while the annual money supply to Guizhou totaled 3.194 billion Yuan, signaling that the money held by enterprises and individuals as a whole almost equaled the money outflow of the same period. The striking scissors difference in the values between the incoming products and outgoing ones has suffocated Guizhou's economic potential.[①] The increasing dependence of the ethnic minority regions on the economy of the more developed central regions in China has, disappointingly, weakened Guizhou's ability to grow on its own. Although it is understandable for Guizhou, as an economically under-developed province, to bring in advanced technologies and machinery, it becomes a serious problem if Guizhou has to rely on other provinces for the supply of agricultural products especially grains.

A province as poor as Guizhou does not translate into a lower level of consumption. The level of total infrastructure investment is higher than the national average. Such a trend of higher consumption as opposed to lower

① Renduan Hu, Wenzhou Zhang, eds., *Guizhou Economic Development Model* (China Planning Press, August 1989), 179.

production has become more evident since 1960s. In the meantime, a big chunk of investment has not been turned into productivity. This is especially true in money spent on poverty alleviation efforts where most of the monetary input has barely returned anything. Some of the impoverished ethnic regions such as Yaoshan Xiang (an administrative level under county)of Libo County in Guizhou received a total of 600 thousand Yuan [①]in state poverty-alleviation investment in the period from the third Plenary Session of the 11th Central Committee of the CPC to 1983, and yet it remains as a nationally famous poverty region as of now. The local people have started to rely on such supports as a normal source of income. It is apparent that the tremendous economic development activities that lasted many years since Guizhou Province was officially established have produced an unfortunate result: the dependence of Guizhou on the rest of China is increasing but its potential of self-development is shrinking.

In summary, we should not feel over-satisfied with the great progress Guizhou has made compared to its past, but ought to get to know that Guizhou is facing a severe economic situation. Such a serious economic situation is not a result of inadequate supports from the country, nor the absence of advanced technologies. Instead, it is caused by deeper level natural and social environments combined. These factors that have restrained the economic development have long been neglected in the past and are the non-economic restrains this book is commissioned to discuss in a systematic way. Chen Shineng, Governor of Guizhou Province, has rightly pointed it out that the economic development in Guizhou is not only about materials. The transformation of conventional mentality is the top priority.[②] His statement is right to the point. However, we must not forget that conventional mentality did not come out of nowhere. It is the cognitive framework and value propensity shaped by natural and social environments. The switch from conventional to modern mentality requires more than the superficial political mobilization but to start from the social and natural environments where the conventional mentality originated from. Such is not a mission that can be accomplished shortly. Therefore, the problems we discussed in this book can not be solved by simply introducing a few policies, conducting a few tasks or taking a few measures. It demands an all-out effort from all of us who are

① *Ethnic Survey in Yueliangshan Region (*Guizhou Ethnic Research Institute, June 1983), 8, 48.

② Shineng Chen, Governor, "Speech in the Report Meeting of Administrative Agencies Directly under the Provincial Government on Emancipation of Minds," *Guizhou Daily*, August 1994.

willing to get down to the fundamentals.

II The Book: Purposes and Tasks

The research in this book is about numerous complex systems other than a few specific restraining factors. Prior researches of such kind of restraining systems have not offered universally accepted terminologies that we can use in this research. Therefore, we must first coin a term for the object of our research. We have determined to use the Chinese character of "Xiang" to refer to the social and natural entity regulated by the system composed of non-economic restraints that impact economic activities across different ethnic regions. We, by writing this book, attempt to reveal the essences of cross-Xiang economic activities, factors that cause cross-Xiang economic activities to succeed or fail, as well as the solutions to the problems encountered in cross-Xiang economic activities. That is why the book is titled "Principles in Xiangji Operations". The discussions in this book are based on the information collected in Guizhou but the purpose is to uncover the basic scope of economic anthropology and put it into practice.

"Xiang" is an old Chinese character first seen as an inscription on bones or tortoise shells in the Shang Dynasty. It is also an associative compound character that depicts an eye studying a tree, which conveys its original meaning of "observe". Extensively, it carries the meaning of "essence" and "substance" that man can get at by observation. Furthermore, as people understand the essence of things through observation, the result of studying the external characteristics that reflect the essence, this character of Xiang has a more remotely extensive meaning of "appearance". The original meaning of Xiang can be found in *Shijing · Yongfeng · Xiangshu* (the Book of Songs ·Yongfeng ·Observe a Mouse): "When you observe a mouse, you see its skin, but some people don't even know to behave." (It implies the kind of people who, despite their sanctimonious look, often carry out disgraceful and unruly acts.)[①] The second meaning is seen in *Shijing ·Daya ·Wen Wang Zhi Shi · Yupu*: " (King Wen) polished his articles and beautified his appearance." According to *Mao Shi Gu Xun Zhuan* (Annotation and Interpretation of the Book of Songs by Mao), "Xiang is essence of things."[②] In *Xunzi· Feixiang* (Against Physiognomy), Xiang was used in its third meaning, "A man with a

① *Commentaries and Notes on the Thirteen Classics,* Yuan Ruan ed. (Zhonghua Book Company, October 1980), 319 upper part.

② Ibid., 514 lower part.

good heart is a noble man even if he has a repulsive facial appearance. A man is a vile character if he is evil in heart even if he has a charming face."[1]

After Buddhism was introduced in China, masters in the translation of the Buddhist Scriptures picked the third meaning of Xiang to describe things that have the same substance but appear in a different form or state. For instance, the same Buddha may appear in three different forms (states): *Dhammakaya, Sambhogakaya* and *Nirmanakaya*. The term is used in this way to emphasize the coherence in essence and variety in exterior forms. In other parts of the Buddhist Scriptures, "Xiang" is used opposite to "Xing" (essence), where Xiang represents external traits and Xing connotes the internal essence. It is in this sense that the book uses the term Xiang. Every ethnic group has its own traditional culture. Societies regulated under such a traditional culture have a common essence that is presented externally in different forms, such as customs and habits, language, ethics and morals, social education, and religious belief etc. Meanwhile, the natural environment each ethnic group lives in has been processed and transformed by this ethnic group, such as cultivation of wasteland, reforestation, river diversion etc., and is characteristic of the culture of this ethnic group. Therefore it is also a natural entity with the same essence but different external appearances. Subsequently, we think it conforms with the habit in the Chinese language to use Xiang to signify the complex natural and social entity regulated by the culture of each ethnic group.

We are not doing this for the sake of looking creative or different from the others. Examples of using Xiang in this way can be found in scientific fields. "Phase", a term in modern physics and translated as Xiang in Chinese, "carries the meaning of different forms with the same molecule, namely Xiang, such as gas, liquid or solid phase. Each phase has the same molecules that are arranged differently."[2]Such a translation coincides with the way we use this term, both refer to the systems with the same internal nature but different external forms. Human being's economic activities are of the same nature and are conducted to acquire materials from the natural environment for subsistence. However, in terms of each specific ethnic group, the external representation varies. Each of the external forms is like the gas, liquid or solid state of a matter. In modern chemistry, the term *phase* is also widely

[1] Zhikun Guo, *Notes on the Thoughts of Xunzi* (Shanghai: Sanlian Bookstore, September 1991)
[2] *Lexicon of Physics* (Zhongwai Publishing House, May 1979),153

used. For instance, in chemical experiments, phase-transfer reaction [①]refers to chemical reactions between gas and liquid or liquid and solid states, which comes down in one continuous line as the way we use the term in this book.

Each Xiang discussed in this book is a complex of social and natural elements regulated by social cultures, and therefore should have its own components. Generally speaking, it includes at least three sub-systems: 1. The social tradition and culture unique to each ethnic group. 2. The natural environment the ethnic group lives in, which, needless to say, is the result of transformation efforts made by the ethnic group by virtue of its culture. 3. The country that the ethnic group belongs to, as well as the laws and policies enforced by this country and the administrative system it adopts.

Thousands of ethnic groups co-exist in this world and each of them has a unique traditional culture, by which members of each group are bonded together to form a "commonwealth". Every member in each ethnic group is subject to the regulation and restriction of the ethnic culture, while in the same time depends on this culture to acquire conditions for subsistence. Culture is to an ethnic group a means of conquering and transforming nature, a cohesive to bond its people, as well as the power to drive the continuity and development of the nationality. As all the ethnic groups have different cultures, they must operate in different xiangs. In this sense, "xiangji operations" (the operations across xiang) that are the focus of the research in this book refer to the economic activities across different cultures. The restraining forces that an ethnic culture exerts on economic activities are discussed in detail in Chapter Three, Four and Five, "Culture (I, II, III)."

Every ethnic group in the world must occupy a specific living space which, from the perspective of nature, is an objective entity consisting of elements such as landforms, geological conditions, vegetation and climate. These are necessary elements for the relevant ethnic people to process and make use of in their economic activities. Throughout the millions of years since human being appeared on earth, people have not only put these natural objects into use but also modified and transformed them with their own culture. The variety in cultures has resulted in completely different results in the utilization, processing and transformation of natural objects. For instance, a marshland may be transformed into an ideal hunting or fishing ground by ethnic groups that live by hunting and fishing, while it will certainly be

① *Dictionary of Organic Chemistry* (Science Press, 1987), 153 converted by farmers to fertile farmland with developed irrigation systems to ensure stable yields in conditions of both drought and excessive rains. In a modern industrial background, we will do nothing but drain the wetland to prepare it for building concrete structures and factories, thus fundamentally disfiguring the natural environment. Such a transformation of natural environment, while an absolute necessity for related ethnic groups to conduct economic activities, may not be as appropriate or necessary for other ethnic groups. We have to emphasize that the natural environments that are human habitats today have been subjected to human processing and transformation and are hardly pure natural and objective environments any more. Imprinted by the culture of specific ethnic groups, the natural environments have acquired some social attributes and are partially a social product. Such a natural environment that provides a background for the subsistence of ethnic people differs from an objective and pure natural environment, and is called, for the sake of distinguishing between the two in this book, the "ecologic niche" of the specific ethnic group. (Early ethnologists interpreted ecologic niche only as purely natural living space. However, deeper ethnological researches have gradually led people to realize that the external environment surrounding an ethnic group is not purely objective and natural, but rather a result of human processing and transformation. Such an artificial external spatial system that is processed by and corresponds to specific cultures is indeed the ecologic niche for this specific ethnic group, which undoubtedly includes natural and social components that integrate into the living environment, i.e., ecologic niche, for this particular ethnic group.) Economic activities are social activities and living environments are the foundation for the subsistence, continuity and development of a society. Therefore, economic activities carried out by an ethnic group must be closely tied to the living environment of that ethnic group, and xiang must undoubtedly include the "corresponding living environment" as one of its elements. Economic activities across xiangs will certainly be restrained by the living environments of all the ethnic groups concerned, subsequently, a study of cross-xiang operation must not overlook this element.

The majority of the ethnic groups in the world now belong to a country or a region. The cultural operation and formation of living environments of these ethnic groups are regulated by both their own traditional culture and the laws, policies and administrative authorities of the country or region to which they belong. Likewise, countries and their operating functions are a creation of traditional culture. When performing its functions, a state may impede or, in the opposite, facilitate the proper cultural operation of these groups. In the above circumstances, the state and the transition of its policies determine which of these two scenarios plays a major role.

Ethnic groups carry out specific economic activities under the relevant cultural regulation and in specific living environments. Since a country and its administrative authorities have the ability of impacting the cultural operation and the formation of living environments, it can impact the economic activities of the related ethnic groups in a significant way. Consequently, countries and their administrative functions should be another element in the composition of xiang. A research in cross-xiang operation should therefore include the research of the countries each xiang belongs to and their administrative functions. It needs to be pointed out that the three elements, namely culture, living environment and country, are interrelated elements that combine to create a xiang, which is the topic of the research in the book. We must fully understand the three elements before we can unveil workable strategies in cross-xiang operations to make them successful. To ease the effort of writing and reading of this book, we treat the three elements as sub-systems in an over-arching bigger system that is defined as xiang. Among the three elements that are each an integral part of xiang, they have different characteristics and impact the economic activities differently in the direction, intensity and mode. Numerous inner conflicts exist within a xiang whose equilibrium solely depends on the achievement of a balance among these conflicts. Likewise, the success of cross-xiang operations relies on an accurate understanding of the restrictive relationship among these conflicts, through which we can make operable breakthroughs and generalize strategies and solutions.

A generalization on the three elements must start with a profound understanding of the relationship among them, characterized by unity as well as opposition. We may look at the following five aspects: 1. The difference in the energy stored in each element; 2.The difference in the speed of the evolution of each element, or in other words, in the duration that each element lasts stably; 3. The difference in the speed and quantity that each element can input its energy; 4. The way and duration that each element becomes and remains effective; 5. The ability of each element to recover itself and the difference in time that each element needs for the recovery. Below are discussions focusing on the five aspects.

Among all the elements, living environments have the most energy stored in them. Despite the numerous achievements we have made so far in science and technology, no human beings nor ethnic groups in the world are able to change the natural environments completely by political or economic power they have available. No one can turn Tarim Basin into a land that has rain-pours all year round, transforming the desert into rice fields or making Tarim River an exorheic river to avoid soil salinization. Similarly, we can not flatten the hefty and steep mountain ranges in Yunnan-Guizhou Plateau and make them operable for farm tractors, neither can we completely remove the sludge that often obstructs the downriver channels of Yangtze River to make it passable for 100,000 tonnage seagoing vessels and benefit the booming modern industry in this area from the ease of sea transportation. Such a common sense is often overlooked by modern operators who tend to overestimate the power of scientific and technological means they have in hand. They are the ones who often miscalculate in the cross-xiang economic activities.

The amount of energy that an ethnic group can mobilize via its culture, although not as much as that stored in natural environments, far out-competes that made available by specific political or economic projects. Attempts to change the traditional culture of an ethnic group by the force of human often turn out to be unbearably costly and also not so successful as anticipated. Language is a component of ethnic cultures. All the dynasties in the history of China had tried to assimilate the ethnic minority people by consolidating their languages. However, up till today, China is still a country of multi-nationalities who, for the most part, speak their own languages. As early as the first Emperor of Qin Dynasty, attempts to universalize one set of ethics and morals were made,[①] but none of these attempts has discontinued the moral concepts of ethnic minorities until today. In addition, other components of culture such as religious beliefs, arts and crafts, value propensity and ways of accumulating knowledge can not be simplified or unified via political or economic power. "To make use of what is useful" often proves most effective and less likely to cause conflicts among different ethnic groups.

① *Records of the Grand Historian • Biography of First Emperor of Qin*

The source of administrative power of a country usually comes from tax collection, which provides materials and energies that only account for a small portion of the total production of the concerned nationality, between 3%-7%, with the total tax collected no more than 15%. A system that depends on high taxes for an extended period of time will, like killing the goose that lays golden eggs, eventually suffocate the economic life of the nationality. The energy specific economic projects can provide barely matches the taxation of a country for the reason that these projects are often run by financially capable individuals or institutions, who can only operate under the auspice of the administrative system of a country. Therefore, they are no rival of the country in terms of the energy they are able to mobilize and use. Cross-xiang operations are special economic activities because they are operated across different xiangs. On the other hand as they are merely economic activities, when facing unshakable objective facts, the operators can only resort to the energy available to them to make breakthroughs in the complexity created by the mingling three components. How to achieve such a goal is the first theoretical task this book aims to complete.

The three components of xiang vary in the duration that each of them lasts in a stable condition. The speed of change in natural environments is extremely slow. They can remain barely changed for tens or hundreds of thousands of years and can recover automatically from changes resulted from human activities within different length of time once the human activities stop. For example, subtropical monsoon forests have the ability of recovering in 25-40 years after destroyed from deforestation and fire. A river whose route is changed by man will automatically change course and stabilize itself once people stop maintaining the forced route. Some natural environments, though, will never restore to their original appearance once destroyed by human beings. Mountain rocks, for example, can not return to their original form after breaking from explosion, but new soil will form on the exposed rock surface after some time, making it usable again by human beings. Natural environments in such a circulation, although not completely going back to their original state, are renewable from the perspective of human subsistence. In other words, natural environments have the ability of self-recovery. Once recovered, they remain in the stable state continuously and can be used again by human beings as long as in a proper manner, indicating that natural environments are relatively stable systems. The living environment of each ethnic group, being the result of human transformation but not a pure natural environment, is of dual natures. Naturally, it is highly stable just like the natural environment. Socially, it requires constant maintenance by people who can make it usable for man for a long period of time if the maintenance is done properly or who may cause disastrous results by poor maintenance or damage for other reasons. However, even disastrous results, such as the breaking of a dam, desertification of a land, or pasture degradation, are recoverable to some extent by human efforts. On condition of a successful recovery and proper maintenance that follows, the environment can still remain stable continuously and be made usable by man for a duration that usually lasts as long as the relevant culture does.

Ethnic cultures are relatively stable systems that can also continue for a long period in a relatively stable condition. Traditional cultures that coexist in the world will have no problem lasting stably from hundreds to thousands of years. For instance, language (modern Chinese) - a fundamental cultural feature of modern ethnic Han nationality, has lasted at least about one thousand years stably. Some of the customary traditions of the ancient ethnic Hans are hard to find nowadays. One example is "Cold Food Festival" that was constantly talked about in ancient literature but is not celebrated any more among modern Han people. However, enough evidences have proved that a lot of festivals being celebrated now by ethnic Hans have been passed down from hundreds or even thousands of years ago. Similarly, other elements in the Han culture are able to last stably for quite a long period of time. The same is true for the cultures of ethnic minorities in Guizhou. "Jump Flowers", an ethnic Miao tradition, was mentioned in Lao Xue An Biji (Notes Made in the Hut of an Old Scholar) of Lu You of the Southern Song Dynasty. The wax printing, a popular traditional fabric-dyeing technique in the ethnic Buyi and Miao regions was recorded in detail by Zhu Fu of the Southern Song Dynasty in his book titled Ximan Cong Xiao (A Collection of Stories about Barbarians Living inYuanjiang river basin to the west of Dongting Lake). The ethnic Yis have had their own writing system for at least six hundred years. In short, simply based on the information from the ancient literature of the Han nationality, the cultural elements of these ethnic groups have lasted hundreds or even more than one thousand years.

The state power, on the other hand, is quite different. It is a product of social conflicts and can change dramatically with the change in the strength of social groups, international situation, and the need in administrative management. Adjustments of lesser intensity and scale happen all the time. Laws and policies made by states are prone to constant change. They are constantly revised, supplemented or replaced by new ones. It is fair to say that of the three elements in a xiang, this is the one that is the easiest to change and lasts stably for the shortest period of time.

Specific cross-xiang economic activities are subject to the restraints by the degree of stability of the above three elements. The varying duration of stable continuation of the three elements determines that the duration of the restraining force applied by them is different. Economic operations across different xiangs happen all the time. As each specific cross-xiang project is run by financially capable individuals or organizations, who, in a market economy, focus on recovering costs and gaining profit within the shortest time possible. Therefore, the cross-xiang projects inevitably contradict with the three elements in terms of the duration each of them lasts. For instance, if a project involves the change of natural environment, or conflicts with the traditional culture of the ethnic group, or a stability before the project turns profitable cannot be ensured by relevant policies, such a project will almost be certain to encounter difficulties, which will restrain the smooth operation of or even derail the project. How to ensure to keep the background of operation stable, effectively prevent unfavorable barriers, and ensure the project's ability to maximize profits at the least cost possible before the project is complete is the second topic the book is going to discuss.

Both the ecologic niche and the traditional culture of an ethnic group are extremely complex systems, which consist of numerous component factors. The change to any single factor is usually not influential enough to bring significant changes to the living environment or the traditional culture. Such changes, if any, are often very limited in intensity and usually have an entanglement effect, namely, the change in one factor often trigger other dependent factors to change to various extent. It tends to further complicate cross-xiang operations. For the purpose of making the operation smooth, we often need to bring changes to some factors in the traditional culture or living environments. However, due to the entanglement effect, such changes are likely to result in unfavorable changes to other factors, catching the project off guard in unexpected difficulties. Chapter Six of the book will present a discussion in detail with real examples.

Specific cross-xiang activities are different in that they are often simple operations without causing destructive repercussions to the constituent elements of the living environment or the traditional culture of the ethnic groups involved. If rice cultivation is to be promoted among ethnic groups who have never had such an experience, it causes changes to the water supply or land leveling, and culturally promotes and popularizes the relevant cultivation technologies or brings changes to the mode of production. In no circumstances will this affect the climate of the living environment, nor will it result in significant changes to the ethics and morals. Compared with the living environment and traditional culture of the ethnic groups involved, cross-xiang projects are often carried out suddenly in a concentrated manner that brings shocking effect, while the living environment or traditional culture of the ethnic groups concerned tends to respond passively, or demonstrate inertia in their stable continuity. In most cases, changes made to part of the living environment or traditional culture by cross-xiang operations are temporary and are likely to go away once the operations end. To maximize the efficiency of cross-xiang operations in a consistent manner, considerations must be given to the changeability of the parts in the living environment and traditional culture to be impacted by the operations, namely the after-change stability. It is an equally challenging research topic. The third mission of this book is to help the readers fully and craftily make use of the strength already gained in the cross-xiang operations, and identify the best breakthrough points to ensure the long-term and consistent efficiency of the projects.

Natural environments are the evolutionary products of the earth, not subject to the will of mankind. However, all human economic activities depend on natural environments. People can only search from the natural environments for the place to live and grow, select by elimination the objects to process and use, and avoid the natural elements unfavorable to them to ensure economic success. In other words, natural environments impact human activities in a comprehensive but unconscious way, while human beings conduct economic activities with an aim of achieving our goals by smartly searching for and making use of cracks in the mighty natural environment at the cost of small energy input. It is doomed to be a hard-fought battle between small and massive energy, and between consciousness and unconsciousness.

The living environment and traditional culture of any ethnic group are created and constructed by this ethnic group for the purpose of its own subsistence and development. The continuation, development and evolution of such living environment and traditional culture are driven solely by the need for subsistence of this particular ethnic group, but not by that of other ethnic groups. As economic activities across different cultures, cross-xiang operations have to face such a grave reality: they have to concurrently deal with two or more living environments and cultural systems of different propensity in continuation, development and evolution, which are not tailored to the needs of the operators of cross-xiang activities. In this sense, people who run cross-xiang economic activities will have to search for a foothold in totally different living environment systems and cultural systems and learn how to smartly make use of the innate traits of these cultural systems to pave the way for the success of their operations. In the meantime, they have to take into account the innate traits of all the relevant xiangs to ensure that the economic activities are compatible with the living environments and cultural systems without disrupting their normal continuation.

The living environment and culture of each ethnic group are shaped and constructed by the persistent efforts of all members in generations according to the actual needs for the continuation and expansion of this ethnic group. The energy input by the ethnic group for the completion of the shaping and construction is huge and exceeds the amount of energy any individual or organization within the group is capable of controlling. It is therefore unwise for any individual or organization to attempt to counter the living environment system or cultural system the related ethnic group is exposed to. It is advisable for these individuals and organizations to resort to their subjective initiatives to seek auspicious and avoid ominous factors in the existing living environment and cultural system of the ethnic group so as to transform the objective restraints into facilitating conditions.

The living environment system and cultural system of any ethnic group are subject to development. However, such developments are not dependent on the will of individuals or organizations running the operations, but rather on the social need of the entire ethnic group. In other words, the development of the living environment system and cultural system of the related ethnic group usually does not coincide with the intention of the operators of cross-xiang activities. Lower level of coincidence tends to create greater barriers in the operation of these activities and is hardly removable by power-fight. Only through the clever use of the restraints, or by actions purposefully driving the direction of the development can we have a chance of transforming the restrictive factors into driving forces. Unlike an objective natural environment that comes into existence without any human intervention, the living environment and culture of an ethnic group are an outcome of conscious human activities. However, the consciousness does not come from the individuals or organizations running cross-xiang economic activities but rather from the social need of the entire ethnic group.

By contrast, operators of cross-xiang economic activities have a high level of flexibility and motility when it comes to the selection of the mode of operation. They have an infinite number of options to choose from when facing the existing natural environment, the living environment and culture of the related ethnic groups. Instead of competing with these objective existences by sheer force, the operators may consolidate the forces available to them in an extremely rapid speed and launch a sudden strike on the natural environment, the living environment and culture system of the ethnic group. To attack the right spot may prompt these factors to evolve to the benefit of the operators, who can wield the power in their possession and directly convert their will into operable actions. Such an ability of quick and direct response is not a property of the living environment and culture of the related ethnic group. Natural environments respond to cross-xiang operations passively with ambiguous goals, while the living environment and culture of an ethnic group, although able to make active responses to a certain extent, do not target individuals or groups in operation but act intuitively to adjust itself to ensure the subsistence and continuation of the entire ethnic group.

The fourth mission of this book is to discuss and uncover how to develop the flexibility, concentricity, and pertinence in cross-xiang operations run by individuals or organizations to achieve anticipated targets with the strategy of winning with less resources, fewer people or lighter weight.

In essence, all human economic activities will inevitably disturb the objective natural environments. Cross-xiang operations, while presenting no exception, distinguish themselves from the others in that they not only disturb the natural environments the operators are familiar with but also disturb the natural environments where other ethnic groups live. Such a disturbance, although a likely result of the input of a small amount of energy, often produces grave consequences that disrupt future economic activities and is therefore not negligible. Excessive reclamation and cultivation of lands, for example, tend to trigger massive landslides or soil erosion, leading to desertification that turns these lands into barren fields forever. A natural environment subjected to human disturbances may recover after a considerable duration of time that is incomparably longer than the cycle of human economic activities. To ensure the sustainability of human economic activities, we must not wait for the disturbed environment to regain vitality naturally. Instead, a strategy must be put in place at the time when people are planning economic activities. A conscious preservation of natural environments while conducting economic activities is the only way for human beings to keep such activities last steadily. As cross-xiang operations, in particular, necessitate the ability to deal with unfamiliar natural environments, it is extremely critical that a thorough consideration be given to the extremely long-lasting cycle of the recovery of natural environments.

The consequences that result from human activities on natural environments can be disastrous, the degrees of which vary in different regions due to the varying nature of projects. The natural environments in some regions are so fragile that once disrupted are difficult to recover even after a long period of time. For instance, the river valley of Panjiang River in Guizhou Province, characterized with steep slopes composed of limestone rocks with a thin layer of soil on the surface, easily loses water and soil in large areas from land reclamation and cultivation, and is hardly recoverable in a long period of time afterwards. The huge area of exposed rocky mountains we are seeing now in this region is a result of such activities. Different modes of economic activities disrupt natural environments in different level of intensity. The upper reaches of Wujiang River in Guizhou Province was inhabited by ethnic Yi people who lived on animal husbandry before mid-Qing Dynasty and no massive water and soil erosion was reported despite of the steep mountain slopes and loose soils. After the ethnic Hans in large number emigrated into this region and started reclaiming and cultivating the lands from mid-Qing Dynasty, the region became well-known for severe water and soil loss. As cross-xiang operations are carried out in unfamiliar natural environments, they will not be successful if the locations and projects don't fit the environments.

The living environments and traditional cultures of every ethnic groups are enclosed and complete systems that are repellent to external factors. Meanwhile, they can recover at a rapid speed after external factors are removed, usually within years or tens of years. In addition, these living environments and cultures have the ability of self-adjustment and adaptation. External factors are processed, transformed and absorbed to become part of an adjusted yet complete new system. Similar to other economic activities, cross-xiang operations must be carried out in a natural environment on the foundation of a special culture. The difference lies in the fact that cross-xiang operations concern two or more living environments and traditional cultures at the same time, and consideration should be given to the compatibility between the living environments and cultures of all ethnic groups concerned for the operations to be successful. In the event that a cross-xiang project disrupts the living environment or culture of the ethnic group concerned, it faces two options. First, try to avoid the disruption by selecting the least impactful operational practices. Second, proactively direct the living environment and traditional cultural elements concerned to trigger their self-adjustment and adaptation so as to create a social background conducive to the operations.

Comparatively, operators of cross-xiang activities have the most active ability of self-recovery and can recover in the shortest time possible. The last theoretical mission of this book is to discuss and find out how cross-xiang operators can detect the favorable elements in the living environments and cultural systems of the related ethnic groups and, by way of quick response and self-recovery, transform the unfavorable elements into acceptable elements through self-adjustment and turn the restrictive factors into driving forces.

Through the discussion of the above five questions, this book aims to provide a set of guidelines and operating principles for the economic development in the ethnic minority regions, help these minority groups achieve the modernization targets and catch up with the advanced level in other parts of China by taking advantage of the favorable international and domestic environments and putting the limited financial and material resources to best use. As is pointed out in the prior section of the book, cross-xiang operation is a special form of economic activity which exists around the world. It is therefore our hope that this book may offer some assistance in facilitating the interaction between China and the world, and in rationally and effectively learning from the successful experiences of other nations in economic development.

The research in cross-xiang operation is not only about economics, but also relates to the traditional cultures of all ethnic groups concerned, state laws and policies, as well as the objective natural environments where economic activities are exposed to. To accomplish such a mission requires a new interdisciplinary subject - economic anthropology. The theoretical and practical discussions included in this book are conducted under the guidance of this emerging academic discipline.

III Means toward the Ends

The goal of uncovering the laws in economic activities across different cultures and proposing corresponding solutions in this book can not be achieved without referencing the knowledge accumulated and theories constructed in this field, which traditionally fall into the category of cultural anthropology in the West, also known as social anthropology in some countries. The book focuses a key part of its research on economic activities. An academic discipline devoted to the research of human economic behaviors and the laws in economic operations is economics. Traditional economics targeted the economic activities in the developed countries in the West. This book, however, not only studies economic activities in the industrialized world but also those conducted by and between non-industrialized nationalities. Such a distinction in the research objects requires that the application of general principles of economics must be defined specifically to further clarify which of them can or cannot be applied in the researches of this book.

The more direct and relevant theoretical foundation for this book whose researches relate to both cultural anthropology and economics is the interdisciplinary subject of these two, namely the economic anthropology developed since 1930s.[①] Thus, we will first give a brief introduction on the history and fundamental theoretical framework of economic anthropology as well as our evaluation on the current theoretical system of this academic discipline. This book is not about pure theoretical discussions but rather about how economic anthropology can be put into practice. We hope that a

① Zhongnan University of Economics and Law, comp., *Lexicon of Economic Science* (Economic Science Press, December 1987), 359.

set of working principles in economic activities may be produced from our research efforts that offer guidance to relevant administrative authorities, social organizations or individuals when engaging in cross-xiang operations. For this purpose, we also need to tell the readers of the book our methodologies in carrying out the research, from collection of materials to sorting of data, as well as the basis for reaching conclusions, so that the readers can understand in what circumstances or scopes these principles have pragmatic values and significance.

Cultural anthropology is a subject of social science with a long history and has lasted more than one century and a half since its founding. It was first introduced into China over 70 years ago in 1920s. Originally, the human economic activity was not its primary focus but a side topic when other social issues of ethnic groups were discussed. Lewis Henry Morgan (1818-1881), the most celebrated anthropologist whose research mainly focused on family and marriage and origin of private property, only talked about issues related to human economic activities such as inventions in technologies and improvement in tools when he attempted to classify his research contents into different stages.① Researches like this cannot meet the requirements in cross-xiang operations and Morgan was no exception among the anthropologists of his time. Edward Burnett Tylor (1832-1917), an equally well-known anthropologist for instance, was especially interested in the characteristics of natural religions and issues in their development and evolution. Although some human economic activities were discussed in his famous work *Primitive Culture*, they were so fragmented and unsystematic that cannot be used as a complete theoretical foundation and systematic materials in the research of cross-xiang economic activities. ②

As a distinct characteristic, early cultural anthropology viewed "contemporary primitive peoples" or "contemporary backward peoples" as the objects of their studies, who were defined, by the early researchers, as the non-Western ethnic groups spreading across the vast territories in Asia, Africa and Latin America. According to the researchers at the time, these ethnic groups were at the stage tantamount to the early stage in the development of the Western peoples, and the study of these ethnic groups might help explain

① Lewis Henry Morgan, *Ancient Society*, trans. Dongchun Yang et al. (The Commercial Press, August 1977), 10-12.

② Edward Burnett Tylor, *Primitive Culture*, trans. Shusheng Lian (Shanghai Literature and Art Publishing House, August 1992), 25-72.

how man has evolved to the level of the Western peoples. They were believers of the theory that all the ethnic groups in their studies would, in the near future, abandon their traditional culture and draw close to the Western culture under the influence and guidance of the Western civilization. As a result, never in their research methodologies did they give any thought to the issue of a long-term coexistence between the Western and Non-Western peoples, nor did they think of how to construct and maintain an equal and mutually-beneficial relationship across different peoples in the West and other regions. Of course, researches as congenitally deficient as these do not come in handy in our research of cross-xiang operations.

Cultural anthropology inherited such a tradition when it was first introduced into China. Cai Yuanpei, a famous scholar in China, adopted such a methodology and focused his research on the collation and analysis of Chinese ancient books that, he believed, reflected the social and cultural phenomena in the early stage of the Chinese culture and revealed the history of the development of the Chinese culture. [①]The thought of Cai has had such a profound impact on the academia in China that even after the founding of the People's Republic of China, quite a number of scholars still believe that the ethnic groups in the border regions in China that lag behind economically will become equally prosperous and affluent as the developed regions and the ignorant and background situation as a result of class oppression will be gone completely after no more than tens of years of "leap-forward development" under the superior socialist system. This kind of thinking logic is without any doubt against that in the research in this book. As a matter of fact, despite the progress made in the ethnic minority regions in China's border regions, it remains a long-lasting and difficult problem for these regions to catch up with the developed regions and the tremendous efforts we have put in solving it in the past forty-plus years have not made it any easier. Undeniably, the economic gap between the ethnic minority regions and Central China will haunt us in the foreseeable future. It is based on this fact that this book discusses the issue of cross-xiang economic activities and attempts to seek and offer strategies.

Another point that calls for our attention is that, when early cultural anthropologists in the West analyzed the economic activities across different

① Qiwang Hu, "Yuanpei Cai and Ethnology", *Ethnological Study* no. 1 , comp. CUAES (The Ethnic Publishing House, August 1981), 251-260.

ethnic groups, they viewed their own ethnic group as the zenith in the development of nationalities and their ways of economic life as the fate of all peoples in the world. For that reason, the faster non-Western ethnic groups draw close to the Western economy, the higher the level of their economic life. Likewise, to say no to the Western economic life will keep them in the backward and ignorant state forever. Such a perception will naturally lead to the belief that the modernization of non-Western ethnic groups is a process of westernizing their economic activities. People mistakenly believe that such an understanding is true in principle to all ethnic groups, therefore economic activities across ethnic groups must be dealt with by the existing economic concepts and principles prevalent in the West including currency, market, credit, securities etc. Such a research methodology is reflected in China as well where a significant number of Chinese scholars believe that developing the ethnic minority regions in China is to assimilate them with the ethnic Han culture, which has profoundly impacted our policies when the People's Republic of China was first established. Despite the progress we have made in certain degrees, the tremendous efforts we put in many years in the past only produced the disappointing fact that the economic gap between many ethnic minorities and Han nationality widened rather than narrowed. It prompts us to examine whether such a one-way and centralized "evolution and development model" reflects the essence of things. Due to the suspiciousness of the "one-way and centralized" model, we have chosen to conduct the research in cross-xiang operations from the other perspective, a "multi-xiang and diversified" approach.

After World War I, the three traditional schools in the research of cultural anthropology have been put to test by factual challenges. In the 1920s to 1930s, the British colonial empire collapsed; The wave of independence swept the continents in Asia, Africa and Latin America and newly independent countries chose a development path different from that in the Western countries; Socialist ideology prevailed across the globe and the emerging socialist countries walked on the road different from the Western economic development. The three traditional schools did not seem to reflect the reality. Consequently, some insightful cultural anthropologists redirected their research toward the economic activities in the non-Western peoples. Bronislaw Malinowski (1884-1942) was one of these anthropologists whose research was the most significant. After conducting a profound research on the economic activities by the indigenous people on the islands in South Pacific, he discovered "kula ring" exchange and discussed the ways of distributing products among the indigenous people.[1] His work was of a pioneering nature in economic anthropology. Another pioneering scholar was Marcel Mauss (1872-1950) whose research on the relationship between Eskimo's seasonal economic activities and the seasonality in social organizations was ground-breaking and important in the development in economic anthropology.[2] However, the term was coined by neither of them but Karl Polanyi, a Hungarian who dedicated his entire life to the research of this field. In his early years, Karl Polanyi was a political activist and took up key post in the Hungarian government. His academic career started with the research in economics and economic history and was once an editor of the *Austrian Economist*. He moved to Britain in 1930s and engaged in worker's movement while in the meantime propagated the thoughts in economics and economic history that he understood to the British workers. Although his economic theories were deviant to many traditional economists, they profoundly influenced the British working class and made him a highly acclaimed figure. It was based on his prior work that he put forth a series of theories polarized from those of his predecessors. He thought that the creation and development of the form of the British economy was a result of markets, which was not applicable to the ethnic groups in the non-market economies. His first book *The Great Transform*ation was a sheer reflection of such economic thoughts. He argued that the Western economic system was substantially different from the non-Western economic systems, which completely contradicted the "Formalism" in the classical economics and was later labeled as "Substantivism" in economic anthropology by the academia.

After World War II, Polanyi moved to the United States and had devoted his time to the study of ethnography at Columbia University until he passed away in 1964. During this time, his economics thoughts started to mingle tightly with the traditional ethnographic research, giving rise to the systematic theoretical framework of the "Substantivism" school in economic anthropology. In his later works (such as *Trade and Markets in the Early Empires* and *Economy and Civilization),* Polanyi, based his research on the materials previously collected from the indigenous people in West Polynesia,

[1] Zelin Wu, eds., Lexicon *of Anthropology,* s.v. "Kula Trade" (Shanghai Lexicographical Publishing House, May 1991), 587

[2] Ban Yan, *Introduction to Ethnography* (China Social Sciences Press, May 1991), 79-80

pointed out that these people behaved not by the principle of "selfishness" but by "reciprocity" and "redistribution". Markets could not grow in such a society. The "selfishness" Polanyi was using referred to the motives in the market operations in modern Western industrialized societies. He pointed out that the market economy was an exceptional form of human economy, only limited to a restricted number of Western and industrialized societies. Such a form of economy was an economic system composed of individual markets, and was controlled by market prices formed in the trade activities. Such a system was capable of organizing all economic activities in the society in normal situations. However, it was nonetheless existent from the ancient time but was constructed by the fiscal and financial authorities of the government. Therefore, it was by no means the only standard in mankind's economic form but rather a product of mankind's development in history.

Polanyi stated that things that were without any doubt treated as commodities in the Western economic form, such as land, labor work, currency etc., were not necessarily so in the non-Western societies. In such societies, land did not have a monetary value and could be used freely by any individual. To offer manual labor was not in exchange for economic compensation but, in many cases, was to meet the needs for emotional bonding among people, or for reciprocity. The currencies, according to Polanyi, were never heard of in many ethnic groups in non-Western societies. They were made an inseparable part of market commodities in the Western societies by people as well. The readers of this book will find as they read on that these basic facts that Polanyi described are now still commonplace in the ethnic groups in Guizhou.

Polanyi also pointed out that the currency under the Western market economies was merely a part of the culture and was, in essence, quite similar to the language or measurement in the ethnic cultures. The currency itself did not have a supernatural power but was made an intermediary in market trade activities by financial institutions or administrative authorities. Even the price of that intermediary was determined by traditional cultures[1]. This should call for our special attention. The exchange rate between gold and silver that were used as standard currencies in the Western world is well documented, which showed different peoples had different rates. For example, before the

[1] Zhongnan University of Economics and Law, comp., *Lexicon of Economic Science* (Economic Science Press, December 1987), 211-221.

founding of the People's Republic of China, the exchange rate between gold and silver in China was much smaller than that in the international market. China's currency system was based on a silver standard while that in the international market was on a gold standard, resulting in the situation of "devaluation of silver against gold" that cost China's national bourgeoisie tremendously when importing foreign raw materials and equipment. Consequently, Polanyi opposed without any reservation the idea of absolutizing the Western currency system. He insisted that the Western currency system was the product of a certain stage in history and the value of currency in economic activities should only apply to the peoples in the Western world. ①

Based on the above three fundamental perceptions, Polanyi believed that between the West and non-industrialized peoples in other regions, especially those in Oceania, Africa and America, the distribution of products and means of organizing production had nothing to do with markets but were largely carried out in the forms of reciprocal gift-giving and redistribution. In these ethnic groups, ritual exchange of things on regular basis, gift-giving between relatives and mutual help in offering labor work played a decisive role. Even the collective consumption of some items in religious events was of significance in organizing economic activities. Subsequently, he further pointed out that the dominant market economy in the West as well as the economic features derived from the market economy differed from the economic lives of these ethnic groups not only in forms but also in types. Polanyi proposed that human beings exchanged products in three modes, namely by reciprocity, redistribution and market, which after a sharp comparison by Polanyi, reflected a few basically different social means in the distribution of social materials. Although Polanyi sometimes gave the impression that any society was dominated by one of the three modes, his followers in economic anthropology found out that the three modes could co-exist in a single society, and reciprocal and redistributive modes might be universal but a society might likely be dominated by one mode and supplemented by the other two.② Therefore, it is impossible to engage economic lives among different peoples by simplistic means. Furthermore,

① *Concise Dictionary of Social Sciences*, 2nd ed., s.v. "gold standard system" 654, "silver standard system" 936 (Shanghai Lexicographical Publishing House, December 1984)

② Roger M. Keesing, *Cultural Anthropology: A Contemporary Perspective* (Taiwan: Chuliu Publisher), 476.

we should not impose the Western market economics theory and concepts on the peoples of non-market economy. Polanyi even exaggeratingly alerted that such an approach would cause catastrophic consequences to human beings.

Our personal experiences echoed these perceptions and analyses by Polanyi. It was not uncommon in our fieldwork that we received extremely generous hospitality and free services by local people with unproportionate compensation or no compensation at all from us. Such behaviors are hardly explainable by the market principles of exchange at equal values. As a persuasive case, below is an account of some researchers. In 1988 when an American anthropologist came to Xijiang Township of Leishan County in southeast of Guizhou to conduct ethnographic survey, she was repeatedly reminded by her company that the unsophisticated local Miao people might not accept monetary compensation but might, in special occasions, appreciate receiving some gifts. This was proved in her later encounters with the locals. In the visit she paid to a small village of about seven or eight households, she was treated with utmost hospitality by the villagers who received a miserly gift of a few fruit candies from her. The value of given and received items were so different that was hardly explainable by the market principles. It surprised both her and our researchers. The discussions of cross-xiang operations in this book are extracted with our similar emotional experiences as foundation. It is thus natural if some of our points of view coincide with those of Polanyi's.

In addition to Polanyi, George Dalton and Melville Jean Herskovits were also proponents of such views. Herskovits developed on the Cultural Relativism, the thought of his teacher Franz Boas, a well-acclaimed American anthropologist. From the perspective of Cultural Relativism, Herskovits acknowledged that the market economy in the West and other forms of economy in non-Western world each had unique value to their own people, but different forms of economy could not be imposed on all peoples nor be replaced by each other. His thoughts were apparently inherited from and developed on *The Mind of Primitive Man* by Franz Boas. ①

It is our opinion that the similarities in their academic conclusions were related to the personal background of these scholars. Malinowski was born in Poland and Polanyi came from Hungary, both growing up in an unorthodox

① C.A.Tokarev (USSR), *A History of Foreign Ethnography*, trans. Zhengfang Tang (China Social Sciences Publishing House, December 1983), 300-303.

non-Western economic environment. Herskovits spent a significant part of his time in the study of black people and had a profound understanding of the black ethnic peoples in Africa and the Caribbean region. As a result, they did not have any biased predisposition toward forms of non-Western economies, nor would they blindly agree with the other Western economists. With our fieldwork getting deeper, it becomes easier for us to understand the profound reasons of such an academic propensity.

The school contrary to "Substantivism" is labeled as "Formalism" and is represented by Captain James Cook and Edward E. LeClair The theory dictates that our economic components (components of economic lives of the developed peoples in the West, namely the industrial type of economic lives), such as capital, profit, interest and salary, can be applied to all societies. The "formalists" insisted that the economies in a primitive culture and the market economies only differed in form but not in substance. They argued that the differences pointed out by Polanyi were mere exaggerations and did not reflect the substance of human economic lives. Furthermore, the incompatibility between the market economy and non-market economy was the result of an incomplete market economy in the West and a universally applicable economic system could be built by making adjustment and improvement to the current market economy. The "formalist" points of view were by and large influenced by the traditional economic theories and are highly influential in today's academic circle in the West. However, the "formalists" are themselves profoundly influenced by the "substantivists" although they vehemently opposed the thoughts of the later. For instance, they admitted that the Western market economy was incomplete and was in urgent need of adjustment and improvement, which must be made by referencing the forms of economy in non-Western regions. In a nutshell, "formalists" did not deny the differences pointed out by "substantivists" but only felt reluctant to accept the sharp words of the substantivists. Such a moderate disposition was especially evident in the works of LeClair. On the one hand, LeClair believed that an economic theory universally applicable to all ethnic groups in the world could be created. On the other hand, he admitted objectively that the economic theory prevailing in the West was built in a special industrial background and was therefore incomplete. He further claimed that the establishment of a universal economic theory would not be successful without reference to the existing forms of economy in non-market economies. The forms of economy listed by Polanyi, according to LeClair, were merely special forms of the market economy in the West. However, special forms also demand thorough discussion and study. In this sense, there is nothing wrong with Polanyi focusing his research on these special forms.

To further elaborate on the fact that "substantivists" and "formalists" were not as opposing in substance as they looked, we feel necessary to mention Raymond Firth who was a student of Malinowski. Firth was born in New Zealand and later moved to England to teach in University of London. He focused his study mainly in the indigenous peoples in Oceania and Southeast Asia, but he diverted himself from the structural functionalism and shifted toward the research in human behaviors.[①] In economic anthropology, Firth was more of a proponent of "formalism". He argued that the neo-classic mode that dominated the Western world also applied to the economies of an agricultural society, or even more ancient economies. We have reason to believe that his academic thoughts must have something to do with his personal background as well as the era in which he lived. In the heyday of his research activities, the Western world entered the post-WWII era of rapid economic development, which led Firth into the misperception that the Western market economy was rational and universally applicable.

While the debate between "substantivism" and "formalism" in economic anthropology lasted, scholars of new generations kept adding new evidences and materials that supplemented these two opposing views in varied degrees, and resulted in a tendency of them drawing closer. Such a tendency is reflected in the following statement made by Sahlins, a famous contemporary anthropologist as well as the advocate of dual-phase evolution. He said that substantivists were correct in spirit but often made mistakes in practice; They analyzed systems with such an asinine Reletivism that tended to disguise the people's motives and make them incomprehensible. In addition, they sometimes deny the rationality of the people being studied. Formalists, although correct about rationality, often misperceived the systematic structure and value propensity, and misunderstood how economic behaviors are conducted through these structures and value propensities. [②] Sahlins'

① Raymond Firth, *Human Types,* trans. Xiaotong Fei (The Commercial Press, January 1991, Beijing revised edition), 100-113.

② Roger M. Keesing, *Cultural Anthropology: A Contemporary Perspective* (Taiwan: Chuliu Publisher), 488.

statement was appropriate in revealing the pros and cons of the opposing views, but needs revision. In order to analyze cross-xiang economic activities in Guizhou, we feel necessary to get to the reasons why the two schools polarized so that we can make correct choice in our research.

The diverging views were caused by a variety of complicated reasons. In terms of research objects, "substantivists" mostly targeted non-Western ethnic groups in Asia, Africa and Latin America, while the vast majority of proponents of "formalism" were educated systematically with economic theories in the West, and engaged in a long time in the research of economies of the peoples in the West. Their research in other ethnic groups from the non-Western regions was less profound than "substantivists". In terms of the duration of research, "substantivists" employed a synchronic method of research compared to a diachronic method used by "formalists". Cultural discrepancies in cross-ethnic groups that looked prominent and conspicuous to synchronic researchers tended to be overlooked by diachronic researchers. From the academic origin, "substantivists", for the most part, inherited the tradition of cultural anthropology while "formalists" built their theories more on the tradition of economics, especially the tradition from neo-formalism in modern economics. Cultural anthropologists long restrained their research in small-scale communities while by comparison, economists often focused on the economic activities that concerned the entire society. In terms of the goal of research, "substantivists" emphasized that the non-Western ethnic groups and their economic activities did not follow the laws in economy in the West and thus should be treated differently. In the opposite, "formalists" were predispositioned toward the view that the economic activities conducted by the non-Western peoples and the prevailing laws in economy in the West were innately bridgeable, for the purpose of seeking theoretical grounds for the developed countries to carry out global economic activities. Different goals called for diverse focuses. The two schools also differed in research methodology. "Subtantivists" were mostly masterful micro researchers but "formalists" were usually proficient in macro analyses. It is true that all economic activities in the world are essentially in common, which come down to the social activities of exchanging energy and materials between man and nature. This justifies a macro perspective. On the other hand, economic activities of each ethnic group are regulated by their specific cultures. Different cultures determine the substantial differences in economic lives, which appropriates a micro perspective. The topic that faces us is how to integrate the two to attach importance to the substantial uniformity but not to overlook the diversity, so as to drive the prosperity of mankind.

The purpose of our research in this book is to find the best measures in cross-xiang activities so as to promote the shared prosperity among ethnic minority groups in Guizhou. Compared to specific economic activities that last for a very limited duration, the three components of xiang usually last for an extremely extended period of time. In addition, the amount of energy specific economic activities are able to mobilize is far less than that contained in the three components. Therefore, a successful cross-xiang operation does not come from any attempt to change the properties of any component of xiang to suit the need of the project. This indicates that the substantivist perspective must guide our practices in carrying out cross-xiang activities, acknowledging, understanding and taking advantage of such differences across peoples. However, by studying cross-xiang operations, we do not intend to fix the economic lives of ethnic groups in Guizhou to the current level. Instead, it is our hope that our research can lead to their integration into the national socialist market economy, assist them in securing a fair and equal position in economic activities across the country by fully making use of their traditional advantages. To achieve such a goal requires that we discern and acknowledge the substantial coherence between economic activities of ethnic Han regions and those in ethnic minority regions, thus it is necessary for us to accept the rationality at the core of "formalism" from the long-term and overall development perspective. This book has employed a research methodology that combines the two schools in economic anthropology by developing on the rational and abandoning the defective, to reveal the walkable path for the ethnic groups in Guizhou to an economic and social prosperity.

Such an approach has led to the divergence in this book such as material collection, data analysis and drawing conclusions, from both the "substantivism" and "formalism" but at the same time absorbing the merits of the two. When collecting materials, unlike the "substantivists" who focus only on the surveyed communities and attempt to collect all the facts they think are characteristic, we, on top of the cultural and natural characteristics in the surveyed communities, never overlook the impact national laws and policies have on the communities, as well as the impact China's reform, open policy and the transformation into a socialist market economy have on these communities. What has been put at the top priority with regards to material collection is how the surveyed communities have been acculturated by the national trend of development, which coincides with the practices of "formalists".

A great deal of data this book uses come from state statistics. Given the fact that many economic activities in the ethnic minority regions in Guizhou are not conducted via markets and are not incorporated in state statistics, and some are even buried in customs, ritual ceremonies and religious events, we have been extremely cautious and rarely cited data that have not be verified by us. Such a methodology is in line with the reletivism principle that proponents of "substantivists" embraced. In the meantime, we believe that any factual data coming from real economic activities of the ethnic groups are, subject to some data conversion, certainly reflectable in the statistics results. Such a methodology is similar to those employed by "formalist" researchers.

We have adhered to the following three principles when drawing a conclusion: First, never indiscriminately copy the laws of economics believed to exist in the ethnic Han regions in the ethnic minority groups. Second, never absolutize the current modes of economic activities in ethnic minority regions. Third, never treat economic activities across ethnic groups as simple as transferring equipment, technicians and products but rather a process of introducing, transforming and absorbing.

To accomplish this mission, we focused our fieldwork primarily on the 26 ethnic Buyi and Miao communities in Anshun region and the Southwest Guizhou Autonomous Prefecture. We distributed questionnaires to 11 county-level and over 20 township enterprises, and collected back 108 completed questionnaires from these target enterprises, 64 questionnaires on "primitive" agriculture, 89 questionnaires on ethnic people's propensity toward commerce, 380 questionnaires on school education and 12 questionnaires on forestry. We also received help from students of Guizhou Minzu University, who took their summer vacation in 1993 to conduct surveys across the entire province and received 324 completed questionnaires of the above types. In addition, we did 24 interviews and subsequently finished original survey reports. It is based on all these materials combined with the published written materials that this book is completed.

IV Xiangji Operation: Fundamental Concepts

We have already discussed the fundamental concept and components of *xiang* in Section II of this chapter. As *xiangji (cross-xiang) operations* are special economic activities, to facilitate the analyses and discussions that follow, we need to first give a precise definition of cross-xiang operation, and then clarify some fundamental concepts related to cross-xiang operations. Lastly, we must give a thorough analysis of the relationship between non-economic restraints and cross-xiang operations.

As cross-xiang operations are in essence economic activities across xiangs, the operations must concern two or more xiangs, whose characteristics will impact the result of these operations at a level not to be neglected. The research of cross-xiang operations is about finding out how these impacting factors determine the success or failure of economic activities and the effective strategies to ensure the success. What has been discussed in this book only applies to cross-xiang economic activities. Before we start, we need to clarify on the differences between cross-xiang and non-cross-xiang operations so that the readers know where and how to apply the contents in the discussion.

It looks self-explanatory what distinguishes cross-xiang from non-cross-xiang operations. In real economic cases, however, people are faced with complex and changing social environments that tend to blur the boundary between cross-xiang and non-cross-xiang operations. The following examples may provide some insights to us. In the Ming Dynasty after ethnic Han people immigrated into Guizhou, two ways of subsistence started to emerge: the stationed army and immigrants under the control of the Ming Dynasty, and those who escaped from the control of Ming into the ethnic minority regions and lived under the patronage of local hereditary headmen. The former kept a Han lifestyle and cultural tradition while receiving material and technical supplies as well as political protection from the developed ethnic Han regions. As they usually lived in the regions inhabited by multi-ethnic groups, it was natural for them to interact economically with neighboring nationalities on frequent basis. As a result, trade and commercial markets gradually formed around their places of settlement, from which the ethnic Han residents engaged in extensive trade activities with other ethnic minority groups.[1] In the meantime, they hired local people for cultivation or family chores and thus maintained a close employment relationship with ethnic minority people.[2] Likewise, local hereditary headmen hired ethnic Han immigrants to be technicians, home tutors, etc. To settle down in the ethnic minority regions, many Han immigrants often acquired lands and forests previously owned by ethnic groups through purchase, lease, etc., and rent them out to local ethnic minority people. The latter then cultivated and harvested from these lands and paid rents to the Han landowners, who became newly emerged ethnic Han immigrant landowners.[3]

Things were different for those who escaped into the ethnic minority habitats without permission and severed all the ties with the Ming government and the ethnic Han regions in Central China. From then on, all their activities would not cross with the Han culture. Now under the control of local hereditary headmen, these Han immigrants paid taxes, assumed corvee tasks and were subject to the rules of the local rulers. Although they might have retained some Han culture such as speaking Han language, cultivating rice and keeping Han customs and habits, their ties with the ethnic Hans were nevertheless discontinued once and for all. From the perspective of the Ming Dynasty, these people did not exist anymore although some of the outstanding ones were placed on key administrative positions under the rule of the local hereditary headmen, such as Chen En and his son Chen Qiyu [4](in the position of Mukui[5]) under Shuixi Tusi in the late Ming Dynasty. They were the officials of the local regime, attended to the matters of the local ethnic groups and often contended the Ming government. In a nutshell, they were fully integrated in the economic life under the regulation of Tusi of ethnic Yi.

The comparison of the two scenarios reveals distinct differences. The former's subsistence and activities crossed two different cultures and

[1] *General Annals of Guizhou* (Jiajing, the Ming Dynasty) , in the collection of the library of Yunnan University

[2] Jizhong Shi et al. eds., *Veritable Records of the Ming Dynasty • A Compilation of Materials about Guizhou* (Guizhou People's Publishing House, December 1983)

[3] Zizhang Guo, *Records of Guizhou* (the Ming Dynasty), mimeographed edition, in the collection of Guizhou Provincial Library

[4] Mukui is an official rank in the administration of Tu Si (local hereditary headman) of Shuixi Yi ethnic group in Guizhou, equivalent to the third-rank official in the central government.

[5] Hongmo Yu, "Discussion and Proof of the Tombstone of Chen En, Shuixi Mukui of the Ming Dynasty," *Collection of Manuscripts in Guizhou*, no. 1 (1980).

subsequently, the economic activities between them and ethnic minority groups were of the cross-xiang nature. The livelihood of the latter, on the other hand, was entirely exposed in an ethnic minority culture and they had no direct interaction with ethnic Hans. Despite some of the Han cultural characteristics they retained, their economic activities were nothing but the internal matters within the ethnic minorities, and therefore were in the same xiang as the ethnic groups, excluding their economic activities from those of a cross-xiang nature. Whether the operators are separated from their original sphere of culture significantly distinguishes cross-xiang from non-cross-xiang operations.

Cross-xiang activities do not include individual actions either. In Guizhou's history of development, it was not unusual that many ethnic Hans or ethnic minority people migrated to the regions traditionally inhabited by other ethnic groups to make a living. In such a process, if the migrants discontinued their economic ties with the original culture and chose to adjust their economic activities to the new living environment and culture, their economic behaviors were not characterized by the cross-xiang nature, therefore could not be included in cross-xiang operations.

In the efforts to develop Guizhou in the Ming and Qing dynasties, quite a significant number of ethnic Hans moved to the settlement of Miao and Buyi peoples and gave birth to children and grandchildren, creating vast and powerful migrant groups. "Gaoshan Han" (ethnic Hans living in high mountainous regions)[①]in the counties such as Wangmo and Ceheng, for instance, whose ancestors migrated here without the government permission, live in the high mountainous regions right next to the *Tianba* (arable land by a river bank) inhabited by ethnic Buyi and are thus nicknamed. We have had contacts with some of them in the fieldwork. Although they have retained a distinctive Han dialect of western Sichuan, they can not tell when and where their forefathers came to live here, nor do they know if they have any relatives in their native places. They are now living in a region dominated by ethnic Buyi and have lost touch with ethnic Hans in cultural and economic

① "Gaoshan Han" (ethnic Hans who live in high mountainous places) is a term translated literarily from Buyi language in the fieldwork, referring specifically to the Han people who migrated into Buyi habitats in the Ming and Qing dynasties and have since chosen to live in high mountainous places seldom occupied by ethnic Buyi. The lifestyle of "Gaoshan Han" is similar to that of "Peng Min" (people who live in sheds) mentioned in the ancient records of the Qing Dynasty. They lived on growing dry crops. For more information, readers can refer to the notes about "Peng Min" in the *History of the Qing Dynasty*.

interaction. For the sake of subsistence, they have learned to closely interact with local Buyi people and imitate their ways of production and living so that they can co-exist harmoniously. For this reason, they have chosen to live in the places abandoned by ethnic Buyi and often hired by local Buyis as permanent or part-time laborers. As a matter of fact, "Gaoshan Han" implies the meaning of contempt and discrimination in local Buyi language. It is apparent that they have not come to the Buyi region to conduct economic activities based on a Han culture but rather have succumbed and adjusted their behaviors to suit the Buyi culture to survive. Therefore, their economic activities are not classified as cross-xiang operations. Examples like "Gaoshan Han" are easily found across Guizhou Province.

In the Qing Dynasty, Emperor Yongzheng took the measure to replace all local hereditary headmen with the officials sent by the central government (*gai tu wei liu*) in the ethnic Miao and Dong regions in southeast of Guizhou and established the so-called "Six Ting (an administrative level) of Xinjiang."[①] To crack down on the riots from the ethnic minority groups, army garrisons were widely built and massive Han immigrants were transferred into this region. These Han immigrants received extremely favorable treatments from the Qing regime and maintained close ties with their native places. They profited hugely from shipping and selling products made in the Han regions to the Miao and Dong regions but only saw their special political status and position disappear with the fall of the Qing Dynasty. The hatred toward and isolation of these Han people by the locals due to historical reasons drove the ones that were financially or politically advantaged back to the Han regions, leaving behind the lower-level servicemen who could not afford to leave but had to learn how to cope with the locals. Consequently, after more than half a century since Xinhai Revolution, they have been assimilated into the local ethnic groups. Although a smaller number of them insist that they are ethnic Hans, little has remained in their habits and ways of economic life that look similar to those of ethnic Hans.

Xijiang Township of Leishan County used to be a place heavily guarded by the Qing army stationed in a huge military camp with more than 200 households. Not many of them view or report themselves as ethnic Hans now.

① *Knowledge about South Guizhou • Official Ranks*, s.v. "Gu Zhou Tong Zhi," 18 (Guizhou People's Publishing House, December 1992)

Instead, they are closely bound with local Miaos by marriage and are hardly separable in looks from the locals. In this case, people who have been segregated from their own culture have melt into the local culture and therefore their economic activities are no more those of a cross-xiang nature. Opposite examples exist as well. For the ethnic minority people who, for a variety of reasons, have moved into the ethnic Han regions and have adopted a Han way of life, even if they categorize themselves as native Miao or Buyi, or even engaged in fund raising events for the benefit of their ethnic minority regions, these are by no means cross-xiang activities but merely individual charitable acts as long as their normal and constant economic interaction with their ethnic groups is discontinued. Such economic behaviors were conducted in ethnic Han regions in line with Han culture. The transfer of individual properties or wealth to their tribal men for individual but not economic purposes can only be defined as individual behaviors. Any behavior that does not retain a continuous and close relationship with at least two ethnic cultures throughout the entire economic activities does not fall into the category of cross-xiang operations.

If economic activities carried out by an individual across more than two ethnic groups and profits are made out of such economic activities, they are categorized as cross-xiang operations. After the lift of the ban on entering the ethnic Miao regions in the mid Qing Dynasty, a lot of ethnic Hans entered the villages of ethnic Miao or Dong with or without government permission. They followed the local customs to establish family ties (*da lao geng, ren tong zong*) with local ethnic people, or *jie tong nian* as recorded in the Han literature. Afterwards, local ethnic people were hired to cut trees to make rafts, which were shipped along the river to the Han regions for sale in as close as Hunan and Guangxi and as far as Wuhan or Nanjing, amassing huge wealth and creating a group of immigrants called by local Dongs as *liu jia ren.*[①] In the era of Republic of China, this group of immigrants grew so influential that they were capable of leasing the abandoned mountains and hiring local Miaos or Dongs to regenerate forests, gaining tremendous amount of money. With the ability to issue promissory notes, a group of capitalists emerged.

The difference between such activities in forestry and those conducted

① Jicheng Long, "The Absorption of the Dong Culture by Ethnic Han Immigrants in Border Regions of Hunan, Guizhou and Guangxi," *Journal of South-Central College for Nationalities,* no.4 (1994).

by *Gaoshan Han* is obvious. The former could not have be completed within the ring of a single ethnic group and the means and modes of operation involved the contents of ethnic Dong and Miao as well as those of ethnic Han. Moreover, the impact by each ethnic group lasted throughout the entire activities, making such economic behaviors cross-xiang operations. In addition, some ethnic Dongs and Miaos who were enlightened by the ethnic Hans joined the efforts in forest regeneration and lumbering, and then shipped and sold them to the Central Han regions. These ethnic minority people engaged in economic activities across two cultures and therefore their economic behaviors must also be defined as cross-xiang operations.

Cross-xiang economic activities are always organized and run by individuals or specific social groups who make operational decisions on the basis of specific cultural environment and innate characteristics. Meanwhile, any cross-xiang operation must start and end in the same cultural context, while interacting with and adapting to other cultures in the process of operation. The aforementioned lumber trade, for example, starts with operators with certain amount of funds brought in from the Han regions and with the information of supply and demand in the destination Han market, and it ends in fetching profits by selling in the Han regions. While in between the start and end points, the operators must follow the customs and habits of the ethnic Miaos and Dongs in the use of lands suitable for forest regeneration and the hiring of labor, or even perform the ritual ceremony of worshiping the same ancestry as the local customs dictate. The operations cannot complete without such cultural interaction. As a matter of fact, the contents of these cultures have been integrated into the operating activities, the success of which now mostly depends on how the base culture impacts the others it interacts with. Economic activities of this sort fall into our category of cross-xiang operations. Similar examples can be found in the leather trade in northeast Guizhou Province.

The vast territory in the northeast Guizhou Province used to be occupied by *Shuixi Tu Si* (local hereditary headman) in the Ming Dynasty and remained a region with a mixture of farming and animal husbandry. Animals were usually herded by ethnic Yi and Miao people while the large-sized livestock such as ox and horse were often transported to central cities or places along the transportation lines by ethnic Hui people who played a role of cross-xiang operator. The economic activities conducted by Huis involved

Yi, Miao, and Han peoples. To ensure the success of these activities, they had to make necessary adjustments to suit the cultures of above ethnic groups. On the other hand, these adjustments must be preconditioned on the maintenance of the Hui traditional culture, which was dominant throughout the entire process and served as the foundation for assessing the values from the start to the results of these activities. In short, cross-xiang economic activities must be based on the culture of one single ethnic group no matter how many other peoples and completely different environments are related. This is the third characteristic in cross-xiang operations.

As discussed above, any type of cross-xiang operation must come from and base on a specific ethnic culture, which, in essence, is tantamount to the society of that ethnic group as any ethnic group is a social community of people bonded by special cultural values. We have also pointed out that any cross-xiang economic activity must engage in interaction with one or more heterogeneous ethnic groups. For the same reason, they have to interact with other heterogeneous ethnic societies. To facilitate our discussions in the book, we need to give different names to the ethnic groups concerned in cross-xiang operations. The ethnic group based on which cross-xiang operations are conducted is the subjective party and the ethnic groups the cross-xiang operations concern are objective parties.

To distinguish between the subjective and objective parties in cross-xiang operations is not only for the convenience of discussion. More importantly, the roles that the subjective and objective parties play respectively and the restraining forces they have on cross-xiang operations are different. As the starter and initiator of cross-xiang operations, the subjective party determines the mode, value propensity, and result evaluation based on its own ethnic culture. The objective party, on the other hand, is the passive receiver in the operations. Merely for the purpose of ensuring the operational success, the subjective parties must adjust the activities to the hosting cultures. It is unlikely that the mode, value propensity, and result evaluation are completely in sync with the cultures of ethnic groups concerned. In other words, subjective and objective parties play completely different roles in cross-xiang operations. The subjective party is in a proactive position compared to a passive subjective party; the culture of subjective parties is the foundation and benchmark that tries to coordinate with the culture of the objective parties; the society of the subjective party is the start and end points of the operations and those of the objective party are cultural backgrounds that the operations have to be put in.

Any cross-xiang operation must be under the direct control and management of the subjective party that determines the specific projects, raises funds for investments, plans on the necessary technology and equipment based on its own needs, or even evaluates the results by its own standard. The objective party is nonetheless completely passive although it does not decide on the specific projects, the investments, and the selection of equipment and technology. Instead of passively accepting the imposed cross-xiang operations, the objective party reacts to them in accordance with its own cultural needs, either welcome, insist or resist, or even channels the operations in the direction favorable to its own culture, and when necessary, makes use of and absorbs the operations based on the needs of its own culture. These activities of the objective party may have negative or positive impacts on the cross-xiang operations. In other words, the success of cross-xiang operations not only depends on the capacity, effort and determination of the subjective party but also on the cooperation from the objective party. The study of cross-xiang operations may not produce a pragmatic result if the existence of objective parties is overlooked.

Due to the differences in the roles and functions between the subjective and objective parties, they are subject to different restraints in the operations. Many factors may have restraining effects but the following are the most representative: With regards to the subjective party, the capacity it can mobilize and the length of time it lasts are significant in the success of cross-xiang operations. In addition, the technology and equipment under the control of the subjective party and the extent of compatibility with the regions of the objective party are also important. The most critical restraint is how the subjective party understands the objective party as well as the room for adjustment by the subjective party. With regards to the objective party, the degree of compatibility between cross-xiang economic projects and the economic lifestyle unique to its culture directly determines the project's probability of success. The innate lifestyle of the ethnic group has a direct impact on the normal operation and the scope of adjustability of the ethnic culture directly affects the operational efficiency of cross-xiang operations. In a nutshell, the subjective and objective parties restrain the operations in different degrees.

The cross-xiang economic activities constantly dominated by the subjective party throughout the entire process are defined as "one-way" cross-xiang operations. Whereas the status of both parties varies in different projects, they are defined as "two-way" cross-xiang operations. Economic activities conducted by parties from similar cultures with comparable economic strengths are usually of the type of "two-way" cross-xiang operations, otherwise they are "one-way" operations where the party at a higher stage of development often is the subjective party. Whether the cross-xiang operations are "two-way" or "one-way" operation not only depends on the level of economic development and cultural type of the parties involved, but is also closely related to the state laws and policies as well as the political background of the ethnic groups. In a superior political system that real equality of the peoples is attained, it is possible for ethnic groups with different level of economic development from different cultural types to engage in "two-way" cross-xiang operations. The favorable policies currently effective in China provide perfect background for operations of such types.

Coming from different ethnic cultures that are adapted to different natural environments, the subjective and objective parties in cross-xiang operations transform and make use of natural environments in different ways. This is another factor that separates cross-xiang operations from other operations and it determines that the success of cross-xiang operations requires overcoming different natural restraints. In non-cross-xiang operations, difficulties from natural environments can be tackled by the same means and measures. In contrast, the restraints from natural environments in cross-xiang operations can not be fully controlled single-handedly by the means and measures of either the subjective or objective party, but rather by a combination of the strengths of the two. Failure in combining the two or lack of compatibility between the two will give rise to non-economic restraints. Subsequently, it is a must in the discussion of cross-xiang operations to distinguish the living environments between the subjective and objective parties.

Non-economic restraints in cross-xiang operations are mainly caused by cultural differences. The ethnic culture based on which cross-xiang operations are conducted depends on the subjective party and functions best in its original ethnic cultural context. However, cross-xiang operations expose the ethnic culture of the subjective party to the society and living environment it is not used to, thus making it operate in an unfamiliar environment. This is one of the main reasons that cause the common existence of non-economic restraints in cross-xiang operations.

All economic activities in cross-xiang operations are shaped by the ethnic culture of the subjective party. In the original cultural setting, all materials necessary for the operation of economic activities are supplied by stable and complete channels. They often become incomplete and unstable, or totally unavailable, in a heterogeneous cultural environment, which cannot be solved, or costs more by pure economic means. Such a restraint resulted from cultural differences directly affects the normal operation and lowers the efficiency of cross-xiang activities. A thorough analysis of the causes of this restraint and the restraining mechanism can be found in Chapter Six.

Cross-xiang operations are carried out in different ethnic cultures that regulate the groups of people with different life habits, languages, and organizational units in society, thus restraining economic activities in many ways. Difference in language directly increases the difficulty in operation and causes misunderstanding and disagreement among different parties. The size of organizational unit in society has a significant impact on the scale of consumers and thus restrains the supply and demand relationship in the consumer's market as well as consumer psychology. Difference in life habits directly determines the market potential for a variety of products, and puts up special requirements for the products available on the market. Under these restraints, the products traditionally provided by the subjective party may find limited markets in cross-xiang operations while the products needed by the market may have to be produced by the subjective party at much higher costs, thus hugely decreasing the operating efficiency. The analysis on this group of restraints can be found in Chapter Four.

Cultural differences may lead to different structures of social education and create different structures of knowledge and technique, causing huge gaps in the level of school education and that in individual knowledge and technique between people of different ethnic cultures. For economic operations in the same xiang, the level of school and social education does not hinder economic activities as it aligns with corresponding ethnic culture and is concerted with the relevant economic activities. Same is true for social knowledge and technical structure. However, cross-xiang operations face a different situation where economic activities that the subjective party is familiar with and proficient in put up requirements for the quality of workers that usually cannot be met by the other ethnic people. The quality of individual participants is often a factor that restraints the normal operation in cross-xiang economic activities. The analysis about this can be found in Chapter Five.

Cultural differences also cause differences in religious belief, ethics and morals, aesthetics in literature and art as well as other ideological views, which will affect, without being noticed, consumer psychology, interpersonal relationship and propensity in product evaluation, and will, in turn, determine the passion of the related parties to participate in the specific cross-xiang operations and how they evaluate the prospective projects. All these factors will eventually determine if the cross-xiang projects are accepted or declined, in cooperation or with resistance, therefore bringing unforeseeable barriers or restrains to the cross-xiang activities concerned. These analyses are included in Chapter Five.

On top of the non-economic restraints in the above four aspects, the difference in the type of culture between the subjective and objective party in cross-xiang operations will cause another type of non-economic restraints. The interaction between different cultures will give rise to the issue of selecting the way of communication between different cultures and adaptation to each other, as well as the issue of cultural change. These issues may result from economic activities but in most cases have little to do with the economy. All these issues are variables and they may have a cycle of stability inconsistent with the execution of projects. In other words, the social and cultural background that any cross-xiang economic activity concerns may contain many unpredictable factors, adding to the complexity, difficulty and risks of cross-xiang operations. The analysis about these dynamic non-economic restraints can be found in Chapter Three.

As cross-xiang economic activities must be carried out in an unfit natural environment, the difference between natural environments becomes one of the components of non-economic restraints, which can be roughly classified into three parts: potential in natural resources, adaptability of natural environment and spatial distance that operations concern. How these three parts affect the success of cross-xiang operations is discussed in Chapter Six.

Natural resource is a composite indicator that is not only about the availability of a specific resource, but also about how different resources are allocated, the difficulty in acquiring these resources and how stably the resources can be acquired. Variances in these elements produce unexpected hindering effects on specific cross-xiang operations. The availability of a certain natural resource is indeed the prerequisite for cross-xiang operations, but the varying difficulties in acquiring it often result in over-budget in investment. Furthermore, the discord in resource allocation continues to worsen the operating efficiency, and, in a worse case scenario, derails the entire project. The stable supply of natural resources is, in many cases, related to numerous natural conditions that, although not subject to laws of economics, must be stabilized via economic means, which surely decreases operating efficiency. In a nutshell, lack of the support of a particular culture or order, natural resources involved in cross-xiang operations will inevitably force the subjective party to go through the process of re-arranging these resources within its own economic capacity, thus resulting in further burdening the operators and causing the overall efficiency to drop and the investment to expand.

The natural environment that cross-xiang economic activities concern is another factor that potentially restrains the operating efficiency. The culture that cross-xiang economic activities depend on is most effective in the ethnic region. Likewise, economic activities carried out in this ethnic region have developed characteristics that are most adaptable to this region. However, cross-xiang operation means that these economic characteristics developed over a long period of time have to face completely strange natural environments, which will certainly give rise to many incompatible factors. To overcome the difficulties caused by these incompatible factors, cross-xiang operators will need to deal with the following three challenges: increase the difficulty in operation, heighten the need for investment and finally, how to make any adjustment aimed at adapting to the natural environments effective continuously. Among them, the most worrysome is that such hasty actions of adjustments often trigger unforeseeable ecological crises, such as air or water pollution, massive soil erosion, etc. These factors pose threats to the expected long-term effectiveness of these adjustments, and may eventually restrain the results of cross-xiang operations.

The spatial distance that cross-xiang operations concern is another restraint whose effectiveness is long-lasting and can not be overcome by economic power or economic means. A longer distance tends to yield stronger impact. Fundamentally, no human economic activities are made possible without material and energy flow powered at costs. The longer the distance in material and energy flow, the greater the costs. All these must be added to the total costs of the economic activities. Without other measures of lowering cost, an extraordinary long distance will result in the erosion in product competitiveness, putting the sustainability of these activities under question.

The political matters that cross-xiang operations need to face, such as laws, regulations, administrative systems etc., also determine the success of these operations. They may impact the subjective party's decision on scale and mode of investments, but on the other hand can pave the way for the establishment of communication channels among all related parties in cross-xiang activities by administrative measures. More importantly, they can play a role of either promoting or restraining cross-xiang activities through the mighty state economic power and its financial institutions, as well as re-distributing interests among the related parties through macro control and regulation efforts. However, all these can not be achieved without reliance on the cultures of the ethnic groups involved. The policy background cross-xiang operations are exposed to usually can not change the essence of the overall background that these activities are subject to, nor can it change the level of adaptability between the cultures of each ethnic group involved and the living environments of all parties in cross-xiang operations. In comparison, the state may resort to its massive political power and means of macro control and regulation to favor selected parties in the operation so as to even the pressure on the parties of the operation from political background, overcome the difficulties the operators face and ensure the continuity of the operation in an unfavorable situation. The discussion about how a political background may impact cross-xiang economic activities and thus qualifies as a non-economic restraint determining the success of these activities can be found in Chapter Eight.

Guizhou Province is a place inhabited by multi-ethnic groups who have a long history of a lagging-behind regional economy. Among the many attributing factors, the restraints resulting from cross-xiang operations, especially the "one-way" economic activities, have been playing a long-lasting and consistent role. Facing this persistent and hard issue that has long dragged the economic growth in the ethnic minority regions in Guizhou, it remains a critical mission for us and a far-reaching target for this book to uncover the non-economic system that has long restrained the regional economic development by applying theories and methodologies in economic anthropology and abstracting the characteristics in cross-xiang operations in ethnic regions, and in the meantime, to explore the paths and strategies in developing the regional economy and achieve the four modernizations in the ethnic regions by holding fast to the trend and objective facts in the transformation of these ethnic regions toward a socialist market economy. Subsequently, it becomes absolutely essential and necessary for us to grasp the overall characteristics of cross-xiang operations in the ethnic regions in Guizhou, and dissect the history of development in Guizhou from a historical and vertical perspective so as to understand the historical context we are in.

Guizhou's development is a result of concerted efforts by all peoples in the region. Since the ancient time, ethnic minority people have, based on their own culture, lived in, explored, developed and made use of this land for a long period of time. Unfortunately, with the exception of a limited number of them, the ethnic minority people are not able to record in writing what they have accomplished in developing Guizhou due to the lack of their own written languages. As a result, we can only access to the information about their achievements as well as their history in Guizhou's development and evolution with the indirect help from cultural anthropology, sociology and natural sciences, rather than directly from written languages in historical literature. The ethnic Han people have unarguably made significant contributions to the development of Guizhou, and more importantly, the development efforts by ethnic Han are reflected in the historical materials of Han. Therefore, we have to rely more on these materials written in the Han language in our research and this is the main reason why the discussion and research in this book proceed along the mainstream line of development activities conducted by Han immigrants. We ask that the readers of this book forgive us for not focusing more on the achievements made by ethnic minority groups in the development of Guizhou as objective conditions have made it impossible for us to do so.

Chapter Two Development (*Kai Fa*)

In history, the word "development" (*kai fa*) has long been used to refer to all the operating activities carried out by the ethnic Han's central government in ethnic minority regions along the country border. Fundamentally, it implied the use, for the first time, of barbarian lands that had not been edified by civilization. It already contained the basic characteristics displayed by cross-xiang operations, however, it was an exception to cross-xiang operations as it only referred to the "one-way" activities from ethnic Hans to other ethnic groups. Today, things have changed. To achieve modernization by all ethnic groups, what we need are cross-xiang operations in multiple directions, that is, both the development of ethnic regions by ethnic Han people and vice versa, which makes it absolutely necessary for us to, from a pragmatic perspective, dissect in a comprehensive manner all the social and natural factors determining the result of development activities. Consequently, it requires a thorough analysis on the similarities and differences between the present development models and those of the past.

I Development: Its Original Meaning and Transformations

With regards to cross-xiang operations, "development" has been the most telling, and mostly mentioned in ancient Han literature. The word was first used in this way in the *History of the Han Dynasty · Biography of Sun Bao*: "At the moment, Lord Hongyang who was the emperor's uncle, by relying on Li Shang, the prefecture chief of South County, occupied and cultivated the lands measuring several hundreds of *qing* (a Chinese unit of measuring area), many of them were leased and developed by local people from Shaofu." (implying that the emperor's uncle forcefully pocketed the resources of the royal court (including wetlands, forests and pastures etc.) and turned them into his private paddy fields.) [①] Here, the word "develop" had the meaning of turning uncultivated lands into farmlands, with an implication of first use and turning the useless to the useful. The meaning of the compound word came from its components of *kai* and *fa*. *Kai* originally

① (Jin) Shou Chen, (Liu Song) Songzhi Pei, annotation, *The History of the Three Kingdoms • Kingdom of Shu • Biography of Zhuge Liang V* (Beijing: Zhonghua Book Company, April 1975, 6th reprint), 920-921.

meant "to open the door", extensively "to begin", *The Annotation on the History of the Later Han Dynasty· Biography of Feng Yan* stated: "A year starts (*fa*) with spring when all the flowers bloom,"① which used the word *fa* in its extensive meaning. The original meaning of *fa* was "shoot an arrow", and its extensive meaning was open (*kai*). The *Wu Cheng chapter of Shangshu* read: "*fa ju qiao zhi su* (open the Juqiao Warehouse and distribute the grains)," which, according to *Annotation*, "stands for open."② This signifies to open and use the grains not used before; therefore, the compound word formed by the two characters of *kai* and *fa* can only be explained as the first use of the unused object through human efforts.

After the Han Dynasty, the word "develop" tended to be fixed in meaning and has evolved to be a fixed disyllabic word; hence, it has gradually shifted away from its original meaning and has been given a few extensive ones. For example, it has the meaning of "enlightenment and inducement" as was used in the *History of the Northern Dynasties ·Biography of Cui Shan:* "So (I have to) trouble you (Cui Shan) to stay with us all the time to *kai fa* (Under the auspices of the emperor, Cui Shan accompanied, educated and guided the prince in the hope to turn him into a useful person.) the little children"; and the meaning of "display" as used in Vol. 12 of *Yi Wen Lei Ju* (A Compilation of Arts and Narratives by Category) when quoting Huan Tan's *Xin Lun* (New Theory):"Emperor Wu of the Han Dynasty was a noble character with great talents and began to *kai fa* his exalted ambition since his enthronement. His deeds and achievements met the highest standards of both present and past times"; as well as the meaning of "demolish" as used in the *History of the Han Dynasty · Biography of Wang Mang II:* "Both the officials and masses submitted letters to report that eunuchs controlled the *kai fa* (demolishing efforts), which was not uncovered by Shang Shu (a high-ranking government official)." The word *kai fa* was even used to mean "dispose of" as was in Chapter 14 of *A Dream of Red Mansions:* "I meant to pardon you, but it makes disciplining others more difficult if I'm not strict for the first time. I'd rather *kai fa* (dispose of) you." All these different ways of using *kai fa* emphasize the meaning of begin (open) for the first time but ignored another layer in the meaning, that is, making use of what is uncovered by the act of *kai fa*; therefore, they are

① *Twenty-five Histories* vol. 2, *History of the Later Han Dynasty*, 889.

② *Commentaries and Notes on the Thirteen Classics (I), Shangshu Zhengyi* vol.11, Yuan Ruan ed. (Zhonghua Book Company, October 1980), 185.

impertinent to what is discussed in this book.

When the word “develop” is used in association with ethnic regions along China’s borders, it has a meaning similar to that in the *History of the Han Dynasty· Biography of Sun Bao*, which rose in an extremely profound social background. In ancient times, the Han culture perceived the ethnic Han people in Central Plain (Central China) to be the representative of the orthodox civilization while all the other ethnic minority regions along China’s borders that had not been cultivated by the Han culture were viewed unexceptionally as “wasteland and useless people.”① These regions were, as described in the *History of the Han Dynasty· Biography of Sun Bao*, like the barren slopes and grasslands that could only be transformed into fertile and rich farmlands usable to the country for political, financial and military purposes after subjecting to the influence of the Han culture; in other words, the ethnic minority regions should be developed and utilized on the basis of the Han culture. “Develop” used this way has the implied meaning of utilizing natural resources that are located across ethnic groups and cultures, which is closely related to the cross-xiang operations this book discusses. However, this book defines cross-xiang operations more broadly than the traditional development of border regions. Not only do they include the development of ethnic minority regions by the Han culture, but also those between different ethnic groups, or even operations conducted by ethnic groups on the Han regions.

We must point out that, in its evolutionary history, the word “develop”, when used in reference to the operations in ethnic minority regions along the borders, implied an apparent bias of self-centered nationalism. It started with the premise to reject the efforts and achievements that local ethnic peoples already made in using the natural environments they were exposed to. As a matter of fact, despite the differences between the cultures of the ethnic groups in the border regions and the ethnic Han culture, these ethnic groups, for reason of survival and self-development, were similar to their Han counterparts in the processing and transformation of the natural environments. Such creative work should also be classified as a kind of “development”, which had begun long before the ethnic Han culture entered these regions. It is therefore a one-sided point of view with a distinctive national bias if the word “develop” is understood only as creative utilization of the ethnic

① *Twenty-five Histories* vol. 1, *History of the Former Han Dynasty*, 721.

minority regions by the Han culture.

According to *Records of the Grand Historian·Collected Biographies of Barbarians in the Southwest*, a full range of means of livelihood already existed in Guizhou in the Han Dynasty, from settled agriculture, Swidden farming (shifting cultivation), animal husbandry, to hunting and gathering. The ethnic peoples inhabiting in these regions had, in fact, made effective use of the natural resources here and had processed and transformed their living environments in a different way from that of the ethnic Hans. It is recorded in the *History of the Han Dynasty·Collected Biographies of Barbarians in the Southwest* that the offensive launched by Emperor Cheng of the Han Dynasty against the remnants of the defeated troops of Yelang Kingdom during the Heping era (28-25BC) was made a final success only after the water supply channel built by Yelang Kingdom was destroyed,[①] indicating that the ethnic minorities' ability in processing and transforming the natural environments was beyond a primitive level. It is therefore not a true reflection of historical facts if we only view the economic activities carried out by the ethnic Hans following the penetration of the Han culture into these regions as the first use of natural resources but overlooked the processing and transforming efforts made by the local ethnic peoples. The word "develop" used in this way displays a distinctive "one-way" nature, e.g., specifically referring to the Han's development of ethnic minority regions, and thus it should be given a new meaning. All activities conducted by any ethnic group to creatively make use of natural resources for the first time should fall into the category of "development activities". In our research, cross-xiang operations are defined as two-way, sometimes even multiple-way and connected cross-cultural development activities.

Understandably, the word "develop" has long been used under such premises and has had a far-reaching impact on the academic world; consequently, this book that is dedicated to the comprehensive discussion of cross-xiang operations must give an all-inclusive dissection of this concept. For this reason, this chapter will expound, from a vertical historical perspective, all kinds of development activities run by the central government of all the dynasties across a horizon of more than 2000 years in the ethnic minority regions in Guizhou. As the development activities mentioned here are a special form of cross-xiang operating activities, we must first discuss

① *Twenty-five Histories* vol. 1, *History of the Former Han Dynasty*, 721.

the relationship between the development of ethnic regions in Guizhou in history and cross-xiang operations, as well as how it is special.

The development activities of ethnic regions in Guizhou by the central governments of all dynasties lasted more than 2000 years in history, which display a series of common characteristics in essence despite of the seeming differences in aspects such as duration of each development campaign, specific goals and actual results, modes of organization and resulting clashes among ethnic groups. The most telling characteristic is that the vast majority of the development activities are organized by the central government, or run by individuals or organizations under the protection of the central government.

The development of Guizhou started from the Qin Dynasty. After Emperor Qin Shi Huang united China, he sent General Chang Wong to enter Yunnan from Qianwei County (present-day Yibin) by building "a way of five chi (a Chinese unit of measuring length) in width",[①] which ventured into Wumeng Mountain in northwest Guizhou. Afterwards, every feudal dynasty that reached its zenith in state power would put Guizhou development in its agenda, while any languishing dynasty would unexceptionally halt its plan to develop these ethnic regions. Among them, the most representative are the following ones. Emperor Wu of the Han Dynasty began developing the ethnic regions in southwest China. Among the newly established "border counties", Zangke and Qianwei counties governed the territories of ethnic minority regions in Guizhou.[②] Zhuge Liang, the premier of Shu Kingdom in the three-kingdom era, employed a "psychological tactic" in treating the ethnic minorities in Nanzhong region under the guiding principle of "pacifying the ethnic groups in the south, befriending externally with Sun Quan and improving internal governance,"[③] resulting in the simultaneous development of ethnic groups in northwest Guizhou. In the late Tang Dynasty, the central government, enlisted armies from Bashu of Sichuan to march southward, recapturing Bozhou and fostering a local regime as a counterweight against Nanzhao,[④] and in the meantime, conducting some development activities in northern Guizhou. After the southbound migration of the Song Dynasty, the

① *Twenty-five Histories* vol. 1, *Records of the Grand Historian*, 329.

② *Twenty-five Histories* vol. 1, *History of the Former Han Dynasty*, 720.

③ (Jin) Shou Chen, (Liu Song) Songzhi Pei, annotation, *The History of the Three Kingdoms • Kingdom of Shu* vol.4 (Beijing: Zhonghua Book Company, December 1959), 913.

④ Chunyuan Zhou, Yanyu Wang et al., eds., *The Ancient History of Guizhou* (Guizhou People's Publishing House, December 1982) , 127.

protracted war between Song and Jin caused a shortage in war-horses and obstructed the supply of horses from the nomadic peoples in the north. The Southern Song court was forced to purchase war-horses from Dali in the south and subsequently built a market in Hengshan village in Guangxi specifically for horse trading, giving rise to development activities in southwest and south Guizhou.[1] At the end of the Southern Song Dynasty, the Yuan Mongolian Empire attacked Dali to threaten the Southern Song court from the upstream Yangtze River. To prevent the Mongolian army from crossing Guizhou to launch surprise attack to the west flank of the Southern Song Dynasty, the royal court of Song borrowed lands from local influentials in Guizhou along upstream Wuyang River, that is, the Tian's in Sizhou and the Yang's in Bozhou, and constructed military fortresses in Zhenyuan City, marking the first development of ethnic minority regions in southeast Guizhou[2]. Following its unification of the entire China, the Yuan Dynasty erased the difference in administrative division for the first time to install formal administrative establishments such as Bafan Shunyuan Lu and Puding Lu in the back-land of Guizhou, and stationed armies to guard the border, thus intensifying efforts in developing Guizhou. The Ming Dynasty, after overthrowing Yuan, followed its established example to build garrisons across Guizhou and sent military families to guard its borders, systemizing the development efforts by the Han immigrants and eventually leading to the establishment of the administrative province of Guizhou. After Qing overtook the entire country, it abolished Ming's management practice of separating the status of military personnel from that of civilians and putting garrisons in the same administrative level as zhous and counties, and adopted the nationally uniformed administrative system to ethnic minority regions in Guizhou, paving the way for the ethnic Hans to migrate freely to develop Guizhou and thus intensifying civilian development activities in Guizhou. All the aforementioned development activities, no matter when they were carried out, were impossible without the central government's operation and organization, as well as its political protection for civilian developments. Simply put, the central government was the operator that directly run these activities.

With no exceptions, all the development activities in ethnic minority regions in Guizhou in history were carried out based on an ethnic Han culture,

[1] (Song) Chengda Fan, Qiwang Hu, Qin Guangguang, annotation, *Guihaiyuhengzhijiyi Annotation* s.v. "Man Ma"(Sichuan Minzu Publishing House, September 1986), 91.

[2] *Huangping Zhou Annals,* mimeographed edition, in the collection of Guizhou Provincial Library

and produced the effect of transplanting the Han culture in these regions, therefore all displaying the ethnic Han characteristics. This was evidenced by the regions which were developed in history. The economy in ethnic Han regions before the Song Dynasty centered around the Central Shannxi Plain and midstream Yellow River where the Han culture was constructed on the foundation of dry-land agriculture. Such a culture was reflected in the development of Guizhou where most development activities were focused on western and northern regions in Guizhou that were predominantly mountainous in landscape and cold in climate, covered mostly by sparse grasslands that were dotted by small forests. A natural ecology like this provided a good environment for growing crops traditionally planted in the dry-lands in northern China and was also easily accessible for the cattle-powered transportation. Farm tools commonly seen in northern China could be used to their best effect. Consequently, development activities before the Song Dynasty were all based in Bashu, marching from north to south to cross the Wumeng Mountain in the northwest and Dalou Mountain in the north to eventually penetrate deep into the backland of Guizhou. The passage that connected Qianwei with Zangke River were repeatedly constructed in history.[①]

The fall of the Song Dynasty was accompanied by a gradual migration of the ethnic Han economic center to the lower reaches of Yangtze River and the intensive cultivation of rice fields emerged to be the dominate economic foundation. A shift in the focus of the development in Guizhou ensued, reflected in the advancement from the east to Guizhou through water channels. The development of Meishandong and occupation of Chenghui Zhou toward the end of the Northern Song Dynasty preceded such a big shift.[②] The completion of Zhenyuan City in the Southern Song Dynasty symbolized that the ethnic Han power penetrated deep into Guizhou. In the Yuan Dynasty, local hereditary headmen in Guizhou were allowed to pay tributes to the central government by way of the east route via Hunan and Hubei, indicating that the development of Guizhou by advancing westward from the east became matured. Such a mode of development continued till the founding of the People's Republic of China.

A discrepancy in the contents of development is evident too. Prior to the

① *Twenty-five Histories* vol. 2, *History of the Later Han Dynasty*, 1050.
② *Twenty-five Histories* vol. 8, *Biography of Treacherous Court Officials*, 6724.

Song Dynasty, dry-land crops such as millet, broomcorn millet, and wheat were among the primary crops introduced into Guizhou; in the meantime, horses were purchased in huge number from local ethnic peoples. In contrast, after the birth of the Song Dynasty, rice began to dominate the crops brought into Guizhou. All the settlements were built by the riverside, making it easy to reclaim and cultivate rice fields. In the hundreds of years since the Song Dynasty, Han immigrants who came to develop Guizhou lived on operations related to rice, while the ethnic minorities at the moment, with the exception of Buyi and Dong nationalities, were seldom engaged in rice-related activities. Rice planting had been very rare until early Qing Dynasty especially in ethnic Miao and Yi regions.[①] The difference in the content of operations contributed to changes in ethnic relationship. Before the Song Dynasty, ethnic Hans relied more on local influentials in Yi regions. A typical example told the story during the wars launched by Zhuge Liang aimed at pacifying the southern border, where Jihuo, a local tribal chief, helped him by supplying grains to his army.[②] After the Song Dynasty, development efforts were mainly about cultivating rice fields and thus were more dependent on Dong people in the east and Buyi people in central and southern Guizhou. Such a trend was indirectly evidenced by the fact that the Yuan Dynasty established Bafan Shunyuan Lu (a provincial establishment) that controlled central Guizhou. With a governing territory of no larger than the present-day xiang (similar to county), the Buyi local hereditary headman heading this Lu was put in an actual official rank as high as that of Zhou and Fu.[③] All the above characteristics were attributable to the development of the Han culture and were, in essence, a result of ethnic Han's development of ethnic minority regions in Guizhou by virtue of the Han culture.

It is not difficult to tell that all the historical development activities usually were not for economic benefit but for military, political or other purposes. Emperor Wu of the Han Dynasty sent his envoy Tang Meng to Yelang Kingdom in the hope of exploring a secret passage from which the Han army could stage surprise attacks against the separatist forces in

① (Qing) Wen Tian ed, Shuqin Luo annotation, *Book of Guizhou,* s.v. "Miao Customs" (Guizhou People's Publishing House, March 1992) , 18-20.

② Hongmo Yu, "Probe into Jihuo Stone Tablet and Related History," *Guizhou Cultural Relics* , no.2 (1983).

③ (Ming) Lian Song et al., *The History of the Yuan Dynasty V,* s.v. "Barbarian Officials in Bafan Shunyuan" (Zhonghua Book Company, April 1976), 1539.

Nanyue.[①] The support provided by the Tang Dynasty to Yang Duan in his efforts to recover Bozhou was aimed at constraining a growing and more threatening Nanzhao Kindom.[②] The construction of Zhenyuan City toward the end of the Southern Song Dynasty was intended for protecting the heart of the imperial court from being attacked by the Mongolian troop marching along the waterway from the east.

All the above activities served military needs. Although it looked as if the development activities of the Song Dynasty had apparent economic purposes, such as the market set up in Hengshan Village intended for purchasing horses; or the facilities to trade salt for grains built in Chenghui Zhou with a seeming purpose in barter trade, in essence, they were conducted from an overall military strategic perspective. The horses bought in Hengshan Village were all used as war horses that reinforced the military capacity of the Song Dynasty battling against the Jin Dynasty, without worrying about any impact this might have on the economy of ethnic minorities in Guizhou. The grains acquired in the barter trade in Chenghui Zhou, on the other hand, helped strengthen national defense as they were neither shipped into domestic market nor consumed by the state, but rather to backup military supplies at war times. Locally available grains relieved the pressure off the country to transport them to the front and yielded surprising military effect. Therefore, such activities should be viewed as non-economic activities.

The Ming Dynasty witnessed the development of Guizhou in the magnitude never seen in previous times. A massive number of Han military families settled themselves directly in the backlands of Guizhou and began cultivating lands to become self-sufficient residents. Both the number of people involved in economic activities and the length of time they lasted transcended those of previous ages; and these activities permeated directly into the inner lands of Guizhou. The military targets these activities were intended for seemed to have been disguised by the overt economic benefits. What attributed to this situation was that at the infant stage of the Ming Dynasty after its unification of China, the Yuan Dynasty still posed a grave threat and its remnant troops not only endangered the northern frontier of the Ming Dynasty, had Yunnan in their control but also haunted the regions from Qinghai to west Sichuan. The confrontational situation between the Ming and

① *Twenty-five Histories* vol. 1, *History of the Former Han Dynasty*, 720.
② Chunyuan Zhou, Yanyu Wang et al., eds., *The Ancient History of Guizhou,* 127.

Yuan dynasties was similar to that near the end of the Southern Song Dynasty, which forced the Ming ruler to venture all-out to re-take Yunnan and station Mu Ying as a hereditary king to shield Yunnan from surprise attacks by Yuan's remnant troops that threatened the security of the Ming Dynasty from upstream.[①] To establish garrisons and cultivate lands in the ethnic settlements in Guizhou to facilitate defending this region for a long time was aimed at keeping Yunnan connected with central China and fortifying the border defense so that the tragic fall of the Southern Song Dynasty would not be repeated. Again, the seemingly dynamic economic activities were nothing but military deployments in essence.

In addition to the development activities mainly for military purposes as mentioned above, others such as those in the following examples were conducted for political reasons. As politically-driven development activities did not focus on achieving economic targets, the ensuing clashes between different ethnic groups were not a result of conflicting economic interests but rather disputes on political status, humbleness or arrogance with regards to rituals. The massive assault on Yelang Kingdom during the Heping era under the reign of Emperor Cheng of the Han Dynasty was merely triggered by the disrespectful acts by the king of Yelang Kingdom toward the envoy of the Han Dynasty. Du Qin once commented on this event as saying: "If given the fact that those are places where nothing grows and people are useless, our wise emperor should just let it go and not burden the entire China (to conquer them); and we should discontinue our efforts in building counties, give up on their people, disavow their hereditary status and never communicate with them again. However, this is the precedent that our former emperors set, and we should not ruin the achievements we have made in past generations. The best time to eradicate a problem is when it is in its infancy; otherwise, it will inflict heavy damages to the masses if we wait until it runs out of control to fight it."[②] The maker of this statement only considered that bringing Yelang Kingdom to submission had been the great achievement of previous emperors and giving it up easily would hamper the political reputation, but mentioned nothing about the economic benefits that the Han Dynasty could get if Yelang Kingdom succumbed to the Han. After "Wang Mang's Reform", he carried

① (Qing) Tingyu Zhang et.al., *The History of the Ming Dynasty,* s.v. "Biography of Mu Ying" (Zhonghua Book Company, April 1974), 3756-3759.

② *Twenty-five Histories* vol. 1, *History of the Former Han Dynasty* , 720.

out massive military operations against Nanzhong,[①] only resulting in his troops being wiped out entirely. The reason that gave rise to this unfortunate war, to everyone's utter surprise, was his decision to degrade the title conferred by the emperor to the headmen of the ethnic minority groups in Nanzhong. "Wang Mang's Reform" stripped all the titles of "king" that had been previously conferred by former emperors to the ethnic tribal leaders and replaced them with an inferior title of *hou.* A meaningless political action intended for making him conspicuous at home cost the country dearly in the border war against the ethnic groups.[②] It is evident that Wang Mang's attempt was blind and a total failure. Zhuge Liang had made outstanding achievements in developing northwest Guizhou. However, nothing he had implemented was for economic purposes. His decision of not to place Han officials, station Han armies, or levy taxes in the ethnic minority regions in Guizhou but appoint local hereditary headmen to exert control over the territory bore no economic significance to Shu Kingdom. They were, however, deeply calculated and well-thought-of unprecedented actions that were taken by Zhuge Liang with an intention of battling northward and revitalizing the Han imperial court. "Pacifying and appeasing ethnic minorities in the south" was in fact an integral part of his political target. Similarly out of political needs, the Northern Song Dynasty established *Ji Mi*prefectures and counties (loose-control administrative units) in the ethnic minority regions in Guizhou, and offered the same treatment to the tributary envoys from local powers in Guizhou as those from Vietnam, Korea and other foreign countries. The imperial grants received by ethnic minority envoys were almost equal to the tributes they paid, and in special circumstances, were greater than the tributes. The *wu xing fan* (five big families) in ethnic Buyi region in central Guizhou at the time each had a territory smaller than the size of today's *xiang*, but received unproportional grants similar to the others without reference to the value of their tributes.[③] As a result, these local tribal headmen even asked to increase the number of tribute-paying trips, turning paying tributes into effective means of making money. Such acts, judged from the Han's economic perspective, were undoubtedly losing business; however, from a political point of view, they were effective measures in stabilizing the frontiers, enhancing the economic

① Guizhou region in later period, namely "Nanzhong" in the Han Dynasty.
② *Twenty-five Histories* vol. 1, *History of the Former Han Dynasty*, 721.
③ *Twenty-five Histories* vol. 8, *History of the Song Dynasty*, 6785 lower col.

development in the Han regions and reinforcing the political situation at home; therefore, they were quite effective and unquestionably wise measures.

In the eleventh year of Yongle of the Ming Dynasty, Guizhou was officially made a province, which by regular standard should keep self-sufficient financially first and if possible, contribute to the budget of the country. Guizhou, as a matter of fact, never met this requirement during more than five hundred years from the establishment of the province to the fall of the Qing Dynasty. In the early days when Guizhou Province was set up, even the salaries of the local officials in Guizhou would have to be paid out of the pockets of central provinces. ① The establishment of Guizhou Province was merely for political reasons. It had long been subsidized financially. Such a mentality in developing ethnic regions was often reflected in the memorials government officials sent for the Emperor's review, which never talked about the economic gains from establishing Guizhou Province but tried in every way possible to emphasize the political benefits such as popularize the glory of the previous emperors and elevate the image and authority of the imperial court.

Some of the important and profoundly impactful measures in the history of Guizhou's development were, on the surface, aimed at wiping out local forces in ethnic minority regions but essentially were related to the domestic political needs. The well-known *gai tu wei liu* (to replace all local hereditary headmen with the officials appointed from the central government) adopted by Emperor Yongzheng was an example. This measure that attracted tremendous attention was, in essence, merely to ensure the unobstructed passage of the post road, reinforce the border defense in the southwest regions to confront the military pressure of Western Mongolia. Such a nation-wide measure not intended for economic gains had, to the disappointment of many people, added to Guizhou's financial burden. The huge costs associated with the adoption of this measure quickly drained the financial capability of the government and forced it to dissolve the military organizations soon after they were created to shrug off the financial pressure. To accompany this measure, the *Prohibitive Rules in Miao Region,* an imperial decree, was issued that strictly prohibited ethnic Hans from migrating into this region to conduct commercial activities and ethnic

① *Veritable Records of the Ming Dynasty • A Compilation of Materials about Guizhou* (Guizhou People's Publishing House, December 1983) , 534 "Hong 26" , 743-744 "Jia 196" .

minority people from leaving this region without permission,[1] indicating that this development campaign was launched out of the political needs without any economic concerns.

The nature of seeking military and political interests determined that these development activities were not organized based on the need of economic activities, but followed the two distinctive routes: by military organizations; or by political organizations prevailing at the moment. The garrison system of the Ming Dynasty was a typical example of development by military organizations. To develop Guizhou, a large number of garrisons were set up within the local ethnic minority settlements, around which patches of lands were cultivated by Han military immigrants. Anything about these military men, from headcount, management agency, logistics, development fund investment to the way of personnel input, is aligned with the rules of the military establishment of the entire country. It is recorded in the *History of the Ming Dynasty · Soldiers* that the organizational hierarchy of *wei suo* (garrison) in the Ming Dynasty was basically like this:"...discontinue using the official ranks of the Yuan Dynasty, namely *Shumi, Pingzhang, Yuanshuai, Zongguan,* and *Wanhu* and change to *Zhihui* for those who head 5,000 people, *Qianhu* for those who head 1,000 people, *Baihu* for those who head 100 people and *Zongqi* for those who head 50 people, and *Xiaoqi* for those who head 10 people. In strategic places, *Suo* is to be established in every county, and *Wei* is to be established for neighboring counties. Generally, a *Wei* has 5,600 people; a *Qianhu Suo* has 1,120 people; a *Baihu Suo* has 112 people. Each *Suo* has two *Zongqi* and ten *Xiaoqi*. They join to form an army. Soldiers come by way of enlistment, surrender, or people in exile. Enlistment refers to the soldiers who are made permanent residents by offering a piece of land. Surrender are referred to as those who are captives from other countries that were defeated by us. People in exile refer to the people who commit crimes and are sent into exile. Their military status is hereditary."[2] Such a mechanism was almost a total copy from central China to Guizhou region with the only exception, if any, that, compared to other *Wei Suo* that were set up in ethnic Han regions, these were built in ethnic minority regions.

To illustrate the real situation, let's take a look at the related part in Guo

① *Veritable Records of the Qing Dynasty • A Compilation of Materials about Guizhou* (Guizhou People's Publishing House, November 1964) , 329.

② *Twenty-five Histories* vol. 10, *The History of the Ming Dynasty • Soldiers (2)*, 8018.

Zizhang's *Records of Guizhou*, which listed in detail how Wei Suos were equipped under the chapter "Wei Suo Zhi".[①]According to the book, the *Wei Suos* in Guizhou were completely the same as those in other parts of China from organizational hierarchy, appropriation, to ownership of the cultivated land, with perhaps the only exception that the difficult natural environment in Guizhou drove many soldiers away. As these garrisons were all established within ethnic minority settlement regions, it was hard for administrative authorities to subject them to the administrative control, resulting in some uniqueness compared to those in central China. For example, the stationed servicemen were more heavily used, which triggered many to escape. *Guangzhiyi* by Wang Shixing of the late Ming Dynasty has such a statement: "The number of servicemen of this Dynasty was usually inaccurate and thus adding to the burden of ordinary people for nothing. The only exception was the soldiers in the garrisons of Guizhou as well as in Sichuan and Yunnan who were used as postmen and coachmen and thus saved the government a large amount of transportation fees"[②] Wang Shixing spoke highly of the contributions made by the stationed soldiers from the perspective of the imperial dynasty, but his comments revealed the fact that these soldiers assumed heavier laborious tasks that caused many people to desert. This was one of the factors that resulted in insufficient staffing in many garrisons in Guizhou.

For the same reason that local administrative authorities could not impose effective control over these garrisons, army officers of these garrisons tended to acquire lands illegally, take the wealth of local ethnic people by force and enslave the local people to cultivate the lands for them. To legitimize these grabbed lands, they chose to file with administrative authorities and paid taxes accordingly to the state. This was recorded in Guo Zizhang's *Records of Guizhou* under the chapter "Taxes", which discussed in detail the sources of all the taxes paid by the garrisons.

Take the real cases in the development of Guizhou by administrative organizations as an example. In the Han Dynasty, the development of Guizhou was conducted through a corvee system according to the taxation payable by each household. Labor forces were selected from the four

① (Ming) Zizhang Guo, *Records of Guizhou*, mimeographed edition, in the collection of Guizhou Provincial Library

② (Ming) Shixing Wang, Lv Jinglin annotation, *Guangzhiyi* (Zhonghua Book Company, December 1981), 133.

counties in Bashu to construct the passway connecting Bashu with Zangke River. The corvee system in the Han Dynasty dictated that the selected laborers must bring food supplies and necessary tools with them. Due to the long distance and the difficulty in transportation, this development attempt had to be called off.[①] Apparently, the administrative system at the time restrained the efficiency of the development efforts. The failure of this development attempt was not due to the lack of willingness from the ruling class, or of the hard work from the labor force. What caused the task to fail was that the administrative system at the time was not structured to deal with the difficulties in the development.

The political and military nature deeply embedded in these development activities pushed grassroots participation to a secondary priority. Besides, it was difficult for the ethnic Hans who migrated into Guizhou in the early stages of development to maintain their own culture. The failure of these development activities was often followed by either an exodus of Han people out of Guizhou or an assimilation of the Han people into other cultures, which actually cut off their economic ties with the Han regions; therefore, their development activities no longer fell into the category of cross-xiang operations. The operating activities mentioned above, regardless of their specific characteristics, have one thing in common; that is, they have all the elements to qualify as cross-xiang activities. First, they were all carried out between ethnic Han people and minority groups, and were exposed to more than one cultural settings. The garrisons of the Ming Dynasty, for instance, related to ethnic Dong, Buyi, Miao, Yi and Gelao peoples. Second, from a natural environment perspective, all such development activities were conducted in the natural and ecological environments totally different from those in the developed Han regions. The development activities in northwest Guizhou before the Song Dynasty were mostly carried out in grassy mountainous regions with thinly scattered trees, in sharp contrast with the developed ethnic Han regions represented by the Yellow River Alluvial Plain and Guanzhong Plain with easy access to irrigation systems. The center of the development activities after the Song Dynasty shifted to eastern and central Guizhou, where subtropical riverside jungles and small plains surrounded by the mountains in central Guizhou dominated the landscape. In the meantime, the center of ethnic Han culture moved to the mid-lower reaches of Yangtze

① *Twenty-five Histories* vol. 1, 325, col 3-4.

River with dense river networks. Few similarities existed between the regions to be developed and the center of the regions where the operators of the development activities resides in terms of natural and ecological environments. Third, from the perspective of political context, all these activities were operated by the central government in central China while the administrative authorities in the regions to be developed were local ethnic powers. To cope with the administrative architecture of the ethnic minorities, such as *Ze Xi* System of ethnic Yi nationality or *Ting Mu* System of ethnic Buyi nationality, which had little in common with that of the ethnic Han, the central government had to keep the *Ji Mi* status intact, or maintain the *Tu Si* system. As the three major elements that constitute xiang were different between the party who ran these activities and those who were to be developed, these development activities certainly have the fundamental characteristics of cross-xiang operations.

These activities must have been subject to non-economic constraints. Despite the lack of economic viability in most cases, they were indispensable actions by the government at the time on political or military grounds. Government financial subsidies, which were often granted by the state from its tax revenue, were critical to keep these activities sustained. The non-economic constraints emerged, like in other ordinary cross-xiang operations with few exceptions, from the discrepancies in the structures of each relevant *xiang*. Although it seems that these development activities were not organized in pursuit of economic gains, they needed to follow basic laws of economy, such as investment in capital, technology and manpower, and the selection of specific projects. The continuation of these activities also depended on the economic capacity of the operator, and would inevitably impact on the economic lives of the ethnic groups in varied degrees. It often came to our attention when we were analyzing the results of these development activities that such economic impact, which was likely to cause conflicts among ethnic groups, in worst cases might interrupt these activities. Therefore, such development activities are, in essence, special economic activities, that is, cross-xiang economic activities. The superficial differences should not conceal the cross-xiang nature of these activities, and it is for this reason that we include them in our discussion of cross-xiang economic activities.

Needless to say, as special cases in cross-xiang operations, these development activities have some unique characteristics. First, they were unexceptionally one-way activities as the operators were always the ethnic Hans and the related ethnic minority groups were always put in an inferior and to-be-developed position. Second, they were always conducted from the ethnic Han cultural background, that is, to make use of and transform the natural environment out of the needs of Han culture, and the Han cultural principles must be followed even in an incompatible natural or cultural background, and even if doing so meant extra costs. Third, they were usually conducted for non-economic purposes although they were by nature economic activities, which made them significantly different from today's cross-xiang operations that mainly focus on attaining economic goals. Lastly, they were, for the most part, dependent entirely on the tax revenue of the country. Private funds, if any, carried extremely negligible weight throughout the entire process, which diverted hugely from the present-day cross-xiang operating models that embrace the notion of separating enterprise functions from administrative functions and managing the business by economic means. In such a context, we feel absolutely necessary to further summarize and analyze the different modes in which each dynasty developed Guizhou, so as to clarify the differences between these models and the two-way or multiple-way cross-xiang operations we have been advocating.

II Traditional Modes of Development and Literature Review

As "development" (kai fa) is a special form of cross-xiang operations that was carried out in the ethnic minority regions in Guizhou for a long period of time in history, it is therefore necessary, before we begin a thorough discussion of the characteristics of cross-xiang operations, for us to systematically summarize, and to give an approximate classification of the development practices in the history of Guizhou. This will put our analysis of non-economic constraints for development of Guizhou in a definite social context, thus laying a solid foundation for our discussion on the determinants and characteristics of such constraints. As development activities have long been carried out in Guizhou and each had different targets and practices involving many ethnic groups, a summarization of these activities becomes a complicated task. To simplify the work of classification, we will tackle the seemingly complex task by centering around different status and functions of the subjective and objective parties in the operations, supplemented by the depth of penetration into each other's economy. Following such a method, we may initially classify the development history in Guizhou into four basic types: (1) transit development; (2) proxy development; (3) indirect development; and (4) direct development.

The long distance between the central ethnic Han region and Guizhou has kept it off the main military battleground in history. However, Guizhou spans across two large water systems: Yangtze River and Pearl River, along which one can get to the central ethnic Han cultural region in the mid- lower reaches of Yangtze River to the north and another cultural center in the Pearl River Delta region to the south, making it a strategic point from which military actions may be launched against the Han regions indirectly. Situated in the east of Yunnan-Guizhou Plateau with diverse and complex landforms consisting of alpine steppes at high altitude, mid-altitude jungles and pieces of plains as well as low-altitude forests, Guizhou is a region where different arms of the services, military equipment as well as strategic offensive and defensive technologies in different times can be put into use to some extent, but are constrained by both the natural environments and social elements from playing to their full potential as in the central Han regions. For this reason, Guizhou has seldom been involved as a main battleground in history, but has often been used as a place to launch attacks against the flanks of the main battleground and therefore a supportive strategic spot. Although many ethnic groups intertwine against each other in this land, the sheer size and density of the population of each ethnic group determine that the wars among different ethnic groups in this region can barely match, in magnitude, those fought in the central ethnic Han regions. The military actions taken by ethnic Hans, if spilled over to Guizhou, are often limited in scale and duration, indicating that large-scale military confrontations in the Han regions have often affected this region but never turned Guizhou into a military stronghold that anyone finds necessary to defend tenaciously for an extended period of time. Whenever a military need of this nature emerged in the ethnic Han regions, economic development activities often ensued in Guizhou, leading to the "transit economic development".

The "transit development" prevailed primarily in the Qin and Han dynasties. At the time, the central government knew little about Guizhou and the control of ethnic Hans over this region was weak. In addition, the densely populated Han regions had not be subjugated under one ruling regime, making it a special and meaningful strategy to achieve surprising military results by crossing Guizhou stealthily. Under such a circumstance, to develop Guizhou in this mode was both feasible and effective. It also determined that such development activities usually had an adventurous nature, ended abruptly and only left behind some symbolic facilities, the so-called *bian jun* (border county) by historians, after the activities came off their peak. As a representative of this mode, Tang Meng's diplomatic trip to Yelang Kingdom offers a glimpse of some distinct characteristics of this mode of development.

First, such development was usually an adventure carried out without enough knowledge about the subjects to be developed. Tang Meng's trip to Yelang Kingdom was made possible by totally relying on indirect hearsay and inference and by lobbying Emperor Wu of the Han Dynasty who was eager to recover Nanyue shortly. Little was known by the central government about the targeted place at the moment and what happened later further proved that Tang Meng's trip did not yield the expected result, that is, to stage a surprise attack on Nanyue. In fact, inadequate knowledge about Guizhou was not limited to Emperor Wu but spread across the two Han dynasties. Indirect evidences can be found in *The History of the Former Han Dynasty and The History of the Later Han Dynasty,* in which contents about the history and geography of ethnic groups in Guizhou were often a mixture of legendary stories and facts, and records on geographic locations were often inaccurate, causing heated debates among historians up to now.

Second, these development activities usually lasted for a relatively short period of time and often ended abruptly when their primary target was attained or proved to be unattainable,. The idea of coping with Yelang Kingdom this way fueled heated debate within the central government. Central government officials represented by Gongsun Hong and Zhufu Yan were against confronting Yelang Kingdom militarily. In fact, the operations in Yelang became so difficult that the Han Dynasty decided to give up on the military activities toward Yelang soon after they had started. Subsequently, the development activities in Yelang quickly subsided. Tang Meng set out for Yelang in the sixth year of Jianyuan (135 B.C.); in the third year of Yuanshuo (126 B.C.), Gongsun Hong was appointed *Yu Shi Da Fu* (a high-ranking government official), and Emperor Wu of the Han Dynasty accepted his proposal to abandon the project of building a road to Zangke River and "focus on battling *Xiongnu*" (an ancient nationality living to the north of

China).The peak of the development lasted only about ten years before waning.[1] Due to the lack of deep understanding of the targets to be developed, massive but blind mobilization of people and resources was hard to sustain. The following statement of Zhufu Yan is insightful and thus worth discussing: "The proposal to quell Nanyi, pacify Yelang, frustrate Qiangbo, seize territories, build cities and fortresses, penetrate Xiongnu and burn down its capital city pleases the proposal-makers. However, they are for the benefit of the government officials but not a sustainable strategy in running a country. The present-day China is a peaceful country, and it is not advisable to exhaust it by waging wars against states located far away. If we cannot control our infinite desire to offend Xiongnu, our borders won't be secure. If we don't appease the resentment but incite wars again, that will only make ourselves miserable and terrify our neighboring countries. That is not a sustainable strategy. Now everyone in this country is worried about the endless arms race and burdened with subsequent transportation of military supplies. It is true that protracted wars give rise to rebellions and onerous duties create anxiety. In the territory of *wai jun* (far-away counties) that spans thousands of *li* (Chinese unit of length), we have built tens of cities and fortresses which restrain each other and are flanked by vassals, it is detrimental to the country."[2] Aimed at empowering the central government and weakening the vassal states, Zhufu Yan argued fully against provoking border wars simply for making oneself happy temporarily. With regards to the development of regions like Yelang Kingdom, he argued, right to the point, that such efforts would not give expected results even at the cost of resources. Emperor Wu's decision to abandon the project of Zangke River later proved that his statement was correct. The above examples suggest that transit development was, in most cases, a short-term strategy which cannot be sustained.

Third, the subjective and objective parties in such a mode of development often did not have a concerted relationship. The subjective party usually relied on its sheer power to either threaten or lure the objective party to satisfy its needs while the objective party could do nothing but accept it passively. Tang Meng's first trip to Yelang was accompanied by only a few thousand soldiers but the number of people carrying the supplies and army gear totaled more than ten thousand. It was by such a power play

[1] *Twenty-five Histories* vol. 1, 325-326.
[2] *Twenty-five Histories* vol. 1, 326 col 3.

supplemented by heavy bribery that Yelang was forced to submit itself. Afterwards, Yelang repeatedly pulled back from its original position, demonstrating its reluctance to be forced into acceptance. For the central government of the Han Dynasty, the first trip to Yelang was just a beginning. To maintain the result, it had to keep pumping in tremendous material and manpower resources. The four counties in Bashu, the most affected region, was drained in resources by the road construction designed to lead to Zangke River despite the affluence for which they were previously well known.[①] The cost became so high for the country that it had to pull out from the development eventually.

Fourth, these development activities did not have a significant economic impact on either the subjective or objective party. Other than getting to the core of the economic life of the other party, the economic activities between two parties were only limited to the exchange of surplus people and products. Take the case of Yelang as an example, the Han central government as the subjective party of the operation only received, as documented in *Records of the Grand Historian,* some "horses, cattle and slaves" from the ethnic minority regions.[②] The ethnic minority peoples, similarly, took the surplus products such as metal and fabric from ethnic Han regions. The exchanging activities were mostly conducted by influential individuals or organizations from both sides and seldom involved the makers of these products. Such economic activities, in a nutshell, stayed on the surface.

Lastly, the non-economic constraints that disturbed the development in this mode are primarily a result of incompatibility with natural conditions, followed by the emotional confrontation by the objective party in the operation. *Records of the Grand Historian • Collected Biographies of Barbarians in the Southwest* summarized, rightfully, the reasons why the efforts to construct the road to Zangke River had to be discontinued: "At the time when the road connecting the four counties in Bashu and the ethnic peoples to the southwest was being built, the efforts were unsuccessful even after a few years and cost the lives of many people. The situation was worsened by the repeated barbarian rebellions from the southwest. Government troops were then sent in but failed to crack down the rebellions despite the heavy costs incurred."[③] Apparently, it would not be nearly as

① *Twenty-five Histories* vol. 1, 330 col 1.
② *Twenty-five Histories* vol. 1, 329 col 4.
③ *Twenty-five Histories* vol. 1, 330 col 2.

difficult to build a similar road in central Han regions by the Han government as it was in the ethnic minority regions. The key reason lies in the fact that they were exposed to different natural environments. The construction techniques that the Han government was familiar with were acquired to fit the needs of ethnic Han regions, and would require extra costs if they were to be successful in a totally different environment. However, the operators of these activities tended to be unaware of this. Tang Meng lobbied Emperor Wu of the Han Dynasty on the ground that the mighty dynasty and affluent Bashu combined were enough to force the objective party to give in. However, he forgot one basic fact: a powerful Han was built on the affluent central plain, without which its economic power would lose some steam. Bashu, on the other hand, benefited from unequivalent exchange with the ethnic peoples. A disturbance of the fixed relationship attained in a long period would deprive Bashu of its basis for generating massive wealth, let alone spend more on completing this project.

From a cross-xiang operation perspective, this mode of development is certainly short-term based and unsustainable. Retrospectively, we have to admit that at the initial stage of development when little was known about the targets to be developed, such mode of development was necessary and unavoidable in history. Further development activities would have to rely on the experiences and information acquired in this way. Consequently, the short-lived efforts in developing Yelang Kingdom should not be viewed as a total failure but rather a beneficial exploratory practice in the long run.

Another mode of development, "proxy development", emerged after effective improvements were made to the transit development in the following aspects: First, by effectively building a cooperative relationship with the development targets, try to alleviate frictions between the subjective and objective parties to reduce the chance of being constrained by human and social factors. Second, try to avoid overwhelming the other party by pumping in endless human and material resources to ensure the sustainability of the development efforts and the stability of the status of both parties. Furthermore, try not to keep the people from the subjective party stay inside the regions to be developed for a protracted period of time, so as to reduce the constraints resulting from the incompatibility of these people with the natural environments. This mode of development, created by Zhu-ge Liang of the Three-kingdom Period and lasting into the Song Dynasty, was referred to in the ancient books of the Han Dynasty as *Ji Mi* Policy, which, by its original meaning, signaled the inequality between the subjective and objective parties in the operations and conveyed an evident attitude of ethnic discrimination. *Ji*, a headgear for a horse, and *Mi*, a rope pierced into the nose of a cattle, analogized establishing contact and maintaining a relationship. Apparently, in such a mode of development, the objective parties in the operation were treated as subordinates in the hope of winning their cooperation.

The difficulty in executing the mode of proxy development was to secure the cooperation from the development targets. To this end, measures such as utilization of materials, spiritual reformation, duress by force, and abduction in policy were widely used, among which, the strategy of a psychological attack proposed by Ma Su to Zhu-ge Liang was the most classic. The story was recorded in *The History of the Three Kingdoms · Kingdom of Shu · Biography of Ma Su* annotated by Pei Songzhi: "In the third year of Jianxing, when Zhu-ge Liang was about to launch a military strike on Nanzhong, Ma Su saw him off by accompanying him tens of li. Zhu-ge Liang said: 'We have planned this for many years and are still searching for better strategies.' Ma Su responded: 'Relying on its precipitous landscape and remote location, Nanzhong has long been rebellious to us. We may defeat it today but they will come back tomorrow. When they know that our entire country has been mobilized to fight the war against our enemies in the north, they will take the chance to attack us before we know it. To avoid future troubles by killing them all is neither merciful nor achievable in a rush. As the best military tactic is to frustrate the enemy's will to fight rather than to take their cities by force, and fighting a psychological war is more worthwhile than costing the lives of our soldiers, I wish you may win the heart of our opponents.' Zhu-ge Liang adopted Ma Su's tactic and released and pardoned Meng Huo to bring the south under control. Later, they never revolted while Zhu-ge Liang was alive."[①] The so-called psychological war was a strategy in the development activities where the operators tried to win the trust and willingness to cooperate from the development targets by, on the basis of the ethnic Han culture, fostering strengths and circumventing weaknesses. Whether or not the development activities can be successful

① *The History of the Three Kingdoms • Kingdom of Shu* (Zhonghua Book Company, punctuation ed.), 983-984.

depends on how profoundly the subjective party understood its strengths, how accurately it knew the objective party, and how skillful it was in fostering strengths and circumventing weaknesses.

Unlike transit development, proxy development was a long-lasting and stable mode of development. "They never revolted while Zhu-ge Liang was alive." Although Zhu-ge Liang's operation in Nanzhong lasted for less than one year, he was returned with a stable Nanzhong for more than twenty years. This was a typical example. One thing we need to be watchful was that the stable continuity of this mode of development could not be determined only by the tributary records in ancient books as these records only reflected the interactions happening on the high levels of both sides but not those among grassroots. In reality, as long as the *Ji Mi* relationship did not deteriorate into a military confrontation, exchanges among grassroots would never stop. The ethnic Dongxieman living in the back-land of Guizhou in the Tang Dynasty, for instance, only had three tributary records in history, namely, the third year of Zhenguan (629 A.D.), the thirteenth year of Zhenyuan (797 A.D.) and the third year of Jianzhong (782 A.D.).① However, the three tribute-paying trips made by Dongxieman were all rewarded by the envoys being granted official positions and the establishment of *Ji Mi prefectures and counties* in the territories under their control. With such a foundation in place, civilian interactions would continue in a peaceful and stable manner even though the local rulers did not travel to the capital city directly to pay tributes. Another example was the relationship between the two Song dynasties and Dali, which had a record of even smaller number of tribute-paying trips in more than four hundred years.② However, it did not affect the Song imperial court from buying horses, cutlery, and felt rugs from Dali and selling teas, porcelains, silks to it through indirect channels. Civilian trade was never interrupted.③ Therefore, the number of tributary trips was not always an accurate indicator of the level of developmental interactions between the two parties. The suspension of tributary trips did not necessarily bring an end to the development activities, which was why this mode of development was more advantageous than the transit development.

As civilian exchanges, rather than top-level interactions, carried more weight in this mode of development, the economic penetration between the

① *Twenty-five Histories* vol. 5, 4110, lower col.
② *Twenty-five Histories* vol. 8, 6766, col 1-3.
③ (Song) Chengda Fan, *Guihaiyuhengzhijiyi Annotation*, 91.

subjective and objective parties was deeper and wider than the transit mode. The scale of material exchanges between the two parties was subsequently expanded. Zhuge Liang's southern expedition won him the cooperation from the development target, which gave rise to "a mighty military power and prosperous country."[①] This mode of development, in essence, was based on the need of the Han culture and required that the subjective party exert impact on the regions to be developed to create a complementary economy, and greatly enhance the economic influence. Another example was the Song Dynasty that bought horses from Dali. All the ethnic minority peoples between the Song imperial court and Dali, such as Bina (present-day Zhijin County) and Ziqi (located in present-day Southwest Guizhou Autonomous Prefecture) were involved in such activities. Although the operating activities across different peoples in this mode of development mostly concentrated on the border areas, they were no longer one-way activities conducted by the subjective party. Instead, their influence penetrated into specific civilian production items and units.

The key to the stable continuity of this mode of development was how to adjust the interest relationship between the subjective and objective parties, and how to accurately assess each other's capability and to act accordingly. The Song Dynasty, having learned the lesson from a militaristic Tang regime in its late period, leaned toward a moderate and steady way of developing ethnic regions and was reluctant to take a confrontational approach, thus significantly improving the principle of the proxy mode of development. According to *The History of the Song Dynasty · Southern Barbarians (I)*: "The reason for the kings from ancient times to resort to arms against the people in remote and border regions was simply to stabilize the domestic situations by repelling external threats, but not to parade their might. The barbarians in the southwest live in high mountain regions surrounded by the lands of our emperor, that is, Jing, Chu, Ba, Qian (Guizhou), and Wuzhong. If we try to seize their territories where nothing grows at the cost of our affluent resources, what good does it do to us other than exhausting our own people in exchange for those who can do nothing? It may be a short-term solution if we install tribal chiefs of their own to make them control their own people for us. However, lacking long-term strategies to manage these barbarians, they will

① *The History of the Three Kingdoms • Kingdom of Shu* (Zhonghua Book Company, punctuation ed.), 919.

display an inherent nature of wayward animals to either seek revenge for hatred or gather to revolt out of famine. As a result, they will attack administrative authorities in prefectures and counties, or retreat into the backwoods to become bandits. Although they may eventually be suppressed by our military forces, they can cause heavy damages to the people. The Song Dynasty is grounded on culture and education but not in military threat. Neither was it the way our ancient kings pacified the barbarians."① This statement, disregard of its overt glorification of the benevolent rulers and the contempt for ethnic minorities, reveals some significant and valuable points.

First, it admitted that ethnic minority groups had a legitimate right to develop by their own tradition instead of being forced to accept the ethnic Han culture. As we know, one of the fundamental prerequisites for cross-xiang operations to last is the co-existence and continuation of heterogeneous cultures. A long-term stability among parties in cross-xiang operations can not be secured without first acknowledging the right of subsistence and development by the ethnic minority groups. This is a distinctive characteristic displayed by the proxy mode of development.

Second, it based the policy proposals on the ground of stabilizing the development of the ethnic Han regions and creating a peaceful and conducive inter-ethnic group environment without unprincipled interventions in the economic activities of ethnic groups or a "leave-it-alone" attitude. It opposed any massive undertakings or military actions that were merely driven by personal desires, and proved to be a critical principle in building a long-term harmonious relationship across ethnic groups.

Third, it put the demonstration of military power in a very insignificant position. As described in this statement, "The Song Dynasty is grounded on culture and education but not on military threat." Tragedies like Tianbao Rebellion during the Tang Dynasty never happened throughout the history of developing the southwest in the Song Dynasty, which was attributable to the constraints on showing off their military power by the rulers of Song who seldom forced the development targets into submission. They, instead of turning blind to these regions, were more likely to use economic means such as offering generous grants to the tributary envoys from these minority groups. Another measure was to open up the barter trade markets along the borders in an attempt to encourage trade activities among grassroots. Deeper

① *Twenty-five Histories* vol. 8, 6777, col 1-2.

economic penetration and mutual benefit between ethnic Hans and minority groups ensued. One thing we must keep in mind, though, is that ethnic Hans always led the efforts of these development activities under the principles of Han culture; therefore, proxy development, in essence, was still a "one-way" operation.

People used to think that it was irresponsible for the developed regions not to proactively involve in driving the development of ethnic minorities and allow the backward situation in these regions to continue without interference, but the facts proved otherwise. Although during the Song Dynasty, direct interactions between Dali and the Song imperial court were rare, Dali's economy was not suffocated but instead entered a period of prosperity. The Song court, on the other hand, was worry-free from a costly military buildup, and did not suffer heavy losses as the previous regimes. This was a mutual beneficial scenario. Apparently, it is out of the Han ethnocentric misperception that we tend to think that the ethnic minority regions won't be developed without the proactive interference by the Han culture, and it is an irresponsible behavior if the central government won't take any initiative of the interfering sort. We must firmly believe that the ethnic minority peoples, like the Hans, are capable of innovation, and are able to develop themselves consciously, while in the process, necessary aid, support and guidance can not be ignored.

Despite the shallow penetration into the economy and life of the other ethnic groups in similar modes of development, a series of non-economic constraints emerged for different reasons and influenced in different ways as a result of divergence in the principles of running these activities. Generally speaking, as the personnel and the corresponding economic activities in such a mode of development usually did not directly go deep into the heterogeneous cultural regions, the intensity of incompatibility with a different culture and environment was minimized. While the *Ji Mi* policy was adopted, the constraints on development activities caused by natural environments did not break the surface for a long period in history, with the exception of a few cases, such as Tianbao Rebellion of the Tang Dynasty, Nongzhigao Incident and Zhang Chun's development of Meishandong in early Song Dynasty, which were escalated into military confrontations. In addition, a long-standing and stable operational policy reduced the repercussion on specific development activities by the changes in domestic political tug of war. One thing to be noted was that the Song imperial court stuck to its development policy with few changes, took the initiative to encourage civilian interactions and subsequently reduced the frequency of exchanges for political and ritual reasons, thus yielding more effective results. By the same token, the open-up of barter trade markets to facilitate trading activities in the border regions was a wise practice by the Song Dynasty. The major non-economic constraint in this mode of development came from cultural differences, especially where two cultures engaged with each other. A difference in cultural traditions, and subsequently economic lives governed by such cultural traditions, might easily gave rise to disputes about the product components, quality standards, and pricing, etc., causing contentions and conflicts commonly seen in the barter trade markets. ① Different traditional cultures also resulted in the difference in ethics, morals, habits and customs in life, which, if not dealt with properly, were likely to spiral into tensions, complications and frictions, or even disturbed the normal operation of the development activities. In a nutshell, a large proportion of this type of activities were hampered by non-economic constraints resulting from cultural differences. The impacts are deep and long-lasting.

The above two modes of development had one thing in common: both were centered around the developed ethnic Han regions and radiated outward to influence the other regions. Such a pattern underwent a great change in the Yuan Dynasty. The establishment of the Mongolian Yuan Empire and its unification of China did not begin in the developed Han regions but from the remote ethnic minority regions. Consequently, it differed from previous dynasties in the way of unifying China in that it encircled the ethnic Han regions from outside before finally seizing control over the entire country. This great change had a far-reaching impact on the development of Guizhou. At the time when the Yuan government was planning to develop Guizhou, Yuannan, to further west of Guizhou and more distant from the center of ethnic Han regions, was a strategic place that had already been stationed and heavily guarded by the close relatives of the Yuan monarch.② The regions in Guizhou that used to be in the *Ji Mi* state were tightly circled by Yuan-controlled territories, making the continuation of proxy development a blind and meaningless option. Out of the political and military needs of

① (Song) Chengda Fan, *Guihaiyuhengzhijiyi Annotation*, 208.

② *The History of the Yuan Dynasty* • Table of Kings (Zhonghua Book Company, punctuation ed.), 2735-2749.

opening up the roads to and staying unobstructedly connected with Yunnan, the Empire of Yuan felt it inevitable to send troops to station in and develop Guizhou,[①] bringing an end to most proxy development activities and replaced them with a new mode of development - indirect development.

The major indicator that separated indirect development from proxy development was that the economic interactions between subjective and objective parties in an indirect development were not limited to the areas where relevant ethnic groups bordered each other; instead, people from the subjective party in an indirect development lived, in a status of permanent residents, deep inside the habitats of the objective party. No unified culture, however, emerged out of this situation, but rather, each evolved along the course of its traditional culture in parallel with the other and jointly contributed to the development activities of this region. Although both parties are exposed to the same natural environment, each chose to process and transform the natural environment by conducting different economic activities. The interactions between two parties happened primarily in trading needed products and referencing technologies from each other. Indirect development was not preconditioned on transforming the economic lifestyle of the other party. How long could the parallel evolution last depended on how each culture progressed relative to the other. As long as the culture of the subjective party and that of the objective party evolve concurrently, this mode of development could continue. We used to be misled by the presumption that once a novelty was made accessible to the ethnic minority groups, they could quickly catch up and learn to do it themselves, which would soon transform their backward economic lifestyle into modern ones. In fact, this proves to be an unrealistic hypothesis that overly simplified the process of accepting a heterogeneous culture by an ethnic group and equaled an extremely complex development process to an issue of learning. Furthermore, this misperception seemed to hold that advanced things were like a panacea that could be copied in the places of all kinds of environments. A close read of how Han scholars of the late Ming Dynasty described the economic lives of the ethnic minority groups in Guizhou will offer some help in banishing such a simplified logic. In the year of Wanli of the Ming Dynasty, Guizhou Governor (*xun fu*) Guo Zizhang published a book entitled *Records of Guizhou*, which included ten poems by Jiang Jinzhi under the collective heading of "Assorted Poems about

① *The History of the Yuan Dynasty • Geography* (Zhonghua Book Company, punctuation ed.), 1539.

Central Guizhou." These poems objectively depicted the state of the economic life of the ethnic minority peoples in central Guizhou, and truly reflected how they were developed in parallel with that of the Han people in central Guizhou. These poems were quoted below:

One

On my way home to Dingzhou, I looked back at Guizhou, my gaze being intercepted by the Spring cloud. I could hum verses when surrounded by lush green mountains and the passing egrets reminded me of the places I'd been to. Although indigenous girls with flowers on their heads smiled to them bashfully, soldiers sent from afar could only frown. The rugged and never-ending roads were dreadful even to Li Bai and Yang Shen (two great poets who were said to have traveled to Guizhou).

Two

Traveling all the way to the West, I saw half of the houses deserted and families separated after the war, and nothing delighted me. The only state road meandered in the surrounding mountains that were inhabited by barbarians. Government officials sitting remotely in the royal capital knew nothing but optimistically discussed the situation that even we were unsure about. As an envoy appointed by the central government, I felt lonely and hopeless, let alone those in exile.

Three

Continuous mountains and deep valleys dwarfed the lonely travelers. Going eastward, local dialects were heard to mingle with the language spoken by ethnic Hans who also adopted some customs of local Miaos. Cultivation was done by slash-and-burn, and everyone left home with a hacking knife as a tool. Ravaged by the rebel forces, most thatched cottages were abandoned.

Four

Geographically said to have been under the state of Yelang, the landscape was dominated by endless mountains and valleys, where people of different ethnicity cohabited and traded in local markets. Beautiful ethnic Dong girls were adept at embroidery and brocade, but Gelao women had their hair cut short and could not wear hair accessories. The locals who viewed fish and salt as delicacy never had the luxury to eat mackerels.

Five

When can we see the end of these mountains and fortresses and stop the seemingly endless wandering? Solitude villages made smoke from cooking seem cold, and army stations would otherwise seem deserted if without a few flying flags. The sky was blocked by lofty mountains that muffled the sound of southbound wild geese. Only monkeys haunted the thick clouds. How I wish that the Han government not constrain the local barbarians with unnecessary and over-elaborated formalities!

Six

Local minority people lived in shabby thatched cottages and moved around, competing against each other when in Spring on slash-and-burn cultivation. Only faint drumbeat echoed in desolate villages. Army stations seemed deserted with half slanted flags. Outside merchants rushed in to chase precious minerals and stones. How I wish the emperor would not demand and plunder simply by looking at the local chronicles.

Seven

(Guizhou is) a perilous region with sparsely-allocated people and scarce resources, it produced skinny horses and crippled sheep. Aboriginal women wore seashells threaded by colorful ribbon as ornaments, and soldiers wore uniforms made of locally-produced fabric. Burn marks were seen on the precipices but it only took a rain to turn them green. Meals cooked with grains harvested a year before tasted extremely delicious. This was the way locals accumulated family wealth, on which the government relied to fill its granaries.

Eight

(Guizhou is) surrounded by precipitous mountains with only one passage. Although guardians scattered in the wilderness, they would not prevent unruly Miao bandits from relentlessly seizing the chopping knifes from lonely travelers. We had hoped that the royal troops could have easily suppressed the rebellion, only to find that our soldiers stationed here were under siege by Chief Yang (a rebel leader).

Nine

Looking west at the endless road leading toward the state of Luoshi, the royal capital was already a world away. The soldiers were accompanied only by the moon. The warhorses were so spent but they could only drop to the ground at sunset. The fortresses were attached even at daytime, why should we surprise that no wines were to be found in brothels. How I wish that the expelled government officials be pardoned and permitted to return home by the emperor, as they had been soaked in loneliness for too long.

Ten

The surrounding mountain peaks, in the form of halberd or loop, were impossible to climb. At time of rain and wind, evil spirits could be heard to howl; and during a clear day, you should be able to hear the sound of celestial beings playing pipes. The local Miaos were constantly in the move, who could deliver the official peace-making documents to all of them? (That was why) when urgent military missions were commanded, the general and his soldiers all turned gloomy.

Although a complete verification of what was described in these poems was not the topic of this book, we find it necessary to give them a brief explanation. The regions covered by these poems are the areas surrounding present-day Guiyang, the busiest and most prosperous city in Guizhou, as well as areas along the Hunan-Guizhou Expressway. The contents of these poems were mostly about the lives and production activities of the ethnic peoples who lived in these areas. Most ethnic groups at the moment were in the stage of development labeled as "slash-and-burn cultivation", and regular rice growing was barely seen. In the meantime, the Han immigrants who relied on the only transportation line to stay connected with ethnic Han central regions kept their own economic lifestyle that, although completely different from the surrounding ones, continued stably and uninterruptedly in parallel with each other. In nearly three hundred years since ethnic Hans began migrating into central Guizhou in large numbers until the time when Jiang Jinzhi wrote these poems, no substantial changes happened to the process of parallel evolution between Han and other ethnic groups. It proved that it was possible for the indirect mode of development to continue stably in a long term. It is therefore groundless in history and non-sensical in practice to assume that the introduction of advanced technology and mode of production will lead to a natural and rapid adoption of the new mode of production and the abandonment of the traditional ones by the objective parties in the development.

Needless to say, the penetration of economic activities between the subjective and objective parties in the indirect development was much deeper and wider than that in the previous two modes, but it should not be interpreted as the subjective party's arbitrarily imposing its own will on the objective party to change the economic lifestyle of the later. It was repeatedly proved by the historical documents of the Ming and early Qing dynasties that although the Han immigrants living in Guizhou received the support and financial subsidy from the government and were able to build economic ties directly with producers of ethnic minority groups without having to go through the local hereditary headmen, they could only ensure to keep the Han cultural traditions themselves but could not force the Han cultural standards upon ethnic groups during the mutual economic penetration. For example, the Ming Dynasty did not mechanically follow the regular practices in the developed Han regions when collecting taxes in ethnic minority regions. Instead, it allowed the ethnic minority people to pay taxes with the products they made. Consequently, the *Tu Si* of the ethnic groups near Guiyang were permitted to substitute teas and horses for regular monetary tributes. In fact, the economic penetration between ethnic Hans and other minority groups in this mode of development was achieved primarily by the penetration of products. The garrisons crowed with Han residents often became trade hubs across different ethnic groups. Products that were common in the Han regions such as metals, porcelains, and salt penetrated into ethnic groups; in exchange, local specialties of different ethnic groups such as leather, utensils, lacquers, horses and felts from ethnic Yis, lumbers and teas from ethnic Miao and Dong, rice and forestry by-products from ethnic Buyis flew into the Han regions. Compared with proxy development, indirect development usually involved a flow of products in a greater magnitude and number of types, and happened more frequently.

The status of the subjective and objective parties in the indirect development was determined by political, military and other non-productive factors. The subjective party would lose its status without the support from administration or constant financial supplies enabled by the administrative power, or powerful military backup. That explained why the indirect development activities in Guizhou were mostly driven by military needs and conducted by military immigrants in the beginning. As is widely known to everyone, Han immigrants often received financial subsidies from the government, which, added to the political and military spending, amounted to a massive cost to the feudal state. When the indirect development became a well-established practice, however, the feudal state often viewed it as the expense it had to pay to carry on the glory of territory-expansion by their previous generations, even when the regime was on the verge of a meltdown. In the late Ming Dynasty when the regime was dragged into deep trouble by the protracted war against the late Jin Dynasty in the north and the peasant revolts inside the country, it had to levy heavy taxes to make the ends meet, further sucking the lifeblood of ethnic Han people. However, it did not reduce the financial support and military supplies to Guizhou, which was in the middle of a ten-year-long "She An Rebellion" at the moment. To reinforce the result of cracking down the rebellion in the fourth year of Chongzhen (1631), more garrisons were constructed and more soldiers were enlisted to station in these garrisons in Guizhou as planned by Zhu Xieyuan, who was then the Governor of Guizhou[①], sending the country into a deeper financial abyss. Such a measure was necessary at the time when chaotic political situation inside the country weakened its control on Guizhou. Without the protection from the central government, ethnic Han immigrants who had settled in Guizhou would escape back home in central Han regions, thus putting the indirect development of Guizhou to a complete and abrupt halt. It was for the same reason that Zhu Xieyuan distributed, for free, the lands confiscated from the rebellious *Tu Si* to the willing Han immigrants. Understandably, the government never reduced its political and military backing like this even when the country was in life-threatening crises; otherwise, the fruits gained from indirect development would evaporate overnight.

It is likely that some Han immigrants might have entered Guizhou before the central government organized indirect development activities. During the indirect development, some Han immigrants, both military personnel and civilians, might have escaped the control of the imperial court

① *The History of the Ming Dynasty • Collected Biographies • Zhu Xieyuan* (Zhonghua Book Company, punctuation ed.), 6446 - 6447.

to live under the protection of big or small *Tu Si*[①]. It seems that these people were also developing Guizhou without government support. Such was a misled understanding. The people who broke away from the Han culture would have to live by the mode of production and under the governance of the culture of a particular ethnic group. The production technologies that they had in possession would not be nearly as effective due to the severance from the Han culture. In essence, they had no choice but to be assimilated into the ethnic culture. The difference, if any, was merely the result of different levels of assimilation. Therefore, it is inappropriate to perceive the level of advancement in production technologies as the determinant of the status of subjective or objective parties in the indirect development. It was impossible to secure a subjective status in the development without the backup by political and military powers.

Likewise, indirect development was constrained by many non-economic factors. As indirect development must rely on political and military support, the change in policies was very critical in extending or suspending the development activities. The fact that large-scale indirect development in Guizhou had not happened until the Yuan Dynasty was exclusively the result of a great change in strategic situation that forced the Yuan regime to put more weight on developing Guizhou. For the same reason, the indirect development efforts in the Yuan and Ming dynasties mainly concentrated along the transportation lines and barely touched the southeast Guizhou. The reduction in the intensity of indirect development in Guizhou in the mid-Ming Dynasty was also a result of policy change, when the imperial court did not act quickly enough in response to the military personnel shortage commonly seen in each garrison in Guizhou as a result of a severe and widespread army desertion problem.[②] The Ming central government at the moment was in an all-out war against wo kou (the Japanese pirates) and deployed a majority of its military forces in the southeast coastal region, with barely any reserve left to reinforce Guizhou.

Natural condition was another big constraint on indirect development. As a region with predominantly steep and high mountain landforms, sparse cultivated lands, poor irrigation systems, low temperature and changing

① *The History of the Ming Dynasty • Collected Biographies • Guizhou Tu Si,* see materials about Qiyu Chen (Zhonghua Book Company, punctuation ed.), 8174.

② *Veritable Records of the Ming Dynasty • A Compilation of Materials about Guizhou*, 722,1053,1108, 1009, 1136.

climate that were hard to predict, Guizhou was not an ideal place for growing rice. The local indigenous people, with the exception of ethnic Dong, Buyi and Shui peoples, did not cultivate rice. With the indirect development came a huge number of ethnic Han immigrants, who faced grave challenges when trying to grow rice, which was what they were adept at doing. Despite the land appropriated to them by the government, these Han immigrants found it hard to live on growing rice in these lands and had to rely on other parts of China for food supply. Due to the constraints by natural conditions, the Han immigrants using traditional method of cultivation harvested so little that barely covered the input they made in the lands. Consequently, it caused a devastating shortage of grain on the one hand; and on the other hand, many lands that were appropriated to them by the government were left uncultivated. Many Han immigrants had to live on doing business rather than farming. Unarguably, the results of indirect development depended, to a large extent, on how successful the traditional way of cultivation was adjusted to suit the new natural environment. As all the indirect development activities throughout the Ming Dynasty were subsidized by the government, the Han immigrants in Guizhou never put the need of adjusting their traditional way of cultivation to adapt to the new environment as their top priority. Such a situation did not change until the end of the Ming Dynasty when the Han immigrants, although living on farming, could not produce enough grains for themselves. The efficiency in agricultural production remained at a low level.

The biggest drag on indirect development was the cultural differences across ethnic groups. The ethnic Han people migrating into Guizhou with the wave of development were exposed to the surrounding indigenous cultures that were sharply different from theirs, depriving them of the social foundation that enabled them to carry out economic activities in a stable environment, as they did in the ethnic Han regions. In the case that such a way of living encountered barriers, these Han immigrants could not handle them by making necessary adjustments to adapt to local conditions, but rather had to rely on supports from central Han regions. The problem got so harsh that, although the Han immigrants had settled in Guizhou, it was very difficult for them to build any close relationship with the local ethnic people. Instead, their living space was stranded to near the transportation lines or inside the garrisons simply for the ease of receiving supplies from the Han regions, thus creating a sharp cultural contrast separated by the walls of these garrisons. As Wang Shixing put it, all the activities of the Han immigrants were conducted inside garrisons and local administrative governments only focused on the duty of collecting taxes and corvee without bothering themselves by disputes within ethnic minority groups. [①] Apparently, garrisons in such circumstances were tuned into single "cultural island" isolated from each other and from their surroundings. Lacking the social and economic foundation, these isolated islands could do nothing about solving the numerous difficulties encountered in normal economic activities; in the contrary, they easily became the targets in social turmoils. The fact that the Han immigrants were nearly wiped out in the "She An Rebellion" mirrored the impasse that these Han settlements were in.

The large-scale direct development in Guizhou did not happen until after the mid-Qing Dynasty, which was symbolized by the following three indicators. First, the ethnic Han residents outnumbered ethnic minority people in Guizhou. Second, no "raw territories" that had not been touched by the Han culture could be found in Guizhou anymore. Third, despite the continuation of the financial subsidies from the central government to Guizhou, ethnic Han new arrivals could settle down in absence of these subsidies. Following the emergence of these trends, Han immigrants began setting foot deep into the ethnic minority settlements and independently built Han villages within an unlimited vast territory. The major difference that separated direct development from indirect development was that the development goals were not achieved by the influence on the ethnic minority group's economic lifestyle through product radiation, but rather by integrating the ethnic minority groups and the ethnic Han people into a same economic entity. During the process, the Han economic lifestyle was subjected to a certain level of adaptation to the new environment that drifted apart, to a certain extent, from that in the central Han regions; while the ethnic minority groups started to draw closer to the Han culture. Unlike indirect development where economic lives of different parties evolved in parallel without much crossing, the parties in a direct development tended to approximate to and converge with each other, which narrowed the gap between the two in economic interests. We need to point out that such a scenario has only existed in central cities or along the transportation lines but has not appeared in remote areas where development activities have never

① *Guangzhiyi,* 133.

been undertaken in such a manner. In a direct development, people from both the subjective and objective parties are involved in frequent and deep interactions that blur the border concept. In sharp contrast, indirect development focuses on material exchanges that are often restrained to the areas where different ethnic groups border each other.

The emergence of these new characteristics has not changed the essence of direct development activities. They are "one-way" activities based on the Han culture, aiming at building an area subordinate to the developed Han cultural regions. From a perspective of means of operation, the ethnic Han residents are still the subjective parties in the development, whose mission was to induce the ethnic minority economies to develop for the benefit of the Han culture. The utilization of resources is completely by the standards of the Han culture without taking into account of whether the allocation of resources satisfies the need of a sustainable development. As a result, they create a homogeneous economic lifestyle instead of the coexistence of diversified economies. After all, none of the shortages, such as deficiency in resource utilization, ecological degradation, and unsatisfactory economic efficiency, that are inherent in one-way development activities is riddled by the direct development.

Although the continuation of direct development does not rely on the political and military protection as does that of indirect development, it, similarly, depends on support from developed Han regions primarily in the form of economic support. Unstable political and economic situations in the developed Han regions will affect the execution and steady continuation of direct development activities. What calls for our close attention is that the purpose of this mode of development is to create an economic region subordinate to the Han culture, resulting in the lack of stability in the speed of economic development. In a long-term horizon, Guizhou has lagged behind the developed Han regions.

Direct development activities in Guizhou had lasted until before the founding of the People's Republic of China. Here, we will not elaborate on the pros and cons of this mode of development as they are discernable simply by field investigations. Detailed discussions about these field investigations can be found in later chapters of this book. To facilitate the comparison between direct development and the aforementioned three other modes, we hereby briefly list the primary constraints on this mode of development. Any change in political, economic and military situations in central ethnic Han regions will have a more direct impact on the progress and effectiveness of the direct development activities than those of the other three that tend to have a slower but more inertial response. The regions associated with direct development activities will respond to any political, economic or military changes occurring in the developed Han regions at a slower speed but lasting in a longer period than the developed Han regions. In extreme cases, the intensity of the response from the developing regions may surpass that in the developed Han regions, producing a heavier blow on the development activities in the ethnic minority regions. These scenarios do not exist in the above three modes of development. Constraints from natural environments begin to evolve into sizable ecological crises under the direct mode of development. To some extent, the pace of direct development is forced into a deceleration not by human factors but by the intolerable natural environments, which also contributed to the failure to achieve the expected results for development activities in Guizhou. In direct development, unlike the other three modes of development, the cultural differences across different ethnic groups do not manifest themselves by way of direct ethnic confrontation or friction, but rather by the force of potential containment that causes the operating efficiency to fall. What people see in direct development are usually the failure of specific project or operating enterprise, while in the above three modes of development, what we see are usually the debates over the national development policies.

The four modes of development introduced above are an abstract summary that may not reflect all the development activities that vary dramatically due to the massive territory and numerous ethnic groups in Guizhou. Therefore, we need to keep the following aspects in mind when trying to understand and use these modes of development. First, the discussion is made in the order of the first appearance of a specific mode of development. The appearance of a new mode is not necessarily a signal of the complete phaseout of an old one. As a matter of fact, within the sphere of the entire Guizhou, it is unavoidable to have simultaneously more than one mode of development. We should not understand them as one completely replacing the other. Second, different modes of development have different impact on different ethnic groups due to disparity in their traditional cultures and living environments. It is therefore not appropriate to think that every ethnic group experiences the four modes of development in the same order. Some ethnic groups only underwent one or two modes of development. The ethnic Bunuzhi Yao in Guizhou, for example, has not been subjected to the impact of transit development, while the only mode of development in the Miao settlement in Leishan and Taijiang in southeast Guizhou has been that of indirect development. Third, some regions in Guizhou have been viewed by the ethnic Han people, up to now, as inhabitable places where people cannot survive. Ethnic Hans have barely set foot on these places, thus enabling the ethnic minority people to continue living in their traditions with the need of receiving a quite limited number of tools and necessities from outside. Understandably, none of the above four modes can be applied in the analysis of the economic life in these places. The extreme complexity in the history of development in Guizhou has made it a formidable and onerous task to carry out a thorough analysis of the non-economic constraints in the Guizhou's economic development; therefore, it becomes quite necessary to first clarify the tasks we are about to complete and the difficulties in completing them.

III Realities

The development of ethnic regions in Guizhou has lasted for more than 2000 years. 40 years has passed since the newly founded People's Republic of China began the economic construction in Guizhou, but it remains a tough question as to how to aid this remote and underdeveloped region. Most people still believe that ethnic minority regions are synonymous with poverty, backward and are in urgent need of development and a feasible development strategy. Not to be exaggerating, how to develop the economy of ethnic minority regions has long haunted the administrative authorities in Guizhou, and that's why articles with the titles such as "Alleviate Poverty and Develop Economy," "Subsistence Project" have long occupied the front page of newspapers and magazines. To solve this problem, numerous researches, papers and books have been published and discussed, and we have come up with theories one after another and then rejected each one of them after they are put to the test of practice, most notably the "gradient theory," "counter-gradient theory," "impact development," "radiant development,"etc. The result remains the same: the laggard economy continues in Guizhou. A deepening "reform and opening-up policy" and the shifting emphasis of economic development more toward the coastal regions in the east have widened, other than narrowed, the gap in economy between ethnic minority regions in Guizhou and the developed central Han regions. The gloomy realities are wakening, and it is time for us to consider what are the reasons that have caused the economy of ethnic regions to lag behind, and where do we turn to for the solution.

To answer this question and work out a corresponding strategy, we must first understand the essence of the issue before we can touch its kernel. It is our belief that the laggard economy in ethnic minority regions in Guizhou is a result derived from the characteristics of cross-xiang operations. It has no direct correlation with the amount of effort made by the parties involved, the degree of attentiveness of the administrative authorities, or the size of economic input, but is directly related to the goals and modes of cross-xiang operations as well as the indexes in measuring the level of economy development.

As we emphasize in Chapter One, cross-xiang operations are, in essence, economic activities that must follow the general economic laws. We also point out that cross-xiang operations are special economic activities that are undertaken across different cultural, social and natural backgrounds, which put cross-xiang economic activities in an undeniable objective reality, that is, whether all the phenomena involved in the operating activities are valued equally in terms of describing the level of economic development. As everyone knows, the indexes used to measure the level of economic development vary in different social backgrounds. Mencius, a sage of the ethnic Han nationality, once expressed his philosophy of running a country: "If farmers are not held from cultivation, there will be enough grains; if fine-meshed fishing nets are not used, there will be enough fish and turtles; if trees are cut at the right time, there will be enough lumbers; if there are enough grains, fish and turtles for people to eat and lumbers for people to use, they will have no worries about their life and death, which is the beginning of being a king. If mulberries are planted in a house of five-mu in size, a fifty-year-old will be clothed in silk; if domestic animals are raised and made to mate in time, a seventy-year-old will be fed by meat; If people are not held from cultivating the land of 100-mu, the yield will be enough to feed a household of a few people; if filial piety is taught in school, there will be no grey-haired people with a head-load of things walking on the road. I have never heard of anyone who won't become the king if he enables 70-year-olds to dress in silk and eat meat, and keeps the people from hunger and cold."[1]

The major indicator in Mencius' Utopia is the level of material abundance for each individual in the society with no direct mentioning of currency or market. By contrast, in today's Western world, e.g., the United States of America, the Dow Jones Industrial Average is used as an index of measuring its level of economic development, which reflects the total level of social investment.[2] The rise and fall in stock prices are deemed to be the indicator of the level of social investment. A rising stock price translates into the expansion in investment and thus a higher level of economic development, while a falling stock price symbolizes an economic decline. Stocks, an absolutely necessity in the Western economy, have just been introduced into China, and in Mencius' time, they were unheard of. Apparently, the indicators used to measure social and economic development are different in different social and cultural backgrounds.

We have been facing the same issue in the economic development in ethnic minority regions in Guizhou. As a measure of supporting the economic development in ethnic minority groups in the border regions, the Chinese government introduced "substitute labor for aid" as a poverty-relief initiative, that is, the government sponsored key infrastructure projects and asked the people from disaster-hit or poverty regions to contribute labor hours in exchange for cash payment from the government. The government made the effort in hope of increasing the income of local minority people and driving the infrastructure construction at the state level. In theory, this was a good policy and was in fact very popular in the ethnic Han regions, but it encountered indifference and awkwardness when implemented in ethnic minority regions. Wangmo, a state-level poverty-stricken county, had a per capita income of well below the national average according to reports of economic statistics in China. Contrary to the wish that the introduction of "substitute labor for aid" would be well received by the local ethnic people in Wangmo, unexpectedly, when the road connecting the county center with Zhexiang was constructed, the ethnic Buyi people living along the planned route were unwilling to participate in the construction work and declined the monetary compensation, causing the project to struggle. Eventually, the ethnic Miaos from Ziyun County some hundreds of li away had to be

[1] *Commentaries and Notes on the Thirteen Classics (II)*, 2666.

[2] *A Concise Dictionary of Social Sciences* (Shanghai Lexicographical Publishing House, May 1987, 8th print), 1036.

recruited to complete the project. What was even more puzzling was that the local Buyi people chose to look on idly when the bustling construction was going on by their villages right in front of their very eyes. When we visited these Buyi villages and surveyed them in 1993, we were very surprised when they told us that they had lands and enough grains at home and don't want to make a fool of themselves by running an errand of face-losing nature like this in exchange for some small money. Bear in mind that in China, the standard of measuring the level of economic development is national income, which is calculated by monetary income. However, the ethnic local people only value the grains and foods they have. Direct monetary income is often insignificant to them. In other words, we are encountering a situation of divergent indicators in the measurement of the level of economic development.

Things like this are not uncommon if the characteristics of cross-xiang operations discussed in the previous chapter are taken into account. Unfortunately, they have not attracted our attention as they deserve.

It is widely known that service income is included in the total GDP in the developed Western countries. Service-rendering activities are without any question viewed as an integral part of economy and are given a special term, that is, tertiary industry, which usually generates more income than the first and second industries combined in these countries. China, on the other hand, had not brought the issue of the tertiary industry development on its agenda until the "reform and opening-up policy" was implemented and is still lagging far behind these Western countries in the tertiary industry development up to now. The tertiary industry accounts for a meager percentage of the total GDP in China.

In our fieldwork, we also met the people who had a totally different understanding of service income. We once met a teacher of the Miao ethnic group who was teaching in the Gaopo Miao township merely 50 kilometers away from Guiyang, the capital city of Guizhou. He told us: he left Yunding village, his hometown, to come to work for the township government and live here along with his family of four. While his family was away, his contracted land was cultivated by his neighbor who did everything from cultivation management, harvesting and drying the grains to finally storing the grains in his barn without taking a single grain except for the ones dutifully delivered to the government. Besides, his house was taken care of and kept clean and livable for the return of his family at any time. He once invited us to visit his home with genuine hospitality: "You would think that my house would be trashed while I am away from home all the time. You are wrong. I guarantee you that if you go home with me, you will have no trouble with where you stay and what you eat at all, and you won't feel any inconvenience." It is not necessary for us to verify each one of his words, but we are sure about two things: First, his house is taken care of by someone who does not take any remuneration in return; second, he has not cultivated the land contracted to his family and someone does that for him. It seems that the local people don't have any idea about the concept of service remuneration. Here, inter-personal relationship and ties of friendship are more important to them. To exchange such relationship and feeling for money is shameful. The question is which of the current indicators used in calculating service income can be used here, and if no such indicators can be found, how can the current economic statistics reflect the service income generated in this region. Evidently, our realization of the economic distress in these regions is subject to at least one negligence, that is, labor services in these regions are usually not priced and traded among individuals and therefore the service income in these places are usually recorded as zero.

The current economic system in China strictly separates the means of production from the means of livelihood. In the developed Han regions, farm cattle have, in tradition, been an important component of household assets and have long been treated as important means of production. Such a way of statistics is simply beyond comprehension in modern developed Western countries where animal-driven cultivation of lands is almost non-existent anymore and the horsepower of each farm machine is summed up to measure the level of investment in agriculture. The ethnic minority regions in Guizhou are a sharp contrast. In the remote areas in Anshun and southwest Guizhou, it is common for farmers to own cattle from several to more than ten in number, which are never used to cultivate lands but kept at home to symbolize family wealth, usually served as betrothal presents or sacrifices in religious events instead of being traded for cash or other goods. The same is true for pigs in these regions. Before the "reform and opening-up policy" was executed, a certain number of pigs must be handed over to the country, as was apportioned by the government down to townships and villages. In exchange, local people received slender income in the form of cash at the moment. Such an apportionment has been called off since the beginning of "reform and opening-up policy", but surprisingly, the number of pigs each household feeds and keeps at home has dwindled. The answer, as we are told, is that the only purpose for them to raise pigs at home is to butcher them for the occasion of New Year. Since one or two are enough, it is meaningless for them to feed more.

A comparison of the three economic indicators reveals that they are not inter-replaceable, or will lead to conclusions contradictory to local realities. We cannot, for instance, arrive at the conclusion that one region is in a higher level of agricultural production, or has more massive economic strength than the other simply because the former has more cattle on hand, where as a matter of fact, many of these regions are not yet beyond the slash-and-burn stage. It is even more fallacious if we base on the market price of the cattle they have on hand to determine that they are above the "fairly well-off" level when in fact many of them are classified as poverty-stricken areas up to now.

As the statistics of modern economy are generally based on market prices, the statistic results must, in principle, be validated by the market. Although China was under a planned economy for a protracted period of time, the prices of products were indirectly determined by the market with the exception that the government was inclined to adjusting prices when it felt the need to do so to ensure that the economic construction be undertaken as planned. They were indeed artificial prices but not market prices. However, they were not completely made up but were subject to constant adjustments following market prices; only that these adjustments were not always fully in line with market movements. This was proved by the adjustments in price for products like grain, cotton, oil, steel, and coal under the planned economy. On the other hand, the prices in developed Western countries are completely determined by the supply and demand condition in the market, resulting in repeated fluctuations within a year in the market price of the same product in the same quantity, from as high as double the lowest price to below cost. As the economic statistics are based on market prices, an equal income does not necessarily mean that the product quantity and quality stay unchanged. For the same token, to double the quantity of the same product in the same quality does not always translate into a doubled income; in worst cases, they may sell at a price below cost. These are, by the standard of modern economics, normal phenomena. It was not until the "reform and opening-up policy" was kicked off in China did we abolish the methodology of measuring the operating performance of large and medium-sized state-owned enterprises by the increase in the quantity of products and the book values but through the implementation of a comprehensive economic indicator. Although it had not emphasized the market effect before the "reform and opening-up policy," China had never entirely rejected the role of the market and had cited stable market price as one of our economic achievements. Following the "reform and opening-up policy," the role of the market has received its due affirmation and China's economic statistics are becoming more correlated with market prices. We need to realize, however, that while China is undergoing a market-oriented transformation, we must deal with another situation that seems to be incongruous with market prices in ethnic minority regions in Guizhou.

Located in the Buyi community to the south of Zhenning, Mashan is a region where the four counties of Ziyun, Changshun, Luodian and Wangmo border each other. Local residents use woods and grain stalks exclusively for fueling purposes. As they are directly obtained from their contracted lands or mountains not assigned to anyone without going through the market, local residents don't have such a column as fuel spending, or fuel production when completing statistical surveys. For the same reason, the domestic animals such as pig, cattle or chicken, or even the spending associated with home construction are not reflected in the state statistics. Furthermore, in regions of extreme poverty such as Mashan, statistics in the income from grains often include the corn and the rice of small yields only, but not the side crops such as rice bean, millet, sorghum, or red panicum. Even the local administrative officials can not tell the exact outputs of these side crops. In other words, when we report on the condition of poverty of these regions, we have missed a considerable part of the agricultural outputs, which are significant to the livelihood of the local people but may look penniless to the outsiders. After all, they are results of economic activities and thus an inseparable part of the local economic life. The evaluation of local economic efficiency without taking these side crops into account apparently does not paint a true picture. If we want to reflect them as they are, we will be facing another difficulty, that is, how to price these kinds of products for which there is no local market and to which current economic statistics are not applicable.

The above discussion reveals such an undeniable basic fact: economic indicators for statistical purposes in cross-xiang operations are usually incompatible and often, consciously or unconsciously, distort the facts when used to evaluate the results of cross-xiang operations. As the indicators used to evaluate the success of one-way economic activities conducted in ethnic minority regions in Guizhou in history - the traditional mode of development, are more from a military or political, instead of an economic perspective, such a distortion is negligible. Today when reality requests that cross-xiang operations must be two-way economic activities, such a distortion can no longer be ignored. Therefore, how to face and overcome such a difficulty becomes a matter of great significance that we must address when discussing cross-xiang operations.

By the standard of modern economics, the mode of operation is a structure of production composed of numerous industries and finely-divided type of work. Before the "reform and opening-up policy" was implemented in China, basic industries already existed and were made clear in the national population census although the division was not as fine and numerous as the Western countries. By contrast, there has been no clear-cut division of labor even today in ethnic minority regions in Guizhou where every laborer knows how to work on different type of tasks and, in practice, need to work on multiple types of work simultaneously. This is true even for the households promoted by the government to be specializing in a particular field. They must attend to the jobs in addition to the one they are specialized in. Clearly, work is not organized by division of labor but by coordinating relations among laborers. Consequently, the structure of production is characterized by evident and widespread overlapping types of work, and exchange of products is attained by personal relationship between individuals instead of through commercial channels. A person does not hire other people to help complete a production task that he can not do himself, but rather by the exchange of work with other people, which is made possible through inter-personal relationship. Such an exchange of work is not on monetary basis.

In the ethnic minority regions in Guizhou, especially the remote mountainous areas that are still in the phase of slash-and-burn cultivation, it seems that people also grow crops, raise livestock or work in handicraft industry. A closer analysis often leads to the finding that most of the production work in these regions can be completed by a single worker without the need to cooperate with others. We hereby take the crop farming in Sidazhai Township, Ziyun County as an example to make a brief illustration.

Sidazhai is a township of ethnic Miao where locals predominately live on dry land cropping. We noticed when we paid a visit to a few local Miao households that, first, the land of each household was by no means small in size; but instead of growing one or two crops as ethnic Hans normally do in their hometown, they grew every crop that was useful to them in one piece of land. By our observation, as many as 20 to 30 crops from vegetable, melon, bean, to grain or even cotton might be grown simultaneously in a 15-mu piece of land. We also saw trees planted in the land, including paper mulberry and a variety of fruit trees as well as a considerable number of tung trees. These trees were used either as fodders like paper mulberry and locust tree, or for producing fruits like all the fruit trees. The only exception was tung trees. The locals would bring the fruits of tung trees to the market in exchange for money and then to buy salt with the money received. Nearly everything else was consumed by the household that operated this piece of land. The remainder, if any, might be taken by his neighbors at their own will. The operators didn't seem to mind it as they could do the same thing to other households. In addition to mixing all crops and growing them in one piece of land, the locals, unlike ethnic Hans who usually keep their livestock within densely-fenced cages or dens to prevent them from ruining the crops, often left their domestic animals to feed in the land. After the crops were harvested, big animals like cattle and horse were left unattended to enter the mountains to feed themselves until next spring. It was often the case that the ownership of baby animals that were born while in the wild must be determined by which mother animals they followed. In such a mode of operation, each household usually did not know for sure how much income a specific crop growing in the land could generate. What they reported to the government was usually a small portion of the actual output. For instance, they only reported the output of corn that they collected and stored inside home for winter but not that already consumed. When we visited their villages, we were often treated by the local Miaos with chickens but nobody could answer us when we asked how many chickens they fed each year. They only knew that chickens were butchered whenever there were guests or in special occasions such as wedding ceremonies and funerals. They could always borrow chickens from their neighbors and did not always have to return. Such a mode of production made us aware that there was no division of labor among the households here and the total production was often largely underestimated and as a result could not reflect the real capacity of production. It caught our attention when we were conducting fieldwork in these regions that the locals were capable of firing bricks and tiles, making agricultural tools, and building houses. None of these required hiring artisans from outside the village. The local artisans were, without exception, also very capable in farm work and often took on artisan tasks in slack agricultural seasons without asking for remunerations other than the treatment with meals that often involved meats and wines, on the condition that they would be treated the same way by the others when his family was in need of such helps.

A small sugar factory was constructed in Wangmo County under the state funding. To provide raw materials, the government appealed, in vain, to the local people for planting sugar canes. When failed, it had to persuade the people living some distance away into moving to this region and becoming specialized in planting sugar canes in the lands leased from the local Buyi people near the factory. When we surveyed this region, we found out that in addition to sugar canes, they also planted other crops such as corn, soybean, plantain and vegetables. We were told by the local residents who complained that the sugar factory's irregular production cycles made them worry about subsistence issues if the only thing they planted was sugar canes. In 1993, the yields from the lands cultivated by the specialized sugar cane planters were hardly enough to meet the production need of one month in the factory. Ironically, the efforts made by the government aiming to turn these people into specialized sugar cane planters seemed to have failed.

While many economists have attributed this phenomenon to remnants from a natural economy and the result of a deficient market economy, they fail to interpret one thing: such is not an exceptional phenomenon only visible in remote and poor regions but is seen in places close to the county center, leaving us with no options but to admit that it is not a temporary economic lifestyle and therefore we can not wait for the market to mature before planning on economic projects. To change such a structure of production requires changes to the entire combination of modes of production including cycle of cultivation, individual skill training and integration into the market, etc. Needless to say, it is impossible for individual operators to change the established social reality merely by relying on the economic capacity they have in control. In other words, we hope to veer these local ethnic people onto the path of the market economy so that their economic activities may be integrated into the national or even international economic circulation; however, we feel powerless in face of the combination of modes of production that has lasted for a protracted period in history. This poses another big difficulty to the researchers of modern cross-xiang operations.

Modern economics dictates that the purpose of production is to gain profits from the finished products supplied to the market; put it simply, to maximize profits. Nothing was mentioned about profits in the economic slogan of "to increase productions and ensure supplies" that we chanted before the "reform and opening-up policy." Later, we included the profitability in the indicators measuring the enterprise operating performance as a way of validating the profit-driven behaviors. In the ethnic minority regions in Guizhou, however, things are not quite the same as either of the above. The production activities conducted here barely have anything to do with the market, nor is gaining profits one of the goals of operations. To put it more directly, the production activities in these regions, in essence, are merely for the subsistence of the laborers and their families. Such a conclusion is hard to find only by looking at the statistics results. For example, Liuma region in the south of Zhenning County is rich in raw materials to make the world famous "Liuma tung oil." In 1991 and 1992 when tung oil price skyrocketed, the households here sold tung oil seeds of as many as thousands of jin (Chinese unit of weight equivalent to 500 grams) on average, and easily had a cash income of thousands of Chinese yuan if calculated by the market price at the moment. To our surprise, the surveys we conducted in Banle and Nongpao indicated that this massive income did not end up in investment in pursuit of more profits, or deposited in state-run banks. Instead, people chose to keep the cash at hand or spent it in ritual or social occasions. Nongpao village, located less than five kilometers away from the highway, had an average actual per household income that was enough to afford to build a feeder road connecting the nearby highway with the village, but the road did not materialize. No one in the village proposed to raise funds among the villagers in an effort to make some infrastructure investment such as electricity or running water. The houses had been kept intact for years, even the village school was tumbledown and in urgent need of repair. When we arrived at the village in August 1993, the villagers were working on a deal to sell their 11 precious Phoebes, over one-thousand-year-old trees that made a beautiful scenery, to foreign businessmen at a low cost, in the hope that the foreign businessmen could help build a semi-finished road for the village on their way of shipping the trees out. With the money they had in hand, these villagers could have put in some labor hours to construct the road themselves, a normal thing to do in economic developed regions, without having to sell the rare tree species that were under state protection to lure the others to build the road for them. Such a behavior of disregarding the loss in value and disdaining to organize oneself for the common good of the village is simply beyond the understanding of profit-driven people.

The consumer habits in this region are also puzzling to outsiders. Mashan of Wangmo County, a national poverty-stricken township, is indeed a place in dire poverty if judged by cash income. Many parents here don't even have money to buy text books for their children in primary school. Some consumer habits, though, have puzzled us. For example, residential houses for the farmers in Basai village were all made of high-quality hardwood boards more than 10cm in thickness. The timbers used to build one farm house in this village were more than enough to build three houses of the same size in other places. The same value in use might be attained by saving at least half of the timber used, which could produce a considerable amount of money if sold in the market. However, no one in the village took actions to seek such reasonable income even when they were faced with children who urgently needed text books. In the early 1980s, to tackle the problem of lack of drinking water for both man and domestic animals in dry seasons, the government loaned the village more than 100,000 yuan for a drinking water project. However, the lack of the mechanism to make a maintenance reserve in the local structure of production led the water pipelines made of cast iron to rust badly over ten years after the project was completed. Without another loan from the government, the pipeline would be useless soon. Youmai is another township in Wangmo County where a road was built by state funding to lead directly to Youmai village. Due to the same reason that there was no mechanism in place for the maintenance of this road in the local social structure, heavy rains easily took this road out of service to any vehicle. As a place abundant in tetrapanax papyriferus resources, every household in the village could make hundreds or even over one thousand yuan in cash from selling this medicinal material. Regardless, no one came out to organize the maintenance of the road. Examples like this clearly show that huge investments made by the state do not seem to have been highly valued and cherished by the local people who usually carry out economic activities for the reasons other than gaining profits. As a result, it has not occurred to anyone that the maintenance of the infrastructures paves the way to higher economic profits for the village and for their own families; therefore, the hard-won investments become something irrelevant to the local people.

What is described above makes it clear that these regions are not so poor that cannot raise funds for self-development, or the natural environment so harsh that is not livable, but that the desire to profit and benefit oneself is not overt, making it hard to organize profit-driven investment activities in these regions. The attempt to change the mentality of all the people in the regions will undoubtedly meet with constraints of personal relationship in the society, thus impossible to yield the expected result in a near term. Since we are determined to integrate these regions into national or even international market, the first thing we need to change is people's mindset that is not independent of social environment but rather shaped by the society. Consequently, a change in social structure must happen before the change in people's mindset, and that is not going to happen in the foreseeable future merely through economic investment or ungrounded ideological education. This is another difficulty we face in our research.

The essence of the aforementioned three difficulties and their impacts on cross-xiang operations will be discussed in detail from Chapter Three to Chapter Five. As the incompatibility among heterogeneous ethnic cultures in economic activities has directly given rise to these difficulties, we must have a systematic and thorough understanding of ethnic cultures so that we can further look into the constraining mechanism ethnic cultures have on cross-xiang economic operations. We will carry out the discussions under the title of culture due to the fact that these issues all fall into the category of what cultural anthropologists define as culture. For the ease of reading, we spread the contents into three chapters to avoid flooding the readers with too much information in one single chapter.

Chapter Three Culture (Section I)

Culture is a comprehensive normative system that holds an ethnic group together and coordinates the operation of the society. As each ethnic group has a traditional culture that is distinctive from other ethnic groups that exist concurrently in the world, every ethnic group is an independent social and cultural entity relative to others. As a result, economic activities across different *xiang* are exposed to divergent social backgrounds derived from such different traditional cultures, and therefore must be made compatible to these cultural backgrounds to be successful. Such a compatibility cannot be achieved without extra costs and efforts, which, although not part of the normal economic operations, will have direct impacts on the efficiency of the economic activities. The existence of these impacts, in most cases, directly constrains the effectiveness of cross-xiang operations. Beginning from a discussion of the essence of culture, this chapter analyzes the mechanism of how the traditional cultures of all ethnic groups involved may constrain cross-xiang operations. It goes deeper to look into the composition of ethnic cultures and the differences in economic lifestyles and modes determined by these ethnic cultures, as well as how these differences constrain cross-xiang operations and keep them from attaining the expected results.

I Culture: Essence and Structure

From an economic perspective, cross-xiang operations are by all means economic activities, which requires that they should be carried out by following the laws in economy, and only yield expected results in appropriate social and cultural backgrounds. Besides, cross-xiang operations must be put in a natural background of a supportive nature that can provide necessary natural resources. These, however, are hardly or only partially available to crosss-xiang operations in reality. As a special kind of economic activities, cross-xiang operations span across at least two heterogeneous cultures and have to cope with two or more divergent natural backgrounds. Consequently, it is almost actually impossible to have all the needed social conditions in place. The variances, especially those across cultures, certainly will force these economic activities into trying to balance the innate characteristics of various heterogeneous cultures, and as a result, dampen the operating efficiency as compared with those conducted under the same conditions within a homogeneous *xiang.* Judging by the fact that the same investment, operation, technology and distribution have not yielded similar results, the subjective parties in cross-xiang operations would naturally blame non-economic constraints for the discrepancy from the expected targets in operation. In other words, as cross-xiang operations will, without question, concern heterogeneous cultures, they will certainly be affected by non-economic constraints caused by the existence of divergent cultures. To lead our discussion to a deeper level, we must first systematically probe in "culture", a social phenomenon, to fully understand in what ways it mechanically constrains cross-xiang operation before we may possibly unveil the effective solutions.

The deepening implementation of the "reform and opening-up policy" in China has brought back to life cultural anthropology, or ethnology, that remained dormant for a long period in the past, beginning to attract a widespread heed in the academic circle. Before long, "culture" has become a hot topic in the fields of social science in China, around which scholarly books written in or translated into Chinese start to pile up, making any research in social science seemingly related to the topic of culture. We must realize, however, that the long dormancy of ethnology in China has resulted in a fault between the ethnological research in China and that in the world, and subsequently hindered the academic integration between the two. Putting the issues of a deeper nature aside, the definition and essence of culture are not agreed upon even in most influential scholars in China. Without a broad consensus on this, it is impossible to communicate in the academia on any research in any form that is undertaken at a deeper level, not to mention the possibility of drawing any conclusion with practical values. Therefore, to elaborate on our very own understanding, we attempt to answer the following two questions: 1. What is the essence of culture? 2. How do we define culture? Based on this, we then push the discussion one step further to continue exploring the status and functions of culture in cross-xiang operations.

"Culture" has been a key term in cultural anthropology, or ethnology. In more than 100 years in the past, quite a few scholars whose theories contribute to the establishment of the discipline of ethnology have, based on their own theories and materials they have on hand, illustrated and elaborated on the essence of culture, which have understandably demonstrated both some theoretical inadequacies and values hitherto due to limitations in time and natural endowment. Although for the sake of today's research, we should have preceded our research by thoroughly classifying and summarizing the research results of our predecessors, it is nevertheless a difficult and complex mission that cannot be accomplished by any individual independently. As the purpose of this book is to study cross-xiang operations, it suffices our needs to give a general and brief introduction as below.

Culture is a general system that governs the behaviors of all members in a given society and regulates the material and spiritual life in that society, which concerns nearly all, rather than some, facets of the life of human beings. Culture has long been perceived this way. Edward Tylor, one of the founding figures of ethnology defines culture as not only regulates the material life of human beings but is that complex whole which includes knowledge, belief, art, morals, law, custom, and any other capabilities and habits that fall into the category of spiritual life of human beings. [①] Such a definition has its weaknesses, the most apparent one being the lack of integrity. He does not see the individual element of a culture as an organic and integral component that is interdependent on and constrains each other. To understand this essence of culture is key to cross-xiang operations. It tells us that any economic activity is a social activity conducted in specific cultural backgrounds and an economic activity is a sub-system, or an integral component, of the overall cultural system. Economic activities cannot be conducted without being exposed to a social context; to the contrary, they can only survive by relying on a specific culture, which, in cross-xiang operations, becomes two or more heterogeneous cultures, one of the major substantial differences between cross-xiang and same-xiang operations.

Instead of one homogeneous culture, the human society has numerous cultures that are heterogeneous and develop concurrently to create a diversified picture of mankind. This is one of the fundamental attributes of human being's culture in general. The notion that heterogeneous cultures are relatively independent of each other, remain relatively stable and have divergent value propositions is defined in ethnology as "cultural relativism". It was first brought forward by Boas and later improved and built upon by his student Herskovits to become one of the most fundamental theoretical foundations of ethnology. Boas, in his efforts to counter "environmental

[①]Edward Burnett Tylor, *Primitive Culture*, trans. Lian Shusheng (Shanghai Wenyi Press, June 1992), 1.

determinism" in ethnology, pointed out after flawlessly devised and well-carried-out researches that a relatively independent culture is not determined by any single factor, geographic environment, historical tradition, religion or social system but is shaped eventually by multiple elements combined. The complexity of constraining elements will undoubtedly lead to different cultures with varying degrees of independence and stability, and the inability for different cultures to merge in value proposition.[1] On this basis, Herskovits systemized and improved the cultural relativism to make it an important component of ethnological theories.

Although cultural relativism has been a target of criticism and questioning after World War II, the fact that ethnic groups in today's world, including all developed and developing ethnic groups, have demonstrated a cultural stability and uncrossing value propositions has continued offering fresh evidences in support of this theoretical perception. Understanding this essence of culture is equally important in the cross-xiang research. Exposed to at least two heterogeneous cultures, cross-xiang operations have no choice but to face the following three difficult contradictions: 1. the sharp contradiction between a long continuation of stably lasting heterogeneous cultures and the short-term nature of economic activities; 2. the contradiction between the diversity in coexistent heterogeneous cultures and the homogeneity of specific economic activities; 3. the contradiction between the diversity in the value propositions of heterogeneous cultures and the purity of material forms of economic activities. These contradictions are one of important reasons to subject cross-xiang operations to the impacts of non-economic constraints.

Culture is a complex and organic system composed of numerous elements, i.e. cultural factors, which are mutually interdependent and constraining to form a tightly fit network. All the cultural factors perform their respective functions in a constant movement and combine to service the ethnic group. Such a notion was first proposed by Malinowski[2] and was later developed by people like Radeliffe Brown into the so-called "structural functionalism", which not only establishes as one of the theoretical foundations of ethnology but also infiltrates into other disciplines such as

[1] Zelin Wu, "A Brief Introduction of Boaz and the American Historical School," *Ethnological Study* no. 11 (The Ethnic Publishing House, August 1981), 319-337.
[2] Malinowski, *A Scientific Theory of Culture,* trans. Xiaotong Fei (China Folk Art Publishing House, February 1987), 14.

sociology, economics, religious studies, and linguistics etc., making it one of the most far-reaching and influential schools of thought in the 20th century social science studies.

It's equally unignorable for cross-xiang researchers to realize that culture is an orderly structure with specific social functions.

First of all, the power to initiate an economic activity is not unlimited or can continue infinitely; it aims at accomplishing a pre-set target. As a result, the barriers that cross-xiang operations must face are by no means one or two in number, but a systematic network of barriers.

Second, the mutual interdependence and constraint between the systematic structure of culture and its cultural factors determines that culture does not respond to external stimulation by the strict-sensed one-on-one cause-and-effect mode but by systematic adjustment, rejection and resistance that are complex and perplexing. Even though cross-xiang operations only attempt to accomplish economic targets, the reactions they trigger will definitely expand outside the economic territory, resulting in the further complication of cross-xiang operations. Overlooking such a reality of complication that is sure to happen will see unexpected non-economic constraints to follow one after another.

Third, as the systematic functional network structure of culture concerns a wide array of things, and cultural factors have an extremely complex and seamlessly-structured relationship, the culture of any ethnic group can generate massive energy that easily overpowers that mobilized by a single economic project. Therefore, cross-xiang operators are sent into a stalemate. On the one hand, the economic efficiency is without any doubt disturbed by non-economic constraints if the heterogeneous culture is left intact; on the other hand, the attempt to shake the heterogeneous culture is usually beyond the capacity of the operators and often ends up in the difficulty in attaining expected results in a timely manner although the key elements required by economic activities may be made available on time. It is not so difficult to tell that the organic systematic structure of culture is another fundamental reason that subjects cross-xiang operations to the impact of non-economic constraints.

Fourth, culture is a tool made exclusively for the specific ethnic group. Every ethnic group must rely on its unique culture to conquer, process and transform the natural environment it is exposed to in order to acquire the material foundation for the subsistence of its members, coordinate interpersonal relations among them, and to keep the whole group to live on and reproduce. Lack of such a tool makes it impossible for mankind to develop societies or conquer the nature, but to live, like animals, on one's own. Such a concept was set forth by David Emile Durkheim and Marcel Mauss who first used the term "collective consciousness"[①]and later made it into the popular academic lexicon. It was further developed by Malinowski who saw his theories as built on the fundamental "theory of need", and argued that the culture of an ethnic group is a set of tool needed by this particular ethnic group for its subsistence and continuity.

To understand the essence of culture as a tool exclusively for the use of an ethnic group is a significant breakthrough in ethnological theories. It presents to us a direct corresponding relationship between the culture and the ethnic group it belongs to, and solves the problem of the cultural evaluation, providing keys to many questions in cross-cultural economic activities that have long puzzled us. It used to be that when subjective parties in cross-xiang operations encountered barriers or frustrations, they, without hesitation, blamed the objective parties for their inferior quality, purposeful disturbance, or unwillingness to cooperate, and sometimes they blamed people on their side for the lack of efforts or resolve in operations. Since the acceptance of culture as a tool by the academic circle, people have begun to reflect on whether the means of operations employed in their own culture can be effectively used in a heterogeneous culture. Following this train of thought, it quickly became apparent that in traditional cross-xiang operations, people would unexceptionally copy the items and means of the operations of the subjective parties and seek to accomplish the same operating targets, whose success was constrained by the traditional culture of the subjective parties. A tool's level of efficiency would decrease when used beyond its designed scope of usage. It is therefore natural and understandable if culture, as a tool, is used in a heterogeneous environment. Based on such an understanding, Malinowski suggested that the British colonial regime rule the colonies in an indirect way, i.e., through a continuation of the traditional culture of the colonies. Although Malinowski's stance is totally unacceptable to us as China is a socialist country where every ethnic group is equal in status and no ethnic

① C. A. Tokarev (USSR), *A History of Foreign Ethnography*, trans. Zhengfang Tang (China Social Sciences Press, December 1983), 217-220.

oppression in any form is tolerated, the foundational theory, on which Malinowski made the policy proposal, has a significant value of reference to us. If we copy the exact culture of the subjective parties in cross-xiang operations without giving consideration to the coordination and compatibility between heterogeneous cultures, the cross-xiang activities will no doubt encounter rejection, resistance and blockade from a deeper structure of the heterogeneous culture, which will give rise to a serial non-economic constraints, causing the operating efficiency to fall and the project to fail eventually.

Lastly, culture is established through customs and rules by the ethnic group it is associated with, and is subject to constant improvement and development in actual practice to be shaped and eventually become fixed. Culture does not fall from the sky nor is attained in one stroke; instead, it is gradually passed down in generations among all the members of the ethnic group. In other words, culture is both "inherited" in generations and "learned" by individuals.

The fact that culture is acquired by both inherited and learned behaviors was known to the pioneering figures in ethnology much earlier in time. However, researchers acknowledged it only as undeniable facts and seldom gave much thought to their practical value, nor did they pay much attention to the underlying causes of these facts. With the expansion in the scope and deepening in the contents of ethnological research in recent years, scholars start to notice the practical value of such an attribute of culture, especially the impact of cultural learning process on the personality formation of members of ethnic groups, as well as the inner connection between individual personality and culture, [①] making it possible to deepen the understanding of the essence of principles in cross-xiang operations. Any economic activity must take the basic form of individual activities on the reliance of corresponding cultures to achieve the expected targets through individual efforts and cultural continuation. Cross-xiang operations are no exception in that they are carried out through individual activities. Compared to same-xiang operations, cross-xiang operations have some unique attributes. They concern the people who, due to different cultural heritage and learned cultural behaviors, have divergent personalities that are difficult to integrate

[①] Roger M. Keesing, *Cultural Anthropology: A Contemporary Perspective*, trans. Gongqi Zhang et al. (Taiwan: Chuliu Publisher), 303-306.

with each other, thus shaking the cornerstone for interpersonal communication and profoundly impacting how cross-xiang operations need to be managed. The subjective parties in cross-xiang operations have to face individuals who grow in a heterogeneous culture and thus have divergent perspectives, other than those whom they prone to understand. In other words, throughout the execution of cross-xiang operations, any conflict between the subjective parties and anyone they deal with (by hire or cooperation) goes beyond these individuals and is sure to relate to other people who may look irrelevant from an operating perspective, such as relatives, family members, secular or religious leaders of the community, or even neighbors of the individual involved. A seemingly simple dispute with an individual may provoke an entire group of people, which extremely complicates the managerial situation in cross-xiang operations, and causes unnecessary losses and a sharp fall in economic efficiency. A series of non-economic constraints will become overt and play out to our surprise if we manage the interpersonal relations in cross-xiang operations by blindly copying the means of operation that we are familiar with without acknowledging the inheritance and learning nature of culture, or discerning the relationship between such a nature of culture with the personalities of the individuals involved. This is the underlying reason that keeps cross-xiang operations from making expected progress.

After the elaboration of the essence of ethnic cultures, we need to give culture an accurate definition to facilitate our discussion of cross-xiang operations. Such a definition will definitely have some discrepancy from the one used traditionally in the discipline of ethnology since it is generalized for a specific research topic instead of a highly abstract statement used in academic researches. Here is our definition of culture: Culture is a collection of all relatively stable, independent and aggregate social norms that are established by all the members of a particular social group (meaning ethnic group) in the way of gradually accumulating and practicing customs over a time span of generations, and are continued and developed through learning among group members for the purpose of maintaining the subsistence and development of this particular social group. [1] By this definition, an ethnic group is an "aggregate", or "community" of people. From the perspective of

[1] Tingshuo Yang et al., *Ethnic Culture and the Living Environment*, (Guizhou People's Publishing House, September 1992), 2.

the components of *xiang*, cross-xiang operations are activities that cross both cultures and ethnic groups; therefore, a further discussion of the characteristics of cross-xiang operations is hardly possible without first understanding the internal structure of culture as well as the complex relationship between the internal structure of culture and cross-xiang operating activities.

As mentioned above, culture is a structure of network in order. Due to the complexity of a cultural network, its analysis may be carried out from different angles. To begin with the analysis of how closely related the component factors of a culture are to material lives, we may categorize any specific culture into four different levels, each consisting of a number of different groups of factors named "cultural complex" that are made up of a large number of cultural factors. These cultural factors, cultural complexes and cultural levels are interdependent and constraining within this specific culture and serve, as a whole, this ethnic group. The internal structure revealed from this angle is called the "structure of forms" of culture. Although the structure of forms of each ethnic culture is similar, the components of cultural factors, interrelation and interdependence among cultural factors are different. To help readers better understand the structure of forms in a culture, we will provide a brief illustration on the structure of forms for each ethnic group in the section below.

Generally, every culture is structured at four levels, namely, material, organizational, guidance and emotional components. The two cultural complexes, i.e., the distribution of ethnic cultures[①] and economic lives form the first level, namely, the material level or fundamental level. The second level, namely, the organizational level or coordination level, consists of the three cultural complexes of social organization, language, and custom. The third level, namely, cognitive guidance level or potential level, is made up of knowledge, skill and traditional education in societies. The fourth level composes religion, ethic and moral, ethnic consciousness, and art, and is also called resonance balance level or potential supplementary level.

The first level lays the foundation on which members of the ethnic group can subsist. It is both the material foundation on which the ethnic culture is built and the ground level of the culture itself. It serves as corner stones of the

① The distribution of ethnic culture is the ethnic living environment mentioned in chapter one. The relationship between ethnic living environment and cross-xiang operations will be discussed in chapter six.

entire culture and is thus called fundamental level. The function of the second level is to directly organize subsistence activities among group members, coordinate the processing, usage, transformation and sharing of material products, communicate and cooperate among individuals as well as regulate the generational reproduction of the group members to ensure the long-term continuation of this ethnic group. It is classified as the organizational level due to its relation with social materials. The function of the third level is to offer cognitive guidance to the members of the ethnic group, the carrier of the culture, and activities that happen at all levels of each cultural complexes. From a functional perspective, it is categorized as cognitive guidance level. Due to the fact that the cultural phenomena at this level are not as overt as the above two levels, and only some, but not every, members of the group must understand them so that they can guide the direction of the cultural movement, it is, from the perspective of performance of functions, viewed as a potentially dynamic level and is therefore called potential level. The fourth level supplements the third to distribute the effectiveness and guidance formed in the third level across the entire ethnic group (of course unlike the first and second levels that never stops functioning, the fourth level can only play this role under specific circumstances) to drive a concerted and consistent action by all members of the group, when necessary, to achieve the goal of adjusting the culture as a whole. It has a supplementary function aimed at creating an emotional resonance across all group members so that the effectiveness achieved by the third level can be reinforced and be materialized, and is therefore called potential supplementary level, or resonance balance level.

The below table illustrates the structure of forms of cultures, created for the ease of understanding by the readers.

Level	Cultural Complexes
IV	Religion art ethic and moral
III	Knowledge skill education
II	Social organization language custom
I	Economic living environment (distribution)

The clarification on the structure of cultural forms makes it much easier for us to understand the essence of a variety of non-economic constraints in cross-xiang operations. It also offers principles for us to follow when carrying out analyses and discussions. In a nutshell, the structure of cultural forms is significant in the following five aspects of cross-xiang economic analyses.

First, it enables us to determine how close a relation each non-economic constraint has with cross-xiang operating activities. As cross-xiang economic activities are special economic activities, they are at the fundamental level of the structure of cultural forms and are most directly related to the ethnic living environment of the objective parties in the operations. The different types and forms of economic life of different ethnic groups that cross-xiang economic activities concern have a more direct impact on cross-xiang operations. The cultural complexes at the coordination level such as social organization, language, custom and habit impact the cross-xiang activities in an indirect way, and any non-economic constraint arising from these cultural complexes are understandably indirect constraints. Based on this logic, cultural complexes at the potential level, such as knowledge, skill, social tradition and education etc., are more distantly related to cross-xiang operations, and non-economic constraints arising from them are further apart from cross-xiang operations. The cultural complexes at the potential supplementary level such as religious belief, ethic and moral are even more remotely linked with cross-xiang operations. Naturally, non-economic constraints triggered by these cultural complexes can only bring difficulties to cross-xiang economic activities through multi-layered indirect methods. It calls for our attention that the above analyses only point out how directly or indirectly related a variety of non-economic constraints are to cross-xiang operations without mentioning the actual energy any of these non-economic constraints has; we only point out the ways in which these non-economic constraints disturb cross-xiang operating activities without touching on what destructive damage they are able to do to cross-xiang economic activities. Even the cultural complexes that are most remotely related to cross-xiang operations and impact them in an indirect way can inflict destructive damage that is irreparable. Therefore, the negative role they can play must not be underestimated.

Second, the structure of cultural forms may help us understand the essence of non-economic constraints. Every cultural complex has established major social functions, to which the social functions of the non-economic constraints arising from that particular cultural complex correspond. It leads to the conclusion that as long as we have identified to which structure of cultural forms a non-economic restraint belongs, we get hold of its major social functions, as well as over what social issues it may conflict with specific cross-xiang economic activities. It helps avoid aimless trials and tests.

Third, the structure of cultural forms also aids us in clarifying the relationship of co-movement among many non-economic constraints. For instance, non-economic constraints arising from religious beliefs may seem to have no direct conflict with cross-xiang operations, but they may spread their impact among members of the related ethnic group via the language channel and thus change their attitude toward the cross-xiang activities. They may also directly interfere in these activities through social organizations, or disturb their management via customs and habits. Apparently, any non-economic constraint in cross-xiang operations does not exert impacts on these operations independently but may cause simultaneous movement of other constraints that combine to hinder or drive the execution of cross-xiang operations from different angles and in different ways.

Fourth, the framework of structure of cultural forms can help foresee the probability of the emergence of non-economic constraints. As the structures of cultural forms of all ethnic groups are basically congruent, if evident divergence or discrepancy in a certain cultural complex exists between different ethnic groups in a cross-xiang operation, and such divergence or discrepancy is related to this particular cross-xiang operation, non-economic constrains will without any doubt arise out of this particular cultural complex. Such a cognition enables us to foresee where and what non-economic constraints will emerge even before the cross-xiang operations start, which better prepares us for possible difficulties.

Fifth, the structure of cultural forms also provides valuable insights in dealing with the disturbances caused by specific non-economic constraints. Despite the various ways in which non-economic constraints disturb cross-xiang economic activities, operators usually don't go underneath the reasons on the surface. For example, when workers disobey factory rules, what the management can do is to discipline them by the rules and regulations, which in cross-xiang operations is off the point. Under the guidance of the structure of cultural forms, it becomes easier for the management to figure out what the underlying reason is: are the unruly workers constrained by the ethnic and social organization they belong to, or language barriers cause the misunderstanding of factory rules, or is the social education the specific workers receive in their own ethnic group contradictory to the factory rules? A right-to-the-point solution can easily be found after the underlying reasons are identified. In this regard, the structure of cultural forms provides a guideline to the subjective parties in countering non-economic constraints in cross-xiang operations.

In summary, the structure of cultural forms is a framework that is valuable in many ways to the subjective parties in cross-xiang operations, without making use of which, the operators' attempts to battle non-economic constraints blindly by pure economic measures usually will end up in failure.

II Similarities and Differences in the Economic Life of Human Beings: An Overview

On the basis of a thorough understanding of the essence and structure of culture, our perception on the similarities and differences of the economic life of human being is renewed and that on the core of the argument between the two schools in economic anthropology is deepened. Human beings form into thousands of ethnic groups that are governed by a wide array of cultural rules and live dramatically diversified economic lives. Such a diversification is manifested not only in the level of energy control, but also in the form of materialization when human beings and the nature exchange materials with energies as well as the ratio, scale and means of such exchanges. Due to the extreme complexity of the diversification, the academic world has not been able to agree on a unitary measurement to make the quantifiable analyses possible so far. These objective realities are the foundations of substantialism in economic anthropology. On the other hand, no matter how different human economic lives look, they fit the universal definition that, for the purpose of meeting all their needs in subsistence and reproduction and on the basis the laws of cultural operation, human societies enable the exchange in material and energy between man and nature while the material and energy are in constant movement. Due to the universality in the exchange of material and energy in all human economic lives, ethnic groups that capture more energy and use it more efficiently are able to lure or force other ethnic groups to conduct economic activities by their own norms to some extent by means of partially lowering efficiency. In ethnology, such an ethnic relationship is defined as "acculturation", which provides a foundation for formalism in economic anthropology.

This book focuses on the study of non-economic constraints in cross-xiang operations. However, a striking difference in the understanding of the connotative meaning of non-economic constraints separates us from economists. Principles in economics are theorized based on the ethnic groups and societies with a fully developed market economy, and may prove irrelevant in societies without a market mechanism or a premature market economy. Because of the existence of cross-ethnic-group acculturation, the irrelevancy usually does not manifest itself by an utter denial of the established viewpoints in economics, but rather is reflected in social phenomena outside the sphere of economic life in a way that can hardly be explained by prevailing economic theories. This has given rise to the confusion that the barriers encountered in cross-xiang operations as a result, without a doubt, of divergence in economic lives of different ethnic groups are viewed by economists as disturbances from non-economic constraints and therefore should be classified into non-economic constraints.

To facilitate the communication with academic terminology that has long prevailed, we have chosen, with reluctance, to continue following the pre-existent norms by referring in general to these disturbing factors as non-economic constraints. We have no doubt that these hindering factors are in fact of economic nature resulting from the unavoidable differences in economic activities across different ethnic groups in cross-xiang operations. They are, however, too dramatically different from the economic activities carried out by the subjective parties in cross-xiang operations that they usually find it impossible to categorize these phenomena into the economic activities they are familiar with, and thus often treat them as other social problems instead of economic problems.

The efforts made by the pioneering scholars in ethnology in more than 100 years in the past have made it possible for us to systematically classify and analyze the vastly diversified economic lives of human being. After World War II, the school of neoevolutionism emerged in the United States of America that introduced the theory of "dual evolution" to the evolutionary perspective of ethnic culture. It argued that the development and evolution of every ethnic group in the world was the result of the "general evolution" and "specific evolution" combined, and although they differed in direction, content and result, a specific ethnic group, however, might possibly undergo and therefore have the contents of both of them.[①] This brand new theory on evolution was introduced into China after the Third Plenary Session of the 11th Central Committee of the CPC and received tremendous responses in the academic circle in China. Attempts have been made, by Mr. Tan Minghua, for instance, to build an indicator system that can be used to quantifiably analyze the development in ethnic regions, which will have unfathomable ramifications on the quantifiable ethnological research in China.[②]

The dualism in cultural development determines that the development of economic life, as a component of ethnic culture, has the dualism characteristic. On the one hand, economic lives evolve generally from lower to higher level, displaying a level discrepancy. We may, by following such a clue, distinguish economic lives of ethnic groups in the world and classify them into a few different levels. To continue naming them the same as did by Mr. Tan Minghua, we name the economic life at different levels as different type of economic life, and the difference between different types as "difference in type". The quantifiable level in the control and usage of energy sets types of economic life apart. On the other hand, economic lives of different ethnic groups may have characteristic differences at a horizontal level as a result of specific evolution. Such differences are not of a linear nature across different levels but attributable to different degrees in comprehensive adaptability, which are the ability of specific ethnic group to adjust itself when facing specific natural or social environment. Currently, there has been no term commonly accepted in the academia in China to describe such a difference in economic lives as a result of specific evolution. To facilitate the writing of this book, we hereby name the total results in economic life resulting from specific evolution as differences in mode from the same type of economic life, briefly referred to as "difference in mode" in the economic life of related ethnic groups. In cross-xiang economic activities, the operators may encounter the "difference in type" or "difference in mode", or even both simultaneously, each of the above three scenarios likely to give rise to constraints in cross-xiang operations. From the perspective of subjective parties in cross-xiang operations, such constraints are unquestionably identified as non-economic constraints.

① T. Harding et al., *Culture and Evolution*, trans. Jianjun Han et al.(Zhejiang People's Publishing House, September 1987), 19-31.

② Minghua Tan, "On the Development of Ethnic Groups and Its Measurement," *Ethno-National Studies* no. 5 (1992), 7.

The academic world has not unanimously agreed on the types of ethnic economic life in the world. Victor Barnouw classified economic lives into four types, namely, hunting and gathering, Swidden cultivation, agriculture and industry [①] while Keesing classified them into hunting and gathering, shifting cultivation (Swidden cultivation) and nomadism, conventional agriculture and modern industrial civilization. [②] Despite their popularity in the scholarly world, both are weak in that they have not given a strict connotative definition and a number of issues lack universality and completeness when human economic lives are generalized. We have borrowed Leslie White's method of classification that determines the type of economic life by the amount of energy an ethnic group is able to capture when analyzing different types of economic lives in ethnic minority regions in Guizhou,[③] and classify them into five types, namely, hunting and gathering, Swidden cultivation, animal husbandry, agriculture and industry, which ascend in terms of the level of energy capturing ability by people, and expand in that order in terms of the objects to capture the energy from. This expansion in scope can be easily felt by the direct "participant observation", and therefore this method of classification is more symbolic and easier to operate. Below is a brief illustration of these symbolic characteristics.

Hunting and gathering is the oldest and most rudimentary type of human economic life. Although it is not existent any more in ethnic minority regions in Guizhou, such type of economy was clearly recorded in the ancient literature. *The History of the Wei Dynasty · Biography of Liao Ethnic Group*, for instance, recorded the economic life of ethnic Liao at the moment. [④] In addition, it needs to be pointed out that remnants of this type of economy can be found in some ethnic minority regions in Guizhou even today and they are able to exert considerable constraining forces in the economic life of these ethnic minorities. Systemic surveys and researches carried out recently on ethnic Bunuzhi Yao people in Yaoshan Township, Libo County have echoed this finding. Even in the busiest fall harvest season, once traces of wild animals were detected, the ethnic Yaos in this region would stop their farm work on hand immediately without the slightest hesitation and go into the

① Victor Barnouw. "Ethnology", *A Collection of Researches in the History of Ethnic Groups in Border Regions in Southwestern China,* no. 4.

② Keesing, *Cultural Anthropology: A Contemporary Perspective,* 149-157.

③ Meng Zhang et al., *The Genesis of Mankind* (Sichuan People's Publishing House, June 1987), 256-259.

④ *Twenty-five Histories* vol. 3, *History of the Wei Dynasty* • *Biography of Liao Ethnic Group*, 2429 mountains to hunt animals. They looked assured and unyielding when defending their action: "Crops in the field cannot run but the wild animals only come here once a year. You won't catch them again if you miss them this time."① It is apparent that hunting to them is not a game or recreation but an appropriate economic activity. Former researchers used to interpret this as an indication that these people lagged behind in their ideology and did not take agricultural production seriously, and that kept them in poverty. Such an interpretation is not a reflection of reality because these researchers did not realize that ethnic Hans and Bunuzhi Yaos were in two completely different types of economic life. They also acknowledged agricultural production, but not hunting, as an appropriate means of economic life. After all, it is a traditional point of view arising out of the biased Han ethnocentrism.

Typical hunting and gathering type of economy has the following symbolic characteristics. First, this type of economy acquires the materials needed for the subsistence of human being from the natural lives that are undergoing a natural growth and reproduction by corresponding skills without interfering in the cycle of normal growth and reproduction of natural lives. Second, this type of economic life does not make use of any energy other than biological energy. Third, it barely considers the long-term storage of materials. People usually "look for food while hungry but dump the remainder when fed". The limited number of stored items are usually ornaments and special production tools. Lastly, such a type of economic life hardly requires the possession of natural resources, let alone private possession, which leads to another character: mobility of life.

When cross-xiang operations concern the ethnic groups in this type of economic life, they may encounter barriers that are most likely a result of the above characteristics. For example, Bunuzhi Yao people don't give much value to taking possession of lands, nor respect other people's land ownership, let alone other people's ownership of means of production. They will take, with the slightest hesitation or consciousness of guilt, whatever is given them by others regardless of its value. They believe in the idea that "everyone is entitled to whatever he comes across." In the meantime, they don't see currency as valuable an item as we do; instead, they tend to treasure, to a larger extent, things with higher use value, especially food. After the

① Guizhou Minzu College Survey Group, "Survey Report on Yaoshan Commune in Libo County", *Ethnic Survey in Yueliangshan Region* (Guizhou Ethnic Groups Research Institute)

founding of the People's Republic of China, the ethnic Yaos here have often been "hired" by bait of food to work on laborious tasks such as carry sedan chairs. As a matter of fact, it is not a hire in real term but an enticement and deceit.

Another tough issue is that ethnic groups in the hunting and gathering stage tend to live a carefree life and don't want to be disciplined by strict rules, which is often the source of accusation by outsiders. Modern economic lives are social activities conducted on the foundation of prudently managed investment, market and exchange. The economy will not function normally if the three conditions are not accepted and respected by the ones with whom you are to cooperate. It is because of this that our poverty-relief efforts in Yaoshan lasting more than ten years have not made much progress.

Lastly, we need to solemnly reiterate the fact that today's ethnic Bunuzhi Yaos are not in a typical hunting and gathering type of economy any more. Lack of more appropriate examples, we have chosen them in our case study as they are displaying the characteristics of hunting and gathering remnants, which can provide our readers with a real example to understand the hunting and gathering type of economic life. Similar situations like Bunuzhi Yao exist in many other places in China such as Oroqens in the Northeast, Derungs and Kucongs in Yunnan, and Lhobas in Tibet. Cross-xiang operations that concern these communities will face similar problems.

Another type of economy that is commonly seen in Guizhou is Swidden cultivation, conveniently referred to by our ancestors as "slash-and-burn cultivation" or "cultivation by hoes". In fieldwork, however, it is not difficult for us to notice that "to chop" and "to burn" are not necessarily the characteristics of this type of economy, nor are "hoes" necessarily a symbolic tool of this economic type. We came to the realization in the fieldwork that hoes were never used when working on some projects while in other projects "flood by water" replaced "burn by fire". Ethnic groups in this type of economy in Guizhou include Miao (especially those who speak dialects of Sichuan, Guizhou and Yunnan), Yao, Gelao and the sparsely distributed Buyi and Dong. Although the total number of people from ethnic groups in this type of economy is limited, no more than one million by estimates, their geographic distribution is wide, accounting for one fourth of the province. By the standard of economic statistics currently implemented in China, all the regions where these ethnic minority groups live fall into the category of extreme poverty and are key state poverty-relief targets. Special attention need to be paid to the ethnic Hans who migrated into these regions in an earlier time and have been acculturated into the local ethnic culture. As a result, their type of economic life is very similar to that of the ethnic minority groups. The "*Gaoshan Han*" as is called by ethnic Buyi in Wangmo County is an example.

What substantially separates Swidden cultivation from hunting and gathering is that in Swidden cultivation, people don't merely acquire materials from a completely natural environment but temporarily open up a piece of land by man power or natural power under human control, where they can grow a variety of plants and raise animals for their use at the time of need. As a temporary control on the land of harvest is required in this type of economy, it further expands the scope of use of energy from the type of hunting and gathering. For example, to clean up the land of harvest by burning is, as known to everyone, a means of naturally renewing the plant and animal communities on the land for the need of man. People in this type of economy do not have fixed product storage methods and often grab what they need from the land directly at the time when they need it. Our surveys in Mashan region revealed that the cultivation and harvest seasons in the ethnic Miao areas in this region are one-to-two-month longer than those in agricultural regions, a clear indication of the existence of such a characteristic. Permanent possession of natural resources is not respected in this type of economy except when they are being used. Our fieldwork conducted in Rong village in the northwestern corner of Wangmo County captured quite a few occasions when lands, pastures, or even houses were transferred for free. We also noticed that any attempt to build permanent production facility on the transferred land was unwelcome in the society. Prohibitive behaviors included, for example, planting timber trees that take a long time to grow on the land, or turning the land into permanent rice field etc., which signaled that these lands might become privately owned. Finally, in this type of economy, cultivators usually are in a state of constant movement as a way of balancing out the use of land capacity. As an old Miao proverb goes in places like Qinglong and Guanling: "Every Miao family has as many as one thousand foundations to build home on and ten thousand wells to drink water from."[①]

[①] Feng Liu, "A Reflection on Contemporary Primitive Culture", *Agricultural History of China*, 1995, no.1.

It vividly characterizes this type of economy.

Cross-xiang operations carried out in the regions of ethnic groups that are in a Swidden cultivation type of economy may likely encounter barriers in the following areas.

First, in this type of economy, the seasonality in production is not evident. Planting seeds and harvesting happen almost simultaneously, making it difficult to grasp the laws in the time of product maturity and thus to integrate into the product circulation outside the region. A deeper discussion with more specific examples will be conducted on this issue in next section.

Second, the majority of regions in Guizhou that are currently in the Swidden cultivation type of economy are not suitable for the practice of regular farming. The introduction of agricultural production technologies and operating methods, for instance, will do more harm than good to the regions represented by Mashan that have a landscape of predominantly stony desertification, Beipanjiang River Valley characterized with a typically seasonal foehn climate, or the alpine Wumeng Mountain region. Unfortunately, many poverty-relief workers now still focus their efforts on trying to bring in the mode of regular agricultural operation into these regions.

Third, people in this type of economy whose production does not coincide with the cycle of the agricultural type are reluctant to be restricted by the disciplines of the later, resulting in numerous difficulties in the management of cross-xiang operations. More critically, it is characterized by the "economy of food production," i.e., the economy operates around the supply of food instead of a stable possession of means of production; therefore, any investment in cash or materialized means of production will not easily lead to an accumulation of means of materials, but will, due to the characteristics of this type of economy, be turned into consumer items. That provides an answer to the question a lot of poverty-relief workers have been wailfully puzzled: "why are the endless investments we have made not giving us any return?"

The primary difference between animal husbandry and Swidden cultivation is that the former directly controls the products that are produced, namely the domestic animals, other than a certain piece of land in natural environment. To achieve this goal, the only technical advancement people in this type of economy have to make is to domesticate and control herbivores.

The need for them to process and transform natural environment is only limited to maintaining the pasture, marking the grazing route or protecting water resources, etc. With the realization of direct control of live animals in large number, people in this type of economy are able to make use of the animal energy in massive scale and by plan, in addition to the use of the biological energy from human and food, significantly enhancing the ability of energy control to a much higher level than the former two types. Previously, some scholars inappropriately named the "animal husbandry type of economy" as "nomadic economy," for the reason that migration among pastures in the "animal husbandry economy" is often a periodical behavior that happens at a "fixed" time, compared with the rambling "hunting and gathering type" that may happen at any time. Besides, "migration" is not a necessary characteristic in the "animal husbandry economy". As far as Guizhou province is concerned, seasonal migration among pastures has remained as a characteristic until today. Live animals, animal leather and wool are among the major products of animal husbandry type of economy which enables the products to gather quickly and move flexibly that begin to appear in bulk with limited variety. Although the animal husbandry type of economy has made the products' access to the market easier, it cannot solve the problem of long-distance transportation, especially the issue of ensuring the product quality after leaving the pastures. In this type of economy, pasture is one of the most important means of production, but a mechanism of keeping a pasture under one's stable control is not in place to establish the norms of stable possession of means of production. In addition, the long-distance seasonal migration characterizes this type of economy, causing the control on pastures even weaker and a weak point in the entire operation of economy. This contributes to the sensitive issue that this type of economy is subject to detriment when it coexists closely with agricultural type of economy. Once the completeness of pastures is not safeguarded, this economy is likely to shrink and the chance of establishing a stable and supplementary cross-xiang operating relationship becomes slim.

In Guizhou province, ethnic groups that are in this type of economy are represented by ethnic Yi and "*Caijiaren*" (family of Cai) in northwestern Guizhou. According to ancient literature, the ethnic Yi groups had been in an economic type of typical animal husbandry until the Qing Dynasty decided to replace all local hereditary headmen with the officials sent by the central government in the territories under the control of *Shuixi Tusi*. Afterwards, a huge number of ethnic Hans flocked into these territories and began to turn the pastures into croplands at the heavy cost of ethnic Yi both in people and lands, thus discontinuing the traditional way of life of ethnic Yi people and causing some of them to be acculturated by the Han culture and shift to operating an alpine agriculture. The previous animal husbandry economy was a seasonal type of vertical grazing that benefited the ecological balance and water and soil conservation in this region. The immigration of a huge number of ethnic Hans and the ensuing reclamation of lands by them and "to abandon animal husbandry and shift to agriculture" by ethnic Yis, however, have so far triggered massive soil erosion and kicked the local ecological environment out of balance. A further discussion on this topic can be found in chapter six under the title of "background".

What is most threatening to the cross-xiang operations that concern an animal husbandry type of economy is the incompatibility in the use of land resources, i.e., croplands rival against pastures for lands, water resources etc., and demand a long-term and stable occupation of them, which contradicts with the essential characteristics of an animal husbandry type of economy and keeps the cross-xiang operations from carrying on if effective measures are not identified to bring it back to balance. Currently, a small percentage of ethnic Yis in Guizhou are still in the animal husbandry economy but croplands scatter along their normal grazing routes, resulting in a prolonged distance in grazing and a deterioration of grasslands. Besides, grasslands that used to fit seasonal needs are kept out of balance and the economic efficiency is dramatically decreased. The second difficulty in cross-xiang operations is the conflicts in the way the means of production is occupied. One of the fundamental characteristics of the animal husbandry economy is that pastures are not stably and directly occupied. To the contrary, the investments made by subjective parties in cross-xiang operations are preconditioned on stable and continuous occupation of land resources. The unstable and seasonable use of grasslands presents intolerable risks to the investors and makes the operators feel difficult to manage and control. Finally, the operation of this type of economy is subject to a certain degree of mobility which also causes many barriers to cross-xiang operations.

In Guizhou province, the ethnic Buyi, Dong, and Shui peoples are representatives of the agricultural economy. Although these ethnic minorities are in the same type of economy as the ethnic Hans, they are divergent in mode. We hereby give a brief illustration of the fundamental traits of agricultural type of economy. An agricultural economy requires a solid and permanent change to natural landscape, by the power of man or nature, to reclaim and cultivate the lands suitable for continuous agricultural use, on which only a limited number of fully domesticated crops are allowed to grow, with all other plants being treated as weeds and completely eradicated. To ensure the prolonged and continuous use of the croplands, this type of economy has to rely heavily on animal power as well as water power and chemical energy to meet the need of bringing complete changes to natural landscapes. Energy inputs of this nature must be continued to maintain the changes to natural landscapes and water supplies, eradicate the growth of plants and animals other than the desired crops on the lands, continue fertilizing these lands to keep its productivity, and guard against natural disasters. Needless to say, the agricultural type of economy has a much higher level of energy control and usage than the prior three types. Products begin to be stored in limited varieties but large quantities, and the period of time during which these products are transported is made longer than their annual cycle of production, and long-distance transportation far from the place of origin becomes available. In addition, as the means of production in this type of economy is the man-made result through massive energy inputs that can be used continuously in a prolonged period of time, the lands, one of the major means of production, have a steady transferable value. This separates the agricultural type of economy from the previous three types, and is most likely the source of potential troubles when the agricultural economy encounters the other three in cross-xiang operations. Lastly, this type of economy has grown to be highly stylized and demonstrates an apparent seasonality. With the establishment of complete farming settlements, it is easy for this type of economy to migrate into the next type.

The industrial type of economy is a way of production in a fully man-controlled production environment. It requires the elimination of interruptions caused by natural environments as much as possible, and dictates that the entire economic activities are conducted in unnatural artificial structures. Modern large industrial and mining enterprises are best examples of this type of economy. The industrial economy also includes agricultural and animal-raising production but is sharply contrasted against the agricultural and animal husbandry types of economy in that it absolutely cements the possession and usage of croplands and pastures, subjects the tasks ranging from cropland fertilization, control and treatment of plant disease and insect pests, water supplies, to plowing of croplands to human control, and completes these tasks by inputting thermal, chemical and mechanical energies. Large ranches in the United States of America offer typical examples in industrialized agricultural production where the recovery of soil productivity is achieved almost by machines instead of manpower, and biocenosis hardly has any impact on the recovery of soil productivity. In Netherlands, not only are ranches absolutely fixed in animal husbandry, but also are the boundaries of the movement of animals; even the animal fodders are industry-produced. Machines have replaced almost all human work in the operation. This can be viewed as a typical example of industrialized animal farming.

It is clear from the above examples that the industrialized production is detached from natural environments. The production environment is maintained completely by the use of energy fully in man's control. As a result, the industrialized agricultural and animal-raising production is uneconomical as the inputs outpace the yields. That explains why the country has to put huge amount of money in agricultural subsidies. At the moment, ethnic groups in an industrialized type of economy meet their needs by heavily depending on chemical energies produced by oil and coals, supplemented by water resources and, in exceptional cases, by biological energies, but are still in energy shortage. Consequently, they are putting tremendous efforts in developing atomic energy to quench the thirst for increasing demand for energy. The ultimate expansion in the use of energy characterizes this type of economy. As the production in this type of economy is conducted in a man-made environment that significantly increases the purity and fineness of finished products, therefore considerably prolonging the duration of product storage and making the ultra long-distance transportation and ultra long-cycle trade possible. With the ecological environments being artificially controlled, densely populated human settlements are built. The rise and development of modern cities is another trait of this type of economy. All the above traits are unique to the industrial type of economy and are thus sources for potential conflicts that are likely to give rise to a series of non-economic constraints when ethnic groups in an industrial type of economy engage in cross-xiang operations with ethnic groups in other types of economy.

The ethnic Han people, the predominant ethnic group in China, were basically in the agricultural type of economy before the founding of the People's Republic of China. In the past 40 years afterwards, despite the significant progress that has been made in some regions and the large number of industrialized enterprises and corresponding technologies that have been introduced, they have fully survived and displayed vitality only in some parts of the country. Industrialization has not been realized across the entire ethnic Han regions and it does not seem that such a goal will be accomplished within a short period of time. Up to now, cross-xiang economic activities carried out in the remote border regions in China such as ethnic minority groups in Guizhou are still dominated by the principles of agricultural type of economy. Among the massive number of cases that modern industrial enterprises are introduced into the vast Western China, few are successful. Some of the enterprises, although physically moved to the west, barely have any interactions with the surrounding ethnic minority people and communities. To keep these enterprises in operation, the government first has to continue allocating financial and fiscal subsidies to offset the losses caused by the deficient production in these enterprises; the enterprises themselves, on the other hand, have always tried to build a social background they need, and as a result, have turned them into "enterprise islands" that are isolated from the surrounding people and communities. With the deepening of "reform and opening-up policy", the transformation of these enterprises is put on top priority, yet the result has been far from satisfactory even after over ten years of tremendous efforts. From the perspective of cross-xiang economic operations, it is not difficult to see that the dilemma these enterprises are in is caused by their failure to facilitate a smooth integration among different types of economy in cross-xiang operations. Simple changes or repairs are not the solution to the problem. The problem of integration across different types of economies must be tackled at the root, which may mean that, inevitably, a considerable percentage of enterprises of such nature have to be given up or moved out of the ethnic minority regions.

As the majority of ethnic Han people in China are now in the agricultural type of economy, it is based on the assumption that the subjective parties in cross-xiang operations are ethnic groups in the agricultural economy that we have drawn the previous conclusions on the non-economic constraints that are typically seen in the cross-xiang operations involving, respectively, the hunting and gathering, Swidden cultivation and animal husbandry types of economy. However, cross-xiang operations as two-way activities will cause a series of non-economic constraints from the perspective of an agricultural ethnic group just as ethnic groups in hunting and gathering, Swidden cultivation and animal husbandry types of economy will encounter other non-economic constraints when they engage in economic activities with agricultural ethnic Han people. Given the fact that ethnic groups in the Swidden cultivation are in a large population and are geographically distributed across wide territories in Guizhou, and are classified as subjects from state or provincial key poverty-stricken regions, we will take them as examples to carry out an analysis on the non-economic restraints that they will be subject to when engaging in cross-xiang economic activities with agricultural ethnic peoples.

Making products is the major goal in economic activities. The products produced by the ethnic groups in Swidden cultivation type of economy are limited in number and thus hard to gather in large bulk, diversified but inconsistent in varieties, and distributed across a vast territory, making it impossible within the economic circle of this type of economy to gather a specific product by the commercially minimum quantity and meet the basic requirements on product quality. In our fieldwork in Ziyun, Wangmo, Zhenfeng, and Ceheng counties, we constantly heard complaints from local ethnic Miaos that their products didn't sell, or the price for the only product that sold fluctuated dramatically but it was always them that were hurt by the price fluctuation. Currently, the products produced by dispersed Swidden cultivation could only circulate in small-scale rural markets, and the products that didn't sell were left rotten and discarded. The development in the ethnic Han regions has raised the bars on the minimum quantity and standardized quality of the products, making the access of the traditional products from these ethnic minority regions to domestic markets even more difficult, and further deteriorating the state of poverty in these regions.

In terms of the quality of people, the agricultural economy demands that people settle in a specific place, around which technologies and skills are devised. The Swidden cultivation is different in that its production has a certain degree of mobility and is insignificant in operating cycles. As a result, the people who work in this type of economy are not trained for a specific expertise, but instead are required to make use, more intensely and widely, of the techniques related to the knowledge in their possession about animals and plants. People who have been grown to get used to this type of economy are often viewed, when seeking employment opportunities in agricultural regions, as technically under-qualified, undisciplined and only fit for coarse and inferior manual work. It tends to psychologically frustrate these people who can't help but feel resentful for their seemingly low social status.

The techniques and skills that people from Swidden cultivation economy are familiar with become useless when they come to the agricultural regions, forcing them to learn from the beginning if they want to find jobs in the ethnic Han regions. That, however, is not supported by the educational facility currently available to them. Even if the educational facility were improved to equip them with the needed techniques and skills for landing jobs in the ethnic Han regions, that would not help the poverty-relief projects to run in the expected fashion. Today, a lot of people who are responsible for poverty-relief projects in these regions are enthusiastic about introducing the agricultural technologies, fertilizers, pesticides, and fine breeds that they think are advanced into these poverty-stricken regions without seeing that in the Swidden cultivation regions in Guizhou, not only are large agricultural machines not able to play a role, but in some regions even the cattle-powered wooden plows can not be used. Without fixed croplands, the large quantity of fertilizer and pesticide only yields unproportionately small returns. Consequently, instead of increasing income, these technologies have added to the economic burdens on the local ethnic people. The promotion of fine breeds has been beset by similar problems. The special conditions needed for the cultivation of any fine breed hardly exist in the vast Swidden cultivation regions in Guizhou. In our fieldwork in Zhenning County, we witnessed an interesting incident.

The mountainous regions around Liuma Township of Zhenning County are inhabited predominantly by ethnic Miaos who, after years of efforts by the county government, started planting the improved variety of corns in the regions. However, the landscape of the regions is dominated by high mountains and steep slopes coupled with extremely thin soils. As a result, the leaves of the corns would dry out and wither if it did not rain in three consecutive days, and the cobs of the corns were in a size no larger than that of a chicken egg. After noticing this phenomenon, the staff from the Guizhou

Academy of Forestry took some of the seeds and planted them on the field used for experimenting new plants for their own use. It turned out that the cobs grew to more than one chi (a Chinese unit of length equivalent to 33.3cm) there. The ethnic Miao people thought that these were new superior varieties of corn and would pay a high price to buy them, or even risk stealing the seeds when they could not buy them. What followed was then predictable.

It is because the natural backgrounds in the Swidden cultivation regions in Guizhou are not congruent with the agricultural production technologies that the repeated attempts to introduce improved varieties of crops ended up in failure. Understandably, the ethnic Miao people voiced their discontent that surprised the government departments responsible for the promotion of technologies. First, they complained that these departments imposed on them some "new technologies" not so effective as advertised. Second, the technical departments did not care about them and sometimes even cheated them on purpose. The third thing they complained about was the fertilizer that seemed overpriced and did not return them with the expected outcome. Some people from these technical departments always responded to these complaints with accusations that these ethnic Miao people were innately conservative, ignorant, and unwilling to accept new technologies. We now realize, after understanding the diverging directions in technological development between the Swidden cultivation and the agricultural type of economy, that what lie at the core of these conflicts and underlie the accusations are the inevitable results from the non-economic constraints arising out of the differences in the types of economy. Both sides in this debate did not argue to the point.

Both types of economy are not congruent either with regards to the use of natural resources. The ethnic groups that are now still in the Swidden cultivation economy such as Miao, Yao and Gelao do not view their habitats as unlivable as the ethnic Hans do. Although they envy the *Dabazi* (large intermontane basin) inhabited by their Han and Buyi counterparts for the thick and rich soils and abundant water resources, they have never thought of abandoning their homes and moving to live in those *Dabazi* for the following three reasons:

First, these *Dabazi* are densely populated and developed areas rather than unoccupied territories. They have to compete with other ethnic groups for living spaces that are already heavily crowed, and apparently they are not the rivals of the other more populated and capable ethnic groups. To settle in these *Dabazi* permanently is not possible, as they understand, even if they can move to the *Dabazi* with the help of the local government. In fact, we were told in field surveys that even before the move began, other residents of *Dabazi* had already started driving them out. Incidents of forced flight happened constantly in counties such as Zhenning and Guanling, which could not be stopped even by the people's government.[①] It tells how difficult it may get to make ethnic minority people change their living environments.

Second, the ways of production in which the ethnic groups in the Swidden cultivation economy conduct their economic activities are still effective till today. They will have no difficulty in providing for their subsistence as long as there are enough hillside fields for fallowing. If the rice fields in *Dabazi* and hillside fields in their hometown are both simultaneously available to them, they will always put the majority of their efforts in the hillside fields and leave the rice fields unattended.

Third, these ethnic groups are fully aware, and thus feel secure, that the ethnic groups in agricultural economy are, without any doubt, unable to survive or settle down in their living environments. An old Miao proverb is a vivid reflection of such a mentality: "Miaos may not win a fight but can always win the game of hiding."

Lastly, it is for the above reason that the ethnic groups in the Swidden cultivation economy usually do not seek to establish stable economic ties with other ethnic groups but choose to seal themselves off from the others.

The above four reasons have contributed to the loss of confidence in these regions by both the government officials and agricultural technicians who insist that these regions are not inhabitable to modern people and should be completely abandoned, and the local residents should be moved to other places with better natural environments. As a matter of fact, these proposals are not new and have been tested in the mountainous regions in southern Ningxia Hui Autonomous Region. Now, Guangdong province is planning on moving several hundreds of thousands of residents living in the mountainous regions in the north out of the region. In Guizhou, similar recommendations have been made. The government of Libo County in Guizhou once tried to convince the ethnic Yaos living in Yaoshan region to move out of the

① Yuan Zong, "The Cultural Connotation of Place Names in Ethnic Miao Region," *Miao Studies*, no. 3, Jinping Li ed. (Guizhou People's Publishing House, December 1994), 213 extremely poor and infertile Yaoshan mountains and settle in the better-conditioned Jialiang region, but the initiative has never materialized due to the willingness of the ethnic Yaos to cooperate. We believe that the above proposals are doomed to fail simply because of the following three weaknesses to which we have not found a solution.

First, the astronomical costs associated with such a gigantic migration project are not affordable by the country, nor are the conflicts caused among ethnic groups solvable.

Second, the production techniques and skills as well as the knowledge of the emigrants will become invalid and useless in other regions. To ensure the subsistence of these people, all kinds of training must be provided to them from the details of daily life to ideological thinking and perceptions, from production techniques and skills to customs and habits, all based on the cultural requirements of the agricultural Han ethnic group. It is both an overwhelming burden for the agricultural ethnic group and a spiritual and psychological coercion to the ethnic minority emigrants. Either one can easily crush us.

Third and most critically, the people who made such proposals have not taken into account the fact that ethnic groups are communities of "live" people, which will keep growing until they fill up the entire living space. Even if we have tried everything we can to move 99% of the residents out, it takes as short as one century for the remaining 1% to reproduce themselves and create, by their ethnic culture, another poverty-stricken region exactly the same as the current one. Are we expecting to be returned with another impoverished mountainous region in one-century's time with all the efforts and pains we have been through? If not, why are we doing it now?

In a nutshell, differences in the types of economy are systematic, which give rise to unavoidable constraints easily seen in cross-xiang operations. Only by facing the realty to explore the possibility of integration between different types of economy can we find the solutions to alleviate the effects of these constraints.

III Barriers in the Integration of Xiangji Products

The last section is a comprehensive introduction of the differences in the type of economy among different ethnic groups, and the constraints resulting from these differences on cross-xiang operations. In this section, we will focus on other differences in the economic lives of each ethnic group, namely the "differences in mode" and their constraining effects on cross-xiang operations, followed by an analysis on how the differences in type and mode have created barriers in the integration of product circulation in cross-xiang operations.

Ethnic groups in the same type of economy are not identical in their respective economic lives. They demonstrate another kind of differences, namely the differences in adaptability to specific living environments as a result of specific evolution, or adaptability differences. For example, the rice cultivation agriculture of the ethnic Han regions has been developed to adapt to the plains in the middle and lower reaches of Yangtze River and Pearl River that are densely scattered by rivers and lakes; and the agricultural economy of the ethnic Buyi people has risen to fit the landscape of highlands, river valleys and *Bazi*, while that of the ethnic Dongs has grown out of a living environment characterized by the alternating landscapes between low mountain hills, river valleys and *Bazi*. Although they are all in the agricultural economy, each has distinguishing characteristics in the product composition, cultivation technology, land possession and the primary direction of natural resource processing and transformation etc., but each has been able to continue and develop independently to build glorious past of their own. To help our readers further understand the contents in the differences in mode, we hereby provide a brief comparative analysis of the three ethnic groups that are most closely related to the development in Guizhou.

All the three ethnic groups are distributed in a region which can be turned into massive rice fields that are more than enough to meet the needs of the normal operation of an agricultural economy. A closer inspection reveals, however, that the differences in the living environments among the three of them are evident and un-negligible. The kernel ethnic Hans live on a massive plain where rivers and lakes densely scatter. The only thing that needs to be done is to build dams and embankments to separate water systems from rice fields to make large patches of rice fields. As they live in the mid-to-downstream river basins, the fertile soils that are rushed with the river current naturally deposit in this region to add more humus to the soil, fertilizing it even without the efforts from human beings. In addition, the distinctive four seasons with a relatively shorter high-temperature season in a year (specifically the middle to lower reaches of the Yangtze River) has reduced the effect of oxidation on the soil, keeping the soil productive most of the time. This region is prone to be hard-hit by floods. On the other hand, the massive reclamation and cultivation of rice fields has dramatically decreased the number of grasslands, making it increasingly difficult to raise farm cattle. This explains why the Han culture put such an emphasis on farm cattle. The shortage of farm cattle got worse since the beginning of this century, however, it has been partially relieved by other forms of production power with the introduction of modernized industries and mechanized farming, and the popularization of electric irrigation and drainage. In addition, one thing that needs to be brought to our attention is that in the mediaeval times, the Huai River basin that had once been very prosperous was heavily salinized after it was flooded by the Yellow River that changed course into Huai River to flow east into the sea and sediments began to form in this region. Consequently, the conditions for agricultural production in this region have become so irreversibly deteriorated by the technologies available today. The prosperity of the Huai River basin may only exist in our memories.

The ethnic Dongs are a different story. Located on the *Bazi* of the river valley, the crop fields drain well and the locals never need to worry about the salinization of the soils or massive flooding. The crop fields here, however, are separated and cannot expand into a large one. Rice fields of different altitudes can only be turned into strip-shaped terraces, causing ethnic Dongs to disperse and their villages to be smaller and less populated than those of ethnic Hans. The varying altitudes make it impossible to plant one single crop across all the fields. It is an advantage, though, to ethnic Dongs to be able to produce crops of different varieties at the same time but it is hard for them to bring one single product to a minimum volume. As a result, ethnic Dongs can not rival the ethnic Hans commercially on the supply of large quantity of grains. The real strength that ethnic Dongs have is not in the cultivation of rice fields but in the low mountain hills that house the largest man-made forests in southern China. The fortunes that ethnic Dongs have made in the past two hundred years are mostly attributable to the timber trade and export of forest and timber by-products, which witnessed the rise of a few large groups of a capitalist nature at the turn of the century.

Ethnic Buyi and Dong in Guizhou are similar in that they both operate rice fields in the *Bazi* and the advantages and disadvantages of these rice fields are basically the same. On thing that disadvantages the ethnic Buyi region is that the rivers and streams in its territory do not directly flow into the central ethnic Han regions and thus are not ideal for the shipping of timbers, which explains why the ethnic Buyi group has not developed a "business of timber and grains concurrently" when the other natural environments in the ethnic Buyi region are similar to those in the ethnic Dong region. In addition, the *Bazi* where Buyi people live are usually located in mid-mountain areas, causing a greater variation in relative altitude and an inferior condition for growing man-made timber forests. These are the reasons why ethnic Buyi people have put a majority of their efforts in the development of rice fields and kept most of the primitive forests preserved and not used for the production of timbers while mainly growing tung and fruit trees on gentle slopes. Like ethnic Dongs, Buyi people have constructed their rice fields in strip-shape terraces. Each *Bazi* is kept in a half-sealed state, where, with the exception of land shortages resulted from population growth, natural disasters that affect large areas have rarely occurred. The level of fertility in the soils remains very stable as they depend on the surface run-offs for the supply of organic fertility. Traditionally, these soils are sources for steady yields of grains even after being used continuously without fertilization.

The difference in living environments has also contributed to the different ways of land occupation in the three ethnic groups. In the ethnic Han regions, a majority of lands are privately owned and can be traded without any restrictions. The litigation arising from disputes on land transfer has never ended. By contrast, the occupation of lands in the ethnic Dong and Buyi regions is restricted by the extended families. A Bazi area is usually occupied by members from one or several extended families, and the transfer of lands does not take effect merely by the decision of the party involved, but also requires sanctions from his family and neighbors. Normally, lands are not permitted to sell to the people from outside the village especially from other ethnic groups. Although the three ethnic groups entered the rice cultivation agriculture by settlement at about the same time, the polarization between the rich and poor is much more evident in the ethnic Han regions than the other two due to the existence of such a difference in the ways of land occupation. In the Ming and Qing dynasties, the lands were so highly centralized that it was possible and necessary for the Ming government to decide to uniformly measure the lands and compile "fish scale books" (land registration books)[1]in an effort to bring them to a centralized management by "ascertaining the hills and plots". The ethnic Dong and Buyi regions, on the other hand, had never had their lands measured by the government until the fall of the Qing Dynasty, and all feudal land taxes were collected conventionally by mu (a Chinese unit of area).[2] Our surveys in the ethnic Buyi regions recorded a considerable gap between the actual area of the lands assigned to farmers by contract and the area they reported in the manual of contracted lands, the actual area of lands being greater than the reported area. The two ethnic groups have both documented infrequent transfer of land ownership, and the cultivation of rice fields has continued in the traditional method until today. The cultivation system in the ethnic Han regions, in comparison, has undergone dramatic changes.

Another commonality shared by the ethnic Buyi and Dong is that the cultivation of rice fields is primarily for the use of the farmers themselves and only a small portion of rice is for sale. The two ethnic groups don't sell things on land but from the mountains. To ship a large quantity of timbers out of the region by the ethnic Dongs is a typical example, while the products sold by the ethnic Buyi people focus on tung oil, dried fruits and cattle.

The places where the two ethnic groups produce products for sale in other areas are in fact public-owned lands. It came to our attention when we conducted surveys in Liuma of Zhenning that the big producers of tung oil in the major production region in Liuma, such as Nongpao, Ximan and Liangtian villages, harvest from the tung tree forests that are actually open to everyone who plant trees and harvest the fruits as long as the lands are not being used by other people. Whoever plants tung seeds in the land will automatically be entitled to operating on the land. Likewise, the right will be lost if the tung tree forests need to be renewed but the former operators don't have labor resources before new tung trees are planted on this land by other people (must be members of the family or the village).

The timber tycoons in the ethnic Dong regions before the founding of the People's Republic of China were created not because they were in possession of massive areas of forests but, more importantly, because they had the ability of shipping the logs provided by his neighbors and fellowmen

[1] Bozan Jian, *Outline of the Chinese History*, (People's Publishing House, January 1967), 167-176.
[2] Shu Zhang, *Book of Guizhou Continued*

out of the regions by rafting and sell them successfully. They accumulated their wealth by winning in channel instead of in production. The log production was a traditional process and thus identical in nature; therefore, although the trade of timber accounted for a significant percentage in ethnic Dong's economic life, it did not bring dramatic changes to the conventional way of occupying lands, nor did it lead to the high degree of land concentration as was seen in the ethnic Han regions.

The technological improvement to the cultivation in the ethnic Han regions primarily focuses on increasing the yield per unit area of fields and the cropping index, as well as ensuring the steady yields of crops. Therefore, water conservancy constructions and related technologies are prioritized at a very high level, and the farmers would volunteer to contribute to the construction and maintenance of the water conservancy projects that mainly include building and maintaining the embankments. Intensive cultivation characterizes the rice cultivation in these regions, resulting in a yield of crops on a per unit area basis far exceeding that in the developed countries in the West today. The Buyi people cultivate the rice fields differently; they barely use the fields for multiple cropping in a year and hardly cultivate the rice fields nearly as intensively and meticulously as their ethnic Han counterparts. Until today, a lot of them are still choosing not to use fertilizers especially the human feces to improve the productivity. The small-season cultivation has, after years of efforts in education and persuasion, seen some moderate progress in recent years. The key reason for this is that the Buyi region has huge mountain grasslands and forests where people invest little but will benefit a lot by raising domestic animals that spend the winter on the rice fields. The incomes they gain by animal farming in the winter rice fields have far outpaced those they can get by winter cropping. Our local surveys recorded how the ethnic Buyi people viewed the small-season cultivation. They were consistent in alleging that they as well as the neighboring villages never enclosed the domestic animals such as cattle, horse, pig, and chicken but would let them feed on the rice fields, which made small-season cultivation a wasted effort. Many ethnic Hans perceive this as a backward thinking. However, if the value of the livestock is added to the value from grains, we have to admit that such a conventional cultivation practiced by ethnic Buyi people is not necessarily backward. This is especially true when the rising prices of livestock under the situation of "reform and opening-up policy" have unleashed its potential.

Such a cultivation system also contributes to a slack and long winter season among the ethnic Buyi people, and gives rise to intensive commercial activities in the form of local markets, especially the interactive commercial activities with the ethnic Han and Miao groups as a traditional side work. Such a phenomenon was recorded in ancient literature of the Han Dynasty. It sounds reasonable when Chen Ding, author of *Qianyouji* (Notes from Travel in Guizhou), analogized this kind of activities to the business activities conducted by Huizhou businessmen in the developed Han regions.[①]

Similarly, to increase per-unit-area yield of crops has not been the priority of the ethnic Dong groups in their traditional cultivation. The massive wealth they have fetched from the sale of large quantity of timbers to other areas has limited their requirements for rice fields to merely meeting the demands of family consumption. The leading efforts in technological improvements have been put in perfecting reforestation technologies. This was fully described in *Li Ping Fu Zhi* (Annals of Liping Fu),[②] which illustrated that the ethnic Dong people had amassed a full set of advanced experiences and superb techniques from selecting seeds, growing seedlings, field plantation, to maintenance of cedar trees. They still have values in promotion and reference even in today. The favorable living environments and such techniques developed throughout its history make it easy for the ethnic Dong group to get out of poverty and become wealthier, build a well-off society or even realize the four modernizations as long as the policies are devised in support of these efforts.

The above three differences determine that the three ethnic groups have different structures in the products in and out of their specific regions when engaging in cross-xiang operations. The products sold from the ethnic Han regions into Buyi and Dong regions traditionally focus on metal tools, salt, silk, and cotton fabric, while logs and forest products account for the majority of the products shipped from the ethnic Dong to Han regions. Buyi people often sell economic forest products and livestock to the Han regions. It calls for our special attention that rice, the symbolic crop of the agricultural civilization, has surprisingly not been a major product in cross-xiang operations. After the establishment of modern industry, the Han regions have

① *Book of Guizhou • Book of Guizhou Continued • Record of Guizhou • Language of Guizhou* (Guizhou People's Publishing House, March 1992), 424.

② *Liping Fu Annals*, in the collection of Guizhou Provincial Library, woodblock print started shipping modern industrial products into the ethnic Buyi and Dong regions. In the meantime, due to an inflexible polices in the Buyi and Dong regions, their product structures have not changed much, or in other words, the traditional means of production in these two ethnic groups have not been optimized. For instance, the processing of forest products in ethnic Dong regions so far has not been uplifted to the level of modern industry. Even the paper-making industry built with timbers as its foundation and the refinement and processing of forest chemical products has remained in a dispersed state. Similar situations have been observed in the deep processing of tung oil and spice industries in the Buyi regions. As a result, the products shipped out of these ethnic minority regions are far lower in value than the products from the Han regions and the gap is widening, keeping these ethnic regions in poverty for an extended period of time. The current proposals and strategies still over-emphasize the importance of introducing technologies from the Han regions but under-estimate the value of the traditional economies of these ethnic minority groups, thus are of little use in reinforcing and making use of the mutually supplementary economic relations that have long existed between ethnic Han and these minority groups. From an operational perspective, even if the technologies are successfully introduced into these regions, the prolonged distance in transportation and the restriction by other natural factors will disadvantage the products made in these ethnic regions and put them in an inferior position when competing against similar products made in the ethnic Han regions; therefore, introduction of technologies will not play an effective and beneficial role in driving the economic development of the two ethnic groups.

To facilitate our readers to understand, we name the ethnic Han's traditional economy as rice field intensive economy in plains with river network, the ethnic Dong's traditional economy as forest-grain mixed economy in lower intermontane basins, and the ethnic Buyi economy as farming, forestry and animal husbandry mixed economy in mid-mountain riverside intermontane basins. The differences among them are differences in mode, which are equally important to cross-xiang operators as they directly constrain the type of products, scale of bulk of products, quality standard as well as the channels and means of gathering products. In cross-xiang operations, these differences affect the level of difficulty in the integration of different economies and hinder the operations. More importantly, the differences in mode result from cultural differences, and due to the fact that culture is a complete system, such differences may cause other cultural complexes in the cultural structure to change correspondingly, which also bring unexpected effects on cross-xiang operations.

Difference in mode does not happen only to agricultural type of economy, but also to the type of animal husbandry, Swidden cultivation and hunting and gathering, even to the industrial type of economy. Among them, the effects caused by difference in mode on the Swidden type of economy are especially far-reaching to the economic development in the ethnic minority regions in Guizhou. For this reason, we will spend some extra time to discuss the differences in mode in the Swidden type of economy in ethnic groups in Guizhou and give a brief comparison between the animal husbandry, hunting and gathering types of economy and similar types of economy in other parts of the country.

The Swidden type of economy in Guizhou can be classified in general into three modes: dry-land cultivation in mid-mountains, dry-land cultivation in alpine mountains and rice cultivation, which are practiced in different clans of ethnic Miaos as well as ethnic Gelao and Yao groups. The dry-land cultivation in mid-mountains prevails mainly in the regions who speak western Miao dialects and is basically characterized by "slash-and-burn". It primarily surrounds the places where highland pastures and forests border each other and takes the form of burning the fields and directly sowing seeds by manpower, simple dibbling, or even broadcast sowing with no cattle used in principle. Among the main crops are corn, myotonin, millet, sorghum, and panicum. People also raise cattle as meaty foods or for religious ritual purposes and seldom use them in cultivation. Other than Miao, the ethnic Gelao and Yao groups in Guizhou are also in this mode of economy. The dry-land Swidden cultivation in alpine mountains is practiced primarily by the ethnic Miaos who speak Northeast Yunnan sub-dialect. Buckwheat, potato, and wheat-type of crops are widely grown in this economy, accompanied by herding of large livestock. Instead of burning, manpower is used to plow or hoe the fields. Rice cultivation in lower intermontane basins scatter in Liping, Rongjiang, and Congjiang of Guizhou where rice fields are plowed by man, and rice is the predominant corp, mixed with economic forests. Farm cattle are raised mainly for the purpose sacrificial ceremonies.

The hunting and gathering economy in Guizhou, although mostly in the form of remnants, is unique to some extent. For example, the ethnic Bunuzhi Yao people around Libo and Dushan mainly hunt the animals that cross their territories in seasonal migration by "chase hunting". The Miaos who speak the Western Yunnan dialect, in comparison, hunt the animals that come to the riverside to drink water by "ambush". Both are very different from the ethnic Oroqens in northern China who usually hunt by "trap" and "round up".

The animal husbandry economy in Guizhou takes the form of herding that varies in altitude by season, i.e., go up on the mountains in summer and come down to the river valley in winter, which is different from the ethnic Mongolians in China who tend to move in the north-south direction by season. Such a way of herding in Guizhou makes it easy to integrate with the agricultural type of economy when the lowland pastures are left vacant in summer. When animals leave the highland pastures in fall, the growth of winter crops is not affected, making it easy to merge with the Swidden cultivation practiced by ethnic Miaos in this region, thus giving rise to the mode of economy that mixes agriculture with animal husbandry.

The differences in type and mode of economic lives between ethnic groups concerned in cross-xiang operations are relatively stable and long lasting, which, naturally, will impact the cross-xiang operations continuously, the most evident being the impact on the percentage of commercialization of products by each party. As is widely known, commodity is a key subject of research in the study of economics. However, products made by ethnic groups concerned in cross-xiang operations may not be fully converted into commodities but will only be commercialized when the products are acceptable by the traditional culture of the other party. A continuous and stable cross-xiang operation is often conditioned on a wider compatibility of products between different parties. Furthermore, to ensure that a cross-xiang operation be developed into the type of a supplementary nature requires that the products in actual circulation remain balanced in the total incoming and outgoing values. The achievement of this goal does not depend, to a large extent, on the wish of the subjective parties, but on the characteristics of the traditional culture of each party involved. Here, before we can discuss how the differences in type and mode of economy of each related party in cross-xiang operations impact the commercialization of products of these ethnic groups, some new concepts must be introduced, i.e., product component, compatibility and integration.

As a result of the differences in the type and mode of the economic lives, each ethnic group in cross-xiang economic operations has, based on its own traditional economic life, produces special products that are difficult to integrate into the economic life of the other parties, mainly in the following four aspects: First, product portfolio; second, steady supply of each product; third, the value of each unit quantity of product; fourth, the added value that is needed for each unit product to access the market of the other parties. Any change that happens to any of the above four parts is enough to affect the access of the products from one party to the economic circle of the other party, the product commercialization and market value realization; in other words, enough to give rise to the constraints in economic activities. To discuss how products are converted into commodities in cross-xiang operations requires that we conduct a comprehensive analysis of the above four elements, which combine to form a comprehensive system that we name as the commodity convertibility ratio of the indigenous ethnic products in cross-xiang operations. We have noticed when we analyze the differences in the mode of economic lives in ethnic Buyi, Dong and Han peoples that other than the fact rice has been the predominant agricultural crop, the three ethnic groups produce a divergent variety of products. The silk, cotton fabric, metal tool and porcelain that are commonplace items in the ethnic Han regions are rarely made in Buyi and Dong regions. By contrast, the log and forest by-products account for the majority of the economic output in ethnic Dong regions but they can not be produced in large quantity in the ethnic Han regions. The livestock and economic forestry products commonly seen in the ethnic Buyi regions can not be found in the product portfolios of both ethnic Han and Dong groups. The divergence in the type of economy has an even more telling impact on product portfolios. Our surveys in Mashan and Huashan regions in Guizhou suggested that the local Miaos and ethnic Hans produced completely different economic products. A statistic conducted over the biggest four villages showed that a Miao household produced as many as 21 varieties of grains alone on the field contracted to the family, which in addition to the familiar core, sorghrum, and millet, also included myotonin, panicum, amaranth seeds, and sesame as well as several varieties of beans. The number of varieties of grains alone is hardly imaginable in the developed Han regions. We should keep it in mind that on top of these varieties of grains, the cultivated fields of the Swidden cultivation type of economy produce almost all necessities in life, animal fodder, plant fiber used for making fabrics such as cotton, hemp, and paper mulberry bark; as well as vegetables and fruits for the consumption of the farmer household. Economically useful plants such as tea that must be planted in special-purpose plantations in the ethnic Han regions may also grow in the same fields. Some natural stuff that are deemed completely useless in the ethnic Han regions such as cicada pupa, bee pupa, and longhorn beetle larvae are harvested along with other agricultural products and are consumed by the children as a nutrient supplement of protein. Such a diversified product component structure posts a sharp contrast against unitary product structure in the normal agricultural Han regions. Not surprisingly, from an ethnic Han economic perspective, the per capita grain output in these ethnic minority regions is unbearably low and is far from enough to feed the population. However, instead of being starved to death, the local people look strong and able-bodied. The mistake we have made is that our statistics only reflect a small portion of their output, namely the output of the variety of grains acceptable to the ethnic Hans as food, but exclude all the others, making such statistics a distortion of the real economic life in the ethnic minority regions.

To reinforce the sharp contrast in product components, we feel it necessary to mention the special tax phenomenon in the history of Guizhou. In the Ming Dynasty, the Yunwu Tea (cloud and mist tea), produced in the Miao region in present-day central Guizhou, served as a tribute to the royal court and was supplied by the nine *Zhangguansi* (department of officials) under Guiyang Fu that governed the ethnic Miao regions in the Ming Dynasty, which also supplied horses. [①] It is a known fact by recent surveys and through the analysis of ancient literature that ethnic Miaos living in this region were in the Swidden type of economy without designated tea plantations. The local Buyi people were mainly in the agricultural type of economy and did not have vast ranches either. These products designated as royal tributes by the Ming Dynasty were by-products from the fields of agricultural cultivation: tea grew in the hilly areas that could be burned to prepare the lands for cropping, and horses came from the public grasslands that belonged to extended families. They only accounted for a very limited portion of the product portfolios of these ethnic groups, i.e., those that were

① Zizhang Guo, *Record of Guizhou* • *On Tributes and Taxes*, mimeographed edition, in the collection of Guizhou Provincial Library accepted by ethnic Hans and also easy to transport. Another example of levying taxes that would surprise the people today was the dried bird meats used as taxes paid to Nandan *Tu Si* by the ethnic Bunuzhi Yao people in today's Libo County. One of the primary tributes made by the ethnic Yi *Tu Si* in northwestern Guizhou in the Yuan Dynasty was felts.① The above three examples indicate that the differences in the type of economy would undoubtedly lead to un-overlapping product portfolios among different ethnic groups, meaning that only a tiny percentage of them can enter the cross-xiang circulation. In a market economy, only these products can be converted into commodities.

The differences in economic lives among each ethnic group also contribute to the difference in the scale of the bulk of products. Generally speaking, the higher the type of economic life, the purer the product component and the greater the bulk of products. Rice, silk, tea, and porcelain became products in bulk quantity in the developed Han regions as early as the medieval times. Ethnic Dongs started to produce logs in large quantities in the mid-Ming Dynasty. ② The "Liuma" tung oil, a high quality product of the ethnic Buyi region, began to be shipped out of the region with Guanling Huajiang (previously under the control of Muyi *Tu Si*) as hubs after the mid-Qing Dynasty. ③ By contrast, the Yunwu tea in central Guizhou could not be produced in large quantities for a long period in time despite its popularity. The dried bird meats unique to the Yanshan region were never and are still not a mass production, nor will they be in the future. Our field surveys have revealed that most of the products in Mashan and Huashan in Guizhou province cannot meet the minimum requirement of quantity necessary for being shipped outside the region. After the measure to "replace the local hereditary headmen with officials appointed by the central government" was adopted in the Qing Dynasty under the reign of Yongzheng, cotton and hemp planting was enthusiastically promoted by the government in these two regions, resulting in a Huashan region specializing in the outgoing bulk cottons and a Mashan region specializing in the outgoing bulk hemp. The former locates in the area bordering the four present-day counties

① *Twenty-five Histories* vol. 9, *History of the Yuan Dynasty • Biography of Yuan Shizu,* 7283.

② Shengzhi Pan, "The Glory and Hidden Worries of Liuma Tung Oil," *Guizhou Ethnic Studies*, no. 1, 1996

③ *Memoir of the Qing Dynasty • A Compilation of Materials about Guizhou* (Guizhou People's Publishing House, November 1964) , 21-24.

of Zhenning, Zhenfeng, Wangmo and Ziyun, while the latter locates in the areas bordering the four present-day counties of Ziyun, Changshun, Luodian and Wangmo. It was not until then did the ethnic Miaos who were in the Swidden type of economy start to ship locally produced items in bulk, but the shipping of other products has remained negligible till today. Based on the quantity of products shipped out of the region, poverty is not a present-day phenomenon. The fact is also evidenced by the results of the surveys we conducted in Yaoshan. Now, Bunuzhi Yaos only sell a limited quantity of timbers in the market, while the majority of products they produce are hardly seen even in local village markets due to their extreme dispersion that makes it impossible to gather.

In a nutshell, the per capita output of products for the ethnic groups in the Swidden cultivation may not be less than the ethnic groups in agricultural economy. However, many of the products are not produced in bulk, nor can they be stored for an extended period of time due to the lack of a storage mechanism in this type of economy, they, consequently, cannot circulate as commodities under most circumstances in cross-xiang operations.

Another critical factor that limits the product's chance of entering the market circulation is the unit value. It takes different amount of labor work to make the same product by ethnic groups in different type or mode of economy. The work required of ethnic Miaos to produce the same quantity of millet is much less than that of Buyi or Dong peoples, while the work required of ethnic Miaos and Yaos to produce the same quantity of rice is several times more than ethnic Buyi and Han groups. Such a situation may have arisen from natural or cultural factors, yet in a well-circulated market, the price of rice cannot differ beyond a reasonable variance due to the similarity in the use value of rice. In other words, in a common market in cross-xiang operations, different ethnic groups are compensated differently for the same products.

The labor input in unit product in the Swidden economy is usually lower than that in the agricultural economy. We observed in Dalang Village of Ziyun County that the labor input in growing millet by the locals was only limited to burning weeds and sowing seeds in the fields before they could harvest. Any of the work that was performed by ethnic Hans such as cultivating, tillage or weeding, or fertilizing, was omitted. Although the output per *mu* (666 m^2) of land was merely a little over 100 *jin* (one half kilogram), it wouldn't be a problem for a laborer to be responsible for tens of *mu* of lands provided that there were enough cultivated lands for them.

Another example came from Dayi Village of Wangmo County where the local ethnic Buyi people were in the Swidden cultivation type of economy before 1960s. Given an abundant supply of cultivated lands, they could produce grains enough for 3-4 years in one-year's time. By this standard, the input-output efficiency might not be lower than the average level in the agricultural economy.

These products produced in the ethnic minority regions may yield higher than we originally estimate as long as they can enter the common market in cross-xiang operations. The real difficulties, however, lie in the fact that, as discussed above, they are hard to enter the market for failure to meet the minimal requirements in quantity. In addition, more values must be added to these products before they can enter the market. Consequently, they end up in costing more than the same products made in the ethnic Han regions. Both natural and cultural elements may give rise to the added values, eventually driving up the cost of these products. As far as natural elements are concerned, the Swidden cultivation is usually practiced in remote and mountainous regions without easy access by transportation, usually causing the costs in the collection, shipping, and transportation of products to be higher than the value of the products themselves. We will have deeper discussions on this issue in the chapter headed with "background". From the perspective of social elements, the dispersed locations of production, inconsistency in the type and quality of products require that human efforts be put in the collection and necessary processing of products, causing the added values to possibly exceed the value of the products themselves before they can be put in the market for sale. For this reason, in the Swidden cultivation regions that we surveyed, a considerable portion of locally produced products, other than those consumed by the locals, decayed or expired and their values were thus lost. In the meantime, this region is classified as one of the poorest regions in China according to the statistics result by national standards.

The differences in the type and mode of economy also give rise to the issue of product incompatibility. It is natural that the production of an ethnic group is subject to the cultural tradition of that particular ethnic group and is in line with the economic type and mode that ethnic group is in. Only in this fashion can the products be successfully consumed and become valuable in this cultural setting. For instance, the tradition in the practice of Chinese medicine in ethnic Han regions has created an industry chain from the collection, planting, processing to distribution of the Chinese medicinal materials in its economic life. However, when engaging in the cross-xiang economic activities with an ethnic group that does not accept the traditional Chinese medicines, all these industries and the corresponding products are hard to circulate among the people of this ethnic group. This is what we call lack of product compatibility. Similarly, the products accepted in the ethnic Miao traditions may be viewed as taboos and thus totally unacceptable to other ethnic groups. The ethnic Miaos, as we mention earlier for example, often view the pupa and larva of a variety of insects as normal products and thus harvest them accordingly. They are, however, totally unacceptable by the ethnic Han standards. As another example, the ethnic Bunuzhi Yao people often feed on field mice and have accumulated in their practice a full range of knowledge and tools about the steps and skills in catching the field mice. The mice caught this way can be eaten directly or made dried meat for easy storage. These products likewise can not be accepted by either ethnic Buyi or Han peoples. Similar cases are countless. It is impossible for the products that are not acceptable by the other parties in cross-xiang operations to enter the distribution channels; or to put it this way, incompatible products will undoubtedly be ruled out from the commodity list in real cross-xiang operations, thus giving rise to factors that constrain the economic activities.

Life habits partially explain why products are incompatible. The ethnic Buyi people eat dogs while most Miaos refuse to do so. Ethnic Hui people do not eat pork, yet it is a major source of meat for ethnic Hans. The incompatibility issue may also be attributable to the lack of necessary material conditions for the proper function of products. Electrical appliances, for example, are popular in ethnic Han regions but they are not acceptable to ethnic minority people who live in the regions without stable source of power or with no power at all. On the other hand, some products that are normal to Miao and Buyi people, such as indigo used in wax printing of fabrics, is of no use in the ethnic Han regions where chemical dyes are widely used, and is therefore an unacceptable product.

In general, the compatibility of the products, and when compatible, the variance in the useful value of products both amount to constraining factors that may hinder the smooth cross-xiang operations. To ensure such a smooth operation, we must introduce a new concept - product integration ratio, as a way of comprehensively measuring how the differences in the type and mode of economy in different ethnic groups give rise to the barriers in the product circulation as well as the size of the barriers. Product integration ratio refers to the percentage of the products made by one ethnic group in normally functional economic conditions that can enter the channel of consumption (including the market) of the other party over the gross social products. A greater value in the ratio signals a greater potential in cross-xiang economic activities across different ethnic groups, and vice versa. In the development of the ethnic minority regions in Guizhou, the product integration ratio of the ethnic Hans is usually greater than that of other ethnic minority groups. An ethnic group in a lower type of economy tends to have a lower product integration ratio when engaging in cross-xiang operations with the ethnic Han group, and therefore is inevitably put in an inferior position. Generally speaking, the lower the level of energy control by an ethnic group, the lower its ratio when engaging in cross-xiang operations with ethnic Hans. The ethnic Han product integration ratio in Buyi societies, for example, does not vary much from the ethnic Buyi product integration ratio in Han societies. However, the variance becomes much greater if the ethnic Buyi is replaced by Miao. It will be more difficult for commodities to circulate in the societies of other parties when a greater variance exists in the product integration ratios of the two parties. Therefore, one thing that must be done when planning cross-xiang operations is to accurately estimate the product integration ratios, and to ensure the ratios of both parties concerned in cross-xiang operations be close to each other if the operations are to continue successfully. Only by doing so can we achieve an equilibrium between the total value of outgoing products of one party and that of incoming products of the other, which lays the foundation for cross-xiang operations to last steadily. Based on the above analyses, an accurate estimate of product integration ratio usually requires that we survey and hold the following item data:

(I) Product components in the ethnic groups concerned

(II) Minimum quantity in the supply of each kind of product

(III) Additional costs for a specific product to enter the market of the other party

(IV) Unit value of each product

(V) Product compatibility

With these data at hand, we may calculate the percentage of each item over the gross social products. It becomes easy then for us to take all these percentages into account to estimate the product integration ratio of a specific ethnic group when engaging in cross-xiang operations with other related ethnic groups, thus offering guidance for these cross-xiang operations to be conducted successfully.

IV Different Types and Different Modes: the Meaning in Economics

In the previous two sections of this chapter, we put forth two important concepts, i.e., the type and mode of economic life of different ethnic groups, and a few specific questions that we must address when analyzing the cross-xiang economic activities using these two concepts. To facilitate following discussions, we feel necessary to remind our readers of another important content we talked about in the first section of this chapter: the economic life of each ethnic group is only a component of the traditional culture of this ethic group, and a discussion of economic issues without taking into account of the other cultural components will lead to false and groundless conclusions. Many economic issues are in fact a manifestation of deep-rooted cultural factors instead of the economic activity itself. We cannot clarify economic issues before we have a profound understanding of the cultural network. Since World War II, many renowned economists have thought otherwise. The difference in academic traditions and personal academic history has led these economists to take another route when discussing the modernization in developing countries. However, the difference in type and mode of economy is an objective fact. Regardless of the situations in the beginning of the research of ethnic economic development, the flaws in the research methodology will be exposed with the elapse of time, and new methodologies will emerge by making revisions to prior conclusions and methodologies before new conclusions are drawn that reflect realities. We are glad to see that many economists have, in recent years, come to the conclusions that are gradually approaching our train of thought to some extent. The purpose of this section is to further emphasize on the significance of the differences in the type and mode of economy on the research of ethnic economic development through a review of prior economics theories.

Classical economics is developed around the two big subjects of microeconomics and macroeconomics. The former studies how to achieve economic objects through operation and commodity production under the assumption of a perfect market, while the latter emphasizes on how to tackle the economic problems such as economic fluctuation, unemployment and inflation through control and adjustment measures in order to achieve a stable economic growth. With the expansion of the world market, developed countries have to engage in close economic relations with developing countries, which either don't have a perfect market, have a different financial system from the developed countries, or don't have the "unemployment" as defined by the West, causing the classical economics to be out of reach of new economic activities. Therefore, a sub-discipline of economics emerged in the 1940s that is aimed at solving the economic problems unique to the developing nations and is now called "development economics."

The foundational works in the development economics include *Problems of Industrialization of Eastern and South-Eastern Europe* (1943) by Paul Rosenstein-Rodan, *World Economic Development* (1944) by Eugene Staley, and *The Industrialization of Backward Areas* (1943) by K. Mandelbaum, which symbolizes that it becomes a fact that development economics is extended into the research of the economic life in low-income nations.

The post-WWII era witnessed the independence of many former colonial countries whose economic development attracted increasing attention from academia, thus fueling the rapid development in development economics and the rise of many famous economists. Among them were W. Arthur Lewis, Theodore Schultz and Gunnar Myrdal whose remarkable achievements won them the Nobel Prize in Economics. A revisit to their research methodologies and conclusions will greatly deepen our understanding of cross-xiang operations and be valuable in deepening the understanding and broadening our vision with regards to the classification of economic types and modes of each ethnic group as well as the role it plays in the economics research.

Lewis's major contribution is the introduction of what came to be called "Dual Sector Model". He classifies industrial sector and traditional agricultural sector to different economic categories, namely two different types of economy, which differ in the mode of labor supply. In developing countries, these two modes co-exist to give rise to the dual economic structure. Lewis holds that industrialization is the way for developing countries to achieve economic success, to grow the gross domestic products rapidly and to become developed. The key to industrialization is capital accumulation. To point to the direction of capital accumulation for developing countries, Lewis starts his analysis with the supply of labor. It is his view that the agricultural sector has a limited amount of land to cultivate, and the marginal product of an additional farmer is assumed to be zero as the law of diminishing marginal returns has run its course due to the fixed input, land. As a result, the agricultural sector has a quantity of farm workers that are not contributing to agricultural output since their marginal productivity is close to zero, or even in negative territory, making it possible to have an unlimited supply of labor. "Some writers have noticed the existence of 'disguised' unemployment in the agricultural sector, and have made it clear that the lands owned by individual families are so few that if some of the family members get a job in other places, the remaining members can still cultivate the lands without any problem."① Based on this perception of labor supply in the traditional agricultural sector, Lewis points out that the industrial sector will have access to unlimited supply of labor if it is willing to pay the labor with a salary slightly higher than what they need for subsistence, and that enterprises may have a high marginal productivity, gain huge profits and thus accumulate capital by relying on these cheap labors. His theory of development is, to put it in a more straightforward way, "to take advantage of the huge quantity of farmers who are in disguised unemployment in the agricultural sector and keep their salaries at a lower level to provide support in the capital accumulation for modern industrial sector."②

Lewis' arduous and tenacious efforts in the exploration of a development path for developing nations are commendable and his theory is right to the point in a certain aspect of the economic development studies and is thus of great reference value. We have to point out, however, that he seems to have oversimplified the issues he studies. Take the labor issue that is the focus of his study as an example. Apparently, it is not an issue as simple as counting

① Arthur Lewis, *Dualism in Economy*, trans. Wei Shi, (Beijing College of Economics Press, March 1989), 3.

② Sifu Cai, Yansheng Zhang, ed. *An Introduction to Development Economics*, (Beijing College of Economics Press, March 1992), 8.

the heads of people, but must be related to the quality and perceptions of labor, interpersonal labor relations as well as such deeper level questions as the possibility of unlimited supply of labor force by the traditional subsistence sector without disrupting its original production mechanism. The capital accumulation, for another example, is likewise not an economic advantage that is completely dependent on the profits, which may not be fully converted into productivity or investment. The decisive element that determines if profits may be converted into investment is the social mechanism instead of how much profit there is. In fact, the aid provided by the developed countries to the developing countries, although quite limited, may benefit the receiving countries to some extent if the aid can be fully converted into investment. A closer observation reveals, however, that such a considerable part of aid in limited quantity, after entering the societies of the receivers and put into operations, usually is not used to make investments but simply consumed. If we cannot put an effective social mechanism in place in the developing countries to convert each dollar received into investment, we cannot guarantee the capital accumulation even though the enterprises are profitable.

The oversimplification in Lewis' theory is also reflected in the structure he puts together for the developing countries marching toward modernization. His point of view that to follow the footstep of the developed countries is the only way for developing countries to modernize themselves is neither materialistic nor dialectic. In reality, economic development can be achieved by different means in different nations and economic evolution is both diversified and multi-faceted. No economic goals can be reached simply by utter imitation. This has been a consensus in the academia of economics in China and is reflected in its comment on Lewis' theory: "The classical development economics theory introduced by Lewis perceives the path that the capitalist countries in the West walked in the 17th and 18th centuries as the only way for the developing countries to build modernization. In other words, he views the capitalism to be the only way of achieving economic development." In the meantime, Lewis' theory rejects "the diversity in the economic development approach and thus repudiates the possibility and superiority of the socialist economic development."[①] Consequently, it is

① Department of Economics, Peking University, comp., *Foreign Economics Review* II (Shanghai People's Publishing House, August 1982), 123.

inappropriate and unrealistic for us to mechanically apply Lewis' theory and approach when trying to solve the problems we run into in economic development in ethnic regions in China.

With the knowledge of the different types and modes of economic life in ethnic groups, we think that Lewis' theory of attributing the gap in economy only to a difference between industrial and agricultural sectors is far from convincing. From a vertical point of view, developing nations are in fact in different levels of development, which determines that their development must follow different paths and is not merely a problem of migrating from traditional agriculture to an industrial sector. Horizontally, even for the nations that are in the same level of economic development, they have demonstrated different patterns in the economic life. The Western Europe, North America and Japan, although all rank among developed nations, have diverse economic lives. Japan, for example, has retained such a considerable portion of its cultural tradition while going through the process of industrialization that the Japanese enterprises differ dramatically in structure from its American counterparts judging from any angle. Needless to say, how can the developing nations that endeavor to attain industrialization achieve such a goal by following one mode of industrial culture? Therefore, the discussion of modernization in developing nations must be carried out by taking into account of specific situations rather than attempting to fit everything in one model.

Following the Third Plenary Session of the 11th Central Committee of the Communist Party of China, China has announced its grand vision of building a socialist country with the Chinese characteristics, signaling a successful conceptualization of giving specific analysis to specific issues on our way to modernization. Therefore, to identify each ethnic group's economic type and mode becomes extremely necessary and pragmatic before we formulate the development plan for these ethnic minority groups. To tell the truth, these ideas of ours are not groundless imaginations but are enlightened by and built upon Lewis' analysis of the "dual sector economic structure."

People coming from ethnic groups in different economic type or mode tend to perceive the issue of labor surplus differently. It is completely from the perspective of an industrialized society of developed nations that Lewis draws the conclusion that the traditional cultural sector is able to provide unlimited surplus labor forces. If we shift to another angle and look at the vacation of as long as more than one month in a year, merely five working days in a week and six working hours in a day in an industrialized society, what conclusions can we draw otherwise? As a matter of fact, many farmers in traditional agricultural societies would without a doubt view the employment in an industrial society an easy job with a lot of spare time and view outsourcing the household chores such as cooking and childcare a symbol of sloth. In summary, the issue of surplus labor force must also be thought of and treated specifically. A worker from a traditional agricultural society who enters an industrial society needs to be adjusted to such a society in the way of thinking and knowledge structure. To retain such labor force, constant and systematic trainings must be provided to the workers as well as their children, which means enormous costs to the industrial society. To put it in an easier-to-understand language, all this costs money, without which these workers cannot take root in the industrial sector. If such costs are considered, the hypothesis of supply of unlimited labor force at the cost of minimum wage will prove to be false, and thus putting the possibility of capital accumulation on the low wage basis under serious doubt.

Now let's think about the issue of capital accumulation. According to Lewis, a capital accumulation can be realized as long as the country accumulates all the profits gained from the marginal productivity created by a low wage. This conclusion is also questionable. Capital accumulation will ultimately be constrained by the economic type and mode. Accumulation of profits does not necessarily translate into the capitals needed by industrial enterprises. In fact, ethnic groups in different type and mode of economy differ in their way of accumulating, distributing and consuming wealth. The "banquet to show off one's wealth", for example, is a way of accumulating wealth as well as a way of doing things by the Indians in North America. The Tibetans in China accumulate wealth by giving their hard-earned money to the temples. The ethnic Miaos in Guizhou province often spend all their money on jewelries for their children. Although counties such as Taijiang, Leishan and Jianhe where ethnic Miaos settle are on the top of the list of the poorest counties in the country, any silver jewelry supplied by the country to the market will be made out of stock in a buying spree by the locals, which is also a way of accumulating wealth by the majority of local people. In the above three cases, there is wealth, and the wealth is accumulated, but unfortunately the accumulated wealth is not converted into the productivity as expected by Lewis. Therefore, the perception that industrialization can be realized as long as there is wealth that can be accumulated by effective means is too good to be true. The profits made by enterprises won't automatically lead to industrialization if such a channel and way of accumulating wealth, or the way to treat wealth is not changed. This is where we divert from Lewis. It is our belief that Lewis' theory has some value of reference but it should be one of a few ways. The reality is much more complicated. To solely rely on the profits gained from the supply of cheaper labor is not enough to solve the problem of modernizing the ethnic groups in a developing stage.

Unlike Lewis, Schultz points out another way for the developing countries to develop their economy. Contrary to the points of view of Lewis, Schultz's theory is based on the following two points: First, he does not view the traditional cultural sector as a burden but rather a valuable sector of production for the economic growth. He insists that the developing countries cannot become industrialized if the development of the traditional agriculture is overlooked. Second, unlike Lewis who indiscriminately treats the surplus labor force from the traditional agricultural sector, Schultz highly emphasizes on the importance of training to improve quality of labor. To stress the importance of the labor quality in the economic growth, Schultz conceptualizes the term "human capital". Instead of simplifying the capital accumulation to be a mere accumulation of monetary capital, he views the improvement in the physique and quality of labor as capital accumulation as well, thus fully affirming the role of people on economic development. Based on this perspective, Schultz sharply criticizes the foreign aid policies adopted by the American government for quite a long time that, argued Schultz, in fact selfishly dump surplus agricultural products into developing countries. Such aids yield a result of purposefully suppressing the price of grains in the countries receiving aids and thus depriving these countries of the chance to develop local agriculture and eventually suffocating the traditional agriculture. As a result, the aid-receiving countries, due to an under-developed industrial sector and an ever weakening agricultural sector on which they subsist, will shrink into economically crippled countries that can not survive without alms from developed countries.

In his well-acclaimed book *Economic Growth and Agriculture*, Schultz affirms the value of the traditional agriculture in the economic development by citing Mexico in the 1940-1960s as an example of successful economic development. The growth in the agricultural sector in Mexico, as pointed out by Schultz, depend on two traditional elements of production, namely the increase in the area of cultivated lands and the growth in employment. The growth in agriculture has not hindered the growth, but instead, fueled the growth in industry, and thus has been comprehensively rewarded in economic terms. Today, we feel very necessary to re-read and understand his book by putting it in the context of the real agricultural production in ethnic minority regions in Guizhou.

"Despite the weak agricultural performance in the majority of Latin American countries, Mexico's agricultural sector was exceptionally successful and thus highly enlightening. It grew by more than 5% annually from 1940-1962, and its agricultural output increased by over 8% annually from 1963-1965. No other countries in Latin America experienced such a high growth rate. The success in the agricultural sector in Mexico was not at the cost of its industrial development; To the contrary, economic stimulus resulted in fast growth in both agriculture and industry. Although most of the growth in the agricultural sector was achieved due to an increase in the two conventional elements of production, i.e., the area of cultivated land and the jobs in agriculture, ample evidences suggested a constant rise in agricultural productivity since the mid 1950s. Between 1950 and 1960, agricultural yields on per acre basis increased significantly as a result of agricultural modernization, of which heavy investment in irrigation systems was an integral part. In 1950, the execution of the water power resource plan brought the total volume of water used in land irrigation to 6.5 billion cubic meters, and the number climbed to 17.5 cubic meters in 1960. The fertilizer supply and usage grew even faster. Rockefeller Foundation – Mexican Government Research Plan also contributed to the success, which yielded an annual ROI of 290% since the early 1940s. More importantly, most Mexican farmers were not hurt by the inefficient prices in agricultural products and elements of production that had strong effects of economic stimulus on the increase of agricultural production, to which the farmers responded astonishingly. We can learn a lot from Mexico in this matter. It gives us some hope that more countries in Latin America will remember it when time goes by." ①

① Theodore W. Shultz, *Economic Growth and Agriculture*, trans. Xibao Guo, Kainian Tong (Beijing College of Economics Press, February 1991),175-176.

In this part, Schultz talks about the successful experiences in Mexico and brings up two thought-provoking questions: the great contributions that the investment in Mexico, especially in agricultural research, makes to the recovery and development of traditional agriculture, which has fueled heated debates in the scholarly world in China and it is not necessary for us to reiterate. Second, the farmers in Mexico have not been subject to the damage of inefficient agricultural products and factor prices, enabling the traditional agriculture to last successfully and generating enormous economic benefits. This issue has not received widespread attention from the academia in China. However, such an issue is critical to the economic development in ethnic minority regions as the existence of inefficient agricultural products and factor prices is fatal to ethnic minority groups that are in a non-industrial economy. It not only prevents these people from accumulating capital for reproduction, but more importantly, it dampens the enthusiasm and subjective initiative critically needed by the ethnic groups to carry out production, resulting in the abandonment of the projects for self-subsistence to pursue economic income that is more remotely possible to them. One of the essences in Marxism is that it highly values the people's subjective initiative and asserts that nothing can disrupt the economic development more than the hurt on the subjective initiative of the labor force. We will further discuss this topic in chapter nine titled "solutions".

The issue of "human capital" demands our special attention as well. The concept enables us to expand the meaning of "capital" and helps us make correct estimation on the labor value in non-industrial economy, which is of significant importance in accurately evaluating the labor quality of ethnic minority groups. The economists in the West have now further extended the concept of "human capital" and applied this concept in the non-industrial field. It greatly helps us in carrying out our task in the book, and to this end, we feel necessary to briefly introduce the basic definition and history of evolution in "human capital".

Human capital is a term relative to physical capital and non-human capital. It refers to the capital that is reflected in human beings that can be used to generate income in the future. By the definition of R. G. Lipsey and P. O. Steiner, human capital is reflected in the form of skill and knowledge, etc., on a person rather than on a machine. The major components of human capital are health care and education.[1] Schultz, based on the definition of human capital, further clarifies the difference between "human capital" and "physical capital", acknowledges its status in economic lives, and points out the role of education and technology in the increase of "human capital." In his book *Human Capital, Education and Economic Growth*, the American economist Stanley L. Engerman further supplements to and develops on the definition of "human capital". "Schultz thinks that human capital as a form of capital differs from physical materials in that it cannot be traded, nor held as an asset; but it functions like physical materials to play a productive role in economy, and increase domestic income. Engerman continues to argue that the viewpoint that the ownership of human capital can not be transferred, or a human capital can not be inherited and traded as a physical asset is not universally applicable in all human capitals in the society but is only applicable to free labors. Human capital exists even in a slave society, on slaves in particular, but the return on the human capital belongs to the master of the slaves, not to the slaves themselves."[2]

The above quotations have illustrated the foundational concept of "human capital". We need to remind our readers, however, that it is from a perspective of the labor quality in an industrial economy that the discussions of "human capital" are carried out. It does not include the requirements on the labor quality in other forms of economy, or in other words, it is not entirely compatible with the requirements on the labor quality in other types of economy. In fact, different types of economy have different requirements on the physique and quality of the labor force. An excellent hunter may not be a good farmer, and likewise, an excellent shepherd is not necessarily a qualified truck driver. To understand this difference is a critical principle in the discussion of the topic of the book - the economic development in the ethnic groups in a non-industrial economy. Our readers will have a better understanding of this after finishing chapter five of the book.

Another uniqueness in Schultz's economics thought is that, unlike other economists prior to him who tended to fill their books with grandiloquent slogans such as fair competition and humanitarian aid, he discloses the facts by unveiling what is hidden underneath the policies by the American government. Notably, these are not problems that only happen in America but

[1] *Foreign Economics Review* II, 3.
[2] *Foreign Economics Review* II, 7-8.

are universal throughout the world, and they reflect the utter selfishness of the industrialized countries when they develop economic ties with non-industrial countries. Schultz's book provides valuable insider materials for us to understand the essence in the economic interaction between ethnic groups or nations that are in different types of economy, which cause, at a profound level, a variety of disputes in the world market such as trade wars, trade disputes between the South and the North, and the Uruguay round of negotiation etc. A revisit to Schultz's statements keeps us clearheaded in dealing with economic issues across ethnic groups.

"The agricultural committee in Congress requires that the Department of Agriculture impose a series of restrictive measures when providing aids in agricultural development to other countries. What's troubling is the hypothetical threat that these countries may produce agricultural products that compete with us; therefore, we are in possession of a historical inheritance in legislation, i.e., we've declined the important joint venture operations with foreign countries in crop improvement imagined by Henry Wallace (who had foreseen the favorable possibility in conducting cooperation with neighboring countries), and we don't admit to rely on cooperation with other countries for obtaining generic varieties of many specific plants (including wheat, corn). The US Department of Agriculture has long been instructed to find a way of exporting more subsidized and encouraged agricultural products without worrying about the impacts that these activities may have on economic stimuli (needed for incenting farmers of these countries to increase agricultural production)" ①

Sensible politicians have gradually come to realize that the dumping policy on agricultural products in America has inflicted heavy loss on developing countries. Insightful scholars have become aware of the long-lasting damage it has done to the world. The dumping policy of this nature thus is a target of all criticism. Schultz goes one step further to unmask the deceptive and distasteful nature of such a policy: "It is not difficult for us to turn our surplus agricultural products into international assets. By doing so, however, we are not deceiving others but ourselves. We may continue pretending that we are well-intentioned, yet intelligent and knowledgeable foreign leaders won't be fooled by us. They know it from the beginning that

① Theodore Shultz, *Economic Growth and Agriculture*, 21.

our foreign policies have been devised to suit our domestic needs."[1]

Despite the tremendous value Schultz's economics thoughts have provided, he is congruent with Lewis by classifying economies into a dual-sector structure, i.e., his thoughts presume the opposition between the industrial economy and traditional agricultural economy. The establishment of the theoretical framework on the type and mode of human economic life will significantly expand and enrich Schultz's thoughts. It enables us to see that to developing nations, the traditional agriculture has immeasurable values and it is by no means a drag on the industrial modernization. In the meantime, traditional animal husbandry and Swidden cultivation also have values and won't dampen the efforts by the ethnic groups to build a modern society as long as they are dealt with property. In light of Schultz's economics thoughts, we have to show our admiration for the foresight and sagacity of our country that implements a fundamental policy on the ground of agriculture. We need to admit, though, that we must do more than that. We have to acknowledge that in some ethnic minority regions in this country, the economic life has not reached the level of traditional agriculture, and if we don't admit in theory that the type of economy they are in now have values, we will lose directions in our poverty-relief efforts in these regions, consciously or unconsciously, ending up feeling helpless or unnecessarily doing things that we are not supposed to do. The job of expanding Schultz's economics thoughts in this field has historically been put on the shoulders of the Chinese social scientists.

Schultz's theory on "human capital" needs to be expanded as well. As Schultz and his followers discuss "human capital" mainly from a perspective of the industrial economy, their explanation of "human capital" can never include all connotations of this term. The indicators to measure the quality of human beings must differ in different types and modes of economy. In fact, it is not uncommon even among developed countries that people may experience difficulty in seeking employment, or unemployment by highly skilled high-tech professionals, as a result of the existence of varied modes of economy that causes a mismatch between job requirements and job seekers' qualifications. It is possible that these countries may try to solve the unemployment issue by re-training these people, it is, however, a costly and inefficient behavior from the perspective of invest (in education, scientific

[1] Theodore Shultz, *Economic Growth and Agriculture*, 25.

research etc.) and output. A discussion of "human capital" is incomplete if such an issue is overlooked. The incompatibility in "human capital" becomes even more evident when we attempt to broaden our vision to other types and modes of economy. Therefore, when dissecting various non-economic factors constraining the economic development in each ethnic group, we must not underestimate the difference in the mode and type of economy, the incompatibility in "human capital" caused by this difference and the negative impacts such a difference may have on the economic development of the related ethnic groups.

China is a socialist country and has made it a national policy by laws and regulations to support the economic development in ethnic minority regions. Although things like the developed countries have done that put national interests of the developing countries in jeopardy will never happen in China, a lack of deeper understanding of economic type and mode may lead to unintentional damage to the interests of ethnic minority groups by the formulation and execution of inappropriate policies. It becomes a mission for us who engage in the research of the ethnic economic development to ensure that unfortunate things like this not happen. We believe that with the safeguard by the superior socialism, as long as our research reflects the real situation and such a research is put in practice without delay, it is possible for us to remove the disturbances caused by these negative factors to the economic development in ethnic regions. To ensure our research is done properly, Karl Gunnar Myrdal's research achievements may offer some value of reference.

Before we give a thorough review of Gunnar Myrdal's economics thoughts, we feel necessary to reiterate the goal of this book: to comprehensively analyze the non-economic constraints in the economic development of ethnic minority regions. Our research methodology is that of modern cultural anthropology, especially the economic anthropology, instead of the conventional economics. As a highly achieved economist, Myrdal carries out his research from the angle and by the methodology of classical economics. Although many of his researches have led him to the same conclusions as cultural anthropology, he claims that cultural anthropological methodologies are of no use in the economic research in developing nations. He argues that cultural anthropologists always restrain their research to small communities through "static" observations in the hope of finding how the people in backward regions live and subsist, which is not compatible with the overall characteristics of economic activities.[①] His understanding is not entirely senseless, yet what he describes is the situation before WWII and is not a true reflection of the modern cultural anthropology. It is not difficult for our readers to find out from the below introduction that some of the academic conclusions by Myrdal are in sync with those of modern cultural anthropology. While accepting Myrdal's insightful thoughts, we must be cautious not to exclude the cultural anthropology from the research of economic development in ethnic regions.

The research methods employed by Myrdal are completely opposite to those employed by classical economists. He firmly opposes the way that the classical economists statically analyze economic behaviors and economic results. Instead, he maintains to conduct a dynamic analysis on economic activities and, to this end, conceptualize that economic activities are a "causational dynamic process". He is also in disagreement with classical economists who often restrain the discussion of economic issues to economy and proposes an aggregate analysis methodology. It is Myrdal's view that the economic development is impacted not only by the economic activities themselves, but also by other factors such as natural environment, culture and institution etc. To ethnic groups that are in the developing stage, the restraining effects caused by established institutions are especially important. He asserts in his book that institutional reform is more important than direct economic reforms. Based on the changes he makes to the above two research methodologies, Myrdal puts forth the "circular cumulative causation model" in economic development, where he emphasizes the mutual restraining and mutual dependent relations among numerous factors in economic development. We would like to mention that Myrdal's aggregate analysis and dynamic analysis are, in essence, different presentations of the same content as the overall cultural perspective and cultural dynamic balance perspective in modern cultural anthropology. As Myrdal's economics theory stresses the research on institutions as well as the impact by institutions on the economic development, the economics thoughts represented by him are later called "neo-institutional economic school". With regards to Myrdal's research methodology, Fu Yincai's summary has some value of reference.

① (Sweden) Myrdal, *The Challenge of World Poverty: A World Anti-Poverty Program in Outline,* trans. Chaoyang Gu et al. (Beijing College of Economics Press, December 1991), 5.

"Institutional economics studies the emergence, development and roles of economic institutions. It views modern economy as a changing institution and that economic development is closely associated with impacts from all social phenomena, stretching its subject of research beyond the classical economics and moving closer to sociology. Neo-institutional economic school proposes to revolutionize the foundational methodologies in modern economics theories. The economists from this school perceive that the constant technological innovations have brought constant evolution to capitalist social institutions and social structures. As capitalism is a "causational dynamic process", economists must study change and process but not the static cross section of the economy, and that is a progressive and comprehensive methodology. Myrdal emphasizes that economic analyses must be related to the social and institutional factors by a progressive method, based on which he further puts forth the "circular cumulative causation model" for the research of the issues facing developing nations. The core of the "circular cumulative causation model" is: In a dynamic social process, all social and economic factors are causally interrelated. Meanwhile, the change to one social and economic factor will cause change to another social and economic factor whereas the second-level changes will reversely drive the initial change, resulting in the economy developing along the direction of the initial change. The relationship among various social and economic factors is not of an equilibrium nature or tend to reach an equilibrium, but rather operates circularly, not simply circular but with the cumulative effect."①

The most relevant and valuable part of Myrdal's economics is the principle of analyzing specific environment by specific method and handling specific issue with specific treatment, and the new perspective deriving from this principle about the promotion and transplant of scientific and technological achievements. Also, the conditions under which economic terminologies are applied to under-developed nations are significant. Although Myrdal insists that the economic growth in developing countries is dependent on the introduction of science and technology, unlike his predecessors, he has not absolutized science and technology but rather states that the advanced science and technology in the modern Western world are specifically targeted to developed countries and must be subject to a

① Yincai Fu, *Contemporary Western Economics Theories* (Yunnan People's Publishing House, October 1985), 260-261.

re-engineering process if they are to be introduced into the developing countries. Only by introducing the scientific and technological achievements that specifically suit the developing countries can they play an effective role in driving the economic growth. Such a comment is specifically applicable in correcting the mistakes we make in the poverty-relief work in China. Reading his remarks again provokes us to think deeply: "The agricultural technologies in under-developed countries must be made highly labor intensive while those in developed countries have been improved to be extremely labor-saving. This fact indicates that, unlike in the industrial sectors where modern technologies can be directly introduced and used, it is much more important for the agricultural technologies be tailored to suit the different percentages of elements in under-developed countries before they can be used in these countries." He further points out that "Some special technologies, such as cow artificial fertilization, new methods to prevent plant diseases and insect pests and to exterminate rats, are adoptable, yet even these technologies often must go through complete adjustment. Even more critically needed are new researches, although they are often based on the fundamental researches conducted by the developed countries." "In addition, modern agricultural technologies invented by developed countries are meticulous and localized researches on climate, soil and seeds etc., and are mainly applicable to the countries in temperate regions. Therefore, it becomes an urgent task to carry out intensive researches of the same type for the tropical and subtropical regions where the majority of developing countries are located."① To some extent, Myrdal's statements have implied the extremely important theoretical perception that technologies must be "nationalized" and "localized". In the meantime, having realized the importance and difficulty in the technological promotion, he writes: "It is only a beginning of the agricultural reform that some reasonable and suitable agricultural technologies are made available. We must direct millions of farmers to use these new technologies. Small-scale experiments, regardless of how successful they are, are a mere beginning."②

With regards to the latter, Myrdal clearly stresses by the use of his economics research methods that conventional economics terminologies and concepts are established in the background of fully developed markets, and

① Myrdal, *The Challenge of World Poverty: A World Anti-Poverty Program in Outline,* 87.

② idem

thus can not draw correct conclusions when used in ethnic groups in an immature market, as these terminologies have left the environments where they are applicable. Myrdal uses the economic terms such as "unemployment" and "underemployment" as examples to illustrate that they, when used in less-developed countries, either lack economically practical meaning or lead us to conclusions that have completely different meanings. It is very necessary to read closely what he writes in his book: "In the developed countries, it may be meaningful to analyze the economy and arrive at sounding conclusions by the pure 'economic' terms, e.g., total number of employment and unemployment, saving, investment and industry; demand, supply and price that are on the condition of a market and a fairly effective market, because these concepts, models and the theories that bond these terms together are a reflection of the reality in developed countries." "These methods, however, can not be used in less developed countries unless at the cost of digressing from the topic and thus making serious mistakes. In the absence of a fully competitive market or no market competition at all, we should not use the above mentioned presumed (and many other) 'economic' terms."[①] Despite Myrdal's denial, these theories, to some extent, have concerned the issue of "relativism". These thoughts are interchangeable with the cultural relativism in cultural anthropology, and are a result of logical reasoning of cultural relativism in the field of the science of economics. As a school of thought developed by Boaz, Herskovits and other scholars, cultural relativism is a useful tool in accurately understanding and dealing with heterogeneous ethnic groups, including the economic activities of these heterogeneous ethnic groups.

The researches in this book also benefit from other key academic thoughts of Myrdal. Unlike Walt Whitman Rostow who believes in "the Stages of Economic Growth", Myrdal thinks that every country is so dramatically different in social and historical conditions, geography, climate, population density and growth rate that developing countries don't follow the same route in industrialization as the developed countries. The rationality of the core contents implied by the non-linear development perspective will be easier for our readers to understand by referencing to the analyses on the dual evolution in the first and second sections of this chapter. Myrdal also opposes Paul A. Samuelson's viewpoint that uses per capita income as the only

① idem

indicator of economic growth. He stresses that economic development is a comprehensive process of social evolution and must take into account of the constraints by and possible cooperation from social culture. This perspective guides our research throughout the entire book, to which our readers' attention is called for when reading later chapters.

The classification of economic types and modes is not an economic issue only. As economy functions as the foundation of all cultural activities, divergent economic types and modes will, without a doubt, give rise to and shape corresponding cultural characteristics. To more effectively organize production, culture, on the other hand, must adjust the living environment and existing economic type and mode to which it is exposed to. In addition to the relativity demonstrated by the main direction and scope of promotion of science and technology as pointed out by Myrdal, some social phenomena that are related to economic lives also have the nature of relativity. It is extremely detrimental if we mechanically copy or imitate other practices without taking into account of specific situations in the research of ethnic economic development. Therefore, to clarify the economic type and mode of the ethnic groups that for us to avoid making such mistakes. The detailed discussion of specific cases in this matter can be found in chapter nine "solutions".

Cross-xiang operations are bi-lateral economic activities, and thus the subjective and objective parties both have decisive impacts on their success or failure. An analysis of the economic type and mode shall, in principle, include the following two aspects: On the one hand, to clarify the type and mode of economy that the subjective party is in. On the other hand, to clarify on the type and mode of economy that the objective party is in so that we can understand the strengths and weaknesses of both parties in the operation, and play the strengths of both parties to the full and avoid their weaknesses, jointly contributing to the attainment of the operational targets. For this reason, a fundamental perception must be brought to everyone's due attention: Every economic type or mode functions well in the most congenial environment and operates poorly in a constraining living space. No single type or mode is perfect. If a certain type or mode of economy is imposed forcefully on other ethnic group in cross-xiang operations, the results will definitely prove unsatisfactory. This is the most fundamental reason why we must give a thorough and full analysis of the economic type and mode of each party involved in cross-xiang operations and why we emphasize the classification between the types and modes in economic lives.

Chapter Four Culture (II)

This chapter focuses on discussing how the three "cultural complexes" on the level of ethnic cultural organization, i.e., custom, language, and social organization, impact cross-xiang operations. The customs of objective parties in cross-xiang operations directly constrain interpersonal relations among its members, whereas the subjective parties demand new interpersonal relations to be established to cater to the needs of such operations. What lies in the core of these interpersonal relations is the relationship between employers and employees, and that between managers and the managed. Differing in major contents and the relationship they maintain, the two kinds of relations may hinder the cross-xiang operations if they are not made compatible with each other. From the perspective of the subjective party in cross-xiang operations, a set of solutions is critically needed that do not collide head-on with the customs of the objective party, nor jeopardize the execution of the rules in operation management either. We will show our readers by the following analyses that such solutions are available to us.

Cross-xiang operations are not possible without exchange of information carried by means of specific languages. The fact that the subjective and objective parties speak different languages impedes the understanding and communication between them. It is not as simple as an issue of translation, but also that of conceptual integration and divergent values. Only by fully taking into account of these factors can the subjective and objective parties accurately and truly exchange information, understand and grasp the positions and intentions of the other party, therefore enabling the relevant information to be of service to both parties. The analyses we have conducted tell us that these barriers can be removed as long as both parties acknowledge the importance of conceptual integration and try to attain such an integration in practice by thoughtful planning and progressive execution. Most problems we have run into around the communication of information in cross-xiang operations are caused by the inadequate understanding but not an inability in actuality. The social organizations of the objective parties in cross-xiang operations are an objective social existence and will not change for the ongoing cross-xiang operations. They can hinder or facilitate the smooth operation in cross-xiang activities; therefore it is a challenge for the subjective party to coordinate with them. To do this, we must first admit that they exist objectively, then try to identify, through meticulous surveying, the points where a mutual compatibility can be attained, and eventually find feasible ways of coordination. Only by doing so can the subjective party turn the social organizations of the objective party into mutually supplementary and beneficial factors, and prevent them from disrupting the normal cross-xiang operations.

I Constraints Triggered by Local Customs

Every ethnic group has its own traditions and customs that are norms in interpersonal interactions established through practices and customs in the continuing history of this ethnic group. Interpersonal lives in an ethnic group depend on material supplies, which are governed by the economic activities of that particular ethnic group. In this sense, the differences in the type and mode of economic life among different ethnic groups that we have discussed above will have profound impacts on the traditions and customs of the related ethnic groups. The traditions and customs, on the other hand, serve the corresponding economic lives and combine to safeguard the continuation and development of the ethnic group concerned by means of coordinating interpersonal relations. Naturally, the traditions and customs of each ethnic group will have different impacts on cross-xiang operations, sometimes pushing and sometimes dragging the operations. A comprehensive analysis of the specifics of the projects and of the ethnic groups is required before we can draw a sound conclusion about under what circumstances a pushing or dragging force may come into play.

All traditions and customs of each ethnic group will have un-negligible impacts on the four elements that any economic activity cannot do without, i.e., investment, technology, manpower and market due to the fact that traditions and customs, within the overall ethnic cultural structure, play the social role of regulating consumption, coordinating interpersonal relations, organizing accumulation of social wealth, and governing re-distribution of materials in the society, etc. Therefore, traditions and customs of a particular ethnic group usually are congruent with its economic activities but are often irrelevant to, or even conflicting with, the economic activities of other ethnic groups. As cross-xiang operations must be carried out across more than one ethnic culture, they are sure to bring inconsistency or conflicts among traditions and customs of different ethnic groups involved in the operations.

Examples like this were recorded in ancient literatures. *Han Fei Zi* told such a story: A man living in the Central Plains was good at making shoes and his wife was good at making hats. The couple decided to migrate to the Kingdom of Yue to make a living. Before they hit the road, a friend who became aware of their plan came to tell them that the people living in the Kingdom of Yue walked on bare foot with tattoos on their bodies and disheveled hair. They neither needed shoes nor hats. You wouldn't find demands for your skills. [①] Examples like this are not rare in today's efforts in developing Guizhou.

Huajiang Township of Guanling County is located at the "throat" of Yunnan-Guizhou road and it used to be a large township where businessmen gathered to exchange commodities that were radiated to nearby Miao and Buyi regions by trade caravans. Both ethnic groups are well known for widespread alcoholic drinking and a vast consumption of white spirit, creating a highly potential white spirit market. Before the "reform and opening-up policy", this place was packed with liquor stores and wine shops that contributed tax revenue as much as RMB 500,000 to 600,000 each year to the county government. The majority of product made in these liquor stores and wine shops, however, was mild spirit below 20 degree with the exception of a small quantity of distilled liquor that was stored in wine cellars for a few years before being sold primarily to the Han businessmen who travelled a long way here. Such an operation consistently yielded satisfactory economic benefits in its long history. After the "reform and opening-up policy", in-charge authorities determined, merely by the highly reputable Huajiang Cellar Liquor, to invest in building a large and new liquor distillery, amounting to, after several revisions to the original plan, more than RMB8 million in total investment. Unfortunately, the first output of liquor from the distillery coincided with the shrinkage in the market for high-degree liquor that swept across the entire country. As a result, numerous bottles of liquor could not sell and the 8-million massive investment was reduced to a pile of scrap iron. The total investment of over 8 million yuan was, by the way, more than the total fiscal revenue of the county during the same year when the investment was made.

By sharp contrast, the employees who were sent home after the suspension of the production in the distillery started distilling liquors in the

① Zhonglin Zhou, et al. eds., *Han Fei Index,* s.v. "Shuo Lin Shang" 22, 27 (Zhonghua Book Company, May 1982), 772 traditional way, and began selling them to the locals as well as the Miao and Buyi settlements in nearby Zhexiang, Niuchang, Baiceng, Liuma, Yongning and Gangwu through transshipment by Buyi traders. The business was as prosperous as before the distillery was opened. To better understand what caused the distillery to fail, and to track the channels and directions in the sale of these liquors, we interviewed some Buyi businessmen who exclusively traded on Huajiang liquor in Shangguan and Pochan. They told us that they would travel to Huajiang to replenish stocks every time there was a local fair (once in every 12 days), and carried the liquors on caravan to sell in every ethnic Miao and Buyi township and county. Although the liquor's unit selling price was merely a few cents more than its purchasing price, these businessmen made considerable profits by diluting the highly concentrated liquor they purchased (about 30 degree) with the same volume of water. It was a welcomed practice in the ethnic Buyi and Miao regions as the locals had the habit of consuming liquor instead of tea when receiving guests, or casually chatting with friends. In these occasions, milder spirits (usually less than 15 degree) were enough to enhance the atmosphere but not over intoxicating. Some Buyi businessmen even admitted to us that they sometimes would buy in the slow-moving high-degree liquors produced in state-run distilleries at lower prices and resell after diluting by water, thus fetching larger profits.

Similar things happened in Yanhe liquor distillery in Guizhou. After the "reform and opening-up policy" was implemented, under the influence of the prevailing trend of upgrading commodities by improving their packaging, the distillery was once lost in the attempts to upgrade its product by over-packaging and prolonging cellar storage time. In 1988, it learnt the lesson and abandoned the strategy of over-packaging and stretched cellar storage time, and began to sell unpackaged liquor. Such a shift in strategy catered to the consumption habits of local people and successfully reduced inventory, helping the distillery weather the storm of a stagnant liquor market.

The above two cases reflect one thing in common: the supply and demand situation in an ethnic market is, to a large extent, restrained by the traditions and customs of this ethnic group. Different ethnic groups have different customs that will undoubtedly put up specific requirements for how the same product should be supplied. To ensure that a particular product sells well in all the ethnic regions in cross-xiang operations, special attention must be given to the quality, packaging, distribution channels and mode of sale of the product. A common perception is seen among all the people who are in charge of the economic development in ethnic minority regions: ethnic regions are backward and the only way to change it is by introducing and installing the most advanced and modern technology and equipment in these regions. As a reflection of this guiding perspective, Huajiang Liquor Distillery abandoned the profitable traditional distilleries and shifted to building a modern factory. People also think that ethnic minority regions are desperately poor with negligible disposable cash income, and thus don't have the necessary purchasing power. As a result, modern factories are built to make products with the developed Han regions as target market, and the packaging, specifications, and quality standards are designed to follow those in the large and medium state-owned enterprises. The employees from Huajiang Liquor Distillery, after the suspension of production, began setting up and managing distilleries individually and making products widely popular in the market. It provides a direct answer to such an unrealistic perspective. A mighty factor built under this guiding principle naturally stands out in the ethnic regions, causing the factory management consider themselves no ordinary being and distain working with the small vendors and businessmen from the local ethnic groups, nor willing to listen to their feedback of information. The factory is thus turned into an "isolated island" without the willingness or channels of communicating with the local communities. We learnt from surveys that these minority businessmen, speaking local dialects and quite familiar with the local customs and habits, were fully aware of the allocation of local villages and their different purchasing capabilities; some of them were even relatives of the people to whom they supply liquors by marriage or kinship, and therefore, were quite flexible in selling techniques and knew how to make a sale by catering to local habits and tastes. We met a woman in Pochan who was an NPC representative of Guanling County. In addition to the farm work on her land, this Buyi woman made a fortune exclusively by selling Huajiang liquor across all the villages in the four counties of Guanling, Zhenning, Zhenfeng and Qinglong. She told us that she had the information about which household from which village might possibly have a wedding ceremony on a particular day, or a massive religious gathering would be held, and she would prepare necessary supplies accordingly and thus was never worried about the salability of her products. She was also very flexible in the method of selling and would accept anything from regular supply of goods, credit sale, barter trade, advance payment, to exchange of labor. Subsequently, she could sell averagely 600 to 800 jin (half a kilogram) liquor in a six-day period and make a profit between 200 to 300 yuan. This example shows that our efforts in developing ethnic economy are doomed to fail if we only build factories and run them in enclosed circumstances instead of relying on knowledgeable local businessmen.

Certainly, Huajiang Liquor Distillery is not the only factory that is built and run under this guiding philosophy. In the visit to Wangmo Sugar Refinery and Zhenfeng Baiceng Sugar Refinery, our talks with the management of these factories gave us the same impression. Unexceptionally, these factory managers focused their conversation on the national sugar refinery market and complained about inadequate support from the county government while in the meantime attributed the unprofitability of their factories to the small scale and working capital shortage in their factories. They seldom mentioned the factory's sugarcane bases or the ethnic Buyi people who worked on these bases to produce and supply sugarcanes to the factory. We once asked the locals for their feedback on the products from the sugar refinery and were surprised by their answers: the local Buyi and Miao people bought, without exception, the brown sugar (red sugar in local language) produced by small local refineries in occasions such as receiving guests, presenting gifts and consumption in holidays for reason of the auspicious word "red" that was associated with the red sugar. The white granulated sugar made by the factory barely had any demand in local markets other than occasional purchases by city or town residents, forcing the factory to ship their products to the markets in Guiyang and Anshun some 300 kilometers away. When conducting field surveys in the above counties, we were often mistaken by the owners of small brown sugar refineries for businessmen that came to buy their brown sugar and were approached proactively by them. After we identified ourselves and inquired about the local brown sugar production, these owners of small refineries told us that local Buyi and Miao people had the habit of consuming home-made brown sugars both for the reason of auspiciousness and as food additives to enhance its color. The local demand for brown sugar was huge and the locally produced brown sugars were even sold through private channels to the markets in northwest of Guizhou. However, after the establishment of the modern sugar refinery, sugarcane farmers were refrained from refining sugars to ensure raw material supply to the factory, putting private sugar refinery business into operational difficulties. In addition, restrictive measures on the trade of brown sugar imposed by the local government, heavy taxes, inability to make timely delivery, and the obstruction of original sales channels all contributed to the decrease in the profitability of sugar refinery and destabilization of sugarcane fields. Among the many reasons that caused the difficulties facing these two sugar refineries, totally ignoring the consumption habits of local ethnic minority people and blindly targeting the markets in the developed regions as the only sales market was one mistake that should not have been made and must not be forgiven.

In fact, it would have been easy for these modern factories to out-compete the local sugar mills if they were willing to make slight modifications to the production technique so that they could make brown sugars popular among local people. The operators of these factories, by following the above-mentioned guidelines, never thought of switching strategy but instead put all their efforts in expanding factories, lobbying for more investment to fund new projects, and keeping adding new variety of foods made out of white sugar. While we were conducting field research in Wangmo, the leaders of Sanglang, a township under Wangmo County, were busy putting together a plan in the hope to attract aid loans from Bank of Asia to build a larger and more technologically advanced sugar refinery. How could they ensure that the new refinery would be profitable while the existing ones were struggling to break even? We learnt from our conversations with the local people in Southwest Guizhou and Anshun region that many food products produced in the food processing factories in these places barely had any local demand, primarily because these products were not produced in consideration of local customs and traditions, and as a result, had to compete in the ethnic Han regions some hundreds of, or even over one thousand kilometers away. These factories and mines were doomed to fail even before they were put into operation.

Enterprises have been built and managed in the ethnic minority regions in Guizhou in a fixed model, i.e., the state contributing investment, local government contributing lands, local people contributing labor, and upper-level government authorities appointing operating personnel after factories are completed. The model is created and followed to ensure that these factories are mostly likely be owned by the state. Although the deepening "reform and opening-up policy" has established the legitimacy of private ownership in enterprises, and has shaken the old enterprise management philosophy, the inertia effect remains. The thought of boosting ethnic economy naturally leads to the construction of large enterprises, which demands more investment, but no one wants to spend some time finding out how to bring the existing enterprises back to life by changing strategies. It is a common misperception that the ethnic minority regions are poor and there is nothing they can do without allocation of funds from the upper-level government, but the funds, if any, could not be turned into investment. People view the ethnic minority regions in Guizhou as so poor that people are incapable of raising funds in setting up enterprises of their own, which warrants a deeper and necessary study. By the standards of current statistics, most ethnic regions in Guizhou are below the poverty line, yet our prior discussions reveal that the accumulation and use of wealth by an ethnic group is the result of regulation by the traditions and customs of this ethnic group. An ethnic group that has a seemingly low average income may be able to accumulate a sizable amount of wealth as long as its traditions and customs tend to create a favorable environment for the accumulation of wealth that can be used in special circumstances including making investment in plants and factories when necessary. To further elaborate on this issue, we will take the silverware accumulation by the ethnic Miao in Southeast Guizhou as an example to dissect the fact that money in various forms can be accumulated in poor regions.

The ethnic Miao people in Huangping, Shibing, Leishan, Taijiang, and Jianhe counties in Southeast Guizhou treasure silver jewelries, and every female in an ordinary family owns silver jewelries from tens to hundreds of Liang (a weight unit equivalent to 50 grams) on average. Other than the vast amount of silverwares accumulated, the Miao settlements also have their own silver jewelry making industry. Dagou of Leishan and Jiaoxia of Taijiang are famous silversmith villages, each boasting more than 100 artisans in making silver jewelries and silverwares. However, there are no silver mines across the entire region and all the silver used to make jewelries has to be shipped in from outside the region. In the Qing Dynasty when silver was used equivalent to tax payment, ethnic Miao people would sell local produce picked from the nearby mountains in exchange for silver ingots that were later turned into silver jewelries. A massive quantity of silver accumulated in this region and consequently exited circulation as a result of the Miao customs, and has been reserved until today. In the period of Republic of China, Dayang (a hard currency made of silver) was used in making payment, and for the same reason, ethnic Miaos would melt the Dayang received as payment and turned them into silver jewelries. The rapid industrial development after the founding of the People's Republic of China increasingly drove up the demand for silver in both the domestic and international markets. The ethnic Miao people, out of the same customs and traditions, continued buying and accumulating silverwares in this region, pushing up the purchasing price of Dayang by 30-40 folds. Currently, silversmiths in the Miao region would trade RMB40-50 for one Dayang issued in the third year of the Republic of China, a process fully in line with the Gresham's Law in the history of economics.[①]

Gresham's Law states that in a dual standard monetary system, a good coin made of precious metals will be driven out of circulation by bad coins and thus accumulates as a result. According to this Law, in the Qing Dynasty and Republic of China period where bronze and silver coins as well as paper money were used at the same time, it was predictable that precious silver ingots or silver coins would eventually exit circulation. Due to the tradition among ethnic Miaos who were extremely enthusiastic about owning silver jewelries, the silverwares kept flowing into the Miao regions through a variety of channels and became a way of wealth accumulation by the ethnic Miao people. For the same reason, these silverwares that were kept by ethnic Miaos would not be sent back into circulation but became idle funds. The analysis of how such a custom impacted the efficiency of economic operations makes it clear to us that it is not absolutely impossible for the ethnic groups living in poverty-stricken regions to accumulate wealth. The most difficult problem is how to convert these idle funds into capitals that can be invested in economic activities.

The traditions and customs of an ethnic group may help build wealth, and also contribute to the redistribution of wealth among members of the

① *A Concise Dictionary of Social Sciences* (Shanghai Lexicographical Publishing House, May 1987,9th reprint), 830 ethnic group. The ethnic Miao people have retained the custom of "*Chi Gu Zang*" that is a grand ritual ceremony to worship family ancestors. Despite the slight differences in how it is labeled among different Miao tribes, the contents of the ritual ceremony are completely the same. The ceremony is held once every 12 years in the ethnic Miao settlements in Southeast Guizhou that must be attended by all members in the family and congratulated by all relatives of the family by marriage, numbering as many as thousands of people. In the ceremony, buffalos, cattle and pigs are sacrificed and are distributed among family members to eat. One time of "*Chi Gu Zang*" may cost from as little as several thousand yuan to as much as tens of thousands of yuan, ① and it takes several years for the ethnic Miao people who usually are frugal and in a state of poverty to save enough for one such ritual activity. No modern economic activity may be carried out without capital accumulation. Such a customary practice, however, may drain the vast amount of capital that is hard earned and frugally saved for a long period of time within as short as a few days, which is a totally absurd act from the perspective of modern economic activities. If the capital can be directed into investing in economic construction, it will be out of question for the people in such poverty-stricken regions to accumulate enough capital for investment.

The greatest difficulty in diverting the accumulated capital in businesses is how to change the perception of ethnic Miao people about honor. In central Guizhou, every time a "*Chi Gu Zang*" ("killing the cattle to worship ancestors" in local language) is held, an honorary title is added to the name of the sponsor of the event. Many ethnic Miao people are willing to pursue such an honor of being remembered in the generations to come at the cost of the wealth of the entire family. ② An ethnic Miao government official at Pilin village of Gaopo county who came from a family that was so poor as to receive government aid every year was able to put aside enough money to buy a *Gu Zang* Ox worthy of hundreds of yuan, in exchange only for such a title. Professor Wu Zelin, a late ethnologist, already conducted profound surveys on the rituals in Yangwang township of Guiding county, ③ based on which we took part in an ancestor worshipping ceremony held here and

① Chaolong Li et al. eds., *The Minority Folk-Customs in Guizhou* (Guizhou Education Press, September 1995), 380-400.

② *General Annals of Guizhou • Longli Wei*, handwritten version in the collection of Guizhou Library.

③ *A Collection of Papers in Memory of Zelin Wu* (Hubei Science& Technology Press, September 1988), 185.

observed that more than ten oxen that in total were worth tens of thousands of yuan were slaughtered on the scene. They lost the fortune that could have been used to make production investment to receive, in exchange, the honor of being remembered.

In addition to "Chi Gu Zang," ethnic Miaos also observe other holidays such as Lusheng (a local musical instrument) Festival, Longchuan (dragon boat) Festival and Tiaohua (dancing and singing) Festival etc. The particular village that holds such an event is also responsible for accommodating the people who came from other places to attend the event. On average, each household in the host village receives tens or even hundreds of guests at the cost of hundreds of yuan per day, yet the host households don't have any complaint about sharing their hard-earned assets and money among their family members. Such a customary practice of sharing wealth among family members in holidays has made wealth sharing and equal distribution a prevailing mentality among ethnic Miao people, which eventually hinders the sizable accumulation of social wealth and prevents its conversion into investment.

In addition to ethnic Miao, Buyi people also have a similar tradition. We noticed when we were conducting fieldwork in Wangmo county that most Buyi people lived in an extended family environment. People living in the same village were usually members of the same family. Among them, to have a closer emotional bond was more important than to make extra money. Fruits borne from a privately-owned fruit tree were barely offered for sale on the market but often open to all villagers to pick. People gladly invited their fellowmen in the village to share any delicacies they have or make, the inviters being generous and the invitees feeling no hesitation. Without a doubt, the interpersonal relationship was a harmonious one among the villagers, but it suppressed the growth of small merchants and businessmen as well. We observed at Shabao village of Zhenning county that in such a village of nearly one hundred households, there was no mom and pop stores. Villagers had to travel to the fair several lis away to buy even the small things such as match, cigarette, and kerosene. A further investigation revealed that villagers had once opened such stores, but the attempts ended up in failure as the customers, namely the neighbors in the village, often owed money that the shop owners felt reluctant to collect. Eventually the stores had to be closed. As a matter of fact, the behavior of the villagers was not ill-intentioned but was merely a reflection of the interpersonal relationship characterized by sharing of personal wealth and assets. From an operational perspective, such a custom apparently can not tolerate the emergence of small merchants in the village, let alone to expand the stores by investing more capital accumulated through hard work. We now understand why ethnic Buyi people, as recorded in history, were adept at doing business.

Doing business in the Buyi style is, in essence, a commercial behavior that treats people who are classified as internal and external differently. While feeling shamed to "make profit" on the people from within the family, ethnic Buyi people are no easy bargains when dealing with people from other families, other villages, especially from other ethnic groups. The Buyi people we surveyed alleged that they would rather do business with people of other ethnic groups, other than those of their own ethnicity, for fear that they might be caught up emotionally and lose money. Our observation in local markets also proved such statements. Some Buyi merchants who sold things in local markets always tried to avoid their fellowmen and acquaintances and attempted to sell their goods to strangers, especially the ethnic Hans who were from outside the region. Such a customary practice, on the one hand, restrained the wealth accumulation and capital expansion. On the other hand, it makes it possible to unite the entire family and amass all the wealth within the family to direct the investment to the trade with other ethnic groups. With regards to the first scenario, what happened in Huangla township of Anshun city is also thought-provoking.

In history, Huangla township has the mask-engraving tradition for the performers of Dixi opera. The income of Huangla artisans increased sharply following the introduction of Anshun Dixi opera to other parts of the country and to the world. Under the recommendation of ethnic committee in Anshun city, one of the artisans travelled to many big and medium cities in the country to demonstrate his skill. After his return, his home was constantly filled with friends and guests, the reception of whom exhausted all his money within less than one month. Although he seemed to have incurred a heavy loss on a monetary perspective, he received help in the form of labor by all villagers when he was renovating his house. As a result, he saved more than half of the cost needed to renovate a house of similar size. It shows that to lead such a custom to a market economy, the key is not about the custom itself that has long been an objective existence, but about how to guide such a custom to make it suit the need of a market economy.

The second scenario was mentioned in ancient records, and our fieldwork has offered fresh examples. People from the same village accompanied each other to the local market and often aided each other in trade activities, either serving as a broker or pretending to be a buyer to inflate the selling price for their fellowmen. This is indicative that ethnic Buyi were able to unite under the influence of such a custom to play a greater role in the market, but the difficulty is that their limited vision has prevented them from amassing greater power, thus only able to seek unstable advantages in the local markets and can not enter larger domestic market. In addition, such a custom is likely to grow into a habit of bullying the ethnic Miao people who are in a weaker economic position.

In his work *Dual-Sector Economy* that won his the Nobel Prize, the American economist Lewis stated that labor surplus was a constant state under a "closed economy", under which, the normal function of the social economy would not be affected even if a considerable percentage of people left for opportunities in other places. Hence, the capitalists were able to find unlimited supply of cheap labors as long as they offered wages slightly higher than what these labors had previously made. An ideal "marginal effect" might be created by taking advantage of this wage gap to help capitalists gain maximum profits.[①] Lewis, based on the modern economics models in the West, focused his analysis on ensuring the continued economic growth to maintain the vigorousness of the modern western economic system. However, he seemed intentional to have avoided two equally tough questions: First, in a "closed economy", other than the people who left for opportunities in other places, how did the people who stayed pursue their economic life? Second, how did the dual-sector structure created by the people who left and those who stayed function?

The answer to the first question is self-evident. The "closed economy" that capital faces will continue functioning the same among the people who stay. It is for the purpose of gaining profit rather than assuming any obligation on the conventional economy of another ethnic group that capital hires labors. Obviously, we will not follow the same practice. In addition to seeking economic benefits, our investment in ethnic minority regions is also tasked with the goal of driving the rapid economic development in these

① *Dual-Sector Economy* (Beijing College of Economics Press, March 1989), 9-12.

regions, eventually attaining the goal of joint prosperity and modernization across all ethnicities in China. In other words, while we expect economic returns from the investments we make in ethnic minority regions, we are also required to radiate the prosperity brought about by these investments across the entire ethnic regions. To this end, we must not overlook or avoid the existence of conventional economic system that will undoubtedly last into the future.

With regards to the second question, we must admit that it has been a long-lasting practice in the human being's inter-ethnic relations that some people from a "closed economy" choose to leave and subsist in other economies. In the history of Guizhou's development, it was not uncommon that some ethnic minority people chose to depend on the feudal state for a living, either serving as a clerk at a remote post, or a horsekeeper, even enlisting in the military or pursing an official career by taking the imperial examination. Such a way of subsistence has never discontinued and it is natural that some of them have been hired by other ethnic groups as labors. These people, however, should not be deemed as fully assimilated into other ethnic groups and totally delinked from their original ethnic group. Some of them have maintained close ties with members from their original ethnic group, retained their original ethnic consciousness and continued, in varying degrees, to be governed by their original culture. At times when they are economically stranded, or have achieved their goal by accumulating certain amount of wealth, they may choose to go back and live in their original ethnic group. Such a situation will frustrate the people who make investment in ethnic minority regions even more for the apparent reason that investors who feel that their goal of making profit can not be achieved will likely withdraw the investment they make or totally abandon the projects. To the operators of enterprises, it is an extra burden for them to deal with the difficulties caused by the dual-sector structure. In a "closed economy", all labors understand this and temporarily accept the disciplinary restrictions imposed by capital. This, however, does not necessarily mean that they have abandoned their original culture, nor does it indicate that these people have given up their ultimate reliance on their original culture. Although we are not sure if this is true to every person who chooses to make a living in other ethnic environment, as least a considerable portion of them view their work in other ethnic settings a temporary means of subsistence, hence, it is hard for them to fully comply with the rules of conduct in the enterprises they work for.

The above analysis reveals a fact that, when making investment in a "closed economy", or in under-developed ethnic regions, the investors must face a "dual-sector" economic structure that will not change by the mere fact of investment. The people who are involved in such a "dual-sector" economic structure demonstrate a dual-structured character: They follow the restrictions in their original culture, and in the meantime, they must temporarily abide by the disciplinary restrictions imposed by the investors. The co-existence of a dual-sector economic structure and the dual character of the personnel have given rise to the difficulties in labor management for the investment made in the ethnic regions in Guizhou, or in Lewis' terminology, in "closed economies". Here, we will discuss the constraints in the people management and training from the perspective of ethnic customs and traditions.

Like other economic activities, cross-xiang operations must put labor employment and training into consideration. The investing activities in ethnic minority regions in Guizhou in the past years have mainly been conducted in two modes. One can be labeled as "placement type". The modern enterprises established in Guizhou during the "construction of third-tier provinces and regions" period fall into this category. It also includes the state-invested railway, highway, power, and mining enterprises. The other mode may be shortened as "borrowed type". The local enterprises sponsored by county or prefecture government in Guizhou, or the state-funded enterprises constructed and run by the government at the county or prefecture level, falls into this category.

The overwhelming majority of people working in a "placement type" of enterprises are immigrants from Han regions who live in an exclusively Han cultural environment and are not affected, in principle, by the traditions and customs of surrounding ethnic minorities. In addition to a total reliance on appropriation of funds by the state, these enterprises must depend on self-service to ensure a Han cultural living condition in the community. Needless to say, such enterprises will be increasingly burdened and the situation is worsened by the "inbreeding" within the enterprises that causes them to lose vigor and operational efficiency. With the high tide of "reform and opening-up policy" came the proposal of "converting military-oriented enterprises into civilian operations". Such a measure aimed at easing our difficulties has forced these enterprises of former "isolated islands" to interact more closely with the ethnic communities they are surrounded by. As a result, the traditions and customs of these ethnic groups inevitably spill over and infiltrate within the enterprises, forcing them to face the ramifications of these customs and traditions. In recent years, disputes and conflicts between these enterprises and local ethnic communities over the issues of marriage and differing customs and traditions are becoming more frequent and intense, making the management of these enterprises an increasingly complex and difficult task for the managers. Subsequently, many enterprises have in recent years requested to move to near transportation hubs or central cities for the reason of, on top of economic factors, getting closer to Han cultural regions and getting rid of the influence of customs and traditions of ethnic minorities.

In fact, the "three-line construction" period was not the first time that witnessed these "placement type" of enterprises ended in this way. The garrisons and settlements constructed by the feudal state in history were similar in that the people involved were either assimilated by the local ethnic groups or escaped from these places and returned to the Han regions when a weakening state power resulted in a loosening grip on these posts. The personnel working for the enterprises established by capitalist countries in their colonies were put in the same situation at the time when colonial empires collapsed. It is evident that to operate enterprises in developing ethnic minority regions must face the conflicts in customs and traditions caused by the dual-sector structure. To deal with these conflicts means a decrease in enterprise efficiency as well as a further managerial complication, both of which were against the original intention when we establish these enterprises in ethnic minority regions.

In "borrowed type" of enterprises where people from different ethnic groups must work together, the divergence in ethnic customs and traditions naturally becomes a direct constraint in the enterprise management. All the enterprises we surveyed faced the same issue with a difference merely in the way of dealing with it and subsequent results. Now we first compare two enterprises of completely different nature: Wangmo Sugar Refinery and Zhenfeng Baiceng Sugar Refinery. Ethnic Buyi people accounted for a majority of employees at Wangmo Sugar Refinery. With the exception of several managerial and technical positions that were filled by people from

Han regions, nearly half of other positions, from the head to ordinary employees of the factory, remained occupied by ethnic Buyi employees since it was established. The farmers who made up of the majority of employees in the bases that supplied raw materials to the factory were the local Han people – the so-called "*Gaoshanhan*" who were mobilized by the local government to move to the nearby region and plant sugarcanes on the lands leased from local Buyi people. Ethnic Buyi or Miao were rarely seen in the base. The employee makeup in Baiceng Sugar Refinery was a complete opposite. The people who worked in the factory mostly came from outside the region, with ethnic Hans taking the biggest share. In the raw material base, the majority of workers were local Buyi, followed by local ethnic Hans, who had their own lands and owned small refineries to make brown sugar before the factory was constructed. The different employee composition in the two factories was reflected in the management structure of the factories. Many Buyi holidays in Wangmo county, such as "Guoliaonian" (a local holiday after Chinese Spring Festival) and "Sanyuesan" (a festival on March 3rd according to the Chinese lunar calendar) happen to fall within the high production season of the factory. "Guoliaonian" starts on the 25th day of the twelfth month of the lunar calendar and lasts over 20 days into the 15th day of the following month, taking nearly one fifth of the production season of the factory. During the period of "Guoliaonian", factory workers would go home to join family reunion, friends gathering, entertaining guests every day and were often drunk from drinking alcohol. For the employees whose homes were far from the factory, they often disregarded the factory disciplines and left work for almost half a month. Even those who stayed for work would be busy receiving their relatives and friends and would come to work drunk. Such a conflict between ethnic customs and factory rules could not be tolerated by any factory head of course. However, any manager in the factory could not shrug off the impact of the ethnic customs and would be slack in enforcing factory rules as long as he was of the Buyi ethnicity. A former head of the factory once bragged about the fact that he was addressed by factory employees as their brother and uncle to indicate that he had a good and harmonious relationship with his employees. We were not nearly as happy as he was because we knew that by the Buyi customs, such an address must indicate that he would be a guest in all ethnic holidays and family celebrations by all the employees in the factory. When Buyi employees were in the holiday of "Guoliaonian", he would join the celebration and would not be exceptional when everybody else came to work drunk. Such a factory head meant that factory rules would not be strictly enforced. A joke about a vice secretary of the factory who repeated factory rules in front of all employees is still talked about until now. When making a speech at an all-employee meeting, he said that anyone who violated factory rules by coming to work drunk would be subject to severe punishment. He continued by explaining that he also drank alcohol while working but was never drunk, which sparked an outcry in the audience. Although factory leaders repeatedly told the county government that the factory operated smoothly, we knew from the quantity of purchased raw materials and sales of finished products that the factory never operated in its full capacity, one of the major reasons being the difficulty in management and the semi-crippled factory operation resulting from ethnic customs and traditions.

To the contrary, Baiceng Sugar Refinery is distant from Zhenfeng county and ethnic Hans made up of the majority of the factory employees. As a result, ethnic Buyi customs and traditions were not influential, which generally guaranteed the full attendance in high production seasons, although it could not guarantee the operation in full capacity. Another difficulty also caused the factory to operate in partial capacity. The raw material base of this factory, mainly made up of Buyi farmers, was often hindered by the shortage in labor in harvesting seasons. Ethnic Buyi farmers would not give up on their holidays while the ethnic Miao people who were hired from other places to harvest sugarcanes also returned home for holidays. Consequently, although factory employees were present to operate all the machines, the shortage in raw materials determined that the efficiency of the factory could not be enhanced.

The sugarcane plantations that supplied raw materials to Wangmo Sugar Refinery were different. All the workers here were hired from outside the region and they lived entirely on the income from selling sugarcanes. Consequently, holidays were never a reason that disrupted harvesting. However, their efforts might also be wasted. While the factory was operating in limited capacity, factory managers were afraid of over-stocking sugarcanes or worried that the sugarcanes in storage might go bad to incur losses. Due to the inability of the factory to match its production capacity with sugarcane harvesting seasons, the sugarcane fields that had been under fast expansion shrank tremendously to less than one third of the original size. As a result, the factory owed a total of over RMB 800,000 on purchase of sugarcanes from the farmers, who, for reason of subsistence, had to sell the "white slip" (a hand-written receipt evidencing the payment owed to the holder of the slip) at 70% or even half of its face value. The farmers here also hired a large number of ethnic Miaos to help harvest sugarcanes, and they also run the risk of labor shortage in holiday seasons. It seemed clear that the "dual-sector" structure and the "dual-character" employees already became one of the key constraints in the normal operation of the factories. We don't think that the disturbance caused by the ethnic customs and traditions in the "dual-sector" economic structure is an unsurmountable constraint. Countless examples of ethnic minority people hired by Han immigrants as labor were recorded in the history of Guizhou's development. Crops such as corn and potato were introduced by Han immigrants to Guizhou in the feudal age. These high-yield crops and the related cultivation technologies apparently were grasped by the ethnic minority groups in the dual-sector economic structure, which proves that it is totally achievable for us to spread advanced technologies in ethnic minorities regions in a dual-sector structure and to enable them to take root and survive in the conventional economic life in these regions. Although ancient literature did not elaborate on the details of how Han immigrants adjusted themselves to local customs, fragments of records are available. According to *General Annals of Guizhou* completed in the Qing Dynasty under the reign of Kangxi, white Miaos (ethnic Miaos now living in the region bordering Guiyang, Longli and Huishui) were in constant moves and were often out of control, thus causing losses to ethnic Han landowners.① Such a scenario is not completely distinct in today's ethnic minority regions in Guizhou, and still prevails among the Bunuzhi Yao in Libo and those Yao people who speak Sichuan, Guizhou and Yunnan dialects, posing numerous difficulties in the management of people and stability of investment in the economic development in these regions. How to appropriately handle these old problems has become a practical issue that calls for our immediate attention. We also notice in our fieldwork that some private enterprises have gained valuable experiences in this regard that may be referenced by others.

An owner of a small enterprise in Houchang township of Ziyun county,

① (Qing • Kangxi) *General Annals of Guizhou* "White Miao" under "Miao", mimeo version in the collection of Guizhou Library.

whose employees included both Han immigrants and local Buyi and Miao people, revealed his management tips: first trained the people from each ethnic group who were willing to cooperate with him, then they would recruit and train other members from their own ethnic group, thus achieving the goal of self-management within each ethnic group. The owner was only in charge of the supply of goods and technology, purchase of finished products at a price corresponding to the value of these products, and overall coordination among employees of all ethnic groups. In his primary business of food processing and construction material processing, the gathering of crops and distribution of finished products were assumed by contact persons from each ethnic group, while the production and sale of construction materials (concrete brick and tile) were also conducted by contact persons of each ethnic group. Such a mechanism ensured the raw material supply and sale of finished products despite the existence of a variety of complicated ritual and ceremonial procedures in each ethnic group, as these contact persons were quite knowledgeable about and well prepared for these events. It turned out that local customs did not have a shocking impact on his business as they did to the above two factories, and as a result, his business was a success.

In a nutshell, the impacts from ethnic customs and traditions on the establishment of enterprises, propogation of new technologies and conduct of commercial activities must not be overlooked, yet the non-economic constraints of this nature are not unsurmountable. The key to the success lies in how to make the best use of the power in one's own ethnic culture to attain the goal of mutual-adjustment and mutual-accommodation in a dual-sector economic structure.

II Reception and Application of Information

Ethnic languages are barriers that cross-xiang operations often come across. Different ethnic languages that co-exist in cross-xiang operations intensify the difficulty in interpersonal communication. The difficulty in translation may lead to misunderstanding and eventually directly reduce the operating efficiency. Such barriers to cross-xiang operations, however, are overt obstacles that stay on the surface. Language-related barriers at a deeper level come from the "inner language" system in the mind of members of each ethnic group, which, according to the research by linguists, grows out of accumulation in life and in actual practice of language and plays a key role in human beings' acquisition of the ability to accurately express themselves and understand others. Before one speaks, he/she organizes his language within the "inner language" system in his/her mind. The listener restores the contents in the voice message he/she captures within his/her "inner language" system. [1] According to the theory of Ferdinand de Saussure, it is not extremely difficult for members from different ethnic groups to learn, understand some simple languages and follow the instructions from each other, although it may not be very easy. It is, however, well beyond the ability of ordinary people or even the experts who have engaged in language translation for years if it is to fully understand the flawless logical thinking, complex scientific and technological principles or the subtle change in personal emotions. Subsequently, to analyze comprehensively the impacts of languages on cross-xiang operations, we must examine from two angles.

What direct impacts do language barriers have on cross-xiang operations?

More importantly, how do the differences between the "inner language" systems of different ethnic groups constrain the ability of these ethic groups to receive the useful economic information from within and outside the country? In addition, ethnic minority groups build their own knowledge base by accepting the knowledge of modern natural science, and integrating it with its own conventional knowledge and experience. To ethnic minority groups in Guizhou, the barriers caused by language difference have a more far-reaching and latent impacts on their modernization, and therefore are easier to be overlooked. We will provide a systematic analysis in the above three aspects with the help of the real-life examples we collected from our fieldwork.

The constraining effects that language differences have on cross-xiang economic activities are most easily discernable in rural markets. Our surveys on the sense of business among different ethnic groups indicated that 70% of Miao women were reluctant to buy things from the people of another ethnicity in the market. They often asked their husbands or acquaintances to buy for them. This scenario was attributable to many factors including influences of traditional ethics, fear of strangers, but more importantly, the language barriers. More than half of the women in all the Miao settlements and a few Buyi settlements in Guizhou do not speak Mandarin. Business in

[1] Ferdinand de Saussure, *Ecrits de Linguistique generale* (The Commercial Press, November 1980), 43-47.

the markets in the Buyi settlements in Wangmo, Zhenfeng, Ceheng and Luodian etc. is conducted in Buyi language and Mandarin is only spoken when a Han businessman is involved. Under such a circumstance, being able to speak a number of languages is a must to conduct business without help from others. We also notice from our surveys that the Han businessmen who have long been conducting business in counties such as Wangmo, Cengheng and Zhenfeng usually can speak Buyi language, and the ethnic Miaos, especially the young and middle-aged ones, all understand Buyi language, which is more frequently used as an intermediary language and is thus more valuable from a usage perspective. The variety in languages tends to annoy the people involved in the communication and is often a source of suspicion. According to many local Han businessmen, one can easily be tricked if he/she does not understand Buyi language. The "shielding effect" of language, among other reasons, mainly contributes to such a psychological thinking. When different languages are involved, it is often the case that people from the same ethnic group first negotiate in their own language before they bargain with the people from other ethnic groups. Consequently, it is not uncommon to see that in the same market, all Buyi traders ask for exactly the same price, so do the Miao traders, and they usually are not open for negotiation. No wonder they are constantly complained by the Han traders as too foolish to reduce the asking price even if it means no sale for them. In fact, these Han people have drawn such a conclusion without realizing that such a situation is closely related to the language barriers and is the result of the "shielding effect" when different languages collide with each other.

We disagree with some researchers on the "shielding effect" of language. These researchers, who deeply worry about how language difference has prevented ethnic minority people from conducting business activities smoothly, have advocated to encourage, promote or even force these minority people to learn Mandarin, believing that it will remove the language barriers on their way to modernization. We do not agree for the following three reasons:

First, it is quite common that people speak different languages interchangeably in trading activities around the world and it is always the case that initiators of trading activities proactively learn to speak the languages of the people they trade with. It has never happened in history that people must learn and speak one language in trading activities. Furthermore, to allow the co-existence of different languages has never suppressed trading activities. In the ethnic minority regions in Guizhou, people started to trade in the languages of Buyi, Miao, Dong, Shui and other ethnic groups interchangeably a long time ago and such a practice has been accepted by all the people involved. It is thus nonsensical to request that everyone speak Mandarin to facilitate trade.

Second, every language is a relatively stable dynamic balance system. To expect that people from ethnic minority groups learn and master Mandarin as proficiently as ordinary ethnic Hans requires that they receive constant trainings in Mandarin on daily basis, which costs disproportionately higher than return. As a matter of fact, the numerous dialects in the ethnic Han regions[①] and the complex jargons combine to make it hard enough even for a Han businessman not to be disturbed when he travels around the country to conduct business, let alone the ethnic minority people. Unarguably, every individual conducts trading activities within a certain radius that is determined by the economic condition he is in and the nature of his business. It is also true that not everyone needs to expand his business all over the world or needs to directly deal with people who speak other languages. Therefore, businessmen only need to grasp the language the he uses the most based on his immediate needs. As Buyi language is more often used than Mandarin in the rural markets in Buyi settlements in southern Zhenning county and other counties such as Wangmo, Ceheng, Luodian and Zhenfeng, to be able to speak Buyi language is enough for traders in these regions. This is why many Han businessmen from outside the region are proficient in Buyi language. The fact that most Miao women don't understand other languages and thus cannot access the markets is not merely a language issue but a phenomenon derived from an under-developed rural market in the Miao region. Subsequently, we should push to develop Miao markets instead of asking everyone to learn another language.

Third, language is only a media for human interactions. The change of language can not replace the economic development and it may not drive the economic development either. For many Han early immigrants who chose to settle in southwest Guizhou, namely the "Gaoshanhan" mentioned earlier in this book, they don't have much difficulty communicating with other ethnic

① Xueliang Ma, "On Ethnic Written Languages and Bi-lingual Education", *Guizhou Ethnic Studies*, no. 2, 1986, 25-26.

Han people, yet their economic strength is much lower than that of local Buyi people. We can not help but ask: are we certain that being able to speak Mandarin guarantees an economic improvement? The ethnic Buyi people in the region of Longguang in Anlong county abandoned Buyi language during the period of Republic of China and switched to speaking Mandarin. Now, the majority of them can not even speak Buyi language, but are they much more advanced in economic development than their ethnic counterparts in other places? As a matter of fact, at the time when they decided to abandon Buyi language, they also gave up their right to make use of the economic strength unique to ethnic Buyi group, which is not necessarily a good thing for them. Similar examples can be found in other countries. American Indians, for instance, have mostly lost the ability of speaking their native language and can only speak English now, yet they are still at the bottom of the social hierarchy in the US. The fact that they are citizens of the most developed nation in the world has not lifted their standard of living significantly higher than that in developing countries. Apparently, it is impossible to achieve the goal of economic development simply by pushing Mandarin as a means of overcoming language barriers in trade activities.

The "shielding effect" of language works in both ways. It increases the difficulty for the ethnic minority people to get to know the ethnic Han societies and accept the modern science and technology through the media of Han language. On the other hand, it deteriorates the insufficient knowledge of the Hans on economic situations in ethnic minority regions. Such a result must be perceived dialectically. Modern advanced science and technology may be learned through media other than Mandarin. Furthermore, if the academic terminologies and theories learned through Mandarin can not be integrated into the languages of local ethnic groups, such modern science and technology can not spread across the entire ethnic community; therefore, mastering and accepting the advanced science and technology becomes an individual achievement rather than translating into the success of the entire ethnic group. When two languages interact, each permeates into the other in a different degree (a gap in permeation), i.e., the chance of using the language spoken by the more economically developed party as a media in the interaction tends to be greater. To put it more plainly, an extremely small percent of ethnic Hans in Guizhou can speak ethnic minority languages while the percentage of the ethnic people who can speak Mandarin is much larger.

As a result of such a gap in language permeation, ethnic minority people know about the economic situation of ethnic Hans much better than the latter knows about the former, which, in the initial phase of economic development, yields advantages that far outweigh the disadvantages because it helps the ethnic minority groups take initiatives to play their advantages to the full and avoid the impacts of the weaknesses in economic activities. The fact that such a favorable side of the "shielding effect" of language has not manifested itself is due to another reason: the difference in the type and mode of economy between the Han and ethnic minority regions determines that some cross-xiang operations have "one-way" nature where ethnic Hans are always the subjective party while the ethnic minority groups are always the objective party. Subsequently, a mechanism has not emerged in the ethnic minority societies that can collect, process and eventually make use of the economic information of the Han society through the language as a bridge, thus keeping the "shielding effect" of language from playing a favorable role.

We have found real cases among the ethnic minority groups in Guizhou who have effectively made use of the "shielding effect" of language in the collection and processing of economic information of the other ethnic groups. When we discussed the sales channels of Huajiang liquor in Guanling county in previous sections, we mentioned the Buyi traders of Huajiang liquor who already did the work of systematically collecting the supply and demand information in the liquor market and thus outcompeted the Han counterparts to occupy a monopolized position in the local liquor market. Historic documents reveal that the Buyi traders have long been doing this. The fact that ethnic Buyi have long been playing the intermediary role in the trade between ethnic Miao and Han people while ethnic Hui have been playing similar function in the trade between ethnic Yi and Han people demonstrates how successful they are in information collection and processing. Today, with the ending of "one-way" cross-xiang operations, ethnic minorities have begun to show an enthusiasm in developing local economy and receiving the economic information in the Han regions; therefore, to develop the value and function of information resources in the ethnic minority economy calls for full attention from the academia.

Mr. Yu Shi was the first one among the researchers of the ethnic economic development in Guizhou to make the following statement about the value and function of developing the information resources: "Modern systems science tells us that any economic system is positioned in a space that changes with time. It interacts with and impacts on surrounding environments through the flow of logistics, energy and information, functions through exchange of information and has a close mutual dependency on information exchange. The connections between all elements and layers inside the economic system are also a process of information exchange and transfer. Therefore, only by including ethnic minority economic systems in the dissipative structure and constantly introducing entropy flow – information flow can we stabilize the development of ethnic minority economic system and adjust it to the change of environments."[①] Although a consensus has been gradually reached about the correctness of this statement, people are divergent in how to develop the information resources in ethnic minority regions. As a matter of fact, information as a resource has long grabbed people's attention. The fact that information theory did not become a new scientific discipline until this century does not indicate that people overlooked its importance. To facilitate the development of Guizhou, many local chronicles were compiled by our ancestors and each dedicated a special chapter to the local ethnic groups – "Chronicles of Indigenous Miao". Collected in these chronicles was the cultural and social information about ethnic minorities. Today, ethnic minorities must collect and process economic information about ethnic Hans for the purpose of developing their local economy. They must compile "Chronicles of Ethnic Han" based on their own needs, or even collect and make use of economic information about ethnicities in other countries and put together their own "*Zhu Fan Zhi*" (Chronicles of Other Ethnic Groups). This is a requirement by the times we are in and the need to achieve modernization. Scholars are apparently diverging on this issue and the gap is even wider with regards to how to successfully carry out the work of information development.

What comes to some people's mind when talking about information development is to set up information agency and information transmission center, which is naturally followed by the demand in money, headcount and people. This is a traditional thinking under the political background of combination of government function and enterprise management. With the deepening of "reform and opening-up policy", institutional reform and

① Shi Yu, "Vigorously Develop Information Resources to Drive the Ethnic Economic Takeoff," *Guizhou Ethnic Studies*, no. 2, 1987, 9.

separation of government function from enterprise management has made it impossible to continue. After all, this traditional thinking is a result of mistaking causes for effects. We believe that the establishment of information agency must be preceded by finding values out of the information collection and the commercialization of information, which lays the economic foundation and ensures the sustainability of such an agency.

The key to making the collection of information useful depends on the profound and systematic understanding by the collectors and processors of information on the subjects they serve. Experts and scholars from other ethnic groups may not be very helpful in this regard. We say so not because we look down upon these experts and scholars but because social science researches are characterized by timeliness and pertinence and will not be applicable at all time. For the same reason, scientific researches have the best scope of application and thus will not work for everyone at equal level of effectiveness. Scholars from other ethnic groups can not replace those from within the ethnic group. This is first an issue of where you should start. The scholars from other ethnic groups start his work from the need of his own ethnicity while those from within the ethnic group know what is needed and feasible in their own ethnic group. Only the information collected and processed from this perspective can be accepted and adopted by this ethnic group. Take the minority people from Guizhou who travel to work in the southeast coast in China as an example. Some of these people have secured a firm foothold in these regions and have accumulated tremendous experience in dealing with ethnic Han people in central China. Some, of course, are badly frustrated in their endeavor and have to return home in despair. Information about these people and their experiences is extremely valuable to the ethnic minority people who are making similar adventure plans. We have no doubt that it will be treasured and adopted rapidly among ethnic groups if the information is collected, sorted and transmitted effectively to them. However, before these migrant workers from ethnic minority regions grow strong enough to bring shocking waves to the Han economy in southeast coastal regions, or cause disputes among different ethnic groups, they will not be noticed by the scholars from other ethnic groups, such as the Han scholars. In such a circumstance, they are looked at as a group of labors that come from some remote and backward villages. The information collected and sorted under such a guidance by Han scholars, if any, must be irrelevant and thus useless to the ethnic minorities in Guizhou unless it is screened and sorted by the scholars from within these ethnic groups. Such information, however, will not spread and become useful across the ethnic minority groups if it is not translated into local languages.

Information work is about sorting and transmitting information with a high degree of pertinence. In today's world, information comes from an extremely wide variety of sources. No user of information can look for what he/she needs by searching through every piece of information; therefore, today's information work must be carried out in layers to narrow the scope of material searching. To achieve this, we must first understand the needs of the subjects we serve and sort the materials accordingly. In other words, only by knowing ourselves can we clarify on how to know the others. We are not sure if the ethnic groups in Guizhou really know themselves. We noticed in our fieldwork that many places in the region are named differently in local ethnic languages from those marked on the maps, and many people have Mandarin names that are different from what they are called in their own language. It tells us that any information sorted and processed only by the Mandarin names of people and places will not be transmitted to ethnic people. For similar reasons, the local people won't have a clue about what is happening to their relatives far away from them only by the information in Mandarin. It shows that the current way of collecting information about ethnic minority people exclusively in Mandarin only benefits the Han people but proves useless to minority people. While the ethnic minorities have not yet had complete and systematic materials of themselves, let alone understand what information they need from the external world. To make it truly useful to ethnic minorities in Guizhou, such as Miao and Buyi, the information must be collected and sorted by ethnic scholars and it must be done in local language. Modern information work must also be combined with corresponding mass media to ensure the rapid transmission and supply of specific information. It is a must that we pay attention to integrating ethnic minority languages with modern massive media, which brings about the issue of written languages of the minority groups. Since the founding of the People's Republic of China, we have made significant progress in this aspect by creating the Latin-style phonetic writing for several ethnic groups in Guizhou and by conducting training classes. Currently, the biggest regret is that we have not brought the progress into application, or at least we have not prioritized it as we should have. Arguments are still continuing among academia and the governments over the issues of "bilingual teaching", the promotion of "dual languages" and the usefulness of ethnic minority written languages. In this regard, we should feel thankful to Mr. Ma Xueliang, a respectable predecessor in linguistics in China, for his article in the research of dual languages.[①] The article euphemistically expresses his point of view without confronting anyone, and clarifies on the imperativeness of co-existence of dual written languages as well as the usefulness of ethnic written languages, while at the same time elaborates on the value of ethnic Han language in economic activities. Mr. Ma's article indicates that the most urgent thing to do now is not to debate but to act. It is foreseeable that ethnic minority people will be more than willing to learn and practice their own language without being pushed by us or oked by experts if they find out that mastering their own language can really help them receive valuable economic information. Subsequently, the discussion on bi-language or multi-language system will be removed off the meeting tables and practiced in society, ending the debate that lasted for decades. We do not attempt to prove the real value of the bi-language system in logic, but want to present a real story that was published in *Guizhou Ethnic News*.

A Miao young woman who came to the southeast coast to make a living went astray and was kidnapped by gangsters. Under the heavy surveillance, she could not pass any message to her relatives in her remote hometown. It suddenly occurred to her that she had learned the Miao written language, in which she wrote down what had happened to her when the control was slack. As the gangsters who watched over her did not recognize Miao language and mistook it for English, the message was eventually passed to her relatives and she was thus rescued. No matter what you have read out of this story, one thing is certain that ethnic minority languages can not be replaced by any other language in terms of serving their own ethnicities. Such a story, if spread rapidly in the Miao language, will undoubtedly spark the enthusiasm among ethnic minority peoples in learning and practicing their own languages.

We have no doubt that to understand the value and status of an ethnic language in the information work of that particular ethnic group is one thing, yet there is a long way to go before we can turn that understanding into

[①] Xueliang Ma, "On Ethnic Written Languages and Bi-lingual Education", 27-31.

reality. The most effective way of making it shorter is by the ethnic cultural self-operation that adjusts its ethnic culture to new things to give birth to the information service institutions. To achieve this goal, we must make the ethnic people aware that "one-way" cross-xiang operations are not reliable and must be switched to "two-way" type of operations. In other words, they must not wait for the ethnic Han people to develop these regions; instead, they must go out to understand more about the Han society as well as themselves consciously and systematically, base on which, an information service institution of their own can be established. Unarguably, some ethnic people must become proficient in Mandarin in this process (not everyone must learn to speak Mandarin, just as in the case of ethnic Hans learning to speak English. It is a waste of resources and efforts of people to make everyone learn to speak English). However, the purpose of becoming proficient in Mandarin is to facilitate the transmission of Han economic information to ethnic regions, but not for the purpose of becoming a Han; therefore, ethnic languages must remain in a predominant position while Mandarin being a subordinate one. After we ascertain such a predominant-subordinate status in the "bi-language" system, it becomes easy for us to detect the elements from traditional ethnic cultures that are valuable in the economic information transmission. The singing festival popular among ethnic Dong and Buyi people, for instance, has many usable values. Traditionally, a majority of songs sung in the singing festival were about love stories and heroic figures in history. It will be natural if new elements are introduced in these festivals that may include stories about heroes in modern times, businessmen who succeed on the market, modern ethnic figures who have unique experiences in other ethnic regions and thus have an admonishing implication etc. Stories told this way may have the effect of spreading the economic information from the Han regions across these ethnic groups. Once ethnic people have the drive to get hold of more Han economic information out of the need in their economic activities, the information buried in this form of entertainment is likely to be turned into texts written in ethnic languages. Such a value in the texts used in the singing festival, once captured by ethnic economic operators, becomes the social foundation from which the information institutions serving this ethnic group will grow. Information institutions that are established this way are apparently more suitable to the local ethnicity and thus easier to be accepted by ethnic people than those funded by the state and run by the people in a bureaucratic organization.

Today's economic development in Guizhou is indeed disturbed and constrained by the lack of accurate information. As we mention earlier in the book that every ethnic Buyi and Miao trader does not show any willingness to negotiate in the local markets. It comes down to the issue of lack of accurate information, which forces the local traders to price their commodities on the basis of inadequate information. The speed of information transmission can not catch up with that in price fluctuation, resulting in the deviation of quoted prices from reality. If a uniform price among traders across the same ethnic group is based on a reliable means of information collection and transmission, it becomes an acceptable and unanimous action of quoting price instead of a blindly concerted behavior that is complained and ridiculed by the Han counterparts. By then, the "shielding effect" of ethnic languages will work to the actual economic benefit. The ethnic minority traders won't accept the predominant position by the Han businessmen and wait for them to come; instead, they will endeavor to fetch the income and price they deserve by playing a role of a subject party in cross-xiang operations. That will be the day when ethnic minority people truly have their fate of economic development in control and the economic equality among different ethnic groups is achieved.

It is apparent that the economic development in ethnic minority regions in Guizhou is constrained by language-related factors. About the essence of these constraints, our perception differs significantly from the traditional one. It is our belief that the constraints are given rise to not by the ethnic language itself, but by the fact that its application has not been expanded to suit the development at the time; not by the lack of useful value in the ethnic language, but because it has not been integrated with the ethnic social culture, thus resulting in the over-dependence on Mandarin by ethnic groups. Such an over-dependence has deprived the ethnic people of a subjective position and has given rise to the constraints. The problem does not come from the very trade among ethnic groups in cross-xiang operations, but from the fact that the trade among ethnic groups has not shifted from a "one-way" type to a "multiple-way" type in cross-xiang operations following the achievement of ethnic equality, resulting in the lack of information service system formed within each ethnic group and thus giving rise to the constraints in information.

Understanding the essence of these constraints has rendered the debate over ethnic language meaningless. The key question remains as to how to integrate ethnic languages with the social culture of these regions. Once such an integrated system is put into operation, it will enable the ethnic people to create and improve the information institutions that serve their own needs.

With regards to the constraints of ethnic languages on the economic development in ethnic regions, one thing that has long been overlooked is the irreplaceability of ethnic languages in accepting modern advanced science and technology. We will not repeat what have been repeatedly said and written about the valuable role modern science and technology plays in driving the economic development in ethnic regions. It is however quite necessary for us to study in which language modern science and technology should be carried. Some people argue that since the introduction of modern science and technology has been systematically completed by the Han language, and a considerable percentage of ethnic minority people in Guizhou have grasped Mandarin (in fact less than one third of ethnic people truly grasped Mandarin), to become proficient in Mandarin is the solution to all problems. Such an argument should be put to more than statistical test. The current surveys on language are not based on a scientific definition of "proficiency in Mandarin". Conclusions such as the one we have made that about one third of ethnic people have truly grasped Mandarin are drawn by vague and unspecific standards, i.e., being able to understand and conduct daily conversations in Mandarin. However, one in such a level of proficiency in Mandarin is a long distance away from being able to fully and completely understand modern natural science, let alone to achieve the goal of unobstructed spread of modern natural science among ethnic groups. We will elaborate on the irreplaceability of ethnic mother tongues in accepting modern natural science by a few examples we came across in fieldwork.

It came to our attention that the ethnic students who already grasped their mother tongue and were studying Mandarin in school did worse in subjects of science than in literary ones. The largest gap was around 20 to 40 points and would continue to widen when the students grew older and were not completed isolated from their mother tongue; otherwise, the trend continued for 3-5 years before the gap began to narrow and eventually bridged.

Due to the existence of such a gap, among the ethnic students in

Guizhou who take the national college entrance examination, those who apply for liberal arts majors are over four folds of the ones who apply for science majors. Less than 20% of the students who are in a science major can continue communicating in their mother tongue. Among the ethnic college graduates and working government officials who are of a minority ethnicity, less than 30% have a job of technical nature, a considerable percent of which can not speak ethnic languages any more. Such a gap seems to have made it extremely difficult for ethnic minority students to pursue a science career; consequently, most of them are not able to return to their hometown after graduating from college to contribute to the economic construction of their ethnic regions. On the contrary, they must stay in the Han regions and compete with other Han students for limited job opportunities. As a result, technical experts who are critically needed to fuel the economic take-off in ethnic regions must be hired from Han regions at massive costs. In 1983 to 1985, many autonomous ethnic counties in Guizhou witnessed the heavy loss of science teachers in middle schools and had to pay double wages to hire the retired teachers from Han regions. Today, the gap is not narrowing. In counties such as Ziyun, Wangmo and Zhenfeng, nearly all students who are able to get admitted into a science major in college are not locally educated but have spent years in taking extra tutoring in places such as Xingyi and Anshun. It is not difficult to see that the gap between the number of students who pursue a liberal arts major and those a science major continues to widen, yet all of the students have no problem reading and writing Mandarin.

Educators disagree on what has caused the gap commonly seen between liberal arts and science students. Some people attribute that to the IQ difference, i.e., ethnic minority people are not as gifted in learning science as ethnic Hans. Others view it as a result of insufficient teaching conditions and believe that the gap may be easily erased as long as investments are made in staff and equipment in schools in ethnic minority regions. Some people argue that it is an issue of vision and the gap will naturally disappear if these ethnic students are not stranded in rural and remote areas but are exposed to a natural scientific environment. We think that neither of the three can fully explain the root cause and essence of such a gap. In essence, the gap is a result of the inability of "inner language" system in the ethnic minority languages to effectively integrate with the concepts in modern natural science.

To think that ethnic minority regions are not gifted in science is an utter bias. We may not need to carry out an experiment to prove this. Just think about what the Westerners say some one hundred years ago about the Chinese ability to learn modern science. They were certain that the Chinese language is designed to facilitate visualized but not logical thinking, therefore it is absolutely impossible for the Chinese to grasp the subtle natural science developed in the West. It turned out, however, that the Chinese have begun to systematically translate the natural science works since the Westernization Movement. With the foundation laid by the pioneers including Yan Fu, Hua Hengfang, Xu Shou and Li Shanlan, a full set of natural science textbooks in the Chinese language were made available by 1930s, symbolized by the publication of the full set of college textbooks that were authorized by Ministry of Education of Republic of China. Nearly at the same time, natural scientists of ethnic Han nationality began to be known on the world platform. We have to point out that all these outstanding people in modern science started their education from the *Four Books* and the *Five Classics*, but none of them grew in England and started primary education in English. Biological researches conclude that ethnic differences do not correspond with differences in IQ. If ethnic Han people can systematically introduce and digest modern natural science, any other ethnic group in China can. The only difference is the start time and the social background when these natural scientific theories were introduced. From the perspective of social system, today's ethnic minorities face much less resistance than the ethnic Hans when introducing western modern science. Therefore, it is totally groundless to make the judgment based on the IQ of an ethnic group.

The fact that schools in ethnic minority regions are poorly equipped is an undeniable fact, which is an urgent problem for governments at all levels to solve. However, insufficient equipment does not explain why ethnic students tend to underperform in science-related subjects as early as grade one and two when lower-grade math does not depend on modern experimental equipment at all. We also notice that schools in ethnic Han regions differ in the level of experimental equipment, but it does not lead to the same gap as in ethnic regions. Apparently, this can not be explained by variance in teaching equipment.

The issue of vision is also a pragmatic one. Undeniably, ethnic students have long lived in rural villages and thus lacked real sense of modern scientific achievements. However, we want to go one step further to ask: do people who are exposed to natural scientific achievements in daily basis really understand scientific theories? How many children who play computer games every day understand computer languages? How many people who listen to weather forecast everyday have the basic meteorological knowledge? How many city residents who rely on motor vehicles everyday know the difference between gasoline and diesel engine?

The study of natural science subjects is a highly abstract brain work, in which experimental equipment and exposure to scientific achievements only play a supplementary role. Scientific knowledge is even more so to an ethnic group in its introduction and absorption of modern science. Any breakthrough in modern science, when it is first published, was only accessible to a limited number of people. The most advanced atomic reactor, for instance, is only owned by a small number of countries, however, it does not keep the ethnic groups with written language from accepting this theory and translating it into its own language, thus benefiting every member in its ethnic group who is willing to learn.

We were lucky to have obtained some interesting materials in the fieldwork. We participated in a few lessons of grade three math class where students used uniform national textbooks. (Most of the math teachers in grade one and two were local ethnic teachers paid by local people.) While the class was in session, teachers always read a sentence in Mandarin followed by a translation in Miao language, and then explained the concepts in Miao language. Many concepts that were no brainers to Han students became messy. The concept of "zero", for example, does not exist in any Miao dialect. A literal translation has exactly the same meaning of "nothing" in Mandarin. Students were confused why "nothing" took a space in calculation and could not make sense in their local language. Other concepts such as "digit", "single digits", and "tens digits" were described by different teachers in their own way. Some of them described it as "room", some described as "grid", others "seat". Although students seemed to have understood these concepts, it occurred to us later that these problems were never solved. These students would continue using their mother tongue in their lifetime while teachers were likely to change. Each teacher explained the same concept discretionally and none of them could establish a stable connection with a specific concept in their own mother tongue. With the study of these subjects going deeper, such confusion would keep accumulating. The flawlessly logical connections between these concepts would become unbearably messy and hard to understand. By now, nobody could help them any more. Ethnic Han teachers in senior grades could only point out their mistakes but were clueless why they made such mistakes. We think that this is the underlying reason that causes the ethnic students to lag behind in science-related subject.

When we were conducting fieldwork in Wangmo county, a government official asked us a surprising question. As a graduate from department of ethnic language at Guizhou Ethnic College, he was proficient in Buyi language and Mandarin and had engaged in the translation of Buyi language into Mandarin. He was given a tough job from the family planning office of the county government: to translate the birth control propaganda materials into Buyi language. After receiving the task, he spent nearly one year and visited all knowledgeable senior people in the county, trying in vain to find out how to accurately translate the male and female reproductive organs into Buyi language. Our answer to his question was: The translated scientific concepts and terminologies became acceptable in local people by custom. The Han Chinese encountered the same problem when they began to translate Western natural science classics. The element "zinc" in Mendeleev's Periodic Table, for example, bewildered the Chinese pioneering chemists in the first place. Their original translation of "*wo qian*" (short lead) or "*bai qian*"(white lead) did not match their names in English. To ensure the completeness and logic in the naming convention of elements, it was impossible to put *wo qian* in the Periodic Table. They eventually came to the solution to coin the character "Xin" that did not exist in *Kangxi Dictionary* by following the structural logic in Chinese characters and the pronunciation of the initial letter z in the word "zinc", thus bringing the task of translation to a successful conclusion. With the popularization of chemistry education, the word "Xin" has become an accepted Chinese character and has taken root in the "inner language" of the Chinese people, while the traditional name "*wo qian*" and "*bai qian*" in Chinese are lost in history. Similar to the translation of male and female reproductive organs, early Chinese translators run into the same problem when trying to translate the structure of eyeball. Before the translation was completed, the terms such as macula, retina, lens and blind spot that are high-frequent academic terms in modern Chinese anatomy textbooks were nowhere to be found in any Chinese dictionary. They were coined by the first Chinese translator in accordance with the law of Chinese word-building and were later universally accepted in the Chinese community. You happen to be the first one in your ethnic group. You will need to think of a new word in Buyi language easily understood and accepted by the Buyi people according to the law of word-building in Buyi language and the shape and other characteristics of the original words. This is the first step of your work. With the spread of the materials you put together, these names will become customarily accepted by Buyi people and will take root among them. Given the fact that you may not be the only one that is doing the work, a Buyi organization authorized to approve academic terms needs to be established. The ethnic language education steering committees at all levels are best candidates for this job. As to whether they are capable of doing this job, we can not answer nor offer any help.

We were not sure if we answered to his satisfaction. We felt profoundly, however, that his question was of great significance. If a designated organization or group of people is authorized to standardize the modern scientific and technological terms in Buyi language, the problems encountered by the Miao primary students in math-learning would not have been so severe, nor would the gap in the academic performance between liberal arts and science have been so wide. It would have been much easier for modern natural science to spread across the ethnic groups and the technical talents from ethnic minority groups would not have felt wasted if returning to their ethnic group.

While we did surveys on the Swidden cultivation in Sidazhai village of Ziyun county, one thing prompted us to think deeply. A local ethic Miao, who was trying to describe the useful plants he could harvest from the fields, mentioned successively more than 100 plants and tens of animals. Unfortunately, as none of the people in our team understood the sub-dialect of Miao in Mashan, we could not identify most of these names in reality and had to ask him to support his account in Mandarin and drawings. Surprisingly, as an educated young man who had systematically learnt biology and had lived and worked in Miao regions, he never used any basic biological concepts and terminologies in his conversation with us. For example, when he mentioned the larva of a kind of cicada that local Miao people fed on, it took him several minutes describing the appearance of the insect without using any basic zoological terms to make his description simpler and more straightforward. It seemed obvious that not only the Miao children or teenagers did not associate modern scientific terms and concepts with their mother tongue, even the people who received middle-school education were not able to do so. We are doubtful that Miao intellectuals like him, even if they can memorize all the materials to publicize science and technology, can solve the problem of disconnection between the contents in these materials and production activities in real life. Fundamentally, it is an issue of how to integrate scientific and technological terminologies with the local ethnic languages, which is not an exception but universal and impacting-all issue. Without solving the problem of integration between modern science and technology terms and their ethnic language, any effort in intensifying the publicity of natural science and technology will not turn them into productivity.

It is an irrefutable truth that science and technology are primary productive forces, which hold, like all other truths, on certain conditions. Ethnic Han college students would not be in current situation if ethnic Han as a nationality had not completed the integration between its mother tongue and modern science and technology, or the Han population in hundreds of millions had not learnt foreign languages and received education in modern science. Now it is time for these ethnic groups to decide what to do. To turn science and technology into real primary productive forces, the ethnic groups must do what the Han people did earlier and be determined to push the localization of modern scientific knowledge to fully integrate ethnic languages with modern scientific language; otherwise, ethnic groups will always be hindered by the difficulty in the introduction of science and technology. Instead of becoming a primary force in driving economic development, modern science and technology may become a constraint in the economic development. Our surveys suggest that such constraints are continuing to hinder the economic development of these ethnicities.

III Societies, Property Rights and Production Organizations

Social organizations are a “cultural complex” at the organizational level in the ethnic cultural system, and are close, in social functions, to ethnic traditions and customs. Although constructed to coordinate interpersonal relations, they differ dramatically in means and scope. Social organizations coordinate interpersonal relations through enforceable means while traditions and customs do so by commonly accepted social rules and traditional norms observed by entire ethnic group to lead human behaviors. Social organizations impact mostly on the most general and fundamental rules of conduct while traditions and customs function in subtlety and may relate to very complex situations. The coordinating actions by social organizations tend to be final and binding while traditions and customs lead individual behaviors without a binding force and tend to allow individuals to have a certain degree of freedom in execution. Therefore, these two "cultural complexes" are easy to be separated in principle, yet they may be interpenetrative to a specific ethnic culture.

Such a phenomenon of interpenetration between social organizations and traditions and customs is easily noticeable when we compare the works by different ethnologists, who differ in the classification of groups of cultural elements. Some ethnologists classify a society into a male-female society, family, kinship group, social group and interest group; even political organizations are classified as social organizations. ① Other ethnologists define social organizations in a broader way and include economic systems and laws in social organizational systems. ② Such a difference in classification is attributable to the differences among these ethnologists in the definition and concept of social organizations, as well as inheritance of different systems in classical ethnological research. As the core of our discussion in the book is cross-xiang operations, we define the boundary of social organizations as the collection of social beings that are directly related to production organizations. Family members assume corresponding social obligations that are, to a certain extent, compulsory and relatively stable; consequently, we discuss families in this book as a cultural component of social organizations.

The interpersonal relations that social organizations coordinate include the contents in two aspects: relations between people, and between people and the material world; on the other hand, interpersonal relations formed as a result of human reproduction. The former are the major research topic of this book due to their direct relations with human economic activities as well as a

① （US）Carol Ember, *Cultural Anthropology*, trans. Du Ze (Liaoning People's Publishing House, February 1988), Ch.8-13.

② Roger M. Keesing, *Cultural Anthropology: A Contemporary Perspective,* trans. Jiayun Yu, Gong Zhang (Taiwan: Chuliu Publisher)

cultural reality that cross-xiang economic activities may touch easily. The interpersonal relations formed as a result of human reproduction, on the other hand, will also be discussed in a certain degree due to their relevance to the issue of property inheritance and the likelihood of being indirectly touched in cross-xiang operations. Facing the ethnic groups involved in cross-xiang economic activities with different forms of social organizations, if the subjective party only considers the characteristics of their own social organizations, it will, without a doubt, lead to the resistance in economic activities, the intensity of which primarily depends on the compatibility of the corresponding social organizations on each side: the higher the compatibility, the lower the resistance, and vice versa.

The most noticeable constraints triggered by differences in social organizations are the rights and obligations of these social organizations in the ownership and disposal of natural resources. As mentioned earlier in the book, the ethnic Miao people who speak western Miao dialect in Guizhou do not have a permanent settlement until now. Their villages are, to certain extent, mobile and are built in principle around extended family groups. The lands, although cultivated by individual households, are owned in name by the entire village, or the extended family. In these villages, the trade and lease of lands do not strictly follow any laws, nor are carried out in the forms as they are by the ethnic Han people. The land left behind by a household who has moved out of the village entirely may be cultivated by any member of the extended family without having to pay any rent, nor should the land be returned later. In case a household from the extended family moves in under permission, all the households in the village may rearrange the lands and set aside a piece for the new household to cultivate. The household contract responsibility system currently implemented in these villages only exists in name and merely symbolizes the responsibility of turning in grains as a tax by each household. The information about which lands are transferred to which households in the extended family is constantly changing and usually does not match with what is written in the contract. The situations may vary to some extent. Generally, paddy fields are relatively fixed but dry lands are subject to much greater and more frequent changes. These ethnic Miao people live in a region often hard hit by severe water-and-soil-losing disasters caused by a landscape dominated by high and steep mountains, making it a tough job to protect ecological environments by "conceding cultivated lands to forestry". Such a relationship in land ownership, however, does not provide any help in achieving the goal of "sealing hillsides to facilitate afforestation". For the lands that are contracted in the name of law to individual household, the household only has the right of use but without the right of disposal for a longer period. Once the household plant trees on these lands to convert them into forest, it means that the household as well as other households in the extended family will lose the legitimate right to cultivate on these lands in decades before the trees grow big enough to be chopped. It is completely intolerable in the local customary laws in these villages.

It was at Rong village of Barao township in Wangmo county when we identified a chance to break through the relations between such social organizations and land ownership. The local Miao person who was hired by us as a guide and a translator was planning on moving out and building a new village. When he asked us where and how he should move, we asked why he decided to move. He answered: "This village has too many old rules and won't be open to accept new things." It sparked our interest, knowing that he was a village school teacher paid by the local people. Our insistence revealed that the land that he was contracted to was a sloped plot where the sun was blocked by nearby high mountains for most of the time in a day, making it hard for any crops to grow. Consequently, he decided to plant white poplars in hope of chopping them down and getting some lumbers later, only to see his moves opposed by all his brothers and cousins in the extended family. They feared that once the land was planted with white poplars, it would be inaccessible in later years to other households who want to cultivate on this land and thus the land would become privately owned. In the fieldwork in Qinglong and Guanling counties, we came across several occasions when lands were transferred without making any payment to brothers from the same extended family regardless of what was stipulated in the legal documents authorizing the contract of this land. In Cuojiwan village of Zhenning county, we paid visits to all the cultivated lands of this Miao village that scattered a few hillsides nearby, and saw with our very eyes the plots of land that were fallow, abandoned or cultivated successively for a period of one to three years under a Swidden cultivation, witnessing again what really happened to the lands under a joint ownership by the village. According to the people from the ethnic work committee of this county, a few households had left the village and gone to live in newly built villages in Jinggangshan of

Jiangxi province, some remaining unseen till now. However, our surveys suggested that all lands had been put to use by following the locally observed rules in land ownership and mode of production. It further proved the similarities in the ownership of land across all the Miao people in this region.

Such a uniqueness in the use of lands by the ethnic Miao people in these regions is rarely reported in the academia, even though its impact and constraint on the planning of land resources and implementation of water and soil conservation plans are obvious and therefore must not be overlooked. The good side of such a land ownership relations is that under such circumstances, no household will be left with no land to cultivate, nor will lands be abandoned for a long time out of shortage in manpower. The imbalance in the use of lands seen in Dong and Buyi regions can never happen here. The instability in villages and cultivated lands may amount to a constraint that hinders the state efforts in the development of ethnic minority regions, and therefore must be given much attention. Currently, the governments in relevant townships and counties are calling for "converting mountain slopes to terraced fields" and a comprehensive treatment of forests, cultivated fields and roads. They may run the risk of ending up on a scrap of paper if we can not identify a way to streamline policies and customary laws in these villages. The work and achievements that are clearly written on the statistical materials are nowhere to be found in fieldwork.

The ownership of natural resources in the Dong and Buyi societies is quite different from that in the Miao societies in the west. The cultivated lands, especially the paddy fields, in these two ethnic groups have been completely assigned to specific households in principle, and are therefore inheritable by the descendants of these households. The priced transfer, trade and lease of lands are generally well documented. It came to our attention while conducting fieldwork in these communities that some title deeds of land had the original record of land ownership in the Ming dynasty. In Qiantao township of Guiyang city, we found a stone tablet that was inscribed on how a plot of land was transferred in the fourth year of Kangxi by the ethnic Buyi to the descendants of stationed army in the Ming dynasty. [①] At Pingpo village of Daba township in Huishui county, we found a stone sculpture on a hillside that detailed a land dispute that was brought to the

① Recorded by the writer of the book from fieldwork.

arbitration of Guiyang Fu in the 25th year of Wanli in the Ming dynasty. ① The party who lost the case was a local Buyi household while the winning party was a Miao family who owned a bullfight place some 20 li away from the cultivated land in dispute. The losing party was demanded by the verdict to return this land to the Miao family who could use it as a bullfighting ground. In this case, the ethnic Miao appeared in an extended family while the ethnic Buyi appeared in individual household, fully demonstrating the significant difference in the ownership of land between the two ethnic groups. Similar cases were also found in Yashui and Baijin in Huishui county, where the bullfighting grounds and *Tiaohua* grounds owned by Miao families were surrounded by paddy fields of ethnic Buyi people who intended to cannibalize these grounds by stealthily planting in these grounds, thus giving rise to disputes over property rights. The Ming and Qing governments, for the purpose of maintaining local stability, did everything in their capacity to keep the status quo and strictly prohibited these Buyi families from cannibalizing these Miao "enclaves". Most of the verdicts were documented by inscribed tablets. These disputes, however, have lasted till today. When the system of output-related contract operation in these regions was implemented, many Buyi people repeatedly asked of the county government to convert these "enclaves" into paddy fields. Such a request was objected to by the Miao officials represented by the county ethnic committees, and thus dragged on for years without a resolution and had to be shelved eventually. Behind the continuous disputes over property rights was the divergent way of property ownership between ethnic Miao and Buyi peoples. The paddy fields had been owned by individual Buyi households and the history in the transfer of titles to them remains clear among local people, despite the implementation of the system of output-related contract operation, which was viewed by the Buyi people as merely a change of name. To the contrary, the lands in the Miao communities remain under a joint ownership of the entire extended family.

In the Buyi and Dong regions, all the hillside lands other than the paddy fields are, in principle, public lands that can be used by all households in the village but should not be turned to private properties. When negotiating a lease of these lands with other ethnic groups, it must be handled by the entire extended family instead of specific households and the income from lease is

① "Postscript to Cliff Inscriptions in Dog House of Pigong", *Guiyang Annals*. no.3.

shared by the all family members. The ethnic Buyi group use these hillside lands roughly in three ways: first, the forest lands behind the village are sealed indefinitely in the form of *fengshui* forest and are not to be chopped down nor developed for other purposes even if the forests have overgrown. These lands are called "*houlong*" (backyard dragon) in Buyi and bear a religious symbolic meaning for the protection of the entire village. Second, all the public lands owned by all households in the village, including pasture, firewood-producing and lumber-producing forests, must be disposed of by following customary rules. Before the "cultural revolution", stone tablets detailing these customary rules were commonly seen in nearly every Buyi village. Third, each household is entitled to cultivating and harvesting the non-public lands, without restrictions, but should not permanently occupy, trade or lease these lands. Now, most of the trees of economic value and dry-fruit producing trees are developed on these lands.

Such a set of rules regulating the use of hillside lands in Buyi communities has an impact on today's economic development that is not to be neglected. The development of raw material bases for world-famous Liuma tung oil in Zhenning is an example. We noticed when conducting surveys in Nongpao, Ximan and Liangtian of Zhenning county that all the tung trees were planted and harvested by individual households. Any land that was left idle might be developed by any other household into tung tree forest with the income from selling tung oil kept by the developer. Such a flexibility in land ownership and usage yielded direct positive results on the production of Liuma tung oil.

First of all, the suitable lands for tung forest are distributed among individual households purely based on the availability of labor force in each household, ensuring that these lands are not wasted but made full use of. Secondly, disputes over the rights to the forests are rarely seen as they are sanctioned by all the related households in the village. In case of rare disputes, they don't need to be brought to state judiciary system but can be solved through coordination within the village. Lastly, since these lands are in principle owned by the entire extended family, the income from the tung forests is not exclusive to the operating households. By custom, the forests are open, after most of the tung seeds are harvested, to poor families with weak labor force to pick the remaining ones thus allocating some of the income to these families.

The above three characteristics have given rise to a social element most critical in the production of quality tung oil. To pick and harvest tung seeds stealthily rarely happens in these regions, which enables the tung seeds to fall from trees after they are fully ripe and successfully enter the period of dormancy before they are harvested. These tung seeds that are in the period of dormancy have a higher tung oil content and eleostearic acid after made into tung oil, and a low oleic acid and linoleic acid content that prevents tung oil from forming films. Coatings made from this kind of tung oil have a good film-forming property and have a much better stability and insulativity than the tung oil produced in other regions. This is one of the most important reasons for the success of Liuma tung oil, which is also totally dependent on the form of ownership in the lands suitable for planting trees implemented in the village organizations in the Buyi communities. We have noticed in our surveys that the tung seeds growing in the regions where ethnic Buyi people interacted with other ethnic groups on a frequent basis, or even in state-sponsored tung forests, were often harvested before they fully matured to avoid being stolen. As a result, the tung seeds produced in these regions, despite state sponsorship in some places, could not rival those produced in Liuma in both quality and economic benefit.

Ethnic Dong people have a similar form of land ownership as that of Buyi, but a different traditional economic life style. Up until the eve before the founding of the People's Republic of China, ethnic Dong people had practiced an economic style of "interplanting of crops and trees" with a priority on forest. The operation of forest plantations, as the predominant form of their economic life, was carried out on hillside lands jointly owned by the extended family in the village. Consequently, the phenomenon seen in Liuma manifested in the means of production in commercial forest plantations. In recent five centuries, ethnic Dong made tremendous progress in forest plantations development and many business tycoons were given birth to. [①] To a certain degree, the land ownership was created on the basis of such unique social organizations. The man-made operational forests have the following four unique characteristics compared to the agricultural economic style of exclusively paddy fields.

First, the operation of forest plantations is a long cycled business,

① One of the series of books on ethnic issues compiled by the State Ethnic Affairs Commission, Series of Books of Materials from Investigations on Ethnic Minority Groups in China, *Investigations on Ethnic Dong Societies* (Guizhou Ethnic Press, Februrary 1988), 30-33.

depending on the natural geographic characteristics of the forests and the projects in operation. Regardless, a cycle takes at least 10 years and may be protracted into half a century, of which the Korean pine forests in Lesser Khingan Mountains were an example. For the man-made Chinese fir forests in the ethic Dong regions in Guizhou, the production cycle is dramatically shortened due to a superior geographic location and the abundant knowledge and techniques acquired by the Dong people in the operation. However, it still takes more than 8 years the shortest, much longer than the production cycle of rice fields, i.e., once or twice a year. The protracted production cycle determines that the forests must be operated in fragments and in successive order and can not be harvested at one time, making it absolutely necessary to maintain a land ownership that lasts long and stably. Under a public ownership of land by the entire extended family in the village, the trade, mortgage or lease of lands by individuals or households are prohibited. The transfer of ownership must be decided by all relevant families in the village. Before the founding of the People's Republic of China, this right was performed by the respected seniors in each village who represented the entire extended family. It guaranteed the continuous stability of forest land ownership in a long period and the smooth operation of the forests.

Second, compared to paddy fields that can be as small as one mu (a Chinese unit of area) or several fens (a Chinese unit of area), forest plantations must be operated in a massive area of at least tens or thousands of hectares due to the prolonged production cycle of forests and lumbers. To ensure the continuation of production and balanced input of labor, the forest lands must be managed by plots based on different production cycles. A small area, once segmented into different production plots, will be too small for minimum labor input and thus unprofitable. In the forestry operation, the requirements for labor input differ dramatically in different stages of the life cycle of trees: the stage of forestation requires the most, followed by the stage of harvest. It takes 70% of the entire production cycle from the stage of sealing the forest to logging, and the gap in labor input is hard to bridge. The residents in forest areas are hardly self-sufficient in food supply. In addition, the annual output of lumber is limited; with the best at 3 cubic meters and generally around 1 cubic meter in southeast of Guizhou. A limited area of forest makes it hard for the people who live on forests to subsist. For similar reasons, the organization of labor input in the forest regions is not possible without a certain production scale. Consequently, in a successful forest plantation operation, each production unit must have a large area of forest lands and a large production organization. The public ownership of forest lands by the extended families in ethnic Dong regions ensures the scale and large area in forestry operation, which is one of the social factors that contribute to the dynamic forestry operation in these regions.

Some foreign countries also provide successful examples in planting forests in large area and scale. The forest plantation in Canada, Finland and US under independent accounting has a much larger scale than ours, which is advantageous in many ways. First, it takes advantage of the ecological potential in the natural growth of trees and thus reduces the input of manpower. Second, forests in massive area facilitate their protection and management, making it easier for implementing fire and insect-prevention measures that may be completed by putting the manpower and materials to concentrative use. Third, it rationalizes the use of natural resources including climate, land, and water source and reduces the waste in natural resources as a result of decentralized operation. Fourth, it makes it possible to take advantage of the strength in financing and can wait for a favorite market price to log the trees, thus increasing operational efficiency. Fifth, it benefits the further development into deeper processing of forest products to increase the efficiency of wood usage, thus adding values to the operational performance within the group. The forest bases for the papermaking industry in the US and Canada do not only produce paper, but also sell some logs, and a large quantity of organic chemical products. Slovakia successfully turned an unlogged forest into a world famous hunting ground for tourists. All of the above were made possible on the basis of a large-scale forestry operation. [①]

Thirdly, the operation of forest plantations is multi-project comprehensive industry. As we discussed in the previous chapter, the ethnic Dong people are in an agricultural economic type, one of the basic characteristics of which, as we mentioned earlier, is limited number of economic projects and large quantity in the yield. The forest plantation in the Dong regions also has such characteristics. The primary product from these forests is lumber. However, unlike the rice field cultivation by the ethnic Hans in brooky regions, the economy of Dong people has largely tilted

① Yuxiao Long, "What Shackles the Marketization of Ethnic Forestry Economy", *Guizhou Ethnic Studies*, no. 3, 1993, 38.

toward forestry, as a result, the innate characteristics of forestry production must have great impact on the economic life of the Dong people. Forestry production, especially the man-made forestry operation, yields a variety of products that, in addition to the primary product lumber, include forestry by-products, natural animals and plants that yield considerable returns. Before the man-made forestry operation entered the stage of intensive operation, these forestry by-products could only be shared among specific households in accordance with customary rules and were not reflected in statistics. The march toward modernization will bring the multi-project forestry operation in Dong regions on the agenda. In foreign countries, forestry production is also associated with hunting, tourism, processing of forestry by-products, breeding of rare animals and gathering and processing of Chinese medicinal materials etc. The successful cases that can offer some reference include the Korean ginseng, breeding of elephants and monkeys in Thailand, the extraction of turpentine and advanced aromatic oil in the United States, the production of eucalyptus oil in Australia, production of camphor in early Taiwan of China and the hunting and tourism in forests in Slovakia. They provide examples for ethnic Dong people to follow in their pursuit of modernization. To deepen the intensive operation and modernization in forestry operation, they need to consider transitioning from the forestry product processing to industrialization that includes papermaking, processing of fiberboard, wood, and forest chemical products. It requires that the current basic model of agricultural economic type be replaced with a unified industrial production model that gives rise to the large scale and unified social productivity.

The traditional land ownership in forest plantations in ethnic Dong regions played a facilitating role in the development of forestation, and had the effect of compatibility and coordination in the multi-project comprehensive forestry operation in history. However, the tendency in forest plantations toward building an intensified and modernized multi-project comprehensive industry is posing increasing challenges to such a compatibility, raising a directional and urgent question for the ethnic Dongs in their efforts to try to deepen the forestry development.

Fourth, forest plantations must be operated in a fully enclosed environment. The operators of forest plantations in foreign countries are in complete possession and have uninterrupted rights of operation of the forests.

With an independent right of supervision and control, the operators have the right to prohibit any unauthorized person from entering the forest region. At time of high risk of forest fire, they also have the right to unconditionally decline entry into the forest region to anyone, impose strict control over the use of fire by the people other than their employees, thus making the protection of forests simple, easy and highly effective. The disasters caused by forest fire after the founding of the People's Republic of China were bitter results from the practice of un-enclosed operation of forest. In the countries with a developed forestry, the enclosed operation has minimized the interruption from other industries and personnel to the lowest level and ensured the lasting stability and high efficiency in forestry operation, in particular, effectively prevented unlawful felling of trees and illegal hunting and mining of animals and plants in the forest region.

Take the production of rosin and turpentine in the US as an example. The large-area enclosed operation has enabled the operators of the forests to make an overall arrangement to collect rosin one year before logging the trees, which increases the income from forestry by-products but does not reduce the quantity of lumber. A diversified business is not possible without enclosed operation because the production of forestry by-products requires a vast area and frequent long-distance transportation of small-quantity products. For example, the medicinal materials from the forest are gathered over a vast territory to reach the minimum commercial quantity. The labor input in these products usually takes the form of irregular and non-mechanical force in transportation. The forestry management regulations effective now only apply to mechanical transportation of products in butch and therefore seem irrelevant to the operation of forestry by-products. If the forest is not fully enclosed, we can not prevent illegal hunting, gathering or use of wild animals and plants, which not only hurts the rights and interests of forestry operators, but may also destroys the resources of the country. In the worst case scenario, it may lead to the extinction of certain animal and plant species in the forest region and cause severe ecological crisis.

A fully enclosed operation simplifies and unifies the forestry management. It is the pre-condition for the effective prevention of natural disasters in the forest region. In the meantime, it is the most effective measure of reducing the cost of forest protection, and a must for eradicating destructive behaviors by people. The disasters and destructions caused by people in the forest regions in China are severe and visible in Jinping county, a key forestry county in Guizhou province. The forest area that was burnt by forest fires from 1980 to 1984 in Jinping reduced to about 5000 mu a year but increased sharply to over 10,000 mu in 1985. In the first half of 1986 alone, over 12,000 mu was destroyed by fire. [1] In 1983, the county broke the record of excessive deforestation since the founding of the People's Republic of China. According to the statistics by the county Forestry Bureau, about 200,000 cubic meters of wood were felled, which was well over the annual plan of 13,000 cubic meters in the county. The logging quantity in 1985 was estimated by the county Forestry Society to be around 400,000 cubic meters, accounting for approximately one tenths of the total volume of wood in the forests of the county. [2] The devastating destruction to the forest regions in the 1980s was a direct result of the forest ownership being broken into households, causing the forests to mix with farmlands, adjacent to township enterprises and the construction projects invested by the state to cross the forest region. The economic tide, in particular, brought speculative individuals from all over the country to sneak in the forest region and steal logs for the purpose of making exorbitant profits. This is the source of all evils that threaten the enclosed operation of the forest region.

The above four basic characteristics in the forestry operation are general in nature. The fact that forest plantations in the ethnic Dong region in southeast Guizhou rapidly emerged to be a predominant industry in the region is closely related to the ethnic Dong's traditional ownership of land resources. It is safe to say that the forest plantations could not have been created, let alone developed, without the social safeguard on the basis of the traditional public ownership of the forest-suitable lands shared by the extended family in the village. A revisit to the history in the commercial forest plantations has significant values for us to deepen our understanding of the relationship between the social and human background and forestry plantations.

The ethnic Dong group completely entered the agricultural type of economy in the 10th century at the latest when cultivation of rice fields was the primary operation and the surrounding forest-suitable lands remained clad by virgin forests. The Song dynasty treated the ethnic Dong group as

[1] Yougeng Yang, "A Discussion of the Successes and Failures in the Forestry Reform in Jinping and the Reasons", *Guizhou Ethnic Studies*, no. 1, 1989, 43-44.

[2] Idem

"soldiers of a vassal state" and used them in farming and border defense. The Dong people who accepted such arrangement by the Song dynasty were called "*dong ding*", [①] and the ethnic Miao people who lived in the surrounding hillsides and virgin forest regions were called "*san qiao*" at the moment, which was derived from the rules of the Song dynasty: the territories that were "*san qiao*" (three shovels) away up the hills surrounding the intermontane basin were allocated to the "uncivilized" people to live, and the "*dong ding dong min*"(cave men) who were registered by the government must not step onto these territories.[②] The ethnic Dongs had long lived in these regions and cultivated rice fields, fully driving the development of private land ownership and postponing the ownership of the hillside forests. The Song court that moved south intensified the development and management of the Dong regions while ethnic Dong people began developing the regions up the river streams. The Dong villages began to closely interact with Miao people and intensified the development and exploitation of the virgin forests, and expanded the operation of the economic forests originally on the gentle slopes toward the virgin forests up the mountains, laying the foundation for the transition of the ethnic Dongs to a forestry-predominant economy.

The unification of China by the Yuan dynasty completely opened up the south and eastbound water channels along Wuyang, Duliu and Qingshui rivers from inner Guizhou, making it possible to transport logs along the rivers. The uncertainty in the traditional ownership of virgin forests near Dong villages made it the only way to develop virgin forests in the form of a joint ownership shared by geographically adjacent families, which formed the historical foundation for the public ownership of forest-suitable lands by the extended family in a village. After the 14th century, the economic prosperity in the early Ming dynasty resulted in the expansion of farm lands in the core ethnic Han regions and drained up the forest resources. In the meantime, conditions were ripe for the surplus lumbers from the virgin forests in the ethnic Dong regions to be shipped out and sold to Han regions, after meeting the demand for Dong people. Although not many evidences are found in the ancient Han literatures about the sporadic sales of logs to other regions by the Dong people, the expropriation of wood for royal usage was documented in

① *Twenty-five Histories* vol. 8, *History of the Song Dynasty • Biography of Barbarians*

② *Liping Fu Annals*, in the collection of Guizhou Provincial Library, woodblock print

History of the Ming Dynasty and *Veritable Records of the Ming Dynasty.* ① Recent research suggests that Jinping region in Guizhou began to ship and sell cedarwood in batches in late Ming dynasty, which attracted Han businessmen from other regions to join the operation. ② The sharp rise in the sale of logs to other regions caused the virgin forests near the river wharfs convenient for floating the log-rafts out of the region to dwindle, thus bringing the forest plantation onto the agenda. As the virgin forests in the ethnic Dong regions had been initially owned jointly by the extended family in a village, such a form of ownership was kept unchanged for the renewed forests planted by people, giving rise to the way of production organization characterized by a joint ownership of the forest-suitable lands, joint forestry operation and shared profits. It is apparent that such a production organization was built on the social foundation of a joint ownership by the extended family in a village, without which, forest plantations would not have been possible. The forestry operation in the ethnic Dong regions grew to a considerable size in the Qing dynasty.

Based on our surveys and historical records, the forest plantations in the ethnic Dong regions have the three following characteristics

First, the forest lands are cleared by slash-and-burn. Trees and crops are planted together during the period of afforestation, which helps purify the type of trees in the forest by clearing up the undesired trees, thus increasing the economic benefit of timber forests. To mix the trees and crops together increases the yield of crop to effectively solve the food supply in the forest region. It also loosens the soil, adds up the soil layer, and fertilizes the soil, therefore facilitating the enclosure of young trees to shorten the period of time needed for forest enclosure. In addition, to mix the trees and crops together attracts the natural enemies of pests in the forest region and thus helps control and treat forest disease and pests later. Given the fact that ethnic Dongs mingle with the Miao people who are in the Swidden cultivation, it is reasonable to deduce that such a characteristic in the forestry production was a result of interactions between the two cultures, the introduction of some positive elements in the Swidden cultivation, and the absorption and digestion of the modes of agricultural production.

Second, the forestry production in the ethnic Dong region is organized

① *Veritable Records of the Ming Dynasty • A Compilation of Materials about Guizhou,* see the part under "*Huang Mu*" in Memoir of Wanli.

② Xun Long, "The Forestry Economy in Dong Societies", *Guizhou Ethnic Studies*, no. 2, 1992, 29.

and maintained primarily by customary rules enforced across all villages, which, from our survey results, are very stringent. The stealthy logging and forest fire caused by negligence are subject to stern punishment. Moreover, to pick dead tree branches to be used as firewood during the forest maintenance and protection period is subject to capital punishment – to burn the perpetrator to death in public, which is also enforceable on their own relatives. These customary rules are enforced by seniors in the villages or clan chiefs who reach verdicts exactly in accordance with the customary rules without pardon. Any dispute over the ownership of forest is to be solved between villages through fiscal fight or by the rules. In fact, the social organizations composed of villages are rudimentary production unit in the forest plantation of the Dong people, while families participate in the production activities as part of the village.

Third, the forest plantations in the ethnic Dong regions are an inter-ethnicity supplementary economic structure based on coordinated operation across different ethnic groups. In the early Qing dynasty, an inter-ethnicity economic structure with ethnic Dongs as a leading force along with other ethnic groups began to surface. Ethnic Miaos living outside the Dong forest plantations received support from Dong people in technology and capital. The ethnic Han immigrants played a role of "setter" of the Dong products as well as a "transporter" of daily necessities from Han into Dong regions. The value of such a supplementary support in providing commercial channel to the development of forest plantations in Dong regions should not be underestimated. The logs shipped out of the Dong regions also supported the economic development in the Han regions and gave birth to quite a number of Han tycoons in forestry. It is worth mentioning that the fat profits in timber trade also lured some Han millionaires who entered the forest operation in the form of leasing and acquisition. The leasing and acquisition of the forest lands were also conducted through a village made up of families. The lessors of forest-suitable lands were the extended families in each village represented by village seniors or tribal chiefs, historically referred to as "owner of the mountain" while the lessees of the Han nationality were historically referred to as "operator". The relationship between both parties was similar, to a certain extent, to the "leasing agricultural operator" in the West. The existence of "operator" deepened the inter-ethnicity supplementary relationship in the forest plantations. The Dong forest regions in west Hunan province are also habitats of a large number of ethnic Tujia people who aided Dong people in their forestry development by supplying grains and offering abundance of skills and experiences in the operation of economic forest. On the other hand, the forestry provides a lot of jobs opportunities to Tujia people. Such a multi-ethnicity supplementary economic structure lays a foundation for the prosperity of forest plantations in the Dong regions.[①]

The above three characteristics were developed on a solid social and human foundation and were safeguarded by a stable mutual-dependency across ethnic groups. The geographic proximity between ethnic Dong forest regions and the core Han regions makes it easy for the direct shipping of logs in raft into Han regions to fill the timber shortage. In addition, the low production cost in timber production and steady supply of timber fueled the expansion of forestry in ethnic Dong regions, giving birth to the large commercial groups similar to Syndicates before the founding of the People's Republic of China. These large commercial groups established a chain business that encompassed forestry, logging, gathering and collection, and sale of timbers to other regions. In the meantime, bureaucratic capitals started to make investments in the timber trade in the Dong forest regions. All the four big banks in Republic of China, for instance, funded forestry operations in Dong regions, symbolizing the considerable potential in the development of forest plantations in the Dong regions.

The potential in forest plantations in ethnic Dong regions is built on a solid social and traditional foundation and attributable to the ownership of forest lands, which is fundamentally congruent with and meet the requirements of the four basic characteristics in forestry production. The joint ownership shared by the families in the village is a collective land ownership that is based on the foundation of specific families and villages, and stabilized by customary rules. Therefore, it is difficult for any individual to change, nor can the ownership be separated into pieces, ensuring the long-term stability of the forestry ownership. Dagui village where we conducted fieldwork is a remote small village of Gaoniang township in Tianzhu county. It has two big extended families by the last name of Long and Pan. Before the founding of the People's Republic of China, the two extended families at the village each had forest lands of several thousands of mu separated by clear-cut borders, which are still in the memory of members

① *Investigation on the History of Dong Societies* (Guizhou Ethnic Press, November 1988), 41.

at least 50 years of age from the two families. According to these old people from this village, the timbers used in the government structures before the founding of the People's Republic of China, such as township office and granary, mostly came from the forests that belonged to Long and Pan families at Dagui village. Calculated from the inscriptions on the tombstones of the two families, they began to settle at this village some 150 years ago, and their ownership of the forest lands had remained unchanged until the "land reform" in the early stage of the People's Republic of China. It is inferable that the ownership of forest lands belonging to Long and Pan families had remained stable for at least 120 years. The continuous and long-term stability in the ownership of forest lands has ensured that the requirements in operating forest plantations be met.

Not only did the forestry ownership in the Dong region last stably, but the forests were huge and covered a discontinued vast territory even in the Qing dynasty. According to the statistics of the Dong forest regions in Jinping county in the early period of the People's Republic of China, the tycoons of ethnic minority groups in the operation of timber, such as Yao Baiwan (Yukui), Jiang Zhiyuan, controlled the forestry production in a few counties in southeast Guizhou. They started by acquiring individual mountains clad with forests and organized large-scale centralized transportation, thus making exorbitant profits. The fact that it took them merely ten to twenty years to achieve this scale of economy was rarely seen even in the developed Han regions. [①] Unlike the overnight millionaires in the Han regions who usually had to rely on political power, these minority timber tycoons did not have any political clout to start with, nor did they have the social status that could jumpstart their initial efforts. What attributed to their fast emergence has been discussed before. We are in the opinion that the fundamental reasons that contributed to their unbelievably fast rise were the following: The forest lands previously owned by each extended family in Dong villages were large in size; the forest mountains were connected into an even larger territory; and the people in charge of the disposal of forest ownership had authorities. However, their lack of ability to connect with Han businessmen made the transportation and selling of timber to other regions difficult. In the periods of Qianlong (1736-1795) and Jiaqing (1796-1820) of the Qing dynasty, the

① Yougeng Yang, "The Impacts and Roles of Ethnic Han on the Development of Ethnic Minority Forest Region in Qingshui Jiang (I)", *Guizhou Ethnic Studies*, no. 2, 1993, 52.

timber supply to the Han regions was in severe shortage. While the Han people tried hard to reach the forest regions of the ethnic Dong group, the timber tycoons of the minority people appeared at this critical moment. With unique personal background and thorough understanding of the Dong regions, they quickly emerged to act as the middlemen in the timber trade. By now, what they only needed to do was to communicate with the village heads before they could organize the shipment of massive quantity of logs to Han regions by rafting and quickly accumulated vast amount of wealth. In other words, these minority timber tycoons could not have made such an impressive achievement without the operation of large forest lands originally owned by each individual Dong village. The large-scale operation over a vast and uninterrupted territory was the natural result of the joint ownership held by the villages made up of extended families.

The surveys on the Dong forestry in the early period of the People's Republic of China were carried out to serve one primary purpose: prove the existence of class exploitation. Under such a guiding principle, the contracts related to timber trade were selectively collected to reflect the intensity of class exploitation, thus might not be a true reflection of the forestry operations that covered a large and uninterrupted territory. Regardless, a comparison of these survey materials reveals the characteristics of large and uninterrupted operation in the forest plantations. In the contracts collected for the survey, each concerned the transfer of hundreds to thousands of trees, indicating that the forest lands concerned were in considerably large areas. Another thing that needs to be considered is that the two parties in these contracts were originally in the relationship of lessor and lessee. The contract was about transferring forest ownership to the lessor, whose overall forests occupied an area that was several or tens of the area covered by the contract. It offers a supporting evidence that the forest lands operated by ethnic Dongs were large and uninterrupted.

We found an individual case in the survey that was convincing. During the period of the Northern Expedition, Wang Tianpei (Dong ethnicity), a senior military officer in the national evolutionary army, was born into a poor family and was once a tenant and a child cowherd for Long Taihai, a rich and influential family at Mushan village in Gaoniang. Wang Tianpei's father, out of destitution, stole and sold some logs from the forests jointly owned by the extended family in the village. It provoked the outrage of the entire extended family who filed a lawsuit against his father (for violating customary laws), and consequently put him in jail. It unveils the fact that even for the families who were destitute and could hardly survive, stealthily stealing and selling the publicly-owned wood was an act prohibited by customary laws, indicating that public ownership of the forest lands had long been honored and maintained. It is for this reason that the large scale and uninterrupted forestry in the Dong regions was fully protected. Examples like this make it easier for us to understand why the minority timber tycoons emerged so abruptly and why the ownership transfer covered in the lease contracts was in such a considerable scale.

The to-be-improved social hierarchy and social constraints have prevented the diversified operation in the traditional forestry in the Dong regions from developing into a deeper and broader level. However, the different ownerships in forest lands and crop fields run stably in parallel to create a dual-system production structure characterized by "producing food from cultivated fields and generating wealth from forest lands". To a certain extent, such a dual-system structure was an early form of diversified operation. In addition, the artificial afforestation in the Dong regions introduced certain elements of Swidden cultivation that made it a historical tradition to mix trees with grains, a fact that can also be viewed as the initial stage in diversified operation. In addition, ethnic Dong people are also engaged in animal husbandry and handicraft, which lays a foundation for diversified forestry operation. What they need is to deepen the integration with modern economy.

The enclosed forest operation is not only a direction in the future but was also practiced in the Dong region long time ago. The separate planting of grains and trees was made possible as grains were not grown in the forest regions and forests were operated by families, each having a clearcut border with the others. Nobody from outside the family was allowed to step foot on the forest region and the family members were subject to the governing of customary laws when inside the forest region. Therefore, the enclosed forestry operation has in essence almost reached such a state under the framework of joint ownership by extended family of a village. In addition, the supplementary relations across ethnic groups were reflected in all stages of the timber operation, especially in its sales channels. The ethnic Han timber businessmen who were responsible for external sales of timber, also known in history as "*shui ke*" (water guest) did not need to have direct interactions with "*shan ke*" (mountain guest), the Dong people who were responsible for forestry operation. The ethnic Hans did not need to enter the forests to purchase logs. They did so through the middlemen, who themselves did not need to enter the forest regions but only talked with village heads. Ordinary Dong people directly took part in felling trees, moved them to the riverside and made rafts. They usually did not enter the Han regions. The chained structure of production and sale existing among the "*shan ke*", "*qian ke*" and "*shui ke*" guaranteed the enclosed forestry operation. In a nutshell, such a guarantee was the result of a joint ownership by the extended family in a village.

Since the founding of the People's Republic of China, the Party and people's government have attached great importance and provided all-out support to the economic development in the ethnic regions, and have done a lot of work and made impressive progress for the Dong traditional forestry. Generally, the achievements in the following four aspects are complete a success.

First, we have attained ethnic equality, eradicated the ethnic oppression that had lasted thousands of years, and erased the estrangement among ethnic groups, laying a solid social foundation for the development of Dong traditional forestry as well as broadening the vision of Dong people and subjecting them to the influence of modernization in the world.

Second, we have eradicated the local tyrants that had bullied the local people, destroyed the shackles that had restrained the development of Dong traditional forestry, and turned the majority of Dong forest farmers into the master of their own life.

Third, the Party and the people's government has implemented the preferential policy and mobilized the manpower, materials and financial strength to make the largest and broadest infrastructure investment in the Dong forest regions. The construction of highways and railways, treatment of water ways, and erection of power grids are now happening across the entire forest region, laying the material foundation for the Dong traditional forestry to modernization.

Lastly, the massive popularization of cultural education has created a wealth of ethnic people with knowledge and skills for the development of Dong traditional forestry. The development in modern science and technology has made it possible for the integration between modern achievements in forestry science and technology. We are making mistakes if we overlook these successes.

Neither is it a perspective of dialectical materialism if we only emphasize successes but neglect failures. These failures, if not uprooted, will likely inflate to overshadow our successes and result in a protracted stagnation in the development of Dong forestry. Objectively, we have faced numerous difficulties if we want to have a comprehensive and profound understanding, within a short period of time, of all ethnic groups due to the vast territory and diversified ethnic backgrounds in China, to which most of the mistakes we have made in policies executed in the Dong forest regions are attributable. As China is predominantly an ethnic Han society and the economy in Han regions has been dominating, from a perspective of national economy, we have to put the characteristics in the Han economic operation on top priority; consequently, it is unavoidable that we sometimes neglect the economic attributes of ethnic minorities when imposing a nationwide economic policy of macro control and regulation. These reasons of subjective nature have caused us to only focus on the commonalities between ethnic Han and ethnic minorities when carrying out scientific researches, but overlook the differences between them, thus deliberately minimized these differences and made mistakes.

Since the founding of the People's Republic of China, we have made many mistakes when formulating policies on the Dong traditional forestry, which were primarily caused by our misperception in how to operate traditional forestry in the Dong regions. We mistakenly treated the traditional forest plantations in Dong regions the same as the virgin forests. Such a mistake has attracted the wide attention in the academic circle. In the discussion of the forestry production in southeast Guizhou (mainly the Dong traditional forestry production), the following four aspects of uniqueness were correctly summarized. First, the forests are collectively but not publicly owned. Second, the forests are planted by man but not naturally grown. Third, the trees are planted and felled by farmers and the timbers they make are agricultural products, but not industrial products. Fourth, the economic structure is a combination of forestry and agriculture. [①] In summary, the

① Wangyuan Zhang, "Streamline the Relationship and Expedite the Reform in Collectively-Owned Forest Regions – Investigations on the Forest Regions in Southeast Guizhou Prefecture", *Guizhou Ethnic Studies*, no. 4, 1988, 56-63.

Dong traditional forestry is a socially organized long-term plantation derived from an agricultural type of economy. The policy that had long been executed in this region by the state was to treat the forests as unclaimed properties and used them without compensation following an announcement of state ownership. Such was the foundation for the "*yi ping er diao*" (equalitarianism and indiscriminate transfer of resources) that was intensively implemented in the 1950s and lasted until 1980s, resulting in the shrinking forest production, worsening ecological resources and impoverished forest farmers in the Dong region.

Another fundamental in policy-making was to treat the forestry operation as mining that was operated by state-owned industrial enterprises, but not as a long-term agricultural operation. Mines are non-renewable resources after one-time exploitation without the need to compensate anyone except for the wages of the workers and investment on mining equipment and power. To the contrary, for an agricultural operation, especially long-term agriculture, it's required the manual work by the farmers, deposits to cover risks in agricultural production as well as investment for re-production should be paid. To manage an agricultural operation, especially that of a long-term nature, by the means of managing a mining industrial operation only takes into account the one-time expenses in cost accounting but totally ignores the objective existence and necessity in making long-term investment. All the forestry administrative authorities are, until now, structured in accordance with such a fundamental principle. Consequently, despite repeated institutional reforms, the percentage in the total revenue that is allocated as income to forestry farmers has kept decreasing. In comparison, all the forestry administrative authorities including the commercial and industrial forestry enterprises have benefited tremendously from the "reform and opening-up policies" and have made profits that have been on constant rise each year. As a result, they have grown unrestrictively into greedy, cumbersome and gigantic interested groups.

It is another mistake that we overlooked the fact that forest plantations in this region were production entities with the nature of social organization instead of isolated and enclosed owner-peasants. Consequently, the polices implemented in this region were all based on the misperception of equalizing these production entities to the individual farmers in ethnic Han regions. For example, in the early stage of the People's Republic of China, the "land reform" here separated the forest lands that had been under the ownership of extended families in a village into plots and assigned them to individual households. In fact, the separation of the vast forests into household-owned plots would destruct forest plantation and hinder its development as it could only be operated on vast and uninterrupted territories. The cooperatives and people's communes established by following examples in the ethnic Han regions were entirely off the point as the ownership of the forests here had already been of a collective nature and not fully converted into private assets. The establishment of people's communes was like unnecessarily adding one administrative and operational agency on top of the previous agency that had operated the production organization. The policy of "focusing on grain production" that was later implemented shifted the focus of the newly added administrative agency to the crop lands that accounted for only 5% of the area of the forest lands. As a result, the forest lands that had been in proper management were thrown out of control, and were since operated by the state forestry authority that treated the forest plantations as virgin forests, thus giving rise to a forestry measure that only stressed harvesting but neglected planting of trees.

For similar reasons, when we kicked off "the contract system with remuneration linked to output" after the "reform and opening-up policy", we did the same thing as to separate the forest plantations into small plots and contracted them to individual households. This destroyed the foundation critically needed in the production in forest plantations – a large scale operation that covered a massive and undisrupted territory. It also made it impossible to completely close the forest lands. More importantly, the system was devised to suit agricultural lands, where crops are planted and harvested once or twice a year; consequently, a contract term ranging from 3 or 5 years to 30 or 50 years did not make a big difference on agricultural operation. The forest operation, on the other hand, was different. The forestry, as a long-term process, must be operated by plots, and continuous and steady input must be made in planting, protecting, nurturing, managing and logging trees to ensure steady yields. In other words, unlike the agricultural production that was carried out in strict cycles in different seasons, the forestry production was done continuously and in cycle, which would be put in danger once the forests were separated into plots and contracted to individual households. The implementation of such a policy was in essence out of misunderstanding of the forest plantations in Dong regions, the disastrous consequences of which have attracted attention from some scholars[①] who have rung the bell on the perilous environment that the forest plantations in southeast Guizhou were exposed to. They have pointed out that the depletion in forest resources, loss in water and soil and the ensuing exhaustion of water source and extreme fuel shortage have severely impacted the economic development in southeast Guizhou. Although the intensity of the problems has been brought to our attention, the solutions to these problems stay on the surface level. In fact, it would not have been difficult to find the right solution if we adhered to the fundamental principle of "reform and opening-up policy" and kept in mind the characteristics of forest plantations. Since the collective ownership is one of the legitimate ownerships in the primary stage of socialism and a successful forest plantation requires large-scale and collective operation, why do we have to unyieldingly separate the forests into small plots and contract them to individual households? Since the goal of "reform and opening-up policy" is to drive the transformation into the socialist market economy and the operation of forest plantations is already a market behavior, why do we need to block the channels between forest farmers and the market by forcibly inserting a variety of forestry administrative authorities and the so-called forest-industry-commerce consortiums? Isn't it a reflection of "reform and opening-up policy" by allowing the direct negotiation between farmers and buyers, from whose activities the state may levy taxes? The separation of government functions from enterprise management should mean that the forestry administrative authorities in each level only have the power of administration but not operation. The currently prevailing mechanism that farmers first sell timbers to the forestry administrative authorities who then resell them to the buyers is, in fact, an interference in the operation and a disregard of the principle of separating government functions from enterprise management. The forest-industry-commerce consortiums, if they are established as an enterprise, should compete with forest farmers and be allowed to go bankrupt if they fail on the market. Under no circumstances should they be given an administrative type of power to intervene in the forestry operation by forcing farmers to sell products to them. The forest farmers, who are legitimate operators, should have the right to determine if

[①] Qianxian He, "Investigations on a Few Issues Regarding the Production and Construction in Southeast Guizhou", *Guizhou Ethnic Studies*, no. 4, 1984, 136-140.

they sell to the consortiums or not. Furthermore, forest plantation is a long-term operating process where operators can independently complete the production cycles ranging from planting, nurturing, intertilling, protecting, managing the forests, to logging, transporting and selling products. The forest farmers are more than capable of taking care of all these steps in the process without the encouragement, supervision and investment from the forestry administrative authorities as long as they are ensured of a legitimate right of operation.

In summary, the key to the revitalization of Dong forest plantations is to acknowledge their unique characteristics, based on which specific policies that distinguish from those designed for agricultural cultivation need to be put in place. Otherwise, an indiscriminate approach will not be abandoned and the forest plantations will not be operated appropriately no matter how much subsidies and support the government provides to them and how many poverty-relief efforts we put in them. This is evidenced by the poverty-stricken counties that account for a majority of forest-abundant counties in southeast Guizhou. Our continuous poverty-relief efforts have not lifted any of them out of poverty.

We have discussed previously the roles social organizations in the three ethnic groups in Guizhou have played in their respective economic development. These social organizations, as an integral part of the traditional cultures of these ethnic groups, are relatively stable as are the cultures themselves. Despite the several political movements we underwent across the entire country since the founding of the People's Republic of China, these social organizations are tenacious in producing significant impacts on the economic life. Our attempts to develop the economies in these regions by the traditional Han culture are activities with a cross-xiang nature, and are thus the subjects of our discussion of cross-xiang operation in this book. The cultural differences between Han and these ethnic groups as well as the difference derived thereof in social organizations will, without a doubt, create conflicts that are hard to reconcile, thus giving rise to constraints in cross-xiang operations. These constraints have offset our efforts in developing the economies in these regions and yielded little results in return to our heavy inputs in these regions. Without change in the mentality and formulation and implementation of new policies that are specific to these ethnic groups based on our understanding of traditional social organizations of these ethnic groups, the goal of revitalizing ethnic economies will drift even farther away from us. The mere adoption of economic measures without policies specific to each ethnic region can not change the traditional social structure in each ethnic society, nor will more economic favoritism be turned into productivity in these societies, but simply be consumed and evaporated.

Chapter V   Culture (Section III)

Education, science and technology, ethics and morals, and religious belief fall into the category of spiritual life in ethnic culture. Although they primarily play a role of governing and coordinating ethnic group members' social behaviors and do not directly impact the economy, they have an indirect influence on the economic activities of this ethnic group by impacting human being's social behaviors. Such an indirect impact is covert and long-lasting, and thus can not be offset simply by direct administrative or economic measures but rather by long-term education and lead. A specific cross-xiang operation usually can not last infinitely and must be subject to the restriction of investment capacity and operational objective, therefore is unable to circle around the spiritual life style of the objective parties protractedly. Only by identifying the connecting points and the mutual compatibility that can be taken advantage of on the basis of accepting the objective reality can we turn unfavorable elements into the conditions that meet the operational requirements. This is what we should always remember when dealing with non-economic constraints in the spiritual life style of the objective parties. Our discussion in this chapter is carried out around this main topic that will lead to the suggestions that the key to handling the education of objective parties in cross-xiang operations is to coordinate the relations between the original social education in each ethnic group and schooling; the key to handling the traditional science and technology of the objective parties is to integrate them with the concepts of modern science and technology. To handle the differences in religious beliefs, on the one hand, we must respect and tolerate these differences, and on the other hand, we must search for possible points to break through. As the ethics and morals of the objective parties hardly overlap with requirements in the management of modern enterprises, the key to handling it is to search for the points where the two parties connect with each other, based on which we may plan, manage and operate. All these will be discussed in detail with the support of the analyses of typical cases.

I Keys and Locks in the Promotion of Science and Technology

It is a common knowledge that science and technology is primary productivity, without which the economic development, national revitalization, and societal progress can not be achieved. We noticed in our fieldwork, however, that another common knowledge, i.e., the pertinence in the promotion of science and technology, had long been overlooked. It is a social progress that the science and technology is selectively accepted, digested and absorbed by its receivers. The relationship is like the key to a lock. If the science and technology we promote does not provide the key to the lock – the various needs in ethnic groups, our efforts are likely to miss the targets, causing manpower and material resources to be wasted or even backfire.

To improve the effectiveness of promoting science and technology in ethnic regions, we must first understand the essence of science. Science is the aggregation of all social activities conducted by human beings aimed at understanding the objective world, as well as the cognitive framework, experience and knowledge derived from these activities. Therefore, science is a human cognitive system that is so vast that nobody is able to, or need to completely understand. Each social group can only understand a small part of it that is relevant to itself based on its actual needs. In a broader sense, ethnic groups are social groups made up of individuals, whose need for scientific knowledge is only limited to a small part, but not all the contents of it. It naturally becomes an issue of selection, processing, adjustment, transformation and utilization. This job can only be done by the members within the ethnic group but not by members of any other ethnic groups. The most relevant and prominent issue in cross-xiang operations is how to make use of the science and technology. Our efforts in promoting science and technology will likely be derailed without clarifying on this point. Unfortunately, the "sweeping approach" that characterized our previous mass movements has contaminated our work in scientific and technological promotions that have been undertaken by indiscriminately introducing a specific technology across all regions without taking into account the specific subjects and feasibility, resulting in unexpected and unwanted consequences.

Mashan district in Guizhou province is a highly petrified limestone mountainous region with barely any surface run-off. Over 70% of natural rainfall permeates into the underground cavity, which drains up even the drinking water and turns it into a region of extreme poverty despite a considerably high precipitation in the region, mostly over 1,000 mm per year. Successful technologies and experiences suitable for agricultural plains become much less effective in such a mountainous region. While conducting field surveys in Dalang and Zongdi in Ziyun county, we found out that the corns planted by local farmers varied dramatically, including "*baimaya*" and "*jinhuanghou*" that were introduced in the early stage of the People's Republic of China, hybrid corns that are recently developed, the sticky corns of local breeds, and the corns with abundant cobs, reflecting our efforts in promoting the fine breeds for many years in the past. The varieties that were eliminated by the Hans in the inlands because of variety degeneration have been kept and planted by local ethnic people until today. Although it looks confusing to us, a close analysis helps unveil the reasons. The growing conditions in this region are harsh for any crop we introduce: the extremely thin soil determines that the corn leaves may roll from drought if it does not rain in three consecutive days; nor does it meet the basic requirements for the root system of these fine breeds to fully develop. Consequently, any fine breed we have introduced produced similar results – the corns growing from between rocks in the size of a chicken egg. As these corn seeds are all promoted by the government, they are happily accepted by the local farmers. However, the actual effect from such a promotion is barely satisfactory.

As mentioned earlier in the book, when the technical people from the government took the corn seeds retained by the local farmers and planted them in the better-conditioned *bazi,* the results were unexceptionally good and satisfactory. Ironically, the local farmers would then chase the technical department for the "fine breeds".

Similar problems exist in the work of technological promotion in Mashan in addition to the promotion of fine breeds. To turn the hillside with thin soils into leveled terraces requires such a tremendous labor and material input that was hardly affordable by the locals. However, a uniform instruction is also followed in Mashan, the result of which is not unimaginable. Take the use of fertilizer as another example. As the key factor that hinders the growth of crops is the thin soil and subsequent poor water-retaining capacity instead of low soil fertility, the use of fertilizer will not create the same effect as in the *baqu*. To the contrary, an over-concentration of fertilizer in the crevices of rocks will suffocate the growth of microorganisms in the soil and disturb the mechanism for the soil to regain fertility automatically. As a result, the use of fertilizer keeps increasing and crops will not grow in some regions without fertilizer. Nobody in the technical departments in the government has calculated and verified if the return justifies the input. In the meantime, the local Miaos could do nothing but accept it passively.

It came to our attention when we conducted fieldwork in Mashan of Ziyun county that, instead of increasing with the vast supply of fertilizer, the grain yield had long lingered at a low level. As the local Miao people put it, "Using fertilizer is like smoking opium. You can not quit once you are addicted. We don't even know what to eat if the government stops subsidizing us in the fertilizer."

As mentioned above, the ethnic Miaos are in the Swidden cultivation type of economy. Instead of feeding on a limited variety of grains, they live in a natural environment with many varieties of plants and animals, and harvest whichever is ripe and consume whichever is harvested. Such a way of surviving on different varieties interchangeably makes mature agricultural technologies irrelevant. In comparison, the seemingly primitive technologies and experiences may prove more useful. For example, the amaranthaceous plants, such as *tianxingmi*, are treated as weeds and removed in agricultural regions. They are, however, viewed as precious plants and kept to grow naturally in the cultivated fields: used as vegetables when they are tender, fodder when old; the seeds are eaten as grains and straws used as fuels. In such circumstances, it does more harm than good to use herbicide in these fields.

It is our opinion that such a reality requires that we search for a new key to the lock in the economic development in these regions. We saw in Mashan with our very eyes that local Miaos caught locusts as meals, and collected inchworms and ailanthus to supplement the main dish. Given the local production tradition and dietary habits, why don't we follow the tradition and try to win over their cooperation in opening up a new road to promote science and technology? For instance, why don't we sponsor the research in growing a variety of plants and in finding the best combination among these different varieties? It has long been a tradition among the local people to try to benefit from the best combination of varieties. It is likely to help increase the rate of commercialization if we can find a way of effectively growing a specific variety in a region, as a part of combination of varieties, that is not grown or is not economically viable in other regions. The aforementioned plants such as tianxingmi, myotonin, konjac, or even medicinal materials such as platycodon grandiflorum, asparagus fern, codonopsis pilosula, and Chinese yam can grow normally without largely affecting the yield of corn. Now, these plants that are grown as by-products and consumed as foods, crops or fodders only may produce a much better commercial efficiency if we can bring them to the domestic market as specialty foods or medicinal materials rather than rely on income from corns only. In addition to the domestication of horse, cattle, goat, chicken, dog, and pig, all other local animals that are easily domesticated should be raised as new livestock varieties through scientific research, and introduced into domestic and global markets as specialty animal products. For example, the reckless hunting and killing of wild animals in recent years has infested this region with rats. Other rodents such as rabbits and bamboo rats, like rats, are likely to reproduce massively and grow naturally in this region, and can be turned into regular specialty animal products as long as their population can be controlled within a reasonable size through planned capture by humans. A better economic benefit is foreseeable if they can be domesticated. Another example is the abundant resource of insects. Local Miaos have accumulated a wealth of knowledge and experience in keeping scoliids and feeding on their pupae, making it feasible to fully domesticate scoliids with an input of some efforts in scientific research. Our personal experience in tasting such a uniquely flavored delicacy in the restaurants in Ziyun county convinced us that it would not be problematic for them to enter the domestic specialty food market. It is possible that escargot, which has been introduced from foreign countries into ethnic Han regions, may be introduced to breed in the wild of the Mashan region after some scientific selective breeding. In addition, as many as hundreds of local animals that can feed in natural environments have the potential of contributing to the local economic revival if scientific researches are carried out to make systematic plans on the hunting of these animals, and to develop effective means in the domestication and stocking of them.

Unfortunately, the narrow-minded governmental departments responsible for allocating resources in scientific research are still restrained by the Han mode of agriculture. As a result, they are unable to explore the scientific orientation that suit these regions from a wider angle and a higher platform, but instead, demand that these regions adopt the perceived advanced technologies in the way described by an old proverb: to cut the feet to suit the shoes. Unsurprisingly, whenever we run into such ethnic groups in cross-xiang operations, we can do nothing but complain about their ignorance and backwardness, helplessly allowing the constraint resulting from divergent knowledge and experience from both sides to run its course. The situation could have been better and the constraints could have been turned into favorable forces driving the local economy if we shift our paradigm and introduce and promote science and technology based on the reality in local societies.

The need to open up our mind does not only exist in the production organization and operation but also in the development of natural resources. As a region in severe shortage of water without normal supply of drinking water, Mashan has been announced as a place uninhabitable for modern people and therefore abandoned by our technical staff. The administrative departments, out of anxiety to solve the problem once and for all, have demanded to search for water sources for the people in Mashan. The technical departments, after receiving the task, chose to deploy troops to carry out explorative, designing and planning activities over a massive territory, based on which some water diversion and conservation projects have been constructed. Now, although some of these projects continue to operate to yield some benefits, the majority of them can neither divert nor conserve water due to the lack of water resources. We spotted projects like this in Dalang of Ziyun, Rong village and Youmai in Wangmo. Technical people are often heard saying that karst caves are everywhere in Mashan region, making it difficult to build reservoirs and other water-conservation projects. The completion of water-diversion works does not steady water supply due to extremely lack of surface run-offs in this region. To pump underground water up is too costly and non-economical given the high lift and resulting huge energy consumption. We are not trying to deny that these are true statements. However, we need to point out that these scientific conclusions are drawn from the Han regions, or research orientations in economically developed regions, and may be misleading when applied in other regions. We must point out that there are many places like Mashan in Guizhou: Yaoshan, Lao village in Libo, the steep rocky hills in the middle reaches of Beipan River, some human habitats in the mountainous regions in southern and central Zhenning, or even in places that are close to central cities such as Yanla, Sangushui and Yongke in southwestern Anshun and Duobunong and Geli in Zhenning. If we act upon such a scientific conclusion, we will have to abandon all these places including the mountainous regions in Daloushan of Zunyi region, which is a relatively developed region in economy and education in Guizhou.

Sadly, we are unable to refute such a grim scientific conclusion by proposing better scientific solutions. Our professional interest, however, has exposed us to real examples of how some nations in the world have managed to survive in deserts, which we want to introduce to our readers in the hope that they may provoke some new thoughts in easing the drinking water difficulty in Mashan.

In the Sahara Desert, some minority ethnic groups obtain drinking water by making use of the drastic day and night temperature change. They first build a hollow structure with stones to allow the natural flow of air. The drastic change in temperature condenses the moisture in the air to produce drinking water. Some Indians living in the desert in North America have learned to squeeze the root of Compositae growing in the desert for drinks. The Mexican Indians often drink the juice secreted from the cut on the pedicels of Tequila. Some minority ethnic groups in the south border of the Sahara Desert in Africa squeeze drinks from plants of Cactaceae and Crassulaceae, or even from the abdominal cavity of frogs that are dormant in summer. Although we are not sure whether these practices are copiable in regions like Mashan, they are valuable at least in helping us broaden our vision in scientific researches that now only focus on building water conservancy projects.

We observed an abundance in the variety of plants in Mashan region where cactaceae and crassulaceae plants grow naturally and varieties of crucifer and compositae plants grow in greater number of varieties. Local people often eat radish as a way of quenching thirst at the time of drinking water shortage. If examples like this can be expanded and our scientific researches can be directed to focus on screening the varieties of plants that have higher water content, grow fast and are non-poisonous and sweet-tasting, the success of growing these plants on arid hillsides can be expected. At least they can be an alternative to drinking water for domestic animals if not for people. It is also possible if we can take advantage of the numerous karst caves in Mashan where the natural air ventilation through these caves whose moisture and temperature contrast sharply against those outside the caves has the effect of water condensation. Some ethnic Miaos in Ziyun county are still living in caves and drinking the water condensed in this way. It is promising that the efficiency of water condensation may be improved by certain scientific methods. Although these measures may not completely solve the problem of water shortage, they provide supplementary means for the local people to survive the harsh dry season. The water cellars that we visited in Wachang village in Mashan were supplied solely by the water dripping from the roof top. Our host in Mashan had a water cellar that contained as much as 21 tons of water, enough to survive the dry season. The only problem was poor water quality. In such a circumstance, why can't our technical people conduct research to help improve the water quality and prevent microbial growth by chemical, physical or biological method?

The Dong forest plantation is another area in urgent need of scientific development. The forestry research in China largely follows the research mechanism in the West that prioritizes its research projects on mechanization of forestry operation, and intensive management in the prevention and treatment of plant diseases and insect pests as well as the prevention of natural disasters in the forests. With regards to the cultivation of varieties of trees, the research has been focused primarily on developing the varieties suitable for cold temperate zones. In reality, the forestry plantations in the Dong region are mostly on the hillsides where heavy machineries are not operable and the trees planted are vertically distributed and extremely diverse. The largest difference, however, comes from human cultural background. The complex composition of nationalities in the forest plantations in the Dong region makes it hard to follow the practice in the developed countries that are characterized with a highly purified variety of trees and a totally-closed operation. As a result, it is hardly possible for these plantations to copy the forestry technologies prevailing in the Western countries that lead in the forestry science and technology. The forest plantations that produce raw materials for the paper making industry at DuPont, for instance, are fully machinery-operated. Some of the heavy logging machines weigh between one to two hundred tons, and are hardly usable in the forest plantations in the Dong region. The trees in Canadian forestry are predominantly frost-resisting coniferous species that are lower in annual yield of timber – only half of that of "eight-year cedars", the fast-growing variety popular in the Dong forest plantations. The vast land in Canada makes the lower yield of timber an ignorable factor. To the contrary, the smaller per capita forest area in the Dong forestry plantations determines that consideration of and research on how to increase the yield of timber a must. In a nutshell, the forestry plantations in the Dong region are unique in natural background, operational tradition and human cultural background. Consequently, the forestry-related scientific researches must be carried out by ourselves. To indiscriminately copy the practices in the developed countries is no solution to our problem.

We have come to realize in our fieldwork that many issues in the scientific research and promotion of technologies in this region are blind spots in current forestry research.

First, over-dependence on traditional commercial tree species in the screening, domestication and utilization of natural resources of tree species. Despite the abundant tree types that naturally grow in the Dong forest plantations, the trees shipped out of this region concentrate on a limited varieties such as pine, fir, empress tree, bamboo, ailanthus altissima, and sweetgum. In fact, precious species of trees grow in the forests in southeastern Guizhou, including China fir, a national class one protected tree species; 15 class two protected tree species such as gingko, Fujian cypress, Rhoiptelea chiliantha, Angiospermae, Tetracentron and Tsoongiodendron odorum; 20 class three protected tree species such as Phoebe Zhennan, Fujian Phoebe Zhennan, Pteroceltis tatarinowii, Semiliquidambar cathayensis Chang and Ormosia hosiei.[①] According to the statistics by the forestry research institute, there are as many as 39 fast growing tree species that have economic values in this region. [②] We can see from the comparison that many tree species are under-utilized and there is ample room in this regard for scientific researches to play a role. For example, China has announced to prohibit the use of naphthalene balls as insect-resist agents and requires to replace them with Camphor. Taiwan, the current major producer of Camphor in the world, has depleted in its Camphor resources. As southeastern Guizhou is a place suitable for the growth of Camphor trees, it is a meaningful and promising research topic to find out how to extract Camphor from the Camphor trees selectively bred for the region that has a poor transportation infrastructure.

Second, the research on how to rationalize plant communities and the overall arrangement of fire trenches and transportation lines in the forestry

① Office for Compilation of Annals of Forestry in the Southeast Guizhou Miao and Dong Autonomous Prefecture, comp., *Annals of Forestry in the Southeast Guizhou Miao and Dong Autonomous Prefecture* (China Forestry Publishing House, 1990), 26-33.

② Idem

plantations needs to be deepened. Southeastern Guizhou is a place suitable for the growth of many types of trees, which differ in production conditions, economic values and measures of management and protection. Therefore, it is quite necessary to carry out research on how to rationalize the plant communities in the plantations by manual control to increase economic benefits. In reality, the Dong forestry plantations are traditionally predominated by fir trees without considering how to rationalize plant communities. Scientific researches have long been focused on fir trees but overlooked the rationalization of plant communities.

Traditionally, the forestry plantations in the Dong region are divided along the boundaries determined by the power of extended families in each village but are not well-planned based on the scientific requirements in transportation, fire prevention, forest protection, stocking of plants and animals in the forest. To make up for the sharp decline in the area of forests as a result of failed forestry policies in this region in China, the forestry administrative departments have been busy planting trees within as short a period of time as possible and thus have not put forest planning on the top priority in forestry research. Consequently, a theoretical framework in forestry planning that is specific to southeastern Guizhou has not yet been developed. As the agency that provides guidance for production, the research institute must act immediately to take over the organizing role and start making deployment. Finland in northern Europe has accumulated successful experiences in this regard that may have some value of reference for us. However, they must be digested and absorbed before they can be of use to us. That provides opportunities for the forestry scientific research teams in China to play a significant role.

Third, the research on the stocking of plants and animals in the forest and the protection of rare animals and plants. The forestry plantations in southeastern Guizhou that used to be a paradise for a large number of rare animals have dwindled so sharply that many rare animal species have been put in danger of extinction. Despite the existence of animal-protection laws, the fate of these endangered species will not be changed without the dedication of individuals to specific tasks. The current situation is that the forestry technical departments are emphasizing planting trees but not the comprehensive use of them. Now, it is unfortunate that in the forestry colleges, universities and research institutes in China, there are no departments or standing research organizations exclusively dedicated to forest tourism and hunting. In fact, it is an important way of improving the economic efficiency in the forest region to naturally breed and protect the rare animals, based on which, planned hunting and capturing may be allowed. Slovakia has made great progress in this aspect that can be referenced and introduced by us. It is promising if the forestry research departments in our country intensify the scientific research in this aspect and dedicate to the promotion of new technologies. In addition to the stocking of animals, we must step up our efforts in the research on how to grow rare plants, medicinal herbs and spices in the forests.

Forth, deepen and innovate forestry product processing. It has long been a practice in the forestry plantations in southeastern Guizhou that people emphasize tree planting but overlook processing. As a result, the forestry products in this region have long remained as primary commodities and have not been upgraded to higher levels. We have easily given up on the privilege of product processing, which does not help increase the economic efficiency. So far, the machines used in forestry product processing in southeastern Guizhou are mostly standardized and are thus not suitable for the production conditions in this region. We still have a lot to do to digest and absorb the technologies. Therefore, it remains a long-term goal for the technical people to build an industrial system specifically for the forestry product processing in southeastern Guizhou.

As a layperson, our above comments and suggestions may sound like teaching fish to swim. However, we are sure they are not too distant away from the truth if they can provoke some fresh ideas in the localization and nationalization of scientific research and promotion of technical results in the forests in southeastern Guizhou. On top of natural science, the research in forestry social science and promotion of social science knowledge must be intensified. Here, we only bring up the issue of cost structure and pricing of forestry products. Due to the fact that the sale of agricultural and forestry products was under the state monopoly for a long period in the past and product prices were under state control, it has remained an unanswered question among economists in China how to set price for the labor input by the forestry farmers, and has become an issue of great significance and urgency in economics research while China is undergoing a transformation into a socialist market economy.

Currently, our economic administrative departments are speechless to the complaints by the forestry farmers about the unreasonable price of timber. The unreasonably low price may eventually hurt the enthusiasm of these farmers and lead to the dire consequence of a gloomy forestry if a solution can not be found through systematic economics research.

Blind spots in scientific research and promotion of new technologies also exist in the vast Buyi regions in Guizhou province, which requires immediate adjustment in order to meet the need of economic development in Buyi regions. The rice cultivation in the Buyi regions in Guizhou province is unique despite some similarities to that in the Han regions. Some rare species of rice that grow in the Buyi regions, although lower in yield, have demonstrated irreplaceable superiority in quality. Now our technical departments, out of the propensity of putting quantity at top priority, are doing everything they can to promote hybrid rice. The damage is often concealed when the market of grain is not fully open. Once the control on the grain price is completely lifted, these high-quality species of rice will outcompete the hybrid rice in selling price, from several to more than ten times of the price of hybrid rice for each jin (half a kilogram) and thus producing considerable economic values. In addition, these highly specialized species of rice are precious gene resources from a scientific research perspective, and will have unfathomable scientific value if they are used as parent in breeding. We are fully aware that any scientific research activity is in essence a social activity. Under a planned economy, it was inevitable that scientific research and promotion of new technologies were suppressed as such research activities must be subject to the constraints of social conditions. At the time when China is transitioning into a socialist market economy, scientific research and promotion of technologies in this aspect are pushed to the front in the social development. To win the right of subsistence and the right to speak, technical departments must, instead of waiting for orders from upper-level authorities, take initiatives to undertake such research projects and make necessary efforts in promoting technologies.

Similar situations are seen in ethnic groups other than Buyi and beyond the species of rice: the red and fragrant sticky rice of ethnic Dong, fragrant pigs in the Miao region, Yaoshan chicken of ethnic Bunuzhi Yao, Guanling cattle of Buyi and Miao, Guoxia horses that are almost extinct, pigs used in making cured meat in Weining county, and sticky buckwheat of ethnic Yi are a few examples. They await rescue, selective breeding, optimization and promotion by the scientific research departments. Failure to do so will hinder the economic development in ethnic minority regions and prevent the ethnic groups from establishing a unique status in domestic and international market. Without the successful migration from one-way cross-xiang operations to multi-way operations, the ethnic minority groups may miss the opportunity of economic takeoff as the constraints associated with the promotion of scientific research caused by one-way cross-xiang operations may not be removed effectively.

Cross-xiang economic activities inevitably concern the introduction of technologies, the success of which depends on scientific research and promotion of technologies. As most of the historic development activities in ethnic minority groups in Guizhou took the form of "one-way" cross-xiang operations, the elimination, selection, introduction and promotion of technological achievements were, in most cases, carried out under the guidance of ethnic Han's intrinsic cognitive framework and were thus impertinent and unrealistic. The execution of these technologies was constrained by the natural environment on the one hand, and by the digestion and absorption in the technological promotion on the other hand. Consequently, the technologies introduced were hard to become efficient in the "multi-way" cross-xiang activities. It was often the case that technologies were introduced in history through civilian channels and became successful for unexpected and abnormal reasons, rather than initiated by the people who led the development efforts. These people, who were constrained by "one-way" cross-xiang operations, were often unable to see the real difficulties in the new technologies, let alone to find the way of overcoming these difficulties.

A few crops in the history of development in Guizhou, such as potato, corn, tobacco and sweet potato, were introduced through civilian channels. The most successful example in the introduction of new species that was exclusively undertaken by the operator was the introduction of the Chinese tusser into the Zunyi region. ① Today, if we can target the introduction of new technologies into the ethnic minority regions at bi-way or even multi-way cross-xiang operations, the digestion and absorption of these

① Zhen Zheng (Qing Dynasty), *Zunyi Fu Annals • Farming and Sericulture*, in the collection of Guizhou Provincial Library, woodblock print technologies will have a better chance of success. We hereby bring forth some of our thoughts on possible technological introduction projects based on our field surveys and analyses for reference.

The Buyi people who live in the middle and lower reaches of Beipan River are traditionally in the type of agricultural economy. They primarily cultivate rice fields in *bazi.* This region does not have ideal conditions for wood gathering and shipping as in the Dong regions, and the soils by the river are too thin for growing commercial forests as in the Dong regions, making it hard to have a forestry-grain mixed economic structure. Subsequently, the use of land resources has concentrated on the operation of commercial forestry products. The hillside land resources in this region, similar to that in the ethnic Dong regions, are not fully privatized but are owned by extended families or villages. In other words, the hillside land resources tend to be utilized for commercial forestry production, but are not yet fully capitalized so far. Subject to the effect of foehn wind, the whether in this region is mild and dry in winter and hot and humid in summer, and is very similar to the Mediterranean climate. Such a climate is good for the growth of tung trees. The high-yield of well-known Liuma tung oil is, to a large extent, attributable to such a unique natural climate. Nowadays, inadequate budget has forced the meteorological departments in Guizhou Province to place most of its meteorological stations in the county center that has some distance away from the Beipan river valley, while there are only a few rainfall recording spots affiliated to hydrometric stations scatter in the valleys of Beipan River and its tributaries. As a result, we have not accumulated enough data for the regional small climate in Beipan River valley. We made the above conclusion indirectly based on the distribution of drought-enduring plant communities of Cactaceae and Crassulaceae and historic records from a limited number of hydrological rainfall recording stations. Our surveys reveal that the traditional economic life of Buyi people in this region has the following characteristics: First, the Buyi people were good businessmen in history. Second, their ability in processing commercial crops has reached a certain level, the most representative of which is the extraction of tung oil and the making of brown sugar.

Based on the above analyses, we propose three options for the region to choose from when introducing new crops and planning on economic structure.

First, deep processing of economic forestry products and fiber plants (paper making and textile). The introduction of these technology projects will benefit from a solid cultural and natural foundation and will not encounter much resistance from local Buyi people. They will help regulate the fluctuation in the domestic price of economic forestry products, stabilize the price of economic forestry products in the Buyi region, and ensure a steady income for the ethnic Buyi people. These projects, once introduced and put into operation, will make products that do not require massive transportation and thus are easily accessible to domestic and international markets, given the current poor infrastructure in this region. The difficulty is that the research on the deep processing of tung oil, the major economic forestry product, is inadequate and has not achieved major breakthroughs in the use of tung oil other than as coating. Only a limited number of factories in China are still using tung oil as raw material to make plastics, but the high cost makes it hard to compete with the plastic industry built on the foundation of petroleum if we can not breakthrough in the quality of plastics.

Pollution is the biggest obstacle to run a paper making operation in this region. Located in the upstream of Guangdong and Guangxi, the Beipan River valley may bring disasters to the developed regions in these two provinces once large-scale pollutions occur. One factor, though, may prove to be favorable. In the period of seasonal foehn wind, the river valley has a high evaporation capacity. Therefore, is it possible to recycle the alkali liquor contained in the wastewater from papermaking operations by natural evaporation? Once a breakthrough in this technology is achieved, and given the abundant energy supply and vast raw material bases, the middle and lower reaches of Beipan River may emerge to be a new paper-making center.

Second, make good use of the Mediterranean climate in the region. We may consider introducing to the local Buyi people the commercial crops that grow well in the Mediterranean climate, such as olives from Italy, oil palms from Yugoslavia and Bulgaria, roses from Bulgaria and Turkey, and grapes used in wine-brewing in France. These plants heavily rely on manual work and skills in planting and processing that the local Buyi people are fully capable of doing, and the involvement of large industrial equipment is minimal. For example, olive oil press is exactly the same as oil pressed from local oil camellia, which often goes through the procedure of melting and baking, grinding, boiling, and skimming. The extraction of rose oil is done in a similar way as the extraction of ginger oil in the region. Products made from these commercial plants are high in value and small in size that takes little transportation capacity, and more promising in the international market. Besides, these plants don't take up the cultivated lands and are thus easier to integrate into the prevailing mode of economy of the ethnic Buyi people.

Some natural conditions in the region favor the production and processing of these products. Natural karst caves that are seen all across the region, for example, can be turned into wine cellars as long as the control technology is made available. Another example is the liquor with low alcoholic content that is popular among locals and thus has a huge market potential. However, the introduction and growth of the crops used as raw materials for liquor is not easy in this region due to the extreme shortage in scientific materials and data accumulated specifically for this region and inadequate investment in scientific research and promotion of technologies.

Third, introduce from tropical and subtropical regions into this region spice crops, crops used as raw materials for food additives, and for natural detergent; optimize camphor raw material plants that are original in the region. The scientific research and promotion of technologies in this aspect may release huge economic potential. Now, the demand for natural spice, pigment, detergent and antiseptic substance in domestic and international market is increasing. Although these useful substances don't require complicated technology to abstract, they offer high added values without taking much transportation capacity, and are therefore a good choice for the Buyi people. Also, the planting and processing of these crops will not disrupt the local production pattern. The difficulty still remains as to how to direct scientific researches to focus on this area.

If we can manage to breakthrough from the science and technology perspective along the above thinking, the introduction and domestication of fine species in particular, the local Buyi economy is hopeful to enter a more optimized "binary mode," i.e., to rely on the agriculture in *bazi* as source of food and hillside commercial agriculture as source of income. In other words, agricultural products produced in *bazi* are mainly for the consumption by local ethnic people while economic crops and their processed products from the hillside mainly target domestic and international market for better economic benefit. Such an optimized structure, if put in place, will minimize the need for large-scale state investment, for integration with modern hi-tech and technology, and will reduce the dependence on infrastructure investment on transportation and energy, thus greatly alleviate the constraints caused by inability to integrate in cross-xiang operations. In addition, as these projects have roots and favorable growth environment in the traditional Buyi culture, there will not be grave constraints in terms of digestion and absorption by the ethnic Buyi group. We are able to better serve the economic development in the ethnic regions and enhance the efficiency in cross-xiang operations if our scientific research and promotion of technologies are carried out by following such a thinking.

The research on the hillside production of crops in ethnic Miao and Yao regions is heavily influenced by the agricultural mode of ethnic Han regions, which has caused many disastrous consequences: the cost of production has risen instead of dropped; the products are not unique and thus uncompetitive; the spatial restriction (see next chapter for details) has added to the cost in entrance to domestic and international markets. The poverty-relief efforts in these regions have not yielded expected results. To the contrary, situations in some regions have worsened. The information available to us reveals that scientific researches in foreign countries have drawn conclusions in two aspects that may have some value of reference to us.

The first is the research on dry-land agriculture. The research carried out by foreign countries on agriculture in deserts and semi-arid regions has focused on sand-stabilization technology and selective breeding of drought-enduring species. The mountainous regions inhabited by ethnic Miao group in Guizhou do not have the problem of sand stabilization or the issue of reducing crop evaporation. However, they are faced with two grave issues: First, thin soils and poor water conservancy ability, and the resulting irregular occurrence of drought. Second, some of these regions are subject to seasonal drought in varied degree that are related to the foehn activities occurring in a small region, the worst being Yaoshan and part of Mashan. In terms of the first scenario, the soil surface covering technology used by foreign countries can be referenced with the following technical difficulties. These regions are in low altitude and the cycle of drought is irregular and unpredictable; consequently, wild weeds are a big threat. To remove weeds by manpower is labor-intensive and to remove by herbicide is costly. Three research approaches may be referenced in this regard. First, take advantage of the characteristics in Swidden cultivation and mix the wild plants, especially succulent plants such as crassulaceae, with grains so that they can squeeze the wild grass out. In dry seasons, these plants can cover soil surface to prevent water evaporation in soil surface. At night when temperature gets lower, the succulent leaves of these plants can condense the moisture in the air into water to partially increase the water content in the soil, thus help crops survive the short dry season. The succulent plants can also be made into fodders. Second, intensify the research in the screening and selection of drought-enduring crop species. Experts from other countries have made some progress in this aspect. They have looked beyond the scope of gramineous plants and found some drought-enduring species of grain from Amaranthaceae, Chenopolidaceae, Compositae and Liliaceous plants, which may have some values to be introduced in the region after thorough research. The millet grown by local Miaos and the prosomillet in northern Shaanxi may be considered as well. Third, foreign countries have used the technology of spraying chemical agent and film-forming agent to fight drought. Although these technologies prove to be effective to some extent, they have disadvantages of high cost and heavy pollution. Some minority groups living in the upper reaches of the Yellow River including ethnic Hui, Dongxiang, and Salar, have learned to cover land surface with cobblestones to prevent water evaporation. Compared to the film-forming technologies, it has the benefit of low cost and light pollution, but requires tremendous labor input. How to introduce and make necessary modifications to these drought-prevention technologies and make them more suitable for the mountainous regions of ethnic Miao and Yao is a topic for our scientists and researchers. With regards to the second scenario, we may select and breed short-seasoned species of crops. In dry seasons, we may consider using the cultivated lands as seasonal pastures concurrently to increase the efficiency of land utilization. This has long been practiced by the ethnic Miao and Yao people, based on which further research needs to be carried out to integrate it with modern science and technology to produce social benefit. The investment in the research and promotional activities will be acceptable. Unfortunately, such a research is looked down upon by our scientists and researchers and has not been brought up on the agenda.

Second, intensify the research on the cultivation of steep hillside. The current research by academia in China mainly focuses on agricultural history but overlooks the practical application. In recent years, some people have attempted to further the research on Swidden cultivation and have given some criticism to the traditional research conclusions. However, the research on application is weak due to restrictions by the thinking of “one-way” cross-xiang operation. The most influential perception in the academia still holds that four modernizations can never be realized in such “contemporary primitive agriculture”, namely the Swidden cultivation, and therefore it must be eliminated and replaced with modern agriculture before its economy can take off. Unlike our approach, the research carried out by foreign experts on Latin America follows another perception. They combine agriculture with Swidden cultivation to form a hybrid economy to drive the economic development in the hillside Swidden cultivation nationalities. These researches have led to a fundamental conclusion that such a combination is feasible. Specifically, separate these hillside lands into belt-shaped plots along the contour line and fill the lands between these plots with fast-growing arbors to form arbor belts. These trees help slow down surface runoffs and reduce water and soil loss. Most of the arbor trees are deep-rooted Leguminosae plants that absorb nutrients from deep under the ground surface and store them in their leaves and branches, which are used as fodders or green manure. The feces of cattle that feed on these fodders and the green manure are then returned to the soil to provide necessary nutrients for the growth of crops. Each year, the branches and leaves on the tips of the arbor trees are chopped off to keep them between 1.5 to 3 meters in height, thus ensuring that they don’t block the sunshine and affecting the growth of crops. At time of insufficient fuels, the chopped branches and leaves are burned as fuels and the plant ashes from the burning are retuned back into the soil as fertilizer.

Follow the practice in Swidden cultivation to alternate cultivation and fallow in belt-shaped cultivated lands. The lands are cultivated by slash-and-burn, as in Swidden cultivation, but not by tilling. The seeds are planted by sowing or dibbling. One year after fallow, the lands are also used concurrently as pastures. The soils are fertilized with excrements of animals grazing on the pasture. In addition to the plants that grow wildly on the lands in fallow, we can plant seeds of wild plants and forage artificially to speed up the recovery of soil fertility. The types of crops may be deliberately mixed as is the case in Swidden cultivation.

The introduction of such research accomplishments in China’s academia is confined to the stage of material excerpts. The work on how to apply and promote as well as deepen the research accomplishments has not been put on the agenda. However, based on these material excerpts and the issues identified in our field work, we think that such a research achievement can be promoted in the Swidden cultivation regions of ethnic Miao and Yao groups in Guizhou, or even in Swidden cultivation regions inhabited by many ethnic minority groups in Yunnan. Three points warrant the feasibility of such an approach.

First, these regions are in the traditional Swidden cultivation zone. Such a mode of economy modified from the Swidden cultivation is easily acceptable by these ethnic groups.

Second, such a mode of economy does not require heavy investments and is affordable by local farmers. In the meantime, it relies little on modern chemical fertilizer, pesticide, plastic film, and growth hormone; therefore, there is little barrier for the input of materials in the remote regions inaccessible by public transportation.

Third, such a mode of economy makes it easy for product diversification. It can meet the need of livelihood for the ethnic minority groups in remote and border regions. In addition, it has a minimum requirement on natural conditions and is a best fit for the steep and rocky mountains, mostly the ethnic minority regions along China's border, which are not suitable for normal agricultural operations.

This mode of economy benefits the economic development in the following eight aspects: First, it enables the comprehensive use of lands. Agriculture, animal husbandry, wild animal hunting and plant gathering, firewood supplying can be accomplished in one plot of land. Second, it takes advantage of biological natural circulation to enhance soil fertility and reduce dependence on chemical fertilizer, and minimize pollution from fertilizer, thus maintain a balance in soil capacity and a steady and considerable yield. Third, it benefits the conservation of water and soil in steep hillside and converts steep slopes that can not be used in normal agricultural production to semi-fixed cultivated lands. Fourth, it has obvious advantage in crop protection. To alternate cultivation and fallow on the lands results in the dramatic changes in the types of crops planted each season, making plant diseases and insect pests unlikely to spread over a large area. The leveled belt-shaped forests are natural habitats for the natural enemies of pests that play a role of pest control. Fifth, steady yield of all crops combined at the cost of minimal labor input. In fact, this mode of economy does not require large-scale farmland capital construction. It does not even need to bring complete changes to the natural scenery over a large territory. With less labor input than normal agriculture, farmers are returned with yields that are certainly higher than the maximum yields they can get if they are only engaged in normal agricultural production. Sixth, it plays a role of protecting natural resources and biological diversity. Seventh, it helps direct the ethnic groups in the Swidden cultivation to settle down and thus has administrative values. Eighth, it is compatible with the production of specialty animals and plants, thus helps increase the product commercialization rate in this region. Under proper guidance, a "binary structure" of products may be achieved in this region. While the major type of product is for local consumption, specialty animals and plants, if priced reasonably, are able to access domestic and international markets by small batch.

With regards to this mode of economy, a lot of work needs to be done in the research and promotion of technology. Below are problems in urgent need of solution.

First, develop technologies in the selection of type of trees to be planted in the leveled belt-shaped forests as well as the construction of these forests. Foreign countries often use leguminous plants such as locust and Robinia Idaho. The ethnic Derung group has bred Alnus cremastogyne Burk on the slash-and-burn lands, [①] whose promotion in a larger region remains to be seen. In Guizhou, In addition to Robinia Idaho and the Chinese scholar tree, paper mulberry and mulberry of Moraceae, Castanea mollissima and Rhus chinensis of Fagaceae should be promoted after some research and appraisal.

Second, the structure of types of crops and animals as well as the technology in growing and grazing backup types need to be researched immediately. We can screen the plants and animals that already exist in ethnic minority regions. On the other hand, this mission may be accomplished by domesticating wild plants and animals, such as the scoliid and bamboo rat mentioned earlier. Although the abundance in wild plants and animals makes it easy to find target for the research, the propensity in scientific research in the past has prevented us from doing so. Another approach is by the

① Zhaotao Liang, *Introduction to the Chinese Ethnography* (Yunnan People's Publishing House, 1985), 91.

introduction of external crops.

Third, the research on the social work associated with the transformation of this mode of economy remains heavy, which relates to land ownership, traditional customs and habits of the ethnic minorities as well as relevant state laws and regulations. They await answers from the research in sociology and ethnology.

The above analyses reveal many problems in the scientific research and promotion of technologies, which have hindered the economic development in ethnic minority regions. For many years in the past, our scientific research and promotion of technologies have been influenced and diverted by the thinking of "one-way" cross-xiang operations and thus have left many blind spots. We have not broken away from the restraints of agricultural economy in the selection of research topic, identification of research goals and composition of research teams. In the meantime, we have over-estimated the value of modern technologies and industrial products, and have not given necessary consideration to the current cultural development and economic conditions in each ethnic group in Guizhou. To solve the problem, we must keep in mind the actual need in "multi-way" cross-xiang operations, broaden our thinking, and re-appraise the value of production experience gained by ethnic minority people. Only by making such adjustment can our scientific research and promotion of technologies fully benefit the ethnic economic development.

II Ethnic Education and the Economy: An Interactive Relationship

It has long been debated in the academic community over which comes first in the relationship between ethnic education and economic development. Some people believe that education costs money and that demand can not be met by only relying on state appropriation. Compulsory education will never be achieved in ethnic minority regions without first developing the economy in ethnic regions that can provide sizeable investment in education. Others believe that the backward economy in ethnic regions is a result of poor education and critical shortage of talents. Compulsory education will be illusionary if we don't first put intensive efforts in education to build a talent pool for the economic development. It seems that the opinions are polarizing but they are in essence identical in that both base their arguments on the premise of state budgetary appropriation. People who prioritize economic development ask for state funds for developing production while those who emphasize education are eyeing state funds for promoting education. The conflict between the two would have been solved if the country had enough money for both economic development and ethnic education. In case that fiscal appropriation is not enough, the situation becomes a person whose right hand vies with his left hand for the limited amount of money. It does not make any difference whether the money is spent on the left or the right hand. Same is true between education and economy. Neither education nor economy will be successful in such a situation. The debate has given rise to some compromising proposals. Some suggest, for instance, that education and economy be equally developed while funds for education be fully guaranteed. There are many similar proposals that are in essence trying to strike a balance between the investment in education and that in economy, both coming from state fiscal appropriation. In recent years, we have launched the "Hope Project", which relies on donations from developed regions to accumulate funds in support of the development of ethnic education. Admittedly, the "Hope Project" has indeed played a supporting role to the ethnic education in Guizhou Province and has been rewarded by good social benefit, especially in establishing closer ties between ethnic regions and developed regions. However, anyone who can make meticulous calculation of the gap in fiscal appropriation in ethnic education is able to tell that the "Hope Project" can only be a supplementary measure and can not be used to provide all support to the entire ethnic education. Another channel of collecting educational funds is in the form of educational surcharge based on the state taxation reform. It is a way of collecting educational funds from the entire society and is now implemented across the entire country. In addition, each ethnic region has some unique way of accumulating money for educational purposes. It is clear to us without having to undergo field surveys but simply by logical predication that all the measures combined are not sufficient to completely solve the problem. The surcharges are levied by a certain percentage of the tax collected according to the previous tax system. The developed regions are big contributors of tax money, as a result, are sources of large sum of educational surcharge. In comparison, the ethnic regions in Guizhou lag behind in economy and thus can generate meager tax revenue. Consequently, the collectible educational surcharge is pitifully small. However, the uniform educational system across the country determines that the educational costs can not be too different across regions. Due to historical reasons, developed regions have solid educational foundation and thus the thirst for educational investment does not seem obvious. The ethnic regions in Guizhou Province, however, have a much weaker educational foundation and are extremely thirsty for fiscal investment. Subsidies to education by the same method are enough for the developed regions but are merely a drop in the bucket for the educational administrative organs in ethnic regions in Guizhou. Other than these, we have no better way of raising funds for ethnic education. Now the issue goes back to the starting point: to extend hands for budgetary money from the Central government. The result is obvious.

From another perspective, it becomes easy for us to realize that the relationship between ethnic education and economic development can be harmonious and mutually dependent, and the development of one does not have to come at the cost of the other. Although this relationship varies from region to region, and from nationality to nationality, it has not been substantially affected and impacted by how we label them. The different viewpoints mentioned above are misleading presentations of facts as a result of the forced uniformity in the educational system across the country that has concealed these differences. To further clarify on the relationship between ethnic education and economic development in minority regions in Guizhou, we must set foot on reality to closely study the real relationship between the two in these regions.

Ziyun and Wangmo are two impoverished autonomous counties, on which our fieldwork focused. Each has an annual fiscal revenue in recent years of around six to seven million yuan, and each has a total number of three to four thousand teachers, which translates into a total of seven to eight million yuan in teacher's salary a year if calculated at 2,000 yuan per head on average (about 160 yuan on monthly basis). It is apparent by such simple estimation that the total fiscal revenue generated in the entire county in a year is not enough to cover teacher's salaries, let alone any surplus to spend on other things. Without fiscal subsidy from the state, even the administrative departments at all levels in these counties that are responsible for collecting educational funds can not make ends meet. The economic capability in these counties and how much can be contributed to education are clear and undeniable facts, which always constrains the educational development in these counties no matter how the facts are worded and presented differently.

The compulsory education by the state standard costs a certain amount of money, without which, it is only achievable on paper by fraudulent actions. In our surveys in these counties, we were stunned by the run-down facility in educational infrastructure, discontent and anger voiced by the primary-level teachers especially those paid by local people for delayed payment of salary. We saw with our very eyes a huge number of children of school age who were deprived of education or dropped out of school, and piles of applications filed by the teachers who were teaching in ethnic minority regions for transferring out of these regions. Each government official in charge of education in these regions was well aware of such a situation, yet the reports submitted were all made in full compliance with the requirements by upper-level educational departments. Here, we don't feel necessary to dig how these reports were put together, but the most urgent issue is how to fill the gap between the need in educational funding and actual capacity.

We have never been optimistic because the way to fill such a gap is not in sight now, nor will it be in the next 30 – 50 years if we continue down the current path. To completely solve this problem requires that we accept the reality and abandon the traditional thinking of educational development by a uniform measure and mode, and take the approach of selecting the way of education that best fits the actuality of each ethnic group in different regions.

We have discussed in previous chapters that the types and modes of economic life differ dramatically among different ethnic groups in Guizhou, and people from different ethnic groups have divergent understanding and perception on education. The education talked about by our education administrative department refers to the education in schools, which is funded by the state and attended by students sent over by their parents. We have to keep in mind that another form of social education exists in ethnic regions: children are educated by the people from older or same generations to acquire abilities to survive in the society. This form of education, regardless of official recognition or funding, will continue existing and being effective as it fits and is mutually dependent on the local economic life. It is made possible fully by local economic activities, creates talent pools to support these activities, and goes hand in hand with local economic life. In contrast, the former form of education has been struggling in ethnic regions simply because it is not embedded in the economic life of the ethnic minority but comes down to how much surplus from the economy in developed regions can be allocated by the state to these regions. In fact, all the hot topics discussed in the ethnic education such as insufficient funds, unstable teaching staff, backward teaching facility and equipment, and unsatisfactory teaching quality are in essence an issue of funding from state fiscal budget. In other words, it is an issue of whether the developed regions can provide enough funding for the regular compulsory education in all ethnic regions. It is not about whether the gap exists but about how big it is. Although the problem is seen in ethnic regions, it is not caused by ethnic regions but by developed regions. It is half solved if the state can provide enough funding for operating schools by national standards. To the contrary, the gap will never been bridged without adequate state funding for the schools that are run by following national standards. As a result, education administrative departments at all levels can only do what they are capable of doing with what they have in hand, and to make up things that they are not capable of doing to avoid being accountable.

Every ethnic minority intellectual who is holding an official position in the government has a clear memory of how he or she came out of the formal school education. Those who received good school education before the founding of the People's Republic of China were funded either by their parents who held high hopes for their children and were willing to spend family fortunes to send their children to foreign schools in the hope that they could be offered governmental positions and rise above their peers or by donations from various charities, or as a result of forced concession made by the National Government. The intellectuals who grew up in the initial phase of the People's Republic of China were, without exception, fully funded by the people's government, which included everything from textbooks, tuitions, foods and lodging. It was not a great barrier in the 1950s as the ethnic minority children who had a chance of being selected and admitted into school were quite limited in number and the state funding was leaning largely toward ethnic education. However, the increasing number of minority people entering the workforce has worsened the situation. Fewer ethnic students can now be funded by the government and the schools in ethnic minority regions especially primary ethnic schools are not able to receive any state funding. Consequently, these schools are funded by local people and teachers can not be given a public servant status. They earn minimum wages, usually 20-30 or 40-50 yuan a month, and are often delayed. We cannot blame them for the attitude of the students in school. Therefore, the gap between the educational target the government hopes to achieve and the ability in state educational funding has been an old and lasting question. As long as we aim at school education and the costs are covered only by state funding, the gap will keep widening with the increasing number of minority students who receive compulsory education, and can never been bridged. .

An imagination used to guide the planning on ethnic education. For a long period in the past, we firmly believed that with the realization of ethnic equality and the socialist system, we were able to quickly eradicate the impoverished and backward situation in ethnic minority regions and turn these regions into places like in the central Han regions that could support school education with their own economic capacity. Therefore, the conflict in demand and supply in the ethnic education could be resolved once and for all. However, things did not turn out as simply as we imagined. It is until recently that impoverished counties are all over the place in ethnic regions in Guizhou and poverty-relief still tops our agenda. Our previous prediction has not become reality, indicating that the school education in ethnic regions is doomed to fail. By origin, the difficulties that face today's ethnic education is not a new problem but an old one.

An old problem must be solved by seeking answers from the original root cause, i.e., how to integrate the school education we aim at with the social education that already exists in each ethnic region. A better integration means that the social education in ethnic regions may be fully utilized and the local economy is developed well enough to provide ample support to school education; consequently, the reliance of school education on government fiscal revenue can be lifted to a certain extent. The better the integration, the less the reliance on the state and the more relieved the difficulties facing the school education in ethnic minority regions. To achieve such a goal, the ethnic education must be integrated in and be handled by following the principle of cross-xiang operations. Such an approach will not be compatible with the current one unless a change in perception occurs. Based on materials we collected in fieldwork and by referencing statements made by relevant experts and scholars, we will discuss the contents of such an incompatibility below.

Let's first look at the issue of teacher. According to our educational system, teacher's wages are paid in cash by the government. It will not be a problem of course if the country can afford to pay all its teachers. If the six-year compulsory education is implemented in all ethnic minority regions as is a nation-wide standard, about two million ethnic students out of all children of school age in Guizhou will be put in school, which produces the need of 50 thousand teachers based on the 1:40 teach-student ratio and translates into a total expenditure of 100 million in teacher's wage on an average of two thousand yuan per head per annum. It is a number arrived at by factoring in the minimum teacher's wage, and yet it is a mission impossible at least in the near future. The greatest difficulty comes from ethnic minority regions in Guizhou Province, the settlement of ethnic people in particular, that are still in a self-sufficient natural economy, or even in a production-food economy, i.e., local production for local consumption, and have little or no relationship with currency. In a few regions, people don't conduct any cash transaction other than in purchasing iron farm tools. They paid all local taxes in kind. Even if the government can send teachers to school, the locals can not collect enough cash to support these teachers. If we change the perspective and allow local ethnic people to fund these teachers with materials, such as timber, grain, and cattle etc., it may offer a feasible solution to the problem. We saw how schools were run in Huamigu village of Qinglong county. Students turned in 15 jin of corns and one chicken each year. A school was run in this way by a Miao veteran and his wife in their home. New problems arose after the school was open. The first was teacher's qualification. Neither of them graduated from a teacher's training school and was thus not qualified for a formal teaching position. To become a qualified and government-registered teacher requires passage of all qualification exams and the availability of formal headcount. Secondly, how to acquire the teaching equipment? Textbooks and stationeries were paid out of the ethnic expenses in cash by the county ethnic affairs committee, which apparently could not afford more such schools. Thirdly, how to get the recognition from the educational administrative department? There is no readily available answer in the regulations of the educational administrative departments on what kind of certificate the students who graduate from such schools would get. These schools would not last long if the above three questions could not be solved. Now, the nature of the issue has changed: the locals are able to set up schools but they are not able to get our recognition, while the schools we plan to set up can not be fully funded by us and the locals can not afford them either. The problem remains.

We've found out from our surveys that it is very common that local ethnic people paid teachers in kind, which was acceptable to a majority of local people. For example, when teachers in Wangmo county were delayed in salary payment, many teachers who were not on official government headcount subsisted on donations from local people. However, it only works for teachers who come from the same village or who have family in the same region. For the teachers who are trained at different kinds of schools run by the government, especially those who came from outside the region, they arrange their life by the Han standard and culture. Even if they are willing to make sacrifice, how will their family members react to such a decision? In what kind of culture will their children grow up and leave this region? All these questions are beyond the scope of the educational administrative departments.

In a nutshell, in order to make local ethnic people provide funding for the teachers of the schools recognized by us, we must break the rules in current educational regulations with regards to teacher qualification, norms in teaching management or even teacher's individual life, and construct new standards based on the cultural life of each ethnic group. In other words, the educational system that is universally implemented across the country must be modified to suit the current social condition of each ethnic group.

Now let's take a look at what is in the teachers' mind. In today's educational system, teachers are trained by normal schools of each level that are planned and constructed following the ethnic Han mode. To receive education in these schools, students must think and live by the Han standard. Even minority students wish to set up a family in the city, live on monthly wages, and receive awards from the government if they work hard and have some achievements. To ask them to settle in ethnic minority regions means that they must abandon all their wishes and live a life that they have never imagined to live before. They may be forced by administrative orders to spend some time in ethnic regions, but they will always be an outsider in the local ethnic life. Physically living in ethnic regions does not keep their mind away from the Han cultural life in the city.

All the primary schools in ethnic settlements we visited kept changing teachers. Gangwumucheng Primary School in Guanling county had once made notable progress in teaching but now only has one teacher to stay. He is from the local region and his wife is a peasant. His home is inside the school. Although they also yearn for the life in the city, they can not leave. All other teachers who had taught in the school, over 20 in total, have been transferred out, some of them have not even showed up in the school before taking positions in other places even though they were assigned to work here after graduating from Zhenning Normal School. In exceptional cases, even transfer procedures were completed by administrative officials on behalf of the transferred teachers.

Among the teachers in Ziyun, Zhenning and Wangmo counties who once taught in schools in ethnic regions and received our interviews, some of them were transferred to the county center, or at least to the schools closer to the county center. They told us that they were counting days when teaching in schools of ethnic regions. Nothing in their life, from basic livelihood necessities, culture and entertainment, to normal social interactions, could meet their basic requirement. Although they were there to teach, they spent much more time in taking care of their daily life than on teaching-related matters. Every day, they wished to be transferred out and were counting the days. We spotted hundreds of applications filed by teachers for job transfer at the Education Bureau in Ziyun county. More than 80% of teachers who took official teacher headcounts in the ethnic regions in the county, namely those who were eligible for applying for job transfer, were busy with this matter. How can we expect a stable and high quality teaching staff under such a circumstance? Dalang village in Ziyun county is located in a heavily petrified mountainous region in Mashan, and is well known throughout the county for its utter poverty. Although the local government had amassed all its resources to construct a good primary school by local standards, no formal teacher was willing to come here to teach. All the teachers in the school grew up and were trained locally, and were thus locally paid due to the difficulty for them to be turned into a formal teacher headcount. Any teacher who graduated from a normal school outside the region could easily become a candidate for the principal as long as he/she worked here dutifully for two years.

An ethnic Han teacher who graduated from Zhenning Normal School has been teaching here for a few years and, needless to say, has become the actual principal of the school. It is surprising and commendable that he has made up his mind to give up on the life in cities and willingly become a member of the local Miao people by marrying an indigenous girl. His proposal was declined by the parents of the girl for a simple reason: the Han teacher should never leave Dalang. It is not difficult to tell that such a condition reflects, in essence, the issue of accepting a heterogeneous culture, namely to turn him into a real Miao. Such a request that looks easy to satisfy is in fact extremely difficult to fulfill as it signals the abandonment of entire life style that his entire school education has instilled into him. Neither can it be, from any perspective, openly discussed as it is impossible for any law in China to regulate the issue of accepting a heterogeneous culture by contract. Problems like this reveal a severe crack in the educational system currently in place in China: our teachers are trained by following the Han mode of culture while ethnic education puts up a requirement for teachers to live in practice by the rules of another culture. Such a cultural conflict fundamentally contributes to the instable teaching staff in these regions.

Solutions are available but are, like the issue of teacher's wage, sure to shake the fundamental issue of a universally implemented educational system across the country. For example, we may ask that ethnic teachers to "go back to where they come from", which solves the problem of incompatibility between teacher's life and the local society as long as the prospective ethnic teachers don't break their promise and insist to stay in the city. To make it happen, two premises must be addressed. First, we must admit that the Han culture is not necessarily the only mode of culture in school education, thus keeping these ethnic students respectful for and confident in their own culture and willing to dedicate their entire life to their ethnicity. Second, we must find points for these returning students to survive in schools and to make the locals accept them, follow their lead and offer them the social status they deserve. Third, we must ensure that the schools they run be accepted not only by us but by local people who are willing to provide support to them. The success of the above three points is also preconditioned on a diversion from the current educational system. We must keep in mind that parents send their children to school eventually for the purpose of making a living. Young people in ethnic settlements in Guizhou don't rely on school education to get jobs or make a living unless it is for working in Han regions as government officials. To ensure that these ethnic students are able to come out and go back and worrilessly teach in school, we must align schools in ethnic regions with the employment and subsistence of ethnic young people. Only by doing so can we find points for school education to grow and win the social status for the returning teachers to have a foothold. All these are not compatible with current educational system and are way beyond the ability of the educational administrative departments. Without the removal of this difficulty, the Han teachers wouldn't feel worry-free in teaching in these schools. Even the ethnic teachers would eye for the cities in the Han regions. They stay only because they have nowhere to go. It is apparent that teachers in such a mentality are not able to provide high quality educational services. In this sense, to run ethnic education successfully requires us to acknowledge that the entire education in China must contain the equal treatment of education of different cultural contents. Ethnic education demands, in essence, diversified modes of education that sharply oppose the educational system implemented universally across the country.

Now let's talk about the teacher's quality. With an educational system currently in place that must be inflexibly implemented, the requirements on teacher's quality are also inflexible with no room for exceptions. Teacher's quality is determined by the diplomatic certificates they receive and confirmed by all kinds of exams. The whole system is implemented by the Han standard. Intellectuals who grow up in their own cultural context, if failing to pass any of these indicators, will score zero in the evaluation of teacher's quality.

In southeast Guizhou, we have broadcasted in ethnic language, tested printing reading materials in ethnic written language or even launched massive anti-illiteracy campaign. Such measures have helped counties such as Huangping and Shibing lower their illiteracy rate to near zero. However, how should the quality of these people who are engaged in these educational activities be measured remains a question. In ethnic Han regions, a TV announcer must at least graduate from a technical secondary school if not from colleges or universities. An editor or reviewer of articles must have at least a graduation certificate from a junior college if not a normal college or university, and anyone who is able to participate in anti-illiteracy campaigns must at least graduate from a secondary normal school. These ethnic people who have worked hard in reducing illiteracy rate in their own ethnic group, if unable to reach a certain level in mastering Han culture, would be viewed as unqualified. This is true in reality. Without a certificate in Han language, the people mentioned above who have worked on ethnic language-related missions would not be assigned a salaried job, and would not be guaranteed a permanent job but always be part-timers. They can only live on allowances that almost all come from ethnic expenses and hardly have anything to do with educational appropriation.

Facing such a dilemma, any ethnic educator who has grown up in his own ethnic culture would do anything to obtain a diploma in the Han language. If this trend continues, who are willing to work on the ethnic language? If no one works on the education in ethnic language, how can we popularize the culture critically needed in the ethnic economic life? This is the fundamental reason why ethnic language education has been shelved in counties such as Shibing, Huangping and Songtao after they made the achievement of illiterate-free counties.

In summary, to keep ethnic teachers who engage in ethnic education hopeful, we must certify their level of knowledge and capacity, which requires that we bring the indicators from heterogeneous nationalities into the certifying process. Any knowledge that is accepted by the ethnic people must be included in the certifying system even though it is not based on the Han culture. To do so, the current certifying system indiscriminately applied across the country must be reformed. However, such a task is not commissioned to any education administrative agency in this country so far. In Guizhou Province, no agency or individual from the Provincial Education Commission and County Education Bureau is authorized to provide certification on the qualification of ethnic language teachers, nor are they able to seek corresponding treatment by virtue of such certification, if any. Understandably, ethnic language teachers were thus viewed valueless and abandoned after being used in attaining the honor of illiterate-free county.

More complicated issues follow. In addition to ethnic language education, how should the grades in the subjects that are taught in ethnic languages such as math, physics, biology and chemistry be converted? How should the qualification of teachers in these subjects be converted? Keep in mind that Yan Fu, who was the first one to introduce the theory of evolution into China, should be equivalent by current standard to a member of Chinese Academy of Sciences. By comparison, for any ethnic intellectual who is able to translate middle school textbooks into ethnic languages that can be used in the teaching, can we offer him/her a title of professor by our standard of qualification certification? If possible, ethnic teachers would be willing to work hard to improve their quality without us racking our brains to acknowledge that indirectly. Of course, it means there will be more than one set of indicators to measure teacher's qualification.

We've found out in our fieldwork that many ethnic teachers are enthusiastic about improving their quality and have managed to reach quite a considerably high level. Yang Tongsheng, a teacher at the Second Middle School in Shicheng County, translated all the texts in ancient Chinese into the Miao language, in which he taught with an acclaimed effect. Put aside the quality of his translation, the work itself and the result alone would have won him a highest teaching title in middle school. In practice, however, many difficulties prevented this from happening, the most critical of which was that the level of school education he had received in the Han region restrained him and excluded his achievement from current certification indicators of academic and teaching qualification. Subsequently, he was treated no differently from anyone else. If so, who would be willing to do such things and how would ethnic teaching quality be improved? The teacher quality can not be treated with a universal approach. If certified by this indiscriminately universal approach, it would only stifle the development of ethnic knowledge and make it impossible to take root in the school educational system, and thus lose the opportunity of solving the problem of teacher's qualification.

With regards to teaching contents, state-complied textbooks are used across the entire country. These textbooks are in essence compiled by ethnic Han cultural standards without taking into account of the differences in the type and mode of economic life that undeniably exist in ethnic regions in Guizhou Province. These differences inevitably cause needs for knowledge by different degree of urgency, which is not reflected in the state-complied textbooks. The forced use of these textbooks will, without a doubt, be met with difficulties. Some contents in science are never experienced and thus do not have any value of application in these regions. They can only be used as a "knocker on the door" when applying for schools of higher level. English class is an example. The foundation of the structure of knowledge for some disciplines is not in ethnic minority regions but in Han regions. Students who've learned such knowledge will find nowhere to use it unless they enter ethnic Han regions or when advanced technologies from ethnic Han regions are introduced into the ethnic regions. Such knowledge is not necessary if ethnic students choose to stay and conduct local production activities in the ethnic regions. The subjects of Chinese language and history are such examples. To the contrary, the ethnic language, although being used everyday by ethnic students, is not seen anywhere in the state-complied textbooks. Even though ethnic languages are included in the ethnic education, they are never treated by the leaders from educational administrative departments as required courses. To put it in their language: "The ethnic language is a walking stick and we learn it to better learn the Han language", which puts the ethnic language to an inferior position forever. It comes down to the fact that the ethnic language is never an independent course. The contents in urgent need are not incorporated in textbooks but those that are not in need are forced in.

The experience in the Yanbian Korean Autonomous Prefecture offers some values in this aspect. Although the ethnic Korean language is used in teaching, it has not affected the Korean students' language level but surprisingly, pushed it higher than the average level in developed Han regions. It convinces us that once we incorporate the course of ethnic language in the contents of language learning, the ethnic students' language level will be significantly improved. The knowledge to be acquired from natural science courses, such as math, physics, and chemistry, is not only needed by ethnic Hans but also by the ethnic minority groups. Three factors have contributed to lower scores in these subjects by ethnic students than their counterparts in the Han regions: First, as these textbooks are written in ethnic Han language, the less satisfactory level of Han language by these ethnic students has impaired their understanding of these subjects. Second, the integration of academic terms in natural science into local ethnic language as was analyzed earlier when we discussed language issues, which, if not solved completely, will result in many loopholes in these students' knowledge structure even after they graduate from college. Third, nationalization of natural science. As the culture of each ethnic group is exposed to different natural environments from those in the Han regions, they have different needs for natural science, which can not be reflected in the state-compiled textbooks. It forces ethnic minority students to learn things that are quite uncommon in their daily life, while the things that they are very familiar with can not be learned in class. For instance, Dong children before school age have accessed the knowledge about animal and plant that is much more than contained in middle school textbook of biology. When forced to learn things they are not familiar with, their academic performance will surely be affected. Even if they've done a good job in learning these subjects, it can not be utilized in the economic life of their ethnic group. Some ethnic Dong forestry professionals have admitted to us that even they can not directly link the scientific names of some plants to their names in Dong language. How can we expect them to communicate with ethnic Dong people in the forestry development if their knowledge is learnt in this way? Apparently, it is impossible to improve the ethnic group's level of natural science without knowledge nationalization.

In any rate, the contents in school education in ethnic minority regions must not be determined exclusively by the Han culture. Instead, they must be compiled with adequate flexibility to allow adjustment by each ethnic group based on its specific needs. Only by doing so can we ensure that ethnic students learn well and make use of what they learn in class in their production and life. To make it happen, the first thing we need to do is to break the uniformity in textbook usage so that potentials in teaching contents in ethnic minority regions can be further exploited. The learning of foreign language, for instance, is now weighing heavily on English. In fact, it can be much more than that and should by no means be limited to English alone. Ethnic Buyi people in Guizhou, whose mother tongue is understood as much as 60% in Thailand, Laos and Shan State of Burma in Southeast Asia, have the ability of speaking foreign languages as long as light trainings are provided to them. If Thai and Lao are taught as a foreign language instead of English, it will be more practical and students will learn faster, which will greatly benefit the efforts by China in developing the Southeast Asian nations. Mother tongues of other ethnic minority groups are similar to Buyi language to some extent. A majority of our efforts and resources will be wasted if we continue forcing these ethnic students to learn English. Why can not we reform our foreign language education and be more open to other non-English speaking countries.

With regards to the education in natural science-related subjects, countries in the world have been following different modes and chosen teaching contents based on their specific needs. Despite a vast territory and huge differences in natural resources, the state-compiled textbooks in China have focused on heavy industries and put biology in an inferior position. Such an arrangement of teaching contents is disadvantageous to ethnic groups in Guizhou whose thirst for knowledge in biology and natural geography is not quenched by the state-compiled textbooks. Such a dilemma exists in the learning of natural science subjects as well. How can we expect ethnic students to enthusiastically learn natural science subjects if they don't feel the knowledge is needed and beneficial?

Ethnic Huis are good businessmen. They can not take advantage of such an economic strength as the state-compiled textbooks for compulsory education do not have room for any course in business. It is even more difficult for them to explore the trade market in the Arab world by relying on their strengths in traditional culture and religion. Apparently, a state-compiled textbook can not meet the needs in linking the teaching contents to the society of each ethnic group.

Finally, let's look at the issue of teaching system. In China, the teaching system is universally implemented across the country. The arrangement of academic years, division of semesters and the school schedule are all made based on the central cities in ethnic Han regions and thus don't fit the arrangement in production and work schedule in ethnic regions in Guizhou. We only look at how many years an ethnic student has registered in school without worrying about what he has learned. If a student has registered in three years in school, we will acknowledge that he is a third grader regardless if he has learned what a third grader needs to learn. It is, therefore, not uncommon to see that many ethnic students can not converse in Chinese even after they graduate from primary school.

School schedules are often in conflict with local production activities. For example, our summer vacation happens to be a slack farming season and farmers are often busy with farming when students need to be in school. Even for the schools in ethnic regions, they must follow the national rule without any room for flexibility and adjustment. As a result, the actual teaching hours in these schools are often less than 70% of the hours required by the state, to which the educational administrative departments can do nothing to stop it. We have seen many cases in our fieldwork where the result in education is discounted largely due to the incompatibility between our educational system and local societies.

In the region that borders the four counties of Ziyun, Wangmo, Zhenfeng and Zhenning, local fairs open on 12-zodiac-sign basis when schools close on Sundays following the state work schedule. Consequently, the schools in this region must observe the schedules of both the state and the local people. To take a day off work on Sundays is a must for teachers as many of them would need to take this time to visit their families and purchase daily necessities. On the other hand, to take the local fair day off is a must for both the locals as well as teachers as it is the only time for them to buy local necessities such as vegetables. Also, many parents would need their children to attend to matters in the fair on those days. As a result, the number of no-school days in these schools more than doubles those in cities or towns, and therefore, the number of teaching hours in these schools is much lower than those in cities and towns. In addition, ethnic holidays take quite a lot of effective teaching hours if they don't happen to coincide with national holidays. Natural condition is also a constraint. As ethnic residents tend to live in a large dispersed area, schools must start later and end earlier, causing many effective teaching hours to be wasted on the road between school and student's homes. All these factors combine to have significantly reduced effective teaching hours. It is clear that a uniform teaching system has ended up in disparity among regions. Such a system determines that the time of effective education received by students must vary across regions and nationalities. To force a uniform teaching system in remote ethnic minority settlements as in cities and towns only leads to a heavy discount on the contents students learn from schools.

In a nutshell, under a uniform educational system across the country, the school education in ethnic minority regions in Guizhou is essentially an education that is disconnected from the cultural background of each ethnic group. The maintenance of such an education exclusively relies on state appropriation, while ethnic societies are barely capable of providing any support. From the perspective of the teaching result, the basic requirements in compulsory education can not be met and students who've received such education often are not needed in local societies. To solve this problem, the only possible solution is to allow local people to administer the education based on their actual needs and feasibility. Undoubtedly, it requires to break the system that is universally implemented across the country. Whether it is permitted or not is the key to the success of ethnic education.

We are not the first one to propose that ethnic education should not be framed by the uniform school education across China but organized according to the type of economic structure of the culture of each ethnic group. It has already attracted attention from insightful scholars, but not from the educational administrative departments.

In essence, an educational system that is universally implemented across the country evolved from the ancient imperial examinations and for this reason has been questioned by Mr. Tao Xingzhi, a renowned educator from previous generation in China. The power of this system, however, is too big to budge and has therefore lasted till today. A revisit to Mr. Tao's statement about the uniform system seems necessary for us to reflect on its weaknesses.

Mr. Tao said: "Education officials in China like uniformity because it is easy, but reality does not allow them to do so...People are still dreaming to make it work now. (They insist that) Education popularization across the entire country must be done in written language, and that's why we are seeing education of Mongolians be carried out in ethnic Han language and education of Tibetans be carried out in ethnic Han language. It is like expecting the Yellow River to turn clear in one's lifetime. We must now wake up to the fact that the fastest way to popularize modern education is by using the languages people are speaking and characters people are writing in each ethnic group. This way, teachers are easier to find and it saves us a lot of trouble. It also prevents people across different ethnic groups from being suspicious of each other and generates interests within each ethnic group in popularizing education. The progress is soon to be seen. "[①]

What Mr. Tao opposed in this statement is what we are still doing now. The underlying reason, to be frank, is the lingering Han culture-centric mentality, which is intolerable by ethnic equality.

The educational system that is universally implemented across the country restricts the development of school education in ethnic regions as well as the economic development in Guizhou Province. Students coming out of this educational system would forget everything they've learned in school if they can not get a job in ethnic Han regions or be offered a position in local government, let alone make positive contributions to local economic development. However, if we plan the ethnic school education on the ground of the society and culture of this particular region, just as we proposed, we will face other problems where a lot of education administrative officials will, from the Han cultural-centric perspective consciously or unconsciously, raise such questions: Can ethnic people manage their own education given their

① *Selected Works of Tao Xingzhi on Education* (Educational Science Publishing House, 1981), 179-180.

backward society and low quality of people? Can the local economy be developed without the help and support from the Han culture? We need to discuss these questions in the following three aspects: first, the basic understanding of this issue in the academic world across the globe; second, the history in the development of school education; third, the development in ethnic school education since the 20th century.

First, let's look at mother-tongue teaching. China is not the only one that faces such an issue. Instead, there has been consensus among linguists around the world that ethnic school education needs to be planned in mother tongues and modern scientific knowledge needs to be taught in mother tongues. A conclusion was reached as early as 1951 in an expert meeting sponsored by UNESCO that stated "the best language in child education is their mother tongue." In another expert meeting held 30 years later, UNESCO arrived at a unified conclusion on mother-tongue education: "Mother tongues are the best means of education, best tools in cultural inheritance and effective weapons in eliminating illiteracy and ignorance, and in fighting discrimination and poverty." Contrary to the perspective embraced by experts from around the world, academia in China still insists that ethnic language serves only as a "walking stick" for learning the Han language, which is a substantial issue rather than an issue of insufficient understanding. It comes down to the question of whether ethnic language is able to become the tool in understanding and accepting modern science. We don't need to directly answer that question but simply remind the suspicious people of the agonizing history some 100 years ago when the Chinese language was derided by Western powers. Please don't inflict the same humiliation we were through on today's ethnic minority groups.

Quite a number of nations in today's world have realized economic takeoff by virtue of mother-tongue education. As two such examples, Republic of Korea and Thailand were in similar economic situation as China before 1950s, while the economic capacity in Thailand was much lower than the level in China. Now, both are ahead of us in terms of economic capacity and are among the "four little dragons in Asia". Republic of Korea has insisted on Korean-langue education and has ruled out the Chinese language in its education. The rapid economic development in Republic of Korea is an utter denial to the argument that only by education based on the Han culture can we push ethnic minority groups into modernization. In Thailand, the Thai mother tongue, a language that is directly communicable with people who speak the Buyi language in Guizhou Province, has been dominating its national education. If Thailand is able to become one of the "four little dragons", why can't the ethnic Buyi people achieve comparable economic result and realize modernization through an education in Buyi language?

As is universal across all ethnicities, school education is a social phenomenon that did not appear until human society reached a certain level of development. Private schools of Han ethnicity matured at the time of Confucius as a "scholar" class emerged that needed to be trained specifically to prepare them for feudal governmental positions. The Han modern school education originated from the "Westernization Movement" at the end of the 19th century that was aimed at filling the gap between the Han traditional culture and modern application, and training the people that were needed to grasp the natural science introduced from the West. We should keep in mind that the charter for the earliest modern school in China was authorized to become effective by the emperor at the moment. ①

Similarly, the emergence of social classes in foreign countries made the previous social education unfit and gave rise to schools – a social organization specifically developed to train new work force. The recent works by Li Qilong on the educational development in West Germany affirmed this point. ②

Ethnic school education has not yet been developed independently in Guizhou not because these ethnic groups don't need their own education, or they are not able to develop their own education, but simply because social classes in these ethnicities have not been developed to that level, or they have been developed to the level where ethnic education is needed but the "reform and opening-up" policy has not offered enough support. For the former, ethnic Miao group is an example. The Miao people who speak the western Miao dialect have long been in a production-consumption or natural economy with an unconspicuous division of labor in society. Social education is enough for training young workforce. Consequently, social organization, in the form of school, is difficult to be independently developed in such a society. After the founding of the People's Republic of China, the matter of

① Xincheng Shu, comp., *Materials on Modern Educational History in China II* (People's Education Press, 1981), 394-399, 400-410.

② Qilong Li, *Education and Economic Development in West Germany* (People's Education Press, 2nd edition 1981), 4.

establishing ethnic schools would have been brought on the agenda at least in 1960s if we had not messed with political movements everyday but put efforts in deepening the division of labor in the Miao society so that people who were specialized in business, handicraft, ethnic medication or education could have been developed in the societies in these regions, because the new Miao characters were created successfully and people who had been in a profession of non-production-consumption already existed in 1960s. Unfortunately, we have not continued down this path and have ended up in current situation. The ethnic Buyi and Dong groups in Guizhou, however, had similar social classes as ethnic Han group. They set up many private schools and community-based schools that charged no tuition to students by following the school-running practice in Han regions to prepare local people for taking governmental positions outside the region. As ethnic Han people did after the "Hundred Days' Reform", ethnic Buyi and Dong people started building their own foreign-style schools, which, of course, were operated by the Han standard and mode. This was because ethnic equality was not a reality at the moment. Regardless, in many Buyi and Dong schools, people started recording ethnic educational activities in Han characters, suggesting that the enthusiasm and foundation for running ethnic schools were already in place. The situation changed in the late period of the Republic of China. To press for his goal shortened as "theory of evolution" and "theory of great harmony", Yang Sen who headed the administrative government in Guizhou at the moment prohibited by administrative orders ethnic minorities from speaking their own languages or writing their own characters, therefore severely dampening the ethnic minority's enthusiasm in running ethnic schools. Although all ethnic groups were made equal after the founding of the People's Republic of China, a series of political campaigns were launched based on the actual need in the Han regions. As a result, social and economic development in ethnic regions down the original path was discontinued and was veered to become affiliated to the political needs of ethnic Hans, and eventually replaced by the Han culture. It is apparent that the two ethnic groups are fully capable of developing their own school education as long as we abandon the uniform educational system in the country.

Many countries and regions in Asia, Africa and Latin America were colonies of imperial countries before WWII. After they became independent countries following the end of WWII, the issue of national education was naturally put on agenda. In the mean time, the educational system of each colonizing country gradually phased out of the newly established educational system. During this prolonged process, these countries of former colonies developed science and technology and elevated the industrial level by virtue of their own educational system.

Take Southeast Asia as an example. Countries in the Indo-China Peninsula before WWII completely followed the Anglo-French educational system. After gaining independence following the end of WWII, Vietnam purged French influence and started to operate a school education in its own language, developing an integrated educational system that encompassed education from primary schools to universities. Ethnic Chinese in Singapore, a former British colony, began to raise funds to set up Chinese universities after the independence of Singapore. Later, the Chinese language was announced the first national language by administrative orders, thus fully nationalizing its educational system. Thailand, a country that used to rely on Buddhist temples as institutions for compulsory education, gradually opened up schools since the end of WWII, and basically nationalized its educational system by the 1960s. Indonesia followed a similar path. All these countries made progress in economic development at the same time of nationalizing their national educational system. They were in similar situations as ethnic minority groups in China before the nationalization of their educational system. For instance, the ethnic Dai group in Xishuangbanna is similar to Thais. The aboriginals in Shan State of Burma are similar to ethnic Dai in Dehong. What is different is that the ethnic groups in China have not had their own ethnic education, nor has the ethnic economy taken off. Their economic capacity is not only weaker than that in Thailand and Singapore but also weaker than the average level in ethnic Han regions. This proves that without ethnic education, ethnic regions in China are hard to achieve the economic takeoff as the uniform Han culture, if implemented universally across the country, is insufficient to support the massive development in ethnic economy.

While nationalization of education is a must, the goal is not easy to achieve in any ethnic group or nation. Setting the goal is not difficult to be accepted by us emotionally, but more factors need to be considered and more adjustments need to be made before the nationalization of education benefits the economic takeoff of this particular ethnic group or nation. Among the numerous and complex factors, the following demand our special attention.

First, the social education that already exists in a particular ethnic group is one of them. To totally dump it is fast and easy, but in the meantime it removes the social foundation that is valuable for the newly established educational system, and makes it more difficult for the masses in the society to accept it. As the ethnic language in the ethnic Buyi region in Guizhou has not been accepted in the normal school education for a long time in the past, most of Buyi people take a wait-and-see attitude toward the education in Buyi language. However, the "*Lao Mo Gong*" in the Buyi community have shown great interest in the learning of the Buyi language. "Lao Mo Gong" in Ziyun and Wangmo counties once approached Guizhou Minzu College to learn the Buyi language so that they could translate the classics in Buyi into the ethnic language. As these "*Lao Mo Gong*" are highly respected and are viewed as "intellectuals" in the local community, their acts make it easier to include the Buyi language in the local social educational system. Once such a social foundation is put in place, running ethnic school education will be welcomed and fully supported by the local society, thus making it easy to administer school education.

Each ethnic group has its own social educational system. The division of labor and profession among different ethnic societies to varied degrees has simply created different, some favorable and others less favorable, environment for schools to be operated in these regions. The social education in each ethnic society has some values. Taking advantage of these values in current social educational system of each ethnic group will help in the planning of school education. As the publications used during the campaign to wipe out illiteracy with the Miao language in counties in Shibing and Huangping were not aligned with corresponding school educational system, people felt it useless to learn the Miao language; therefore their attitude toward the campaign alternated between enthusiasm and indifference. To the surprise of the people who organized the campaign, ethnic Miao people, without relying on the educational system or waiting for the Miao language to enter ordinary schools, found a place where the Miao language could grow in the social education. They recorded many lyrics in the Miao written langue while singing folk songs in antiphonal style, and accumulated a lot of folk songs and ballads in this way, which helped them win in the antiphonal singing and thus enhanced the local people's enthusiasm in learning the Miao language. Such an experience convinces us that social education of each ethnic group will give birth to school education. How to make use of the social education becomes the key.

Second, the school education must be combined with social and economic activities of the ethnic group so that it directly benefits the social and economic development of this particular ethnic group. By doing so, we don't need to worry that the school education won't develop or local ethnic societies won't be able to support it. Here we will briefly introduce our basic viewpoints in this regard with the school education in the Dong region as an example.

Ethnic Dongs, a farming nationality that is specialized in operating forest plantations, are in an economy characterized as "a combined operation of forests and grains" and "grains as food are for local consumption and forests provide extra source of income", the basic contents of which were explained in the previous chapter. So far, no middle schools or departments in institutions of higher learning have been specifically dedicated to serving the unique form of economy in the ethnic Dong region, let alone in primary education. Given the fact that the ethnic Dongs are a large nationality with more than two million people who spread across 21 counties in 3 provinces, and operate tens of thousands of square kilometers of forest plantations, it is absolutely necessary to set up a school educational system ranging from primary schools to institutions of higher learning specifically for them. Historically, before the founding of the People's Republic of China, the ethnic Dong community already had its own capitalists in forestry, a society that was separated into social classes of mountain owners, property owners and planters, professional worker's groups in operating boats or making rafts with wood logs. They combined to have laid a solid foundation for running schools of vocational education. In the meantime, the Dong society had already had its own schools which were set up for the learning of the Han language to prepare Dong children for taking governmental positions outside the region. With a change in perception in the ethnic society, it is possible to link the teaching contents of these schools to the social and economic activities in the ethnic group.

Ethnic Dong's production experience reveals that they have accumulated the knowledge and created a systematic theory in operating forestry plantations over the many years of production in the past. To set up forestry schools for ethnic Dongs offers a chance for us to summarize these experiences, bring them to the level of modern science and technology and promote them across the entire ethnic group so that they can play a greater role in supporting the economic takeoff in the ethnic group. We have noticed that the United States began to operate forestry plantations in the 1920s, much later than the ethnic Dongs did despite its highly developed economy. It is very unfortunate that many silviculturists in China focus on the United States when talking about forestry plantations but forget that ethnic minorities in China have had a much longer history in forestry plantations. These silviculturists, however, are not to be blamed because the forestry in the Dong regions so far has never been given a status it should have been, nor has it been summarized into systematic theories. A lot of experience and knowledge in Dong's forestry plantations are kept not in the works of silviculturists but in the materials collected from surveys in ethnic regions. It is, however, never too late to begin the work of planning the educational system about ethnic Dong's forestry operation. As long as it is permitted by state polices, and there is room for some flexibility in implementing the uniform educational system, it is both necessary and feasible for each ethnic group to develop its own school education. Like the ethnic Dongs, the Buyi, Yi and Shui peoples in Guizhou may establish their own school educational system based on the need of their own ethnic economy.

Lastly, enough heed must be given to how to integrate the inherent knowledge of each ethnic group with modern scientific knowledge before we can talk about how to effectively operate school education in ethnic regions. The importance of this task has been discussed previously and here we are only addressing the issue of methodology. The system of modern natural science is developed and enriched by the efforts of people from different ethnic groups in the world over a long period of time, and has been accepted and acknowledged by most of them across the world. From an economical perspective, the development of modern school education by each ethnic group is not to independently construct a disciplinary system, but instead, to focus on how to integrate its own ethnic culture with modern science. To do this, the followings must be taken care of.

First, standardize academic terms. This mission can not be accomplished without relying on administrative power to establish the authoritative organization to review and approve academic terms. Such an organization must be associated with local autonomous governments to guarantee its authority.

Second, establish translation agencies and technology introduction agencies. To play a more effective role, these agencies must fully understand the ethnic people that they serve and know what they really need. In the meantime, they must be fully aware of what are available from other places in the world that can be used by this ethnicity to ensure the pertinence and innovativeness in their work of introduction.

Third, China has established a full set of regulations on academic title certification, which should be followed by certifying ethnic minority scholars who grow up in an ethnic culture. However, characteristics of ethnic cultures must be taken into account in such a process to ensure that the real academic level be reflected and the national certification process be aligned with. Such a certification mechanism offers hope to ethnic scholars and enables the development and growth of scientific and technological talent teams in ethnic regions.

We believe that the conflict between school education and ethnic economic development may be resolved as long as ethnic education is developed. It is likely that the situation caused by the uniform educational system is reversed and the ethnic economic development is assisted by school education, which will be welcomed and supported by local ethnic societies, thus alleviates the burden on the country to provide sole funding to school education.

III Invisible Nets

Although it seems that the cultural complexes that are made up of spiritual elements such as ethical perceptions, beliefs and ethnic awareness of an ethnic group do not have a close relationship with the economic activities of this ethnic group, they are an integral and inseparable part of the overall cultural structure. Therefore, the existence of these elements ultimately facilitates the traditional economic structure and its functioning. As cross-xiang economic activities unavoidably deal with new form of economy, introduce new technologies, and build up new interpersonal relationship, the cultural complexes composed of these internal and external elements will resist, restrict or directly conflict with such heterogeneous economic activities. The resulting inharmonious phenomena are almost present everywhere in cross-xiang economic activities, and often do not depend on direct economic interests. Although they don't seem to directly aim at economic activities, they may in fact bring immeasurable losses to these economic activities. To cross-xiang activities, these cultural complexes are like invisible nets - omnipresent but not directly conflicting economically.

The ethnic Miao group that live in western Guizhou Province, as discussed earlier in the book, are in the Swidden cultivation type of economy. The ethic perceptions that exist to maintain such an economic lifestyle show corresponding characteristics: the ethnic Miaos don't have the notion of "parochialism" and are not resistant to migration. They view it a normal act to abandon homeland and build new homes in other places. Constantly craving for and seeking more inhabitable settlements has governed their attitude toward men and things and has controlled their views on right and wrong. For this reason, they don't feel humiliated for not holding on to their homeland. Instead, as the Miao proverb goes that "Every Miao family has as many as one thousand foundations to build home on and ten thousand wells to drink water from", they often brag about feeling at home anywhere they go. Perhaps under such a guidance, the ethnic Miaos have never had the motivation to build heavily fortified and gorgeous villages, but everything seems to be made for temporary use and await being moved at all time. Miao people believe that the world is big enough for them to move around and settle. Such a perception has profoundly influenced Miaos and is constantly reflected in the statements of some administrative officials.

A vice director from the Ethnic Affairs Committee in Guanling county was directly involved in the work to talk the Miao people who had moved out of this region to Baise in Guangxi Province into returning to this county. When interviewed, he said straightforwardly: "I wouldn't have done it if I were not ordered to do so. They lived a better life in Guangxi than in Guanling. To see them being bullied by the people from other ethnic groups after coming back here makes me feel sad." Apparently, he not only fully understood such a pattern of frequent movement but consented to it in heart.

Under the influence of such an ethic perception that does not view migration a forced and painful thing to do, the ethnic Miaos are often reluctant to directly confront other ethnic groups by forming powerful groups. We observed real cases in our fieldwork where the interests of ethnic Miao people were violated. Instead of defending their own interests by risking their lives, or seeking help from laws or governments, these Miao people simply chose to leave this place and easily gave up on the fruits of their hard work.

A member from Zhenning County Political Consultative Conference (CPCC) spent ten years leading ethnic Miaos in planting trees and turning barren mountains into forestry plantations and thus received honorary award from the related governments. However, when they were bullied by other ethnic groups and their plantations were taken by cannibalization, he did not choose to report to the county government to seek legal or administrative protection, but rather led the members of the entire extended family to move to the mountains in Jinggangshan some thousands of miles away where they reclaimed wastelands, planted trees, and cultivated lands to be self-sufficient. Knowing this, a group of government officials led by a deputy county chief went to Jinggangshan to talk them into returning home. For fear of causing a bad political influence, this CPCC member returned to Zhenning with some people. When all this was over, a vice director from the Ethnic Affairs Committee of the county told us: "These Miao people were very welcome and highly spoken of by the local government after they arrived in Jiangxi because they did not ask for aid, fertilizer or pesticide from the state but rather cultivated the wasteland that yielded good crops. They were promoted as good examples among local Han people for being hard-working and self-dependent." In fact, we had been deeply impressed by the tenacious, persistent, and hardworking spirit demonstrated by ethnic Miao people when fighting harsh natural environments. It is because of this that we refuse to accept such a judgment that ethnic Miaos are too timid and lack of courage of confrontation. Their braveness is not toward people but is toward nature. We need to think what we can do for these unsophisticated and peace-loving Miao people? Our investigations in these regions show that most of the places inhabited by ethnic Miaos are steep and rocky mountainous regions where other peoples can not make use of. Where ethnic Miaos can live, other ethnic groups can hardly set foot on. It is often out of slender economic interests that they wantonly bully Miaos. Usually, the lands they seize from ethnic Miao people are quickly abandoned. Judging by the consequence, these are often viewed as minor things by the local administrative governments who are unlikely to intervene unless they extend into other provinces. It is for this reason that we think that simple implementation of "contract with remuneration linked to output" is far from enough. It is necessary to establish a mechanism of permanent usage of land in the regions inhabited by such ethnic groups and to ban any individuals or groups from infringing on these lands so that the idea of settlement can be placed inside the mind of ethnic Miao people before we can talk about further development. If a uniform policy is implemented as is in the Han regions that only guarantees a stability of land usage for 30 or 50 years, it in essence will have a consequence of discouraging Miao people from settling down. If the use of land remains unchanged for extra-long time that is consistent with administrative division of the ethnic autonomous township, and don't be afraid that the territory of a township is too small, it only helps establish the idea of settlement among ethnic Miao people, which offers footholds for further development activities. Such a proposal, however, differs significantly from the current practice of "abolishing districts and combining townships". Regardless, it should be acceptable to us to implement special policies over specific ethnic groups in specific regions if we truly stick to the principle of approaching specific issues on a case-by-case basis.

Unlike ethnic Miaos, in the Buyi ethics, homeland is highly valued, from which people are always reluctant to migrate. They view village, rice field and water source as fundamentals for subsistence and never would want to yield an inch of land or even a tiny bit of self-interests, which make them similar to ethnic Hans and Dongs. Dominated by such a perspective, ethnic Buyi people value their self-interests and the ownership of lands and always act accordingly without thinking much about whether their actions are allowed or supported by governing policies. When conducting field surveys at Mashan township in Wangmo county, we came across one thing that seemed inexplicable to outsiders. A local Miao resident decided to follow his mother's will and bury her in a cave far from the cultivated lands nearby. His decision was strongly opposed by his Buyi neighbors who tried to stop the use of this cave as a graveyard by threatening to kill themselves under the excuse that this mountain was once owned by his family before the founding of the People's Republic of China even though it has since not been occupied or used by anyone. Luckily, the township government intervened to rule according to relevant policies that the use of the cave as a graveyard did not affect production nor harmed anyone as it was not contracted or owned by anyone. The matter was thus brought to an end by the local government denouncing the actions of the Buyi family involved as groundless and unreasonable.

The conclusion of the specific case does not solve all the hidden but similar troubles. Historically, the ethnic Miao people migrated from place to place. The fact that they must have lived in a much wider and larger territory than other ethnic groups can be verified by early tombs of Miao that are seen across all villages. However, ethnic Miaos don't value the ownership of lands. It is even more difficult for them to receive titles to the lands from the government. By contrast, once a Buyi village was built, it often remained unchanged for hundreds of years. It was not difficult for the Buyi people to acquire titles to all the lands nearby by the collusion of the local government. In a culture that values homeland and averts migration, such an act of willful monopolization in land ownership is echoed and supported by all the people in the ethnic Buyi group. The political reforms that have taken place after the founding of the People's Republic of China only touch specific matters or things but have not shaken up the ethics embedded deeply at the bottom of the heart, which may surface at any time in the form of land disputes. Without a fundamental solution, the mere implementation of the "output-related contract system" is not able to eliminate such disputes that are given rise to by divergent ethics.

Based on the culture that values homeland and averts migration, Buyi villages may last hundreds of years, which is the source to another characteristic in Buyi ethics, i.e., they treat people who are inside or outside the group differently. They tend to shy away from gaining profit from the people who are inside their circle and attach great importance to invest in interpersonal relationship, while not willing to yield even a tiny bit of interests to others, sometimes even unscrupulously as shown in exceptional cases. Such an ethic has resulted in very complicated constraints in cross-xiang operations. On the one hand, it hinders the overall development in the Buyi region as the behavior of the Buyi people is more influenced by the power of individual villages. A government official at Sanglang township in Wangmo county repelled the officials from a Miao background or even those people who came from other Buyi families. Such a behavioral pattern has largely weakened the overall economic strength of the Buyi group and dampened its competitiveness in domestic markets. On the other hand, as people put the interests of individual family or village above those of the entire ethnic group, it has significantly restricted their vision in economic activities. People tend to focus exclusively on their own village and would rather get rich or become poor together, which makes it difficult for the Buyi people to grow healthily within its ethnic group by relying on the collective power and the advantage of their ethnicity.

It was mentioned in many ancient literatures that ethnic Buyi people were good businessmen. We have further realized with the knowledge of such an ethic that ethnic Buyi people are good businessmen only when they deal with people from other ethnic groups or other Buyi families, and are only in the activities of reselling what they have purchased from others, rather than in the participation of market competition on the foundation of the industries that already exist within the ethnic group. As a result, these commercial activities are conducted on such a fragile ground that it is difficult to accumulate capital for the long time in the past. Any profits gained from these activities are quickly spent to build and maintain the interpersonal relationship in the village of extended families.

The perception that values homeland and averts migration also results in the inclination among ethnic Buyi people to look down upon non-farming work. A strong familial bond has traditionally given them a full sense of security, but has also resulted in insufficient risk awareness. They tend to think that farming is the most stable, reliable and noble work, all other types of work are looked down upon in the Buyi society. Commercial activities are viewed as individual conducts and not as work. Such an ethic is reflected especially in their unwillingness to offer labor service in exchange for money. They are extremely reluctant to go out and get paid jobs or even hired by factories or mining enterprises as long as they have things to eat, wear and use at home.

To aid impoverished counties such as Wangmo, the state government has replaced the outright monetary grant with employment opportunities. While such a measure is very welcome among the ethnic Miao people who view the opportunities a normal means of subsistence, the Buyi people disregard it as they think it humiliating to offer labor service in exchange for salary. As an example, the state-invested highway connecting Zhexiang township and Wangmo county was constructed by attempting to pay the locals in exchange for their labor work. Surprisingly, nobody in nearby Buyi village would want to take the job even when salary was offered, the progress of the construction was thus delayed. Finally, ethnic Miaos who lived near the border of

Wangmo and Ziyun had to be hired to do the digging while the nearby Buyi people leisurely watched on. Due to the existence of such an ethic perception, people living in the Buyi settlements don't take working in factories and mining enterprises seriously unless it is a government official position. Seeking employment outside the region does not appeal to them. To change such a perspective, individual efforts are far from enough. They key is how to guide the Buyi people in broadening their horizon to realize that a much bigger market is out there that can provides much greater economic potential than sticking to a few acres of land. It requires that we start with creating a team of business-oriented people in the Buyi region who are not content with switch trade in a restricted area but turn their eyes on the much bigger market for development.

Due to the influence from timber selling into other regions, capital accumulation and risk awareness have become an integral part of the traditional ethics of the ethnic Dong group, which often combine with the familial awareness in land ownership to give rise to a powerful social strength. Such a view of ethics makes it easy for the integration with modern market economy, mentally prepares locals for market competition and lays a solid social foundation for the unification of powers across the entire ethnic group. In the past few years, the seven counties in the east of Southeast Guizhou Autonomous Prefecture were able to unite themselves, without direction or guidance from the government, to conduct cross-provincial border trade activities to strive for the economic benefits for the entire Dong regions. It is worth noting that these private economic activities were not developed in the direction of the administrative structure of the autonomous prefecture. Specifically, they were not centered around the capital of the autonomous prefecture but targeted the Dong regions outside Guizhou Province or central Han regions. As such a direction in economic development is somewhat related to the economic activities of the Dong people, it is thus predictable that the economic development in these Dong regions is likely to lead other ethnic groups in Guizhou Province in both economic potential and growth rate.

On the down side, such an ethical view does not grow on the foundation of individuals but on villages of extended families, which differs from the Han ethics in a market economy that is based on individual operations. As capital was accumulated and risk was shared by the entire family, and it is closely related to the land ownership, economic groups that emerged in such an environment could be gigantic. In history, the fight between different Dong groups in Jinping region for the access to the river portended such a trend of development, which posed challenges to law enforcement for fear of provoking mass revolts. The open plunders of the gold mines in Tianzhu and Jinping counties that have happened in recent years are of a similar nature. The law enforcement has felt difficult to deal with such incidents, but they will only get worse. To bring these incidents under the legal framework does not depend only on the law itself. They must be restrained by the ethnical views of the Dong people. To achieve this, instead of waiting for things to happen to take legal actions, we must guide the direction in the development of Dong ethics. No matter how these ethical views develop in the future, we must not underestimate their existence when we plan cross-xiang operations and economic development in Dong regions because they have profound social foundation and historical original and will have far-reaching impacts on the economic development in the Dong regions.

An important target in the "reform and opening-up" is to establish a socialist market economy, the impacts on which by traditional ethical views in different ethnic groups vary. For the ethnic Miaos in western Guizhou and the Bunuzhi Yaos in southern Guizhou, their commercial activities have long been highly underdeveloped, which are mostly limited to trade in livelihood necessities in nearby local fairs. Traditionally, they viewed doing business a way of seizing other people's money, and therefore business men were looked down upon by them. Ethnic Miaos firmly hold such a view and it has a huge barrier in their efforts to develop a market economy. They, however, view differently on offering labor service in exchange for money from other ethnic groups. They think that a hired laborer is a normal means of subsistence, subsequently, it is normal for ethnic Miaos to work as migrant workers when they are not in busy farming season. In the sugar refineries in Wangmo and Baiceng, most of the workers hired to harvest sugar canes are Miao people. The Miaos in Gangwu of Guanling county take another form of labor. They travel to city centers to practice medicine and sell drugs. The development in the "reform and opening-up" is witnessing an increasing number of Miao people from Gangwu township to seek outside labor work. To put in their own language, they have set foot on all the provinces and districts in China other than Taiwan. Although by the standard of common people, selling drugs is a commercial activity, local Miaos think that compared to drugs that are cheap and are available everywhere in the mountains, practicing medicine is more important. They are offering a service but not reselling products, therefore, practicing medicine in their view is not a business conduct and is thus acceptable while trading is not. How much income has such a practice generated is hard to tell as it is not included in state statistics. Some Miao local doctors we've interviewed have told us frankly that it is easy to make enough money to cover food and lodging by such a trip, and if lucky, they can bring back some extra cash of as much as several thousand yuan. They all think that practicing medicine is a reliable channel of making money as it does not cost any money, nor involve any risks.

The tradition of shying away from talking business does not exist only in the Miao region in the west but also in the Miao settlements in southeast Guizhou. It is extremely rare for the Miao people who live in settlements far away from the transportation lines to do business away from home. In recent years when the southeast costal regions are in urgent need of labors, many Miao people from southeast Guizhou have chosen to come as migrant workers but rarely as businessmen. Migrant workers are viewed as a temporary means of subsistence and they will return home regardless of the result. Due to the restraints by such a traditional perspective, a sizable team of businessmen have not been developed in the Miao regions although the "reform and opening-up" policy has brought big changes to the Miao society. How to grow such a team remains a key topic in the economic development in Miao regions.

Unlike ethnic Miaos, Buyi people have a strong sense of business. As described in their own language, even when they bring a bottle of wine to visit relatives, they would stop to try selling it if it happens to be a market day. Under such an influence, many Buyi people started participating in commercial activities along key transportation lines or by wharfs and ports since the implementation of the "reform and opening-up" policy. Commercial activities grew larger in scale in Zhexiang township of Wangmo county, Huangguoshu township of Zhenning county and Duanqiao township of Guanling county, and contributed significantly to the prosperity of local economy. These activities, however, were never commercial behaviors driven by the business needs in individuals but, as we discussed earlier in the book, were unexceptionally subject to the rules of villages of extended families. They were mainly conducted between different ethnic groups, at least between different extended families. It was very rare that business was conducted between members of the same extended family. Consequently, such commercial activities were characteristic of family group: While in the market, members from the same extended family communicated with each other to push up prices and form price alliances even at the cost of losses by individuals, which often puzzled and annoyed their counterparts from other ethnic groups. Some of the large-scale economic development projects sponsored by Wangmo county government were aborted due to the influence of such ethnical views. The failure in the attempt by Wangmo county to plant winter garlic in Dayi and Kanbian was an example.

The project was led by the government and the money to buy garlic seeds was loaned from the bank by the county ethnic affairs committee. The trouble began when the potential buyer was contacted. As the buyer did not agree to the asking price, all the garlics already loaded on the trucks were unloaded. The Buyi people all demanded a uniform price with no one willing to yield, which failed to make the selling. All the garlics from a good harvest then went bad and were thus dumped. The bank loan has not been repaid until today.

The unique way of doing business in Buyi communities has been detected by the Buyi ethnic government officials. In meetings with directors of ethnic affairs committee in the counties of Southwest Guizhou Autonomous Prefecture, they summarized it in this way: "The Buyi people are extremely inflexible when doing business. Everybody from the same village would ask for the same price as in the central cities without any room for negotiation. Who would want your stuff if they come all the way to here but end up with no profit to make? The Buyi people, on the other hand, are happy to see that people from their own village eat and use anything at will. We are puzzled, as everyone else, by this kind of behavior." Such an ethical view needs to be analyzed dialectically. Just as these Buyi officials said, its weakness is obvious. On the other hand, if the Buyi people are guided to venture out of this region and conduct business activities in a larger arena by relying on the family or village power, the annoyances mentioned above will be turned into powerful economic strength that will enhance the competitiveness and risk tolerance rather than hinder their economic activities. The real obstacle is that the vision of Buyi people is too narrow. They restrict their activities only within the local markets and are reluctant to trade with members from their own extended family. They would rather do business with Han businessmen than have any business interactions with members from their extended family. If this obstacle is removed, Buyi's advantage in commerce will help them rise in the domestic market just as the timber trade in the Dong regions. The key to make this happen is how to guide the Buyi people to proactively engage in cross-xiang operations and put their products into the domestic market.

Among all the ethnic minority groups in Guizhou, ethnic Hui people embrace a business ethic that is easiest to integrate with modern markets. They never look down upon businessmen and view commercial activities normal means of subsistence. Even before the "reform and opening-up" policy was implemented, a considerable percentage of Hui people were engaged in business activities in varied forms. After the "reform and opening-up", the team of businessmen has grown even larger. However, ethnic Hui has not emerged as a nationality by virtue of commerce because their commercial background has been constrained by some other elements mainly in the following three aspects: First, they have not been able to enter the international market but are restricted within a small region. Second, traditionally, the main business of the Hui people was to transship and resell cattle and animal hide and skin from the pastures in northwestern Guizhou. Such a business has lost the source in raw materials as a result of the policy that prioritized grain production over everything else, which crippled the animal husbandry. Third, the commercial channels of the Hui group need to be recovered and improved. In a nutshell, there are many things to do before the potential advantages in Hui's business ethnics can be made to play a greater role in business activities.

The goal of cross-xiang operations is to attract each ethnic group to participate in economic activities that reflect the characteristics of this group so that they can take advantage of their strengths to seize a unique position in these economic activities. Therefore, how ethnic groups view themselves and others will have a direct impact on the participation of these cross-xiang operations. Among all the ethnic minority groups in Guizhou, ethnic Miao group has the largest population and is the one with the most apparent ethnic self-awareness especially in the Miao settlements. In their perceptions, although the ethnic Hans are affluent, their behaviors are not always appropriate. For instance, ethnic Miao would be very surprised and annoyed when they see that in Han families, people from different generations sit together in front of a TV and watch TV programs on love stories. They believe that "looking for partners" or "dating" should happen between young people and must be kept away from their parents or siblings. It is against their ethics if all of them sit together and watch such programs. Under such an influence, ethnic Miaos always feel reluctant to adjust themselves to living in Han regions although they also envy the affluence of these regions. They would always think about going back home if they make enough money in the Han regions.

For similar reasons, if a Miao girl marries a man of Han nationality, most of her fellowmen would think she chooses to marry a man from another ethnicity because nobody in ethnic Miao group wants her. The Miao people who come to live in Han regions tend to feel uneasy and lost but they would feel assured and thus talk and behave in confidence when in their hometown. Anybody from any ethnic background who offends Miao people or hurts their interests will become the target of mass condemnation and assault by all the Miao people.

Unlike the Miaos, the Buyi people not only feel at ease when in their own settlements but more importantly, they are self-conceited and proud. Instead of envying the ethnic Hans who come all the way to Buyi region to make money, they tend to think that these Han people work the dirty and exhausting jobs, are low in social class, and thus their behaviors are not worth following. They feel it easy to handle these Han businessmen because this is "their territory". For the same reason, the Buyi people think that the fact that Miao people leave their native place and travel a long way to work on temporary labor jobs is out of poverty and despair. They themselves, in comparison, live a rich, happy and worry-free life. They don't think that the prosperity in the Han regions is a result of Han's capability but because ethnic Hans have taken a favorable geographical position. They could have made the same achievement as Hans if they were in that position. Therefore, they don't admire some of the practices by the Han people.

It has been long in history that ethnic Dong people have engaged with Hans; consequently, they are confident when dealing with Han people. They are not afraid of hiring Han people. To them, a Han individual is easy to manage. They are just fearful that ethnic Hans may cause trouble to them with the help of administrative powers. Unlike the Buyi group, Dong people are not afraid of venturing in the Han regions and are confident that they can handle the situation no matter how cunning the Han people are. Currently, the Dong youth have been motivated to try their luck in the Han regions despite being discouraged by people of old generations. Basically, ethnic Dong people view the Miao people as hardworking, unsophisticated and trustworthy who live in a less favorable environment. As a result, it is easy for Dong people to form alliances with Miao people when dealing with the Hans. Likewise, Miao people have a considerably high level of trust in Dong group. Of course, people within the ethnic Dong group vary. Those from the tribes in the south are not as close in the relationship with Miaos.

For historical reasons, Buyi people primarily focus their activities in the Han regions in Guangxi and Guangdong. However, most of them don't like the hustle and bustle in central cities and feel more comfortable living a quiet and stable life in their hometown. Consequently, not many ethnic Buyi people have chosen to live in Guangxi and Guangdong. To them, making money in the Han regions is a temporary thing to do mainly for demonstrating their ability. In our field surveys in Wangmo, we came across an interesting thing. A girl from Sichuan who had come to live in Wangmo to do business for many years married a Buyi man who was a government official. By the time we travelled to Wangmo, a tung oil factory that had been contracted to her had made her a lot of money. With such a status in the family, she proposed a few times to bring her husband's sister with her to go to Guangdong to make big money. However, her repeated attempts in persuading the family failed for a simple reason: Girls are not supposed to go out. It brings risk and more importantly, loses value in social status if she keeps showing her face in public. In the regions where the ethnic Miao and Buyi mingle together, they share a common pattern of behavior: Both like to interact with ethnic Hans but are cautious when interacting with each other.

Different ethnic groups demonstrate differing values for engaging in economic activities. Ethnic Miao people participate in business activities mainly for the reason of direct acquisition of consumer products. They don't care much about reserving and accumulating cash, and seldom pay attention to long-term investment. They often think about selling things only when they are in need of money. It is very rare in the Miao group that people choose to do business simply for the sake of making money. Out of the 61 stores in the local market in Leyuan township in Wangmo county, only one is owned by Miao family, all the others are split between ethnic Han and Buyi people. Although the township is fully surrounded by Miao-inhabited mountains, and Miao residents frequent the local market, they come to the market only to sell products that grow on their farms and animal products with very exceptional cases where people come to resell what they have bought from other people. In southeast Guizhou where a large Miao population lives together, people who are in the business of large-scale switch trade are mostly non-Miao people. In the markets in Kaili, most of the Miao people come to sell agricultural products from their farms and the majority of stores are operated by ethnic Han people. Such a phenomenon is directly related, in addition to historical reasons, to the perception that it is more reliable to depend on lands for subsistence. How to foster the risk awareness in ethnic Miao people to guide them to actively participate in business competition becomes a big topic if we want to introduce the market mechanism in the Miao society.

Contrary to the ethnic Miao, the Buyi people are active market participants. They highly value the ability to make money in the market. To lose money in commerce is viewed as incapable. However, the business ethics endorsed by the Buyi group in commercial activities are different from Hans. Instead of solely chasing after individual wealth, they bring human relationship to these activities where they attach great importance to the maintenance of relationship with members of their extended family or businessmen from the same ethnic group, and would not sacrifice harmonious interpersonal relationship for individual interests. Subsequently, many Buyi businessmen would rather travel a long way to other regions so that they can make money from people of other ethnic groups or from other regions. They think that it is straightforward and trouble-free to deal with ethnic Han businessmen. By contrast, many Han businessmen who do business in Buyi regions complain that Buyi people are no good business counterparts who are too inflexible and not easy to deal with.

The business awareness is encouraged and highly spoken of in the Dong community. The youth in ethnic Dong group grow in such an environment and are thus not fearful of competing in the market. Anyone who demonstrates any talent in business is highly commended by seniors in the group. External businessmen usually are welcome in Dong regions. Generally, the scale of trade conducted in local markets in the Dong regions is much larger than that in the Miao regions.

In summary, the impact of ethic views of an ethnic group on economic activities of that ethnical group is not to be ignored, which has pros and cons. The key to success is how to play the strengths to the full and overcome the weaknesses. Individuals who participate in the operations are usually biased when making intuitive judgment on other ethnic groups. Therefore, we must be impartial and understand the overall structure when analyzing factors contributing to successes or causing failures.

IV The Unavoidable Problem

Religious belief is not merely a spiritual activity in individual ideology, but should also be a social activity. No matter what kind of religious belief an individual has, how deep or shallow such a belief is, it impacts not only on the spiritual life of the individual but is also reflected in interpersonal relations and cause social impact, and of course, will play a role in the economic life of the individual. The universality of religious belief makes the impact it has on economic life unavoidable. Needless to say, the impacts of religious viewpoints on economic activities have specific characteristics and must not be equalized with the impacts from other elements. Generally, religious impacts on economic activities are covert. People usually will not bring religious beliefs on the table and debate with others in logic. In the contrary, they will insist on their beliefs via other channels and refuse to accept reasonable decisions.

Religion impacts the economy abruptly, which makes it difficult to prepare for it in advance. To the subjective party in cross-xiang operations, the impacts always come unexpectedly and are hard to coordinate positions of opposite parties by reasoning.

The impacts of religion on economic activities may implicate other matters. Once an economic activity is viewed by local people as conflicting with their religious beliefs, similar activities are affected. For this reason, to remove the disturbances caused by religious beliefs in actual economic activities is much more difficult than the removal of other disturbing factors.

The basic situation of religious beliefs of each ethnic group in Guizhou is the result of development over a long history. For specific ethnic group, it is hard to fully understand it by the summarization of a few simple sentences. Here we can only provide a general explanation as a reference for cross-xiang operators in principle.

In history, ethnic groups of Miao, Buyi, Dong, Yi and Shui in Guizhou all believed in natural religion with slightly varied contents and forms. In Yi and Buyi groups, for instance, people in religion-related careers already emerged and they usually enjoyed a high social status. These ethnic groups would consult "*Bi Mo*" and "*Mo Gong*" on all matters of varying degree of importance before a decision was made. In ethnic Miao groups, however, religious activities were usually hosted by members from within the extended family and dedicated religious people did not emerge in the society.

Different ethnic groups also differ in the scope of religious activities. The religious activities in ethnic Miao communities are mostly carried out around extended families, whose members may join from near or far, turning these activities into mass events. The religious activities of Buyi and Dong, in comparison, are organized by villages and the taboos established by these religious activities must be strictly enforced throughout the entire village, which does not involve as large an area as ethnic Miaos. Religious events of the Miao and Yao can be very frequent, and may happen for reasons such as a sick family member, or something big happens within the family that is in need of a decision. The Buyi and Dong religious events are generally held in slack farming seasons following an established schedule.

Religions from out of the region have some impacts on ethnic groups in Guizhou to a certain degree. The Buddhism and Taoism introduced from the Han cultural regions have impacted almost every ethnic group to varying extent but have not become a religion of the entire ethnic group. Before the eve of the founding of the People's Republic of China, only a very small number of ethnic people, mostly individuals, were converted into Buddhists or Taoists. Although ethnic people were involved in the construction of all the temples in the Ming and Qing dynasties, or participated in religious activities in Guizhou, no theocratic class emerged out of these activities. The founding of the People's Republic of China witnessed the waning of Buddhist or Taoist activities. However, some of the religious rituals from these two religions have infiltrated the religious activities of ethnic groups. For instance, the belief in samsara and reincarnation in the Buddhism is also reflected in the religious activities in Miao, Dong and Buyi groups. The amulets to avoid evil spirit are also reflected in the religion of Yao. In addition, Fengshui and divination that are not related to either Buddhism or Taoism but are widely practiced in the Han regions are very popular in the Buyi and Dong regions. The way of divination that is prevailing in the ethnic Shui people is quite similar to that in the Han region. In the Sidazhai village of Ziyun county, local people have independently developed a full set of divination method, which is similar in contents to that in the Han regions. Certainly, these ethnic people have not accepted the religious thoughts in Buddhism and Taoism in a systematic way but have added the contents characteristic of their own ethnicity with their own interpretation. For example, the "April 8th" Buddhist Congregation in the Han regions is not a religious festival in these ethnic regions any more but is turned into an ordinary ethnic holiday. Some religious rituals practiced in "Yu Lan Hui" by the Buddhists in ethnic Han regions, such as dying and cooking the Umi rice, do not bear any religious significance but serve as a normal food in holidays among Buyi and Miao people. Therefore, ethnic religions should be interpreted, only in the research of origins, as being impacted by the Buddhism or taking some forms in the Buddhism but not as being totally accepted by these ethnic groups.

Western religions began to enter China after the Opium War. Foreign priests had lived in ethnic minority regions and had created religious communities that were quite influential in certain areas, and had exerted considerable impacts on ethnic economy and societies. The spread of Christianity in Shimenkan township of Weining county once had provoked widespread reactions within China and in the world. Quite a considerable percentage of Miao people in this region are still Christians. Catholicism is also influential in this region and some of Miao and Buyi people in Guiyang, Guiding, Anshun and Puding today are Catholics. Foreign missionary activities were also seen in Panghai township in Kaili city before the founding of the People's Republic of China. As a result, some Miao people in this region are now Christians.

The ethnic Hui people who are Islamic are different in religious belief from other nationalities. First, among all the ethnic groups, Islam, unlike other religions that are practiced across different ethnic groups, is practiced only by Hui people. Second, different from the other nationalities, Sunna, the Islamic principles, is observed in Hui's daily life. The ban on eating pork, for example, is strictly enforced by the entire ethnic group. Second, the uniformity in religious belief across the entire Hui group has established a certain corresponding relationship between religious organizations and social organizations in Hui communities. The imams in Islam are highly respected among Hui people. As Guizhou is an inland province, the interactions between Hui people in Guizhou and Islamic people from other countries are not as close as those living in the border regions in China. Neither are they so concentrated as ethnic Hui people in these border regions. However, the coherence between religion and ethnicity demonstrated in Hui communities has produced a close relationship between Hui's economic life and religious belief. When engaging in economic interactions with other ethnic groups, Hui people strictly observe Sunna and seldom conduct activities prohibited by it.

Religious beliefs impact the economic life of all ethnic groups directly or indirectly. The depletion of labor and material in religious activities has apparent restraining effect on the capital accumulation and expansion of investment in production in the ethnic groups concerned. During *Chi Gu Zang*, a way of worshipping ancestors by the Miao people, not only a large number of animals are slaughtered, it also depletes tremendous labor and money. In addition, such religious activities must be prepared for several years in advance, which restricts the economic life of the relevant family members for an extended period of time.

The religious ceremonies of the natural religion practiced by ethnic people in Guizhou are characteristically exclusive. For example, when ethnic Dong and Buyi people are in "*Sao Zhai*"(sweeping the village), nobody from outside the village is allowed to enter the village, as in the family religious ceremonies to avert a misfortune or disaster where outsiders are banned. The normal economic activities among different ethnic groups often are interrupted by unexpected religious activities. To try to make decisions on economic life by way of religious activities may end up in the delay in production and cause heavy losses. Although this has been studied by many people and is discernible to ordinary people, the inertial continuation in religion may become a constraint under such circumstances. It is critical for the operators in cross-xiang activities to be fully aware of the covertness, abruptness and implication of religious impacts.

Many parts in the Buyi and Miao regions in Guizhou are good pastures, where bulls are raised in many families. Such a condition may have been turned into huge production potential and help increase income for the Miao and Buyi people. However, as bulls are widely used as sacrifices in the Miao and Buyi religious events, they seldom enter the market. Even if they are traded in the market, it is only for the purpose of changing hands between the people from the same ethnicity or across different ethnic minorities. They are seldom sold in the Han regions in bulk and exchanged for money to accumulate as capital. Although it seems that these ethnic people, due to lack of commercial awareness, prefer accumulating physical materials than paper money, a further study on the underlying reasons unveils their connection to religious activities, which is often covert.

To foster the "Fengshui" for Buyi villages, "Fengshui Forests" are enclosed where trees are not allowed to be felled even when they are mature, thus causing a big waste of resources. Although it seems that it does not conflict with the normal life in Buyi societies, by a deep analysis of the resource utilization rate, we can not deny the potential negative impacts on the economic life. A strange thing caught our attention in Youmai township of Wangmo county. The trees in the forest in the Yao graveyard were not allowed to be felled, and even the dry branches and fallen leaves were prohibited from being picked and gathered. Nobody from the village was willing to cooperate when trees needed to be felled for the road construction. Eventually people from other ethnic groups had to be summoned to do the job. Such a phenomenon is not uncommon in the ethnic minority regions in Guizhou. Many state infrastructure projects have been delayed when religious taboos are concerned. Although they seem to have been attributable to ethnic customs and perceptions, after all, it comes down to the issue of religious beliefs.

The impacts of religion on economic life sometimes may appear unexpectedly and therefore catch the people involved off guard. In Buyi regions, many disputes have arisen and dragged on from fighting over the "dragon veins" of the house foundations. In an inexplicable lawsuit that we came across in Nongpao village of Liuma in Zhenning county, two Buyi farmers brawled over the "dragon vein" of house foundation. It escalated into physical fighting that injured one man and kept him away from work for a month. The party who caused the injury was ordered to compensate the injured for 800 yuan. We were told that all relatives from both sides were mobilized in an attempt to win the case. As neighbors from the same extended family who were not hostile toward each other, neither side had predicted such a grave consequence before the renovation of the houses. The incident was surprising to both parties involved and the judiciary departments that the case was submitted to. Out of the reason that it was hard to get to the real reason for the dispute and neither side was willing to tell, the case was treated as a regular neighborly dispute and thus hastily closed.

Similar things that happened in state-sponsored construction projects were much more complex and caused much heavier losses. When a road connecting Wangmo county center to Zhexiang that would pass through Linlou village was constructed, after the reconnaissance was completed and the project was about to begin, villagers started to protest and demand that the road be rerouted from passing through the village to crossing the mountain ridge in the back of the village. It turned out that these villagers blew the water outlet of a spring with explosives in order to increase the volume of water gushing out of the spring. Surprisingly, the explosion channeled the water downward into the karst cave and thus caused more severe drinking water shortage. People unanimously agreed that the explosion must have damaged the "dragon vein" and thus triggered the disaster. Subsequently, when the villagers learnt that the road construction would have to use explosives, they feared that the "dragon veins" might have been affected again. Therefore, they insisted that the government revise the plan to reroute the road. As a result, heavy losses were incurred with added costs in reconnaissance, designing and construction. However, it turned out that the villagers were the ones who suffered the most. The re-routed road is so far away from the village that the villagers must carry the products they produced a long way to the roadside to sell, thus causing unnecessary costs in labor. Now, the villagers demand the road be rerouted again to pass through the village only to be rejected because the government does not have such a budget any more.

The constraints of religious belief on economic activities are usually not effective to specific economic project, or a specific phase in an economic activity, but rather on all production phases or even several economic projects concurrently. As a result, operators in cross-xiang economic activities feel lost when dealing with specific issues. When we were conducting surveys in Yaoshan of Lizhi county, we came across an incident that involved the move of an entire village, which frustrated the local administrative government. To solve the water shortage in Yaoshan, the local government built a big water pond in an attempt to provide drinking water for villagers and cattle in a small natural village near Yingpan village. Unfortunately, a little girl who played by the water accidentally fell into the pond and was drowned. The ethnic Yao people from the village concluded by following their religious beliefs that the place had been haunted by evil spirits, and decided, after the religious ceremony to avert the evil spirit, to move. As a result, the water pond that cost the local government a lot to build and the fields that had been cultivated for many years had to be abandoned. The move required that new village be built from scratch and barren lands be reclaimed, which affected the economic life of that village for a number of consecutive years. Even the administrative reporting relationship had to be adjusted. The incident makes it clear that the effect of an isolated event may spread to economic projects and social organizations that seem to be disconnected from each other due to the implication of the effect by religious belief. Under such a circumstance, it is apparently not possible to convince ethnic minority people not to expand those effects to other unrelated matters. Administrative departments have tried in vain to keep things like this from happening. The losses resulted from this are not remediable if the operators in cross-xiang activities do not fully understand or prepare for it. It is our opinion that the best solution is for the doer to undo what has been done, namely to directly impacting the people who are in charge of the religious events and to divert the conclusion they make when hosting ceremonies to avert the evil spirits, so that they won't harm the economic activities while achieving the same result of pacifying all the villagers by other means or forms.

In the Miao settlements in west Guizhou Province, many ancient funeral customs and corresponding religious ceremonies have remained in local funeral activities, such as "second funeral", "xuanguan funeral", "cliff funeral", "cold funeral" as well as tomb sweeping activities participated by all family members in mid-Spring. The religious activities usually do not occur on regular basis but are often related to unexpected incidents such as a dream or frustration in life by the person involved, an epidemic disease or natural disaster. Once a family determines to initiate such religious activities, it usually implicates all the members in the family as well as other families associated by marriage, which will affect the regular economic activities of these families. Some religious activities even require that the entire village sealed from the outside world, thus affecting more people than the ones involved in the activities and causing losses much greater than those directly consumed in the activities.

With regards to the economic loss caused by these religious activities, ethnic Miao people interpret it this way: "These religious activities are planned long ahead of time based on our economic ability. They won't affect our life or production." However, it is not the case in reality. The hosts of these religious activities focus their attention on affirming their social status and gaining corresponding economic income. The people who initiate and sponsor these activities are to seek peace of mind. The participants of these activities, frankly speaking, come for entertainment, or simply for the feast. The three kinds of people who are have different motives and demands would collaborate once unexpected things happen, and would totally forget about their regular production, life and reputation in external economic relations. We run into a few large-scale religious activities in the busy farming seasons in our fieldwork.

The situation in the Miao settlements in southeast Guizhou is similar, only that they implicate administrative government officials and cause even heavier and unfathomable losses. A few years ago when the mother of a government official in Dadi township of Leishan county died, the wizard said after some calculation that the body must remain unburied for seven days and seven nights. It was in the summer farming season where people should be busy with harvesting and planting, the local township government was faced with a general election, and the provincial government was calling on a mass discussion on how to increase income and get rich. Despite all these, a decision was made to make it a huge and grand funeral. All the people related to this official – relatives, friends, subordinates and superiors, immediately stopped what they were doing to gather at the township government. The two meals before the burial ceremony to cover more than three hundred dinner tables alone cost over ten thousand yuan. It was almost impossible to estimate the loss caused to production and work. This was just an example of how unexpected religious activities could cause unfathomable and irremediable losses especially in reputation if economic activities of huge monetary value are involved.

The above analysis makes it clear that religious activities can cause enormous impacts on the economy. We must not, however, arrive at the conclusion that the economic loss can be avoided only by completely eliminating religion. Such a uniform and inflexible approach will not yield the desired result, but in the contrary, will cause more severe consequences. Since religion is an objective and undeniable social phenomenon, we must look for solutions on the precondition of acknowledging its objective existence. The best plan is to bring these religious activities under our control and to make use of them. The second best plan is to avoid severe consequences by proactively guiding these activities after they happen. To directly intervene by wielding administrative power is the worst case scenario, but unfortunately has long been preferred by our administrative officials as it is easy to do without much preparatory work or taking any responsibility for the result. The operators of cross-xiang economic activities, due to the lack of administrative intervention capability, and inability to counteract the strength of the overall ethnic society, may only end up in ruining these economic activities unless the best plan is implemented. To this end, each operator of cross-xiang activities must not only focus on the economic activities themselves but also try to fully and deeply understand the ethnic religions that affect economic activities. More importantly, they must not treat religions from their own perspective, or be governed by individual preferences, but be confident in controlling and utilizing these religious activities, and ensure that they don't conflict with cross-xiang operations in practice.

As a social phenomenon, religions impact the society in many, and sometimes good ways as long as they are brought under control and guidance. By our observation, we may take advantage of religion in the following aspects. First, it is universal. Religious activities may implicate members of every social class and every age group in the societies, thus giving rise to a massive social power and gathering of a vast quantity of materials. Given such a circumstance, these manpower and materials gathered under the name of religion may be utilized by us as long as the related social activities including economic activities are acceptable by these religions.

In the feudal age, it was not uncommon for Buddhist and Taoist temples in the Han regions to run schools that charged no tuitions to students. Religious temple fairs usually had the function of a trade market. Many projects of public interests were made possible by the manpower and materials gathered under religious name. New operating projects may be benefited and promoted by a favorable social environment created by the interpretation of the people of religious background. Quite a number of cases that have produced positive effects have been recorded in the practice of religion among different ethnic groups in Guizhou.

In Shimenkan of Weining, a desolate and remote place, modern schools, hospitals and other public undertakings were established thanks to the spread of Christianity. Priests also help create the written language for local Miao people, guided them in afforestation to change the production environment, which not only positively impacted production, but also brought significant changes to Miao's life style.

In the Dong regions in southeast Guizhou, every village of extended families pays tributes to its own "*Sa Sui*". It seems that this is for the purpose of asking for blessing from *Sa Sui* to protect the entire village. In fact, the ritual ceremony of *Sa Sui* has the effect of coordinating interpersonal relations, reinforcing the rules and customs in the village and directly maintaining and organization production. It proves to be more effective and easier to be accepted by members in the society than direct administrative intervention or direct award and punishment. Temples of Mazu scatter along Qingshui River and Duliu River that are the main waterways for the shipping timbers out of the Dong regions. These temples were originally built by family groups that were involved in the trade of timber to pray to Mazu for the safe journey down the river and successful selling of timbers. Before the founding of the People's Republic of China, these religious places had played a role of balancing these family powers to coordinate and organize the shipping and selling of timbers. When dealing with religious issues in the past, we only emphasized on the superstitious nature of religion but ignored that it was an objective and undeniable social phenomenon, and accused that all religions introduced from foreign countries were aggressive in motivation and consequence. Under such a guideline that was more based on emotions and perceptions rather than practices, we indiscriminately "prohibited" and "destroyed" all religions and be tolerant only when forced to. It hurt people more than it did to the religion itself. As a result, religions practiced at the village level tended to get out of control, which suffocated the positive side of religion, and pushed the negative side further underground and thus more difficult to predict, prevent and deal with.

Second, religions may be practiced across different ethnic groups, therefore, religious groups have an irreplaceable role to play in connecting the economic life across ethnic groups. Religious activities may impact every aspect of the social life of the entire nationality to different extent, which contributes significantly to the exploitation of product markets across different nationalities if properly guided. Each ethnic culture is an integrated social system that can last in a relatively stable condition following its own laws in normal situations. Consequently, the contents of the economic projects that are an advantage in one ethnic group are not easily acceptable in the society of another ethnic group. The communication between heterogeneous ethnic groups may be more effective if a common religion or even a religious ceremony of that religion is used as a medium. Shimenkan of Weining mentioned earlier in the book is well-known among domestic religious organizations. Even those from Europe are aware of the ethnic Miao people due to connections among religious groups.

As discussed earlier in the book, the Miao and Yao people in Guizhou are still in the Swidden cultivation and the lands in these regions are not privatized among individuals. However, the inscriptions on the tablets we found in Yunwu township in Guiding, Gaopo township in Guiyang and Huajiang township in Guanling reveal that privatization of land and fixed operation were first seen in Buddhist temples in these regions. In other words, the land ownership in the Han regions began to grow in these ethnic regions through Buddhist temples. If land relationship was successfully transplanted through the medium of Buddhist temples, we have reason to believe that other economic activities and production relationship can be successfully transplanted in ethnic regions through religious relations. In Guizhou Province, direct connections with foreign countries have not been established. Trade in animal products with Islamic countries such as Iraq must be conducted via the channels of state foreign trade. As foreign importers require that export products must be handled by Muslims and must not be mixed with meat products banned by Islamic taboos, disputes constantly arose. If the Hui religious organizations in Guizhou Province are permitted to build ties directly with these Islamic states, a commercial channel irreplaceable by any government agency may be established to facilitate the foreign trade in Guizhou, and thus prevent disputes from happening. In a nutshell, religion has an irreplaceable value in connecting economies across ethnic groups, and may largely benefit the economic development in ethnic regions if used properly.

Lastly, religion is highly compatible and has strong adaptability to the changes in social life. Fundamentally, it is attributable to the fact that religious beliefs are highly abstract spiritual activities. Religious doctrines may be substantially revised and freshly interpreted at different time and in different regions to adapt to different social backgrounds and changing social life as long as the fundamentals are maintained. We did not fully understand this characteristic and only saw religion as spiritual opium but did not realize that it actively participated in social life and adapted to social background. As the result of historical development, the religion we see today has transformed from its early forms to adjust to the needs of different life. Different ethnic groups in different regions subject to different social backgrounds have revised and interpreted the religious doctrines differently. This is one of the fundamental reasons that we see so many religious sects in today's world. To put it in a more straightforward way, as each religion is separated into many sects, we can always find one that will provide assistance in our mission no matter which ethnic group we face and which geographic environment we are exposed to. Due to the reason that religious doctrines have ample room for interpretation, it can infiltrate in almost everywhere in ethnic regions in Guizhou as long as we don't resort to administrative intervention. This is why each ethnic region in Guizhou Province was subject to religious impacts in varying degrees before the founding of the People's Republic of China. Although significant changes have occurred in the background of economic development in ethnic regions and the goals in our development have changed today, religion can survive in this environment. It brings up two issues: First, how to treat the existence of religion. Second, should we make use of religion?

For the first issue, it must be viewed from a materialistic perspective. Since religion is an objective social existence, we must honestly admit that it is a social phenomenon. Besides, it is explicitly announced in our Constitution that citizens of China have freedom of religion. Although we don't advocate religion or encourage religious beliefs among ethnic people, we must give serious consideration to how to deal with religious organizations under the Constitutional principles once a religion has been practiced by many ethnic people. Specifically we must consider if religious activities will disturb ethnic economic development, and if yes, we need to further consider how to minimize such disturbances. In summary, as religion has been an active social participant, and the economic development is a large scale social activity, we must therefore consider how these two are related and what kind of connection we should have with religions.

About the latter, we think that religion can be used for the fundamental reason that religious doctrines are to a large extent subject to revision. As long as our economic development activities have powerful social vigor, religion will lean toward our preferred direction for the sake of its own survival. The "*Chi Gu Zang*" religious activities in the Miao regions, as described previously, cost a lot live cattle, which does not help accumulate wealth. However, the development of commodity economy in the Miao regions near central cities or transportation lines has brought some changes to such a situation. We have learnt that ethnic Miao people in Xiaba of Guiyang city and Baxiang of Longli county have begun to abandon the practice of using live bulls as sacrifice. The entire religious ceremony remains unchanged with the only exception that bulls as sacrifices are not slaughtered. Instead, a handful of bull hair is cut from the bull and burned in fire to symbolize the slaughter of bulls. This is an indication that religions can be very flexible and adaptive. Of course, such a practice has met with some resistance by local people who said to us in regret: "We are left with the bull horns as souvenirs from our ancestors but we have nothing to pass down to our children." In response, we tried to comfort them by saying: "Your ancestors had bigger pastures and more bulls. Losing one or two bulls did not make a difference. Now we have new forestry plantations and farm lands, the bulls you have are only enough for farming. It is a big waste if they are slaughtered. It is easy if you want to leave something for your children. Since there are many stonemasons among you, simply put up a monument after each sacrificial ceremony and carve a bull horn out of it. You can also carve the names of the people who participated in the ceremony. Isn't it more reliable than trying to memorize all the names of the people in the ceremony as was done by your ancestors?" They were very content with our explanation and said that they would do as we suggested.

We realize from this incident that the vast pastures in the Miao regions in west Guizhou Province are ideal place for raising cattle. In some ethnic townships, the number of bulls owned by local people exceeds one bull per person in average, but they are mainly used in sacrificial ceremonies and as betrothal presents in marriages, thus are hard to become commodities to produce more economic benefits. If we can follow such a practice to convince the people that host religious activities so that they can change the ritual in the sacrificial ceremonies to keep the live cattle and turn them into commodities, it will help local products access the domestic markets. Religious doctrines do not remain eternal and religious rituals are subject to revision. It is possible for us to minimize the negative impacts of religion and enable it to play a bigger role in the economic development in ethnic regions if it is guided properly.

Needless to say, obstacles are ahead of us, which may arise from subjective or objective causes. Subjectively, religious doctrines and ceremonial rituals have strong inertial force and are hard to change within short period of time. We need to be patient in carrying out ideological work and establish close relationship with people of religion to win their trust so that they will be willing to cooperate with us, thus better serving the ethnic economic development. In addition, it is extremely critical for us to broaden the horizon of these people of religion. We are certain that they would accept our suggestions if they see that revisions are made to the same religion in other places and are convinced that our suggestions are for the benefit of local people. They would help us work with local people to make things done by taking advantage of their reputation among local people.

Objectively speaking, our administrative officials have been taking a restrictive stance toward religion. They've always thought that religion is a superstitious activity and must be harmful. They would choose to keep a distance from religion if it can not be fully banned, for fear that they are blamed for encouraging religious activities. Such a simplified understanding and behavior is in essence not a materialist practice. As a social phenomenon that exists naturally, religion has a social foundation that can not be banned by executive orders, nor be avoided. A true materialist must admit its objective existence, try to understand it more profoundly and search for ways of making the best use of the circumstances so that it works to our benefit.

Chapter Six On Background

This chapter focuses on discussing the impacts of the natural conditions in each "*xiang*" on actual efficiency of cross-xiang operations. These natural conditions include those that exist naturally as well as the secondary elements that are shaped by the social culture in each "*xiang*", which demonstrate different levels of stability that are determined by different factors. Both of these natural conditions contain the amount of energy that far exceeds that under the control of cross-xiang operators. Therefore, cross-xiang operators must not try to fight natural backgrounds in cross-xiang operations with their operational capacity. Instead, they must take into account of the pre-existing natural conditions when planning the projects and measures to achieve operational success.

The goal of this chapter is to provide the operators of cross-xiang activities a full set of guiding principles in evaluating the existing natural conditions and determining how to use these conditions, so as to help cross-xiang operators achieve operational targets. It also discusses the spatial distance in cross-xiang operations and its impacts on expanding operational investment, as a reminder to cross-xiang operators of the existence of constraints caused by such a space attenuation, and pay enough attention to such constraints when planning specific cross-xiang operational activities.

I Similarities and Differences in the Background of Cross-xiang Operations: An Overview

All human activities must be carried out in specific natural conditions, which directly determine the effectiveness of economic activities. We must keep in mind, however, that the quality of natural conditions is a result of evaluating how they impact specific economic project in a specific human culture. In other words, a good natural condition is the result of analysis and statistics by the specific social indicators that are made by summarizing and extracting a specific culture. People from different ethnic groups may arrive at different conclusions about the same natural conditions in different economic projects. Therefore, whether a natural condition is favorable or not is relative and specific, and there is no such thing as universal standard across all the ethnic groups on how to measure natural background.

The nature of cross-xiang operations determines that activities across different *xiang* must be carried out in two completely different natural conditions. Any specific cross-xiang economic activity must be carried out by specific operators based on the requirements of the specific ethnic culture. As a result, generally speaking, cross-xiang activities are sure to encounter unfavorable but unavoidable natural conditions. To ensure the success of cross-xiang operations, we must understand the type of natural conditions, the relationship between ethnic culture and natural conditions, and how a difference in natural condition constrains the effectiveness of cross-xiang operations, so that we can provide a set of methods in analyzing and utilizing natural conditions to help the operators turn the negative factors into positive ones and understand and make use of natural conditions at a deeper level.

The natural conditions that human economic activities are exposed to are roughly made up of two parts: pure natural background, and secondary artificial natural background. Pure natural background is the sum of all natural elements that objectively existed before the existence of human economic activities. Secondary artificial natural background is the sum of all man-made objective environments that are a result of human processing and transformation according to specific culture of the pure natural background over a long period of human economic activities. For instance, in natural forests that have never been inhabited by human beings, its climate, landform, vegetation, hydrology, soil, rock and mineral resources are all syntheses of pure natural elements that exist naturally. There are different syntheses in different regions on the surface of the earth. For the need of scientific research, we may classify, analyze and inspect these regions by their different characteristics so that we know and understand them more profoundly. These syntheses of natural conditions are pure natural backgrounds. They don't have the innate characteristics any more after being processed or transformed by mankind, but will demonstrate a series of non-natural characteristics that are made to meet the needs of human economic activities. In a prairie that has been inhabited by nomadic people for some time, roads for pasturing, and signs along the route of pasturing will surely appear. In the meantime, it will be separated into different pasturing areas, the water source will be transformed, and temporary residential settlements will be established. These characteristics are all created by human economic activities and are thus secondary artificial backgrounds. If the same prairie is occupied by a farming nationality, it will, after some time, be turned into farmlands with irrigation and road network. Villages, or even markets, temples and entertainment places will be built on the land. All the plants on the land surface will be treated as weeds and completely exterminated. All wild animals that trample on crops will be wiped out. These landscapes are not natural but the result of human economic activities, the aggregation of which give rise to another type of artificial background. If the same prairie falls into the hand of an industrial nationality, we will see another picture where factories and cities will be built that are packed with water supply and sewerage works, highways, railroads and airports, barely leaving any trace of protogenetic natural elements. They are also the result of human activities and have combined to create another type of secondary natural background.

These environments for human subsistence are shaped by human processing and transformation by virtue of specific cultures. Consequently, they are social products with social attributes. To separate them from the pure natural backgrounds, we hereby name them "living environments". It is self-evident that living environments are specific to nationalities and cultures, therefore they are unique to each specific nationality, and each nationality has a unique living environment. Culturally, living environments are the product as well as an extension of culture. Ultimately, they are a component of culture.

In the first chapter, we pointed out that natural backgrounds are a necessary component of "*xiang*". As cross-xiang operations are characterized with economic activities across different *xiang*, it means that these economic activities must be carried out in more than two different backgrounds. Due to the differing nature of pure natural backgrounds and artificial secondary environments – living environments, they impact cross-xiang operations differently. To facilitate our writing, we will discuss the constraining force of pure natural backgrounds and ethnic living environments on cross-xiang operations.

Human beings, along with human economic activities, began to appear on this planet more than several million years ago. The coexistence of all the nationalities in the world has lasted several hundred or even one thousand years. Each nationality has been shaping and transforming its living environment by virtue of its culture for so many years in the past that there are not many pure natural backgrounds left in the world. However, such pure natural background can be found in the regions where modern technology has not been able to conquer, such as Antarctica, tundra in Arctic Circle, desert in northern Tibet and Sahara. In addition, even in the regions where modern people conduct frequent economic activities, there will be places that are left untouched in the human transformation of natural backgrounds due to different cultural characteristics. Although these untouched places are not completely natural, the change is so small that it would not affect the conclusion of our discussion. Therefore, we may treat these places as pure natural backgrounds. Some of such examples are Leigong Mountain and interior Moon Mountain in Guizhou Province, the steep slope along the deep south and north Pan River valley, and the completely petrified barren mountains in Mashan region. Although these regions are not completely beyond the reach of human activities, the impacts of these activities are so weak that they are almost negligible in our analysis. Subsequently, we think it reasonable to treat these regions as protogenetic natural backgrounds.

The majority of the backgrounds that people face in cross-xiang operations in Guizhou are secondary artificial living environments that differ enormously. As a multi-ethnic region, Guizhou is home to ethnic Han, as well as Miao, Buyi, Dong, Yi, Shui, Tujia, Gelao, Yao and other minority groups. Each ethnic group processes and transforms natural environments by its own traditional culture, thus giving rise to characteristic living environments. Ethnic Buyi group, in many situations for instance, always cultivate large rice fields in the intermontane basins in the valley and build villages along the borders of these intermontane basins, forming residential settlements in the shape of "chained beads" along the river valley. Ethnic Miao group, especially those in west and south Guizhou, often reclaim large dry lands or fallow lands on the mountain slopes while building scattered settlements of villages on the hillsides. These two living environments shaped by two ethnic groups, simply by the appearance, are very different, and have different impacts on the operational efficiency in cross-xiang activities. The same is also true about other ethnic groups and the living environments that they created, which must also be seriously considered and handled when we plan cross-xiang economic activities.

In addition to natural background and living environment, a third background, i.e., spatial background, exits. All human economic activities must bring with them the movement of materials and people across spaces, which requires extra energy. When economic activities are carried out in the same “xiang”, such a movement of materials and people is a normal component of cultural operation and does not need operators to input extra energy. In cross-xiang operations, however, things are different, where the product, material, equipment, power, and people have different useful values or are not directly available in different “xiang”. For the former, relevant products must be moved to another “xiang” to realize their useful values, while in the latter, the materials and people that are needed must be sent over to another “xiang” to ensure the normal operation of economic activities. To put it in another way, sometimes in cross-xiang operations, one-way transportation of materials and people and excessive non-production related transportation are needed on top of the normal exchange of materials and people. The energy consumed in such transportation will undoubtedly be multiplied with the increase in spatial distance across each “xiang” in cross-xiang operations, inevitably resulting in the hike of costs of production and a subsequent decrease of operating efficiency before the related products are put into use. Such a decrease in operating efficiency is called spatial attenuation in cross-xiang operating efficiency and will be covered in detail in the fourth part of this chapter.

In a nutshell, cross-xiang backgrounds in general include three major elements, i.e., natural background, living environment and spatial background. They differ in nature and have different restraining effects on cross-xiang operations, which must be discussed separately to come up with solutions specific to each background. A specific cross-xiang activity will undoubtedly concern the three elements concurrently in the related “xiang”. Which of the three elements will have a more direct and bigger impact on this activity depends on the traditional culture in the relevant “xiang” and is directly related to the characteristics of such project, and must be analyzed specifically.

Natural background is a result of the combined action by natural forces. The natural backgrounds in each “xiang” have mutually constraining relations with the geographic location, landform, ecological community of animals and plants, meteorological condition, and geological conditions. Compared to the enormous energy contained in such mutually constraining force, the energy and lasting duration that each cross-xiang activity is able to mobilize is too limited. Therefore, the capacity in cross-xiang operations must not, in principle, be used in an attempt to directly change the natural background but may only be used in the operation of cross-xiang activities. In other words, to bring fundamental changes to natural backgrounds should not be listed as one of the missions to be accomplished in cross-xiang operations. Instead, we may only discriminately select the natural backgrounds that have the least constraining impacts on cross-xiang operations. As Josue de Castro said in his book *The Geography of Hunger*, it is absolutely possible to grow rice on the top of the Himalayas regardless of costs, but the location of rice fields is fixed and can not be changed by people if costs are factored in.[①] For this reason, any project in cross-xiang economic activities must be determined based on the specific natural background. If ethnic minority regions in Guizhou Province are short of the natural background needed, in principle, the corresponding cross-xiang economic project should not by carried out, unless this project is equipped with special measures to minimize the loss in operating efficiency resulted from an unfavorable natural background. For instance, we should by no means plan to establish rubber plantations in Guizhou, or to introduce Korean pines in the Dong regions where natural background suitable for such projects does not exist. Even though these projects have the potential for generating high profits, they must not be implemented and the advanced technology associated with these projects are not implementable in these regions in Guizhou. The Miao habitats in west Guizhou have a short season of plentiful rainfall, which does not guarantee the water source for the planting of late rice. The temperature drops significantly when the late rice is ripe, making it hard to seed. The efforts of blindly promoting the double cropping rice in these regions ended up in failure, unexceptionally attributable to the constraints by natural backgrounds with least direct relationship with the size of investment by investors or the amount of effort by operators.

Living environments are shaped by specific cultures. As in cross-xiang operations, economic activities are carried out across cultures, they are sure to encounter two or more different living environments. Any specific economic activity, however, has a unique and specific living environment that it suits the best, without which the operating efficiency will decrease accordingly. In the Buyi regions in Guizhou, for instance, the large rice fields make it seem very similar to the living environments in the developed Han regions. A closer look reveals that the differences between these two regions

① (Brazil) Josue de Castro, *The Geography of Hunger* (Sanlian Bookstore, December 1959)

are huge. Half of rice fields in the Buyi regions are terraced fields that mainly rely on natural rainfall instead of irrigation canals for the supply of water, which can not be guaranteed when introducing the improved variety of rice from the Han regions. The problem is especially apparent in the introduction of short-straw varieties. The water stored in the fields must not be too deep in transplanting but it will be short of water after tillering, making the improved varieties of rice from the Han regions unable to yield the expected results. It gives away the underlying reasons why the Buyi people traditionally planted high-straw rice varieties. The resistance met by technical departments when promoting the improved short-straw varieties of rice is not exclusively for the conservativeness of the local people but also for the underlying constraining effect by the living environments shaped by the Buyi culture.

Similar things are also commonly seen in the river valleys of northwest Guizhou Province. Before 1960s, rice was grown for only one season. After the harvest, the rice fields were left unattended for the entire winter and domestic animals were allowed in to feed on these fields. It looked that the cropping index in these regions was low, which seemed extensive from a pure agricultural economic perspective. However, a deeper analysis finds that each Miao, Buyi and Yi household in this region had a much greater number of cattle than the households in pure agricultural regions. In the winter, an ample supply of fodders must be guaranteed for these cattle. If these rice fields were not used as pastures in the winter, the number of cattle raised would not grow. Before the founding of the People's Republic of China, northwest Guizhou was a place that exported a vast number of live cattle, as well as raw hides and bristles, and animal products in this region had a huge economic value. Therefore, the evaluation of economic efficiency in the region of such an extensive cultivation must not be made by only looking at the cropping index but should also taking the income from animal products into account. Once we noticed this, we would soon discover that the pastures and farm lands here were self-looped in structure. People in this region were in an operational mode of seasonal vertical pasturing. In the summer, animals were herded atop the mountains and the river valleys were left to grow rice, while in the winter when the temperature in the mountain dropped and the supply of water was drained, animals were herded back to the river valley. The flocking of a large number of animals in the river valley made the small-season cultivation difficult. To grow small-season rice would largely decrease the grazing capacity of the lands. In 1960s, represented by the slogan of "prioritize grains over everything else", we started promoting small-season cultivation. Although it witnessed some increase in the income from cultivated lands, the gain was more than offset by a sharp drop in the income from animal products. From the perspective of an overall economic efficiency, it did more harm than good. We came across another living environment in this region, i.e., the special living environment where farming was combined with pasturing by the Miao, Buyi and Yi people and the grazing shifted vertically on the mountains with the change in season, which was not like the living environments in the developed Han regions. Therefore, the overall economic efficiency will drop if we force the promotion of any advanced technology from the Han region without taking into account the integral structure of such a living environment. If we blindly copy the successful experience from other ethnic regions to an existing living environment without adequate and proper research, we would jeopardize rather than drive the economic development in this region. Apparently, the existing living environments in the ethnic minority regions in Guizhou are objective facts that are shaped and processed by specific cultures. In situations where economic activities are carried out simply by a good hope and the movement of advanced experience from external regions without being respectful for reality, the existing living environments will become invisible nets that constrain cross-xiang operations.

As the operators and objects in cross-xiang operations are located in different "xiang" inevitably, the movement of materials and people in cross-xiang operations can not be accomplished in the same "xiang". As a result, the movement of materials and people are not equalized in both ways, and thus will cause empty load in one direction, which will increase the percentage in invalid transportation in cross-xiang economic activities, and will increase the product costs and dampen the product compatibility. The increase of costs is directly proportional to the distance between the two parties: the longer the distance, the higher the percentage of invalid transportation, and vice versa. This is another non-economic constraint that should not be overlooked in cross-xiang operations. The decrease in efficiency caused by this kind of non-economic constraint is the spatial efficiency attenuation as aforementioned. It should be brought to the attention of our readers that spatial efficiency attenuation has long been noticed by senior economists. The “differential rent” discussed in Marx’s *The Capital* is in essence one form of spatial efficiency attenuation.

In the early period after the founding of the People’s Republic of China, we planned the domestic economic build-up under such an assumption that the fact that modern commerce and industry in China had leaned toward the coastal region in southeast China was a result of the colonial and semi-colonial rule in the Chinese society, and what we need to do after the founding of new China was to attain the economic balance between the inland and coastal region. To achieve this goal, we deliberately intensified investment in the inland and reduced that in the southeast coastal region. In 1960s, for strategic reasons, we implemented the policy of the “third front movement” and began to make heavy infrastructural investment in the west of China. As this policy was not made, for both the reason and goal, from the perspective of economic benefit, it was not fair to evaluate the result of this policy simply by its economic results. However, as the purpose of this book is to discuss cross-xiang operations and to deal with economic issues especially the aftermath of existing economic facts, and at a time when we are transforming into a socialist market economy, we will discuss cross-xiang operations from an economic perspective only and will not reiterate how successful these policies were in the strategic and political aspect.

Guizhou is located in the under-developed regions in the west of China and is a key province in the “third front movement”. As time passed and situations changed, a look-back at the economic results of the modern enterprises in ethnic minority regions in Guizhou makes it easier to demonstrate the constraining force of spatial efficiency attenuation. These enterprises have been in operation in Guizhou for more than 20 years, but the majority of them have been relying on state subsidies to survive. Although measures to convert military-oriented enterprises to civilian production have been taken in recent years, we have not been able to pull these enterprises out of red. Some of these enterprises are equipped with people and equipment that were taken from similar factories and mines in coastal regions but their operating efficiency has never reached the level in these factories and mines. The situation was caused by many complex reasons, among which, the constraining effects from spatial efficiency attenuation was a major one. It is not what this book is able to do to analyze all the individual enterprises, but to point out the general problem of a low economic efficiency across these enterprises is what we must do by writing this book. We can start by looking at the railroad transportation condition in Guizhou. In 1950s, Guizhou Province began to build four major railways connecting Guizhou with neighboring provinces, which were directly operated by the branch of Guiyang Railway Bureau. Although the total railway mileage operated by the branch of Guiyang Railway Bureau was greater than that operated by the branch of any neighboring province, the passenger and freight transportation volume was lower. Also, the trains always got in with full load of goods but got out empty. One of the major reasons that contributed to such a fact was that all raw materials and equipment needed by these enterprises and livelihood necessities for people working in these modern enterprises mostly came from the central Han regions, and finished products must be shipped back to these regions for sale. Both the start and end point of materials were in the central Han regions, but production was in the remote ethnic minority regions. As the spatial distance across different *xiang* was artificially expanded, the spatial efficiency attenuation effect kicked in and meaninglessly boosted the product costs and thus largely weakened the competitiveness of these enterprises. Such a spatial efficiency attenuation will keep impacting on these enterprises even after they are converted to civilian production. To ensure the vitality in these enterprises, we must take other measures to reduce the rise in costs that is caused in single-direction transportation.

It is apparent that spatial efficiency attenuation effect is a long-term non-economic element that constrains the economic efficiency in modern enterprises that are alone and far into the ethnic minority regions. Unless we put enough efforts in the research of this element and find the best solution, enterprises in similar situations will not be dragged out of the operational inefficiency.

To specific cross-xiang operations, the three major elements that make up of the background in cross-xiang operations are concurrent and mutually restraining. They combine to impact economic activities with the only difference in the level of impact and the form of efficiency attenuation. Therefore, to ensure the success of cross-xiang operations, we must find effective solutions by concurrently taking the three elements into account. It is not enough to focus on one or two elements, or only notice the existence of but overlook the correlation between these elements. To provide systematic measures to help understand the backgrounds in cross-xiang operations, we will discuss in the following sections of this chapter the nature and constraining mechanism of natural background, living environment and spatial background, followed by a comprehensive analysis of how they transform into each other, so as to enable our readers to systematically acquire all the knowledge on the analysis of the backgrounds in cross-xiang operations.

II Natural Backgrounds: Essence and Constraining Mechanism

We made it clear in the previous section that pure natural background contains enormous energy that is not nearly rivaled by the energy under the control of the operators of cross-xiang activities. The only thing that these operators can do when facing the powerful natural backgrounds is to discriminately select the best investment places to carry out operational activities after meticulous investigation and analysis. Two things must be considered when making the selections: First, the pure natural backgrounds in the places of investment. Second, characteristics of the culture that the investors are in. Conditions that are compatible with the above two standards must be selected to serve as the foundation for investment. To achieve this goal, operators must deepen the understanding of the pure natural background in cross-xiang operations to complete the investigation of the following three aspects by taking their own cultural characteristics into account. First, the comprehensive guarantee ability of the targets to be selected must be given enough attention; Second, the ability of the targets to remain continuously stable; Third, to determine the integratability of the pure natural background with the cross-xiang economic activity.

In the same-xiang economic activities in a fully-developed market, the foundation for the survival of enterprises is supported by a stable market. In cross-xiang operations, however, the operators of the investment projects are in a relatively developed social market while the objects that the operations concern are usually in the ethnic minority regions with a less developed market. This is commonly seen in the development activities in ethnic minority regions in Guizhou. The normal operation of an economic activity requires very complex backgrounds, which usually can be provided by the market and may be settled in a uniform currency if the activity is carried out within one *xiang*. In cross-xiang operations, if the investment market is not fully developed, the conditions that are needed for the normal operation of relevant economic projects can only be met by the enterprises themselves through non-economic measures. It requires that when selecting investment places, we must ensure as much as possible that the pure natural backgrounds in these places have the potential comprehensive support ability to satisfy the majority natural conditions needed by this project. The higher the comprehensive support ability, the higher likelihood of a normal operation. We hereby take the example of the sugar cane base for Baiceng Suger Refinery in Zhenfeng county to explain the essence of the comprehensive support ability of the pure natural background as well as the constraining mechanism on the modern manufacturing and mining enterprises.

The climate in Beipan River valley in Zhenfeng county is characterized by scorching heat in the summer and little precipitation in the winter, and is suitable for growing sugar canes and increasing their sugar content. Traditionally, Beipan River valley was home to sugar cane plantations and sugar press mills. Brown sugars made in indigenous methods have been a traditional local product sold to other regions and have been a source of huge economic income for this region. To take advantage of this tradition and enhance the Buyi economy in this region, the government invested to build the first modern sugar refinery in Baiceng, which has begun production and generated tax revenue for the local government after many years of efforts. In this sense, it is successful. However, the cost in this factory has long been higher than that in the factories in Guangdong and Fujian, making the economic efficiency lag behind in a long time. For this reason, the leaders in the factory have repeatedly submitted reports to authorities in the county and prefecture to ask for more investment so that they can expand the factory and increase the productivity.

Our investigation and analysis reveals that the fundamental reason for the costs of this factory to stay at a high level is not the inability of the factory leaders, the technical conditions, or the size of the factory, but rather the natural conditions that the factory is exposed to, especially the natural conditions in its sugar cane base. Such a natural condition can not be changed by expanding investment; therefore, expansion in the size of factory can not fundamentally solve the problem.

Located along the Beipan River valley, the sugar cane fields in the sugar cane base of Baiceng Sugar Refinery is less than 10 kilometers in the widest, and less than 1 kilometer in the narrowest, but more than 80 kilometers in length. Such a huge gap between width and length is not seen in similar sugar refineries in Guangdong and Fujian where sugar cane bases evenly scatter around the refineries, roughly in circles, each having an approximately equal distance from the refinery, and much shorter than that in Baiceng Sugar Refinery. The below simple calculation makes the point clear.

In the costal regions, the sugar cane yield is around 5 tons per mu. On the assumption that the refinery can consume 600 tons each day, this refinery needs a total of 108,000 tons of sugar canes in one season of production. As all the plantations scatter evenly around the refinery roughly in circles, the longest distance between sugar cane base and the refinery is about

$$\sqrt{\frac{180 \times 600}{\pi \times 5 \times 1500}} = 2.14$$

kilometers.

In the Beipan River valley in Zhenfeng, the sugar cane plantations are roughly in two curved lines.

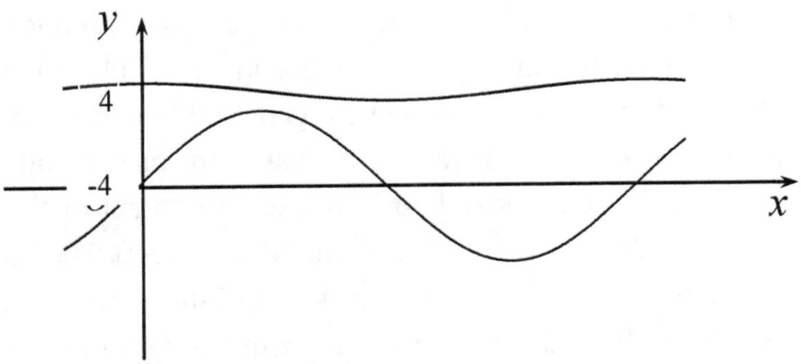

Between Y=(1 / 2)COS(x / 4)+5 and y=4cos(x / 4—3 / 2). The sugar cane yield is 2 tons per mu. The refinery is located in the center of the valley, if it consumes the same quantity of sugar cane as in the coastal regions, the direct line between the farthest sugar cane supply point and the refinery may be calculated by such a formula:

$$1500\times 2\times\int_0^x (1/2\cos x/4+5)-4\cos(x/4-3/2)dx=5400$$

X = 7.82 kilometers, and the average sugar cane supply distance in the costal regions and the river valley regions is 2. 14(2 / 3)=1. 43 kilometers and 4 kilometers respectively.

It is apparent from the above calculation that with the same production capacity, Baiceng Sugar Refinery has a transportation capacity that nearly triples that in similar refineries in Guangdong and Fujian, which will certainly add to the cost of products of Baiceng Sugar Refinery and will directly constrain its improvement of economic efficiency. A further expansion of the refinery will require the expansion of sugar cane base that can only expand along the river valley in the upstream or downstream direction. Such an expansion will further add to the burden on transportation and thus offset the benefit resulted from the expansion of the refinery. In other words, the pure natural background that Baiceng Sugar Refinery is exposed to has fundamentally constrained the actual efficiency and expansion of the refinery. The economic efficiency calculated by pure economic indicators after the expansion are not attainable.

The sugar cane base of Baiceng Sugar Refinery is also subject to the impact of the local climate. Scattering on the hillside with a difference in elevation of over 300 meters, different sugar cane fields differ in sugar content, maturity season, and growth period. The sugar canes growing in the fields at the bottom of the valley have high sugar content, mature earlier and a higher yield. By contrast, the fields on the top of the valley produce sugar canes that are lower in yield and sugar content, and must rely on manual transportation. These differences determined by geographic conditions have directly constrained the quality of raw materials and processing costs. According to the "ministry-issued standards", the sugar content of the sugar canes used as raw materials for sugar refinery should be at least 9%, however, the actual sugar content of the sugar canes from some of the bases of Baiceng Sugar Refinery is below 8%, which mostly come from the high-elevation and thin-soiled sugar cane fields. Simply, the natural geographic condition has kept the quality of raw materials from being further improved. Under the current circumstances, the refinery has no choice but use the low-quality sugar canes, resulting in a thin profit and low competitiveness. A further expansion will only worsen the situation.

To be close to the base of raw material, the refinery has to be placed in the Beipan River valley that is far from the county center and major transportation lines. All the raw materials, equipment and people must be shipped on a road that is badly-conditioned with many curves and steep slopes, which also creates heavy burden for the refinery, especially the transportation of fuels that relentlessly adds to the production cost of the refinery. It is apparent that a location far from major transportation lines is a big constraint on these factories. A manager from the department of equipment in this refinery once told us that during the busy production season in 1992-1993, a part on the machine broke. As no one in the factory was able to repair it, it took five days for someone to travel to Anshun and come back to the refinery simply to repair this part. The loss would have been a lot less if the refinery were located near the county center or transportation lines.

In fact, the refinery has encountered many other difficulties out of the reason of pure natural backgrounds, which may not be a problem in the same *xiang* but are all exposed in cross-xiang economic activities. In same-xiang operations, all relevant conditions required in each enterprise can be met in the interactive relationship across enterprises through the stable relations between the market and relevant enterprises. In cross-xiang operations, however, these enterprises are in a business with no other alternatives. The quality standards are not up to the factories. To tighten the standards may cause delay in the supply of raw materials or maintenance in equipment, thus bringing all pure natural environments to the surface. The unsatisfactory economic results in these small factories are attributable to the factors other than blaming on the poor management unconditionally.

A comprehensive analysis of the natural conditions of Baiceng Sugar Refinery tells us that no economic project is based on one natural condition only, but on an aggregation of conditions that are mutually constraining. Thus, a decision that is made simply based on one or two natural conditions is highly risky and rather reckless. In ethnic minority regions in Guizhou, factories as well as projects in farming and pasturing all follow the same law. The forestry scientific research department in Guizhou is now conducting research in the introduction of eucalyptus. It is not problematic to introduce eucalyptus in the river valley in south Guizhou if judged by regular meteorological conditions and soil texture. Given its high economic value, the introduction of eucalyptus in the poverty-relief efforts is gladly accepted by the administrative, science and research departments and other relevant processing enterprises. However, they have overlooked one important natural element, i.e., the fluctuation in meteorological elements.

Guizhou is an inland province subject to the influence of monsoon and cold winds, causing the meteorological elements in Guizhou to fluctuate drastically. Precipitation in extreme years may fluctuate more than 50% from regular years. In exceptional cases, the temperature nose dives from 20℃ to -2℃ within 24 hours when strong cold winds from the north sweep across the region. In the low-elevation mountainous river valley in the south, although the average January temperature in regular years is higher than 4℃ to 6℃, it may drop below 0℃ for several consecutive days in the years of extreme weather. In east Australia and the south Pacific Islands that are in the oceanic climate zone and are home to eucalyptus, the temperature and precipitation barely fluctuate and it is impossible for the temperature to plummet within a short period of time. Guizhou dos not have such a condition. As a result, although the introduction of eucalyptus may be successful temporarily, a sudden drop in temperature may wipe out all of previous efforts. Such things have happened before in China. In a blizzard in early 1980s, more than half of the eucalyptus trees that had grown tens of years in Kunming died. It indicates that among all natural conditions, one is enough to derail the entire operation if it is not compatible with the cross-xiang activity.

The reproduction and plantation of asexual cedars is now being promoted in southeast Guizhou Province. Despite its unquestionable economic value, these trees are threatened by plant diseases and insect pests. In the forest made up of one type of trees, an abrupt outburst of plant disease and insect pests may destroy all the trees in tens of thousand of hectares. Asexually reproduced cedars are vulnerable to attack by plant disease and insect pests. It takes explorative efforts that span across a long period of time to find out which disease or insects they are susceptible to. Now our technical departments have not had a thorough understanding of all these natural conditions. If we force the implementation of such projects by administrative power, given the fact that we have not totally eliminated the mass movement impact in organizing economic activities, we may end up in disaster relief rather than poverty relief once these trees are attacked by plant disease and insect pests. When planning on the long-term projects such as the renewal of variety of trees and animals, it will be extremely dangerous if we don't consider the risk elements in the natural conditions and are not prepared for the worst. Unfortunately, we tend to overestimate the superior natural conditions under regular circumstances but underestimate the role of comprehensive evaluation of natural conditions, especially overlook the risk elements of the natural conditions when we conduct economic development planning for ethnic minority regions. Needless to say, such a planning is not fool-proof.

We have stressed repeatedly that the energy contained in natural environments is enormous and can not be rivaled by the energy under the control of cross-xiang operators. This, however, is only one facet of the problem. Another important facet needs to be taken into account when selecting cross-xiang projects. Although the energy under the operator's control is minimal compared to the natural environment, it may disrupt the natural balance and thus turn the originally positive natural conditions into negative ones when we don't fully understand how natural laws operate. These dynamic changes to natural environments caused by human actions should not be underestimated.

To build the sugar refinery in Qinglong county, some heavy machines need to be shipped to the site. As the Beipan River was not passable by ships with such heavy load, the stones in the middle of the river had to be blown to clear the water channel for these heavy machines. What ensued the explosion disappointed the constructors. The removal of the stone by the explosion sped up the currents in the section near Hetang of Maokou River and shifted the course of the river to its west bank, flooding a large area of fertile lands in the Hetang area and gravely damaging the area previously planned as sugar cane base. The measures originally perceived to be positive to the sugar refinery now worked against it.

Many rivers in Guizhou Plateau are the outcome of long-term operation of natural environments. We must be extremely cautious when economic development projects involve the change of river course, because even a small change may trigger a series of changes along the original river course. Such a chain reaction will not only bring unexpected results to the economic project itself, but will also cause losses to other economic departments, the rice fields on the river banks being the most threatened. It has happened quite a few times that rice fields along the river in the Buyi region in Guizhou have been flooded, which, to a large extent, are caused by the change in river course and the ensuing change to erosion surface as a result that the stones from mountain cutting and pile-ups from factory construction have changed the river course. The fertile lands in Panjiang village of Guanling county have been collapsed from erosion at an average speed of 5-7 meters each year for the reason that the pile-ups up the river, especially the cinders from coal wash, have caused the erosion surface of Beipan River to shift from the west to east bank. Similar things have happened in Leyuan and Naye of Wangmo county in recent years. In addition to the change of river course, the water and soil conservation is another sensitive issue. We all know that to plant trees and grow grass is a key measure in water and soil reservation, but an equally important issue which is always ignored is the destructive power of seasonal flooding to the water and soil reservation. Guizhou is a region with widespread limestone distribution. The landform of Southwest Guizhou Autonomous Prefecture, a representative of this landform, can be classified into erosional and corrosional landforms. Erosional landform, by its form, can be classified into terraces and flood plains. Across the entire prefecture especially in the northwest and southeast, erosion gullies are distributed, to varied degrees, in parallel or in the shape of braches. Flood plains are distributed, to varied degrees, on both sides of the river. Corrosional landforms are widely distributed across the entire prefecture and can be classified, by its degree of development, into erosional landform represented by needle karst, torso mountain and low-lying land and corrosional landforms represented by peak cluster and low-lying land. The lands appear in the form of beacon hill, fluid bowl, channeling, silo, isolated peak, peak clusters and peak forests, and karst caves, in between are intermittent streams but not perennial flows. ① The instability of erosional landform has been discussed earlier in the book. The instability of corrosional landform, especially the instability of water and soil systems, is different from erosinonal landform. Mashan region is a typical example of corrosional landform. In regions around Mashan, there are no surface runoffs but only rocky mountains and withered grass in most of the time in a year. However, the torrential floods in storming seasons that are very limited in a year have the stunning destructive power. We witnessed an abrupt torrential flooding in Basai village in Mashan township in Wangmo county. After the torrential rainfall in two and half hours, the outburst of mountain torrents flooded all low-lying lands, bringing with them rocks and landslides that destroyed the stone bunkers built to block the flood. The water disappeared into karst caves in as short as one hour, only leaving debris behind. We are told by the locals that things like this happen

① *Planning on the Comprehensive Agricultural Regions in Southwest Guizhou Buyi and Miao Autonomous Prefecture* (Guizhou People's Publishing House, November 1989), 6.

two to three times a year and flood come in different directions. The soils in the newly cultivated terrace may get carried away with the flood at any time, taking with them all the efforts in the past.

Now, the administrative departments in some regions are pushing ahead the movement of "converting mountain slopes into terraces" by offering some subsidies, which has generated widespread enthusiasm among local people. Although we have recorded four incidents of death or body injuries when local people worked on "converting mountain slopes into terraces", the local people view it as fight for subsistence and development and thus are participating without any reservation. Their enthusiasm has not been affected at all even the promised subsidies are not delivered. We have witnessed the achievements of "converting mountain slopes into terraces" in Dalang and Hongyan of Ziyun county and Mashan and Barao in Wangmo county. Unfortunately, the local people have not been given any scientific guidance and their work has not been conducted under an overall plan on the landforms. Most of them have invested a lot of money and labor in building low stone walls around their own terrace in an attempt to shield these newly built terraces from the ravage of abrupt mountain torrential torrents. However, to their surprise, as these terraces are misplaced and the short stone walls have diverted the direction of the torrential torrents, they have intensified the scouring force that has destroyed many terraces. The cycle continues till today.

We have observed that when cultivating the lands reclaimed by slash and burn, ethnic Miao people would keep a plot of unattended land above the land to be cultivated, where wild grasses grew. We were told that wild grasses were used for covering house roofs. A further observation revealed that it was an effective way of minimizing the scouring force of the torrential torrents. However, "to convert mountain slopes into terraces" that is pushed now requires to level up large plots of land. Local people have followed the instructions from the administrative departments and at the same time believed that stone walls are able to block the mountain torrents. Therefore, they have abandoned the traditional practice and begun to build large-area terraces walled by stones. What they do not expect is the terraces are more likely to be destroyed. We think after some analyses that the enormous power contained in the outburst of torrential torrents can not be diminished simply by changing the landforms that are a result of long-term natural development.

Instead, the change only exposes the weakness, or even intensifies the scouring force of the torrents. By contrast, if a grass land is reserved above the cultivated land, as grasses are perennial plants with twisted roots underground, they can hold the soil together and conserve water. When torrents become too strong, they can pass through the grasses, which can slow the speed of torrents but not block them or divert their direction. Besides, the grasses won't be overturned and uprooted, and thus the cultivated lands below are protected. We realize from the comparison of two situations that to inappropriately change the existing landforms without taking into account the non-stability and abruptness in natural conditions, our efforts would produce the results contrary to our wishes, and may be more harmful and cause more damage than the traditional water and soil conservation measures.

The water source in corrosional landform is another non-stable system. To inappropriately change the system by human efforts and mistakenly copy experiences in water regulation from other regions will destroy the status in water supply. In the example mentioned earlier in the book, people in Linlou village of Wangmo county blew the water outlet with explosives in an attempt to increase the volume of water supply only to find that the well water infiltrates into the karst caves. Many working teams in Mashan used the same methods from other regions indiscriminately to help the local people find sources of water. They built water ponds near the water source or dug deep down the water outlet, in the hope that these methods would help people in Mashan solve the problem of drinking water shortage. However, they overlooked one principle issue: Mashan is a place with thick calcite and iceland spar ledge that are prone to crack when pressured, therefore it is extremely risky to dig open the karst cave or underground rivers underneath the stratum. The few sources of surface water are mostly formed because these cracks are blocked by the sediments washed down with currents. Such mini water outlets used to be the source of drinking water for people in Mashan. Any vibration from construction or pressure from the water pond itself will re-open these cracks, as a result, the original water outlets can not continue supplying water or even totally disappear. These examples make it very clear that the water sources in Mashan are very unstable and to blindly introduce the water facility from other regions may yield unexpected results.

Guizhou is a place with widespread limestone distribution. Limestone erosional landform and corrosional landform dominate the landscape of the entire province with Mashan being a typical region of dense distribution of corrosional landform. In fact, the problems encountered in Mashan also exist in the more developed region along the line from Guiyang to Anshun. In central Guizhou where wider erosional basins can be turned into vast farmlands, problems seen in Mashan also exist in varied degrees in the regions outside the intermontane basins in the river valley. The limestone mountainous regions surrounding these basins are mostly inhabited by ethnic Miao. The land surface is severely corroded and cracked. Soils are carried away by rainfalls, leaving only a small amount of soils in limestone cracks. Before human intervention, shrubs can grow very slowly from these cracks, but it takes much longer time for them to grow again if the environment is destroyed by man. As all the movements launched after the founding of the People's Republic of China such as the land reform concern the regular cultivated lands, mountains like this are left untouched. However, in the period that "put grain production over anything else", local people reclaimed and cultivated the lands improperly and trees were chopped excessively to be used as firewood, resulting in the exposure of rocks in large areas. Such a phenomenon of limestone mountain petrification is commonly seen across the economically developed central Guizhou region, and reveals that improper human intervention will bring devastating results to ecological environments. It has been proved by facts that reclamation and cultivation does not fit such a special region because the ground vegetation in these regions is fragile, thus giving rise to unstable elements. Human economic activities must be carried out under the premise of conserving the above ground vegetation to prevent the natural background from further deteriorating. We are not against all economic activities in these regions. Some economic projects, if handled properly, will be beneficial to us. For instance, to raise goats and plant economic forests will have such a result without large-scale petrification. Unfortunately, we have reclaimed and cultivated the lands as we do in other farmlands and have caused irretrievable petrification in large areas, thus making these natural backgrounds meaningless from an economic perspective.

When carrying out research on cross-xiang operations, researchers from older generations tend to classify human economic life into two opposing categories: the developed and civilized economic life style vs. the backward and primitive economic life style. The previous analyses have made it clear that such an approach is not a reflection of reality. In fact, different types of economy evaluate and make use of natural backgrounds differently and different modes of economy have different requirements for natural conditions. These requirements are pertinent to some extent, which, if not satisfied, will be subject to apparent constraints, result in sharp drop in operational efficiency or trigger ecological crisis, and may bring the relevant economic activities to a halt. To demonstrate the dependence relationship between specific economic life and pure natural background, we name the smoothness of such a dependence relationship the integrality between economic life and natural background. The higher the integrality, the less constrained the economic activities are subject to, and vice versa.

Integrality is an undeniable fact between man and nature. To further understand the essence of integrality from a macro perspective, we think it necessary to revisit how older-generation anthropologists explain the dialectical relationship between man and nature. Raymond Firth stated in his renowned book *Human Types*: First, environments apparently constrain human life to a great extent. Second, any environment will, to a certain extent, force people who live in it to accept a material life style. Third, environments provide materials for people's needs while widely constraining people's achievements. Fourth, environments have subtle impacts on people's cultural life. [①]

The above four points made by Firth have basically summarized the various dependence relationships between human economic activities and pure natural backgrounds. His more insightful statement is reflected in his full acknowledgement on the creativity of the "tribal people"- less developed nationalities, in their economic life. After commending the great achievements the developed nationalities had made in conquering nature, he further wrote: the difference between developed nationalities and less-developed ones in making use of science is in degree but not in essence. Tribal people that are backward in culture have their own technical and scientific knowledge and tools. They can handle the environments, are confident that they can overpower nature in most cases.[②] In this statement, Firth fully acknowledged human being's creativity. He pointed out that

① Raymond Firth, *Human Types,* trans. Xiaotong Fei (The Commercial Press, 2nd edition, September 1991), 38-39.

② Raymond Firth, *Human Types,* 40.

human creativity can transform nature to the benefit of people. In the meantime, human beings can not leave nature and can not get rid of the constraints by nature. This tells us from a macro perspective that man and nature are in a constraining and counter-constraining relationship, and man is dominating in the relationship. With such an understanding and by referencing the previous discussions on the economic type and mode of each ethnic group, we are able to further specify and deepen this perception of Firth.

We can separate the natural backgrounds in Guizhou into different regions, or even into several sub-regions. After comprehensive comparisons, we can further tell that not all specific economic activities can be carried out normally in all these regions. The highly petrified mountainous regions in Mashan, for instance, are hardly able to be turned into rice fields. Even if rice is planted in some fields, they will not yield expected economic benefit due to the instable natural background, indicating that rice field cultivation has a very low integrality in this region. Another example is the Beipan River valley that we mentioned earlier. It is an economically viable option to grow rice in the erosional river basins. However, they can not be used as winter pastures for goats as the high humidity in the winter is likely to cause disease on goats. Besides, the swamps are impassible to goat flocks. We can arrive at the conclusion that this region has a high integrality for rice fields but low integrality for goat pasturing.

As different pure natural backgrounds are concerned in cross-xiang operations, operators must consider the integrality of the regions concerned to which the cross-xiang project is exposed, because this is an important constraint that determines the success of the project. The following principle may help our readers determine the integrality of the concerned regions. Generally, the higher the type of economy, the narrower the region with the best integrality. To the contrary, the lower the type of economy, the wider the region that is suitable for relatively extensive operations. For instance, the pure natural background that suits the Swidden type of economy may not be suitable for the economy of animal husbandry, while the pure natural background that can be used by the economy of animal husbandry is, for the most part, not suitable for the agricultural type of economy. According to this basic principle, we may infer the following experience that may offer some reference value. All the regions in Guizhou have undergone developmental activities by different ethnic groups, while different types of economy have a different level of integrality, and economic capacity tends to rise as a result of the type of economy moving up to a higher level; therefore, the regions that remain in a lower type of economy usually have a lower integrality with the higher type of economy, and economic projects selected from a higher type of economy, without a doubt, will have a lower integrality in these regions. For example, the integrality and probability of success must be low if we want to introduce projects from an agricultural type of economy into a Swidden cultivation economy such as the Mashan region and inland Yueliang mountain. To the contrary, operational projects selected from the Mashan region tend to have a higher integrality and can operate normally but are rarely subject to the constraints by natural environments in northwest Guizhou that has a mixed economy of agriculture and animal husbandry, as well as the agricultural region in central Guizhou.

In addition to the type of economy, the difference in the mode of economy also affects the integrality of the region concerned in cross-xiang operations, and thus restrains the result of operation. However, there are some differences between the two. The change in integrality caused by the type of economy relates to the difference in the cultural structure of the concerned ethnic groups; therefore, to make the adjustment in this aspect affects a wider range and it is hard to manage all factors at the same time. Generally, it is not easy to handle the relationship between the development projects and natural environments. For the changes in integrality caused by differences in the mode of economy, as the cultural structures in the relevant ethnicities are similar, economic activities carried out by relevant parties are similar in nature, and the value propensity of each relevant ethnicity in the economic activities are similar, it is a lot easier to adjust the economic project to the natural background concerned, which in most cases, only involves surface-level adjustments such as technical operation, production management and resource utilization etc.

To further illustrate, we hereby use the example of the introduction of an agricultural research achievement in Guizhou in recent years to compare the differences in the nature of the change in integrality caused by the above two reasons. Given that the river valleys in south Guizhou Province are warm in the winter with plenty of sunlight, and rice fields in the local Buyi region are usually in fallow at this time of the year, some agricultural experts tested growing vegetables in the counties such as Luodian and Wangmo. The tests were successful and the project quickly moved into the stage of local promotion. In just a few years, the technology was implemented not only in the Buyi settlements in the counties in south Guizhou but also in the middle reach of Beipan River and Dabang River, bringing vast economic benefit to these regions. While this technology was tested in the Miao regions, although the technical difficulties were mostly solved, the project did not yield the same economic result as in the intermontane basins of the Buyi Regions. Our investigation suggests that such a technology quickly spread among the Buyi people without having to resort to administrative authority. The Buyi people were quick in mastering the technology, turning it into bulk production, and sending the products to the markets.

Things were different in the Miao regions. Pressed by the administrative departments and encouraged by the technical departments, some Miao villages accepted this technology. However, only a few households chose to grow these vegetables, and thus they were not produced in bulk and could not enter the market. The technology was also accepted in Gaopo township in Guiyang where villagers successfully grew peas as vegetables, but they were not produced in bulk and were not brought to the market. About this question, we asked a former township official who was once in charge of this work and whose answer was intriguing: "This is a new technology, new product, and everybody likes it. It is common in the Miao community that your neighbors would come to your fields to pick some simply to have a taste, and there is nothing left to sell in the market. We have to wait until every household grows it so that we have enough left to sell in the market." We can further speculate, based on his statement, that the villagers felt that to grow peas in the fields only benefited the neighbors. Who knows how many years it would take before the products can access to the market if the local economy is run by such rule?

Such a sharp contrast may be explained by the difference in the traditional economic life concerned in the projects. The ethnic Buyi group was, in tradition, in the agricultural type of economy. Although the project to grow vegetables in the winter was proposed based on the economic needs in the Han regions, it fit the Buyi culture in terms of how the natural resources were utilized; therefore, it won the full cooperation from the Buyi people. To the contrary, as the culture on which the proposed project was based was different from the traditional culture of Miao, it was hard for us to find a point for the growth of the introduced technology from the perspective of how the traditional culture made use of the natural resources. As a result, the success was only limited to individual or household level. When the proposed projects concern the use of natural resources, it is thus very necessary for us to inspect the characteristics of the type and mode of the economic life of the related ethnic groups so that we can find the best option.

Above, we have discussed the three facets of the issue on the relationship between cross-xiang operations and natural backgrounds. We must point out that the three facets are not isolated but mutual constraining. To make the right selection, we must take the three facets into account before we find the project that has the highest economic value and is most stable. Therefore, any right choice in the operation must be the result of a discriminate screening and selection after thorough consideration of all factors and indicators. It won't make the problems go away if we only eye on the upsides of limited projects, indicators, or the natural environments.

After a thorough consideration of the above three facets, we can easily find that any economic activity has the environment it fits the best and worst, as well as the neutral environment that it fits for the most part. Such a difference in the degree of adaptability, to specific economic activities, is apparently exclusive. As human economic life is the result of regulation by specific ethnic culture, such an exclusivity in economic activities is thus an exclusivity of relevant ethnic culture. The regions that produce the best economic results for an ethnic group, or are the most economically developed, must be the region where the culture of this ethnic group best suits the pure natural background. This region is the living environment of this ethnic group that we mentioned earlier. Apparently, no cross-xiang operational activities are carried out in pure natural backgrounds but in the living environments of other ethnic groups. As we all know, the living environment of an ethnic group is a secondary environment processed and transformed by the culture of this ethnic group. Needless to say, to carry out economic activities in the living environment of a heterogeneous ethnic group, we must first acknowledge the existence of the living environment of relevant ethnic group, and consider if the proposed project is compatible and in sync with the living environment of the relevant ethnic group. To this end, we need to further discuss the issue of compatibility in the living environments across different ethnic groups in cross-xiang operations.

III Analysis of Compatibility across Heterogeneous Living Environments

As mentioned earlier, cross-xiang operations in most cases are not carried out in pure natural backgrounds but in the secondary living environments processed and transformed by other ethnic groups. As such secondary living environments are processed through social activities and thus have specific social cultural characteristics, cross-xiang operations will concern not only natural conditions but also a series of relevant social issues. These social issues are grounded on specific heterogeneous cultures and have solid and profound social foundations, which cross-xiang operators do not need nor are able to fundamentally change. To make cross-xiang operations successful, the wisest thing to do is to become compatible with such secondary cultural backgrounds, i.e., the living environments of related ethnic groups, so that cross-xiang operations may be successful at a limited cost, or even become harmonious to the largest extent possible with these heterogeneous living environments to win the effective cooperation from these heterogeneous living environments. For this reason, cross-xiang operators must bring the living environments concerned in cross-xiang operations to inspection before the cross-xiang operations start. Only by fully understanding the compatibility between the heterogeneous living environment and that of the operator's ethnic group can we significantly minimize the constraint caused by the heterogeneous living environment or find the best way to deal with the constraints.

In principle, the economic activities proposed by cross-xiang operators based on the economic characteristics of their own ethnic groups will surely encounter many unfavorable elements from heterogeneous living environments. These heterogeneous living environments have been processed and transformed to possess specific social attributes, which are difficult to overlap with the social attributes the proposed economic projects are based on. Such a non-overlapping characteristic often gives rise to non-economic constraints. However, given that the living environment of any ethnic group is a complex sub-system that is shaped by the existing culture to meet the need of this culture, but not without any principle, the natural environment after processing and transformation must have left plenty of room untouched.

Therefore, as long as we perform deep analysis on these differences, we can find the natural conditions that can be used, or the natural resources that, although having been processed or used, can be re-used or used in another level. Given these circumstances, we have reason to believe that there must be room for compatibility with heterogeneous living environments that cross-xiang operators concern. The key is how to treat and use such a compatibility.

The above analysis suggests that natural backgrounds and living environments are different in nature, formation mechanism and constraining effects on cross-xiang operations. It requires that we treat them separately and specifically when working on the solutions. Therefore, we must take different actions, and more importantly, take different approaches when working on the solutions. In terms of natural backgrounds, the key is about how to understand them correctively and comprehensively to make use of them effectively. In terms of living environments, as they directly relate to the existing economic life of the ethnic groups concerned, we must face the co-existence of heterogeneous economic lives and find a way of achieving compatibility across them. The key is, in the existing living environment, how to make economic life compatible in terms of the use of natural resources.

Natural backgrounds contain enormous energy that stay stable for an extended period of time. No optional projects in cross-xiang operations can fundamentally change their inherent characteristics to make them benefit the operation. Nor should we expect miracles in cross-xiang operations that give rise to new characteristics that favor this operation. Cross-xiang operators must honestly accept the existence of all natural characteristics and plan their actions accordingly. Once the project is selected, the strengths and weaknesses are fixed and will remain so as the operation continues. In a nutshell, natural backgrounds are the fundamental constraining system in cross-xiang operations.

Living environments are not like natural backgrounds. Although living environments contain enormous energy that lasts stably for an extended period of time, they have social attributes and the change in social culture may prompt them to make partial changes to adapt to the need in social development. It seems that the partial changeability in living environments makes them easier to manage than natural backgrounds because they provide some room for us to work with after all. However, things may not be as simple as they look.

The social attributes of living environments determine that they don't change with the needs of cross-xiang operators but with the specific culture to which they belong. It needs to be pointed out that in general, they may change in three possible directions: First, become less favorable to the implementation of the cross-xiang project. Second, become more favorable to the implementation of the cross-xiang project. Third, in most cases, some aspects become more favorable and others become less favorable. Although prior investigation and analysis may offer some insights, more would manifest themselves after the cross-xiang operations begin, which unquestionably adds to the difficulty in the control of living environments. Therefore, to manage the constraints resulted from the differences in living environments requires more than a mere understanding of the characteristics of existing living environments, but also constant dynamic analysis of the living environments of the concerned heterogeneous ethnic group and timely adjustment on such environments.

As living environments are characterized with an overall stability and partial changeability, they constrain cross-xiang operations in a different way from natural backgrounds. In addition to the options, living environments would impact the process of cross-xiang operations by constantly posing new challenges to create more fluctuations in economic efficiency and eventually constraining the effectiveness of cross-xiang operations. Such a new and protracted battle is different from natural backgrounds in composition and it is composed of objective natural elements as well as human elements. Cross-xiang operators need to deal with constraints caused by actions of people.

Due to differences between natural backgrounds and living environments in the constraining effects on cross-xiang operations, failure to realize them or mistake one for the other would give rise to unnecessary loss. At least some of the development projects in ethnic minority regions in Guizhou did not yield the results that had been expected for this reason. For instance, people rushed to build fruit bases when they saw a natural background that had plenty of sunlight, perfect heat and soil conditions for growing oranges, only to find after the fruits were ripe that they could not gather and ship the fruits to the markets or transportation lines. Then they realized that cultural conditions were also needed on top of natural conditions for the success of fruit bases. In this case, what was lacking was the components in living environments such as transportation infrastructure and allocation of markets. Another example was in southern Guizhou. When people noticed that the Buyi rice fields in the intermontane basin in the river valley were left idle for nearly two thirds of the time in a year, they promoted across the vast territory to grow rice for two seasons in a year. However, due to insufficient cumulative temperature in many places, the temperature already dropped before the late rice matured. When people implemented development projects like these, they only emphasized on the advantages in living environments, but ignored that it was the natural background that played a fundamental constraining role. Therefore, to blindly substitute living environments for natural backgrounds is not going to yield expected results.

We've only solved half of the problems if we can clearly define the boundary between natural backgrounds and living environments, and separately evaluate their advantages and disadvantages. To solve the other half of the problems depends on our correct application of the materials in hand. When talking about the development plans for the ethnic regions now, everyone knows to repeatedly quote the data now available on natural conditions, but has overlooked the equally important job of data authentication. People have consciously or unconsciously ignored the principle that these data must be applied pertinently, comprehensively and stably. As a result, the plans that sound flawless and logical would give rise to many unexpected problems, and lead to the total failure of the development plan. As natural backgrounds consist of many elements that are complex and difficult to be illustrated completely, we hereby only use the application of meteorological data as an example for the purpose of our analysis in the hope to help our readers draw inferences from such analysis for their specific needs.

The landscapes that dominate ethnic minority regions in Guizhou are mountains that are deeply cut by rivers. Places separated by only one mountain or river may have completely different climates. However, most of the meteorological stations in the province concentrate in county centers, on which we have to depend to get meteorological data. From our surveys, we had some real sense about how these data were impertinent to the ethnic settlements.

In October 1993 when we were in fieldwork in Wangmo county, we were surprised to see local Miao people dry the grains by burning firewood before they could turn in the grains to the state as an agricultural tax. We later found out that the harvest season in this region happened to be concurrent with rainy seasons that kept the harvested grains from drying up. A lot of corns rot in the fields before being picked. Local people complained that the money and labor they spent on drying up the grains were more than that they could get from selling them. Besides, as the grains could not be carried down the mountain in time, they would get wet again. Sometimes, it took a few more days for the grains to dry up after they were carried to the grain stations before they could meet the requirements of the station. The total cost of turning in these grains far exceeded their value, which was not economical for both the state and the farmers. All the requests by the Miao officials were turned down. It seems that our administrative departments were confident with the meteorological data they had on hand that they already knew everything without the need to understand the hardship of local people.

We saw a different picture in Kanbian and Wongdao that are less than 50 kilometers in a straight-line distance away from Mashan. Tall succulent plants that belong to cactus family were seen everywhere and were used as fence by local Buyi people, indicating this was a place that had a long dry and warm season in a year. This region was called "flower mountain" in history and was a famous cotton-producing region. As cotton matures well in dry weather conditions, it indicates that the long dry season must appear in the fall and winter in this region. Such a characteristic in climate sharply contrasts Mashan. As a matter of fact, Mashan is located on the windward mountain slope facing south while Kanbian is on the north side of the mountain. The warm and wet air coming from the south in the fall and winter seasons climbs with the rising elevation of the mountain to form fogdrops. After it climbs over the mountain, it quickly goes down to warm up the temperature and dry up the air, creating the seasonal foehn climate in the region near Kanbian. Such a complex microclimate causes difficulties to cross-xiang operators if they mechanically use the meteorological data obtained from the meteorological stations of the county when discussing the climate of the investment project.

Climate is a complex natural system. For the convenience of comparison, regular meteorological observation only collects some general data. However, specific operations have special requirements on weather conditions that can not be satisfied by regular meteorological observation but have to rely on specific observation and data accumulation.

Tung trees are widely planted in southern China and tung oil is an important export product. However, only Liuma tung oil is internationally renowned, which, in addition to the unique Buyi cultural conditions, is closely related to the unique weather conditions, landform and environment in Liuma. Liuma region is a river valley basin surrounded by mountains. For the reasons mentioned above, Liuma, like Kanbian, is subject to the seasonal foehn. When the tung seeds are ripe, it happens to be in the continuous high-temperature dry season, expediting the fallen tung seeds to enter a after-ripening. A large amount of eleostearic acid synthesizes and stores inside the seeds before they go into dormancy. To press oil from the seeds in dormancy has the benefit of high oil yield and high eleostearic acid content. The coating made from such tung oil is stable in film-forming with good insulating property, and is thus well received in the international market.

In previous years when Liuma tung oil was in its heyday, many counties shouted the slogan "to get rich by planting tung trees". However, the meteorological data currently available can not answer the question: How big is the area that has the environment and weather condition that best suits the growth of tung trees? We were lucky to have been given access to the data collected by the precipitation station that belonged to Beipan River hydrometric station, from which we obtained the precipitation records by month in six consecutive years in Liuma. The records showed that in this region, the precipitation was extremely low from October to next March with the lowest a merely 18 mm and highest merely 36 mm. Such limited data are far from enough to determine if a region has the best weather conditions for the production of Liuma tung oil. Other data including surface temperature, dew point, relative humidity between day and night, sunlight, and accumulated temperature must be available to make the decision, yet they are not available anywhere. Current meteorological stations are not equipped to collect some of these data and to add them in the observation contents means that new stations bigger than the current county-level stations must be built.

The central Miaoling mountain range in Guizhou is home to cloud and mist Maojian tea, which has very special requirements on weather conditions. The tea leaves must bud in the misty mountainous regions with high humidity.

They are extremely cold-resistant and can bud even in rime or spring snow, but are extremely irresistant to drought. To determine if a place is suitable for cloud and mist Maojian tea, the number of misty days in spring must be included in the contents of observation. Unfortunately, such is a very unimportant item in a regular meteorological station.

In summary, every specific cross-xiang operation, when it concerns the use of meteorological data, will require some specific observation contents which can not be fully satisfied by a regular meteorological station now.

Guizhou is in the monsoon region. The intensity of monsoon and the advance or delay in the shift of monsoon season may cause the weather conditions to fluctuate abnormally. It takes a long time for us to understand and record how weather conditions fluctuate. Such a basic requirement can not be met in the ethnic minority regions in Guizhou. Therefore, our development plans are unavoidably showing a certain degree of blindness when it comes to weather-related matters. The risk is extremely high in the planning of long-term planting or breeding projects. Over a long period in the past, when we planed the expansion of paddy fields, we seldom noticed the deviation from the average annual precipitation; we often overlooked the cold-air outbreak when introducing tropical and sub-tropical varieties; we often overlooked the danger of hail when introducing small-season cultivation over large mountainous areas. It was often the case that we started things first and waited for disasters to happen before we were forced to deal with the aftermath.

Wangmo county is a major producer of Chinese bananas that are resistant to sudden drop in temperature in the winter. The yield is relatively stable even in extreme cold weather. Instead of putting efforts in breeding improved variety of Chinese bananas, expanding cultivated area and increasing yields based on existing advantage in planting, the local administrative departments in agricultural technology were enthusiastic in introducing improved variety of bananas. Such an approach was highly risky and involved a large amount of work as it did not take the fluctuation in weather conditions into account, which indicated that many technical people have insufficient knowledge about the fluctuation in weather conditions, let alone to accumulate meteorological data in this aspect.

When shaping their own living environments, each ethnic group generally carries out transformation in three levels. First purposefully make selections in the complex pure natural backgrounds, eliminating those of little value and retaining those that are valuable to its ethnic culture; then carry out specific transforming activities over the selected targets to make them useful. This is a corresponding process. Third, the measures and methods used in the corresponding process must be incorporated into the related cultural system to make them harmonious with existing social life. By doing so, the processing and transformation can be grounded on the society and last continuously, and eventually transform the entire environment into the condition suitable for the subsistence of the ethnic group. This is an adjusting process. These are three interrelated and chained processes with clearly-defined levels. To make our discussion on the characteristics of living environments more specific, we will follow these three processes and use examples to analyze the characteristics and evolution process in the living environments of ethnic Yi group. For the purpose of comparison, we will also bring the process of how modern Han people shaped their living environment in Yangtze River delta into our discussion.

A complete description of the ethnic Yi's traditional type of economy is not found in the Han ancient literature before the Ming dynasty, but we are able to arrive at the conclusion from the circumstantial evidences of the following four aspects that the ethnic Yi society was in an animal husbandry type of economy. First, according to ancient literatures from the Song dynasty such as *Gui Hai Yu Heng Zhi*, Pina (present-day Zhijin county) that was near the Yi settlements that used to be a transfer place to sell horses from Dali to the Southern Song dynasty. Second, it was recorded in the *History of Yuan* that the primary tributes of Yixibuxue (later under the rule of Shuixi, present-day northwest Guizhou) to the royal court were horses and rain felts. Third, it was mentioned in the *Veritable Records of the Ming Dynasty* that Shuixi *Tu Si* once aided the Ming dynasty in its battle in Yunnan by offering one thousand horses, and that horses remained throughout the entire Ming dynasty as Shuixi's primary tribute. Fourth, according to (Hongzhi) *Guizhou Tujingxinzhi*, local Yi people liked to clad them with wrapping felt and feed mainly on meat and oat flour. The above four records proved, from different angles, that traditionally the ethnic Yi community was in an economy of animal husbandry, but they did not offer any detail about the characteristics of such an economy. These characteristics can only be unveiled indirectly from these ancient literatures by combining the natural characteristics of ethnic Yi settlements with the help of ethnological approaches.

Wumeng mountain range is in the Yi settlements where the landscape is dominated by high mountains, steep slopes and deeply-cut river valleys. The upstream Wu River and Pan River meander in the region. The lowest elevation is about 600 meters and the highest in the Wumeng mountain peak is above 2000 meters. Such a natural circumstance requires animals to move from pastures in different seasons. In the winter, the high-elevation pastures are often hit by heavy snow storms and thus turn extremely cold with all the grass withered. As a result, animals must be herded to pastures in lower river valley to be shielded from the cold. In the summer, the high-elevation pastures have abundance of fresh grass, water source and a mild and pleasantly cold weather, which is best for the growth of animals and fallowing. By contrast, the low-elevation river valleys are in extreme hot weather conditions and are exposed to flooding, making it easy for animal diseases to spread and thus not a good place of grazing. Shaped by such an environment, ethnic Yi people had the tradition of vertical grazing that "go up in the summer and get down in the winter". To make such a practice successful, ethnic Yi people had carried out targeted transformation to the natural environment that they lived in. They planned pastures for the rotation between summers and winters, which were results of discriminate selection of existing natural environments, primarily by taking into account the type of grass, and the convenience for the animal movements. The corresponding transformation of the pastures mainly included the extermination of harmful plants, the capturing and killing of harmful animals and the maintenance of water sources for the raised animals. In addition, roads had to be cleared for the passing of animals and road signs had to be put up. The adjustment and processing of natural backgrounds mainly included temporary settlements established for grazing and fences for the protection of the animals. All the above activities combined to create an artificial secondary environment that fully satisfied the need of Yi's economic life in animal husbandry.

The uniqueness in the secondary living environment of the ethnic Yi community can be further highlighted by the comparison with the Han's secondary living environment in Yangtze River delta. To meet the needs in rice production, ethnic Han people have cultivated and turned the plains crisscrossed by waterways in the Yangtze River delta and Taihu Basin into permanent rice fields. These rice fields need to be maintained by complicated irrigation canals, water gates and flood control dams, which are, in essence, human efforts to convert these regions into shallow swamps suitable for planting rice. By comparison, the ethnic Yi people would never keep such a shallow swamp in the river valleys. Instead, they would clear the way for the river water to flow into the river valley to make the land suitable for winter pasturing and they would do everything possible to level up the river shoals to make it easy for animals to drink water. It is apparent that the two ethnic groups have taken completely different approaches in processing natural rivers.

The soils have been processed by different approaches as well. To ensure the growth of rice – the primary product, the ethnic Han people must plough deep into the soils and exterminate all weeds. The ethnic Yi people, on the other hand, do not plough deep into the soils and would maintain the growth of weeds as much as possible to provide cattle with fodders. They, however, have to uproot the shrubs that keep the grazing grass from growing. The two ethnic groups have demonstrated different processing propensity. They, too, have taken different approaches with the selection of animals to raise. To meet the needs of moving across pastures, the Yi people choose to raise animals that are easy to move such as cattle, goat and horse. By contrast, the ethnic Han people, due to their settlement lifestyle, mostly choose to feed pigs but rarely sheep, that are kept in pens, with the exception of oxen for cultivation and horses for transportation.

As the two ethnic groups process the natural environment in different directions, when they come across each other for economic, political or military reasons, they must consider how to make the use of natural resources compatible with each other: to ensure the co-existence of the two ethnic groups, and at the same time, to ensure that the ethnic cultures and traditional lives of the two ethnic groups, after adjustments, last in relative stability. Such things happened in the Ming dynasty.

The Ming government, for the purpose of safeguarding the state courier route running across the entire Guizhou, had to send a huge number of Han people to station in the guarding posts along the state courier route either as civilians or military servicemen. To provide support to these people, the Ming government had to assign lands around these stations to the Han people so that they could cultivate these lands to provide supplies of food. As a result, it was inevitable for the Han people who penetrated deep into the Yi region to collide and interact with the heterogeneous Yi culture. It was then that the issue of compatibility across heterogeneous cultures was brought onto the agenda, and as a result, the economic lives of both sides underwent changes in order to achieve compatibility in mutual coordination and interaction.

On the side of Yi people, the traditional animal husbandry gradually became impacted by agriculture, thus evolved into a mixed economy of agriculture and animal husbandry. Some traces of change in the economic life of ethnic Yi were reflected in the fragmentary documentations of the Ming dynasty. Although crop farming appeared in the Yi region at the moment, it was basically in the "slash-and-burn" state. ① To meet the need in the mixed economy, the Yi people had a unique way of utilizing land resources. The cultivated lands were located in the barren lands on the hillsides that were not good for pasturing, which was clearly described in the *Annal of Yunnan*: "(people) lived in the high and rocky mountains and cultivated the barren lands to grow sweet and bitter buckwheat for self-subsistence." ② These words were valuable in that they told us that the majority of cultivated lands in the Yi region were located on the top of the plateau that was barren and dry with sparse grass. Given that farming was supplementary to the animal husbandry in the Yi region, to use land resources this way apparently had two advantages: First, save the hillsides where grasses grew well as pastures. Second, the sparse grasses growing on the top of the plateau made the "slash-and-burn" style easier.

As mentioned above, the main crops in ethnic Yi's "slash-and-burn" were buckwheat and oat, which was documented in Vol.34 of *Shu Zhong Guang Ji as* "(people) ate cakes made from buckwheat as main food." As a plant of polygonaceae, buckwheat grows in extremely short period of time and is very drought-enduring. Its seeds are edible and straws can be used as fodders, and is thus a crop that can be used in both crop farming and animal husbandry. Buckwheat and oat are two major farming crops that are related to the mixed structure of farming and animal husbandry, as only such crops can grow on the barren high mountains so that they won't occupy the land for pasturing while at the same time provide animal fodders.

Ethnic Yi people mainly grew barley and oat at the time, as was

① Yingliang Jiang, eds., *The History of Ethnic Groups in China II* (Sichuan Minzu Publishing House October 1990), 168.
② (Ming) Wenzheng Liu, *History of Yunnan*, (Yunnan Education Publishing House, December 1991), 995.

indirectly reflected in the ancient literatures of the Ming dynasty. Among the 13 provinces in the Ming dynasty, Guizhou was the only one in the south that was permitted to "replace rice with buckwheat and oat" to pay "summer tax". ① Given the limited number of household in Guizhou in the Ming dynasty and most of the tax revenue came from the attributes by all the *Tu Si*, this exceptional treatment was granted primarily based on the produces in the fields of big Tu Si, especially the most influential Shuixi Tu Si. In the Yi regions, the summer pastures were left in fallow in the winter. To grow the winter crops such as buckwheat and oat did not affect pasturing. It was an effective way of increasing the utilization index of summer pastures, and the inevitable outcome of a mixed economy of farming and animal husbandry, as well as the outcome of the innovative use of technologies introduced.

After living in the same region for a long period of time with the Han civilians and servicemen, ethnic Yi people achieved some new breakthroughs in the mixed type of economy and started to grow rice in small quantity, which was documented in the Qing dynasty: "The unruly Pisha barbarians (Yi people) lived by plundering. The local influential households did not save money but had many animals such as bull and sheep as well as slaves. They migrated at any time. Seven tenths of them grew crops on the hillside and three tenths cultivated paddy fields. The paddy fields were mostly cultivated lands. People would climb to the hillsides after they finished cultivating the paddy fields and came down at the time of harvest." ② This passage was the most complete explanation of Yi's mode of production after the Qing government implemented the policy to replace all local hereditary headmen with the officials sent by the central government. It clearly indicated that the ethnic Yi community was mainly in the animal husbandry economy. The most important way of accumulating wealth was by keeping as many cattle and sheep as possible. People carried out production by a vertical pasturing characterized by "down in the winter and up in the summer". Although there were a limited number of paddy fields, people did not intertill and would only come down the mountain to rush to harvest the crops. They only cut the panicles but left the straws in the fields for the winter pasturing. Although dry land crops were planted over large areas, the fact that they coexisted with a

① *The History of the Ming Dynasty,* s.v. "Shi Huo Zhi" (Zhonghua Book Company, 2nd edition, March 1984), 1894.

② (Qing • Qianlong) *Annals of Dongchuan Fu Vol 8* s.v. "Hukou" "Fuzhongren", in the collection of the library of Yunnan University large number of animals indicated that these crops were planted in the spaces between pastures. The traditional guiding principle in the use of land resources remained in force.

As a key measure in its development efforts, the Ming government stationed a large number of Han people in the garrisons in the Yi regions, which, from the perspective of cross-xiang operations, was unquestionably a "one-way" development strategy. Traditionally, the Han economic life style was rice field cultivation around Han settlements. It was a sharp contrast to the traditional Yi economic life. How to handle the conflict between the two in natural resource utilization became the key to the successful continuation of this means of development. The strategy taken by the Ming government included three major aspects. First, most of the Han immigrants were stationed in the river valleys along the courier route that were suitable for growing rice. Second, they tried not to intervene in the domestic affairs of the Yi people and not to touch the Yi's inherent life style, for which the only condition was that the local *Tu Si* protected the passability of the courier route. Third, the traditional cultivation method in the garrisons was adjusted to a certain extent to make it compatible with the traditional Yi economic life style.

All the courier routes and garrisons of the Ming dynasty in northwest Guizhou were located in the Yi settlements. They were set up after the *Tu Si* of the Yi group were lured into supporting the construction. The famous "nine posts in Long Chang", was completed after the Emperor Taizu of the Ming dynasty personally appeased She Xiang, the female *Tu Si,* and won her support. The setup of the garrison in Annan was directly related to Pu'an *Tu Si*'s submission to the Ming government. To avoid confrontation between the stationed Han immigrants and local Yi people, the Ming government enforced strict and inflexible laws to prevent Han immigrants from leaving the courier routes and garrisons without permission. In addition, it intimidated and threatened the Han immigrants so that they did not dare to leave their stations and enter the Yi regions. The *Ji Yao Chao Huang* of the early Ming dynasty had specific description about this: "If someone was sent over to the stationed army, he had the mission of telling the servicemen about the fate of the escapees. All servicemen who escaped from the station were either killed by the barbarians in the deep mountains or shackled and forced to cultivate lands." [1] By these means, the Ming government firmly put the Han immigrants under control in the narrow courier routes and the river valleys suitable for rice cultivation. It is apparent that these river valleys were winter pastures of the Yi group and were only for temporary and seasonal use in the Yi's normal life style. Such an arrangement ensured compatibility between the two sides in their economic lives and prevented confrontations between them in the use of land resources.

Although the immigration of a large number of Han people into the Yi regions had added heavy burdens to the military supplies, the Ming government took a very flexible attitude toward Yi *Tu Si*, or even totally indulgent with regards to tax payment, for the purpose of stabilizing its relationship with ethnic Yi groups. To allow the use of buckwheat and oat as tax payment was an obvious example. In addition, the tax obligations of each *Tu Si* were estimated by self-submission and voluntary fulfillment. Those who could not fulfill the obligations that were self-submitted were repeatedly relieved or exempted and were seldom severely punished. [2] The *Tu Si*, after receiving these preferential treatments from the Ming government, were willing to return the government with loyalty. As a result, the courier routes in the Yi region were kept unobstructed and were free from robbers and bandits throughout the entire Ming dynasty.[3] The Ming government had never sent troops to the Yi regions except during the period to put down the "She-An Rebellion" in the late Ming dynasty.[4]

The implementation of these strategies largely kept the two ethnic groups in peace and never led to any armed confrontation except for the disputes arising out of the possession and utilization of natural resources.

The ancient literatures of the Ming dynasty mostly focused on political and military events but seldom directly mentioned the production conditions of the Han people who migrated into the Yi regions. Fortunately, the descendents of these Han immigrants now still keep the Ming characteristics in their production. In today's ethnological surveys, we can roughly restore the style of cultivation of the Ming dynasty from the remaining production characteristics.

[1] *The History of Ethnic Groups in China II,* 167-168.

[2] *Veritable Records of the Ming Dynasty • A Compilation of Materials about Guizhou,* s.v. "Memoir of Hongwu"

[3] Zizhang Guo, *Record of Guizhou* (the Ming Dynasty), mimeographed edition, in the collection of Guizhou Provincial Library

[4] *The History of the Ming Dynasty,* s.v. "Biography of Wang Sanshan" (Zhonghua Book Company)

The Han people who live in Guanling, Qinglong, Pu'an, Liupanshui region and southern Bijie region are demonstrating apparent characteristics in the following four aspects in rice cultivation. First, the Han residents have a unique way of cultivating rice. They don't use *Ta Dou* (local tool for harvesting rice) and only cut the panicles. These panicles are then bundled and carried home, then threshed on slabstones. Most of the straws are not cut but instead left in the fields. Second, the rice fields after harvesting are left unattended to allow domestic animals to feed on, thus are used as winter pastures. Third, the fields are drained during harvesting. They are not submerged in water, nor are ploughed in the winter. Fourth, all rice fields are not ploughed until cultivation when the remaining straws are turned and put under the soil without burning. Such a farming system is completely different from that in the Han regions or the rice cultivation of the surrounding ethnic groups. [①] Unlike the ethnic Miao people who use picking knives to cut panicles, the Han farmers use reaping hooks. Compared to ethnic Buyi people who dry or stack the rice straws after they are cut, the Han farmers leave the rice straws in the field uncut. Compared to the ethnic Yi group who mainly grow buckwheat and oat and raise animals, the rice cultivation takes a much larger share in ethnic Han's economy. Its differences from ethnic Han people in central China are more obvious. They don't double crop, or grow small-season rice, nor gather rice straws for fodders. Based on these situations, we think that these characteristics are neither direct continuation of the Han traditional means of cultivation, nor a mode of production merely introduced from any ethnic minority, but rather an evolutionary adjustment that is made by these Han immigrants to make it compatible with the ethnic groups concerned, especially ethnic Yi, in the resource utilization.

Such an inference corresponded to the distribution of this farming system and the continuation of the culture of relevant ethnic group. Geographically, such a farming system concentrated in southern Liupanshui, the north of the three counties of Guanling, Qinglong and Pu'an, and partially in Anshun, Puding and Zhijin counties. Such a distribution, from an evolutionary geographic perspective, had two obvious characteristics: First, it scattered along the courier routes in the Ming dynasty especially the garrison areas. Second, it was popular in the areas under the control of Yi *Tu Si*. The

① Shengzhi Pan, "Residual of the Supplementary Structure of A Multi-ethnic Economy", *Guizhou Social Studies*, no. 4, 1995.

two distributive characteristics suggest that such a farming system was related to the ethnic Yi group and also to the Han immigrants in the Ming dynasty. In terms of the ethnic groups that implemented such a system, the majority of them were the Han immigrant groups who entered the ethnic Yi region in different ways in the Ming dynasty, such as military households in the Ming dynasty, namely the "big-footed Han people" nicknamed by local minority people, and civilian households who migrated and settled in Guizhou, namely the "small-footed Han people" in the local language, the "*Li Min Zi Ren*" referred to in the ancient literatures of the Han dynasty, as well as the civilian and military households that escaped from the Han settlements and were later under the protection of the Yi *Tu Si* in the Ming dynasty, namely the so-called "Chuanqing people" mentioned in the literatures of the Qing dynasty. Among them, the military households in the Ming dynasty had other names to address their different origins. For instance, the "trumpet people" who came from the ethnic Miao people in west Hunan, and the "Tunbao people" who had served in the Yuan army and later surrendered. In addition to the descendents of the Han immigrants, the ethnic Miao and Buyi people who were under the control of Yi *Tu Si* in the Ming dynasty were also in such a production system. The "Meng Leng" and "Meng Zhang" of the Miao group (the former literarily means "flag Miao" and the latter means "intermontane basin Miao") partially followed such a practice. Given that such a farming system prevailed primarily in the Han immigrant communities, and the people who practiced such a cultivation system were not subject to the jurisdiction of Yi *Tu Si* but were protected and their activities were restrained by Yi *Tu Si*, the goal of adjustment by this farming system was to achieve compatibility with the Yi's traditional economic life but not being acculturated by the Yi culture.

A comparison between the basic characteristics of this farming system and the traditional mode of production in the ethnic Yi groups makes it easy to find the actual significance of the existence of such a farming system. First, in the farming system, rice straws are kept in the fields, which helped turn rice fields into winter pastures. In fact, most of the rice fields cultivated by the stationed servicemen and civilians in the Ming dynasty were in the winter pastures in the Yi regions, apparently for the purpose of achieving compatibility with winter pasturing of the Yi people. Second, such a farming system ensured the harvesting of rice and symbolized a compromise by the Yi people to the Ming servicemen and civilians. By doing so, the ethnic Yi people achieved the compatibility in economic lifestyle with the Han servicemen and civilians. Third, although ethnic Han people lost the benefit of small-season cultivation, the grazing of a large number of domestic animals in the fields in the winter enhanced organic fertilization in the soils and thus ensured the yield in the big-season. On the side of the Yi people, the straws left in the fields provided a source of plentiful fodders for the winter animals, which benefited both sides. Lastly, this mutually supplementary way of land utilization also assisted product exchanges between the two ethnic groups. Therefore, we have reason to say that such a supplementary use of land resources increased the ability in compatibility between economic lives of both sides, and was thus an ideal mode of cross-xiang operations. It is a rare and commendable success if we are able to accomplish this when planning cross-xiang operations.

The successful implementation of this mode of development is premised on the parallel continuation of the economic lifestyle of both parties. Following the policy by the Qing government to replace all local hereditary headmen with the officials sent by the central government, the Yi influence was driven out of the political platform in this region and the Qing government distributed the lands confiscated from *Tu Si* to the people who made contributions in the campaign as rewards, resulting in the Han households beginning to settle in the Yi traditional pastures. Due to the drastic change in the political background, the issue of compatibility between the economic lifestyle of ethnic Yi and Han groups was overlooked. The newly arrived Han immigrants completely followed the Han traditional economic lifestyle to reclaim and cultivate pastures and turned them into farm lands. Furthermore, the Qing government started to implement a uniform taxation policy indiscriminately across ethnic groups. Consequently, some ethnic minority groups began to follow the Han practice to reclaim and cultivate pastures. As a result, the original supplementary economic relation between ethnic groups was gradually abandoned. As the pastures, especially steep hillsides, were converted, water and soil loss began to spread across large areas in northwest Guizhou, with upper reaches of Wujiang River being the hardest-hit region that became well-known in the country. This, to a certain extent, was directly attributable to the drastic change in the farming system.

Looking back at the evolutionary process in the development of northwest Guizhou, the following four aspects have reference values in planning cross-xiang operations today. First, in cross-xiang operations, there is no "one-size-fits-all" project as it concerns the natural background that has not been touched by original economic projects. Without transformation and adjustment, the project will be subject to constraints from natural background, which will decrease economic efficiency and may give rise to ecological deterioration. Second, as the heterogeneous economic lifestyle concerned in cross-xiang operations is the result of adjustment to natural environments over a long period of time, it must have an indomitable vitality and must be profoundly studied so that we can take advantage of its strengths. What we must avoid doing is emotional reasoning and simply view this economic lifestyle as backward and think it must be abandoned to start all over again. Third, cross-xiang operations are bilateral economic activities and the compatibility between the economic lifestyles of both parties is the necessary and sufficient condition for the operational success. Therefore, inflexibly sticking to the economic lifestyle of one party is harmful. Fourth, it is impossible that the economic life of any ethnic group can make use of the natural resources for one hundred percent. While processing and transforming natural resources, both parties must have left some areas that are not utilized due to the differences between two parties in discriminately selecting, corresponding to and adjusting natural resources. We are likely to find the effective point for the integration and for economic growth of the two parties to ensure that both parties may gain from cross-xiang operations as long as it is handled properly.

No matter what project is selected by the operators in the cross-xiang activities, they must ensure that the modes of resource utilization be compatible. This must be treated as a fundamental principle in dealing with secondary natural environments. As the heterogeneous economic life that cross-xiang operations concern is highly adaptable and dynamic in its living environment, it is unwise to recklessly change such a scenario by the operating capacity. Unfortunately, such a fundamental principle is often overlooked by the subjective parties in actual cross-xiang operation. As a result, heterogeneous living environment that the operation concerns have given rise to a series of non-economic elements that constrain cross-xiang operations and have substantially dampened the operating efficiency.

When we conducted fieldwork in the sugarcane bases of Wangmo Sugar Refinery, a section chief of the Refinery complained to us about the local Buyi people. He said: "The Buyi people here are conservative and are not willing to plant sugarcanes in the rice fields, so the sugarcane bases are built on the hillside that have a yield of around two to three tons per mu. If sugarcanes are planted in rice fields, the unit yield can be increased to about five tons. It will not only double the income but will be easier to transport and therefore is good to the factory and the farmers themselves. We've tried everything to convince them but are not successful." This statement was representative of the thoughts of many people. However, such a thinking reflected many unrealistic elements given the Buyi tradition in the utilization of resources of cultivated lands. Although rice field cultivation was the traditional mode of production as well as the major food for subsistence in the Buyi region, the natural environments in the Buyi settlements that could be converted into rice fields were only constrained to the bottom in the river valley. The per capita area of cultivated land in the region was small, and the growing period of sugarcanes was long, making it impossible for the interplanting or rotational planting of sugarcanes and crops. To grow sugarcanes in rice fields would cause conflicts between crops and sugarcanes. To protect the interests of factories must come at the expense of the efficiency of grain production. Even if the local market was well developed and the households specialized in sugarcane planting were able to trade sugarcanes for grains, the price ratio between grain and sugarcane as well as the transportation of bulk grains must be taken into consideration. The local market in this county was, as a matter of fact, far from mature. If we forced the Buyi people to grow sugarcanes in the rice fields, from the perspective of the Refinery, the economic activities between the Refinery and Buyi farmers would not be compatible. Now, it was an ideal situation for the Refinery to have sugarcane bases in the hillsides, which of course was disadvantageous to the expansion of the Refinery and enhancement of operating efficiency. Accordingly, we have reason to say that the project was problematic from the beginning. People only considered the fact that the region was a good place for growing sugarcanes but failed to realize it is difficult to make sugarcane planting compatible with Buyi traditional mode of resource utilization. Consequently, to build sugar refineries in this region must be subject to severe restrictions and production techniques must be adjusted accordingly.

Such a weakness in the stage of project selection would, to a certain extent, constrain the operating efficiency of the factory for a long time.

Comparatively, to grow vegetables is a much better choice than growing sugarcanes in the rice fields in the winter for the following three reasons: First, the growing period for vegetables is short and the idle rice fields in the winter are used, which is highly compatible with the Buyi traditional production. Second, the products produced this way have both market value and direct consumption value. The producers have more room to make decisions on their own; therefore, it is easier for local Buyi people to accept. Third, to grow vegetables can increase the content of organic fertilizer in the rice fields, enhance the breathability of soils in the rice fields, expedite the decomposition of organism, and thus has a direct effect on the increase of fertility of rice fields. As it does no harm but only good to the big-season production, it is compatible with big-season primary production in terms of soil fertility maintenance. One of the important reasons for the current rapid popularity of growing winter vegetables in the rice fields across all the counties in south Guizhou is the high compatibility between such a project and the mode of resource utilization in the Buyi region.

Another successful project in cross-xiang operation was the introduction of litsea cubeba in the Miao mountainous regions. As mentioned previously in the book, the ethnic Miao people in south Anshun region and the northeastern part of Southwest Guizhou Autonomous Prefecture still practiced Swidden cultivation. In such a type of production, the lands need to fallow where wild grasses and litsea cubeba were grown concurrently, and it was not contradictory to the fallow of lands. Litsea cubeba plants could also be burned to fertilize the fields; therefore, to grow litsea cubeba was very compatible with the traditional type of cultivation. The litsea cubeba, while occupying the lands, did not conflict with the grains growing on the lands. Consequently, the utilization of land resource was mutually compatible. In addition, the refinery of litsea cubeba oil was similar in operation to the local traditional roast wine technique. Such a project was easy to be compatible with the local Miao production in the resource utilization and production operation, which was the fundamental reason for the litsea cubeba to spread rapidly and widely in the Miao region. Now, the wave of litsea cubeba planting has waned, for the reason that has nothing to do with compatibility in resource utilization, but market price fluctuation and ineffective control by related administrative departments, as well as the delay in the project of deep processing of litsea cubeba seeds. The real lesson we've learnt from this is: the lack of options in the selection of operational projects, and the delay in subsequent projects. We are sure that similar projects will yield better economic benefit if we can learn from these lessons.

As the compatibility in the project options mainly concerns the specific living environment, the same option may demonstrate very different level of compatibility in cross-xiang operations of different ethnic groups. Liuma tung oil is a famous brand in Guizhou and an important export product in the Buyi region in Guizhou. The tung tree planting in its early stage in the Buyi region was restrained to self-consumption. After it became famous, the officials in the local and county governments put forth the slogan of "to get rich by planting tung trees" and began to plant tung trees in large areas. However, the implementation of such a measure that aimed at developing the local economy was received differently among the Miao and Buyi people. In the Miao regions, most of the mountains that were suitable for the planting of tung trees were in the Swidden cultivation in fallow or slash-and-burn. However, tung trees were perennial commercial trees and to plant tung trees in large areas directly conflicted with the fallow cultivation of the lands. In addition, to ethnic Miao people, anything that grew naturally in the land could be picked by anybody, as a result, the promotion of tung trees in the Buyi regions was slow and the tung seeds were often stolen. To harvest the tung seeds before they fully matured inevitably led to the drop in the quality of tung seeds and these tung seeds could not meet the raw material requirements for the production of high quality Liuma tung oil. The situation in Buyi region was different. As the Buyi people primarily lived on rice field cultivation, and the mountains were owned by extended families in the villages, anyone from the family who input manual labor would have the shared right of operation. In addition, the harvest season of tung seeds did not coincide with the harvest season of rice, and therefore to operate tung tree plantations did not conflict with rice field cultivation. The mountains were not subject to slash-and-burn, and the products as a result of individual manual labor were respected by all the villagers, making it possible for tung seeds to fully mature and drop from the trees before they were picked and taken home. The high compatibility between tung seed production and Buyi primary production contributed directly to the high yield of high quality

Liuma tung oil. From the perspective of natural resource utilization, as the living environment of the Buyi people provided perfect point for growth in the production of tung seeds, the tung tree planting was promoted widely across the Buyi region and quickly went into bulk production. It is apparent from the comparison of the two ethnic groups that the same cross-xiang project will yield different results in living environments of different ethnic groups. Now, although the operation of tung tree plantation is perplexed by price fluctuation, the project has solid natural and living environment foundation, and thus remains to have huge potentials in production, and will surely play a significant role in driving the economic development in the Buyi regions as long as the price can be kept stable.

In summary, the living environment that each ethnic group is exposed to is shaped by this ethnic group and thus encompasses social characteristics. To ensure the success of the cross-xiang project, operators must analyze and inspect the compatibility between the proposed project and the living environment of the relevant ethnic groups. Lacking such compatibility, the project will have no value of implementation.

IV Spatial Attenuation and Investment Expansion

In addition to pure natural background and the living environment of relevant ethnic groups, the spatial distance that the operation concerns may also have negative impacts on cross-xiang operations in the three aspects. As the necessary equipment and personnel are provided by the subjective party in cross-xiang operations, the increase in the distance concerned in the operations will inevitably push up the cost in transportation, and will eventually drive up product costs and lower the operational efficiency. In terms of the supply of raw materials and product distribution in the operation, the wider the area that is concerned, the higher the added costs to meet the demand in raw material supply and product distribution. They will eventually lead to a higher product cost and lower efficiency. In terms of the need in the social life of the personnel who participate in the operation in a heterogeneous cultural environment, the wider the spatial range to meet the need of normal life, the higher the added costs to be spent in the operation. Such added cost is another important element that makes up the total cost of the product. The above three aspects are all related to the spatial distance and range concerned in the operational activities and will unexceptionally lead to the increase in product costs or the amount of investment, and the decrease in operating efficiency. Therefore, they combine to be referred to as the "spatial attenuation" in cross-xiang economic efficiency. As cross-xiang operations must be subject to the effect of spatial attenuation, we hereby refer to it as "spatial attenuation effect" in cross-xiang operations.

In the same-xiang economic activities, the spatial distance and range in economic operations may also impact the result of the operation. However, as the entire economic activity is carried out in the same cultural setting and similar natural background, the impacts of spatial distance and range on operations must be in the multi-direction and multi-project form. As culture has the integral and systematic nature, impacts from different directions and in different contents will surely offset each other to a certain extent in the cultural integration and adjustment, and bring the absolute value of the sum of these impacts to near zero. The negative impacts of spatial distance on the same-xiang economic activities will not manifest except in special circumstances.

Any enterprise that is in normal operation must be supplied with all kinds of raw materials, equipment and power, and in the mean time, must distribute their products across the range that is coverable by the enterprise. The completion of this process relies on transportation. In same-xiang economic activities, raw materials come from different directions across different distances. The products work in reversed direction. They all start from the enterprise and go in different directions across different distances. Enterprises have a large room in selection in terms of the combination of transportation in the above two situations, and they can make the absolute value of the sum of the random combination to near zero by selecting the location of the factory. After such a state is reached, the transportation capacity wasted on no-load runs would be minimized significantly. That is the ideal result that can be achieved by the selection of the factory's site. Of course, such a goal is not fully achievable in reality but can only partially minimize the invalid loss in transportation. In addition, as the operation is carried out in the same xiang and is subject to the regulation of the same culture, even if the result is not the most ideal, the loss caused by invalid transportation generally can be offset by other operational measures. Therefore, in same-xiang operations, the loss caused by such invalid transportation will not evolve into constraints on the operation of an enterprise in good operating conditions. In other words, enterprises may offset the negative impacts by changing the means of operation if such constraints arise.

Things are very different in cross-xiang operations. As the projects are determined by the subjective party in the operation, it is only in the living environment of the subjective party that the need to gather the necessary raw materials and to distribute the products can be met. The need can not be fully met in other xiang. Now, two new elements that do not exist in same-xiang operations emerge. First, the percentage of the materials that need to be transported across different xiang: the higher the percentage, the bigger the volume in cross-xiang transportation, and the higher the percentage of no-load run in transportation, and the bigger of the share of wasted capacity in total service transportation cost. Second, a longer distance between the site of the enterprise and the living environment of the subjective party in the operation signals a longer distance in the no-load run in the transportation service of the factory. In other words, in cross-xiang operations, the total volume of transportation for the service of the enterprise must include the extra loss caused by invalid transportation as a result of prolonged distance in the operation, and the value of the loss is directly proportional to the volume and distance in the transportation. We will analyze how these elements specifically constrain the operating enterprise efficiency by the following examples. For example, to build and operate a cotton spinning mill in an ethnic minority region that does not produce cotton, different varieties of materials are needed ranging from cotton, starch for starching yarns, fuels used as power, and the dyes for printing and dyeing etc. No matter how many varieties of materials and how many quantities for each variety are needed, there must be a part of the materials that must be provided from the living environment of the subjective party in the operation. For the ethnic minority regions in Guizhou that do not produce cotton, apparently, cotton must be provided from the living environments of the subjective parties in the operations, namely the Han regions, and the total quantity of cotton that need to be shipped into the region will, without any doubt, take a considerable percent in the total quantity of materials that need to be shipped into the enterprise. The transportation cost within this percentage must contain three added values. First, the additional transportation cost to cover the prolonged distance from the Han region. Second, the unavoidable additional cost due to the inability to minimize the no-load run in the transportation by choosing the site of factory. Third, the unavoidable additional cost in storage and quality-assurance due to the prolonged transportation lines. The following formula can be used to calculate the inevitable additional cost in transportation due to the prolonged distance for the factories that are located in the ethnic minority regions.

$$F2=Mw\ [Fj\cdot(L1-L2)+Fk\cdot(L1+Fb)]$$

F2 denotes the total cost to cover the extra prolonged transportation in cross-xiang operations. Mw denotes the total tonnage of raw materials that the enterprise must obtain from the subjective party in the operation. Fj denotes the average shipping rate per ton-kilometer. Ll represents the total distance that the raw materials must travel to arrive in the factory located in ethnic minority regions. L2 represents the distance that the raw materials must travel to arrive in the factory if it is located in the Han region under normal circumstances. Fk represents the additional costs in no-load run in transportation per kilometer. Fb denotes the additional costs in storage and quality-assurance in the transportation of raw materials.

The formula indicates that while the shipping rate and the additional costs in no-load run in transportation per kilometer remain constant, the longer the distance between the enterprise and the living environment of the subjective party in the cross-xiang operations, the higher the additional costs; meanwhile, the bigger the quantity in the raw materials transported from the subjective party, the higher the added costs. In cross-xiang operations, the spatial distance between the subject party and objective party, namely Ll in the formula, becomes a constant once the objective party is fixed, and will remain unchanged throughout the entire process of operation. The subjective party in cross-xiang operations must carry out the economic activities on the premise of acknowledging the reality, which means that as long as raw materials must be supplied from and provided by the subjective party, such an additional cost in transportation will continue to exist and make up of the cost of products.

To lower the additional cost, the only change that subjective parties can make is the total tonnage of the supplied raw materials, namely the Mw in the formula. The smaller the value, the lower the additional cost in product costs. For this reason, to measure whether an enterprise in cross-xiang operations is dynamic, we must consider the percentage of raw material supply and demand, i.e.,

$$K = Mw / Mz$$

K represents the efficiency constant due to the selections of the enterprise, and Mw represents the total tonnage of raw materials that must be supplied by the subjective party, which is fixed when the project is determined by the enterprise. Mz denotes the total tonnage of all the materials shipped into the enterprise. In the cotton spinning mill mentioned above, for instance, cotton was supplied from the Han regions; therefore, the Mz and Mw of the factory is fixed, and then the value K of this factory naturally becomes fixed. It is easy to tell that if we choose a cotton mill project, the value K would be a big percentage. The only way to lower the value K is to choose to invest in an enterprise that requires less raw material supply from the subjective party in the operation. To build a paper mill in the ethnic minority regions in Guizhou, for example, will be a different story. As the raw materials necessary for papermaking such as wood, Chinese alpine rush, bamboo etc., can be sourced locally, and only the raw materials such as alkali and bleach have to be supplied from the Han regions, Mw that impacts the value K will decrease accordingly, making the value K a small percentage and the total additional cost in transportation to drop considerably. However, as the spatial distance can not be changed, such an additional cost in transportation, namely F2, will exist forever no matter which project is selected. We can only reduce the quantity but not totally eliminate it.

By analyzing the additional cost in the transportation of raw materials, we can tell that the increase of spatial distance in cross-xiang operations will inevitably result in the drop in operating efficiency, which is a component of the efficiency attenuation in cross-xiang operation. In addition, the distribution of products and provision of equipment maintenance parts also cause efficiency attenuation. However, it is much more difficult to use mathematical formula to describe the laws that the efficiency attenuation follows in these situations than in the case of transportation of raw materials into the factory. As this book is only about illustrating the existence of non-economic constraints, we will overlook the mathematical induction at the operational level.

A factory must keep unobstructed communication with external world to ensure its normal operation. However, the modes to keep unobstructed exchange of materials are different in same-xiang and cross-xiang operations.

In the same-xiang operations, the enterprises rely on the overall society that is established on the same culture. As mentioned previously, culture has a network structure that is a system in itself, therefore, the society it governs and the exchange of materials inside the society are also an orderly network structure. For instance, if the enterprise operates in an ethnic society that has a fully developed market, all the materials needed by the factory including price, quality, and supply of goods will not fluctuate considerably. In the meantime, the products produced by the factory may be distributed in the society through the market channel over the network of commodity demand through cultural operation.

Cross-xiang operations are different from same-xiang operations in two aspects. First, the materials needed by the enterprise include two parts. One part, due to incompatibility with cultural network of the objective party, can only be supplied from the raw material bases outside the objective living environments and distributed outside the living environment of the objective party. The percentage between the two parts is a constant, which directly impacts the operational efficiency. Second, the materials that must be provided from outside the objective party's living environment and products that must be distributed outside the objective party's living environment must be exchanged in the living environments of other ethnic groups. There must be a distance between the site of the enterprise and the point where the materials are exchanged. The extra cost for the materials to travel across this space, due to the lack of cultural reliance, must be covered by the enterprise itself.

Material exchanges that serve the factory must be completed within a coverage. Specifically, a raw material must be supplied to the factory from a corresponding area of supply; a product must be distributed to a certain area. In same-xiang operations, people can choose the best location for building the factory after comprehensively considering the material exchange coverage to make these coverage overlap, so as to ensure the material movement inside and outside the factory, increase effective cost and lower ineffective costs. The attempts by these enterprises are fully reliant on the same cultural network. Cross-xiang operations are different. The materials that move into and from the factory are separated into two parts. Some are completed within the living environment of the objective party and others are completed within the living environment of the subjective party. Therefore, the location of the factory must be determined by taking the two parts into consideration. On the one hand, to make the material exchange completed in the living environment of the objective party more effective, the factory must be built close to the center of the overlapping coverage in material supply and product distribution. In principle, such a way of selecting factory location is similar to that in same-xiang operations. On the other hand, as some material exchanges in these enterprises must be completed in the heterogeneous living environment, operators tend to select a location that nears that heterogeneous living environment to reduce the distance of invalid transportation. Needless to say, the full superposition between the two is impossible in reality. Therefore, no matter how the spatial distance changes under the condition of keeping the cross-xiang operations running, the operations will not produce the same results as in same-xiang operations and will inevitably cause obstacles due to the spatial location of the enterprise. The extra cost as a result of obstacles is a component of the spatial efficiency attenuation.

In cross-xiang operations, the spatial location of the enterprise also negatively impacts the level in which the normal social life of the people involved in the operation is ensured. In same-xiang operations, the requirement of the people in the enterprise is the same as the entire society, which can be fully met no matter where the factory is located. For instance, the social service for the enterprise personnel can be furnished without extra effort by the enterprise. The interpersonal relationship between all the people inside and outside the enterprise can be dealt with without any extra attempt from the enterprise. Things are different in cross-xiang operations. In normal situations, the people from the enterprise in cross-xiang operation are made up of two components: those that come from the subjective party and those from the objective party. The requirements to meet the normal social life for these two kinds of people are quite different due to restrictions by their respective culture, which results in the un-superposition in the social activities of these two kinds of people. Therefore, the selection of spatial location of the enterprise must take the different needs of both parties into consideration, but can not be fully determined by the operational needs of the factory. Subsequently, the operating efficiency of the factory is subject to restriction to certain extent. Now, in the enterprises established in the ethnic minority groups in Guizhou, this issue is handled roughly by the following two methods: First, to build the factory into a society. A number of large and medium state-owned enterprises in Guizhou have taken this method. They have built their own hospitals, schools, stores, kindergartens, and livelihood service facility etc., pushing up the non-production related costs and reducing the efficiency of the enterprise. Another method is to relax the management of the factory to satisfy the need of the people in the enterprise in their social life, which is taken by many county-level enterprises. The county-level small and medium enterprises mentioned earlier, for instance, have taken a permissive attitude toward the minority employees for their conducts in violation of factory rules due to ethnic social activities. Neither of the above two methods can bring the social life requirements of the employees from different ethnic groups into consideration at the same time, which would impact the operating efficiency of the enterprise. It is apparent that in cross-xiang operations, the location of the enterprise can never be as ideal as in same-xiang operations. This is another reason that the spatial location of enterprise constrains the results of the operation.

The efficiency attenuation caused by the above three aspects is the inevitable drop in efficiency if the cross-xiang operators build one or two isolated factories in the living environment of the objective party. One of the major reasons for the drop in efficiency, as discussed above, is related to the change in spatial difference of the enterprise. To reverse this unfavorable investment consequence, Western economists came up with the "big-push" theory in the hope to create the mutual dependence and mutual stimulation among enterprises and thus increase their operating efficiency through one-time investment by a bunch of enterprises.

Paul Rosenstein-Rodan, the most influential advocate of the theory, first put forward the theory of the "big-push" in his article *Problems of Industrialization of Eastern and South-Eastern Europe* in 1943. According to the theory, large-scale investment and infrastructural construction is necessary in the initial stage of economic development to benefit from an economy of scale and the external economy. He states that it is the most appropriate way to improve the situation of uneven income distribution across different regions in the world by increasing the income in the backward regions at a higher rate than the wealthy regions. Meanwhile, he thinks that economy is an integral process and is inseparable. The "big-push" approach helps balance the development in all sectors so that they can serve each other and be each other's customers, thus achieving balance in supply and demand. He further illustrates by example: An under-developed country initially builds a modern shoe factory that hires unemployed workers. The supply and demand of these shoes will not be a problem if the income of these workers is all spent on buying shoes. As a matter of fact, only a small part of the income is spent in buying shoes, which slows down the sale of the shoes. Subsequently, the investment in other sectors must follow that in the shoe factory to create a massive market from which all factories can benefit. In addition, the "big-push" measures also help reduce cost. With production activities across factories, the emergence of specialized factories that provides centralized service in warehousing, shipping, cleaning, safety and protection etc. will eventually lower the cost of each factory. In this sense, the "big-push" approach will improve the status of developing countries to bridge the gap in the income between developing and developed countries.①

Although the "big-push" theory was put forward by Western economists on the industrialization of developing countries, similar theories have been advocated in the poverty-relief efforts in the ethnic minority regions in China, which is "impulse type" of poverty-relief efforts. Specifically, it means to invest massive manpower, material and money at one time in a restricted area to support multi-projects in the hope to break the closure of traditional economy and build a foundation for the self-development in these regions. However, similar practices have run into difficulties in reality as money and manpower is always in shortage. The more difficult thing is that the spatial efficiency attenuation in cross-xiang operations can never be eliminated no matter how the investment is made. Therefore, such a practice can only mitigate the attenuation to some extent. The existence of spatial efficiency attenuation apparently will put the enterprises in ethnic regions in a disadvantageous position when competing in the national market. In addition, these enterprises are put in a fierce market competition while in their initial stage of operation without a well-established internal operation procedure, adding to the disadvantages that these enterprises are subject to. For these reasons, we think that these enterprises must solve the problem by dealing with the spatial efficiency attenuation instead of fighting recklessly by absolute capacity, to put it more specifically, completely abandon the "one-way" mode of operation and replace it with "bi-way" or "multi-way"

① Yincai Fu, *Basic Western Economic Theories* (Yunnan People's Publishing House, October 1985), 254.

mode of operation. We will further discuss this issue in chapter nine *Solutions.*

The spatial efficiency attenuation effect not only restrains the efficiency of the enterprises in ethnic regions, it also causes the scale of investment in the ethnic regions to expand and makes it impossible for the initial investment to realize the desired value. Among many reasons that cause the initial investment to expand, the following four aspects demand our close attention: first, loss in spatial displacement; second, loss in supplementary investment; third, loss in operational stability; fourth, loss in life assurance.

In same-xiang operations, the cost to be spent in the establishment and movement of enterprises is a fixed amount in a stable economy. However, to run similar enterprises in cross-xiang operations costs more in investment due to enterprise spatial displacement. In addition to the prolonged enterprise spatial distance that results in the increase in the costs in enterprise equipment transportation, more importantly, cross-xiang activities are carried out across cultures. Different cultures provide different social conditions for the establishment of enterprises. As a result, the problems that can be successfully solved in same-xiang operations require extra monetary input in cross-xiang environments to create social conditions similar to those in same-xiang operations. For example, to build a factory in same-xiang environment simply requires to buy a land that provides favorable conditions for the operation. In cross-xiang environments, however, that does not symbolize the ending of the problem as more social conditions are to be met before the factory can operate successfully. For the manufacturing and mining enterprises that demand a large quantity of water, the distribution of water resources in the site of the factory must be compatible with existing water system for the farm lands. To achieve this, extra money must be spent by the factory to make changes to current water channels, make the arrangement for the compatibility between the factory and original water systems instead of simply connecting water supply pipes and signing water supply contracts as is the case in same-xiang operations. In addition to water supply, other conditions such as road to and from the factory, and the impacts by the existence of the factory on the traditional production etc., all require extra investment from the factory to ensure that they are compatible with the local living environment. Such a spatial displacement on the cultural foundation leads to the increase in the transportation cost for the newly established enterprises as well as in the total investment in equipment and introduction of technologies. As a result, same amount of investment will not expand, but in fact, reduce the scale of production.

In same-xiang operations, the supply and demand mechanism that supports the operation of the enterprise may be created through interaction and cooperation with other enterprises. For instance, in the situation where an enterprise uses the products from a few other enterprises with which a partnership exists as its raw materials, what usually needs is a corresponding supply contract. Things are very different in cross-xiang operations, especially when one isolated enterprise is to be built. A mere supply contract can not guarantee the supply of raw materials; instead, it requires that the enterprise largely broaden its supply and distribution system. Another example is the road leading into the factory. Usually it is not a problem in same-xiang environments where the fundamental road structure is well in place and it will not cost much for the factory to construct a secondary road leading to the factory especially when the cost can be shared among a few factories. In cross-xiang operations, the factory can not be put into operation without putting in additional investment in constructing this secondary road, which in normal cases can only be undertaken by the factory alone and can not be shared by other partners. In fact, in cross-xiang operations, the spatial displacement of the factory has prolonged the spatial distance in the supply of auxiliary equipment to the factory and the service provided by the factory, thus adding to the burden of auxiliary equipment and investment expansion. Furthermore, enterprises in cross-xiang operations will face difficulties in inadequate and unsupportive auxiliary equipment, forcing them to spend huge amount of investment to build self-service capacities.

In the county-level enterprises we visited in our fieldwork, it was commonplace for them to independently build roads, machine repair factories, power plants, vehicle fleet and storage facility etc. The investments they spent on building these factories and facilities were, in exceptional cases, almost equal to the investment in building the factory. Such an expansion in investment cost a huge amount of money, and more importantly, the capacity created by these investments only served one factory and yielded extremely low efficiency, thus intensifying the burden on the enterprise management and forcing the enterprise to carry the debt burden continuously. All kinds of supportive facilities were built while many manufacturing and mining enterprises were constructed, which, after put into operation for a while, had to be sold by auction to pay the debt. Facing the harsh reality, people tried to solve the problem of investment expansion by opening up more channels for capital investment, establishing centralized supportive enterprises. Such an approach focused on one side of the problem, namely to share the investment in and the benefit of supportive facilities among a few enterprise. However, it overlooked the other side of the problem, namely the un-synchronization in the introduction of investment. Therefore, the administrative departments had to spend a large amount of money on infrastructure construction for the targeted enterprises before they made the investment in the region. Often, the promise on investments was not delivered in time or even would never be delivered. Consequently, the supportive facilities that cost huge amount of money to build could not produce the desired benefit and thus would give rise to new and invalid investment.

It is not difficult for us to tell from the above analysis that the expansion of investment in supportive facilities to better enterprises operating environments is an objective fact that is unavoidable in cross-xiang operations. From the negative perspective, such an expansion can only be constrained by careful and meticulous planning. We should not expect to eliminate the related investment by making another related investment. On the positive side, related investments apparently are the result of different social backgrounds, and the fundamental way of eliminating related investment is, instead of mechanically copying the design of established enterprise by the subjective party in cross-xiang operations, find the point of growth for the investment project and screen and select the project accordingly based on the specific social conditions, i.e., the actual social conditions of objective party in cross-xiang operations.

Another grave issue that the isolated enterprises established in cross-xiang operations must face is that the operational stability can not be guaranteed. In same-xiang operations, general mechanical failures can be fixed by coordination among enterprises. Even the replacement of spare parts can be satisfied by the market and usually will not shut down the factory as a result of mechanical breakdown. Isolated enterprises are different. A mechanical failure may shut down the factory for a long time partially due to the difficulty in supply as a result of prolonged spatial distance, and partially due to the difficulty as a result of mismatch in enterprise technical staff. More importantly, it is about the background in which the society operates. To remove these obstacles, the enterprise also needs to provide self-service to improve operational stability usually in the following way: purchase and store a huge number of spare parts and raw materials that are subject to constant shortage, or even pay a competitive salary to technical staffs only to let them wait for the mechanical failures to happen. They directly increase the investment and tie up the working capital of the enterprise and lead to the expansion of investment by the enterprises.

Another approach is to enlarge the supply in supporting equipment or even set up factories of supporting nature by increasing investment on the foundation of a modern enterprise. Like the above approach, such a practice also relies on making related investments to enhance the operating stability of the factory. Given that these enterprises can never depend on their own capacity to meet all social conditions needed for the operation of the enterprise, it is ultimately a passive approach.

It is our belief that instability in enterprise operation is caused by insufficient social conditions. To solve the problem proactively, we must improve the social conditions and search for the foundation for enterprise subsistence based on the specific social conditions. In this respect, the tung oil pressing businesses run by local ethnic people in Wangmo county have some experience to offer. The oil press machines they use are very simple and clumsy, most of which are eliminated by factory in the Han regions. Despite their low operating efficiency, these machines have a high level of stability. All supporting equipment and spare parts are locally procured, which guarantees the continuous operation of these enterprises, but in the mean time, causes product quality issues. These oil pressing businesses attempt to solve this problem by making use of the traditional experience in production. As they don't have modern baking machines, and even if they do, the maintenance of these machines is very difficult, they would rely on interpersonal relations within the ethnic group and ask that local farmers only supply the tung seeds that have been dried under the blazing sun for an extended period of time. These raw materials meet the requirements for pressing after some simple baking, which ensures that the water content in these seeds won't exceed the maximum. Another example: as these pressing businesses don't have purification equipment, they would add plant ash while boiling the tung seeds and then keep it stay still for a while to reduce the content of free organic acid and protein in the tung oil, which can also bring the finished product up to "the quality standard issued by the ministry". The operational stability is also increased without the complicated machines and equipment. Despite the low yield and the labor input which doubles that in specialized enterprises, these small businesses survive the competition against these modern specialized enterprises. Although massive investments have been made in counties such as Zhenning, Wangmo and Huangping in constructing modern tung oil pressing factories, the total tung oil pressing capacity by these small private businesses almost equals that of these factories with a much small capital. From this perspective, these oil pressing businesses have outcompeted the big factories. It proves that in cross-xiang operations, to focus only on the size, advanced technology and a standardized operation will delink the operation from the background in operation and result in the inefficiency of the limited investment.

The difference in the social life of the people who participate in cross-xiang operations, and the spatial displacement in the work zones not only constrain enterprise operating efficiency but also make it impossible for these enterprises to achieve expected operating targets and cause expansion in investment. Enterprises in cross-xiang operations often operate in the regions without a guaranteed social life environment, and people who work for these enterprises must relatively concentrate as required by the enterprises. As the concentrated people can not receive support from the society, they must rely on the enterprises themselves to meet the need of basic social life. In same-xiang operations, the basic needs in the livelihood of the employees can be provided from the society. In cross-xiang operations, however, these needs must be satisfied by the enterprises, which forces the enterprises to make non-productive investment to help relieve the employees from these worries. Although such an investment is part of the enterprise assets, it won't make any profit but can only be depleted. It is in essence a gift to the employees. The investment expansion is purely a capital sediment. Although the capital increased this way looks very necessary for stabilizing enterprise production, it is a waste in investment for the enterprise. Therefore, it becomes essential to cut this extra investment in cross-xiang investment activities. The key lies in the control of composition of people, namely to employ people from the objective party in the operations as much as possible. Such an approach is constrained by both the objective and subjective parties in different contents. From the perspective of enterprise actual effect, the more people from the objective party, the less amount in service-related investment, but other problems such as quality of people, interpersonal relations in the society and disturbances by traditional social perceptions arise. On the other hand, if more people are from the subjective party, the scale of service-related investment will inevitably be expanded. In a nutshell, to follow the "one-way" investment approach only slows down the service-related investment, and has to wait for the growth point to emerge in the society of the objective party, which can never be achieved by the "one-way" mode of cross-xiang operations.

The spatial efficiency attenuation effect is caused by the prolonged spatial distance, and is worsened by the difference across cultures. The constraints created by the spatial efficiency attenuation not only impact the enterprise's long-term operating efficiency, but also drive up the enterprise's extra amount of investment. Such a non-productive related investment results in waste in investment. In the meantime, it adds long-term burdens on the financial conditions of the enterprise that is already under strains. The fundamental solutions include: first, change the traditional mode of operation by mobilizing the subjective initiative of the objective party in the operation. Generally speaking, the efficiency attenuation resulted from a prolonged spatial distance is minimized primarily by cutting the transportation volume of raw materials and products by enterprise selections. Second, increase the level of compatibility between the cultures of both parties in the operation through a comprehensive analysis of both cultures to effectively change the concentration of raw materials and the way of product distribution, thus further relieving the attenuation. The spatial efficiency attenuation as a result of cultural differences is tackled primarily by changing the means of operation by the enterprise to attain compatibility across related cultures. Lastly, these measures must be supplemented by efforts to improve the relationship between the enterprise and the society to lower the spatial attenuation ratio, thus effectively improve the living environment of the enterprise.

Chapter VII On Capacity

Some people believe that economic development always relies on economic capacity, which is equivalent to the monetary input. Modern economists have broken the tradition by coining the concept of "human capital". However, it is not enough as a considerable part of ethnic regions in Guizhou are still in a self-sufficient or natural economy, many social products can not access the market or be priced, thus the input of pure monetary capital does not necessarily result in new productivity. In these regions, the understanding of "people quality", and also of the "human capital", is different from that in the economic developed regions. For the purpose of analyzing cross-xiang operations in western China, we will conduct a comprehensive study of operational capacity of the subjective and objective parties in cross-xiang operations from three perspectives: compilation of operational capacity indicator, evaluation of operational capacity and the elements that impact the effectiveness of operational capacity. It is our hope that these analyses may help our readers master the method of correctly evaluating the capacities of the subjective and objective parties in cross-xiang operations.

I Components of Economic Capacity

In "same-xiang" economic activities, investment, equipment, people and project are essential and inevitable elements of operation. These elements are also involved in cross-xiang operations. However, as cross-xiang operations inevitably concern more than two heterogeneous economic backgrounds, these elements encompass more complex content than those in "same-xiang" operations, which requires that these concepts be extended in connotation to certain extent to meet the need of cross-xiang operating activity analysis. Investment, by the definition in modern economics, often refers to the monetary input that forms part of the capital. It is meaningful only when used in a fully-developed market economy, because in a less-developed market, not all material foundations related to economic activities can be valued in monetary terms. As a result, monetary input alone can not solve all the problems. We have known from the previous texts that a considerable number of ethnic groups and ethnic regions in Guizhou are still in a self-sufficient or natural economy with an under-developed market economy. Even if sufficient monetary input is made in cross-xiang economic activities that concern these ethnic groups or ethnic regions, only a part of it may be converted into capital, which does not necessarily guarantee the success of the operation. For instance, as the ethnic Miao regions in west Guizhou are in the Swidden cultivation type of economy, their product distribution and resource utilization have distinct characteristics of a self-sufficient economy, and the land resources are not priced and are thus available to be used but not owned by anyone, nor can anyone refuse other people to use them. As a result, cross-xiang operational activities that concern these ethnic regions are sure to face the following three difficulties:

First, in ethnic Han regions, the land resources can be kept in the absolute control of the operators during operation by paying a certain amount of money, through purchase or lease, when the land is needed. Things are different in the ethnic Miao regions in west Guizhou. As lands are not privatized, the first difficulty in the purchase and lease of lands is with whom to go through the purchasing or leasing formalities. The ensuing question is whether such a contract is legally effective. The lease of land is understood by the locals as temporary use and is not equivalent to a permission of measures of privatization. Lastly, how to distribute the income from the leasing or purchasing of lands among households in the village. In case of any problem in the three stages, even if a contract is signed, it does not guarantee a complete control of land resources by the operator.

Second, the utilization of land resources in these ethnic regions also gives rise to the pricing issue. As mentioned previously in the book, the utilization and transfer of lands in these regions are free. The monetary payment made by cross-xiang operators is for the purpose of securing the absolute control over the land during the period of usage, but such a payment is often viewed by the local Miao people as a surprise money due to the local tradition that land transfer is carried out without a monetary consideration. As to the absolute control of the land requested by the operators, the local people have never thought of respecting it. We have noticed from our fieldwork that some of the roads that administrative departments invested in building were used less frequently after “annul districts and merge townships”, and subsequently, nearby local people treated them as idle lands that were cultivated into farm lands. The local administrative authorities tried to stop it repeatedly but were in vain; therefore, they often blamed the local people for their ignorance. However, the fundamental reason was that these local people were simply following their cultural traditions, but did not understand the meaning of "land appropriation" at all. To make them fully understand "land appropriation" and "leasing of land", we must first help them establish the concept of "land ownership", which is not attainable in a short time. Cross-xiang operators will inevitably face such a problem in reality: The absolute control of the lands is not guaranteed even if they have followed the practice in the Han region and have paid the rent or purchase money. Such a guaranteed control can only be obtained by trying everything to please the local people to win their cooperation, which may be more costly than the rent or the money paid to purchase the land. Wangmo Sugar Refinery encountered a similar problem when it built the raw material base.

As local Buyi people refused to plant sugarcanes due to low factory purchase price, the local administrative departments had to mobilize the local so-called "Gaoshan Han" to lease the lands collectively owned by the Buyi villages to plant sugarcanes. In such a background, the ownership of these lands was very complex: Some were owned by the production team, some were appropriated by the county or commune to the forest plantations, and some were expropriated by enterprises and public institutions. The lands were leased to these "Gaoshan Han" at extremely low rent, about 2 to 4 yuan per mu, under the strong administrative influence. For the reasons mentioned above, the use of lands across the Buyi community was free. The low-rent deal was eventually forced upon the Buyi people by the administrative pressure, but things got more complicated later. In addition to the request to raise rents, what troubled the cross-xiang operators more was that these Buyi people, after receiving the rents, didn't think that they were obligated to respect the right of the "Gaoshan Han" to operate the sugarcane plantations. Instead, they would do anything to the lands as they would like because they thought that they were the owners of the lands. Consequently, it was not uncommon to see that cattle were herded in the fields; sugarcanes plantations were destroyed by slash-and-burns; or mature sugarcanes were willfully picked by villagers without the permission of the planters. Similar disputes were brought up to the county government, which was too far away to handle these disputes. When they were brought up to the Refinery, it tried to stop them for the protection of its own interests but failed as it did not want to offend the Buyi people who lived in the local community. Disputes over the right of land use may disrupt the operation of the raw material bases at any time if they are not solved properly.

Third, the form of purchase and lease is another huge issue. As the complete system in land transfer and lease is not in place in these ethnic regions, people don't know how to make the corresponding land transfer and lease formalities complete, making it extremely difficult to obtain the right of control over the needed lands. For the long time in the past, the lands used by the state-run enterprises have been acquired by administrative appropriation and requisition, which is the source of many troubles in the future although it looks convenient at the moment. The local people would not respect the right to use the lands even after they have been requisitioned and appropriated, and they would not hesitate to put these lands into use as long as the construction has not been kicked off or part of the lands are left idle. It is for this very reason that a piece of land may need to be requisitioned and appropriated repeatedly for the state-run enterprises. In the Dong and Buyi regions where the paddy fields are already privatized, it is much easier for the cash deal in the land purchase and lease. To the contrary, lands that are collectively owned by extended families may be used without paying any compensation as long as a good relationship is maintained. However, the right of control over the lands is not respected, which is intolerable to the operators.

It becomes apparent from the above discussion that the meaning of investment in cross-xiang operations is different from that in "same-xiang" operations. The mere monetary input can not solve all the problems. It must be supported by other means to ensure the operating efficiency of investment. Although the limited space in the book has restrained our discussion to the land resources, our readers may draw inferences and apply them in similar issues that exist in other cases of investments. Certainly, in addition to investment issues, we are facing similar problems in the selection of investment, utilization of equipment and employment of personnel. We must remain conscious that these terminologies have been given an extended connotation when used in cross-xiang operation contexts and therefore must be understood beyond the original meaning in economics. As the foundation of similar concepts in cross-xiang operations, we feel necessary to carry out a comprehensive analysis of the economic capacity that is often talked about so that we can have a basic understanding of the connotation and extension in the meaning of these terminologies.

When talking about economic activities, people would always think about the economic capacity, and would first look at the specific monetary accumulation. For the reasons mentioned above, we have realized that mere monetary input is not the solution to all the problems, and it must be accompanied by the work that does not involve monetary input to ensure the success of the operating activities. The reason for us to conduct such work is that monetary accumulation does not fully reflect the economic capacity of one ethnic group relative to the other. Other more complex elements must be taken into account when the real economic capacity of an ethnic group can not be completely converted into monetary values. For instance, how is the economic capacity of each ethnic group reflected in material form? In other words, what are the real differences in the material form of the economic life of each ethnic group? Another example is the way of conversion between economic capacities of different ethnic groups: how can the material form that is a reflection of the economic capacity of different ethnic groups be converted? In addition, we must also consider by which rules the conversion between the economic capacities of different ethnic groups is attained. This is the issue about the rules in regulation and control, by which economic capacities of different ethnic groups are converted. Only after the comprehensive analysis of these characteristics can we have an accurate judgment on the economic capacity of one ethnic group relative to the others.

We have found in the human history that the standards in measuring the economic capacity of an ethnic group differ dramatically in different times and across different ethnic groups. In ancient China, "sufficient grains and soldiers" were the symbol of a prosperous and powerful nation in the ethnic Han regions. ① Later feudal dynasties added the tax-paying households and number of people who had labor or military service obligations as the symbol of national prosperity. ② The ethnic minorities in the Mongolian Plateau also used the "cattle population" to measure the economic capacity. In modern times, with the emergence of modern industry, grains, households, cattle population are abandoned as the indicators of the economic capacity and are replaced with a series of new measurements.

Between the mid-19th century and the beginning of WWII, Western powers used in succession the output of certain material products as the

① *Annotations on the Thirteen Classics* (II), vol. 12, *Yan Yuan • Zigong Discussing Policies* (Zhonghua Book Company, 2nd print, December 1982), 2505 middle part.

② *Twenty-five Histories* vol. 1, col. 3, *The History of the Former Han Dynasty • Shi Huo Zhi*, 476.

material standards in measuring the economic capacity of an ethnic group. For instance, to use total "tonnage" of all merchant ships or the output of "three acids and two alkalis" to measure the economic capacity of a nation or an ethnic group. At the moment, a higher output of sulfuric acid, nitric acid, hydrochloric acid, sodium carbonate, and caustic soda symbolized a higher level of industrialization and subsequently the economic capacity of a country. Later, people began to use the output of "steel" and "oil" to measure the economic capacity of an ethnic group. After WWII, the level of oil consumption, output of plastics, the production of computers etc., were used successively as indicators of the economic capacity of a country. It is clear in the above examples that the economic capacity of an ethnic group can not be evaluated fully by the currency holdings but must be supported by a certain quantity of material products. These material products used as economic capacity indicators are material form of evaluation of the ethnic economic capacity.

It is discernable that the standards used in evaluating the economic capacity are different in different times and across different ethnic groups. Therefore, when analyzing the economic capacity of the ethnic groups that participate in cross-xiang operations in Guizhou, we should not focus only on the monetary accumulation but should also take the material form of economic evaluation of these ethnic groups into account.

In the history of Guizhou, all the major ethnic groups experienced the Swidden cultivation, a self-sufficient economy where all the material products, grains, fuels, and clothes that were daily necessities of people were locally produced and consumed, and were never exchanged across different ethnic groups, thus were not included as indicators of economic capacity. Under such circumstances, the most valuable product was cattle, which were mainly used as sacrificial or ceremonial items. As similar situations existed in the ethnic Miao, Buyi and Yi regions, the cattle population became one of the major indicators in the measurement of the economic capacity of these ethnic groups.

According to the *New History of Tang*, in the Buyi community in central Guizhou, events such as betrothals offered for engagement or compensation offered in case of criminal offenses were all priced by the number of cattle.[①] It was recorded in the book *Xi Man Cong Xiao* that the ethnic Miao in east

① *Twenty-five Histories* vol. 5, col. 3 - 4, 4110.

Guizhou in the Song dynasty used cattle and liquor as pricing indictors in occasions such as sacrificial ceremonies and presenting betrothals. According to *The History of the Ming Dynasty · Biography of Tu Si in Guizhou,* the major tribute paid by the *Shuixi An Shi*, one of the big Yi *Tu Si,* was horse, which was nicknamed "Shuixi Horse" and was the major type of military horses used by the mountainous regions in southwest Guizhou. Within the regions under the influence of ethnic Yi people, the number of available horses was used as one of the criteria to measure the economic capacity. Consequently, an area that was able to provide one horse was called one "horsehead" or "one horse".[①] Such a region was made a basic-level administrative unit and was named after its typical landscape. Many of these names, such as Liuma (six horses) in Zhenning county, and Matou (horsehead) township in Anshun city, are still used today.

In the period of Kangxi of the Qing dynasty, Guizhou, as the rest of the country, enforced the "land, people and silver system", which requested by administrative orders to use "silver" as standards to measure economic capacity. However, the vast differences in the type and mode of economy across different ethnic groups restrained the application of such a standard to the situations where ethnic Han regions were interacted or the royal court was involved. The original evaluation standard remained unchanged to a large extent within ethnic groups. This was the major reason why in the ethnic Miao regions in southeast Guizhou, a vast quantity of silver stayed in the regions in the form of "jewelry" and thus exited from the economic circulation.

The above examples illustrated that the standards used in evaluating the economic capacity in different ages and across different ethnic groups were not completely dictated by the monetary policies of the central government, but rather followed ethnic traditions for a long time. Therefore, to meet the needs in evaluating the economic capacity of each party in cross-xiang operations, we must use a new set of evaluation approach, which must align the monetary and non-monetary policy evaluation indicators, and the non-monetary indicators must be established on the foundation of the traditional ethnic evaluation method. To achieve this goal, we must carry out thorough studies on the material products that can be used to measure the economic capacity of each ethnic group, i.e., the material form of these

① *Twenty-five Histories* vol. 10, col. 2, 8669.

measurements.

Now, the efforts in poverty relief and economic development in ethnic regions in Guizhou are facing similar problems. While the government officials who are charged with the poverty-relief work in these regions are in control of state loans or cash, they would face unexpected difficulties when the loans and cash are distributed in different ethnic regions. Many local people, who don't know how to use the cash loans, are first frightened. Some, for fear of not being able to repay the loans, don't spend a penny but seal all the cash at home. Smarter ones choose to deposit the poverty-relief money in the bank. Both are against the intention of distributing poverty-relief funds. For the poverty-relief cash, local people choose to spend it on buying livelihood necessities after knowing that it does not need to be repaid. Some government officials attribute such phenomena to local people's ignorance of economic development and others blame their laziness. In fact, neither is right to the point. The real problem is that the intention of distributing the poverty-relief money is, from the beginning, not compatible with the perception of economic life of ethnic minority people. It is our understanding that to develop agriculture must start with the purchase of chemical fertilizer, pesticide, improved variety of crops and new farm tool, while in the perception of the ethnic minority people, these are not critically necessary. To them, seeds are retained and fertilizers are composted by themselves, and the need for pesticide and farm tool is quite limited and not as indispensible as in the Han regions. They think that the cash received to relieve poverty may be better used if spent on improving daily life. As a result, the actual use of the poverty-relief money is also against the original intention. In fact, in the ethnic regions with a self-sufficient or natural economy, cash is not always an absolute necessity and cash input does not have a huge impact on production as long as there are no extreme natural disasters. It is hard for us to determine what these ethnic people lack and really need unless we conduct profound study in the material form of the indicators in evaluating the economic capacity in these regions.

In recent years, the Ethnic Affairs Commissions in all counties are busy with one important job – distribute house-building money to the people in poverty-stricken villages. However, our investigations revealed that these funds were not used as they were intended. It was our original thought that local people could take the money to buy building materials, hire laborers and turn their shabby houses into new residence. As a matter of fact, in the regions and ethnic groups that are in the self-sufficient or natural economy, money is not a necessity in house-building: building materials may be sourced locally and laborers are not hired by cash but only need to be treated with meals. Therefore, house constructions are often delayed even after the house-building money is received. When asked, the responses from the local minority people included: the grains have not been harvested; pigs are still too little to be slaughtered so they don't have enough to treat the people to help build the house. If we had known this, we could have replaced the cash grants with building materials, with which the poverty-stricken households could easily have built the houses under the local social backgrounds.

The above analysis makes it clear that in cross-xiang operations, the function of currency may differ tremendously and, in situations like this, a sufficient supply of currency may not necessarily lead to production capacity. As the people who run the poverty-relief projects and are in charge of the economic development in ethnic regions only have cash funds allocated from the state government in their hands, their way of poverty-relief efforts has been restrained by the form of economic capacity. Consequently, they would consciously or unconsciously copy the mode of economy in the developed Han regions when dealing with the economic development issues in ethnic minority regions. Such an unrealistic and impertinent approach has, to a large extent, resulted in massive input in many poverty-relief projects that yield disproportionately low returns. To change such a situation, these people must thoroughly study the subjects of their work to understand the material forms that are indicators of the economic capacity, from which the point of connecting with the market economy and the best way of assisting the ethnic minority economy can be found, making the efforts in poverty-relief and ethnic economic development more effective.

It is obviously a complex and difficult task to give detailed description of material forms of the ethnic capacity for each ethnic group in each ethnic region without a long-term and focused research. However, it is possible for us to make a summarized introduction in the book. Generally speaking, in west Guizhou, the ethnic Miao and Buyi who live in the mountainous regions use "cattle" or "horse" to measure the economic capacity. The Buyi people living in the intermountane basins measure the economic capacity by the quantity of grains they store in the barns, while the quantity of cedars serves the same purpose among ethnic Dong people. People who work economy-related jobs can not help but always want to translate these material forms of the economic capacity of the ethnic groups into monetary terms. Such a practice does not help reveal the truth as in the regions that are poverty-stricken by our standards, even if each individual has on average more than one cattle, they may ask for poverty-relief grains from the state instead of selling the cattle in exchange for grains and bringing the per capita holding quantity of cattle to the original level through reproduction, as is often the case in the regions with a developed market economy.

Similarly, the Buyi people living in the intermontane basins would not sell the surplus grains they have. One may arrive at a conclusion by observing their daily life that they live a frugal and simple life and are not wealthy at all. They seem to be content with baked soybeans and chilly peppers while drinking liquor. Even some Buyi officials do not understand why their fellowmen are so narrow-minded and so easily satisfied. It seems that they can have a better life if they have a higher and broader vision. In fact, the Buyi people value more on their family assets accumulated over a long time. Despite the seemingly simple lifestyle most of the time in a year, the consumption can be surprisingly high in holidays of slack farming season, especially in occasions such as marriage and funerals. The spending in one of these occasions, if translated into monetary values, may easily exceed ten thousand yuan. However, they don't calculate it this way. Outsiders who see that they don't own high-valued household items such as electrical appliances, or are not enthusiastic about spending wastefully as city dwellers, often think that they are in extreme poverty. In fact, most of the Buyi people we visited were worry-free about daily necessities. Those who were in real difficulty were too lazy to do anything or the result of accidents and disasters. It is thus groundless to say that they don't have the capacity for expanding production simply because they don't have much cash in disposal.

Similar things happened in the Dong regions in southeast Guizhou. Although places such as Liping, Jinping, Tianzhu, Sansui, Congjiang and Rongjiang in southeast Guizhou were classified as poverty-stricken areas, the per capita lands suitable for forestry plantations were more than one hectare for the ethnic Dong people in these counties, which equals to an annual per capita lumber output of between 1.5 to 3 cubic meters if estimated by the current level of afforestation in the Dong regions, and translates into a per capita production that is by no means at the lower end across the country if calculated by the current market price of lumber. For a variety of reasons, the per capita income of the ethnic Dong people in these regions remains low. It does not make much sense if we draw the conclusion that they don't have the economic capacity based on their current cash income. We feel necessary to mention that the Dong ethnic regions were the birth place of quite a number of business tycoons from lumber business before the founding of the People's Republic of China. Their business had reached far into the central Han regions. Even at that moment, the ethnic Hans did not view them as penniless vagrants.

In addition to the material forms of economic activities, the conversion across economic capacities is also an important element to demonstrate the economic capacity of an ethnic group. We have discussed previously in the book that different ethnic groups differ in the material form of their specific economic capacity. The forms in which the economic capacities from different ethnic groups are converted differ dramatically. In general, the conversion is made from the perspective of the subjective party in cross-xiang operations while the material forms and value indicators of the objective party are often ignored. In the Ming dynasty, taxes were paid in kind. As rice was the primary product in the Han regions, it became the indicator in the evaluation of economic capacity. The Ming taxation system explicitly stated that rice was "*ben se*"(direct indicator) and other crops were "*zhe se*"(indirect indicator)[①], under which the ethnic Buyi and Dong groups that had already cultivated large rice fields seemed to have a strong economic capacity, while the ethnic Miao groups that had little or no rice production seemed weaker. Although influential Yi *Tu Si* continuously sent horses as tributes to the royal court and subsequently received imperial grants, these Yi regions were treated as "uncivilized and barbarian places" for the reason that *Tu Si* were not able to provide grains to the imperial government. It is apparent that when the economic capacity of an ethnic group was evaluated in history, the conclusion largely depended on the standards by which the conversion was made.

We encountered situations in our fieldwork where economic capacities were mistakenly converted. In Mashan and Huashan that were famous across the country for their dire poverty, the local government only included corns,

① *Twenty-five Histories* vol. 10, col. 2 - 3, 7982.

the primary grain in the region, in the statistics of grain output. However, it only accounted for 60% of the total grain output in the region. We noticed in our fieldwork that people also grew sorghum, *tianxing* rice along with a variety of beans such as kidney bean, pea, cowpea as well as sweet potato and a variety of vegetables in the corn fields. In addition, the locals also grew millet, red panicum crus, and myotonin etc., in the fields by slash-and-burns. Even though the statistics showed that the average per capita holding of grains in these villages was merely about 100 kg, we did not have the impression of a widespread famine when we visited these villages. Instead, what we saw was people living a peaceful and content life, suggesting that statistical data were not a true reflection of their economic capacity.

Similar things happened in Huashan region as well. As part of Huashan region was the main production area of Liuma tung oil, all the Buyi people here had their own tung tree forest that provided a major source of income. In previous years when the price of tung oil was on the rise, the locals with large tung tree forests even had to hire part-timers by offering 0.3 yuan for each jin (half a kilogram) of tung seeds peeled. The quantity of tung seeds that were sold by each household varied from tens of thousands of jin at the most and thousands of jin at the least, which translated into a per capita income of no less than one thousand yuan simply from selling tung seeds at the price of 1.05 yuan per jin. Regardless, it was classified as a poverty-stricken region. People in Zhenning county in the main Liuma tung oil production area were upset because the county was not labeled as poverty-stricken county and thus was not qualified for any subsidy, which has puzzled us.

Another puzzling phenomenon is: nearly all ethnic regions we visited were agricultural regions, which, according to state policies, must pay agricultural taxes in grains that were calculated at the price of grains regulated by the state. By contrast, grains would sell at a much higher price in the market. Consequently, the tax revenue in these counties looked extremely low, but it would look much reasonable if calculated by market price. Such a calculation method apparently can not accurately reflect the true economic capacity of these regions if our goal is to achieve the transition into a socialist market economy. For the same reason, the domestic animals raised by households in the agricultural regions are not subject to property tax in China's current taxation system, and thus the number of domestic animals is not included in the estimation of the economic capacity. Consequently, the per capita holding of domestic animals in ethnic regions is not reflected in the evaluation of economic capacity at all.

In summary, by current statistical methods for economic capacity evaluation purposes, the incompatibility between the policy orientation and the material form of economic capacity of each ethnic group has resulted in an inaccurate reflection of the true economic capacity of each ethnic group and region.

Each party in cross-xiang operations inevitably participates in interactive economic relations. As the material form of economic capacity indicators differs across different ethnic groups, the production cost may deviate from the estimation of the subjective party. If the material form of economic capacity indicators or the method of conversion between these material forms do not change accordingly, the original approach used to evaluate the economic capacity of each ethnic group will, after a while, deviate from reality and will never be able to reflect the current capacity of each party. Therefore, to accurately evaluate the economic capacity of each ethnic group, we must also bring the element of "form of adjustment" into consideration.

It was not uncommon in the history of economic development in Guizhou that insufficient adjustment led to unexpected results. After the development of Miao regions in southeast Guizhou in the period of Yongzheng, to appease the ethnic Miaos, the Qing government announced to use the locally produced fabric as standard tax payment, which remained unchanged in the mid-Qing dynasty despite the great changes that had happened to the Miao economy and the abandonment of such fabric. It triggered a strange economic phenomenon: after the fabrics were turned in by the local people to the local government, the latter put the fabrics in the market which were sold back to the ethnic Miao people, who bought them only for the purpose of paying taxes. As commented by Qing scholars, the initial goal of "bringing convenience to the people" became a "burden on the people".①

Similar things are happening even in today. In the early period of the People's Republic of China, the government continued to enforce the taxation regulations of the Republic of China: to accept paying agricultural taxes in

① *Book of Guizhou • Recod of Guizhou continued • Language of Guizhou,* s.v. "Tie Di Cun" (Guizhou People's Publishing House, March 1992), 224.

grains. The practice was fully supported by the following reasoning. First, grains were the fundamentals for subsistence and were produced by the farmers themselves; therefore, to turn in grains as a fulfillment of tax obligation was convenient to the farmers and advantageous to the country. On the other hand, as ethnic groups were in a self-sufficient or natural economy with very limited cash income, it was easier for them to pay taxes in grains. However, the ethnic regions in Guizhou occupied a vast area that had extremely different natural environments and ethnic cultural tradition. To apply a uniform tax-paying standard yielded different results across all regions and ethnic groups. The lack of effective and timely adjustment measures made these measures originally designed to provide convenience later become a drag on the local people in some regions and some ethnic groups. Lao Mashan in Wangmo county, located on the southern slope facing the Bay of Bengal and South China Sea, is soaked in continuous rains and mists all year round, making it hard for the grains to dry up naturally. The local Miao people had to dry up the grains by burning up trees they chopped from the forest, which not only wasted energy, time and vast quantity of wood, but also dampened the grains during transportation. The grains would have to wait for a few days after arriving in the state granary before drying up. This problem was reported to the government but failed to bring out any change. As a matter of fact, there were other products, such as cattle and mountain produce, that could be used to pay tax. The problem was easily solved by replacing the grains with something that did not need to be dried up. The lack of flexible adjustment measures in management had made a small problem grow into a long-term burden on the local farmers and resulted in unnecessary damage to the ecological environments. Many treeless mountains we saw in Mashan were, to a large extent, the results of drying up the grains by burning trees.

Some phenomena in production came to our attention in our fieldwork. In Miao traditions, the holding of cattle was highly valued in estimating the economic capacity. However, the cost for raising a head of cattle in the vast Miao region in Guizhou varied dramatically. West Guizhou was home to wide mountain grasslands. Part of them are still not in small-season cultivation. The lands were alternated between farmlands and grazing lands, making the cost to raise cattle very low. We were told by local farmers that the cattle were left grazing on the mountain until a calf was born, whose ownership was determined by which cow the calf followed home. It indicated that cattle were very treasured but the labor input in raising them was low. In a few Miao regions in the north and northeast of southeastern Guizhou, the cultivation of farm fields shrank the pastures. As a result, cattle must be enclosed and must be taken care of every day, thus it was much more difficult to raise cattle. As many ethnic Miao people could not afford to raise cattle, they would buy them for cultivation during busy farm seasons and sell them at a loss thereafter. These regions had ceased slaughtering cattle for ancestral worship ceremonies, with a lack of cattle being one of the biggest reasons. In addition to cattle, similar issues exist in rice production and lumber production. If purchased or sold at a nationally uniform price, these products would make profits for some ethnic groups and regions while cause losses to the others. To require that all the regions in the country use the same product in market competition without appropriate measures and price differentials, or allow the price to fluctuate, the economic capacity of some ethnic groups and regions in Guizhou will never be truly and accurately reflected, and it will always be a dream to lift these ethnic people out of poverty.

Despite the differences in the economic capacity, each ethnic group and region has its own strengths. We have no doubt that the economy in ethnic regions will be developed if we can avoid their weaknesses and foster their advantages, which depends on all the above three elements. Only through a comprehensive analysis of the three elements can we find and take the best advantage of the strengths in economic capacity of each party. On the contrary, our development efforts will yield unexpected results and hinder the local economic development if we can not bring all the three elements under consideration, for the reason that in cross-xiang operations, the economic capacity is reflected in many different forms, such as currency, transfer of technology and export of people, as well as the transfer of special products or equipment. Natural resources, as viewed by some people, are a capacity and economic development can be achieved by selling natural resources, to which we don't agree. Natural resources are an objective existence, a part of which had existed before the appearance of mankind on earth. By contrast, cross-xiang operations are social and economic activities, which had not existed until the emergence of ethnic groups. Natural resources are important to human economic activities in that they are the objects that human beings process, transform and make use of by economic activities. Without human economic activities, natural resources are merely objective existence and are meaningless to human beings. On the other hand, all ethnic groups in the world possess certain natural resources. As long as the culture of an ethnic group makes sufficient use of the natural resources in its possession, this particular ethnic group is able to last and develop normally. The reason why some ethnic groups feel that the natural resources in their possession are in shortage is not that they do not have the natural resources but that their consumption of a certain natural resource exceeds its availability. For instance, more than half of the petroleum consumed by the US each year is not produced within the country for the reason that the petroleum needed to ensure the normal function of its culture far exceeds that provided by its living environment. The shortage is in essence a result of over-consumption. Despite the oil resources that are available from within the country, the US would import a huge quantity of oil simply because the sharp contrast in salary between the US and other oil producing countries, which cost much less to produce oil than the US does by making use of high and new technologies. It is therefore not an issue of resource shortage as it seems, but in essence an economic issue, i.e., the issue of production cost. Across the globe, the distribution of specific natural resources tends to be very uneven. For the specific region of an ethnic group, it is always rich in some but poor in others. A comparison between the ethnic regions in Guizhou and developed Han regions makes it easier to understand this point. The ethnic Han people live in the vast middle and lower reaches of Yangtze River plain that offers the uniquely favorable natural resources for creating a place that is abundant in rice and fish. No ethnic region in Guizhou is endowed with such natural resources. By contrast, the Dong regions in Guizhou have the perfect natural resources for forestry plantations. The Buyi and Miao regions in Guizhou are abundant in hydro power resources. The northwest Guizhou is home to the largest coal mines in southern China that can provide enormous energy as well as fundamental raw materials for coal chemistry. The Han costal regions are rich in marine fishery resources and sea salt while the ethnic regions in Guizhou happen to be regions in short of salt, neither can they be turned into a sea fishery production region. The ethnic regions in Guizhou also have large reserves in zinc, lead, mercury, and phosphorite, which are all in shortage in the Han regions. It seems clear that no ethnic group has all the resources necessary for developing production, nor does any ethnic group have no natural resources at all. For this reason, every ethnic group must acquire natural resources from other ethnic groups by all means possible, including political, military, economic and cultural means etc. Due to the limitation in the space of the book, we will only discuss the issue of acquiring natural resources from other ethnic groups through economic means.

When discussing natural resources, some economists often overlook the boundary between natural resources and natural resource products. In fact, these two must not be confused with each other. Natural resources are the form of materials that exist objectively and have not been subjected to human processing, or human labor, and thus can not be priced. Natural resource products, on the other hand, are the results of specific human society's processing of natural resources. Human labor has been input in them, to a certain extent, thus they are priced by the human labor that has been input in them. Therefore, when discussing the economic relations of heterogeneous ethnic groups, we need to be aware that what has been acquired from other ethnic group is not natural resource itself but processed natural resource, i.e., natural resource products. For instance, when Baosteel imports iron mines from Australia, it does not import the mine itself but rather the iron ores that have been explored, developed, crushed, selected, packaged and transported and can be put into direct use. The iron ores are results of human processing on natural resources.

It has been a popular thinking in the discussion of the development of the west: The advantages in eastern China are massive population, advanced technology and developed economy; the advantages in western China are vast lands and abundant resources. The weakness of the East is resource shortage and that of the West is the lagging behind in technology. In fact, such a thinking is not accurate. The abundance in natural resources alone is not the same as economic advantage. To turn the natural resources into economic advantage must first turn them into products through human processing. For instance, although Guizhou is rich in coal mines, they won't become economic advantage unless they are exploited and shipped out of the region. To do this, we must build roads, dig mines, organize exploitation efforts, build coal washeries, and load the coals on the vehicles for transportation. All of them are results of input of human work, which gives the raw coals a price and turns them into economic advantages. Natural resource products, but not natural resources alone, constitute economic capacity in cross-xiang operations. It is therefore inappropriate, from an academic perspective, to treat natural resources and natural resource products equally when examining the economic capacity in cross-xiang operations. Natural resource products should be viewed as one kind of products. Products in economic activities are one of the items that can be used to reflect the economic capacity in cross-xiang activities.

Modern Western economists would always connect economic capacity with monetary input, simply because the targets of their research are regions with highly developed commodity economy. Such an approach is not applicable in the research of the economy in ethnic regions in Guizhou. Just as Polanyi, the founder of economic anthropology, put it, the contents commonly seen in Western economy such as currency, stock, and credit are merely creations of the financial institutions and governments, but not necessarily the contents of all human social activities. ① The above analysis clearly indicates that monetary input alone would not yield expected results for the vast ethnic regions that don't have a fully developed market economy. The ethnic regions in Guizhou demonstrate different levels in the impact. For the ethnic regions around central cities and near transportation lines, monetary input may have better results, and the influence of the developed Han regions on these areas may be greater. By contrast, the monetary input will have smaller impact on the more remote and less developed regions. In some autonomous ethnic prefectures, even state subsidies in millions of yuan could not generate new production capacity. For these ethnic regions, the economic advantages in the developed Han regions do not translate into economic capacity after they are put into the cross-xiang operations. Mr. Liu Jianguo once said: "The fiscal subsidy from the central government on less developed regions is, to a certain extent, an important way of balancing the gap in income across different regions. The fixed-amount fiscal subsidy is mainly for the purpose of covering the expenses in local administrative management and public undertakings. After the deduction of expenses per head and public expenditures, not much is left to be spent on production-related investment. Even for the special-purpose subsidies, only a small part of them can eventually become production-related investment due

① Meng Zhang et al. *The Genesis of Mankind* (Sichuan People's Publishing House, June 1987), 218-219.

to limited amount and restricted purpose of usage.

The six provinces in the border and inland regions in China are all characterized with a vast territory, harsh weather conditions and a small population. In history, they were home to many ethnic minority residents. It remains an issue how the structure of administrative management and the development of social undertakings are to be made in line with the level of local economic development as well as the historical, natural and ethnic characteristics, resulting in the situation where an enormous and clumsy superstructure is built on a fragile economic foundation. From the demand side, fiscal subsidies have indeed stimulated the enhancement of purchasing power and expansion of the market in backward regions. On the supply side, the comparatively smaller increase in savings has not resulted in effective incremental investment and has not effectively driven the steady and continuous economic growth."[①]

To put it more specifically, the capacity (the operational capacity in the form of monetary input) that should have been used to drive the economic development has instead been used in running the economic and political management agencies. As a result, the monetary input has not created new economic capacity but instead has artificially inflated consumption. In some ethnic autonomous prefectures in Guizhou, the office buildings of the local governments are more luxurious than those of the bureau level in the capital city of the province despite the fact that they receive fiscal subsidies every year.

Transfer of technology is indeed able to demonstrate the economic capacity under certain conditions. However, our analysis in section ii of chapter five of this book concludes that the application of science and technology has ethnic characteristics and a specific advanced technology may not yield economical results to all ethnic groups, and thus may not demonstrate the economic capacity to all ethnic groups. As most ethnic regions in Guizhou are primarily in the crop farming type of economy (some are in Swidden cultivation and others are in agriculture), it helps us understand the problem if we compare them with the agriculture in America that is widely recognized as the leader in the world. Today's American agriculture is also called "oil agriculture", which basically is characterized

① Jianguo Liu, "The Dependence on External Poverty-relief Funds in Under-developed Regions and Analysis of Reasons", *Economy and Society*, no. 3, 1991.

with an input of high energy and a balance between the input and output of energy. "Oil has made a great contribution to the increase in the crop yields in the world, yet the cost of oil agriculture is stunning. The energy input in the agriculture in the US increased 3.2 folds from 1940 to 1970 while the ratio of input and output remained 10:10. Such a high energy consumption agriculture is sure to get into trouble when the energy supply is in shortage in the future. On the other hand, the heavy usage of fertilizer and pesticide has destroyed the soil structure and has polluted agricultural products. It is estimated that out of all the pesticides now circulating in the biosphere, the DDT alone has reached 455 thousand tons, threatening the health of human beings."① When we say American agriculture is advanced, the implied but very important premise is that it is only possible in the country or ethnic groups with abundant oil supplies. Unfortunately, China is not one of them, neither are the ethnic groups in Guizhou, which is not able to provide enough output of oil even in 50 years to guarantee food supplies for more than 1 billion Chinese with the US oil agricultural technology. Such an advanced technology can not create economic capacity in the ethnic regions in Guizhou and therefore does not have promotional values. A latent precondition for exported technologies to demonstrate the economic capacity in cross-xiang operations is that it must be able to survive in the specific ethnic society and be digested and absorbed by the specific ethnic group that is the receiver of the technology. Otherwise, any advanced technology can not bring any benefit. The ethnic Han and minority groups in Guizhou are equal with regards to this issue. The advanced technologies from the Han regions are able to survive after being introduced into the ethnic minority regions when they are already accepted by these ethnic groups. The silkworm breeding technology, for instance, was successfully introduced into the Buyi regions and thus demonstrated the Han economic capacity in this aspect. Now, in the forestry plantations being developed in some mountainous areas inhabited by Han people, such as the mountainous region in southern Jiangxi Province, ethnic Dong people may demonstrate their economic capacity when they transfer the traditional plantation technology into these Han regions.

Labor service export in cross-xiang operations is also an important aspect in demonstrating the operating capacity, yet it has long been misunderstood and the introduction of talents is often narrowly restricted to

① "The Pollution-free Agriculture is Growing", *Economy and Society*, no. 3, 1991.

the people with highly advanced technical background. An ethnic society is complex, which is in need of the people with different levels of capability. As He Dongchang, deputy director of the State Education Commission, once said, "What may be needed in the rural areas are those who are equipped with relatively new production techniques under the environment of a commodity economy and are experienced leaders in production or skilled labors. Such people may have a great role to play in rural regions and therefore should be treated as talents on top of doctors and masters. Consequently, we must change the mentality that narrow-mindedly emphasizes on education from an institution of higher learning that exclusively trains people to be government officials in the cities." ① The economic development in Guizhou requires the introduction of a bunch of people with different levels of specialty in techniques or knowledge. It used to be a prevailing thinking across the prefectures and counties in Guizhou Province that it only took one or two experts to formulate the economic development strategy for one ethnic group or region. In fact, these experts have not produced any positive impacts on the economic development in these regions other than leaving behind a few reports on economic strategy. Another key issue regarding the introduction of talents is the relationship between the subjective and objective parties in the introduction. As the goal of introducing the talents is to enable the knowledge and techniques carried by them to take root and survive in the receiving ethnic regions, it requires a screening and discriminative selection process where the receiving ethnic groups are the subjective parties while the people to be selected are the objective parties of the process. Only when the ethnic Han group can provide the people who are needed and also selected by the ethnic groups can we be certain that the Han group has the economic capacity in cross-xiang operations; otherwise, all the doctors and masters would not help.

It is another misconception about labor service introduction that ethnic minority people in Guizhou are of low quality, therefore they can only be laborers to work on odd jobs when migrating to southeast coastal regions and do not create any economic capacity. As a matter of fact, any ethnic society is a complex entirety where people with different levels of techniques are needed, including both mental and manual workers, people who work in

① Dongchang He, "Issues on the Rural-oriented Reform in the Education of All Levels and Categories under Middle County Level", *Study of Township Elementary Education Plan* (People's Education Press, 1st edition, March 1989)

highly technical jobs as well as low tech or even simply non-technical jobs. Now, students with a technical secondary school diploma or even a college degree are feeling pressure in the job market in the southeast coastal regions. In comparison, positions in the nature of ordinary labor such as janitors, constructors, and gardeners are waiting to be filled. Migrant workers from ethnic regions in Guizhou to southeast regions are mostly needed to fill these jobs, and to some extent, they should be viewed as talents as they are critically needed by the local societies. Labor export in this way has affected the economic operation in the ethnic Han regions and has in fact demonstrated the capacity in cross-xiang operations. The thought that people of low quality are surely not able to generate economic capacity is groundless. These migrant workers are, based on the feedback from the southeast coastal regions, welcome and are even hired with higher pays. In the meantime, they can bring the money they make back to their own ethnic groups. What else can it be if this is not a demonstration of economic capacity?

Products are one of the earliest forms that make up of the economic capacity in cross-xiang operations. Ethnic groups had entered into a cross-xiang relationship before the emergence of currency by virtue of products. Nowadays, although currency plays an important role in cross-xiang operations, exchange of products is a critical element in cross-xiang operations, which does not necessarily involve settlement by currency. In the poverty-relief work in Guizhou, physical products such as chemical fertilizer, farm cattle, and fine breed are directly supplied to ethnic minority regions at a price recorded by the state but actually distributed for free to ethnic people. This is a real example of exchange of products without settlement in currency. Although the comprehensive economic capacity of ethnic groups in Guizhou Province is low, quite a number of ethnic products have entered the bigger domestic market, indicating that these ethnic groups may have demonstrated some economic capacity when engaging in cross-xiang operations with ethnic Han regions. People are completely biased to assert that ethnic Han people have a stronger economic capacity while the minority people don't have any simply by the fact that in poverty-relief work in these ethnic regions, local governments often distribute loans and aid funds in these ethnic regions. As a matter of fact, such is the result of a planned economy enforced over a long period in the past, where the relationship between the country and ethnic groups was not established in the form of enterprises but rather administrative departments. The poverty-relief offices of the ethnic affairs commission, for instance, are in reality an administrative department but not an enterprise, and yet they are mostly engaged in unquestionable economic activities where the source of their operational capacity is entangled with fiscal revenue of administrative departments that is appropriated from the upper-level authorities. As a result, the economic capacity they are able to mobilize is quite considerable. For example, they may distribute at one time hundreds of thousands of yuan in areas in Mashan, Yaoshan, and Gaopo of Guiyang city where the population is thousands or tens of thousands. In Yaoshan, to build a primary school for a community of about two thousand people cost 110 thousand yuan. To construct a hydropower station that generated power for merely four to five thousand people in Gaopo ethnic Miao township of Guiyang city cost hundreds of thousands of yuan. Such cases were, in fact, exceptional from an overall perspective. No matter how developed the Han economy is, it can not afford to run cross-xiang operations in this way given the total number of ethnic people in the entire province. To believe that being able to make vast monetary distribution in a small area is a demonstration of one's economic capacity is a tendency of over-generalization. No operator would have chosen to spend money this way if it were the enterprise instead of administrative department that run the operations.

We noticed in our fieldwork that the self-employed businessmen who resold Mashan black goats were profitable in their economic activities with local Miao people, so were the enterprises that did business on locally produced tea in the Miao regions. The state-run forestry departments in the Dong regions gained even more. An apparent evidence was that these departments were able to give out bonuses when other county governments could barely paid out salaries. Some special produces in ethnic regions such as the fragrant pigs produced in Yueliang Mountain region bordering Southeast Guizhou Prefecture and South Guizhou Prefecture have not been put in the market now but have been given out for free or at very low prices to the seniors. Consequently, the economic capacity of these ethnic products in cross-xiang operations has been concealed and thus not attracted attention from the economy-related administrations, nor has it brought any real benefit to the ethnic groups. In the meantime, it makes it impossible for the real operators to try to engage in cross-xiang operations and share profits with these ethnic groups. A dispute that occurred in Gaopo township in Guiyang city was a best illustration.

"Xiaohongnian" (little red sticky), a high-quality variety of rice, was a special produce in the ethnic Miao region in Gaopo township of Guiyang city. It enjoyed a reputation among experts from near and far and was highly demanded on the market. In late 1980s, the township administrative authority followed the practice by other administrative departments and pushed to plant hybrid rice. However, at time of turning in grains as a way of paying agricultural taxes, the state granaries of the township refused to accept the hybrid rice and instead, required that ethnic Miao people turn in the "Xiaohongnian" and then gave them as gifts to their relatives or friends, or even offered them in the market for high prices. A few people from the related government authorities managed to purchase the "Xiaohongnian" at a state-set price by abusing their power in hand. Consequently, the real producers, namely the local Miao people, did not receive any benefit and were even deprived of the right to consume the rice, which prompted the enraged local people to file a joint complaint to boycott such a local rule on taxation and almost gave rise to a collective case of appeal. Although the policy was later abandoned to appease mass anger, the event made it very clear that even without the aid of advanced technologies, the traditional products of ethnic groups were in fact very competitive and the ethnic groups were able to take some shares in both domestic and international market by relying on these products. The fact that the economic capacity of ethnic groups did not materialize was not the fault of the ethnic groups but was the result of the conducts by some administrative authorities who used public office to seek personal gains under the disguise of planned economy. These conducts were an overt infringement on the interests of ethnic groups and were indisputably a violation of the rights of these ethnic groups according to the economic laws and regulations, and therefore should be subject to legal consequences. Mere disciplinary actions apparently were avoiding the important and dwelling on the trivial and were against the goal of supporting the economic development in ethnic regions. To continue doing so would keep the economic capacity contained in the ethnic products from manifesting themselves.

Given the above, we think that even under the current production condition, ethnic minority people are able to demonstrate the economic capacity or even some special potential capacity while engaging in cross-xiang economic activities with Han people by virtue of these products. The fact that such a capacity has long been overlooked by economists in China is somewhat related to the planned economy that has long dominated our society. In a planned economy, products of different qualities are artificially priced the same by policy departments, which causes unfathomable loss to the ethnic groups from suppressed pricing that far outpaces the aid funds appropriated to them. Although it is impossible for us to exhaust all items in detail, the selling of logs in the Dong regions in southeast Guizhou Province alone has illustrated the problem. The forestry departments that have played a mixed role of enterprise and administration have retained the economic benefits far greater than the total aid funds distributed in this prefecture. The attempt to bring the forestry plantations in the Dong regions on the right track will be in vain if the implementation of "reform and opening-up policy" does not touch these administrative authorities.

The exchange and transfer of equipment is also a form of demonstrating the economic capacity. Equipment is an overall display of single technology and the transfer of a complete set of technology is to transfer a set of all single technologies; Therefore, to make the transfer across ethnic groups successful is subject to more constraints than the transfer of a single technology. If the receivers of the equipment are not fully prepared in technology and knowledge, or if the cultures of the receivers do not have the environment for the operation of such equipment, it will not produce the same effect as that on the transferor. In the 1980s, some people asserted that China could buy all the way into modernization, which later proved unrealistic. Such a proposal ignored the fact that the transfer of equipment had to cross heterogeneous cultures and that it cost extra money and efforts to absorb and digest the transferred equipment, which in some cases might exceed the cost in directly buying the same equipment. Many factories in Guizhou Province were entirely moved from the ethnic Han regions and in principle should have yielded the same operating efficiency as the transferring factories. However, it turned out that most of them could not catch up with the operating level in the original factories after running for some time. Guizhou Diesel Engine Factory was moved from Shanghai and after ten years of operation, its cost of production remained higher than that in Shanghai Diesel Engine Factory. Given that Guizhou Diesel Engine Factory, located in the capital city of the province, had such an unsatisfactory result, one can imagine about the performance of the others in ethnic group settlements.

Currently, many "third front construction"[①] enterprises in Guizhou Province that were originally built in the ethnic minority settlements have chosen to move to Guiyang, primarily due to inability to attain the operating targets. It indicates that to forcefully move the "advanced" complete set of equipment to the minority regions without selective screening and consideration will undoubtedly and foreseeably end up in loss in these enterprises. Further boosting efforts by continuing to inject state resources into these enterprises will drag us deeper into the pit.

Above examples tell us that not all advanced equipment in any form is valuable in ethnic regions. Without such a value, the economic capacity of such advanced equipment can not be displayed. This issue has something to do with the relativity of scientific application, which has been covered in section ii of chapter five. One thing we must emphasize is that the ability of the receiving party to digest and absorb the entire set of equipment must be taken into account to make them display the true capacity in cross-xiang operations.

In summary, the economic capacity in cross-xiang operations is demonstrated in different forms. Simply focusing on monetary input or the advanced technology would not reflect the true capacity of each party in cross-xiang operations. It is the issue we have overlooked over the long time in the past while working on the poverty-relief projects, and it is for this reason these poverty-relief efforts were not effective as we had expected. From a perspective of diversified economic capacity, we can see that if the ethnic groups in Guizhou have a chance to participate in "two-way"

[①] "Third-front Construction" was a war-preparing economic policy implemented in 1960s to 1970s by the Chinese government to combat the military threat from the anti-China foreign powers, where the modern manufacturing and mining enterprises originally located in southeast coastal regions, especially the enterprises of military nature, were moved out of the original locations to place in the new sites in the inland regions that scattered in the provinces and autonomous regions in southwest and northwest of China to ensure that we still had basic strategic production capacity when southeast coastal regions were lost to foreign invasions. These manufacturing and mining enterprises were given a military code and were built in mountain valleys or directly inside caves, and the resulting decrease in operating efficiency was subsidized by the country. As these enterprises were located in the strategic "third front" in the planned future counterattack, they were thus referred to in the documents of that time as "third front construction" projects.

cross-xiang operations, their economic capacity is not as low as we expected and they are fully capable of competing in domestic and international markets. The key to their success depends on how we can help them find the right track and guide them through. It is a secondary issue as to how much poverty-relief funding we have for them, or how many people and equipment are introduced and transferred into these regions. Unfortunately, we often mistake the primary issue for secondary issue in the actual poverty-relief work.

II Calculation of Overall Operating Capacities

Previous analysis reveals that, in cross-xiang operations, economic capacity is multi-facet and an accurate estimation of the economic capacity of each party in the operation requires a comprehensive analysis of many indicators. Unfortunately, when evaluating the economic capacity of ethnic regions, we tend to focus on the amount of monetary input, or the introduction of advanced technology, or even on the direct results caused by monetary input alone. For instance, people only look at how many roads, schools or factories are built, but lightly touch whether schools function normally and churn out the people needed by the local community, or whether the factories can make profit. A reflection on these roads, schools, and factories reveals that at least a considerable part of them can not survive on their own and have to depend on the "blood" given by the administrative departments and the support by administrative orders. They would likely be a drag on the local administrative departments rather than a contributor of economic benefit. Consequently, to ensure accurate calculation of the economic capacity of each party in cross-xiang operations, we must acknowledge the fact that economic capacities are demonstrated in various forms which can only be measured by a multi-indicator approach. However, while China is transitioning from the planned socialist economy to a market economy, the prices of many products do not reflect true market prices but are artificially determined by people, and thus the opportunities may not be mature for us to put together the norms in measuring the economic capacity of each party in cross-xiang operations under current situations. To help our readers understand this, we are going to make some further explanations by using grain, a primary produce that all ethnic groups in Guizhou Province can not do without, as an example.

Under a market economy, grain prices fluctuate with the change in supply and demand. The cost in grain production may exceed its market price when supply exceeds demand. Consequently, a large number of grain producers would exit the grain production. Conversely, at the time when the market price is higher than the production cost by a large margin, people who are not engaged in grain production will be attracted to this area. It is not hard to see that the fluctuation in grain price has the effect of adjusting grain production. By observing such a fluctuation in grain, we may indirectly have an overall picture of grain production and collect feedbacks from farmers of ethnic groups and thus indirectly detect the capacity of each ethnic group in grain production. However, the nationwide enforcement of a uniform grain price for the long time in the past makes it unlikely for us to determine what is the real capacity, or the potential, in grain production in the country. We often could not tell that something went wrong with grain production unless there was a large drop in the grain output. As the grain production in China, from the time when we started the system of contracted responsibility linking remuneration to output until 1984, was generally good, some people made the following comparative analysis: "Since the Third Plenary Session of the 11th Central Committee of the Communist Party of China, the grain output has continuously increased sharply, at an annual average rate of 5.6% from 1979 to 1984 and increased averagely by 27.4 billion kilograms each year from 1981 to 1984, reaching a historical high of 407.3 billion kilograms in total output and 400 kilograms in per capita output in 1984. In the meantime, the outputs of cotton, sugar crop and oil crop all broke the highest record in history. "① However, the grain production has begun to drop in 1984, and has never reached the level of 1984 even in a good year, and yet the difficulty in grain selling by the farmers has not eased, coupled with a worsening situation in the abandoning of cultivated lands in some developed regions. What puzzles us even more is that in a poor province as Guizhou where basic needs in subsistence has not been satisfied in some ethnic regions, people have begun to abandon the cultivated lands as well. As a matter of fact, the issue in such severity had happened before 1984 but it had been disguised by the planned economy that enforced a uniform price and supplied farming materials to farmers at the price set by the government; Therefore, it had not

① Zifu Liu, Wang Man, *Where Should We Go* (Guizhou People's Publishing House, October 1990), 5-6.

drawn attention from the economists or in the society.

Under such a grain price policy, the grain production in many ethnic groups in Guizhou displayed the characteristics of circumventing its strengths and fostering its weaknesses. From the perspective of grain varieties, the area of fine varieties of rice developed by local ethnic groups were often reduced while the area for growing hybrid rice kept growing. Despite the increase in grain output, the economic capacity dropped. When the same rice varieties were planted in the ethnic regions as the developed coastal regions, even if the yield per unit area was exactly the same, the rice from the ethnic regions would be less competitive on the market due to the longer distance between the ethnic regions and central cities, which increased the cost in transportation. In addition, the Han regions yielded much larger quantity of rice, which would put the ethnic farmers in a disadvantageous competitive position against the Han farmers. When the grain supply and demand reached a balance, the ethnic farmers were doomed to lose money in business no matter how hardworking they were. Should the ethnic minority farmers not be subject to the price control, the prices for different varieties of rice would differ. Despite the lower output, the selling price for the traditional fine variety of rice produced in the ethnic regions was sure to increase when sold in domestic market as long as its quality was good. Due to the impossibility of expanding the cultivation of such variety of rice, it would always be short supplied and it was likely that its market price could double that of a regular hybrid rice. The rise in price in international market was also foreseeable. Contrary to our constant assertion to guide ethnic minority regions through the transition into a market economy, we have been implementing a grain price policy that in fact weakens the capacity of the ethnic groups in the market competition and pushes them back into a natural economy. Unarguably, this is indeed against the original intention of the poverty-relief policy.

Given the stability in the cultivated area of grains, a uniform grain price often led to a low grain price and high commercial crop price. The lack of subsidy or reward on grains intensified the problem so that ethnic people could not get rich by laboriously growing grains. In contrast, they could make money by opportunistically growing commercial crops. As a result, the shortage in locally produced grains in Guizhou was responded by the shrinkage in the area of rice cultivation, which was disadvantageous to both the country and the ethnic farmers if it continued. The uniform price policy was fatal to the circulation of grain as it made the long-distance shipping and selling of grain unprofitable. With the obstruction in the grain circulation, grain traders would not emerge in ethnic regions and thus commercial capital would not be accumulated, leaving the goal of guiding ethnic minority groups to the market meaningless in essence. In addition, to maintain a uniform grain price required subsidies, which would place a long-lasting burden on the state.

The analysis in the above three aspects makes it clear that a uniform grain price has many hidden troubles, the most threatening of which to the ethnic groups is that it weakens the economic capacity of ethnic groups and hinders them to access the market. The behaviors of ethnic groups in grain production are purely the results of the artificial price. Under such a circumstance, even a thorough and meticulous investigation can only reflect the facts resulting from such false grain price but not the true economic capacity in the grain production by ethnic groups, nor the advantages in grain production. Subsequently, even if we have worked out a set of well-planned indicators for investigation and have collected all data accordingly, we can not find out the real economic capacity of ethnic groups. For this reason, we are unable to provide our readers a set of indicators to measure the economic capacity of the ethnic groups. Regardless, in order to help our readers get a feel of the operating capacity of ethnic groups, we will conduct some analysis on the economic capacity of ethnic groups in Guizhou Province based on the data collected by the state ethnic affairs commission of Guizhou Province from the investigations on ethnic townships by the approaches in ethnology and economics. We will further compare such capacities with the aid funds from the state to see which is greater, and draw conclusions on how much benefit these funds have generated.

Anshun region was the focus of our investigation. The ethnic affairs commission of Guizhou Province provided us with the survey reports that had systematic information on the society and economy in the 25 ethnic townships in this region, based on which we carried out some basic analyses on the social productive capacity of the ethnic groups in this region. The 25 ethnic townships included: Pingba county – Xiaba ethnic Miao and Gelao township, Lege ethnic Miao and Buyi township, Guaduo ethnic Miao township, Lutang ethnic Buyi township, Malu ethnic Buyi and Miao township, Shizi ethnic Hui and Miao township; Puding county – Gumao ethnic Miao township, Xiaodong ethnic Miao and Yi township, Mengzhou ethnic Miao and Gelao township, Maodong ethnic Miao and Gelao township, Longga ethnic Buyi and Miao township, and Houzhai ethnic Buyi township; Xifeng county – Qingshan ethnic Miao township; Qingzhen county – Dongmenqiao ethnic Buyi and Miao township, Longwo ethnic Miao township, and Yaoyan ethnic Miao township; Xiuwen county – Dashi ethnic Buyi township; Kaiyang county – Shitou ethnic Buyi and Miao township, Pingzhai ethnic Miao and Buyi township, and Longguang ethnic Buyi township; Anshun city - Huangla ethnic Buyi township, Yanla ethnic Miao and Buyi township, Longhui ethnic Miao township, Tangshan ethnic Buyi and Miao townshipand Shanmu ethnic Buyi township.

The 25 ethnic townships occupy a total area of 1,036.37 square kilometers, and a total area of cultivated land of 211,697.2 *mu*, out of which 95,448.8 *mu* is *tian,* and 116,248.4 *mu* is *di*. There are a total of 1,250 villager groups, 1,193 natural villages, 42,230 households, and a total population of 196,009, of whom 194,223 are agricultural type and 1,786 are non-agricultural type. 86,376 are ethnic minority people, accounting for 44% of the total population, of whom 39,788 are ethnic Miao, 40,950 are ethnic Buyi, 1,772 are ethnic Gelao, 1,028 are Yi, 16 are Dong, 17 are Shui, 213 are Bai and 5,195 are undetermined.

Land resources: They occupy 116,423.4 *mu* of land of collective ownership, 183,094.5 *mu* of forest land, 163,412.89 *mu* of grassland, and have a total labor population of 97,355. The per capita holding of cultivated land is 1.08 *mu*, translating into 2.174 *mu* per laborer. Based on the assumption that each laborer is able to manage 3-4 *mu* of cultivated land, there will be labor surplus in the 25 townships.

The total value of social production in 1989 was 64,504,043 yuan, and average per capita value of social production was 329.08 yuan; The total industrial output was 12,196,062 yuan with an average per capita value of 62.22 yuan; The total agricultural output was 27,615,589 yuan with an average per capita value of 142.18 yuan; The total production in construction was 2,398,550 yuan; Total production in transportation was 3,358,590 yuan; Total commercial production was 11,296,618 yuan; There were 925 township enterprises that employed a total of 4,201 people, generated a production of 16,337,980 yuan, paid a total tax amount of 1,444,700 yuan, and generated profits of 1,916,300 yuan. Statistics show that 8 out of the 25 townships did not have any township enterprises.

Net economic income was 22,346,885 yuan, 114 yuan on a per capita basis; Dongmenqiao ethnic Buyi and Miao township had a highest per capita net economic income of 640 yuan while the Dashi Buyi township and Yanla ethnic Miao and Buyi township with a per capita net economic income of 10.5 yuan and 9.5 yuan respectively were at the bottom. The total grain output was 45,312.66 tons, translating into a per capita grain output of 249.43 kilograms and a per capita grain ration of 173.029 kilograms. The Pingzhai ethnic Miao and Buyi township of Kaiyang county had the highest per capita grain ration of 309 kilograms while the Qingshan ethnic Miao township of Xifeng county was the lowest with a per capita grain ration of merely 98 kilograms. In 1989, the total grains turned in to the state as a payment of agricultural tax was 7,472.336 tons; the grains retained by the collectives were 137.18 tons, and the capital retained was 504,253 yuan.

In the end of 1989, the total number of large animals was 43,361, out of which 3,744 were cattle, 5,568 were horses, 2,185 were goats, 61,801 were live hogs, and a total of 2,725 animals were sold in the year. Main commercial crops included: 4,297.48 tons of rapeseed, 435.63 tons of tung seeds, 29.362 tons of tea and 475.029 tons of peanuts.

The output of major mineral products included: coal 97,911,430 tons, iron ores 10,000,500 tons, marble 140,000 tons and barite 70,016,000 tons. There was one small hydropower station with an installed capacity of 225 kilowatt that generated 110 kilowatt per hour electricity annually. Total state investment and fund appropriation in 1979 to 1989 was 14,959,017 yuan, out of which 3,526,420 yuan was distributed as ethnic funds; 3,728,200 yuan was spent on infrastructure, 885,600 yuan was distributed as aids; The total amount of loans issued by the state was 13,062,673 yuan, out of which 5,503,073 yuan was issued for development purposes, 3,976.595 tons in state relief grains, 284.74 tons in relief fertilizer, and 8,863 sets of relief clothes and quilts. ①

Some apparent mistakes exist in the above statistics. For instance, in the statistics of land resources, the area of lands was less than the area of cultivated lands by nearly 100,000 *mu*, which must be a statistical error.

① *Compilation of Materials from Surveys on Ethnic Townships in Guizhou Province* (Policy Office, Office of Politics and Laws in Ethnic Affairs Commission of Guizhou Province), 25 - 26.

Regardless, some simple calculations show that the total area of land in the 25 townships is 1,554,450 *mu* and the land resources being used now, including cultivated lands, forestry, grassland, add up to 558,204.5 *mu*, which accounts for a little over one third of the total area of lands. The forestry-suitable lands accounts for about one seventh of the entire area of land. Such a ratio hardly reflects the reality as in these ethnic townships, there are not many large water bodies or rocky mountains that are totally unusable, the residential areas or roads taken even less percentage in the entire area. The aggregate of this can not take two thirds of this total area of lands. As previously discussed in the book, this region belongs to the Miao western dialect region where local people retain apparent characteristics of Swidden cultivation type of economy. Swidden cultivation usually demands a much larger area of land than regular agriculture does. Based on our surveys on similar regions, the ratio between the dry lands and the paddy fields in Swidden cultivation regions ranges from 10 : 1 to 20 : 1. The data provided by above materials showed that the dry lands and paddy fields had a 1.2 : 1 ratio, indicating that the above number of *mu* is, without a doubt, the unit conventionally used by local people but not that used in official statistics.

In some regions in Guizhou, the big gap between the unit conventionally used by local people and that used in official statistics had been noticed by the academia. According to the estimation from Mr. Mou Daiju, the term "cultivated lands" we have used, with the exception of those used for scientific experiment or state-run farms, are a unit conventionally used by local people but not that used in official statistics, the former being larger than the latter. From data collected in typical investigations and aerial surveys, we estimate that the 28,060,000 mu (conventional *mu*) cultivated lands were equivalent to about 50,000,000 mu (used in official statistics), i.e., 1: 1.75. The ratio is greater in mountainous ethnic regions to be over 1:2. [①] Such a gap is more apparent in irregular mountainous regions. We measured the lands in Rongcun of Wangmo county and the results showed that one *mu* in the certificate for contracting the land translated into at least seven *mu*, and 15 mu at most, in actual measurement. Accordingly, we were certain that the data listed above were conventional mu (namely the area listed in the certificate for land contracting) but not actual area of cultivated lands. In

① Daiju Mou, "On the Methods of Ethnic Minority Economic Investigation and Research in Guizhou", *Guizhou Ethnic Studies*, no. 1, 1984, 35.

addition, the material we received listed the ethnic Miao township in Qingshan of Xifeng county as the one with the least per capita grain ration, i.e., 98 kilograms, among the 25 townships. According to our understanding of average grain consumption in ethnic groups, 98 kilogram of grains is unquestionably far from enough for subsistence. To ensure the subsistence of local people, the government must distribute more than one million grains to the local people. In fact, the government could not have done so and the local people have survived without such aid from the government, which can only be explained that some locally produced grains were not included in the statistics, mainly a variety of minor grain crops and sweet potatoes. The fieldwork we have conducted reveals that in regions of Swidden cultivation, the area of cultivated lands is more than ten times of that in regular agricultural regions but the grain output that is included in the statistics only accounts for one third to half of the total agricultural output. It helps us understand why the local people could live on 98 kilograms per capita grain ration a year.

In summary, statistics like this are not a reflection of the reality as they are done by indiscriminately following the statistics methods in agricultural regions, thus do not tell a true story of the economic conditions in the ethnic groups that are in the Swidden cultivation.

A further look at the total value of social production and per capita net income in the above data reveals that per capita value of social production was 329.08 yuan, per capita net income was 114 yuan and per capita grain ration was 173.029 kilograms. The comparison of the three indicators gives away some mismatches. For instance, per capita grain ration in monetary terms exceeded per capita social production. Such a gap was intolerable as the social production was the total value of all products that should include both cash income and cash equivalent of materials, as well as taxes already paid to the state. Apparently, these data were not collected and analyzed by following the norms in social economic statistics but merely adding up all the numbers that were unrelated and submitted from different sources. They certainly would not lead to convincing outcome if used to judge the economic capacity of ethnic minority groups. We think that under current conditions, the cash income by farmers is too fragmented and hard to track while the income in the form of physical goods is more reliable. With regards to the statistics of total social production, too many items are related but many are consumed by the producers themselves without selling through the market, and thus are hard to be converted into monetary values accurately. For example, almost all ethnic groups have the tradition of slaughtering pigs during new year festivals. Each pig would easily produce pork meat that exceeds 50 kilograms that can be converted into more than 300 yuan. This item alone generates at least 60 yuan in per capita production consumption. However, among the 25 townships documented in the above surveys, the Dashi ethnic Buyi township and Yanla ethnic Miao and Buyi township had the lowest per capita net economic income of 10.5 yuan and 9.5 yuan respectively, indicating that such statistics apparently did not include the income generated from the products produced and consumed by local farmers, and very likely only included cash income gained from activities in the market. Therefore, a more reliable method of estimating the economic capacity of these townships is by grain output.

The above data also tell us that in the 11 years from 1979 to 1989, a total of 14,959,017 yuan was invested or appropriated by the state into the 25 townships, equaling an annual average of 1.36 million yuan. In 1989, the annual state investment and appropriation of funds only accounted for 2.1% of total social production, and 10% of total grain output, and 6% of pure economic income. In addition, these ethnic groups also generated a considerable value from commercial crops. In 1989, the output of rapeseeds reached 4,297.48 tons and the outputs of tung oil, tea and peanut were also considerable. The percentage of state investment and fund appropriation over the total agricultural production would become even smaller if the value from these commercial crops were added to the total agricultural production. Due to the change in price and varying methods in statistics, it was very hard to come up with a sound estimation on the income from animal products in these ethnic regions. However, we could indirectly figure out the annual income from animal products by the number of live pigs kept in pens because in these regions, live pigs grew ready for slaughtering within one year and the number of live pigs kept in pens equaled the number of live pigs ready for slaughtering in the same year. The above data indicate that the total number of live pigs kept in pens in the 25 townships was 61,801, which could be used to estimate the number of pigs ready for slaughtering in the same year. Calculated on the assumption of 2.5 yuan per jin and each pig contributed 100 jin of pork, the live pigs alone in these 25 townships generated a value of

15 million yuan, of which the monetary input by the state only accounted for 9%. From these comparisons, one can tell that compared to the total social production, the monetary input by the state in these townships only took a small percentage of less than 10%. The percentage could drop to merely 1% to 2% if we did an accurate calculation of the total social production. To expect a transformation in these townships by such a minimal investment was like trying to put out a fire by a glass of water. The effect of state funding on these regions has long been unrealistically overestimated. In addition, we must point out that the 25 townships turned in a total of 7,472.336 tons of grains as a way of paying agricultural taxes in 1989, which was equivalent to 2.24 million yuan, some 0.88 million yuan more than the overall state investment and fund appropriation. Apparently, these poverty-stricken ethnic townships contributed to the country while receiving aids from it.

For a long time in the past when we conducted research on the economic development in ethnic regions, we always thought that in the regions, the economy was lagging behind, people were of low quality and the productivity was low, thus unable to provide investment for the expansion of reproduction. By making above comparisons in the numbers, we feel necessary to make following clarifications:

First, are the ethnic regions so poor to provide money for the expansion of reproduction? The data comparison we have done above suggests that the annual state funding for these townships was a mere 1.36 million yuan and their total population was 196 thousand people, translating into per capita investment and appropriation of 6.8 yuan. In comparison, the cash equivalent of the per capita volume of grain turned in as a way of paying agricultural taxes was 11.2 yuan. If we really want to raise funds for the expansion of reproduction, simply exempt them from turning in agricultural taxes for a few years would be more effective than the state investment and fund appropriation. To say that ethnic minority regions were too poor to raise funds for the expansion of reproduction simply ignores the facts. The key is that in our current poverty-relief work, we have not helped ethnic people identify the right path to expand reproduction; as a result, even if the ethnic people have disposable funds in hand, they don’t know where to invest and thus cannot accumulate capital. We noticed from our visits that almost all the villages in these regions were passable to carrying horses before the founding of the People’s Republic of China and villagers participated in the economic circulation across the country by way of these horses that carried local produces such as tung oil, animals, animal skins and hikes, raw lacquer or even fresh fruits to Guiyang or nearby markets in exchange for cash. Therefore, it enabled the local people to pay “head tax” on time before the fall of the Qing dynasty. In other words, these local people were not treated as penniless who were waiting to be relieved even in the feudal age. These paths were paved by small pebbles and were all completed by the villagers who invested money and put in labor hours. Based on the population density and construction volume at the moment, per capita construction volume was no less than that in today’s construction of rural roads. This is an example that demonstrates that the expansion of reproduction was not an issue of ethnic people not being able to raise funds but that we did not guide or organize them. It is thus groundless to think that ethnic groups could not be able to raise funds to build a rural road without investment from the country.

Second, people used to think that the government had done too much to help the ethnic minority people, based on which they concluded that all ethnic minority people were of low quality and could not maintain the simplest reproduction without help from the state. This is an absolute prejudice. It is clear from the above comparisons that the relief funding input by the state into the ethnic regions was very limited. The investment made by the country in some key construction projects could be as high as tens or hundreds of millions yuan, and yet they did not necessarily yielded the expected results. In exceptional cases, some projects did not have a normal operation for even one day from the time the project was kicked off to the time it was ended. Given that most of the investment in some key “third front construction” projects was drained on the limited number of employees of these enterprises, the investment the state made on ethnic regions was ignorable. We do not deny that the investment made on ethnic regions has added to the fiscal burden on the country and has some effects on the overall economic construction, about which we will discuss in detail in chapter eight entitled “on policies”. We think that the key to the aid in economic development in ethnic regions is not about how much money has been invested but about the investment efficiency. A good economic efficiency warrants large-scale investment while even small investment is a mistake if it does not yield any benefit. Such is also true to the investments on state-owned enterprises. Unfortunately, our prior efforts in poverty-relief efforts in these ethnic regions often took the form of "spreading ground pepper" over all the area. As a result, vast investment did not convert into new production capacity but was directly consumed. These investments did not bring expected results. It is even farther away from the truth when people say ethnic minority people can not even maintain a simple reproduction without the aid from the state. As we know, most of these ethnic townships are in a natural economy that runs differently from industrial enterprises. Unlike industrial enterprises that can not function without initial investment, a natural economy functions well within an enclosed community where the investment and reproduction alternate. It does not have enough room for large-scale investment and sporadic investments can be handled by the farmers. In addition, under a natural economy, there is no objective pricing standard by monetary term. Many investments are made by relying on interpersonal relations and are completed by gathering of labor force. For example, to build new home, embankment, water canal, and construct inter-village roads are large construction projects to expand reproduction under a natural economy. Even for these large projects, monetary investment is not necessary. In these projects, external monetary investment often can not bring direct benefit and must be converted into physical goods before they can be useful to the construction projects. To think that state investment is a must to maintain reproduction is groundless. In fact, in these ethnic regions, the economy runs by its own laws. Not only simple reproduction but also expansion of reproduction is possible to a certain extent as long as no fundamental changes happen to internal and external backgrounds. For instance, in 1960s when China was in an extreme economic difficulty, some ethnic regions that nowadays look extremely backward and poor could make reproduction continue normally. In places like Dalang and Meichang in Ziyun county, nobody was dead from hunger and even some Han people came here to escape from famine in their hometown. After the economic difficulty was over in the 1960s, seeing the opportunity in the shortage in tobaccos, Yanla township that was mentioned above started to expand the plantation of local tobaccos and later became a well-known place for high-quality local tobaccos. Now, every household in this township has at least thousands or more than ten thousand jin of local tobaccos in storage. The number of "ten-thousand yuan" households is no less than the developed Han regions if the value of these stored tobaccos is calculated at prevailing market prices. It indicates that the expansion of reproduction, or even the introduction of new projects by local fund-raising, is made possible without state investment as long as external environments are favorable.

Third, in the past 11 years, the 25 townships received a total of 885.6 thousand yuan in state poverty-relief funds, 3,976.595 tons in relief grains, 284.74 tons in relief chemical fertilizer and 8,863 sets in relief clothes. As they were not to be repaid by the local people who were receivers of these relief materials or funds, it prompted outsiders to think that local people could not survive without such aids from the state. Further calculations reveal, however, that these relief funds and materials were very limited in quantity that affected only 1% of the entire population with less than one yuan on per capita basis. Such a coverage and quantity in relief efforts are not bigger than those spent in ethnic Han regions. It is thus groundless if we draw the conclusion that these ethnic people could not live without the aid from the state simply by looking at the total amount in relief but ignoring the coverage and per capita relief amount.

In fact, as the subsidies that the country has made in ethnic regions, either in the form of ethnic administrative expenditure or investment, must be managed by administrative authorities instead of enterprises, a part of the subsidies must be spent to cover administrative expenses, leaving those that can be spent on economic construction in the ethnic regions a smaller percentage. To the ethnic minority regions that are in natural economic conditions, the percentage of the subsidies used in investment can not be large. Furthermore, the expansion of reproduction in ethnic minority regions under a natural economy is constrained by the characteristics of the natural economy that is weak in directly making use of monetary investments and turning them into productivity. We noticed in our surveys that in these ethnic regions, people did not know how to spend the loans or did not dare to take loans to use them in developing production, let alone contending for investments or loans. A leader from the CPPCC in Ziyun took out a poverty-relief loan, after no one else from the county was willing to do so, and had to lease the cattle he bought with the loan to villagers to raise, hoping to pay back the loan with the little calves. In many ethnic autonomous counties, of course, people tried all they could to chase after state investments. Zhenning county, for instance, fetched huge investment from the state for the purpose of developing Huangguoshu scenery area and used it to construct many luxury hotels. The money-losing sugar refineries in Wangmo and Zhenfeng counties also vied for state loans that were used in the expansion of the refineries. These loans were not directly related to the development of ethnic regions as these expansion projects were not compatible with the local ethnic economic development and had little contribution to ethnic economy. In addition, these enterprises were mostly underperformed and thus could not help the local ethnic economy, but instead became a drag on ethnic regions. Wangmo Sugar Refinery still owes the locals on the sugarcane purchase money for nearly one million yuan, which means that the refinery has become a drag on the local people. The occupancy rate in the luxury hotels built in Zhenning county remained below 50%, which were hard to maintain a normal function, let alone contribute to fiscal revenues of the county.

Three reasons that are unrelated to the ethnic economic development caused them to contend for state loans.

First, some government officials took it as an opportunity to publicize their political achievement and enhance their personal influence. A government official from Jiuzhou township in Anshun county took out a loan of 200 thousand yuan from the ethnic affairs commission of this county to use in building a hotel and developing local tourism. After our repeated attempts to convince him that this place did not have the necessary conditions for developing tourism, he finally told the truth: "it is unfortunate if I don't leave anything behind after I quit this position."

Second, these counties that received fiscal subsidies for many consecutive years were often on deficit spending and would find it hard to make ends meet in case unforeseen events happened. The state investment would ease the financial difficulties in such situations. These investment projects were usually mismanaged without effective and timely inspection on the results of investment. No one took the responsibility for the protracted investment progress, thus government officials were willing to use state funding to relieve themselves from financial strains while in office. They knew that any future problem, if any, would first have to be faced by their successors.

Lastly, given the increasing "scissors differential" between industrial and agricultural products, and a contrast between a steady agricultural tax revenue and wavering fiscal expenditures in the county, government officials often sought to ease fiscal budget deficit by opening up manufacturing or mining enterprises without giving account of conditions necessary for the success of enterprises. In such a mentality, they could easily be talked into building factories by other people and would seek loans for them. It is a shortsighted behavior rather than for the purpose of developing ethnic economy.

In a nutshell, disregard of these disguising scenarios, we have to admit that the monetary aids that the state put in ethnic regions have produced little effect on the economic development of these regions. Regardless, many people still attribute the slow progress in ethnic economic development to lack of monetary input. It is their opinion that the insufficient fiscal revenue of these ethnic autonomous counties and vast expenditure makes it hard to free up money to spend on ethnic economic development. The below statement was representative of such a thinking: "Low fiscal revenue and large expenditure have caused fund shortage in economic development. According to statistics, in 1989, the per capita fiscal revenue in ethnic regions was 44 yuan and was only 43.8% of the average level in the province. The per capita fiscal expenditure, on the other hand, was 81 yuan, causing a fiscal deficit. As a result, many counties depended on state fiscal subsidies and were short in funds in economic construction."[①] In fact, the key to the low fiscal revenue in these counties was that all these counties, especially the ethnic regions in these counties, were agricultural regions. Due to the existence of "scissors differential" in the prices between industrial and agricultural products, the low fiscal revenue was a result of artificially suppressed agricultural product price. Consequently, the issue must be solved by dealing with the "scissors differential" in price instead of depending on state loans. Certainly, to bridge the gap in the prices between industrial and agricultural products was not within the ability of these counties, but their attempts to acquire state loans may be rewarded with some success. Therefore, such a situation will continue indefinitely. The heavy burden on the state fiscal budget is also difficult to solve. Large fiscal expenditure is a result of massive administrative organization and vast teacher salaries, which depends on our requirements on compulsory education. Either of them can be changed by the efforts of county-level government officials, who otherwise are able to do a better job in determining how to make better use of the

① Jinglong Sun, *The Study of Ethnic Minority Economy In Guizhou* (Guizhou Ethnic Economic Research Institute), 37. *Development Situation of Ethnic Minority Regions in Guizhou and Its Countermeasures*, Guizhou Ethnic Press, 1st edition, September 1991.

investment.

As mentioned previously, these governmental officials kept complaining about the fiscal deficit because they hoped that these enterprises would bring revenue to relieve their fiscal pressure. However, the key to the attainment of this goal was not on investment but on the economic efficiency of these enterprises. All the counties we visited had invested in enterprises to certain extent. The investment came either from the county fiscal revenue or appropriated from the central or provincial governments, and were all considerable in amount. Anshun city spent 8 million yuan to introduce a brick factory that did not make even one single brick. Ziyun county spent over 800 thousand yuan to set up a marble factory that is now left in ruins and has gone bankrupt. In fact, the investment would not have been a problem if all the factories were profitable.

It is absolutely not necessary if the investment is input in agricultural production. As mentioned earlier in the book, under a natural economic condition, monetary input is not very urgent, and the key is to bring agricultural products to the market.

It is in general our point of view that monetary investment is not an effective prescription to take the pressure off the fiscal budget in these ethnic autonomous counties. To help our readers better understand the economic value of monetary investment in ethnic regions, we feel necessary to further discuss on the sources of investment.

The investment capacity in cross-xiang operations come from the surplus in the subjective party's cultural operation. The cultural operation of any ethnic group inevitably generates surplus energy that is more than needed by the culture itself, which is usually stored in the form of physical products, or currency under a developed market economy. More surplus products or appreciation in currency will be created if these stored physical products or currencies can be brought into a heterogeneous culture to participate in its cultural operation, making it necessary for the subjective party in the operation to organize the operations by expanding the economic activities that are subject to its own cultural norms into the heterogeneous ethnic groups, thus enable the cross-xiang operations to last normally. Apparently, the monetary investment in cross-xiang operations has a clear source, which is the surplus energy in the subjective party's cultural operation. To invest such surplus energy in cross-xiang operations, the key is the acceptability of the related cultures and the success of these operations depends on how the subjective parties understand and adjust the investment activities.

The investment in ethnic regions is a kind of cross-xiang operating activity and therefore must follow the natural laws governing cross-xiang operations. However, many researchers in ethnological economy often can not envisage the real source of such investments and have unrealistically high expectations on them. Such a misconception is closely related to the economic system that was put in place after the founding of the People's Republic of China.

Under the planned economy over a long time in the past, the operating profits of any investment and taxation were subject to the uniform planning of administrative departments. It seemed that the investment in the enterprises was all taken care of by administrative departments, making it more like administrative departments performing their official functions than businesses operating the enterprises. The administrative departments perform their functions by following administrative regulations which include the tasks of supporting economic development in ethnic groups. Therefore, people who undertake ethnic enterprises don't hesitate to ask for state investment. They won't skip any chance to acquire the investment without looking at the source of the investment nor caring about the responsibilities they take. When the requests are submitted to the administrative departments, they behave by following the administrative rules but not by economic laws. As a result, they would approve any request as long as it meets the conditions in administrative regulations and the funds are available. After some time, people get used to it and would habitually request to the upper level departments for investments under the excuse of ethnic economic development, turning such investment into a "private coffer" from which they can withdraw money at time without having to take responsibilities.

Economic activities are carried out to gain economic benefit, which requires a study of sources of investment. The material products consumed in the normal operation of any ethnic culture must be enormous while the material surplus from the cultural operation is smaller compared to the consumed material products. For instance, the Han cultural operation must first meet the need of food supply for all its members. The one billion Han population demands one billion jin each day if each one consumes one jin of grain. This is unquestionably a massive number. Subsequently, the grains that are left are not many and in normal situations, they won't exceed more than 10% of the grains already consumed. This example indicates that the funds the Han people can offer for the economic development in the ethnic regions are, in normal situations, no more than 10% of those consumed in the economic operation of their own. Given that Han people must retain a certain amount of surplus capital to prepare for any unfavorable elements and capital turnover, it is likely that the funds available for ethnic regions are 2% to 3% at most. Therefore, it is very unrealistic that the capital needed for ethnic economic development is fully dependent on the surplus from the cultural operation in the Han regions. Instead, ethnic minority people must depend on themselves for the majority of the funds needed.

When talking about self-raised funds, many ethnic government officials felt helpless. They thought that they barely had enough money to cover administrative expenditures, let alone to raise funds for production development. This is in fact a misunderstanding. The shortage in administrative expenditure is the result of a clumsy administrative organization. It is the responsibility of enterprises to raise funds for economic development. What's the use of enterprises if they can do nothing but wait for the administrative departments to provide funds to them instead of generate tax revenue to these administrative departments? They are in fact a demon derived from a system that does not separate administrative functions from enterprises.

Many regions in Guizhou Province are agricultural, forestry or pastoral regions, which in essence are households of farmers and collective enterprises. These enterprises are fully capable of raising funds for self-development. External funding, if any, would help but would not halt the production if without. The situations where administrative departments are charged with investment would be eliminated as long as we can successfully separate administrative functions from enterprises. Helping ethnic regions develop local economy in the form of cross-xiang operations must be an absolute business behavior. To operate enterprises must be equipped with operators, projects, equipment, technology and people. As our poverty-relief work is carried out by basing on developed Han regions to help the economic development in ethnic regions, the operators must be enterprise legal representatives who are very familiar with running enterprises in the Han regions as well as the economic operation in ethnic regions especially the ethnic regions that receive the enterprise. However, the enterprises that currently operate in ethnic regions in Guizhou Province are often the decision by government departments after some simple consultation. Administrative officials often are also the enterprise operators. They neither understand how to run these enterprises in the Han regions nor the economic conditions in ethnic regions. As they are not the legal representatives of the enterprises but "amphibious people", partially officials and partially businessmen, we should not be surprised to see them to fail. These enterprises are thus labeled as "three patting's" enterprises, namely "to make decisions by patting their head, to claim responsibility by patting their chest, and to evade responsibility by patting their bottom". To run the cross-xiang operations successfully requires streamlining the relation of enterprise rights and obligations and establishing the enterprise's legal person status. In addition, if the investment comes from state poverty-relief funds, we must also give consideration of the qualification of the person to be selected, and whether he has the ability to take the responsibility for the economic loss caused by the failure of the enterprises. Now, it is very common for local ethnic autonomous officials to make decisions as well as assume operational positions in these enterprises. They deal with the departments that have money to distribute only when asking for funding from the poverty-relief office of the ethnic affairs commission, which is totally against the principle of cross-xiang operations. Money providers do not have representatives among the operators and would lose control once the money leaves their hands. This is simply throwing money into water rather than investing to run an enterprise.

Problems also exist in these enterprises with regards to technology and equipment. Both the undertaker and operator of these enterprises are appointed by administrative departments. These are the people who are critical to the future of these enterprises, and yet they lack the basic understanding of the equipment, technology and factory management in the ethnic Han regions, nor do they know much about the ethnic economy. The brick making factory in Anshun city that we mentioned earlier in this book incurred losses as the appointed operators and undertakers knew so little about the technology that they were fooled into buying an outdated set of equipment. Although they patted their chests to pledge accountability, they were in fact not accountable for anything. As to how the introduced technologies can be integrated in the local environments, which was key to the success of cross-xiang operations, it probably never flashed in their mind. Without a doubt, the integration of new technology is a tough issue even for the most experienced operators in ethnic Han regions. To leave such a complex issue to the "amphibious people" whose roles are split between an official and a businessman predetermined the failure of these enterprises.

As discussed previously, it is not easy for ethnic Han people to have surplus capitals accumulated from economic activities and the amount, if any, can not be so much that can meet all the requirements. They must be fully managed and utilized if the limited amount of capital is to truly benefit the ethnic economy. The current approach of separating the responsibility of capital management from capital utilization will not manage nor utilize the capitals well. It is thus our opinion that the following three problems must be solved to ensure the better management of poverty-relief funds.

First, the right to determine the establishment of an enterprise. To decide what kind of enterprise is to be established in which ethnic region should be the call of the enterprise legal representative instead of the prefecture or county administrative authorities. Enterprise legal representatives must be recruited by the party that makes the investment, to which the recruited legal representatives should be held accountable. Investors should have an integral right of operation and the administrative authorities at the autonomous prefecture or county level should only have the right to determine if they would accept the investment as well as perform some necessary supporting functions.

Second, the integration of technology. To solve the problem of integration is key to the success of cross-xiang operation. This issue is so complex that not only entrepreneurs of the Han regions but also the informed and knowledgeable experts in economy from the ethnic regions should be relied on to solve. Two opposing attitudes are prevailing on this issue. Some people think that only technicians from the Han regions are to be relied on. The others give preference to local interests and would stuff their own people in the management regardless of their quality. Both are having hindering effects on the technological integration.

Third, the relationship between administrative authorities in the level of autonomous prefecture or county and the enterprises. Administrative authorities should be organizations that regulate enterprises instead of organizations that operate enterprises. They must provide all necessary supports to enterprises but not interfere in the operation of the enterprises. Profitable enterprises should pay taxes in accordance with relevant laws. Failing enterprises must be accountable to the investors and no administrative authorities should be made responsible. Only by handling these three layers of relationship properly can we send the enterprises onto the right track.

As discussed previously in the book, it is not easy to accumulate funds for investment and the amount of funds, if any, is limited. It determines that enterprises in ethnic regions that are invested by such funds can only survive in the areas where Han and ethnic cultures overlap. As a result, these enterprises are of exploratory nature in many cases, and are better kept in small scale and narrower scope, especially the investment expansion as discussed in chapter six. We must not rush to spread successful examples in certain areas. What we must not do when operating enterprises like this is try to change the traditional ethnic culture to adapt to the existence of the enterprises by battling the cultural operation of the entire ethnic culture. This must be followed as a basic principle in running similar enterprises.

As discussed before, the cultural operation of any ethnic group contains enormous material energy. The surplus energy from the Han cultural operation is in no way a rival to the overall cultural power of the ethnic group. Many such enterprises failed in succession because of this, and yet practices that are against this basic principle are still spreading. As an example, all the prefectures and counties in Guizhou Province have set up their own development zones. It is for the enterprise operators to decide in what kind of regions to set up what kind of enterprises. The world is big enough and no matter what conditions an ethnic region is in, there will always be investors who are willing to invest.

First, although the ethnic regions in Guizhou may not have perfect conditions for establishing modern industry, they are in a much better shape than inland Africa. If they can attract foreign investors, why should we worry that no foreign investors would be willing to invest in ethnic regions in Guizhou? The issue is that it takes a long time for foreign investors to know and explore these regions, which includes the stability of state policies and the progress we've made in opening up the local market. This is not an issue that can be rushed for quick results, nor can we talk for the foreign investors. They need time to experience and build the trust in us.

Second, more time should be allowed for foreign investors to have a profound knowledge of the economic situations in ethnic regions so that they can work out an investment strategy. What we can do is to publicize and introduce to help them gain the knowledge more quickly, but should not try to please the investors, which is in essence a form of cheating that can not succeed. We are sure that foreign investors will be able to find a solution as long as we give them an accurate description of the situations in ethnic regions.

Third, despite the fact that investment environment is an objective existence that can not be forged or elevated by human beings, diverging investment environments are not necessarily obstacles to investment. Turmin oil field in Russia is an example. Before the investment was made, the region was barely accessible by paved roads, let alone railroads. Quite a small number of people scattered in the vast land, part of which covered by tundra desert. It was in a much worse condition than ethnic regions in Guizhou Province, and yet foreign capitals came in and turned the operation profitable. Why should we worry about not being appealing to foreign investors because we did not have attractive conditions? Fundamentally, we must be patient to allow enough time for foreign investors to get to know us and make investment decisions, rather than creating some illusionary environments to lure them.

The wide enthusiasm of development zones is an indication that we have taken a wrong direction with regards to the above three issues. When we talk about attracting foreign investment, we are actually hoping to relieve the fiscal burden. Consequently, we can not help but do anything to please foreign investors in the hope of rushing to quick results. It is a mistake that we tend to think that the conditions in ethnic regions are not favorable enough to attract foreign investors, thus would spend vast amount of money in creating more appealing conditions. However, foreign investors are smart and knowledgeable investors, who would not be afraid of any difficulties as long as they can make money out of them. Don't forget that the French investors rode on horses into Yunnan to build the railroad during the Westernization Movement. Why should we take the place of enterprise operators who should be the ones to determine on their operational environments as long as such an environment makes the operation profitable? It is for the purpose of getting some quick money that we have spent such an enormous amount of money in constructing development zones. We have forgotten one basic fact: investment environments are gradually improved along with the development of enterprises, but not entirely constructed before enterprises come. The enterprise environments cost heavily to create. They also cost huge amount of money to maintain. Before we are sure of the investment and are still waiting for the potential investors to acquire the in-depth knowledge on local conditions, we rushed to put these idle infrastructure and equipment in place by spending the valuable poverty-relief funds. Such a practice is indeed tantamount to battling the entire cultural operation with limited capital, and is doomed to fail. Although the fever in constructing development zones has now receded, the equipment and facility need money to maintain, and have become things of little value or interests but can not be got rid of easily. We hope they stay there to remind us of the gap between the energy generated by investment and the ethnic cultural operation, and never to repeat the mistakes of battling with the entire ethnic culture with limited investment.

III Restraints on Operating Capacities

It becomes apparent from the above comparison between operating capacity and ethnic cultural operation that operators of cross-xiang activities must not battle with the ethnic cultural operation in capacity, but should seek steady operating efficiency by identifying the breakthrough point in the heterogeneous culture. However, such an approach takes a long time to develop. An overview of the entire history in the poverty-relief work in ethnic regions reveals that we have repeated the same mistakes in many practices and thoughts related to ethnic economic development over the past 40 years, which are still influencing the poverty-relief work of some government officials in some prefectures and counties. It is therefore necessary to summarize these practices and thoughts before bringing forth our basic opinions on poverty-relief work.

The Party and the government began to make arrangements in the economic development of ethnic regions immediately after the founding of the People's Republic of China. Our approach was based on the conception of class struggle that attributed the backward economic conditions in ethnic regions to class oppression and ethnic oppression, and that the poverty in ethnic regions was caused by the plunder of wealth by the rulers in ethnic regions. The democratic reforms removed the class and ethnic oppression and would make the economic takeoff in ethnic regions an issue of time. Subsequently, our ethnic workers worked diligently trying to save historical materials of the ethnic society for fear that these materials would be lost after decades of economic development in ethnic regions. It was just because we viewed the poverty and backwardness in the ethnic regions a temporary phenomenon that we hardly did any research on how to integrate in heterogeneous cultures but focused our work on relief, for the purpose of helping ethnic groups overcome the temporary difficulties. We did not make policies specifically tailored to ethnic regions. Instead, we launched political campaigns in ethnic regions in Guizhou that were similar to those in Han regions such as: "land reform", "campaigns to suppress bandits and local tyrants", "the struggles against the 'three evils' and 'five evils'", "mutual help and collective movements", and socialist transformation of capitalist industry and commerce. The poverty-relief work in ethnic regions in Guizhou often accompanied the political campaigns and was subordinate to these political campaigns. Only in remote ethnic regions did we see some special practices in ethnic work. For instance, the "democratic reform" was launched in Xishuangbanna in Yunnan and Liangshan in Sichuan but was not launched in other ethnic regions in Guizhou where local ethnic forces were not as concentrated as the above regions. After the campaigns such as "general line", "great leap forward", "people's commune" and "three flags" were proposed, we thought that it was only a problem of "working hard and working smart" to achieve a fast economic growth. As a result, the gap between ethnic regions and Han regions was in fact shelved when the entire nation was intoxicated in the enthusiasm of "work hard so we can run to communism". The ways we carried out economic construction were no different across ethnic regions. Many youths in ethnic regions were talked into moving to the cities and becoming factory workers and those who stayed at home were included in the management mechanism that was a "mixture of politics and society" to engage in collective production. We thought that such practices would bridge the gap between the Han and ethnic regions. However, later development surprised us. In the "three-year hardship", we were forced to fall back on to the traditional practices. Many workers were persuaded back home in the villages. Collective canteens in the rural people's communes had to be stopped and production was re-divided into smaller units, which helped pull through the difficulties.

In the 1960s, ethnic work was again brought back to agenda. However, we continued the old practice by focusing on relief efforts and united front work with people from upper class ethnic societies. Although some of the ethnic autonomous regions that had been annulled were recovered, no fundamental progress was made in the economic development in ethnic regions. The factories, schools and hospitals that were set up in ethnic autonomous regions were often fully invested, constructed and operated by the state. They were completely out of touch with the economic development in ethnic minority regions with the only exception that they were located in ethnic regions. These factories, schools and hospitals were a sharp contrast against the ethnic traditional economy but could never achieve the expected results of coordinated operation with local societies over a long time in the past. Such a contrast became more prominent in later development and the gap was widened to the extent that these enterprises could not get economic support from ethnic societies and therefore could not drive the economic development in ethnic regions; to the contrary, they had to struggle for their own survival. The "cultural revolution" that began in late 1960s shelved the economic development again. It did not resume until mid 1970s. It is safe to say that the economic development in ethnic regions in China before mid 1970s emphasized on poverty-relief and setting examples, which were to attract children of ethnic groups into schools and factories and guide the ethnic groups to catch up with the Han region through setting up factories and schools in ethnic regions. After these years, we came to realize that the mere reliance on poverty-relief and examples would not be enough to develop ethnic economy. It was not until the late 1970s did we begin testing new approaches in ethnic economic development. Given that our country did not have internal or external debt at the moment, some people proposed to buy a modernization with the money China had, namely to achieve the goal of four modernizations through purchasing full sets of equipment. In the meantime, they proposed to drive the ethnic economy and realize the four modernizations by giving the full sets of equipment to them as gifts and introducing technologies into these regions. This was certainly not individual thinking but that of a whole generation. Consequently, although the Third Plenary Session of the 11th Central Committee had made the brilliant decisions, such a guiding principle lasted into the early 1980s. The slogans such as "to get rich begins with building roads", "to aid border regions with knowledge", "poverty-relief by science and technology" and "poverty-relief begins with improving knowledge" etc., are a reflection of such a guiding principle.

In the early 1980s, we carried out activities to develop ethnic economy in the form of paired poverty-relief efforts. Government organs provided aids in finance, materials and technologies to selected ethnic minority regions. For example, the forestry department resumed a forestry school in southeast Guizhou Province by providing all the funding, manpower and materials. Commerce department took the job of communication and contact for the external sale of local produces in Dabieshan Mountain regions. Such a practice, as put by Vice Chairman Tian Jiyun, was: "One way is to carry out development projects in poverty-stricken regions systematically by taking advantage of industries. The other is to mobilize advanced units from advanced regions within the system to jointly conduct development activities by sticking to the principle of reciprocal and mutual benefit." [1] Practices of similar nature were, in essence, symbolized by either of the two words, "*pin*" (to battle with the other in capacity) and "*bao*" (take the responsibility in replace of the other). "*pin*" denotes to battle against the capacity of ethnic cultural operation by the state organs by relying on their financial and technological capacity. Based on the analysis of capacity comparison, we know that results from "*pin*" can not last forever. Nor should we expect a revolving effect that drives the economic development in ethnic regions. The so-called "*bao*" symbolizes a complete movement of capital, technology, equipment and manpower from the Han region to the poverty-relief target regions, and takes over the entire responsibility in economic development in these target regions. No one seriously analyzes the details of economic conditions of the poverty-relief targets. All ethnic regions that are deemed poverty-stricken areas are qualified. There was no time for anyone to carry out deep analysis on how to integrate these elements with the current economic conditions of poverty-relief targets. People were confident that with the advanced technology, equipment, capital and first-class manpower, they would be successful. If such a logic was followed, no matter what slogans were put forth, they did not deviate from the core. Now, by analyzing the following three examples, we hope our readers would be able to draw

[1] *Poverty-relief for the People* (State Council Office of Steering Group in the Economic Development in Poverty-stricken Regions), 6.

some inferences and understand the essence of such practices and find the correct solutions.

"To get rich begins with building roads" was a poverty-relief slogan put forth by the Ministry of Communications,① which meant that poverty-relief work would be made possible if roads were built in the impoverished mountainous regions, and subsequently, people living in the mountainous regions would get rich. If a region already had the fundamental economic foundation, and the only thing missing was the investment for building the roads, the roads, when completed, would lead to economic prosperity and bring economic benefit to local people. However, if the local economy was not fully developed, to build roads would not bring prosperity. The existence of roads might be a problem. It was true in some ethnic regions in Guizhou. We noticed in our fieldwork in southwest Guizhou that the places, such as Barao township in Wangmo county and Jianga township in Zhenning autonomous county, where some county governments were located were not accessible by paved roads. When we were visiting Barao township of Wangmo county, the party secretary of the township told us about his thought. He complained that the county people's government did not solicit their feedbacks when making the decision of "annul districts and merge townships" and thus merged the three townships of Wengdao, Barao and Babian into Barao township. As a result, the place where current township government was located was not accessible by paved roads and did not have electricity. Tens of people from the township government gathered together, making arrangement of daily life a difficult matter. It was their opinion that Barao, Babian and Dajian should be merged into one township and Dajian should be made to house the township government, therefore, the township government was accessible via paved roads and had electricity and markets, which made arranging the daily life of government workers easier. According to him, this would have added one more township that was accessible by paved roads. We will cover the drawbacks caused by "annul districts and merge township" in chapter nine "on solutions". Here, we want to emphasize one issue: where the paved roads are built is a natural result of economic development. In the contrary, the road condition indirectly reflects the level of economic development of a region. If we move the township governments around like moving wood blocks simply to demonstrate the level of

① *Poverty-relief for the People*, 101 -106.

economic development, it would result in a phenomenon where paved roads connect all townships and yet the economic development remains unchanged.

It is a known fact that it costs money to build roads and it also costs money to maintain roads. Without the local economic development reaching a certain level, completed roads may be left abandoned due to insufficient maintenance. As the paved roads we built in remote ethnic regions were often invested by the state or constructed by "offering employment opportunities instead of outright grants" to local people, it was much easier to build the roads than maintain them as long as the project was approved by the upper-level government and money was allocated. Consequently, administrative officials only eyed on building roads and caused many paved roads that had already been opened to close again. The former Mashan township of Wangmo county was an important place of nationwide poverty-relief efforts and thus received many aids from across the country. Paved roads were opened up as early as 1980s. However, the roads need to be maintained, which was difficult for an impoverished township as Mashan that had so little fiscal revenue that could not afford to maintain the roads. As a result, the roads were impassable until they received aid funds from other places. When the roads were passable, most of time they were used by cattle and pedestrians in addition to the jeeps carrying inspecting officials from all government levels. In other words, the roads that were so costly to build were rarely used for the designed purposes with the exception of inspection by government officials and occasional transportation of aid materials. Following the decision to "annul districts and merge townships", former Manshan and Naye townships were merged into Mashan township, and the township government was placed in Naye that was located by the paved road. Subsequently, the road that led to former Mashan township became even less frequently used. No more than one or two vehicles ran on this road in a year. When we set foot on this road, we walked into the wild grasses that were taller than our knees and frogs even leaped into our trouser legs. No roads were in sight. This paved road in Mashan was not the only one that was closed again after put in operation.

We experienced the same in Kanbian township of Wangmo county. A deputy county chief sent a car to take us to Kanbian, but the car started to jolt intensely after it passed Dayi, which forced the driver to slow down and fumble along. In several occasions, half of the road collapsed and our car had to inch by getting close to the steep mountain on the other side of the road. In the middle of the road, a giant rock was lying on the road. To keep the tires of the car from being cut, we had to get off the car and filled the holes on the road with small stones so that we could bypass the giant stone. It took us two and a half hours to cover the distance of 20 kilometers. After we arrived in Kanbian, we were told that this part of road was not included in the territory of road maintenance by the county road transportation bureau, and was thus not under anybody's protection. Although the county government tried to collect some money from local farmers and use it in road maintenance, the regulation by the state council to alleviate farmers' burdens scared them. They had to stop the practice after only one collection. Similar cases were seen in many other places, which we are not going to elaborate here in this book. These examples show clearly that to build roads alone would not bring prosperity to the local people. It is not a difficult thing to build roads with the support from the units that offer poverty-relief funds. The real difficulty is whether the local economy has reached the level enough to support the maintenance of the road. This is a problem that can not be solved simply by building roads.

Realizing that direct input of material and equipment could not achieve the poverty-relief goals, some people advocated that it be more important to "provide aids in knowledge". They believed that local people would be brought out of poverty if they could be trained to become skilled and knowledgeable. Subsequently, specific measures to "provide aids in knowledge" were put forth by relevant units. Some invested in building and running schools; Some put together plans to train teachers; Some set up scholarship foundation to encourage children of ethnic groups to go to school. All of a sudden, people all became enthusiastic about ethnic education. However, problems gradually emerged after the fever continued for a while. The intention of the advocate of "poverty-relief begins with aids in knowledge" was to prepare people for the economic development in ethnic regions, but we should first make sure that these people should be able to stay in these regions. The hard-won educational funding would be totally wasted if the educated people all left. Ethnic Han regions are over-supplied with these people and each year, students who graduate from schools of different kinds and levels are facing fierce competition in the job market. By spending the money raised in the Han regions, we have created the workforce that eventually will come to compete with the Han students for job opportunities. Are we relieving poverty in the ethnic regions or worsening the troubles in the Han regions? People retention is a difficulty. Even if they can be retained, how helpful they are in poverty-relief remains a question. The educational system in China takes the form of a uniform "sweeping approach" across the entire country, or the so-called "exam system", where students of each grade must pass a variety of uniform examinations to be awarded corresponding diploma. In such a system, textbooks, teaching methods or even question types in exams are made standardized as much as possible. China is a country with a vast territory and a large number of ethnic groups, no standardized textbooks can contain everything that is needed by all communities and societies. As a result, many ethnic students who have acquired related diploma feel lost when they go back to the hometown where what they have been taught in school can not be used and what is needed has not been taught in school. After having in-depth conversations with quite a number of ethnic students in our fieldwork, we realized that it was a common mentality among these ethnic students who chose to continue education and leave their hometown for employment or drop out of school if they felt unlikely to get a job in the Han regions, so that they would not have to go through the hardship of education. Such a mentality is hardly in synch with the intentions of the advocates of "poverty-relief begins with aids in knowledge".

We are not simply against the slogan of "poverty-relief begins with aids in knowledge." We believe that it is critically important to first understand what should be included in the "knowledge", without which, provision of aids might not attain the expected poverty-relief goal. As Guizhou Province is home to many ethnic groups that differ dramatically across groups and regions, they demand different knowledge and skills in the development of economy. To ensure that we offer the "knowledge" that is critically needed for poverty-relief in these regions, we must make the textbooks, teaching methods and educational systems fit the specific ethnic regions and groups. Does the current educational model in China have such compatibility? The answer to this question is obvious. The slogan will become meaningless if it is not solved properly.

"To relieve poverty by science and technology" is another slogan that differs dramatically in practice despite its literary uniformity. For instance, some propose to conduct overall technical training; Some insist to intensify research on the resources in ethnic region; Some advocate to improve on the traditional production technology in ethnic regions. Among them, the one that is easiest to promote and accept by ethnic people is to send poverty-relief teams made up of technical experts to teach one or two techniques to ethnic people so that they can turn them into quick money and hopefully can climb out of poverty and get rich.[①] As the value and status of science and technology in the ethnic economic development was systematically analyzed in sector ii of chapter five, we only make one note here. The application of science and technology is distinctively ethnic and regional; subsequently, attempts to relieve poverty by science and technology without taking the traditional culture of the receiving ethnic groups into account will yield no satisfactory results. Without a doubt, many people in these poverty-relief teams are experts in their special fields but are very limited in ethnic knowledge. The projects they have selected are often determined in the Han regions that they are familiar with, and thus often cause unexpected problems in execution. The following are three most prominent problems. First, capacity of market. The hands-on teaching of one special technique (or skill) is for the purpose of enabling the local people to make money and hopefully get rich by engaging in commodity production by making use of this technique or skill. However, commodity production depends on the market. Our technical experts have enthusiastically promoted one technology in every place they visited; as a result, all the people in these places have developed the same product and consequently become competitors against each other. Once the market is saturated for that particular product, all would be drowned. The science and technology team made up of experts from Guizhou Province promoted the technology in early-maturing vegetables in Luodian county, which was a huge success and brought wealth to the region. It later fueled the enthusiasm across all the southern counties in Guizhou. When people flocked to plant early-maturing vegetables, they seemed to have ignored one fundamental fact that the vegetable market in Guizhou Province was not a bottomless pit that could absorb all vegetables as they were produced. In addition, other factors must be considered such as how far that the vegetables could be transported by the current transportation facility in Guizhou, how much it cost and how it affected the total production cost. Therefore, the

① Practices and Discussions on Regional Economic Development (The Cadre Training Center for Poverty-stricken Regions, February 1991), 54 – 56.

production of a certain product or technology alone without studying the market would only make the economic efficiency increasingly lower and eventually would wipe out all the achievements the science and technology team members had made. As a hard lesson, in Rongjiang county of Guizhou Province, a premium variety of orange was once planted over a large territory. After harvest, farmers could not find buyers and the oranges had to be left rotten in the orchards. The promotion of planting pseudo-ginseng in Wangmo county was a total failure and the loans are not repaid even in today. It is an even more severe issue. As science and technology, especially the technological applications, are specific to distinctive time, region and ethnic group, any promotion of such technological applications without giving consideration of the subjects or controlling the sphere of application would result in unexpected results and do more harm than good to ethnic people.

"To aid border regions with knowledge" was first put forth by some democratic parties in China, whose intention was, by taking advantage of the strength in the intensified talents in science and technology, to bring science and technology to the door of the people in ethnic border regions and speed up the economic development in these regions. However, the advocates of this slogan overlooked the basic precondition for the slogan to become effective, and thus were faced with unexpected results. With a limited number of exceptions, activities organized under the influence of this slogan were unsatisfactory in results. It is true that science and technology is the primary productivity. To turn it into actual values, the production departments must accept and become the carrier of science. Science and technology can offer value to the improvement of productivity only through the operation of production department. Unfortunately, when this slogan was put into practice, the production units in ethnic border regions were not independent production entities but extensions of administrative organs of the state that were partially official and partially commercial, and thus were unable to determine what kind of technologies was needed for their own regions, and how to turn the introduced technologies into production. Without solving this problem, the technologies would only be set aside and left ineffective, and the targets receiving the aids could do nothing but accept everything that was given to them. No actions followed. The attempts to "aid border regions with knowledge" brought a series of discussions and speeches on strategy, which were later turned into reports and locked in the drawers in the offices.

Another difficulty is that China has long implemented an indiscriminate mechanism in science and technology research. We have either blindly imported technologies from foreign countries, or blindly attached science and technology research to domestic large and medium enterprises where the attention of researchers was diverted to the supportive researches in the large and medium enterprises in the developed Han regions, and the research projects critically needed for the economic development in ethnic regions have been ignored. The aid providers, due to the lack of capacity, could do nothing but to copy what they were familiar with in the Han regions. For instance, the Swidden cultivation that is still prevailing in some regions in Guizhou is studied by the community of agricultural technology as a subordinate to the agricultural history and the remains of primitive agriculture. Their values are only demonstrated in academic documentation but not in practical economy. The only answer we may get from these researchers on the solutions in the Swidden cultivation is: to completely eliminate it and replace it with modern agriculture. They probably have not seriously considered if the Swidden cultivation was truly replaceable.

The first one that treated the Swidden cultivation as a means of livelihood in a special living environment was Yin Shaoting,[①] who was a scholar that grew up in ethnic border regions instead of an agricultural expert in developed Central Plains. The forestry plantations in the Dong regions in Guizhou, for another example, have been barely studied by the forestry academia. It turns out that ethnologists have accumulated more and solid technical materials in this respect than silviculturists. Our hydraulic experts may know all the specifics about how to build dams and reservoirs. However, nearly all the reservoirs in ethnic regions in Guizhou were built in highly valuable fertile farmlands, which would undoubtedly destroy the slight chance of survival for the crops in the paddy fields. Our hydraulic experts barely gave any thought about that, let alone carried out systematic study on this. These examples indicate that the scientific researchers who have long lived in the central Han regions are not equipped with the necessary knowledge that can be used in aiding the border regions. The have nothing to "sell".

Another problem that hinders the efforts to "aid border regions with

① Shaoting Yin, *A Highly Debatable Cultural Ecological System* (Yunnan People's Publishing House, March 1994), 206-209.

knowledge" is policy integration. Like anywhere else across the country, the lands in ethnic border regions are contracted out to individual farmers, which links the remuneration to output on the lands. According to the relevant policies governing the industry classification, all the economic industries in ethnic regions fall into the agricultural category. The primary products in ethnic regions including grains and commercial crops are included in the monopoly purchase system by the state where administrative departments control all the stages from production to sale of these primary products. By policies, the real operators in production must be specific farming households, but the technical people who come to aid the border regions could not provide consultation in technology to these households and they had to deal with government officials. A good suggestion can not be implemented by farmers but have to wait for the administrative departments to make decisions. In other words, with the technology in their hands, the people who come to help border regions can not find people in need. Others may argue that the technologies may be used in the state-run large and medium enterprises in ethnic border regions. Such a proposal sounds plausible in theory but is infeasible in practice. Many of these enterprises are directly under the control of the central government and are over-supplied with technical people. Obviously, there is no need to aid these enterprises.

For the above three reasons, most of the activities aimed at aiding border regions with knowledge were not successful, with the only exception of the work by experts represented by Fei Xiaotong. However, instead of a result of the efforts to aid border regions with knowledge, the achievement was made because these experts were ethnologists whose knowledge found a fit in these ethnic regions.

"Gradient theory", also known as "gradient displacement law", was one of the theories on the strategy of national economic development that were developed by the academia after the "reform and opening-up" policy was implemented. As it is directly related to the strategies in the long-term economic development in ethnic regions, gradient theory has become one of the hot issues in the research of economic development theory in ethnic regions. There have been heated debates over this theory for a long time in the past, therefore, we feel necessary to give a thorough explanation on the scope of application of this theory and the role it plays in the ethnic economic development.

The basic idea of gradient theory is that the imbalance in the economic development across the country will create a natural gradient effect in the economic and technological capacity in the country. The ethnic border regions have weaker technological capacity and insufficient capital, and thus are slow in the progress of economic development. Many regions still remain in the level of "traditional technology" and backward economy. In addition, a majority of the border regions remain in the ordinary level of "medium technology" while some regions are already equipped with "advanced technology" and solid economic capacity. Therefore, in the implementation of opening-up policy to the outside world, advanced technologies should be first mastered by the advanced coastal regions, and then passed to the regions of "medium technology" and "traditional technology" in a gradient manner (transfer, pass). This would gain more by less cost. [①]

"Gradient theory", a term originally used in geonomics, basically means that the level of difficulty varies when economically developed countries and regions extend hi-tech industries over neighboring regions. To understand this term, we must take the three preconditions into consideration: First, it is a conclusion drawn from the perspective of the operators of the industry extension that radiates from an established center. With the change in the angle and point of observation, the results would be very different. Second, the term is valid on the basis of a certain radiation of industrial technology. A different source of radiation of industrial technology may give rise to very different gradients. For instance, when modern electronic industry is transferring to China, the southeast coastal region is apparently first gradient. Conversely, if dry land animal husbandry is selected, its radiation will start from Xinjiang and Inner Mongolia while southeast coastal region becomes the last gradient. Third, the "gradient theory" is not a strategic theory about the overall situation but merely a development theory for individual industries. The advocates of the "gradient theory" in China apparently applied this theory in the research of the development of ethnic regions in the West to come up with their strategic plans, which was, in the very beginning, against the precondition of the usage of this term. As a result, it caused a heated debate across the country once the theory was put forward. Consequently, some scholars put forward the "counter-gradient theory" that

① Zhenghai Cao, Biao Ma, et al., *A Strategic Vision before Take-off* (The Ethnic Publishing House, 1990), 180 – 181.

alleges that the introduction of advanced technologies must not be restrained to the southeast coastal regions but instead, should start from the ethnic regions in the West so that the West can catch up with and surpass the southeast coastal regions, and thus realize four modernizations in the entire country.

As there have been no established theories in economics and geography on whether the under-developed ethnic regions can surpass the developed regions in economic development, they provide no theoretical nutrient in our discussion of this issue. However, mature theories have been developed in ethnography but unfortunately, have not attracted the attentions of the people who are responsible for ethnic development. As a recommendation, we would like to remind our readers of the "law of evolutionary potential" that recently came up in ethnology. First put forth by American ethnologist Elman R. Service, the core of the theory is so-called "principle of regional discontinuity of progress" and "principle of ethnic discontinuity of progress". The former states that new cultures do not emerge from the previous developed regions but rather from the edges of these developed regions, while the latter asserts that there is often no direct cultural inheritance between two developed countries in different ages. As this theory is put forth for the emergence of new culture instead of a specific industry, for all ethnic groups instead of a specific ethnic group, for all regions in the world instead of a specific region, it has a wide applicability and is thus more appropriate than the "gradient theory" or "counter-gradient theory" if used in analyzing the economic development in the ethnic regions in western China. The theoretical foundation in ethnology resulted from the "gradient theory" will be discussed in detail in the latter part of this section. Here, we will only briefly summarize the above theories about the economic development in the ethnic regions in the west.

Although the above proposals in developing ethnic regions in the west seem divergent on the surface, they are essentially identical in that all are hoping to drive the economic development in the West by relying on the financial and material capacities of the state. Despite the differences in the bases, starting points and ways of solving problems across these proposals, they come down to the point of using the state money to attain their goals. They seem to have forgotten the fundamental principle: state money comes from tax revenues that, no matter how big it is in absolute terms, is a small percentage over GDP. After the majority of the tax revenue is used to maintain the administrative operation of the country, only a small percentage can be used in the economic development of ethnic groups. Compared to the huge gross social product in the economic operation in ethnic regions, this limited amount of capital is far from shaking the economic condition in the ethnic groups, not to mention rapid development. Without the breakthrough in the fundamentals, actions triggered by the above proposals would without a doubt end up aborted due to insufficient investment a while after they began. Even though some results are seen in a few places, their promotion to other places would be aground due to a stagnant economy. Given the huge gap between the supply and demand of capital, we think that the investment from state should not be used to battle against the capacity in the ethnic cultural tradition and economic conditions, but should only be used to stimulate ethnic people to enhance their self-reliance ability, direct the ethnic economy into the domestic and international market, and sponsor development of scientific projects that are immediately needed by the ethnic groups. Any goal beyond these boundaries would be unrealistic. It may not be acceptable to the advocates of these theories if they are told that these theories are not mature in theory. They would be more likely be convinced if we tell them that objectively the country does not have the financial ability to do so. Bringing the consequences into the picture makes it easier for people to understand.

Although it was all over the media that boasted the great achievements we made in the poverty-relief work in the past years, we have to admit that the gap between the economy of the ethnic regions in Guizhou and that of the developed regions in Han regions has been widened rather than narrowed. Despite the reports of actual examples of people being lifted out of poverty, we have also seen real cases of people submerged under the poverty line. In addition, many poverty-stricken counties in Guizhou are still in an impoverished state. Other places still have a long way to go before being completely out of poverty although they've made tremendous progress in economic development. According to the state statistics, many regions in Guizhou are still under the line of subsistence. We've also noticed that many regions were lifted out of poverty simply by resource consumption regardless of ecological crisis, which was not based on solid material ground and would slid back into poverty much faster if the resources are drained. We must think about this issue from a more profound level, and look at the three forms in the loss of non-economic capacity in the poverty-relief work: capacity sediment, non-production-related loss, and loss in production integration.

Capacity sediment is a phenomenon commonly seen in the economic entities in ethnic regions. It is not caused by poverty-relief work but does not change by poverty-relief work either, and has constrained the effectiveness of poverty-relief work. As mentioned in previous text, ethnic Miao group once was in a large trade surplus when it conducted trade with the developed Han regions in the feudal age, However, the money accumulated from the trade surplus was not turned into new productivity but stayed in the form of "ornaments", which has lasted till today. Although Guizhou is an impoverished province, the savings of its rural and urban residents are not low. The ending balance in the savings of rural and urban residents in the entire province in 1987 was 3,073,400 thousand yuan, [①] compared to a total local fiscal revenue of a mere 2,153,967 thousand yuan and a total local fiscal expenditure of 3,160,029 thousand yuan. In other words, the state had to subsidize Guizhou for 1 billion yuan to fill the gap between fiscal revenue and expenditure while the total personal saving tripled the fiscal subsidy. To an impoverished province, it means a huge amount of sediment of money.

Most modern economists in the west would prescribe lowering the bank deposit interest rate as well as the tax rate to turn the funds into capital. These measures are very effective for the regions that have a fully developed market economy, but are not nearly as effective in ethnic regions in Guizhou Province. As discussed earlier in the chapters "on culture", the money stored in the ethnic regions in Guizhou is not for production but for insurance, or as a way of showing off their wealth. No matter how low the interest rate goes, they would deposit the money in the bank to make it idle instead of spending in purchasing production materials to put back in the reproduction. Many economic administrators, out of unconsciousness of this situation, only look at how much capacity is input in developing ethnic regions. They believe that the economic capacity input by the state alone would be able to transform the laggard economy in these ethnic regions. It turned out that the inputs by the state through a lot of strenuous work were either consumed or converted into idle bank deposits and did not benefit the production at all. It becomes obvious that in the ethnic regions in Guizhou, the key to the economic development is not about how much capacity the state has input but rather

① *Guizhou Statistical Yearbook - 1987*, 573

about how to ensure that the input capacity does not sink in the bank accounts but circulates in the production field. Under the circumstances that these issues have not been the focus of academic research now, to emphasize one-sidedly on the input of capacity will only prove invalid and ineffective. In fact, the reality we are dealing with is simple. The fact that current bank deposits can not be converted into productivity and no one would risk taking out loans from the banks makes it clear that what drags the economic development in ethnic regions in Guizhou is not an insufficient capacity but an inadequate use of current capacity. Before we find a solution to this problem, neither the state nor individuals or enterprises should intensify input or dare to set foot blindly on these regions, let alone the foreign enterprises. Now, all the autonomous prefectures and counties in Guizhou are still intoxicated in soliciting domestic and foreign capital into their economic development zones. The question is who would be willing to make such investment with their eyes closed.

Aside from the money sediment, production material also poses prominent problems. During over 40 years of development efforts in ethnic regions, some modern enterprises were established in these ethnic regions. Each county had its own "five small enterprises", namely small chemical fertilizer factory, small agricultural machinery factory, small cement factory, small hardware factory and small power plant. In addition, a few large enterprises were built with state investment in some autonomous prefectures and counties, such as the large enterprises built during the "third front construction" period. Most of these manufacturing and mining enterprises have now gone bankrupt or shifted to other line of business. As a result, the equipment originally purchased for the enterprises, the factories and people trained have mostly sunk in the society and have not yielded any benefit. Although the large state-owned enterprises are still operating, they are not making any profit, and the equipment and people likewise have sunk in the society. To keep these enterprises operate costs the country heavily each year. If we can not find a way to bring these idle equipments operate again but continue soliciting for more investment, how can we ensure that the new investment would not sink again? This indicates that the equipment capacity is also a secondary issue in the economic development of ethnic regions. The key is how to make the current equipment operable and prevent the newly acquired equipments from becoming idle. Unfortunately, such a critical issue has not been fully studied.

Contrary to the capacity input by the state, the traditional production in the ethnic group in Guizhou Province would continue operate profitably regardless of the changes in state policies. Of course, such a profit is, by modern standards, too low. A county can generate no more than a few millions of yuan. However, we need to admit that they are profitable and are thus much better and contribute much more to the country than the modern large state-owned enterprises that depend on huge state subsidies to survive. It prompts us to ask, instead of spending so much money to fill the bottomless pit and turn it into idle funds, why nobody carries out research on how to put the investment in renewing traditional production projects, and on how to identify the point for the modern industry to grow from the traditional economic projects before making proposals on the development of modern industry. To the developed countries in the West, there is indeed no need to carry out such a research as the Western political system determines that it does not need to consider the economic development in the ethnic regions, nor worry about resources. They are capable of reaching out to anywhere in the world to seize all natural resources necessary for their economic development or even buy all the labor force in each technical level, from senior intellectuals to manual labors, by resorting to their economic capacity and military or political might. Things are different in China. The economic development in the ethnic Han regions relies on domestic market for natural resources, specifically the ethnic regions in the west. The natural resources must be turned by social economic activities into resources products, in particular, through the economic operation in ethnic minority regions. Natural resources can not be developed, and the ethnic economy can not be developed that will hurt the supply of natural resources to the Han regions if we don't study ethnic economy or identify the point for the growth of modern enterprises from the traditional economic operations. In summary, we are trying to fill a bottomless pit if we don't solve the issue of economic development in ethnic regions. Capacity sediment is a form of ineffectiveness of state investment in ethnic regions while "non-production-related loss" is another. Due to different cultural backgrounds, and different economic life governed by such cultural backgrounds, these ethnic regions do not utilize the economic capacity as is hoped by the investor of the capacity, but by following the law of their own economic cultural operation when accepting the investment, subsidy and aids from the state. Any capacity input by the state that is beyond the range of the tolerance by the traditional cultural life of these ethnic groups often would not be converted into productivity but instead be consumed. In our fieldwork, we came across situations where local people used the production loans to treat guests rather than to buy production materials. The loans, to the local people, were a result of favor by the other people, so the first thing they would do after receiving the loans was to return the favor. They wouldn't worry about the repayment because in their mind, the production would always continue and the loans would be repaid eventually.

We found some reports that mentioned that some distributed relief items were traded in the market for liquor by ethnic Miao people and agricultural materials such as chemical fertilizer were left idle or resold in exchange for cash. It was simply because the money and materials given from other cultures were unable to change the traditional economic life and thus could not be converted into new productivity but simply consumed.

Non-production-related loss occurs not only in traditional economic life of ethnic groups but also in the manufacturing and mining enterprises established in ethnic regions through state investment. As the ethnic backgrounds in which these enterprises operate are quite different from the original backgrounds, the normal social life of the technical people who have moved into the ethnic regions with there enterprises can not be satisfied, forcing them to provide social services for their employees. As a result, a substantial part of investment has to be wasted in building dormitory, hospital and school etc. but rather than on production. The welfare services undertaken by these enterprises are a form of non-production-related loss commonly seen in these enterprises. Due to the same reason, while in the operation of these enterprises, the maintenance of equipment, supply of spar parts and some special materials all depend on the central cities some hundreds or even thousands of miles away. To maintain the normal production requires extra heavy costs to guarantee the supply of these necessities and technical services, which constitutes another form of non-production-related loss. In addition, these enterprises, materials and markets are usually in the same cultural zones, causing heavy loss by the redundant transportation of raw materials and products and by the waste in transportation capacity. As a result, the production capacity of these enterprises is constrained and their costs remain high, dampening their competitiveness. Although it has not been converted into consumption, the loss goes into the total production cost and directly impact the role the capacity can play, and is therefore a non-production-related loss.

In the nutshell, the existence of non-production-related loss has disabled the invested capacity to be converted into productivity. Instead, it will be consumed or wasted. This is one of the reasons that these investment projects have produced unsatisfactory results for the long time in the past. By simply increasing capacity without effectively reducing non-production-related loss is not going to solve the problem of economic development in ethnic regions.

As discussed in chapter three, ethnic groups in Guizhou are in different economic types and modes, which would inevitably result in the differences in the structure of variety of products, butch quantity, quality standards in different ethnic groups. For the same reason, they have different preferences and tastes for the products provided from outside the region. However, while making investment and introducing technologies in ethnic regions, what we usually do is focusing on the analysis of the details of investment projects, rather than on finding out the product structure and consumer preference in these ethnic regions and including these collected data in the investment plan. The result of totally ignoring the local traditional economy is the creation of many "isolated islands", the enterprises that float outside the local economic life of the ethnic regions. The raw materials needed by these enterprises can not be supplied and the finished products have to be sold outside the regions. Even if they are operated successfully, the added costs in transportation of raw materials and finished products would eat up most of their profits, if any, making it possible for the enterprises to contribute to the local economy.

Huajiang Brewery in Guanling county that we mentioned in chapter four is a typical example of failed product integration. When the brewery was designed, the plan was to create a well-known brand and then seek raw materials to be invested by the state. In fact, from the beginning, they were trying to compete with the large state-owned enterprises. Subsequently, the business plan was not made on the assumption of using the locally produced raw material – corn, and arrangement was not made accordingly. Instead, they put all energy on brewing sample liquors. Even before the winery was completed, the liquor became over-supplied in domestic market, making the supply of raw materials by the state unlikely. Now the winery wanted to shift to traditional way of liquor brewing, but unfortunately it was too late for making arrangement on raw material supplies, and the brewery had to be closed eventually.

The liquor-brewing business in Huajiang of Guanling is based on solid ethnic culture and superior geographic location. All ethnic groups in the region are addicted in liquor and low-degree liquors (with alcoholic content ranging from 15% to 20%) are in large demand. However, local people only buy liquor in bulk but not in bottles. The brewery could have produced liquors that could seize a majority of the local market share if it was willing to cater to the needs of local people, and yet the decision-makers of the brewery did not give any consideration to the integration between its products and local ethnic societies, but instead kept chasing the well-known brand names in the domestic market and competing with them for the Han market, sending itself to a dead road even before the brewery went into operation. Huajiang is located right in the middle of Yunnan-Guizhou highway that is a rest area for passing vehicles. Bulk low-alcohol liquors could be perfect refreshing drinks for the passengers. Despite of all these, decision-makers of the brewery blindly picked the liquors of high alcoholic content as to produce, which found no local market and suffocated its potential market. This brewery, as an example, makes it clear that to establish enterprises in ethnic regions without giving enough heed to how to integrate products with local ethnic societies will inevitably lead to the waste of invested capacity and eventually bankrupt the enterprise.

Nearly all the counties we visited had once set up their own small cement plant. However, none of them could operate normally, one of the reasons being the failure in product integration. Most of the houses in the ethnic regions were of wooden structures and these small cement plants could not produce cements that could be used by large construction projects due to their backward technology, low level and unstable quality. Although it could be used in sporadic local market, the lack of product integration made it impossible for local people to use. We noticed in our surveys that many temporary workers from outside the region made asbestos tiles and precast air bricks with the cement they purchased by illegal means, which could be used immediately. These small plants could have a better chance of survival if they took the production integration into consideration and directly attained the integration between products and the society.

Marble mines have been found in the majority of Anshun region and the counties in Southwest Guizhou Autonomous Prefecture, and many counties established marble plants in the township enterprise fever. Now, fewer are still operating than closed. On top of the mismatch between technical equipment and power, product integration was a direct reason. When these marble plants were planned, they unexceptionally introduced incision and polishing equipments with the production of marble slabs used in construction as targets. As every county invested in building plants, each plant could not be big, making about 1,000 square-meter marble slabs each year with the maximum being around 10,000 square meters. Marble slabs are often used in large-scale construction sites. Modern large-scale structures often demand at least 10,000 square meters each, which must be in the same style, texture and color. The numerous marble plants were mostly small-scale ones whose products were made from marble mines of very different style, texture and color, which no large construction would like to buy. On the other hand, the insufficient working capital of these plants made them very vulnerable and one failed sale effort could force the plants to shut down. The marble plants in Houchang of Ziyun county and Wangmo county that we paid visit to already suspended operation and the equipment all rust away. Nothing left out of the total investment of 810 thousand yuan made in the marble plant in Houchang of Ziyun. In fact, these factories could have walked another path: by relying on the local masons who were supported by some modern equipment, they could have entered the domestic market with single-piece marble artwork, thus solving the problem of product integration. To import slab processing equipment blindly in the beginning of operation was doomed to fail. Similar issues existed in the modern sugar refineries that were invested by Wangmo and Zhenfeng counties. To safeguard the raw material supply, the county governments prohibited, by administrative orders, individuals from making brown sugars and demanded that sugarcane farmers sell sugarcanes to the refineries only. However, the white sugar made by these refineries was not needed in local market and thus had to be sold to other regions. As a matter of fact, these refineries could have been operated more flexibly. For example, they could have collected reasonable processing fees for pressing sugarcanes with their own machines for the farmers, which increased their income, solved the problem of integration between products and local market, and also maintained the traditional brown sugar production thus enrich local farmers and drive the local economy. In case the brown sugar of the sugarcane farmers could not find buyers, the refineries could buy in at lower prices and store it as raw materials. When sugar prices rose and even if it was not in the sugarcane harvesting season, the refineries could use the stored brown sugar as raw materials and turn them by slight processing into white sugar that was demanded in other markets. By taking this approach, the refineries would become the sugar production industry leaders instead of pure processors, and would contribute more to the ethnic economic development.

The ethnic regions we have visited are home to a variety of grains other than wheat and rice, such as myotonin, *tianxing* rice, and sticky millet etc., as well as abundant resources of wild plants: some are raw materials for making spices, some are medicinal materials such as litsea cubeba, polygonum multiflorum etc.; valuable and rare wild animals, such as monkeys in Mashan, bamboo rats in Beipanjiang river region, and a limited number of musk deer and barking deer, and considerable number of pheasants. In addition, it also has a wide variety of snakes. Due to the self-sufficient and natural economy, the abundant resources can only be consumed locally but can not be converted into commodities. In recent years, the emergence of special economic zones has created an increasing demand for valuable and rare plants and animals. Consequently, a lot of lawless businessmen, disregard of the natural resources protection laws of the country, have ventured deep into these ethnic regions to illegally purchase wild animals and plants, and have brought devastating consequences to the local natural resources. The situation has gotten so severe that immediate actions must be taken to stop these conducts. From another perspective, these specialty products and natural resources in the ethnic regions are the source of huge economic wealth, the development of which, if properly organized and effectively managed, may signal a new way of developing local ethnic economy.

To turn potentials into actual benefit, the problem we need to solve first is product integration. The specialty grains other than wheat and rice produced in ethnic regions are put on local markets for sale in gunny bags or in baskets. What are seen in the market are numerous varieties but little quantity, which makes it hard to integrate with the form of trade in other regions as they are not properly packaged, without specifications, quality standards, or even instructions for consumption. Although people may feel interested and may have demand for them, they can not access domestic market due to lack of above measures of integration and appropriate social organizations that play the role of gathering the products that scatter over a large territory.

It is our opinion that to solve the problem of product integration, a coordinating trade organization must be established to keep close contact with local markets across the country, and enable the gathering of these products that spread across a vast territory under the organization that plays the role of grading, determining quality, packaging and attaching description of products. Going through these steps would surely make it possible for these products to access international markets. If a special note is added to the description of products that mentions that these products are 100% free of chemical pesticides or other harmful pollution, they would sell fast and are likely to demand premium price given that people in the developed regions are suffering badly from all kinds of pollutions. Based on this, we can expand production to make these products top sells from the ethnic regions. As to the natural resources of animals and plants, we must follow the regulations in protection laws and combine production and development, and authorize relevant departments to organize local people to hunt or gather these natural resources. At time of right conditions, we may start artificial rearing or cultivation. These resources may become an important component of ethnic economic capacity if managed properly.

We realize that ethnic groups have special capacities in economic development. However, to find out these capacities depends on deep and thorough investigations and researches in ethnic regions. Searches from the perspective of rice field cultivation in the Han regions only would not yield any results. Once we've found out these capacities, the problem of product integration must be solved and capacity sediment and non-production-related loss should be avoided before we can turn these capacities into economic benefit. These issues were seldom brought onto the agenda of research in "one-way" cross-xiang operation. With the emergence of "two-way" or "multi-way" cross-xiang operations, it becomes urgent for us to carry out these researches. We are hopeful that the economic takeoff in ethnic regions can be expected soon if we have done a good job in research and organization.

Chapter Eight On Policy

China was dominated by the planned economy over a long time in the past and is now undergoing the transformation into a market economy, both of which influenced and will continue to influence the economic development in the ethnic regions in Guizhou Province. For this reason, in this chapter we will first give a comprehensive and overall discussion on the pros and cons of these two economic policies as well as their direct or indirect impacts on ethnic regions in Guizhou Province. We think that a "planned economy" and a "planned economy that is out of control" are two different concepts and the slow pace in the economic development in ethnic regions in Guizhou was the result of the planned economy that is out of control but not necessarily that of the planned economy itself. Based on this foundation, we believe that, to push forward the economy in ethnic regions in Guizhou Province, we must first completely remove the negative impacts from the out-of-control planned economy, followed by a planning of cross-xiang economic activities that sticks to the laws in a market economy. In addition, we must be fully aware of the responses to policies in each ethnic cultural tradition and how such responses would impact cross-xiang operations. Different ethnic cultures would yield different responses to policies. A policy that brings positive impacts on one ethnic group may prove ineffective or even negatively effective on another ethnic group. Reality has demanded that diverse, pertinent and, to some extent, flexible development policies be designed and applied in ethnic regions, and the "sweeping" approach that was characteristic of an out-of-control planned economy must be brought to an end as soon as possible.

I Where the Planned Economy Succeed and Fail: An Overview

After the founding of the People's Republic of China, we created a massive economic system by following the socialist economic principle. It had operated until the end of 1970s when we began to realize that the economy in reality had drifted away from the massive economic system we had created to the extent that it had severely hindered the economic development and forced us to start thinking about the issue of "reform". In the meantime, in light of the reality that this massive planned economic system had been kept closed to the outside world for a long time in the past, the issue of "opening up" was subsequently brought up. "Reform" and "opening up" have become two hot topics in the economic life in China since the late 1970s, around which state administrative polices have been designed and executed. In agriculture, a system of contracted responsibility linking remuneration to output was implemented to ensure the right of farmers in the use of land resources and has since stabilized agricultural production. In industry, we started to separate the functions of the government from those of the enterprises by establishing a series of indicators to measure enterprise performance and improving the internal and external environments for enterprise operation, thus making enterprises an independent economic entity instead of an extension of administrative organizations and pushing the manufacturing and mining enterprises onto the right track. In commerce, the monopoly of trade by state-owned commercial enterprises has been terminated and the weight by privately and collectively owned commercial enterprises on commerce has increased, giving rise to a commercial network made up of diversified ownerships. So far, with the exception of some special types of industry such as railroad, aviation, post and telecommunication, other industries have been gradually opened up to enterprises and institutions of various ownerships. All these reforms have been carried out with an aim of transforming China's economy into a socialist market economy.

As the "reform and opening-up policy" was put forward to rectify the departure of the planned economy from the reality in economic operation, and also to achieve the goal of realizing socialist market economy, the pros and cons or even the necessity of the planned economy when we were pursuing the "reform and opening-up" became the focus in the debates in academia. It is our opinion that this issue should be treated differently on a case-by-case basis. To put it more straightforwardly, the "planned economy" and "planned economy that is out of control" are two distinct concepts that should not be confused with each other. Out of this basic understanding, we think that the lagging behind in the ethnic economic development in Guizhou Province over the long time in the past was not primarily the result of the planned economy but instead was due to the planned economy that had been out of control. Our discussion in this section will focus on how the planned economy that had long dominated China went out of control and what negative impacts it had made on ethnic groups in Guizhou. In the meantime, we will also talk about what benefits, and difficulties as well, a socialist market economy would bring to the ethnic economies in Guizhou.

The academic community in China has split in the study of how China's economy should move ahead. Some people believe that the planned economy is a characteristic of socialism and to deny the planned economy is to deny socialism. Others believe that the planned economy has caused tremendous loss to our economy, and would continue to dampen the economic development, let alone to transform it into the socialist market economy if we don't abandon the planned economy. It is their perception that China's economic takeoff will be made possible as long as a market economy is put in place; subsequently, they've complained about the slow progress in the "reform and opening-up" and pushed for the immediate emergence of a market economic mechanism similar to that in the West. These seemingly opposing viewpoints have one thing in common. Both of them have put the market economy to the opposite side of the planned economy and viewed one exclusive of the other. In fact, this is a misperception. What we are discussing here is the state economic system rather than specific individuals or enterprises. To specific operators who either follow the market force or receive instructions from the economic planner, the two can not co-exist at the same time. Things are different to a country that must manage a wide variety of economic entities, face complex domestic economic situations, and take the near-term, mid-term and long-term economic interests of the country into consideration, which demand a state plan. Undoubtedly, any modern country can not do without markets, which existed even at the time when a strict planned economy was enforced in China. From the perspective of a country, a planned economy and market economy should not be put opposite to each other but be treated as two hands in state economic policies; otherwise, we would either be stuck in the mismanaged planned economy or falsely obsessed with the market economy, suggesting that similar theories are groundless.

People are under the impression that the United States of America is a country with a fully developed market economy and private enterprises and is thus an object for others to imitate. Keep in mind, however, that this country is undergoing a stringent economic planning. Take the agricultural production in the US as an example. As the annual yield of grains is more than the US domestic market can consume, international market must be explored, which would inevitably end up in head-on competition with other grain exporting countries and would result in damage to the interests of US agriculture. To ensure the stability of agricultural production and protect the farmers' interests, the US federal government enacted the *1985 Food Safety Act*, which in essence is a food production plan that comprised a wide range of stringent regulations. It had detailed regulations on the scale of production, price and reserves of wheat, rice, dairy products and soy beans etc. To be stringent, it authorized the agricultural minister with all the power to ensure the enforcement of this act. We hereby extract some regulations related to the wheat production in the act as an illustration of the role it played and the value the planning management had in agricultural production: the plan to reduce the cultivation and yield of wheat should kick in when wheat reserve exceeded 1 billion bushel (one bushel = 27.215 kilograms). The percentage of the reduced area of cultivation over the total area of cultivation was: 15% to 22.5% (the target reduced area) in 1986; 20% to 27.5% in 1987; 20% to 30% in 1988 to 1990. To limit the yield of wheat, the minimum price by loan was set to be at US$ 3.55 per bushel, equivalent to 75% of the cost to produce one bushel of wheat. It also set the target prices for different years as a guideline for the farmers to make realistic production plans. The target wheat price per bushel was: US$ 4.38 for 1986 and 1987; US$ 4.29 for 1988, US$4.16 for 1989 and US$ 4 for 1990.

This example demonstrates that most stringent production plans may be executed in countries with highly developed market economy. To think that the planned economy is a complete opposite to the market economy is apparently groundless. What lies in the core of the issue is that what we need to abandon in the "reform and opening-up" is not the planned economy itself but the planned economy that was out of control for many years in the past. Strictly speaking, what caused the ethnic economy in Guizhou to lag behind was not the planned economy itself but rather the planned economy that was a purely man-made economy that stayed on paper and completely delinked from the market. Up to now, we must realize that the planned economy and market economy should be compatible in a country where the operation and production of specific enterprises are guided through the market economy, and economic plans are made based on the actual situations in the market operation. For the problems that can not be solved or the targets that can not be achieved by the market economy, economic plans are necessary to make adjustments and rectifications to prevent market competition from shaking the economic foundation of the country. These two should be supplementary instead of opposing to each other. Even after we are successfully transformed into a market economy, a state economic plan is needed. In other words, the production in some enterprises and departments must also follow the state plans.

For individuals or specific enterprises, it differs whether they are guided by the market or instructed by the economic plans as they are treated differently in production. Market production takes risks and is rewarded with big profit. To the contrary, the planned production takes no risks but is rewarded by low profits, or even at a loss when it is justified to accept subsidies from the state. It is absolutely impossible for us to confuse these two and hope to fetch fat profit while also depending on state subsidies.

The situations in ethnic minority regions in Guizhou are more complex than simply choosing from a planned economy or a market economy, where there are places that can not be regulated by economic plans nor penetrated by the market, or are dominated by a self-sufficient and natural economy. In such economies, surplus products are either abandoned or stored and thus have no chance of trading in the market. The state can not take any of these surplus products without relying on a taxation system. Similarly, it is impossible for products from other regions to access these regions without through the form of support or aid. The debate over a planned economy or a market economy may very likely be irrelevant to these regions no matter how heated it is in other places. Ethnic people in these regions may turn a blind eye to the volatility in the market prices or totally ignore the state economic plans without being forced through state administrative orders. In normal situations, neither the planned economy nor the market economy has any impact on these regions. They, if distorted however, may bring more harm to these regions, which are not immune to such distortions. These regions have not yet recovered from the massive damage inflicted on them in the past years when a distorted planned economy was forced on these regions. This is in fact the primary reason that has caused the economic development in similar ethnic regions to lag behind other places. Likewise, a one-way market economy blindly forced upon the region without effective shield and protection will bring unfathomable loss to the economic development in these regions.

Market economy of some sort had appeared in some ethnic regions in Guizhou before the founding of the People's Republic of China, such as the timber trade in the Dong regions we mentioned earlier in the book. The derailed planned economy in the previous years was essentially the result of an artificially suffocated market economy that brought severe losses to the economy in these regions and left behind numerous hidden troubles, which would continue to remain even after the transformation into the market economy is achieved, preventing the economy from being developed. The issue such as land ownership and organization of operation would not be created, developed and improved in a short time, without which, the economy in these regions would be hindered by these hidden troubles even after the transformation into a market economy is achieved across the country. It is a naïve thinking that a market economy will benefit all ethnic groups equally across the entire country. Policy constraints and their lingering effects on the ethnic economy in similar regions in Guizhou are much more complex than are understood by some economists. Therefore, it is impossible to change the economic landscape of these regions by simply relying on one or two policies without first finding a way of dealing with these constraints properly.

The traditional mode of economy in other ethnic regions in Guizhou was brought under tremendous shock in the past century, and the newly emerged mode of economy was incompatible with local ecological environments. The mere change in economic policies can not bring back the favorable mode of production. For ethnic regions inhabited by multiple ethnic groups such as Yi, Miao, Hui and Han people in northwest Guizhou, rational economic policies must also be supported by administrative force, profound scientific research as well as mutual understanding and tolerance across ethnic groups. A series of economic recovery policies must be executed according to plan and by stage to be effective. The transformation into market economy and improvement of economic policies across all the regions in the country, at most, provide favorable external economic environments but will never replace the internal cause in the economic development. Aside from the above three scenarios, other ethnic regions in Guizhou are in different situations. The Gelao ethnic people that scatter across a wide area in the central and northern Guizhou, for example, do not have an independently regional characteristic economic life. Instead, their economic life is heavily dependent on that of the other ethnic groups. While their own economic strengths can not manifest themselves, they lag behind the economic development of the surrounding ethnic groups. At the time when a distorted planned economy prevailed, the local economy was severely impacted, but it could not adapt to the new socialist market economy and therefore must be treated by special policies. The ethnic Tujia region in northeastern Guizhou Province, especially the Wujiang river valley region, has now switched to the Han mode of economy for subsistence, which has barely enabled the locals to produce any surplus under the local natural conditions. Even if the transformation into the market economy is achieved, we should not expect much in the economic growth potential in lack of strong support from existing local industries.

In a nutshell, due to the huge difference in the traditional modes of economy across ethnic regions in Guizhou, the out-of-control planned economy in past years and the future transformation into the market economy have had and will have different impacts on these regions, and therefore must be analyzed and treated differently. In the following texts, we will first analyze the factors that caused the planned economy to derail in the past years, followed by a discussion of how such an out-of-control planned economy constrained and harmed the economic development in ethnic regions in Guizhou Province.

The economic plans we made in these years are, to a large extent, not based on current economic reality. They overlooked the existing economic capacity of ethnic regions and also turned a blind eye to the differences in the economic development across ethnic regions, and were made completely from the perspective of the ideal of socialist construction. These plans rarely took the coordination of relations across different economic departments into account but emphasized on the output of a few products that were key to the national economy and people's livelihood. For example, they one-sidedly put the output of coal and steel in industry and the yield of grains in agriculture on top priority. People believed at the moment that the high output and yield of these products were an indicator of a powerful and prosperous nation and a demonstration of the superiority of socialism. The slogan of "catching up with and eventually surpassing Britain and the United States in fifteen years" was a reflection of the planned economy that prioritized on the output of single products. Economic activity, as a comprehensive social activity, will lose ground in the society without the rise of the entire economy. The increase in the output of individual products would either end up in inferior quality, or inability to digest for lack of cooperation from other economic departments, thus tying up a large amount of capital and eventually hurting the chance of increasing the output of the products we spent so many efforts in achieving. The fact that the steel production in China remained sluggish in the 1960s was the consequence of a distorted planned economy resulted from our all-out efforts in pushing for a maximum output of single products.

A practicable economic plan must not focus only on the increase in the output of a few single products but rather be made by taking into account the actual demand for each product in the society and the actual production capacity accordingly. In addition to the output of each single product, the plan must also lay out the ratios between different sub-categories in each single product as well as the quality standards for each product. A practicable economic plan is not possible without extensive social surveys and the accumulation of sufficient materials. Unfortunately, these were not available when we made economic plans previously. As a result, people tried to achieve the targets for the products specified in these state plans by "working hard or even risking their lives", but seldom thought about the products not listed in the state plans, causing shortage of these products in the market for a long time in the past. Even for the products that were included in the state plans, it was not uncommon that not all sub-categories were made or the quality was satisfactory. Subsequently, on the demand and supply side in the society, on the one hand, some products piled up in warehouses, and on the other hand, some other products were in extreme shortage. The products in the former situation were usually allocated by plans through the channel of the planned economy. For the latter, the shortage could only be dealt with through the issuance of purchase certificates. It is safe to say that China's planned economy had long been accompanied by the excessive use of all sorts of purchase certificates.

We have made some corrections and improvements to the original planned economy to a certain extent in the past. The mass-movement type of practice typically seen in the 1950s was extinct and replaced with normal enterprise operation and formation of stable channels in production, supply and distribution. However, it remained unchanged in a long time that the economic plan was made under the guidance of seeking to maximize the output of single products. It was in the mind of many people that socialist superiority would not manifest without the continuous growth in the output of single product; therefore, they would take the measure of either "secure" or "uplift" on the primary products. The so-called "secure" was to take all labor force, materials, and equipment necessary to ensure the output of these products. The so-called "uplift" was to produce a single product in a massive scale at the expense of quality or regardless of market demand so as to maintain the superior image of the socialist planned economy. Out of this consideration, although the output of primary products had increased consecutively, the work to support the production facility was not improved in a long time and as a result, the equipment in many state-owned large and medium enterprises have not been upgraded since they were installed and put into operation. It now comes to our realization that, when comparing our industrial structure with that of the developed countries, our industrial structure has been severely disjointed, and the equipment have been outdated, causing the products made in these enterprises to lack the ability of competing in the international market. We had spent all the money that should have been used in industrial adjustment and equipment upgrade in pushing for maximum production of a few single products, which cost the strength for subsequent production.

It should be brought to our attention that the loss of control on the planned economy caused by the pursuit of the output of single products was the consequence of abnormal economic operation over long time in the past. Although the "reform and opening-up" has terminated the compilation of economic plans that was derailed from the economic reality, the abnormal operation can not be reversed by the introduction of a few policies but can only be gradually repaired through long-term market operation. As a deputy secretary of commission of the National People's Congress who has recently conducted surveys in northwest China put it, it is hard for the state-owned large and medium enterprises in these regions to lift themselves out of financial and operational difficulties with their own ability due to heavy social burdens and higher self-service in these enterprises. In fact, the difficulties experienced by the large and medium enterprises in China, not restraining to northwestern regions, was a severe consequence of the out-of-control planned economy as a result of a blind pursuit of maximum output of single products instead of the consequence of the planned economy. Such a consequence is still dragging the economic development in China now.

The planned economy in the past years was aimed at a steady supply of primary livelihood necessities but overlooked the reasonable allocation of cost of production, which was one of the primary reasons for the loss of control in the planned economy. To avoid repeating the miseries before the founding of the People's Republic of China when it was not easy for ordinary people to subsist, we made ensuring the supply of primary livelihood products of the people the primary target when making the economic plans since we started implementing the planned economy. As a result, while trying to maximize the output of some primary products, China's planned economy overlooked the difference and change in the product costs, causing the price of some livelihood necessities, such as grain, fuel, cotton fabric, edible salt and some non-staple food, to remain almost unchanged from the late 1950s to early 1980s. To ensure the subsistence of people in the country, we started implementing the state monopoly of the purchase and distribution of livelihood necessities such as grains from the mid 1950s under the slogan of "develop production and safeguard supply". In the meantime, the markets for the trade of these products were all closed and replaced with state monopoly agencies that were charged with uniformly purchasing and managing these products and selling at a uniform price. Although the practice was well-intentioned, it failed to realize that any product was a social product made at a cost that was subject to constant changes. Artificial prices that were forced upon these products regardless of the costs would inevitably cause huge disparity between the cost and the price. Such a disparity, if carried by the state, would bring unbearable burdens on the country, and if carried by the producers, would undoubtedly dampen their enthusiasm of production. The beneficiaries, on the other hand, would get used to the favoritism and forget about the favor they were done because they could not see cash flow from value-based pricing, thus causing the situation where the loss inflicted on both the state and producers was not appreciated by beneficiaries. The subsidies that the state put for the purpose of stabilizing grain prices was an astronomical figure in China's economic life, which prevented us from putting the limited economic capability in the expansion of economic construction and also directly caused the fiscal loss and the rise in deficit in many provinces and counties. In 1989, the total subsidies in food and oil across the entire country reached RMB 40.8 billion, accounting for approximately 15% of the total budgetary revenue in the year, which was essentially a mere depletion on financial resources and could not contribute to the formation of new production capacity. Regardless, any proposal to reduce or call off these subsidies was contradictory to the guiding principle of safeguarding the basic livelihood of common people and thus would profoundly shake the society. A practice that had not been a must-do in the first place became a policy that people could not live without. Although far-sighted people have realized the troubles of these subsidies, the government authorities flinch when the reform concerns the interests of some people, fearful that city residents may not afford to lose the subsidies. Consequently, with regards to specific practices, some people propose to settle the matter once and for all by completely abandoning the subsidies. Some argue that the reform be phased out in steps to gradually get rid of the subsidies. Others believe that the decision on this issue should be postponed until the economy is developed to a certain level that people's income is increased. Neither of these proposals has solved the fundamental issue. It is a perfectly justified and unquestionable thing for urban residents who have enjoyed the subsidized price of grains for decades to start buying grains at the undistorted prices after the country can no longer afford to do so. As the "reform and opening-up" is a state policy as well as the matter of each one of us, it is thus a right thing for us to lift the burdens off the back of the country and return the benefits that should have been the farmers' to them. When we are chanting that "everyone is responsible for the fate of the country", shouldn't we take the responsibility that we should take? The proposal to gradually abandon the subsidies is in essence not effective. As the price of grains fluctuates all the time, if the subsidies are removed on gradual basis, the subsidies would be offset by the grain price fluctuation. As a result, we would have to start all over again when further steps are taken to get rid of the subsidies, leaving behind a tail that would linger around to hinder the economic operation. The increasing number in such tails would create more factors that impact the path of "reform and opening-up" that would become increasingly narrower. It is our proposal that, in the "reform and opening-up," the reform that we are determined to carry out must be carried out completely without leaving the tail behind. It is in fact an excuse to say that subsidies should not be removed before the economy is fully developed. The fact that the "reform and opening-up" in more than 10 years in the past could not make progress in giant steps was due to the constraints resulting from a out-of-control planned economy such as grain price subsidies. Economic development will not be achieved, and neither will individual income be increased if they are not corrected. The increase of individual income is a relative concept. No matter to which level the economy has been developed, the income would not be increased to everyone's satisfaction.

To purchase grains at a uniform price through state-control channels hurt the farmers the most. When the policy was initially implemented, the grains were purchased basically at the prevailing market price from willing sellers. Most markets were closed and farmers were encouraged to sell grains to the state to support the huge construction efforts in the country. At the time, the majority of the farmers were happy to sell grains to the state, but it gradually turned to "quasi-tax" (surplus grain) that was collected along with the "state tax"(agricultural tax paid in grain) at a price the remained unchanged for decades from that in the 1950s. In comparison, in these decades, the cost to produce grains rose steadily and the gap between the demand and supply widened, which, added by the currency depreciation, made the price paid by the state for purchasing surplus grains symbolic. Before the eve of the "reform and opening-up", farmers who did not have surplus grains were pushed to sell "surplus grains" while those who had surplus grains were prohibited from selling them on the market but had to sell them to the state as "surplus grains". "Surplus grains" became a synonym of acquiring grains at low price from the farmers. Although the governments at all levels now keep talking about reducing farmer's burden, no one was willing to mention anything about this taxation that is apparently a counterfeit. To the contrary, it has been increased rather than decreased and some other taxations have derived from collection of "surplus grains", such as "huanxi grain" and "weiqian grain" etc. The heavy burdens on the farmers have already existed much earlier than today. Right before China started carrying out the "reform and opening-up" policy, the overall burden on the farmers, such as the agricultural tax paid in grains, surplus grains and various kinds of taxes and fees, added up to have exceeded 10% of the farmer's total income. In fact, the losses incurred by the farmers to ensure the food supply to urban residents are hard to estimate in value. It could have been difficult for the fiscal revenue of the state to support such a system long time ago without the huge economic sacrifice made by the farmers. The current fragile foundation for agricultural production and unwillingness to farm lands which has led to many lands abandoned were attributable to the seeds that had long been planted. The development of the agriculture in China will be hopeless forever if these seeds are not exterminated.

The farmer's selling price of grains has long been kept below the production cost, which has made it impossible for farmers to expand reproduction. As farmers can not afford to buy the agricultural materials, the state has to subsidize the production of agricultural materials such as chemical fertilizer, agricultural pesticide, electricity to be used in agricultural production etc. Consequently, any department that is related to the production would unexceptionally seek state subsidies, which gives rise to many dual prices, represented by state-set price, negotiated price, appropriate price, and market price etc., and has long beset the operators of enterprises. In the meantime, price differentials of all sorts have offered shelters and havens for profiteers. The chaos in the price system in the overall national economy caused by the purchase and sale of grains at forced low prices has brought about damage far exceeding the agricultural production departments. Many have touched the fundamental interests of the country. Regardless, the government is not determined to exterminate the system and the issue drags on till today as doing so impacts all urban residents.

To maintain a book balance in fiscal budget, the state also provided fiscal subsidies to other production departments similar to those provided on grains. As a result, the huge gap between the selling price and cost of products became a commonplace phenomenon in the economy in China. These subsidies, also like those on grains, were a forced temporary measure in the first place. However, as our economic plans did not have the ability of receiving feedbacks from the market and adjusting the prices accordingly, the only thing we could have done was to strike balance on paper by manipulating prices when making economic plans. While the plan was executed, the existence of different kinds of subsidies intensified the deviation of the selling price from actual cost of production. Eventually, the plans were made entirely out of touch with actual production and were not reflecting the real prices. It is indisputable that we will never know the true price of our products, our economic plans will stay in paper to remain meaningless, and we will never turn the state-owned enterprises profitable and eliminate the debt chains unless we completely terminate the subsidies. It is based on this that the economists who are advocates of a comprehensive market economy put forward their theory. It is our belief, however, that the issue is not about the plan itself, but rather on the accuracy of the data based on which the plan is made. The data of accurate prices are only available through the market. A fully developed market mechanism that provides real price data makes it both possible and necessary to make the economic plans. It is like giving up eating for fear of choking if we disavow the planned economy because of distorted prices under the planned economy.

Another major reason for the loss of control on the planned economy was that the plans were made under the guiding principle of "dealing with the changing situations with unchanging mechanism". The plan was made simply by statically setting a scale of production and percentage but did not allow room for relevant economic departments to make necessary adjustments and develop independently, which, like the prices that went out of control, did not attract attention from relevant authorities in the beginning but gradually unveiled after operation for a long time. Out of the special background in the world in the early 1950s, China could only open itself to east European countries and USSR, from which equipment and technology were introduced. Although the level of technology in these countries was not the most advanced, we had to plan our industry from such a lower level from the beginning. After the deterioration in the relationship between China and the eastern European countries and USSR, we were left with ourselves to develop our industry, which continued as was planned due to the inability for us to find better benchmark. Such a sealed self-development in technology had lasted until China started opening up to the outside world when it suddenly came to our realization that the industrial equipment we had in hand, although massive in scale and high in value, could not make products that are needed in the international market. If we decided to start all over again, the existing equipment would be totally wasted. Such a dilemma forced us to separate all the industrial enterprises into two categories: the newly introduced equipment was used in export-oriented enterprises that made products for international market while the old equipment was used to make products for domestic consumption. Although the issue unveiled after the "reform and opening-up", it originated from the 1950s. This passive situation in fact was an ostensible phenomenon. More critically, such a long-lasting enclosure in technology directly constrained the making of the national economic plan and forced us to make economic plans from a static perspective unconsciously, which had long lost touch with technical realities and had not been detected for a long time in the past. The depreciation rate for machines and equipment as well as elimination rate for out-of-date products were very low in the economic plans. In the meantime, the reserves that enterprises were supposed to book for technology transformation and equipment upgrade were extremely low. Such a guiding principle determined the fate of the state-owned large and medium enterprises that would end up in aging of equipment and lag in technology. Even if new technology and equipment were introduced, they would soon become out of date before they were digested and incorporated in the existing industrial system. Such a static closure in technology also constrained the researchers and prevented them from catching up with the international technical development. Dealing with the changing situations with unchanging mechanism was not only reflected in technology but also in production management.

In the decades before the "reform and opening-up", many Chinese enterprises expanded production in similar or the same products. The more products they made, the more they piled up in the warehouse. The increase in product quantity resulted in the drop in production efficiency. Changchun Automobile Factory made the vehicles by the brand name of "liberation", some makes and models of which remained unchanged for tens of years. Despite numerous differences in natural environments across different regions, the numerous varieties of agricultural crops and rapid renewal and optimization in China are favorable to the agricultural production in China. However, due to the same constraints caused by "dealing with the changing situations with unchanging mechanism", the crops were purchased, regardless of their quality, at a uniform price. Subsequently, despite the vast territory and abundant resources in China, the varieties of grains circulating on the market decreased and tended to concentrate on a few grains. The varieties of high quality local and special crops were near extinction. Such a reduction of product variety also obstructed channels of circulation. Quality and special products were not distributed but uniform products inundated the market. The original distribution channels for these local quality and special products were blocked successively under such an out-of-control planned economy, making the channels of commercial operation become increasingly narrower. Although tremendous efforts have been put in promoting the local special and quality products after the "reform and opening-up", recovering the traditional distribution channels for these products is not possible in short time.

Both historical and perspective reasons caused the planned economy in China to be out of control. It is not so important to find what or who should be accountable as to eliminate the consequences as soon as possible while ensuring that we are not giving up eating for fear of choking. An out-of-control planned economy has been constraining the economic operation and blocking the road of economic development in ethnic regions in Guizhou. To develop the economy in these regions will remain as a goal without us giving enough attention to the consequences of a derailed planned economy and quickly eliminating the disastrous consequences. As a region where self-sufficient and natural economy prevail, the value and use value of products are realized through the social activities carried out by the producers and their relatives within a small community, and are, in most cases, not demonstrated in the form of price. This is quite different from the developed Han regions, and thus the form and contents of the losses caused by the out-of-control planned economy are also quite different from the Han regions. From a perspective of form, the losses caused by an out-of-control planned economy were, for the most part, reflected in the economic relations being cut off from the outside world, therefore intensifying the stable continuation of the self-sufficient and natural economy in these regions over an extremely long period of time. The prices of the products made in these regions were, when put in the domestic market, often suppressed to the bottom and make them totally unprofitable. As a result, the economic activities in these regions were entirely shut off from the other regions. From a perspective of contents, unlike the ethnic Han regions where, after the planned economy went out of control, state policy instructions replaced economic activities, and the barriers in economic activities were dealt with by state subsidies and the distribution of products was controlled by state-issued ration certificates, in these ethnic regions, state economic instructions could not impact the economic activities but gave rise to social phenomena that crippled the economic operation in these regions and pushed many contents of distorted social activities into the traditional means of production and caused potential operational deterioration. The most severe was the dependence on state subsidies. The control by ration certificates, the unique form of distribution in the planned economy, was turned into a major source of acquiring non-labor income. From an overall perspective, the out-of-control planned economy did less harm on the ethnic regions than on the Han regions. After the out-of-control planned economy was put back on track, however, the Han regions quickly recovered but the ethnic regions could not recover after a long time as the damage caused by the planned economy that was out of control was more latent and deep-rooted on these regions, and thus the change in policy could not replace the recovery of, and in exceptional cases even worsened the background in economic operation.

In order to further clarify the potential impact of an out-of-control planned economy on ethnic regions in Guizhou from an economist's perspective, we feel it absolutely necessary to revisit the statement of the Chinese economist Sun Yefang on relevant planned economy. Subject to the restrictions of specific social environment at the moment, Mr. Sun Yefang could not speak out all his thoughts when making this statement. In this sense, the successors of Mr. Sun, when summarizing his theories, more accurately reflected his real intention. According to Mr. Sun Yefang, planned economy and the law of value had something in common. He argued that it was a Marxist's point of view that from an overall perspective, human societies, no matter what level it is developed to, would always allocate the time of social labor by a certain percentage, and the only thing that changes is the form taken in the allocation of labor time. The planned economy and the law of value are forms in which social labor is allocated by a certain percentage, and to allocate social labor by a certain percentage is the common starting point and objective action of the planned economy and the law of value. We can say that the commonality between the planned economy and the law of value is to allocate labor time by a certain percentage; therefore, "the planned economy and the law of value are compatible with each other, i.e., both can allocate human labor time across different production departments, indicating that the law of value and the socialist planned economy are not repellent to each other."[①] Commonality does not naturally lead to mutual compatibility, which is attainable only by fully understanding the differences between the two and finding the connecting points between the two on the basis of such understanding. According to Mr. Sun, three points are keys to understanding

① "On Yefang Sun's Economic Theory", Reference Room of Institute of Economics of Chinese Academy of Social Sciences, comp. Qingbo Yu "On Planning and the Law of Value" (Economic Science Press, 1984), 158-160.

the differences between the two: "First, the fundamental difference between the planned economy and the law of value in adjusting the distribution of labor time is that one is done consciously and the other spontaneously. Second, when the planned economy and the law of value allocate the social labor time, one does not focus on calculating the average necessary social labor volume and the other must calculate the average necessary social labor volume. Third, when allocating social labor time, the planned economy is subject to human impact while the law of value is not." Based on this profound understanding, Mr. Sun put forth his independent theory on the planned economy: "Only by putting the economic plans on the foundation of the law of value can the plans be made practical and effective."

What's unique about Mr. Sun's theory is that he did not view the planned economy and the market economy as opposing to each other, but rather found a connecting point between the two, which provided the theoretical foundation for our walking the socialist path with the Chinese characteristics, and our transformation into a socialist market economy while maintaining the basic socialist characteristics. Now, it is a misperception of some people who view the market economy as a total denial of planned economy. Such a misperception has brought about very bad influence, which Mr. Sun's theory is a powerful weapon to rectify and it thus bears more practical meaning nowadays. It helps us realize that the mistakes we made in economy in past years were not due to the planned economy itself but due to the fact that the planned economy deviated from reality. They were not mistakes in system but rather those in application, which could be corrected by policy adjustment. It is totally irrational to attribute the economic mistakes of the past years to the planned economy. For this reason, we use the term "out-of-control planned economy" to replace "planned economy" when we analyze the impacts of state economic policies on the development of the ethnic regions in China. As the products from self-sufficient and natural economy do not need to go through markets in most cases, the law of value does not have a role to play. Also, as this kind of economy is a closed economy, the products made in this economy do not circulate across the entire country in most cases. As a result, administrative orders without enforcement power are hard to touch specific phase in production. This is the reason why the ethnic regions in Guizhou suffered less than ethnic Han regions when the planned economy went out of control. However, once these administrative orders were set and systemized, it became well-reasoned to change original mode of production by mandatory orders and the impacts could likely develop into potential constraining factors that lasted over a long period of time. For example, in the period of planned economy, to forcefully change the form of ownership and use of land resources had such profound impacts that could not be recovered and would continue constraining the development of these regions even after the implementation of the system of contracted responsibility linking remuneration to output. The economic subsidies, for another example, that became routine under a planned economy that went out of control would be hard to reverse in people's mind even after the "reform and opening-up" policy was implemented. It is for this reason that we conclude that the impacts of the out-of-control planned economy on the development of ethnic regions in Guizhou, although not direct, were latent and long-term. Our solutions to the economic development in ethnic regions in Guizhou would be irrelevant without fully understanding this point.

Mr. Sun's view not only provides theoretical foundation for the transformation into market economy, but also clarifies the concept of the goal of the transformation, which is to make practical economic plans by following the law of value. Based on this thinking, the selection of policies will have different impacts on Han and ethnic regions in the process of transformation into a market economy. Economists have made numerous discussions on the former, which we are not going to cover here. We feel necessary, however, to expound on the latter. As these regions are still in a self-sufficient and natural economy, they are in a different starting point from the Han region for achieving economic transformation. Some people think that we should not discuss the economic transformation before these regions are developed to the level of Han region. However, environments are constantly changing. "Environments change with time and people should prepare for changes." The maxim by an ancient sage proves to be useful in this situation.

Other people propose to seek the growth points that connect with the socialist market and open a new path to directly introduce the socialist market economy by taking into account the realities and characteristics in ethnic regions. This is a dialectical materialist point of view. While inspecting the existing characteristics of ethnic groups, we should by no means equate the existing self-sufficient and natural economy with the forms of economy that had appeared in the history. Instead, we must realize that the existing forms of economy in these ethnic regions are results of co-existence and adjustment in an out-of-control economy for the long time in the past. It has created new characteristics that had never appeared before. Without fully understanding these new characteristics, we are unable to see the real difficulties for these ethnic groups to transform into a socialist market economy, nor are we able to find practical solutions and help these ethnic groups achieve the transformation into a market economy.

II The Consequences that An Out-of-control Planned Economy Brings to Ethnic Minority Regions

An out-of-control planned economy constrained the economic development in ethnic regions in Guizhou in multiple angles and levels. From the perspective of an overall economic structure, it directly destroyed the diversified production structure and forced the ethnic groups in Guizhou to accomplish the mission planned by the state in the most unfavorable natural and social conditions. In terms of production potential, it put the ethnic economy in Guizhou in a struggling position and thus dampened the resilience of the local ethnic economy. In terms of the economic relations across ethnic groups, it directly disrupted the original connections and the economic supplementary relations that were formed over an extended period of time in the past across ethnic groups, thus giving rise to many barriers for ethnic products to access the market. In terms of the continuation in the traditional economic projects, it disrupted the original form of organizing production and the original structure of production projects in ethnic regions. As a result, the ethnic economy was not able to develop itself based on the actual need and its ability to digest and absorb production technologies introduced from outside the regions. It is reasonable to say that the lagging behind in the economic development in ethnic regions in Guizhou was, for the most part, attributable to an out-of-control planned economy. The natural environments in different ethnic regions were different, and their traditional means of livelihood was different. The economic life across different sub-groups within the same ethnic group could be significantly different. Such an ethnic economic structure could have been a valuable humanistic wealth, by making use of which the ethic groups in Guizhou would have demonstrated the economic strengths in the following five aspects. First, it is able to make use of the natural resources effectively and maximally. Second, it can retain the abundant traditional production techniques and provide a wealth of elements for the construction of a modern production. Third, the difference in the means of livelihood across different ethnic groups and the economic supplementary relations formed over a long period in time could provide solid growth points for the development of a commodity economy and subsequently attain economic alliance across ethnic regions. Fourth, as each ethnic group occupied the best living environment that best fit its traditional culture, the maintenance of ecological resources could have been successfully done through coordination across ethnic groups. Fifth, the co-existence of diversified means of production could have been an important supplement to our economic development and could have been a major source for enriching our economic structure. However, under a planned economy that was out of control, all ethnic groups were forced to arrange production by the same projects, targets and cultivation methods. Consequently, some ethnic groups had to accomplish the production targets assigned by state plans in the most unfavorable production environments.

According to the state plan, agricultural production must ensure the grain yields, which must be dominated in Guizhou by the cultivation of rice. Under such a plan enforced by administrative power, the Dong people who had already commercialized forestry production had to abandon the traditional forestry production and refocus their labor force on the cultivation of limited agricultural field, thus creating a scenario where the production items they were specialized in were not allowed but those they were unfamiliar with were forced to do. In northwestern Guizhou where ethnic Yi and Miao lived together, animal husbandry took a big share in the economic life and livestock, bristles, leather and leather goods etc. had been major exports in the history of Guizhou. To execute the uniform state plan, they had to replace animal husbandry with reclaim of cultivated lands, resulting in massive water and soil loss. Although many lands had been cultivated, the output was very unstable and the traditional animal husbandry was suffocated. In the south of Guizhou that is dominated by the karst landscape and has insufficient surface runoffs, the ethnic Miao and Buyi people who live in this region had long lived on dry land Swidden cultivation. Under the uniform planned economy, local people also developed paddy fields and cultivated rice, which turned out to be barren due to lack of surface runoffs and water resources. The places that could not be turned into paddy fields were replaced with corns, which squeezed out many minor crops that had proved to be highly adoptable in the regions. The output of corns alone was not enough for local consumption. It turned the region that had surplus minor crops to export to a place that was in shortage of grains. Such was especially obvious in today's Mashan. Many ethnic Miao regions in Guizhou had been well-known for making profit from selling teas. The cloud and mist tea produced in central Guizhou had been royal tributes in the Ming dynasty, but the planting and processing of these famous teas dwindled at the time when the country was chanting the slogan of "prioritizing the grain production over everything else". The Nanpan and Beipan River valley in southwest Guizhou had been a major production base and distribution hub of brown sugar, and the brown sugar made in this region had been distributed to northwest Guizhou and the region bordering Sichuan, Yunnan and Tibet. It, however, was abandoned and replaced by the production of grains in the planned economy that went out of control. Raw lacquer had been a major product of the Gelao people and the production of raw lacquer shrank dramatically in the out-of-control planned economy. With the dwindling of these traditional products and their production, many hubs of traditional commodities were suspended and disappeared; subsequently, the trade of medicinal materials in Gangwu township in Guanling county, the trade of livestock and tung oil in Huajiang, the trade of tobacco in Baijin of Huishui county, the trade of timber in Sanjiang of Jinping county and Yuankou of Tianzhu county nearly disappeared. Now, when talking about the "reform and opening-up", people were enthusiastic about commodity economy in ethnic regions but seldom mentioned how the out-of-control planned economy had frustrated the traditional commodity trade in these regions. We need to point out that the diversified economic life in ethnic regions in Guizhou was the essence in the economic development in these regions, without which the further development was not possible. To an ethnic group, to lag behind or be impoverished temporarily was not fearsome, but to lose the potential of further development was. To sacrifice one potential for temporary stability is equivalent to sacrificing the future of an ethnic group. Unfortunately, the planned economy, when out of control, led to the shrinkage of the diversified ethnic economy and played a negative role in this aspect. A diversified economic life has an unfathomable value to all ethnic groups, our country or even the entire human kind. This is an issue that has not attracted the attention from the academic community and therefore is necessary for us to conduct a profound discussion.

When we, guided by the slogan of "prioritizing the grain production over everything else", required that ethnic people follow the mode of production in the Han region, we intended to enable ethnic people to be able to feed themselves. Although it was well intentioned, objectively, it created the undiversified production of grains, which could not give rise to the commodity economy and would only pushed the ethnic groups back to the natural or self-sufficient economy. Such a consequence was apparently contrary to our initial thinking of guiding the ethnic groups toward a market economy. Now, this has drawn the attention from some people in academia who have appealed for emphasizing on the production of minor crops. We need to point out, however, that the abandonment of the production of minor crops was nothing but a disastrous consequence of an out-of-control planned economy.

The relationship between a diversified economic life and market economy is currently a hot topic in the academic community. Here, we feel necessary to further emphasize on this issue. While the planned economy was out of control, ethnic people in Guizhou changed successively their traditional way of economic life, and rice and corn of the same variety as in the Han region were promoted regardless of the local conditions. Subsequently, the products made in the ethnic regions were exactly the same as in the Han regions, but the distance between these ethnic regions and the central regions where the grains were consumed – large and medium cities and sites of manufacturing and mining enterprises was extremely long. According to the results of the discussion in chapter six, due to the effect of the spatial efficiency attenuation, it took extra cost for these products made in ethnic regions to enter the domestic market, which largely weakened the competitiveness of these products in domestic market. While the planned economy was in force, such an extra cost was covered by state subsidies. In a market economy, however, it was put on the producers, making these products unprofitable. Consequently, there were no surplus products left after meeting the demand for self-consumption. However, if these ethnic people produced different variety of grains, or even varieties of rice that matured at different time, such as the hongxiangnuo (red, fragrant, sticky) rice produced in ethnic Dong regions, their use value could not be replaced by other products in the Han regions and, according to the "marginal benefit" theory, would departure significantly from marginal products and therefore fetched a much higher selling price, which not only were able to offset the added cost due to the effect of spatial attenuation, but would generate profits and thus would make more money than the hybrid variety of rice despite the lower output. Local special produces are all over the place in ethnic regions in Guizhou. Things like fragrant pig in Yueliang Mountain regions, sticky millet in Mashan region, the myotonin in Qinglong, jinqian tangerine in Huishui, grazing pig in Weining etc., all could make into the precious agricultural and pastoral products in domestic and international markets. If they could be fully utilized instead of forcing the same product variety across the entire country, they could become highly competitive in the market and would thus contribute to the economic development in the ethnic regions. If we otherwise grow the same produce in the entire country, the produce that is made in ethnic regions would never have a chance to accessing domestic or international markets, which would do more harm than good to the ethnic groups.

The diversified economic life in ethnic regions was a result of adjustment, processing and transformation of specific environment over a long time in the past, and was created to best make use of natural resources and maximize the ratio of input over output, and was the form of production that had the highest efficiency in terms of input and output. The realization of modernization in ethnic regions depends on these outcomes, but would be very uneconomical to completely rely on technologies introduced from outside the region. The most ideal method would be to find out the most suitable path to modernization from the perspective of modernization on the basis of summarizing and systemizing the existing forms of production and by taking advantage of introduced technologies.

After a thorough review of the paths toward modernization in all the developed nations in the world, we must admit that none of them walked a completely identical path as the others. It has been commonplace for all the nations in the world to walk a unique path based on their own characteristics. People in ethnic Han regions are still debating on the path toward modernization even after more than 100 years of exploration. Will ethnic regions that follow the footsteps of the Han people be guaranteed modernization? The planned economy that went out of control for a long time in the past forced all the ethnic regions to imitate how ethnic Han people engaged in agricultural production, which caused the most severe consequence that sacrificed the social foundation, material potential and the creativity impulsion along the way of exploring the path toward modernization by the ethnic groups.

Some people always say that the ethnic regions have a backward economy with low productivity, and that they can not be developed without depending on the introduced advanced production technology and management methods. It is our opinion that it is a one-sided conclusion that is drawn from the perspective of traditional Han ethnic viewpoint and thus can not reflect all the truth. To evaluate things by different indicators may arrive at opposing conclusions. This should apply to our way of treating ethnic groups. The per unit output of grain in ethnic regions in Guizhou apparently is much lower than that in the Han agricultural regions Lake Taihu region, but is not necessarily lower than the output of broom corn millet in northern Shannxi. By the standard of agricultural material consumption, the production in Lake Taihu region would not have lasted even a day without chemical fertilizer, improved variety, chemical pesticide, or herbicide, etc. In comparison, ethnic groups in Guizhou could keep a steady output of grains without chemical fertilizer, pesticide or improved variety from out of the regions but only with the help of a hoe and a chopper. It should not surprise us to see that some ethnic Miao people who migrated out of Zhenning and settle in Jinggangshan were able to turn the hilly areas abandoned by local Han people into arable lands that produced steady yield of crops. When cited as examples in educating the Han people, the local government officials said that these Miao people did not ask for chemical fertilizer or pesticide from the state but totally relied on the hardworking spirit to reclaim the abandoned lands. Although these government officials did not reveal all the facts as they were still evaluating the situation by a single indicator, they were right to have detected some strengths in the ethnic production and were thus more to the point than those scholars who did not hesitate to show their contempt for ethnic people. Isn't it a good thing for the ethnic people in Guizhou to be able to produce agricultural products that are totally free from pollution at the time when the entire world is suffering from heavy pollution from pesticide? Aren't the produces they made this way highly valuable? Some people may argue that the average value of production in these ethnic people in Guizhou is too low, at 30% of that in the developed Han region, and insist that ethnic regions will not be developed unless this situation is changed. Such a view is false in the following three aspects.

First, the way to calculate agricultural output is inaccurate. As we discussed previously in the book, there was no clear distinction between primary and secondary products in the ethnic groups that were in Swidden cultivation. However, our statistics only reflected what we viewed as primary products, which was only a part of production value generated by the labor force in these regions; therefore, the results of the statistics tended to be lower than the actual value.

Second, due to the constraints on the channels of consumption in the society by the traditional culture, the ethnic groups in a self-sufficient economy only produced no more than what they needed, which did not mean that they were not capable of producing more. The statisticians often based on the current per capita output to assert that the labor force in these regions were not able to produce more products. This is a big misunderstanding. If we could clear the channels for the products made in ethnic regions to access the market, the average output of labor force in these regions could be made higher.

Third, the products in ethnic regions are created without the support of social service. All the products are a result of actual individual labor input. By contrast, in the developed Han regions that have developed network of social service, although an individual labor may be able to cultivate two *mu* of rice fields and harvest about ten-thousand jin of grains, it already includes the input from other labor force, such as agricultural pesticide, fertilizer and improved variety etc. Our statistics, however, did not take out this part of the input from other labors, and thus it is absolutely unfair to compare it with the results of purely individual labor input in the ethnic regions.

In summary, to evaluate the value created by each individual labor in ethnic groups based on such incomplete statistics data can not fully reflect the reality of the economic life of these ethnic groups. It is also groundless to think that the traditional economic life of the ethnic groups must be abandoned completely. To the contrary, in some ethnic regions in Guizhou, such as Yueliang Mountain and Mashan regions, where regular agricultural operation can not be carried out, the traditional operation of production is, and will be in a period of time in the future, meaningful, or in other words is un-replaceable by other means of operation. In other region such as Wumeng mountainous region in upstream Wujiang River and the Dong regions in southeast Guizhou that are suitable for forestry plantations, although they can be cultivated into agricultural lands, the economic benefit of doing so will be lower than that generated by the animal husbandry in the ethnic Yi regions or the forestry plantation by the Dong people. Given these elements, we think that the lack of variety in products caused by an out-of-control planned economy not only suffocated the ability for the ethnic groups to maximize their production capacity, but more importantly, failed to foster their strengths and circumvent weaknesses. We must admit that the diversity in the production across different ethnic groups is a must for the joint prosperity of ethnic groups while lack of diversity will deprive their chance of a joint prosperity.

The diversified modes of production are also the elements in creating new productivity. Unexceptionally, all ethnic groups in the world that emerged and prospered at one time in the human history were not able to do so without the interaction and clash among and improvement on the diversified economic life. The rises in the Han history were no exceptions. The establishment of each formidable feudal empire in the Han history was preceded by a period of co-existence, clash, and integration among and improvement on multi-ethnic economy. No powerful feudal states or modern industrial nations were built on a single mode of economic life. Based on these facts, why do we insist that ethnic groups carry out economic activities by imitating our mode of production if we are determined to help them develop the local economy? However, the out-of-control economy for a long time in the past was just the reason that reduced the originally diversified economic life in ethnic regions to singular production of rice or corn. Without a doubt, a simple continuation of the inherent mode of production in ethnic groups would not lead into modernization; Nor would the productivity of ethnic groups leap forward if all ethnic groups continue developing along their respective traditional mode of production without interaction among each other or absorption and improvement from such an interaction. It is for this reason that ethnic groups in Guizhou have developed on their own respective mode of production in parallel for hundreds or even thousands of years, and yet have not achieved a breakthrough. Similarly, if we force ethnic groups to shift their production mode to the Han mode of production by the administrative power, the traditional ethnic mode of production would lose their competitiveness and become an appendant to the Han mode of production, making it impossible any more for different modes of production to interact and clash among and absorb from each other. Under such a circumstance, instead of putting efforts in finding out the strengths and weaknesses of their traditional modes of economy as against that of the Han ethnicity motivated by the possibility of maintaining their own mode of production, the ethnic people would indiscriminately copy the Han mode of production passively. They knew that they would not need to be responsible if they failed and that they could always count on government subsidies. It is clear that the co-existence of multi-cultures is a good thing, and to have expected results from it depends on keeping the entirety of each individual culture and the exchange and digestion from equal positions. To force a mode of production on ethnic groups by policy measures only caused them to lose the traditional mode of production and the status of an independent competitor, which would not only make it impossible to build a new mode of production, but also destroyed the foundation for building the new mode of production – the coexistence of the diversified modes of production.

We have now entered an era that has greatly broadened the vision of ethnic minority groups in Guizhou, who can absorb cultural elements and nutrients from the Han culture as well as all the other ethnic groups in the world when building their own mode of production. The forestry plantations in the Dong regions can be used as an example to best illustrate this point. Finland is an example in the world whose economy was built on forestry plantations. In Finland, all the plantations are divided into different zones and workers rotate in cutting trees in these zones once every 25 years, thus enabling the steady output of lumber each year while keeping the total area of forest unchanged. Besides, all the branches and sawdust are collected and utilized as raw materials for paper-making. Such a mode of production is an ideal target for operators of Dong forestry plantations to learn from and absorb. Slovakia is a country that is experienced operator of hunting in the forestry plantations. All the wild animals in the plantations are accurately monitored and recorded, enabling them to set specific and accurate number of the wild animals that are allowed to be hunted each year. They are even able to control the gender and age of the hunted animals, which stabilizes the number of hunted animals and ensures that the wildlife resources not deteriorate in a long time. Such a way of management can be learned from by the ethnic Dong and be used to significantly enhance the overall economic efficiency of the forestry plantations. The Italians and the ethnic groups in southern Balkan Peninsula have a long tradition and are very experienced in the olive oil business. It is surprising that although the level of industry in these countries and nations are much higher than that in ethnic Dong regions, the method they use in producing olive oil is similar to that used by ethnic Dong people in making tea oil. Both are pure manual operation. The difference is that they distill the olive oil by baking and grounding, followed by boiling and skimming instead of pressing as is used in the Dong regions. The olive oil made in this way has a very high purity without any content of protein or sugar and thus can be stored for a long time and can be eaten by directly spreading on the bread. Due to its fragrant smell and the dark green color, it is also named as "green gold". Given that the tea oil is used as cooking oil in the ethnic Dong region, the pressing method does not affect its use value. However, as such products do not fit the eating habit of the European people, the content of protein and sugar would create a displeasing odor, thus would not suit the European markets. If ethnic Dong people understand this difference and start processing tea oil in the way that the olive oil is processed, they are able to make, without the need of special technology and equipment, the tea oil that is orange yellow in color and fragrant in smell that can be eaten directly, and can compete with the pricy olive oil on the international market. The mode of rice cultivation in the Han regions, such as the breeding of rice seedling, the sophisticated water conservancy facility, and intensive cultivation by the Han people, also has reference value for the ethnic Dong people when building a new mode of production. These are only a few examples. There are many other cultural elements and nutrients that ethnic Dong people can and need to absorb and learn from if they aim at creating a new mode of production that can aid their economic takeoff. However, it won't be made possible without an independent mode of production, their own technical experts, and own social background. Only based on these conditions can they accurately determine what they need to absorb and how to absorb in order to achieve modernization in the ethnic regions. While trying to build a new mode of production, the ethnic groups would not be able to construct the foundation for modernization if they reduce their inherent mode of production to the dependent of another mode of production.

The lack of diversity in the mode of production across the entire country as a result of an out-of-control planned economy not only suffocated the economic development in the ethnic regions but also that in the Han regions. The time when the planned economy went out of control was accompanied by an extreme shortage of products across the country. In the 1960s, the supply of everything was adjusted by ration certificates. Even when people barely had clothes to wear and food to eat, they found nowhere to spend their salary as money could not buy anything without the ration certificates. The GDP plummeted and the economic foundation we put a lot of hard work to build in the 1950s were either suspended or dissolved. The Han regions that had been prosperous now had to worry about the subsistence of the people. In the meantime, the ethnic regions in the most remote and backward areas in Guizhou, as a comparison, were not highly affected by the wave of integration of mode of production due to the dramatic difference in the type and mode of production, and were therefore able to maintain their inherent mode of production. Although their life was also impacted, their basic livelihood was better ensured than that in the developed Han regions. Mashan region that now seems to be in the most difficult situation surprisingly did not have people who died from hunger. The upper reach of Beipan River that is labeled as impoverished region now was able to stealthily buy silk threads with the money saved by selling sunflower seeds at the moment. The people in the Dong, Shui and Buyi regions that are deemed less developed regions now were able to sell the rationed certificates to buy clothes to the Han regions as they were able to plant cotton and weave cloth. At least we can arrive at the conclusion from these examples: these ethnic regions were in a better condition than the developed Han regions in terms of the supply of basic livelihood necessities. The unification in the mode of production brought more grave disasters to the Han regions.

In the 1960s and 1970s, although it seemed that political movements stuck all the country one after another and they restrained the economic development of the Han regions, further studies reveal that the unification in the mode of production caused by the out-of-control planned economy remained to be the primary reason in restraining the economic development in the Han regions. At the time, we were guided in economic development to focus on ensuring supply, which was defined as guaranteeing basic food and clothing by the out-of-control planned economy. Therefore, although on per capita basis, we ranked at the bottom across all indicators in production, some products were overstocked. The actual level of production at the time in the developed Han regions was similar to the level of the ethnic groups in today's Guizhou. In those days, televisions were luxury consumer goods, bicycles were dowries that dreamt by young people and watches were used to replace engagement rings. Such a level of material consumption hardly matches the status of a great country by today's standards. The unification in the mode of production had a surprisingly big constraining effect on the economic development in the Han regions even in the late 1970s when the political atmosphere was relatively loose.

Let's review the movement of educated youth going to the mountainous regions and countryside for two reasons. First, it generated intense social responses in the ethnic Han regions. Second, it was the inevitable outcome of the unification of planned economy, which was designed on a very low level of economic operation at the time. The industries that were critically needed by the society could not be established while the new generation of labor due to propagation of population could not find employment opportunities; therefore, to relieve the pressure off the job market, these new labor force had to be pushed by administrative power to live a self-sufficient life. In essence, it was a retrogression in economic life and an unwilling but forced measure to survive by the Han people.

A series of new reform measures were implemented after the "reform and opening-up" that were aimed at rectifying the bad results caused by the out-of-control planned economy. In agriculture, the implementation of the system of contracted responsibility linking remuneration to output explicitly granted the land ownership to the farmers and has soon corrected the abnormal pattern in agricultural production through operation by the free will of farmer households, bringing the agricultural production back to the diversified mode. The ethnic groups in Guizhou indeed benefited from such a reform. Many traditional operational items were quickly recovered in a short time with policy guarantee. A diversified operation thus became a fact. The enthusiasm in the mid-1980s to set up township enterprises exposed ethnic groups in Guizhou to direct industrial production. Certainly, the main beneficiary of this reform was the Han region as the "sweeping approach" by the system of contracted responsibility linking remuneration to output could not solve the issue of reasonably making use of the land resources completely in the ethnic groups due to their different mode in land ownership from the Han regions.

The pace in the industrial reform was much slower than that in agriculture, mainly due to the ownership of large and medium state-owned enterprises. By the traditional point of view, large and medium state-owned enterprises are symbols of the socialist planned economy. To change the existing mode of operation in the large and medium state-owned enterprises would collide with the planned economy and socialist system. We had realized, from the beginning, the bad consequences of not separating government administration from enterprises, the seriousness of how outdated the equipment in these enterprises were, and the harms the state subsidies did on the state budget and enterprises themselves. However, for fear of bringing damage to others, we were hesitant to carry out reforms in these critical areas. Instead, we chose another path and resorted to special economic zones and the introduction of complete sets of equipment in the hope to create some examples in the new mode of operation to shake the seemingly unshakable large and medium state-owned enterprises, only found later that our efforts did not yield the outcome we desired. As the overall environment of the economic structure in China had been dragged by the planned economy that went out of control, our efforts in these areas did not have supports in the society. The introduced complete sets of equipment, when put into operation, still run in the original mode of operation and thus could not produce the desired efficiency. If any progress was made, other people would follow suit immediately, resulting in repeated introduction of equipment and construction of projects, making the low-efficient operation a common phenomenon. The money used in buying these equipment belonged to the state and responsibility was assumed by administrative departments. The individuals did not take any risk but only had benefit, and might likely be rewarded with a reputation of "reformer". Who wouldn't do it? As to the harm the repeated and low efficient introduction did to the country, the individuals involved in these matters did not consider or could not care less due to the protection from the planned economic tradition. Although the establishment of special economic zones provided a place to display another mode of operation, such a mixed mode of operation had two price systems which made them a paradise for speculation and embezzlement of state funds, and thus causing considerable harms to the overall state economic interests.

Given that the above two approaches were not able to shake the deep-rooted mode of operation in the large and medium state-owned enterprises, we had to slow down the construction scale of special economic zones and increase the number of cities to be opened, and gradually bring the transformation into a market economy to the front stage. The issue of stocks, promulgation of bankruptcy law, auction of partial assets owned by the state-owned enterprises and institutions, relaxation of restrictions on private and individual enterprises and civil servant system were landmarks in the implementation of this measure of reform.

Due to a resistance to the industrial reform, the uniformity in the mode of operation caused by an out-of-control planned economy, the dependence of enterprises on administrative departments, and the control of administrative departments on enterprises in the areas beyond economy have hindered the further development of China's industry. The issues such as outdated equipment, backward technology, and overstaffed organization have lasted till today, which has prevented the production efficiency from further improvement and has given rise to the widespread "triangle debt". Some scholars have made profound analyses on this. Such a status in industrial reform has made a far-reaching impact on the economic development in ethnic regions in Guizhou, which is displayed in the following areas.

First, the structure of all existing industries was constructed to meet the need of a planned economy that went out of control based on the uniform standard while the supply of industrial products that were needed in the development of ethnic economy was not incorporated in the economic plan. In this area, no existing industrial enterprises could offer any help to the ethnic groups and the ethnic regions could not be developed into the market of means of production for the industrial departments in the Han regions. In the meantime, the raw materials for the light industry that the ethnic regions could provide according to the price system of the out-of-control planned economy were still provided to the factories at extremely low prices. Ethnic groups did not receive the value their products deserved and therefore did not have money to buy livelihood materials from the factories in the Han regions. As a result, the trade relations between ethnic groups in Guizhou and the factories in the Han regions remained in a low level for an extended period of time.

Second, despite some preliminary progress made in the recovery of diversified mode of production in ethnic regions, its further development also depends on the market in the Han regions. Without the deepening reform in industrial enterprises and the widened gap in the income of Han people, the special local products produced in small quantity in the ethnic Han regions could not be sold at the price they deserved and thus could not enter domestic or international market. Consequently, these special local products that just recovered could only remain in the ethnic regions to be consumed in the style of a natural economy, and could not become commodities, making capital accumulation impossible for the ethnic regions.

Third, the products in agriculture, forestry, animal husbandry and mineral resources in the ethnic regions in Guizhou now accessed to the market still as primary products. Although some of them were able to enter the international market, the slow progress made in the enterprise reform in the Han regions had limited their ability in absorbing these products, resulting in the products that were exported to the international market subject to fluctuation in the international market. The products that were sold to the Han regions, on the other hand, were severely restricted by the triangular debt of related enterprises, causing a dramatically volatile market price that directly shook the foundation of related products in ethnic regions and seriously hurt the existing production capacity. Take the world famous Liuma tung oil as an example. In the past four years, the price of tung oil per ton fluctuated by a range over 4,000 yuan, while the tung seeds were sold from the local producers at 1.1 yuan per jin at the highest and 0.3 yuan per jin at the lowest. The highest price of myotonin was 2.5 yuan per jin compared to less than 0.6 yuan per jin at its lowest point. Litsea cubeba oil could be sold at 80 yuan per jin at the highest and also at less than 7 yuan per jin at the lowest. Some products that were preliminarily processed mineral resources such as ferrosilicon and antimony white powder were also subject to price volatility following the fluctuation of the international market. In a booming market, more than 10 counties in the province set up factories of antimony white powder and ferroalloy whose operators were figures on the local newspaper. The market turned to sluggish almost in a blink of an eye and the products could not find buyers even at a price below cost, causing the factories to incur heavy debt and were shut down successively. A big country like ours could have provided shelter to these preliminary products from the ethnic regions, but unfortunately the incomplete reform in relevant enterprises made them unable to absorb these products and thus exposed them completely to the fierce international competition. Such a severe volatility shook the economic foundation in these regions.

Fourth, the diversified mode of production that had just recovered in the ethnic regions in Guizhou would, if left to continue in cultural inertia, only carry forward their inherent mode of production. To make them integrate in modern economy and upgrade their production, it is critical and urgent to introduce new scientific and research outcomes, and attract a lot of scientific researchers who are capable by modern standard to carry out pertinent studies. However, as our industrial reform had been under the guidance of attempting to shake the rigid mode of production by importing complete sets of equipment, the focus of the scientific researchers of our country was attracted to the introduction of hi-tech equipment from developed countries. Subsequently, such an urgent need by ethnic groups was totally ignored. With the exception of a very limited number of scientific researchers, few people would concentrate on the research projects for ethnic regions. Until today, most of the research topics related to ethnic regions are of the nature of humanities but not of natural science.

The above four issues are closely related to the completion of industrial enterprise reform in the Han regions. These critical elements that constrain the economic development in ethnic regions in Guizhou would not be brought onto the agenda unless the industrial reform in the Han regions is completed.

Another key barrier in the industrial reform was the continuation of high welfare in inertia. In the out-of-control planned economy, under the slogan of "develop the economy and ensure the supply", we chose to deliberately depress the price of agricultural products to ensure the living standard of urban residents and enterprise employees, and depress the ability to upgrade the equipment in the enterprises to satisfy the need of employee's livelihood and welfare. We would even resort to the state power to contain the price of livelihood products when all the measures could not ensure the need in the welfare of urban residents and enterprise employees. It seemed that the worker's salary in China was lower than that in other countries and they could not afford pricy luxury goods. In fact, the massive coverage of medical and pension funds and low price of livelihood products made their actual standard of living not as low as the low salary suggested it to be. "Engel coefficient" is widely used in the world as a standard for measuring the standard of living in a country. The Engel coefficient for the workers in China during the period of the planned economy, if judged by the nominal salary standard and expenses, would have ranked at the bottom in the world. However, a look at the actual expenses might lead to a different conclusion. The major expenses that foreign workers had including house rent, transportation, entertainment, social insurance, medical expenses, or even utilities and fuels were covered by many large and medium enterprises in China, which were amortized by the enterprises or administrative departments in the production cost. These expenses, by the principle in the enterprise operation in Western countries, would have been paid out of employee salaries, and thus would have made the Engel coefficient not as low as it looked. As a matter of fact, we offered quite generous salary and benefit to our workers given the capability of our country at the moment.

This was a welfare system that was characterized by "eating from the same big pot", i.e., the benefit was shared evenly among all the people, thus making ratio of the actual scale of expense over the total profits in the enterprise greater than that in the developed Western countries. In this sense, the workers and urban residents of China had been used to the welfare provided by an out-of-control planned economy. As such a welfare was evenly spread among all the people and was given in the form of a "hidden salary" under the flag of socialism, the people who received the benefit often did not associate it with the cost of enterprise products and the ability to upgrade its production, but would take it for granted. Once it was cut to some extent, everyone wasted no time to voice their objection. It was in fact way beyond the ability of our national and enterprise capabilities. Any reform that touched these interests would turn it from a simple management issue to that of universal social significance. The most difficult part to streamline the relations in enterprise management is how to get rid of this burden, which has been demonstrated in the difficulties of house reform and reduction of non-production related costs.

A series of new problems emerged from this basis such as the issue of over consumption and enjoyment, who to pay for the worker's pension after the change of an enterprise ownership, and employee social insurance issue etc. The "over consumption and enjoyment", to unrealistically chase the Western level of consumption in the initial stage of the reform, originated in the special economic zones we established and was beyond the level of our national capability. It also reflected the reality at the moment that the outdated equipment were in urgent need of upgrade. Due to the inertial continuation of egalitarian welfare, everyone felt that they should have what the others had. The expansion of over consumption into other areas made it an unacceptable requirement by our national capability. Although the wave of "over consumption" came along with the "reform and opening-up", it put up a new issue for the "reform and opening-up". As a matter of fact, the so-called over consumption did not exist in the Western developed countries for more than 20 years after WWII when every country was busy healing the wounds caused by the war and the standard of living of ordinary workers did not have a huge gap with that of our workers in mid 1950s. The gap became widened in the mid 1960s when we were in the "cultural revolution". Given the time we wasted during the Cultural Revolution, we must seize the opportunity now to develop ourselves, and there was a big price to pay for that. At such a critical moment, if the "over consumption and enjoyment" was advocated and encouraged instead of stressing the personal responsibility in the rise of the country, and requested that enterprises compete against each other on the consumption and enjoyment, how can we accomplish the mission of enterprises system reform? However, we were pressured by people's mentality in the society and thus were hesitant with regards to the measures to take to continue the reform. The housing reform in the cities was an example.

We must also admit that such a hesitation and indetermination was also related to the integrity of some in-charge government officials. We reiterated in the "reform and opening-up" the necessity of combating corruption and building a clean government, combating the excessive and wasteful eating and drinking, extravagant lifestyle, "official profiteering", and junket tour, but none of these was fully implemented and strictly enforced. How can we expect to carry out the reform that was really necessary with determination and resolution and how can we expect ordinary people to willingly tolerate the hardship caused by lower wages for some time for the purpose of national revitalization? These are reasons that entangled our pace in enterprise reform.

The inertial continuation of universal welfare also resulted in high employment rate and low wage. However, latent unemployment was a common phenomenon in all the enterprises. A large number of non-production related staff had nothing to do, workers were under utilized, and most administrative organs and public institutions were over staffed. Although organization optimization was repeatedly brought up, it was not accomplished eventually for the same reason: the placement of the downsized staff. This was an issue of substance that existed when we started the "reform and opening-up" and is still haunting us. If we are not resolute in solving this issue completely, the capital urgently needed for enterprise upgrade would not be accumulated, and the normal enterprise management would stay on paper. In summary, the high welfare caused by an out-of-control planned economy and the state fiscal subsidy have continued as a social inertia until today. We are sure that the "reform and opening-up" in the manufacturing and mining enterprises would not complete if we continue catering to such an unrealistically high-welfare social mentality.

Currently, we are taking an approach of expanding investment in exchange for high growth rate and in the meantime appeasing such a social mentality, which has taken an increasing share of fiscal expenditure and thus must be stopped. However, the expansion of investment is partially for the purpose of pacifying this social mentality and thus can not be totally eradicated. The desire for a high welfare society caused by the out-of-control planned economy and ensuing "over consumption and enjoyment" have prevented the industrial reform from going deeper. Meanwhile, such an outcome from a uniform mode of production has severely crippled the economic development in ethnic regions in Guizhou. As one of the main contents, the high welfare was achieved by depressing the value of agricultural products and huge amount of fiscal subsidies. Currently, nearly all ethnic groups in Guizhou live on crop farming and the breeding industry. If the control on the price of grains is not fully lifted, and the unreasonable tax beyond tax – requisition of surplus grains is not abolished, the true value of the primary products in ethnic regions can not be realized. As a result, the capital needed in the development of production and expansion of area of production in ethnic regions can never been accumulated. The re-production in ethnic regions will not be maintained without subsidies.

The uniformity in the administrative structure in China created clumsy and overstaffed administrative organizations not only in the Han regions but also in the ethnic regions. In a small county with a population of just over 200 thousand, as many as 4,000 to 5,000 were on the payroll in the administrative channels. The annual fiscal revenue in an ethnic autonomous county was not enough to pay the salaries, and all the necessary production construction investments had to be suspended. Everything was allocated to pay salaries, from the investments issued by the upper-level authorities for economic constructions, public institutions, to the house-construction funds allocated after "the districts were abolished to be merged into township". Many counties across the province had to borrow money to pay salaries for many consecutive years. Under such a condition, it became absolutely impossible to make even a tiny investment on ethnic economic construction. How can we expect that local governments could provide any support to the economic development in ethnic regions? It became apparent that "high welfare and high employment rate" could not help ethnic groups. To the contrary, it became a drag on the economic development in ethnic regions. The bad influence of "over consumption and enjoyment" also corrupted some government officials, and damaged the unsophisticated and hardworking nature of ethnic groups in these regions. Consequently, some young people from the ethnic regions began showing contempt for agricultural production and unrealistically pursuing over consumption, casting shadow over the entrepreneurship and revitalization of ethnic economy. The more devastating spiritual damage to the economic development in ethnic regions came from the injustice in welfare benefit under the same socialist system. While the urban residents would not let go of the welfare benefit they received in the out-of-control planned economy, ethnic people had long been kept away from these benefits, which caused the psychological imbalance that was hard to be compensated with limited subsidies and poverty-relief aid from the state. Such a psychological imbalance was a corrosive that dampened the resolution of the ethnic people in revitalizing their economy and a catalyst that pushed them to wait for state aids. In the meantime, they became increasingly dependent on administrative departments, which overshadowed their creativity in economic development. The above factors are constraining the economic development in ethnic regions either spiritually or materially. These non-economic constraints, as an inertial continuation under an out-of-control planned economy, are the result of the execution of such a policy over a long time in the past, and will continue constraining the economic development in ethnic regions in Guizhou as long as the industrial reform is not complete.

In the situation of an out-of-control planned economy that deliberately deflated the price of agricultural products and inflate that of industrial products, rural areas in China began to implement a system of contracted responsibility linking remuneration to output. Although it brought up the agricultural output steadily that reached a record high in 1984, farmer's cash income remained low as the price of agricultural products were still lower than that of industrial products. Consequently, surplus labor began to set up small businesses in the hope of maximizing cash income. In the meantime, the sluggish state-owned enterprises and public institutions witnessed the outflow of technicians and technical managers into small enterprises in rural areas, thus enhancing the technical capacity of small rural enterprises. For the same reason, managers of some state-owned enterprises began to transfer equipment to small rural enterprises openly or stealthily, and thus boosted the level of equipment of these small enterprises. In such a background, these small businesses in rural areas found a foothold amid larger counterparts and gradually grew stronger. This is the history of the development of what are later called township enterprises.

Once they emerged, these township enterprises rose rapidly thanks to a few extremely favorable living conditions they possessed in the out-of-control planned economy.

First, unlike state-owned enterprises, township enterprises did not have heavy welfare burdens and were thus easy to be on the right track from the beginning.

Second, small enterprises operate flexibly. They did not attract people's attention in the beginning, and thus rules of planned economy had little impact on them. They could be put in operation and turn profitable in a short period of time. The transfer of assets and operation were easy in case of operational failure. They were quick in turning profitable than the state-owned enterprises.

Third, small enterprises were close to raw materials and market, and some had their own sales channels, which often made them lead the way in the market and leave the state-owned enterprises far behind.

Also, township enterprises grew in the environment where the prices of agricultural products were deliberately kept low. In particular, the enterprises that used agricultural products as their primary raw materials were able to receive the benefit of a deflated price of agricultural products. A slight mark-up on the price of the raw materials was enough to block the raw material supply channel of the state-owned enterprises. The favorable conditions created by the out-of-control planned economy for state-owned enterprises were, to a large extent, intercepted by these township enterprises before they reached the state-owned enterprises.

Lastly, due to the sluggishness of the state-owned enterprises, township enterprises often appended themselves to these state-owned enterprises in the form of affiliation, appendage, proxy processing etc., which was, in essence, to make use of the large and medium enterprises to lay the foundation for their own development. These favorable conditions designed for state-owned enterprises boosted the rapid development of township enterprises and eventually gave rise to the situation where “small fish ate the big ones”. The essence is on the word “ate”, vividly depicting how township enterprises took advantage of the loopholes in the planned economy and sought growth by hurting the interests of the large and medium enterprises.

The development of township enterprises created economic prosperity in the Han regions but could not do the same thing in the ethnic regions in Guizhou. First, the social foundation for the survival of small enterprises did not exist in the traditional economic life in ethnic regions. Second, these regions were still in the self-sufficient or natural economy where the market economy was not fully developed and the products produced in township enterprises did not have local customers while the export market was constrained by the spatial attenuation effect. Third, the ethnic regions in Guizhou were a long distance away from the sites of large and medium enterprises. Enterprises that were located in these regions were mostly secondary enterprises and were not easy target to be “eaten” and “dug” as did by the township enterprises in the Han regions. Lastly, as the administrative organizations in the prefectures and counties were heavily debt ridden, they had to turn to the township enterprises for new sources of fiscal revenue. As a result, the township enterprises barely started before nailed down. In summary, the development of township enterprises that was viewed as a short cut in rural economic development could hardly benefit the ethnic regions. To the contrary, the economy in ethnic regions was harmed by the negative effect caused by township enterprises. The township enterprises that grew wildly in the Han region often did not meet any resistance or competition in the ethnic regions and thus were able to dump inferior and defective products in these regions before the local government had time to respond. Some ill-disposed businessmen took the chance to fool or deceive the hungry and blind local government officials who were eager to attract external investment. In recent years, it often happened in ethnic regions in Guizhou that people from the Han regions lured the local people into buying out-dated or abandoned equipment or run with the prepayment from local people under the disguise of a contracted project. If these negative impacts brought over by the township enterprises in the developed Han regions could not be curbed, the ethnic regions would not benefit from booming township enterprises and would, even worse, be jeopardized by these enterprises.

To sum up, the uniformity in the mode of production in ethnic regions in Guizhou as a result of an out-of-control planned economy severely damaged the foundation for the economic development in the ethnic regions in Guizhou over a long time in the past, from different angles and in different ways. Ethnic groups, out of constraints in objective environments, did not benefit much from the measures we took to correct the mistakes we committed in the out-of-control planned economy, but rather were hurt by the negative latent impacts derived from them. From the perspective of developing the economy in these ethnic regions in Guizhou, special and effective policy measures are urgently needed. In the meantime, we should speed up the reforms, in particular, to quickly marketize the prices of agricultural products. Simplified solutions could not help the ethnic groups but rather would hurt the economic development and direct economic interests of ethnic groups.

III The Impact that Existing Cultural Environments Have on Economic Development

Close economic relations had existed in ethnic groups in Guizhou, which had been developed over a long history in the past. They were of the nature of mutual supplementary, interconnection, interaction or parallel development. Such an intricate relation across ethnic groups could have formed a solid social and humanistic foundation for the further development of the ethnic economic development, and could have been the humanistic environments for the mutual absorption and exchange across ethnic groups. However, these inter-ethnicity relations were damaged, to a certain extent, in the out-of-control planned economy. Some were suspended; some changed in nature; some were totally destroyed. We had to recover and rebuild new inter-ethnicity relations when we were making plans for the new development in ethnic regions. Before these tasks were completed, the inter-ethnicity relations must have contained a series of elements that constrained the economic development. It was more difficult for us to change the existing cross-ethnicity relations caused by policies by the power of new policies. Furthermore, due to the resistance we encountered in the "reform and opening-up" in the industrial area which made it difficult to deepen the reform in the short period of time, we would not be able to focus on solving these issues for now. Therefore, the latent troubles caused by non-economic constraints should not be overlooked.

These policy-triggered constraints manifest in complex and intricate ways. For the ease of organizing the writing, we will discuss this issue in the four areas: ecological resources maintenance, market formation, introduction of modern equipment, and coordination of inter-ethnicity relations.

Although ethnic groups in Guizhou clashed among each other, before the founding of the People's Republic of China, they basically conducted their own economic activities in a way that was best to themselves and maintained the ecological resources in their own regions by following their own cultural characteristics, thus forming a complex and intricate inter-ethnicity relation with other ethnic groups. In other words, before the founding of the People's Republic of China, large-scale ecological crises similar to the ones we are experiencing now had not appeared despite the sign of a looming ecological deterioration. The current ecological crisis was, for the most part, resulted from the malignant development following an out-of-control planned economy since 1950s. Nowadays, the most obvious ecological crises include a sharp drop in the area of forests, over-reclamation of crop lands and massive loss of water and soil, air pollution, water resources shortage and pollution of water body.

The sharp drop in the forest resources began in the 1950s and deteriorated in the 1970s, which was directly related to the disruption of the traditional inter-ethnicity relations. The forests and lands that were suitable for forestry plantations in Guizhou were largely occupied or operated directly by local ethnic group before the founding of the People's Republic of China. They were either self-consumed by the local ethnic groups or converted into commodities through the established relations across ethnic groups. The excessive deforestation and burning of forests due to unclear ownership of forests was rarely seen. The land reform carried out in the early stage of the People's Republic of China did not handle the issue of ownership of the forests properly out of our ignorance of the fact that a significant part of the regions in Guizhou had been covered by forestry plantations. As a result, the land reform only touched the ownership of farm lands and it was later stipulated in the law that all forests were owned by the state, thus the ownership of the forestry plantations was out of control. Although by law the forests that were not planted by people were owned by the state, they were brought out of control as the state was not capable of direct operation of these forests. The original owners of the forestry plantations could not get around the laws to execute their rights of operation and management while the state did not have the resources to do so either. Subsequently, in the ensuing political movements, with an administrative order from the government of any level, people could exploit the forest resources without having to pay any price or assuming any responsibility, thus triggered the massive destruction of forests. In the early 1950s the government officials from ethnic groups were not available, and yet the Han officials from outside the regions did not understand either the history or the status in the ownership of the forests. Although the forests were, by law, owned by the state after the planned economy was implemented, the actual right to dispose of the forests was in the hands of people's commune and administrative officials in each level, resulting in the destruction of large areas of forests for the iron production in the wave of "three red flags" in the late 1950s. Even in the regions that did not have room for pudding, people chopped down trees as fuels for pudding. When the fever was over, a huge quantity of logs that had been cut were left in the forests to rot.

In our fieldwork, we talked to some people who shared with us their memory of "the great leap-forward" movement. Some senior villagers in Niuchang village of Mashan in Wangmo recalled: "We were expected to 'break the production record' and people were mobilized by the commune to climb to the mountains to fell trees. These trees could not be shipped down the mountain and we could do nothing but let them rot. We ate the mushrooms growing from the rotten trees for more than ten years." We collected similar materials in Chashan and Jialie that border Guiyang and Huishui, as well as Kepu and Kehun in Ziyun. Even worse, the multiple adjustments made to the ownership of the people's commune shifted the people in charge of the forests from the team formed by united a few counties to production teams. The forests that survived the "great pudding" movement were depleted as a result of numerous changes in their ownership. Since then, we have begun to plant trees every year but have never seen the increase in the forest area.

The disruption of inter-ethnicity relations caused massive deforestation, the most representative being the forestry plantations in southeast Guizhou, which was an economic entity created through coordination across ethnic groups. The basic contents included: the virgin forests in the upstream Qingshui River and Duliu River were habitats of the ethnic Miao group and were primarily used to supply large-sized lumbers to the market through the transshipment by the Dong group along the river, while the wildlife products in the forests were mainly resold on the road via ethnic Han merchants. The alpine virgin forests controlled by the ethnic Miao people were, from the perspective of the structure of the forests, served as a natural shelter to the Dong's forestry plantations on the hillside of mid to low-altitude and was an indispensable forest for maintain water sources and prevent the loss of water and soil, and thus directly ensured the normal production in the forestry plantations of the Dong region. Economically, they were sources of supreme varieties of trees for the forestry plantations in the Dong regions, which were dominated by the fast-growing cedars in low-altitude mountains and hilly areas. Technically, these forestry plantations combined the elements of Swidden cultivation of the Miao group and intensive cultivation of the Dong people. Ethnic Dong people employed the method of growing seedlings and transplanting them to the field in forestry plantation. Similar to rice cultivation, intensive care was given in the entire process from growing seedlings from selected seeds, arranging seedbeds, to managing and controlling the seedling. The clearing-up of forestry fields was carried out in the slash–and-burn method copied from ethnic Miao people and looked extensive. Dry-land crops were mixed with the transplanted cedar seedlings and grew together in the early phase of field planting, which, on the one hand, reduced the scouring of surface runoffs and thus helped cedar seedlings to take root. On the other hand, the dry-land crops sheltered the young cedar seedlings from the scorching sunlight, diminished the force of strong wind, and thus ensured the survival of young cedar trees. The decayed straws from the crops enriched the fertility in the soil. In the meantime, such a mixed cultivation yielded some output of crops and increased the income of operation. Only after the forestry plantations were sealed off was the mixed cultivation of agricultural products stopped, symbolizing that the plantations entered the phase of maintenance and conservation. This was a mode that absorbed the strengths from two ethnic groups and proved to be effective, successful and considerably profitable. By such a technology, it only took eight years in the well-conditioned regions for the trees to mature to the size of 20 cm in the diameter at breast height, and produced 8 to 10-cubic-meter lumber each hectare. Such a speed was unattainable even in the countries that are specialized in forestry plantations in the world.

The shipping of lumbers from the Dong regions by rafting was also made possible by coordination across multiple ethnic groups. The water channels on the two rivers were dredged and managed jointly by ethnic Han and Dong groups while the distribution channels in the Han region were maintained primarily by the Han people. The lumbers were shipped down the Duliu River southward, with Liuzhou as a distribution hub, to Wuzhou and Guangzhou at the farthest, or down the Qingshui River, with Yueyang as a distribution hub, over to Nanjing and Shanghai at the farthest. The operators of the rafts were made up of people of multiple ethnic groups including Miao, Dong, Han and Tujia. The forestry plantations of the Dong people were later gradually expanded toward the upstream Duliu River and Qingshui River and subsequently brought the forestry operation to the ethnic Miao and Shui regions, where ethnic Dong and the other two groups conduct joint operations by forming relations of interaction and mutual supplement. Ethnic Miao and Shui people felled the wood on the mountain and shipped them to the riverside where Dong merchants bought them and shipped over the river course through rafting. Sanjiang, Guandong and Jianhe were all used as distribution hubs in lumber trade. In a chimeric form of coordination, ethnic Dong people rented the mountains owned by the Miao group and hired local Miaos to operate plantations and produce lumber. This form of forestry plantations produced quite a number of business tycoons in lumber trade who, up till the eve of the founding of the People's Republic of China, marked up respective sphere of influence or even issued securities to participate in market competition, giving rise to the "coordinated process" in the production and trade of lumber that was led by the Dong and Han group and joined by other relevant groups. In the old societies, such an operational structure across ethnic groups was certainly characterized with exploitation and oppression. Open or secret strife constantly happened across power groups, which might end up in large-scale fight with weapons and cause heavy losses to the production. The lower-class people thus lived a miserable life. However, we realize that such an organizational structure has some value. Above all, it effectively brought together all the relevant ethnic groups that were otherwise sealed from each other and led them to the market. Today, while we stand firm on opposing ethnic oppression and exploitation, and the monopoly of trade by local influential groups, we hope to equally unite all ethnic groups and march toward shared prosperity and wealth.

In the planned economy that went out of control, lumber trade carried out by individuals was treated as capitalist tail and was thus prohibited. The lumbers could only be procured and shipped out of the region by state channels, blocking the distribution channels created by joint efforts across ethnic groups and breaking up the union formed across ethnic groups. Meanwhile, under the slogan of "putting grain production over everything else", locals who worked in forestry plantations were forced to shift to agricultural production. The living environment in the Dong regions was characterized with "90% mountainous region, 5% paddy fields and 5% water body", and the ethnic Dong people have made a living by exchanging lumbers for grains. To switch from forestry plantations to agricultural cultivation and a severe shortage in farm lands forced people to destroy forests and turn them into farm lands, and depended on dry-land crops for subsistence. Since then, ethnic Dong people returned back to the natural economy. To put it more straightforwardly, the out-of-control planned economy forced Dong people to turn back from a commodity economy to a natural economy. The ensuing ecological damage created many latent troubles for the recovery of forestry plantations in the Dong regions. To completely recover the forestry production would be hindered by the soil depletion. The forestry plantations operated by the country was thus plagued by stealthy felling and constant forest fire due to lack of support from local organizations, making it difficult for the maintenance of normal ecological environment. Things like this happened not only in the forestry plantations in the Dong regions, but also in the massive Miao regions in Danjiang River and Qingshui River. The state forestry departments focused on cutting instead of growing trees, and even if some symbolic gestures were made in afforestation, the newly planted trees were hard to survive for the lack of support from local Miao society. As a result, barren mountains are a common view even in today in these regions, suggesting how the ecological environments were damaged.

As Guizhou is the upstream of a few tributaries of Yangtze River and Pearl River with a rugged landscape and relatively high altitude. Subsequently, forests directly impact the size of water resource reserve and the intensity of the erosion of surface runoffs. Lack of vegetation coverage, especially forests coverage on steep hills, would result in massive loss in water and soil and also directly threaten the limited area of paddy fields. It also caused the abrupt rise and fall of water in the rivers, thus flooding the paddy fields in Guizhou and bring many hidden perils to the downstream rivers. The insufficient water resource reserve in Guizhou not only would threaten the construction of manufacturing and mining enterprises as well as farmland capital construction, but also cause deposit of sediments on the river beds in the Han regions. Therefore, the forest coverage is an indicator of ecological condition in Guizhou.

The deforestation and over-reclamation of agricultural lands under the slogan of "prioritizing grain production over everything else" caused serious loss in water and soil in Guizhou. Specifically, it included four important aspects:

The upstream Wujiang River and Beipan River had been used primarily as grazing lands. As discussed in the chapter "on background", when used as grazing lands, the surface of the lands was not ploughed and herbs of perennial root could hold the soil and water. In addition, the steep hills were widely covered by forests, which combined to prevent the Wujiang River and Beipan River regions from massive water and soil losses. After the implementation of "replacing local hereditary headmen with officials sent by the central government from other regions", a large number of Han people moved to this region and the loss of water and soil began to deteriorate, but the area impacted was still limited. Only after the slogan of "prioritizing grain production over everything else" was brought forth did it evolve into a crisis. The direct reason was that this was a region that was not suitable for agricultural cultivation, and yet "prioritizing grain production over everything else" demanded that people grow grains on the barren mountains. They were forced to plough the surface of mountain slopes which took away the protection of soil and water by the herbs of perennial root. It was inevitable that a rainstorm would bring heavy loss of water and soil. Nowadays, exposed rocky mountains were seen across many of these regions, making them one of the regions that are severely afflicted by loss in water and soil and urgently need aids from the state.

In addition to the loss in water and soil, an out-of-control planned economy, more importantly, directly disrupted the economic supplementary relations among ethnic groups in this region. The ethnic Yi and Miao people who had barely farmed lands were forced to work on growing dry-land crops on the fields that were the least suitable for agricultural cultivation. In the meantime, the ethnic groups who had lived on rice cultivation were forced up to the mountains to start cultivating dry lands. The relation among ethnic groups was thus changed from a supplementary nature to a competing one where people strived over limited hillside resources. Now, the situation has been noticed by relevant departments, who have warned on the severity of the loss in water and soil in this region and appealed for returning grain plots to husbandry in large areas. However, the consequences from an out-of-control planned economy have hindered the execution of this plan. The ethnic Yi and Miao people who had lived on animal husbandry had a smaller population and lived in an area other than the steep slopes in the upstream Wujiang River that had been most hard hit by the loss in water and soil. They could not play a significant role due to the limitation on population and geographic location. The Han people, who are the most populated ethnicity, scatter on the steep slopes not suitable for agricultural cultivation and should take most of the tasks in returning grain plots to husbandry. To do this, three difficulties must be overcome. First, overpopulation of the Han people. To return grain plots to husbandry would become meaningless without the emigration of a large number of Han people out of the region. Second, without any experience in animal husbandry, it would not be achieved in a short time if they had to learn from the start. Third, it would be unacceptable for the ethnic Hans who have put tremendous labor in the steep slopes to abandon the lands and give them away to the Yi and Miao people as grazing lands. It would be an astronomical figure if the state has to pay for the price to let the Han people abandon their lands. It is apparent that the restructuring of ethnic relations caused by an out-of-control planned economy has already caused astonishing loss in water and soil, and the social barriers we must overcome in order to alleviate the trend of deteriorating ecological environment are greater than the loss in water and soil.

The restructuring of ethnic relations also caused massive loss in water and soil in southwest Guizhou where ethnic Miao and Buyi people lived together. We mentioned previously in the book the incident where ethnic Miao and Buyi people in the counties of Zhenning and Guanling rivaled for the hillside lands and ethnic Miao people were forced out of the region. Such an incident was a partial reflection of the strained ethnic relations that, in fact, could affect these regions in a much wider and deeper way. Traditionally, ethnic Miao and Buyi people were in a parallel or chimeric relation. The main contents of the former was: Ethnic Miao engaged in the Swidden cultivation on the hillside while the Buyi people engaged in agricultural production on the rice fields in the intermountane basins. They were separated by a region of natural forests and each developed its own economy based on its own cultural tradition. The chimeric relation was prevailing primarily in central Guizhou and northern south Guizhou where the difference in altitudes was relatively small and the rice fields cultivated by Buyi people and the dry lands of the Miao people were not separated clearly but were interlocking with each other, and yet the right of land usage was mutually respected by each other. All local governments in the history did all they could to maintain such a relationship. Although people from these two ethnic groups lived a different economic life, they interacted closely with each other. In the period of an out-of-control economy, the chaos in the land possession caused damage to the natural forests that had separated two different modes of production. In the period when everyone was called to "prioritize grain production over anything else", ethnic Buyi people were forced to reclaim lands up on the mountains, which not only destroyed the publicly-owned forestry lands and grazing lands, but also penetrated deep into the lands that had traditionally been cultivated by Miao people, thus fueling strife for lands between two ethnic groups in some regions and forcing Miao people to escape. With the continuation in the fight for mountainous lands by the Buyi group, the traditional forest lands were destroyed to a certain extent, which resulted in petrification of mountains in many places as these forests often grew in steep slopes that were prone to water scouring and loss in water and soil. The natural scenery we spotted in the Beipan River valley and downstream Dabang River valley was of this type, and it is now very difficult to grow any crops in these regions. Barren slopes dominated both sides along the Pan River that crosses the area bordering Guanling and Zhenfeng counties as the soil has become so thin. As a result of ecological damage caused by man, on the river banks of Pan River across Guanling and Zhenfeng, and along the route of Bangui and Dingtan, we have seen huge areas of exposed rocks, which is hard to recover in a short time by manpower. Despite natural reasons, the irrational reclamation of mountains as a result of the change in ethnic regions was more important in triggering the ecological deterioration that has been happening in these regions.

In central Guizhou where the terrain slopes gently, although the change in the chimeric relation between ethnic Miao and Buyi groups did not cause massive water and soil loss, barren hills expanded rapidly, causing severe deterioration in the ecological background for multiple operation and irreversible harm to the future comprehensive economic development. For instance, the central part of Miaoling mountain ridge was home to the well-known cloud and mist tea and Zhaosi tea. After the forests were destroyed, soil water content was decreased, affecting the quantity and quality of these teas. It also destabilized the water supply into a few rivers flowing down from Miaoling mountain ridge, the most affected being Nanming River in Guiyang, Wengcheng River in Guiding and Lianjiang River in Huishui, which directly affected the water supply to central cities and thus caused irreversible loss to the economic development in these regions.

Over reclamation of farm lands especially rice fields also existed in the upstream of the rivers in southeast and south Guizhou. It destroyed massive forests that served to preserve the upstream source of water and sharply reduced the water in Wuyang River, Qingshui River and Duliu River. Meanwhile, the abrupt rise and fall in these rivers threatened the safety of downstream territories. In our visits to Jiuzhou in Huangpin, Nangao in Danzhai and Dujiang in Sandu, we found it a common phenomenon.

Similarly, it was attributable to the change in the original ethnic relations that forced the ethnic people to vie for the forest lands and cultivate them into farm lands. It was extremely important for the shipping of lumber produced in these regions to have a stable and ample water supply in these rivers. In the past 40 years, the cruising ranges in Wuyang River, Qingshui River and Duliu River have been reduced. Now, we can barely see any boats in Zhenyuan, a place where ships and boats swarmed at the time when the People's Republic of China was established. In the Jiuzhou of Huangping that used to be passable by boat, people can now walk across the river. The Sanjiaotun wharf that was opened in the Qing Dynasty is barely passable by water now.

The change in ethnic relations created some barriers in the development of the market economy. In history, ethnic Hui had been the middlemen in the commodity trade between the ethnic Yi and Miao people in the pasturing area and the Han people, which was severely destroyed in the out-of-control planned economy. Constrained by the single mode of production under the slogan of "prioritizing grain production over everything else", the ethnic Hui people were forced to abandon the business to begin farming. We must point out that the export of large-quantity medicinal materials, leather and domestic animals in the history of Guizhou were all carried out by ethnic Hui as middlemen, and the products made in the Han regions that were distributed in northwest Guizhou were also depended on the Hui businessmen. To perfect such an ethnic relation had irreplaceable positive impacts in history and will continue to do so in today. When we enthusiastically advocate the development of the commodity economy in ethnic regions, we must keep in mind that there used to have such a harmonious ethnic relation in history and the special position ethnic Hui people occupied in this relation of transshipment.

The city of Guiyang is a central city developed in the region inhabited by Miao and Buyi people. It also had close interactions with ethnic Yi group in history. After Guiyang was developed into a central city, the ethnic Miao and Buyi people who had traditionally lived in this region had engaged in transshipment between the Miao and Buyi people in remote areas and the Han central cities over a long period in the past, and thus had played a positive role in the development of commodity economy in the remote Miao and Buyi regions. However, in the out-of-control planned economy, the Miao and Buyi people had to abandon conducting business and switch to farming, and thus the trade relations were brought to a stop. With the subsequent expansion of cities, the Miao and Buyi villages in Guiyang city that used to serve as bridge tower in the trade with ethnic Miao and Buyi in remote regions disappeared. For example, the Miao village in present-day Henanzhuang, the Miao village in Mutouzhai, the Buyi village in Sifanghe, the Buyi village in Xiaohe in Guiyang city, etc., either have disappeared or are disappearing now, which makes it impossible for these villages to play the role of connecting the Han people and ethnic Miao and Buyi living in remote regions in the trade activities.

Guizhou is a multi-ethnicity province and Guiyang is a multi-ethnicity provincial capital. To retain hereditary neighborhoods and market streets of different ethnic groups in the central cities was an important measure to expand the radiation effect of these cities, break the sealing of the natural economy of each ethnic group, and direct these ethnic groups to a market economy, as well as an indispensible long-term strategy in the construction of central cities and a symbol of ethnic equality. Unfortunately, an out-of-control planned economy discontinued the vitality of these ethnic villages in the economic life of each respective ethnic group and forced them to unexceptionally lean to side of the Han culture in economic life. The value of these villages in channeling trade across ethnic groups was lost in the process. After the "reform and opening-up", we were short-sighted when making plans for central cities. As a result, instead of bringing vitality back to these ethnic villages, our massive construction of big cities destroyed these villages. Anshun is similar to Guiyang in this case, which we will not make further elaboration.

In the Ming and Qing dynasties, the Han immigrants who lived in ethnic regions for various reasons had long served to connect the trade relations between ethnic groups and Han people. A considerable number of communities of people in the ethnic relations in Guizhou could be classified in this category. "Liujia people" in southeast Guizhou, "Gaoshan Han" in Southwest Guizhou Prefecture, "Tunbao People" in central Guizhou and "Chuanqing People" in northwest Guizhou all played a role of intermediating trade relations between Han and ethnic groups. As these Han immigrants lived in different regions with different ethnic relations, the roles they played were slightly different. "Liujia people" mainly engaged in lumber trade; "Tunbao people" were primarily retailers between ethnic Miao, Buyi and Han people; “Chuanqing people” played a similar role as Hui group in the trade. All these communities of people, at the time of an out-of-control planned economy, experienced the same trend in the change of their economic life as other relevant ethnic groups: abandoning business and switching to farming. From the perspective of guiding ethnic groups to develop commodity economy, it is a constructive measure in removing the negative consequences resulted from a planned economy and helping ethnic groups break the fence of the natural economy to bring life to traditional means of livelihood.

A normal ethnic relation also ensured the spreading of advanced science and technology and is the social foundation for different ethnic groups to live in harmony, but the change in ethnic relations caused by an out-of-control planned economy had negative impacts on both. Advanced technologies were often introduced from the Han regions into the inlands of ethnic minority regions in history by such an ethnic relation. The corn, tobacco, sweet potato, and potato that are now widely planted in ethnic regions were induced this way. The ceramics and puddling technologies were also spread across ethnic regions from Han regions in this way. Nowadays, to promote advanced science and technology in the ethnic regions, and enhance the ability of these ethnic groups in absorbing and digesting advanced science and technology also relies on recovering and strengthening the inherent ethnic relations.

Although the equality of all ethnic groups has been incorporated in the laws of China, a true equality requires more than legal stipulation. It also depends on a coordinative, understanding and yielding ethnic relation. As mentioned earlier in the book, the dispute over land resources between ethnic Miao and Buyi groups, the “turning farm lands back to pastures” in northwest Guizhou and “turning farm lands back to forests” in southeast Guizhou all concerned the personal interests of many ethnic people and were thus impossible to solve only by legal verdicts. More importantly, the interests of all ethnic groups must be properly protected. Besides simple mediation, it also requires that we conduct profound investigation and research on the economic life of each ethnic group under the theoretical guidance in ethnology, sociology and many other fields of social science; otherwise, we only treat the symptom but not the cause of the consequences of the out-of-control planned economy.

Above all, a disorder in the ethnic relations across ethnic groups in Guizhou as a result of the out-of-control planned economy has produced ill consequences that not only constrain the current economic development in ethnic regions but will also bring latent troubles to ethnic economic development for quite a long time in the future. Therefore, we must envisage the severity and protraction of these ill consequences, and properly deal with the ethnic relations.

The above contents were about the ill consequences from the implementation of an out-of-control planned economy. Of course, they have been gradually resolved and a considerable part of them are remaining issues. What is worrisome is that new problems have emerged in succession before the old ones are solved. Problems related to agriculture have attracted widespread attention in China. As all ethnic groups in Guizhou mostly engage in crop farming and breeding, any mistake in agricultural policies will significantly constrain the development of ethnic groups. The unique social and natural backgrounds in ethnic regions in Guizhou have made these constraints more effective than the Han regions, which reach far beyond the scope of economy in width and depth.

There have been quite a number of valuable books and analyses on the severity of the agricultural situation in China, some of which have revealed the crucial reason in the agricultural development in China. The paper entitled "The Issues and Development Strategies in China's Agriculture" by Ding Zeji is the most representative [①] and it has pointed out four big hidden worries in agriculture in China. First, China's agricultural problems are classified into shallow, medium and deep levels. Those in the shallow level can be solved by adjustments through policies while those in other levels can not be solved in short time even by policy power. Second, the core in the agricultural issues in China was to give too little but demand too much disguisedly instead of openly, especially through the "price scissors" between industrial and agricultural products and "unjustified financial or material levies", as well as excessive demand on agriculture to support the industrial development. Third, the paper also refutes the roundabout strategy that attempts to drive agricultural development by "change from agriculture to non-agriculture status" and township enterprises. Fourth, based on the situation in China, the paper points out that we must execute the strategy of coordinated development between industry and agriculture and between

① Zeji Ding, "China's Agricultural Issues and Development Strategy", *Issues of Agricultural Economy*, no. 7, 1994, 42-46.

urban and rural areas. The four issues discussed in this paper are commonly seen in ethnic regions in Guizhou and there are special cases that are more difficult to deal with. To clarify these special issues is necessary for us to better understand the difficulty in the development in ethnic regions in Guizhou.

With regards to the shallow issues, ethnic regions in Guizhou are nationally impoverished regions, where the fiscal expenditure has long been relied on state subsidies. The execution of wage reform has increasingly inflated the expenses of administrative departments. In these regions, it is impossible to have new source of revenue and to downsize the administrative agencies in a short period of time. Even though upper-level government authorities have ordered not to unjustifiably impose financial or material levies, raise funds, or collect fees, administrative departments would do the same regardless as a way to solve the issues in organizational operation and personal interests. In other words, these practices that hurt the farmers' interests would never stop, or would come back under some other disguises even though they are prohibited by law. Otherwise, how can we expect the administrative organizations that can not survive on their own to implement the agricultural policies?

With regards to the issues in the medium level, the comparative benefit in the production of grain and cotton dropped; the "price scissors" between industrial and agricultural products" widened and the increase of farmer's income slowed. All the three issues deteriorated at the same rate as those in the Han regions, while the deterioration in the following issues directly suffocated the agricultural development in these regions. First, the "price scissors" directly constrained the growth in the income of farmers and herdsmen but could not offset the growth in consumption. Besides, the spatial efficiency attenuation resulted from the special natural environments in these regions would inevitably added to the huge transportation costs for the products made in ethnic regions to access the market, causing a sharp drop in the comparative production efficiency. Second, due to the constraints by the traditional culture, stable business channels did not materialize in ethnic regions in Guizhou and thus the products could not create values except for self-consumption, which would directly reduce the cash income of ethnic local people. More severely, it frustrated the enthusiasm of the local people to develop agricultural and husbandry economy and further widened the gap in the income between the people in ethnic regions and the Han regions. Considering the rise in price, it was likely that the actual income of the local people grew negatively. Lastly, it is well know by everyone that the increase in comparative production would first rely on income and then on science and technology. As discussed previously in the book, the financial difficulties in these regions made it impossible to expand investment in agriculture. The scientific research that is suitable for these regions has not been put on the agenda, and is hard to translate into productivity even if investment is made by the country.

Deeper level issues were more frightening. Ecological environment deterioration, natural resources depletion, and the lagging behind in education would, as in the Han regions, constrain the development of agriculture and animal husbandry for a long time in the future, and would cause vicious cycles in some regions. Take education as an example. In the heat wave of urbanization, young people in some regions who had received some school education chose to leave their hometown, leaving behind only those who were old, weak, ill or disabled to continue the agricultural production. In these regions, it was difficult to develop education and more difficult to keep the results of education. Who else do we expect to revitalize the local agriculture? We encountered a deadlock now when it came to the low agricultural productivity, and the key to the deadlock was disappearing. The depletion in natural resources was even more dangerous. However, solutions to reverse this trend were nowhere to be found. Many administrative departments even chose to evade negatively and abandoned these mountainous regions. However, these lands could never be abandoned in essence as we could not give up on these national territories. Although administrative departments left, the local people had to continue their life and suffer in here.

In summary, the current difficulty that agriculture in China is facing is a national issue, and yet ethnic regions in Guizhou have their own uniqueness. If we continue the "sweeping approach" in terms of policy as we did before, even if it can relieve the constraints on agriculture in the Han regions, the situation will deteriorate continuously in ethnic regions.

The crucial reasons in the agricultural issue caused more severe damage to ethnic regions than Han regions. Although ethnic groups had lighter agricultural tax, they had other heavier burdens than the Han regions. This was caused, on the one hand, by the "sweeping approach" in policy implementation by administrative organizations; consequently, the contribution that farmers in ethnic regions made to administrative organizations relative to the total agricultural income was greater in these ethnic regions than in Han regions. On the other hand, as the officials from administrative departments are paid by the state, their level of consumption is equivalent to that in the cities. The existence of huge "price scissors" prevented local ethnic people from realizing the necessary value by selling their products, and yet they had to provide support to the administrative organizations that are in the same size and the government officials who lived a life at the same standard as in the Han regions, which would inevitably lead to minimization of the input in agriculture. Farmers cultivated lands only to survive but not for development. Such a gap in standard of living frustrated the farmer's enthusiasm in farming and would eventually disable the state of social spirit.

As to practice of transferring labor to the cities and setting up township enterprise in the Han regions, it would encounter severe difficulties as well in the ethnic regions in Guizhou. Due to the reasons that were discussed earlier in the book, such as disintegration of products, lagging behind in education, and impertinent scientific research, to operate township enterprises in ethnic regions would be more difficult than in the Han regions, so would be to transfer massive labor force. To develop agriculture in a roundabout way is itself a mistake, and these ethnic regions don't even have room for such a roundabout approach. Without the implementation of special policies to enable local products to realize their values, the agriculture in these regions would not be developed further.

The currently prevailing methodology in developing agriculture across the country is to mobilize the entire society to conduct poverty-relief and "agriculture-aiding" activities, which is still highly influential now. Whenever talking about developing ethnic regions in Guizhou, people always associate it with government-sponsored poverty-relief initiatives and with requesting preferential policies, but not think about how to help the ethnic regions build the capacity of self-accumulation and self-development. Such an approach totally overlooked the actuality of ethnic regions and did not yield much effect after implemented for many years. The approach we recommended was the opposite. We think that we must first solve the issue of self-accumulation and self-development in the ethnic regions before talking about the development in ethnic regions, and only with such a foundation can the poverty-relief and preferential policies be effective. We name this practice as special solution approach due to its divergence from traditional thinking and practice. It is special not because it is a panacea that can not be understood but because it is different from traditional and customary practice. In fact, the history of mankind suggests that no ethnic group or nation could develop itself by relying on the aids from other peoples. No aids or supports would enhance the vitality of an ethnic group without elevating its own capacity in self-accumulation and self-renewal. Such a capacity makes these aids and supports effective. To "create blood" and "transfuse blood" should be properly prioritized. Specifically, we propose that "create blood" should be put on the first place while "transfuse blood" be put on the second. To put aids and supports in the first place is like put the cart before the horse.

China is a big agricultural country and a big farmer's country. The development of China requires coordination between industry and agriculture and between cities and rural areas. The issue in most regions in Guizhou Province is purely an issue of agriculture and farmers. Without a special solution that develops the economy on the present foundation, industrial development would not have a chance of being brought onto agenda, let alone a coordinated development. The most urgent problem that needs to be solved is how to realize the value of the products made in these regions before we can talk about how to realize the fair market value of these products. Only after the second step is finished and capital is accumulated can we talk about industrial takeoff. What worries us is that there has no feasible solutions to ensure the accomplishment of the above three goals. The existing agricultural policies applied in the Han regions would not be able to solve the agricultural issues in the ethnic groups in Guizhou if they are not tailor made to suit these regions but simply resorting to the "sweeping approach" in "agricultural support" and "agricultural aids". For this reason, we feel it critical and necessary to conduct a profound discussion on what special solutions are needed for the development in ethnic regions in Guizhou.

Chapter Nine On Solutions

A lot of researches have been done on the economic development in ethnic regions, the conclusions of which may be referenced or subject to significant revision with the change in time and situation. In this chapter, we will first carry out an analysis on the international and domestic situations that ethnic groups in Guizhou are in, and will further establish the methods in search of the solutions to ethnic economic development based on these situations. Due to the dramatic differences in the traditional cultures and living environments across different ethnic groups in Guizhou, it is apparently a formidable task to find solutions to the development of each ethnic group; therefore, the goal of this book is to make a systematic explanation on the basic principles in policy making. Our readers may find such principles in section ii and iii of this chapter, based on which they can build specific development strategies by taking into account of specific cultural conditions and living environments as well as related policies of individual ethnic groups.

I A Review on the Methods in Search of Solutions

Right solutions come from an accurate understanding of things and the accurate understanding comes from the right thinking that guides the activities to understand things. Obviously, the unsatisfactory economic development in ethnic regions in Guizhou is a result of inappropriate development policies, which, in essence, is attributable to our failure to fully understand the characteristics of the existing economic life of ethnic groups. The insufficient understanding of the economic life in ethnic regions is caused by our thinking logic that does not reflect the current situation in ethnic economic development in the following three aspects:

First, the perspective from which we see things. For a long time in the past, we have studied the economy from the perspective of the developed Han regions but seldom from that of ethnic groups, nor have we ever seriously reflected on our work. The "sweeping" approach has long dominated our practice in the introduction of policies in ethnic group and has not been corrected until today. It is the result of the perspective from which we observe issues, which has in essence never changed. The widespread "sweeping" approach is merely a manifestation of the inappropriate perspective we take when observing things.

Second, inaccurate estimation of power. We have failed to realize that no matter how good or effective the policies are, their power to mobilize resources in the natural environment and the entire society is limited relative to the overall economic activities. The effectiveness of the solutions lies in the fact that they can, by making use of limited power, bring out, mobilize or even directly control the operation of natural environment, continuation of society and operation of economy that are more powerful than their own. It is therefore unacceptable for us to misjudge ourselves as so powerful to be able to do anything, or so weak not to be able to proactively guide or interfere, but instead wait for the accumulation of power, or try to achieve an imaginary goal by leveraging, without principle, other irrelevant forces. We were once enthusiastic about the poverty-relief measures in ethnic regions, believing that the input of materials, manpower and technology would unquestionably lift the ethnic regions out of poverty. Later, we were controlled by helplessness and frustration, and were demanding for the appropriation of more funds and more investment from the state. The seemingly opposing mentalities were in essence a reflection of failure to accurately estimate the power of policies.

Last is about specific policies. We dealt with poverty issues in the past by "completely taking on what ought to be done by the others". We used to copy what we believed were advanced and replace what we believed were backward in the ethnic regions, only to have overlooked that anything deemed advanced had its own range of applicability and foundation. We failed to realize that anything that deemed backward did not mean that it could not survive or did not have any value, nor should it be completely replaced by what we deemed as advanced. The practice of indiscriminate copying dominated our poverty-relief efforts in the past and we never thought of turning around even after we experienced difficulties. Fundamentally, we treated advanced and backward things in absolutely opposite positions. Such a misperception blocked our vision and disabled us to see the creativity in ethnic groups. We must realize that economically backward regions have their own advantages and values, and it is possible that these regions may be modernized via a new path based on their cultural traditions.

What is at the core of these three manifestations is that we attempted to create a mode of economic life in ethnic regions that was identical to that in the Han developed regions, namely to integrate the ethnic regions and developed Han regions ranging from product, variety, quality, price, technical composition and norm, as well as enterprise organization, management, and evaluation. After all, such a thinking was in essence a continuation of the mode of ethnic economic development in the history of Guizhou, which was a "one-way" cross-xiang operation that developed ethnic regions by relying on the Han culture. It restrained our way of understanding ethnic regions in Guizhou. An over-simplified angle of observation resulted in our overemphasis on pushing ahead in the economic activities in ethnic regions but extremely ignored the necessary adjustment and improvement. In the meantime, we pushed for quantitative economic development but ignored the consequence and efficiency of economic activities, or tried to find out the reasons for the drop in economic efficiency. We tended to attribute any obstacles to weak foundation, poor condition and unsatisfactory quality of people, but totally forgot that the survival of enterprises and success of projects depended on the creative labor work of people but not on putting them in care. What caused such a situation was the lack of incentive in our guiding philosophy that prevented us from guiding the people concerned to accurately understand the economic, natural and humanity characteristics of the ethnic regions, let alone built a mechanism of reward and punishment for this reason.

Similarly, the inability of accurately evaluating the operating capacity led to conclusions that overestimated the power of the subjective party but failed to see the power of the objective party, or the comparative strength of one over the other. In project evaluation stage, we tended to enumerate favorable conditions over-emphatically but were often frustrated and feeling helpless in the stage of project implementation. As a result, many projects were kicked off with everyone being enthusiastic but soon turned to a state of half-death as we cooled off very soon. As a matter of fact, the project feasibility studies only stayed at the conceptual, but not profound level with regards to the understanding of natural, economic and humanity environment. Some of us even thought that economic development was nothing but modern, industrial and scientific, and thus we need not consider the reality in local environment. That explained why we have not gathered data on the actual economic life of ethnic groups in Guizhou that were accepted by the academic community after so many years of development efforts in ethnic regions in Guizhou. This was evidenced by the fact that the examples cited in previous chapters in this book have not grabbed the attention from authorities in charge of economic affairs. Up to now, when it comes to the reality in the economic life of ethnic groups in Guizhou, we have not been able to produce complete and sounding materials other than taking abstractly about their impoverished and backward situation. Under such a background, it is inevitable that operators of economic development in ethnic regions overestimated their own power but underestimated the unfavorable elements. Nor could they be able to see the role the ethnic people played in economic development. Subsequently, they seldom sought cooperation with local people, but instead often blamed on their conservativeness and unwillingness to accept new things. This flawed perception is best described as "good at understanding oneself but bad in understanding the others".

Due to the underestimation of the difficulty and complexity in the economic development in ethnic regions, we often resorted to measures that were of a mere blind imitation that were forced upon the ethnic regions and seldom summarized and made use of inherent tradition, knowledge and experience of these ethnic groups. We mistakenly viewed them as outdated and thus must be abandoned, or even attributed our failure to the existence of these traditions without principle. We often unexceptionally forced the universal mode of economic development upon the ethnic regions without giving consideration of the complex nature of cross-xiang operation in the background of economic activities in these regions. We unexceptionally followed the process of determining equipment, workforce, and project across all ethnic regions, or even distained to collect feedbacks from these ethnic regions. When the projects or enterprises that were invested in encountered difficulties, we would try to keep them alive at any cost including carrying heavy fiscal and financial burdens, but never thought of completely cleaning up the mess, let alone re-planned the entire project from the beginning and took in experts from ethnic groups to improve. To the contrary, we used to segregate the projects and enterprises from local people. In the past decades of economic development in ethnic regions, we never seriously conducted studies, or mobilized manpower and material resources to collect data on the fundamental issues such as how to integrate ongoing projects with existing local economic conditions, and how to make them compatible with existing economic activities in these regions.

The deepening reform and opening-up, increasing improvement to laws and regulations in China and the radical change in the world have determined that the economic situations ethnic groups in Guizhou are facing now have changed completely from those in an out-of-control economy, and as a result, the mode of "one-way" cross-xiang operation that dominated our economy for a long time in the past has to be changed. However, the operating inertia continues and makes it extremely difficult to effect a paradigm shift in people's mind. To help solve such difficulties, we feel it absolutely necessary to clarify the economic background that ethnic groups in Guizhou are in at present.

The first important economic situation that ethnic regions in Guizhou are subject to now is the transformation of the national economy into a socialist market economy. The fundamental theoretical foundations and contents of the transformation were clearly stated in the *Decision of the Central Committee of the Communist Party of China Regarding the Economic System Reform*: The goal of reform is, firstly, to break the traditional conception that puts the planned economy to the opposite of the commodity economy, and realize for certain that the socialist planned economy must consciously utilize the law of value and is a planned commodity economy based on the state ownership. In other words, socialist economy is a combination of planned economy and commodity economy. *Decision* made the following precise and profound statement about this important theoretical issue: "The complete development of market economy is a stage that can not be bypassed in the development of society and economy, as well as a necessary condition for the realization of economic modernization in China." "The intensive development of socialist commodity economy will give rise to blindness to a certain extent and thus must be guided and adjusted by plans and managed by administration, which is achievable under the socialist condition." "A planned economy and the development of commodity economy by making use of the law of value are not mutually repulsive but unified. It is thus mistaken to put them in opposite positions." [①] With the deepening of "reform and opening-up", a consensus has been reached in the academic community that China must transform into the socialist market economy. After the goal is achieved, we will have a fully

① Xiguang Yang, eds., *A Probe into Economic Theories in the New Age* (Guangming Daily Publishing House, February 1982), 345-346.

developed and robust market economy. It is also a socialist market economy with Chinese characteristics where the government has the responsibility and ability to regulate and control the economy and to eliminate the blindness in market economy. Such an economic situation will raise four practical questions for the economic development in ethnic regions in Guizhou.

First, from a market economy perspective, it means that from now on the economic development in ethnic regions must be subject to the constraints of the law of value, which will eliminate any practice characterized as "wait for, depend on and request" to upper level authorities or any economic subsidies made for other purposes. Consequently, all the economic consequences caused by an out-of-control planned economy to ethnic regions will be eliminated sooner or later. To seek self-development in ethnic regions, we must consciously understand and follow the law of value, thus offering a good opportunity for ethnic groups to merge into a market economy.

Second, as the country has the ability of regulation and control and the flexibility to choose means of regulation and control, the request by the ethnic groups in Guizhou to restrain the blindness brought about by market economy especially when such blindness affects the self-interests of ethnic groups is sure to be honored and supported by the country, thus winning valuable time and room for adjustment for the economic development of ethnic groups. However, to enable such a superiority to work for the development of ethnic groups, we must first fully and consciously understand ourselves, other ethnic groups, national economic characteristics and effectively seek to achieve self-development through legal means. All these will provide the most ideal political and economic conditions for ethnic groups to develop their economy by subjective initiative and encourage them to break the sealed mode of economy and participate in market economic activities. On the other hand, ethnic groups also face great challenges. They must abandon the habitual way of doing things and thinking and learn to walk by themselves, to understand the external world, other ethnic groups and characteristics of market economy on their own.

Third, this economic structure confirms the co-existence of diversified forms of economy, which undoubtedly provides the domestic political and social background for ethnic groups in Guizhou that have not entered a market economy to continue their own mode of economy via the path that best fits them and to enter the market at the best timing. In the out-of-control planned economy, ethnic groups in Guizhou that were in non-market economy were forced to follow the uniform mode of economy across the country that distorted their own mode of economy, and lived a distorted economic life in an economic background unfavorable to their own economy. All these will be gone. Now, all ethnic groups in Guizhou are able to make use of the law of value consciously, choose the best opportunity and best mode to integrate into the market economy, which will be protected through state laws and regulations. They may, based on their specific needs, choose to set up economic entities in the form of individual, collective, joint stock or joint ventures, or by self-raised funds, as family-owned or village-owned assets, or by ethnic autonomy, and to achieve integration into domestic and international market at the best time through the most convenient means.

Fourth, under the protection of stable state policies, the economic structure is in an economic environment that stably operates in longer term. Its existence ensures that the economic regulation and adjustment and restructuring in ethnic regions have clear and consistent direction, which will never put their own economy in chaos due to economic fluctuation as was the case in an out-of-control planned economy. This is a valuable opportunity for the economic development in ethnic regions and will, without any doubt, boost the enthusiasm of the ethnic groups and thus maximize their subjective initiatives.

The above four aspects will provide conditions to encourage ethnic groups in Guizhou to actively participate in their economic development. The practice that restrained the economic activities of ethnic groups within the planned economy as was the case in "one-way" cross-xiang operations will be discontinued and replaced with a new era when local ethnic people are able to actively participate in their economic development, which will surely push the "two-way" and "multi-way" cross-xiang operations to the onto the front stage in economy.

With the end of superpowers influencing international situations, the world economy is moving toward multi-polarization and regionalization, which raises a series of new issues for the economic development in ethnic regions in Guizhou. Among them, the following five are the most directly related.

First, the development of multi-polarization and regionalization in the world economy has greatly expanded China's foreign economic relations. The countries and regions that for a long time in the past had no direct economic ties with China established stable economic relations with us. Capital from these countries and regions may be directly invested and technologies and equipment may be imported into ethnic regions in Guizhou. The drip irrigation technology from Israel, for instance, has some values for ethnic regions in Guizhou that were plagued by water shortage. The grassland breeding and sheep raising technology in New Zealand and Australia has some values of reference for the ethnic Yi pasturing areas in northwest Guizhou. The mountainous agriculture in the Andes countries and Gabon of Africa has significance for mountainous ethnic regions in Guizhou. Such a big change in the world economy will greatly expand the horizon of ethnic groups in Guizhou, motivate their enthusiasm in proactively understanding the world economic situation, making it possible for them to select, absorb and digest the fruits of advanced economic development from foreign countries.

Second, the change in world economic situation will increase the frequency of economic activities carried out by China in neighboring countries. As a neighbor of Southeast Asian countries, it's the best direction for Guizhou to develop its economic ties with Southeast Asian countries. Besides, as some ethnic groups in Guizhou have ties of consanguinity with those in Southeast Asian nations, economic projects and products have high compatibility, and resistance in economic integration caused by cultural difference is low. Such a trend in development will help ethnic groups in Guizhou open up market in Southeast Asia. In the meantime, it is an ideal shortcut to introduce capital and technology from Southeast Asia, which provides a valuable opportunity for ethnic regions in Guizhou to develop their economy by taking advantage of their respective cultural tradition. It also ignites the enthusiasm of these ethnic groups to proactively seek to know and understand the external world and pushes them to break the closed economic layout.

Third, with the possible solving of the issue for China's accession to the World Trade Organization in the future, the tariff barriers between China and other countries created for various historical reasons will be eliminated soon, making it easier for the export of products from China and import of products from foreign countries. It is possible for the traditional products made in ethnic regions in Guizhou to enter the international market in their original form, which will greatly drive the process for local ethnic people to open their eyes on the world. Meanwhile, ethnic groups will have more room and autonomy in selecting the technologies and equipment to be imported from other countries. Those that are needed for economic development in ethnic groups in Guizhou will be put in place by the first attempt. Under such a circumstance, the conditions for ethnic groups to understand the world will become more ideal and it will be possible for them to control their own economic development, achieve integration with the world market and adjust their own economic operation.

Fourth, many ethnic groups in Guizhou have a considerable number of people from their own group living across tens of other countries as a Chinese or foreign national. Ethnic Miao people, for example, are found now living in Burma, Thailand, Laos, Vietnam in Southeast Asia, US and Canada in America, France and UK in Europe, and Australia. With the great change in world economic situations, these ethnic people will proactively seek to build economic ties with ethnic groups in Guizhou, which will expand channels of economic relations with their counterparts in other countries, build confidence for them to compete in international markets and solidify the social foundation for them to access to international markets. It will also boost their enthusiasm to proactively participate in cross-xiang operations.

Fifth, China is a socialist country. It is also a developing country with massive economic capacity. The superior socialist system and mighty economic capacity provide powerful protection and shield for the economic development in ethnic groups in Guizhou. As a result, unfavorable elements such as economic fluctuation and monopoly across countries in the world are unable to impact ethnic economy in Guizhou, thus minimizing the impacts of unfavorable elements through efforts of the country and guarding the normal start and healthy development in the ethnic economy in Guizhou.

Above all, the great change in world economic situations produces a driving effect on the economic development in ethnic regions in Guizhou, and is able to boost their enthusiasm in participating in cross-xiang operations. The landscape of ethnic economic development in Guizhou dominated by "one-way" cross-xiang operation is starting to shake, paving the way for the establishment of "two-way" and "multi-way" cross-xiang operations.

In addition to the big change in domestic and international economic situations, other factors such as the examples of economic takeoff in developing nations in recent years, fresh experiences in the poverty-relief efforts in China and the results from modern economics research in developing nation's ethnic economy are enough to provide theoretical as well as empirical support to ethnic groups in Guizhou, who will participate in the "multi-way" cross-xiang operating activities as subjective parties to develop their own economy and to realize modernization through a unique path. After many years of poverty-relief work, the government departments in charge of economic affairs have come to realize that the economic development in ethnic regions can not rely on "blood transfusion" but instead should be on enhancing the ability of "hematopoiesis" in ethnic groups. Although further clarification and specification need to be made on the concept and connotation of "hematopoiesis" function by the academia and government departments in charge of economic affairs, it is quite an achievement for us to have reached a consensus on this point. It brings to an end the traditional "one-way" mode of cross-xiang operations and replaces it with a new mode of development that must be able to motivate ethnic groups to proactively participate in domestic and international economic activities.

With this in mind, to develop the "hematopoiesis" function of the ethnic groups should include four indicators of measurement. First, this ethnic economy has the ability to self-support its stable continuation and development on rolling basis without external economic aids, or in other words, without supply outside the law of value. Second, the ability of continuous recovery and renewal of natural resources in the living environment of each ethnic group under the precondition of ensuring its normal economic operation. Third, the ability to integrate with external environment through self-adjustment, including product, equipment, technology, resource acquisition and utilization etc., especially the ability of accepting, digesting and absorbing external technologies. Fourth, the adaptability of ethnic cultures with the developed economy, or the economy after transformation, has reached a relatively stable state.

We think that we must not overlook any of the four aspects. The attainment of a balance of relative stability among the four aspects is an indicator that this ethnic group has gained the true "hematopoiesis" function. Such an indicator system symbolizes that this ethnic group in essence has attained the qualification to participate in cross-xiang operating activities with the status of a subjective party.

A booming East Asia characterizes today's economic situations, symbolized by the rise of Asian "four little dragons". Thailand, one of the "four little dragons", offers value of reference for the economic development in ethnic regions in Guizhou. Before it became one of the four little dragons, Thailand was a standard agricultural society, a country that defined Buddhism as its state religion and an unquestionably monarchy. It suffered tremendously while developing its economy, which resembled the process of economic development in ethnic regions in Guizhou. Besides, it has ties of consanguinity with some ethnic groups in Guizhou in cultural origin. Other than the fact that Thailand is closer to the sea, it is in no better position than these ethnic groups in Guizhou. As to the factor of proximity to the sea, it is by no means an unbridgeable constraint for the economic development in Guizhou as China is a unified socialist country that has achieved true ethnic equality across ethnic groups. For this reason, the rapid economic takeoff in Thailand offers valuable experiences for these ethnic groups in Guizhou.

One hot topic in modern economics research is the direction of economic development in developing countries. A considerable number of new theories have emerged around this topic and they surely will play a role in the economic development in ethnic regions in Guizhou if we can discard the dross and keep the finer part.

It has long been held by the academic community in China that the traditional products in ethnic groups are primary commodities, in which a lot of labor hours are input but they are sold at low price; therefore, ethnic groups are in a disadvantageous trade position and this can never be changed. Fortunately, the researches carried out by Western economists on north-south trade in a pure market economic context have arrived at a conclusion that is contradictory to our traditional perception. Among the economists who carried out research on north-south trade, Arghiri Emmanuel is the most renowned who thinks that there is a disparity in the economic status between the south and the north. In fact, the disparity in the wages between the south and the north has shown a tendency of expanding. According to statistics from the UN, the ratio of average hourly wage between the south and the north was 1: 4.8 in 1970 but it climbed to 1: 8.1 in 1978 [①] for the reasons

① Min Tang, eds., *Topics in the Fronts of Modern Economics (I)* (The Commercial Press, that: First, in northern countries, there were unions that were expanding, but such unions were non-existent or not playing their role. Second, although labors could not flow freely between the north and the south, capitals could. Therefore, the return on the capitals should be equal in the north and the south. She stated that the powerful unions in the north kept the worker wages at a high level. On the one hand, higher level of wages led to high level of consumption, which further stimulated the expansion in production and advancement in technology, sending the economy to a virtuous cycle. On the other hand, low wages in the south deteriorated conditions for trade and exposed the south to worsening trade environments. To deal with such a reality, she recommended, as one of her policy recommendations, that countries in the south increase taxes on their exports and thus artificially boost the international price of primary products.①

China has the most superior social system, i.e., socialist system, to ensure that Emmanuel's policy proposal be realized. For the economic interests of our country and ethnic groups in Guizhou, it should be an easy thing for us to raise the export price of the primary products, which will not affect our domestic economic operation and will also yield a positive result of the increase in foreign exchange income. In this regard, the hard-line policies implemented in Japan and South Korea were examples of success.

The problem is whether the agricultural and pastural products made in ethnic regions in Guizhou are competitive in the international market. Economists have offered mature theories on this issue. For example, the researches on *marginal propensity to consume* and on "indifference curve" by Pareto all concluded that a new variety of a product that never appeared on the international market could demand a higher selling price. The primary products produced in ethnic regions in Guizhou happen to fall into this category. As we mentioned previously in the book, ethnic regions in Guizhou are home to many superior agricultural and pastural products that are highly competitive on the international market. These products are produced in an environment free from any chemical material and thus can pass any stringent test by the international standard on food. They can easily access to the international market and accumulate capital as long as our government provides necessary protection. It is the developed countries like the US, not

Septembe1989, Beijing), 202-203.

① Chonggui Fang, eds., *Western Economics Study* (Shanghai People's *Publishing House, December 1991), 410-414.*

us, that should be worried about this. When we introduced the theories of Schultz and Myrdal in section iv of chapter iii, the quotations already concerned about the threat posted by the superior agricultural and pastural products made by ethnic groups in developing countries to the mechanically produced agricultural products in the US. Now it becomes clear to us that the superior agricultural and pastural products produced in ethnic regions in Guizhou are not a drag on modernization but instead, should be hit products on the international market and valuable assets for the accumulation of capital.

Another issue raised by Emanuel was the social function of unions. It should not be a problem either in the economic development in Guizhou because of the existence of complete sets of laws governing the autonomy in ethnic regions in China as well as regulations protecting the rights and interests of ethnic groups. As long as we can keep improving the administrations of economic management in ethnic groups, intensifying education of law dissemination, enhancing the level of consciousness and ability in learning and using laws among ethnic people, we can successfully replace the social function played by unions in developing countries, or even better, because we are a socialist country that has achieved ethnic equality. However, another issue that was not mentioned by Emanuel should not be overlooked. Due to the implementation of planned economy in China for a long time in the past, the administrative departments governing foreign trade in China, like all other administrative departments in China, became overstaffed and clumsy, and thus caused inappropriate interception of resources by administrative departments of each level. Today, it still remains an issue whether the majority of profits from selling products made in ethnic regions in Guizhou is allowed to be kept by local people after tax payment. Fortunately, we believe that the reforms that we are carrying out now such as civil servant system and government downsizing will play a positive and effective role in this aspect.

One more ideological issue must be clarified as well. China is a socialist country and it is an inseparable part in our national policy to safeguard the basic need in the livelihood of its residents. Consequently, whenever we talk about large increase in specialty agricultural and pastural products made in ethnic regions, some people would link that to safeguarding the basic need in the livelihood and worry that it would destabilize the economy in developed regions. Admittedly, this is an unnecessary concern. First, these specialty products are low in output and will never be big enough to threaten the developed regions. Second, such products mainly target the high-end consumers in the international market and thus would, in principle, generate pressure on domestic market. Third, even if only a limited amount of products are sold in the domestic market, they are sold primarily to the high-income consumers and thus would not produce any pressure on the people in general. Lastly, such a policy has the nature of supporting the economic development in ethnic regions in the form of aids by following the law of value instead of direct economic subsidies. It is thus feasible from the perspective of the nature of China. Under Emanuel's framework, it is not difficult for us to tell that the background where ethnic regions in Guizhou are in now happens to the best for the subjective parties in the "two-way" and "multi-way" cross-xiang operations.

Among modern economic theories in the West, the "innovation" theory put forward by Joseph Alois Schumpeter is another that is meaningful to us. As a figure whose academic thoughts were extremely complex, Schumpeter has attracted widespread criticism in the Chinese academic society especially through his defense for the capitalist system and his refutation of the Marxist standpoint as well as his disguised replacement of concept of socialism. ① It is by no means a perspective of historical materialism to indiscriminately obliterate the influential academic thoughts from the West, the rational part of which should be treated justly. We may choose to introduce, process, transform, digest and absorb the parts that have value of reference. Schumpeter's "innovation" theory falls into this category.

Some Chinese scholars have summarized the basic contents of the "innovation" theory as follows. According to Schumpeter, "innovation" is the creation of a new production function that is a combination of production elements by a certain ratio: $P = F(A, B, C \ldots N)$, where P denotes output, A, B, C … N denotes the accumulation of productive labor service or production elements. The so-called "innovation" is to introduce a "new combination" of production elements and production conditions into the production system. Specifically, it includes the following five scenarios: First, to introduce a new product or new quality of a certain product; Second, to adopt a new

① (UK) Mark Blaug, Paul Sturges eds., *Who's Who in Economics: A Biographical Dictionary of Major Economists* (Economic Science Press, October 1987), 567.

production method; Third, to open a new market; Fourth, to gain access to the new source of supply of a certain raw material or half-finished product; Fifth, to implement a new form of enterprise organization, e.g., establish a monopoly or break a monopoly. Therefore, "innovation" is an economic rather than a technological term. An invention is not qualified to be labeled as "innovation" unless it is applied in economic activities. By Schumpeter's definition, an inventor may not necessarily be an "innovator", and only those who take risks to be the first to bring an invention in the production system are qualified as "innovator". Schumpeter name the proponents and conductors of "innovative" activities "entrepreneurs" who are the economic subjects in a dynamic economy and are different from the operators and managers who manage an enterprise by traditional methods. Entrepreneurs must be willing to take risks with entrepreneurial spirit, be innovative, and constantly propose and carry out "innovative" activities. ①

Schumpeter's fame in the economist's community in the West won him many followers, some of them developed on his theory to give rise to two new sub-theories. One studied institutional evolution and formation and was given the name of "institutional innovation" economics while the other studied technological evolution and promotion and was thus named "technological innovation" economics. The latter expanded Schumpeter's theory by starting from the research on the technological innovation, monopoly, competition, and the enterprise relationship. It had three major components: First, level of competition, scale of enterprise and power of monopoly were three key elements in determining technological innovation. Level of competition necessitated "technological innovation". Every enterprise must innovate in technology to defeat its competitors, protect and develop itself and gain more profits. Consequently, the fiercer the competition, the more necessary and urgent the technological innovation. The size of the enterprise not only directly affected the ability of "technological innovation" but also affected the size of the market prospect. The bigger the enterprise, the larger the market its technological innovation was able to create. The higher the level of monopoly and the tighter the control it had on the market, the more difficult for other enterprises to imitate, and the more lasting the benefits from the technological innovation. Secondly, an optimal

① Chonggui Fang, Bocheng Yin, eds., *A History of Economics* (Fudan University Press, August 1989), 399-400.

market structure for a technological innovation is one in between monopoly and perfect competition, i.e., a market in a “medium degree of competition”. Thirdly, there were two types of technological innovations under the optimal market structure: those that were driven by monopoly and those driven by competition.

Schumpeter’s “innovation” theory was based on a market of full competition. The economists of “institutional innovation” put forward the second-generation “innovation” theory that was different from Schumpeter’s by introducing institutional evolution into the process of economic growth based on the monopoly and competition theory in a capitalist society. They defined the “institutional evolution” as evolution and reform made to existing systems by innovators for the purpose of gaining extra benefits, such as joint-stock company, union system, social insurance, establishment of state-owned enterprises etc. Factors that affected “institutional innovation” included the change in the size of the market, development in production technology, and the change in the expectation of income by certain social groups, etc. ①

Although it seems that Schumpeter’s “innovation” theory has nothing to do with economic activities by ethnic groups in developing countries as he discussed general laws of economics under the context of a perfect competition, a further analysis on the kernel of this theory reveals that he understood the term “innovation” as one that did not exclude ethnic groups in developing countries from participating in innovation activities. Therefore, in principle, his theory should also apply to developing ethnic groups. The five aspects of “innovation” as illustrated by them, for example, may be partially attainable to ethnic groups in Guizhou even in current situations. Specifically, it is obviously impossible for ethnic groups to adopt new production methods in existing conditions as the traditional culture has not been integrated with modern science. However, it is absolutely doable based on the above analysis if we bring the traditional products produced by ethnic groups to the market so that new markets can be opened up. With regards to the provision of new quality for a certain product, as ethnic groups in Guizhou have long been in a natural or self-sufficient economy, their traditional agricultural and pastural products are completely new to both the international as well as domestic

① Sifu Cai, Yansheng Zhang, eds., *An Introduction to Economics of Development* (Beijing College of Economics Press, March 1992), 141-142.

markets, their access to the market by following the law of value is, in itself, a provision of new quality of a certain product. They have not been able to do this as of today not because of the existing mode of production in ethnic regions, but because of the circulation. As these ethnic groups are in a natural economy with inadequate circulation of commodities, which are under the control of the subjective parties in “one-way” cross-xiang operations, it is natural for the subjective parties to avoid their weaknesses and fully play to their strengths on the targets that they can control from the perspective of protecting their own interests to maintain their position as subjective parties. The agricultural and pastural products produced in ethnic regions are, without any doubt, the weaknesses to the subjective parties in the operation, and as a result, their values are intentionally concealed in circulation. The dispute over the “little red sticky” mentioned earlier in the book that is a specialty product in ethnic Miao regions in Gaopo of Guiyang city provides an evidence in this regard. If these ethnic Miao people were able to directly enter the markets in the developed Han regions by gaining the status of a subjective party in “two-way” cross-xiang operations and were able to play to their own strengths, such specialty products would become new quality of a certain product. In this process, ethnic groups are carrying out “innovations”, and thus the huge profits brought by these innovation activities would remain in their hands.

Gaining the status of the subjective party in cross-xiang operation is, of course, the basic necessary and sufficient condition for achieving innovations similar to the agricultural and pastural products in the market economy, and yet it does not warrant solving all the problems without tackling the issue of integration between certain products and the ethnic culture of the objective party. Schumpeter did not address the necessity of this condition as his discussion revolved around same-xiang instead of cross-xiang operating activities. The analyses in the previous chapters have made it clear that products from heterogeneous ethnic groups would not be turned into commodities without integration in the culture and being included in the consumption channels of the ethnic group concerned, which would render the innovation meaningless. Therefore, this issue must be solved if any traditional product from ethnic groups in Guizhou is to be made the target of innovation in cross-xiang operations. The completion of innovations requires a profound and well-executed research on the culture of objective parties in the operation, followed by screening from their own products the ones that could be targets of integration.

Fragrant pigs, a traditional product in the ethnic Miao region in Yueliang Mountain, were mentioned earlier in the book and have attracted the attention within and outside the country. The sale of breeding pigs alone has generated huge profits. Although it looks like a great success, we view it a disastrous defeat based on the theoretical framework of Schumpeter. These breeding pigs are results of hard work of tens of generations. Before their use value is fully displayed, these pigs are not commodities and thus are not protected by the economic laws and patent laws; therefore, they are not the targets of innovation. Now, this technological invention has become a commodity and fallen under the protection of economic and patent laws. Under such a circumstance, the first thing we should do is to seek the protection of patent laws of the country by applying for patents, other than rush to sell them, or voluntarily slashing price among ethnic Miao people that would hurt the interests of the local people. A trade monopoly alliance needs to be established that controls the sale of breeding pigs at a high price due to the patent. In other words, it relates to one of the five innovation contents, i.e., "a new form of enterprise organization". Unfortunately, no one has ever thought about how this should be done, nor has anyone started to do so. The "entrepreneurs" advocated by Schumpeter have not risen from the parties concerned. In the administrative departments of each level, those that are in charge of ethnic affairs should be the ones that best understand the laws and know how to protect the ethnic interests by these laws, and yet they have not taken any initiatives in this aspect. This is unfortunate. It is apparent that promulgation of laws is not enough to drive the economic development in ethnic regions without the emergence of local representatives who know how to apply these laws.

The theory on "institutional innovation" put forth by Schumpeter's followers also has unfathomable value for the economic development in ethnic regions in Guizhou. It is the view of the theorists of "institutional innovation" that "all reforms to the existing systems that would bring added benefits to the innovators fell into the category of institutional innovation." Our previous analyses indicate that even in current conditions, ethnic groups in Guizhou are likely to become innovators. What are lacking is "institutional innovation" if the innovators are to be the real beneficiaries. Now, the forestry plantations in ethnic Dong regions in Guizhou are following relevant policies implemented since the “reform and opening-up”, i.e., a contract system with remuneration linked to output, which will undoubtedly cause a dispersive right of operation. As we discussed in chapter five, forestry plantations must be run in a massive and closed operation for a long cycle. The dispersive operation does not meet such requirement. Therefore, the revitalization in the forestry plantations in ethnic Dong groups depends on institutional innovation. Apparently, it was based on the general practice in the West that Schumpeter’s followers advocated to initiate institutional innovation through unions, joint-stock companies, social insurance system etc. Given the historical development in ethnic Dong regions, we believe it is an acceptable and easily achievable target of reform to implement an intensive operational mode across villages and communities. Once it is finished, we think it is absolutely attainable for the ethnic Dong people to secure a position of the subjective party in cross-xiang operations. The key to the success of this innovation task also depends on how we may use the laws and regulations currently in force. What the ethnic Dong people are urgently needed now is the “entrepreneurs” advocated by Schumpeter.

In summary, Schumpeter’s “innovation” theory is extremely rich in content and has multiple significances in both theory and practice to the economic development in ethnic regions in Guizhou. The afore-mentioned examples are merely a small part of them. It may not be difficult for our readers to link the innovation in theoretical environment as proposed by the theorists of “technological innovation” to the socialist system and socialist market economy in China, as they are identical to a certain extent when it comes to “innovation”. Due to space limitation and our trust in our readers’ ability to draw inferences about other cases, we will not elaborate on this issue.

From the analysis provided in this session, our readers should realize that ethnic regions in Guizhou are fully capable of becoming a subjective party in cross-xiang operations, which is permitted and protected by the socialist system and related laws in China, and also favored by the current international environment. Consequently, it is our belief that the key strategy in the economic development in ethnic regions in Guizhou is that we must turn the traditional “one-way” cross-xiang operations into “two-way” or “multi-way” operations. “Two-way” cross-xiang operation is a mode where each party in the operation is both the subjective and objective party relative to the other. This mode is made possible by the insurance of the socialist system and the quality of people, namely the "entrepreneur innovators" in Schumpeter's theory. The insurance provided by the social system is well in place in China and any imperfection is believed to be gradually improved in the process of deepening the reform. What is hard to predict is the quality of people, which is missing in the ethnic groups in Guizhou. Therefore, the key solution must be accompanied by specific ones, i.e., the specific strategies aimed at creating innovators. We will leave the discussion of this issue to the following two sessions.

II The Co-existence of Entirety and Disequilibrium

A basic precondition for understanding, namely the relationship between economic activities and the whole society, or the status of economy on overall society, needs to be further clarified before we start the discussion of specific solutions. This issue was addressed in chapter three when we analyzed the cultural structure, and yet we need to further emphasize that all economic activities, regardless of the range and intensify of their influences, are always a tiny component of the entire social system. Economic success does not necessarily symbolize the success of the entire society while economic failure is irreparable by its own force. Eventually, economic problems must be solved through the operation of the entire society. Pure economics researches, macroeconomics or microeconomics, can not bring the entire society, or not even all fields of economics, within the scope of their study. Instead, they can only bring some prominent issues in the economic operation, such as wage, unemployment, inflation, etc., under discussion. The prescriptions they write subsequently are only effectively meaningful within the reach of the government or certain economic power groups within the range of a specific time frame and scope.

Keynes proposed to solve the problem of inflation and unemployment through government intervention. Friedrich A. Hayek, to the contrary, advocated against any government intervention and proposed to curb inflation and bring down unemployment rate by free competition among private banks that are permitted to issue currencies.[①] Facing the same

① *Foreign Economics Review*, compiled by the Department of Economics of Peking University (Shanghai People's Publishing House, February 1982), 294-296.

problem in the markets that are fully mature, they wrote prescriptions that sharply contrasted against each other, which would definitely dumbfound any outsiders. The issue would become much clearer, however, if we view economy as a sub-system in the entire social system and view any blockage in economic activities, such as unemployment, as an even smaller sub-system, just as was reiterated in previous text. The fact that Keynes and Hayek provided different points of views and solutions to the same problem was simply because they were in different social backgrounds where unemployment occurred in different social environments and thus should be treated differently. In fact, this was a natural phenomenon determined by the nature of economics discipline and thus should not be surprising. What is important is that we must not mechanically copy and try to apply their conclusions in our society as we are facing different backgrounds of social entirety.

Another issue is derived from such an understanding, which is the relationship between cross-xiang operating activities and the society of the objective party in cross-xiang operations. The society of any objective party is, without any doubt, a self-improvement system. Any cross-xiang operating project, regardless of the scope it impacts and the economic capacity it mobilizes, can only affect a limited sphere in the economic life. It is therefore unrealistic if enterprises attempt to drive the social development in ethnic regions by individual investment projects. On the other hand, any cross-xiang investment project will not always yield positive effects on the society of the objective party. Lewis was more objective when he admitted that both positive and negative impacts existed regarding this issue. According to him, we had "no reason to expect that traditional departments can always benefit from the expansion of the modern departments; the economic system has the power to benefit as well as hurt the traditional departments, the end result of which may be poles apart under different circumstances. The expansion of modern departments may benefit the traditional departments in four ways, namely, to provide employment opportunities, share physical equipment, disseminate modern ideology and system, and cross-trade, each of which includes some unfavorable elements."① Here, we want to express our appreciation to Lewis for his frankness. His impartial scholarly demeanor helps us understand the objective significance of investment in cross-xiang

① Arthur Lewis, *Dualism in Economy*, (Beijing College of Economics Press, March 1989)

operations and enables us to see the fatal stages that operators in cross-xiang operations tend to overlook, and keeps us from deviating from the right track when making specific solutions.

Honestly, each investor cares about the issue of interests and each has to touch the social system. However, the results of the operation are by no means an issue of pure interests but would trigger a series of other social issues. Hence, investors would leave behind them a chain of social issues at the time of making profits, some of which are good and some are inevitably bad. Since the investors only care about profits, the remaining issues, being good or bad, must be handled by the society of the objective party in the operations. If properly handled, investment can continue; otherwise, no one is able to make further investment. It is the subjective wish of everyone that cross-xiang operations last stably. Therefore, our operating activities have to focus on achieving limited goals, on the things within our capability and be on constant alert whether the negative impacts have gone beyond our control. Once they are out of our control, we are more likely a hindrance than a help. Based on this understanding, specific solutions must be on two parallel footholds. First, we should not replace the role of the objective party in the operations to adjust and control the situation so that a steady social background is to be provided to ensure the continuation of our operation. Only in this way can cross-xiang operations eventually lead to a mutual prosperity across ethnic groups. Second, as any operating activity can only touch a limited sub-system in the society of the objective party, we must not demand that cross-xiang operations resolve all issues and problems, nor should we exaggerate the real benefit of these activities. Instead, we must consider them as they stand, both the good and bad sides of them. In other words, we should not expect to push forward in all the fronts and treat each one of them in the same degree of priority, but should try to focus on one sub-system in the social system of the objective party. Each of the footholds is like one side of a coin and is thus equally important. For the former, we think that specific solutions must be devised to maintain the entirety of the objective party in the operation. For the latter, we must take an approach that pushes forward in different fronts at different speeds.

It now becomes clear to us after going through the previous chapters that any party in cross-xiang operations contains three major elements of culture, background and policy. We have further clarified that culture is a network system with complex structure. Background is the space for cultural operation and it also contains secondary artificial elements that are often shaped by culture. Policy is the behavioral norm enforced by the state within the specific range of time and space. However, consequences of operation will inevitably concern relative culture and background, and will create multiple impacts with contents for which operators can not be fully and completely responsible. Efforts to adjust and control through polices are not able to solve all the issues. They must be digested and absorbed through cultural operation to reach a new round of dynamic equilibrium before a new round of investment can be made. Therefore, to cross-xiang operators, the series of activities in cross-xiang operations always alternate from equilibrium to disequilibrium and then another round of equilibrium. As any cross-xiang operating activity must depend on the objective party to provide a stable social background that is only attainable through cultural operation, it is thus a pre-determined principle to maintain the entirety of objective party to ensure the continuation of any operating activity.

Following this principle, it is easy for us to tell the flaws in our practice of economic development in ethnic regions in recent years. The elements we considered were too limited and artificially viewed as static. For example, when we saw that ethnic regions were very poor, we believed they could not accumulate enough capital for the establishment of modern processing factories, which we also thought could make money. Once such a thinking was turned into a resolution, it was easy to acquire loans in a system like ours. The construction of factory was soon kicked off, only followed by a series of unexpected problems that stunned the operators. Receiving loans of course could enable them to buy equipment, but not necessarily help them find suitable people, nor would it guarantee that the purchased equipment could operate normally in a new environment, or realize their value, or turn the project profitable even after their value was realized. We also hired some employees. The factory could pay them wages but could not control their social relationships. It is obviously impossible for them to be disciplined by the factory without considering their social background. In addition, the supply of raw materials and distribution of products also related to many social issues. None of them was replaceable and was within the total control of the operators. The factories could not offer any help but would have problem surviving in the new environment. As quite a number of government officials in the autonomous prefectures and counties in Guizhou put it, "We are afraid of setting up enterprises as they all ended up dead." This is not a deliberate exaggeration but a reflection of reality in the past that indiscriminately copied the same-xiang operating practices in the cross-xiang operations. When we saw that enterprises made profits in same-xiang operations, we failed to realize that such a profit was obtained in a highly heterogeneous social background. In cross-xiang operations, although the practice remained unchanged, the execution process would touch a complete new society, the reaction of which was totally unpredictable to the operators. It was not until problems rose did we suddenly realize that the capacity we had in hand was not enough to solve these issues. It is thus foreseeable that a considerable number of our development plans would end up in failure despite the laudable motives.

The most reliable method to avoid such a failure is to select the projects that have the least impact on the objective parties in cross-xiang operations, leaving them with enough room for self-adjustment and regulation and allow enough time to digest and absorb our operating activities. People may ask if this is too slow or too passive. Our answer to this question is simple. First, our power is limited and can not take on what ought to be done by ethnic people in their own development. Second, our understanding of ethnic groups and societies is very inadequate and we must deepen our knowledge about them in the process before we take further actions. Third, the issue of development speed should be viewed dialectically. What's the purpose of having a project that moves forward rapidly but can not continue or yield profit? On the contrary, although it looks insignificant from a statistical perspective if we make one factory live on or accomplish one thing, it will be an objective reality in the society of the objective party, play a guiding role, and generate social consequences that can spread across ethnic regions as long as it can survive and last on its own. Consequently, when planning on the social and economic development in the ethnic regions, we should focus on specific target to ensure its survival instead of massive deployment of projects regardless of their sustainability. The former approach would produce much faster and more effective results to the social development in these regions than the latter.

In addition to the strict control on the scale and project in the operations to minimize the level of shock that is brought to the objective parties in cross-xiang operations, we must also give a thorough thought on the issue whether we can find the point for the growth of the project we operates in the society of the objective party. The selection of the projects that have already had a growth point diminishes the shock to the society of the objective party and also significantly brings down the amount of investment. Here, the issue of the size of profit comes into play. It was a common practice in our previous efforts of economic development in ethnic regions that our eyes were glued to the projects with bigger profit (in fact, our forecast) and shorter time to become profitable but distained the trivial matters. However, it turns out that what is critical in the ethnic development is not how much profit we make in a short period of time but about a steady and lasting efficiency. It is no exception to any ethnic group that social development can not be achieved overnight and what matters most is a long-term accumulation. We are not helping the ethnic people if we only stare at the short-term profit but not on its sustainability.

In addition, we must not overlook how mutually compatible a cross-xiang operational project is with the society of the objective party. As any operating activity needs certain objective background to operate, we are isolating ourselves if we don't take the compatibility issue into account. We will hurt ourselves and damage the others if we try to force our way by relying on the sheer capacity.

In a nutshell, the above three specific solutions are to accomplish one ultimate goal, which is to put the objective parties in cross-xiang operations and ourselves in the position of a cooperator. We must not act like a savior who comes here to save the objective parties. This is at the core of operating in entirety that we have mentioned. Certainly, it may look too abstract to talk about the principles. Hence, we feel it absolutely necessary to elaborate systematically with a specific example. Here, we will provide some analysis of the land issue that is relevant in all cross-xiang operations.

All human economic activities are inseparable from lands. It is well known to all that economists in generations from David Ricardo to Schultz all attached great importance to the value of land resources. While we also acknowledge the value of lands, we have noticed that different modes and types of economy make use of land resources differently. Any cross-xiang operating activity needs to have a way of making use of land resources. In cross-xiang operations, the use of land resources is not determined exclusively by the subjective parties but must bring in the factor of how the objective parties use lands. Failure to do so will likely subject the subjective parties to direct boycott and disrupt the inherent economic life of the objective parties, either causing the subjective parties unable to make use of the lands or discontinuing the normal economic life of the objective parties. The subjective parties are often helpless when facing such a situation, which will endanger the normal operation and development of economic activities and would eventually create many unexpected burdens for them while not helping the ethnic groups at all. Guizhou Province has encountered many difficulties of this nature in recent years.

As everyone knows, a system of contracted responsibility linking remuneration to output is in place across the rural areas in China. Such a policy is absolutely necessary and also extremely effective in the Han developed regions, but encounters different situations in ethnic regions in Guizhou. As discussed earlier in the book, the ethnic Dong forestry plantations in southeast Guizhou are famous forestry plantations in southern China. The traditional culture of ethnic Dong people has been highly adapted to such a mode of economic life that is dominated by operating forestry plantations. We have also pointed out that forestry plantations must be operated in a vast area that must be closed for a long cycle time. Therefore, a simple implementation of the system of contracted responsibility linking remuneration to output will undoubtedly lead to the dispersion of land resources and instability in the right of operation of lands regardless of our announcement of keeping the policy unchanged for 30 or 50 years. Besides, such a system is linked to the agricultural output and agricultural tax, but forestry plantations would not start yielding products after tens of years and the products come in large quantity once it begins. No matter how we've adjusted our measures or what promises we've made, we can not satisfy the basic conditions for the operation of forestry plantations for the fundamental reason that the implementation of such a system in such a social background has blown a strike on the entirety of the Dong traditional culture. Although some ethnic Dong people have followed their traditional practice of production to keep planting trees, such a heroic behavior has not been reacted by corresponding social cooperation and thus has not translated into a primary industry in the society. Most of the farmers can only focus on cultivating the lands contracted to them but can not work on forestry plantations. In the meantime, although the country has invested heavily in operating various kinds of forestry plantations, some of which have yielded profits, such a practice puts the country in a position antagonistic to previous forestry farmers. Now, many state-run forestry plantations are plagued with stealthy felling of trees, some even openly, and are in constant danger of forest fire. Needless to say, these problems can be traced back to the previous forestry farmers. By this token, what is critical is neither about the attitude of the upper level governments nor about the amount of investment, but about whether we are able to create the necessary and sufficient conditions in the society for the forestry to operate on its own. With such conditions in place, the forestry in the Dong regions would be developed naturally due to the forestry tradition in these regions; otherwise, the forestry would not be developed regardless of how skillful ethnic Dong people are in forestry operation. The implementation of the system of contracted responsibility linking remuneration to output does nothing but shakes the social foundation for the forestry operation, and frustrates all our efforts in developing forestry plantations in these regions.

Facing such a reality, we think that it is necessary to terminate the system of contracted responsibility linking remuneration to output and activate another set of policies specifically tailored to forestry development, which must include the following contents: First, declare the state ownership of the forestry lands with infinite duration of the right to use these lands under one condition that they must be used for forestry plantations and not for any other purpose. Second, forestry lands must be contracted on hereditary basis by at least a certain scale to a collective group such as a community, a village or several villages, and must not be transferred for a price. The contracted right should be revoked once the original operator leaves the contracted lands to work in other business. Third, an impaired and complete right to operate the forestry lands must be granted to the forestry farmers to make them real legal representatives who are entitled to all the proceeds from the lands after taxes are paid. Fourth, as the forestry lands are contracted to collectives that apparently have their own internal organizations such as religious groups, communities and individuals who later hire workers to operate etc., the government must not intervene in these organizations but only needs to ensure that they really operate forestry plantations. Fifth, the existing forestry administrative departments should be transformed into service organizations and should not be given the right of an administrative privilege or right of management. The execution of these policies would surely drive the development of forestry plantations in these regions.

In the ethnic Miao regions in west Guizhou, the system of contracted responsibilities linking remuneration to output have met different problems from the Dong forestry regions. As the local Miao people in these regions are still in a Swidden cultivation and the right to operate a certain piece of land is not fixed, whether the system is in place or not can not ensure that the corresponding piece of land is being cultivated, let alone to ensure that it is cultivated by a specific household. The system of contracted responsibilities linking remuneration to output is, in fact, a basis for levying taxes rather than a production mechanism. Moreover, the "intermittent" use of these lands enables other ethnic groups to occupy and use these lands while they are in fallow, which has caused confrontations among ethnic groups and resulted in the flight of Miao people from these regions, as was mentioned earlier in the book. As ethnic Miao people do not think of the right of operation a big deal to them, the implementation of the system of contracted responsibilities linking remuneration to output does not help them, nor does it stop the escalation of civil disputes over land usage. We mentioned in chapter five that we may give rise to a new type of economy in the non-agricultural regions if scientific researches lead to the relative stability in the sphere of land usage in a Swidden cultivation mode of economy.

Following this train of thought, we think that to the ethnic Miao people in this region, other than mechanically push to implement the system of contracted responsibilities linking remuneration to output, we must devise specific land policies with the following contents. First, clarify in the form of policy that local Miao people have the right to infinitely use the lands not suitable for agricultural farming. Second, correspondingly, the tax may be levied by specifying a certain quantity of physical products that is to remain unchanged for a long time. Specific methods should be worked out by local Miao people internally. Third, disputes over lands may be resolved through consultation on the condition that the existing interests of ethnic Miao people are not hurt. Fourth, the economic development in these Miao regions should be achieved through the enhancement of efficiency in production by scientific researches, but not through forcing them to "turn hillsides into terraced fields", or plant rice. Nor should we force them to change their traditional mode of cultivation, or fix the segregation of lands by administrative orders. These proposals are aimed at maintaining the entirety of the economic life of these ethnic groups and, based on this, to ensure the flexibility in positively guiding their production. Only by doing so can we make sure that our policies are adapted to their local specifics and eventually be implemented.

It is widely agreed for the sake of ecological protection that we must return the grain plots to husbandry in the upper reaches of Wujiang River in northwest Guizhou. To put such a consensus into practice, the issue of the system of contracted responsibilities linking remuneration to output is in the way as well. The lands that are turned from grain plots into pasture apparently can not be contracted to individual households or linked to corresponding state taxation, making the target of returning grain plots to husbandry a meaningless term if the system is forced. More complicatedly, what should we do with the grain fields that scatter in the pastural lands? Should they be contracted to the cultivator or the herdsman? If to the former, who should be responsible for the loss caused from grazing? If to the latter, the herdsmen have to be treated by two different policies, which makes it difficult to implement. New policies must be introduced to tackle this issue, and they must include the following contents. First, the pasture must be planned for the need of animal husbandry. Winter pasture, summer pasture, and nomadic routes must be stabilized on a relative basis, and must be operated in full by ethnic groups who are in the animal husbandry business. Second, taxes must not be levied on the basis of area of lands but on the number of animals owned. Third, ensure that agriculture, husbandry and forestry be compatible with each other in these regions. This point is discussed in chapter six, which may be referenced. Fourth, lands with specific purposes must be strictly followed and should not be used for other purposes. This is completely out of the need of ecological protection while at the same time taking into consideration of the traditional practice in animal husbandry in ethnic Yi and Miao people in the regions.

Some people may feel the above three specific solutions are appeasement or are allowing the free fall of ethnic people in these regions. Our answer to such reaction is: The traditional mode of economic life of each ethnic group is an entirety that can not be easily changed with the introduction of a few policies, investment on a few projects or provision of a small amount of subsidies; otherwise, we could have done that with our efforts in the past tens of years. What we can do is only limited to creating a policy background that enables the continuation of their traditional economic life and thus does not turn them into the burden of the country or the objects of state remedies. The development of these ethnic groups is not made possible by land policies only but has to depend on other supporting policies.

We make such policies due to other reasons. We think that traditional economic life is an entirety, which must be maintained to stabilize the life of these ethnic groups. If we can not ensure the continuity of their economic life style, we will not have a stable social background that is the foundation of further social development. Besides, if the existing life style can not last normally, these ethnic people would have to depend on the reliefs from the state, which is not capable of feeding them all. We need to say that to implement such policies is a forced choice under current circumstances. To replace policies with feelings out of good wishes is not feasible. Although we have only elaborated on the policies regarding the management of land resources in this chapter, more specific policies need to be made based on the principle of development as an entirety. As our readers may draw inferences about other cases from what we cover in this and other chapters, we will not elaborate further. However, we need to remind our readers that no matter what development policies you propose for the ethnic regions, it is critical that the entirety in the inherent economic life of these ethnic groups must be kept as much as possible. Any attempt to resort to mass movements by mobilizing a vast number of people and materials but does not treat ethnic people as an equal partner is doomed to fail. It is not enough to solve the problem, however, if our attention is only on the entirety of the economic life in these ethnic regions as it would lead to another practice, i.e., to push forward on all fronts, the so-called "big push theory" in the academic community in the West. As we discussed in previous chapters, this approach is based on the theory that economic activities are an entirety and investments on individual projects would not have impacts on this entirety. Therefore, a comprehensive push across projects and industries is needed to generate better effects. It is self-evident that the "big push theory" is constructed on the foundation that the objective parties in the operations are to be transformed. This is similar to the thinking that many people in China who work on poverty-relief efforts have. They favor an "impulse" type of poverty-relief and hope to gather all the economic capacity available in hand to launch "quick battles" in the ethnic regions, only to find that end results are unsatisfactory. Learning from these lessons, we believe that we must respect the entirety in the economic life of ethnic groups, and in the meantime must take a disequilibrium approach to gradually build progress.

We made our proposals out of the considerations in the following three aspects: First, the economic lives across ethnic groups in Guizhou are different and thus one approach does not meet all requirements. Each ethnic group needs one key to its economic development. We can not meet our expectations if our capacities are utilized in equilibrium across all fronts. Second, the internal economic structure in each ethnic group is extremely complex, therefore, among different components in the same economic system, some are easy to integrate with the cross-xiang operating projects, and some are not. As a result, some operating projects have favorable points for growth and others don't. From the perspective of operating efficiency, we can only choose the projects that are easy to survive instead of pushing all the projects forward out of the convenience of the subjective party in the operations. Third, the development of ethnic regions depends mainly on the power of their own while the external forces are only supplementary. As long as the economic activities can survive and are accepted by ethnic groups, they would drive the development in other areas. The survival of one project is a triumph to us. To move multiple projects forward at the same time would be difficult for us as well as for the ethnic groups

The approach of moving forward in disequilibrium ensures that we can focus on gradually deepening our understanding on ethnic groups in the operational process, so that we can find the best method to reinforce our achievements and are easy for us to seek cooperation with ethnic groups. To put it more simply, to move forward in disequilibrium means that we would find the key that restrains the development of each ethnic group and make it our main target of offensive, which must be the projects within our capability. Once we are successful, these projects can be operated by the force of each ethnic group and generate rolling effects that would drive the social and economic development in ethnic regions. It saves our efforts and is easier for ethnic groups to accept, thus yielding better results than taking on what ought to be done by themselves. The key to moving forward in disequilibrium is to form a partnership with ethnic groups on the specific projects that have the most apparent driving force and are easiest for us to execute while ensuring the entirety of economic operation in related ethnic groups. It does not mean that we can not execute a few projects at the same time, but to do so is not for the purpose of disrupting the economic life of ethnic groups, nor purely for the convenience of our operation, but instead, because we can find favorable points for the growth of these projects and we can reach a partnership on these projects across ethnic groups.

A considerable number of development plans we are executing now in ethnic regions are conflicting with this principle. Currently, many of our poverty-relief and development plans and working targets are made by different administrative departments, enterprises or public institutions separately without communicating with each other. For instance, educational departments often set hard targets on education such as how many schools to be built, how many students to be admitted and what educational level to be reached etc. Transportation departments put together their own plans that include how many roads to build, which villages are to be connected, and what standards should these roads meet etc. The agricultural departments have their own plans as well that specify a specific output for a certain year, which improved variety to be introduced and promoted, the specific area of hillsides to be converted into terraced lands etc. The administrative departments on the county level only care about how much fiscal revenue or tax money they can collect each year and the target per capita income etc. However, those who make plans often do not know if these plans are executable or how to accurately collect data on the results from the implementation of these plans. The ethnic people, on the other hand, can only follow orders and do whatever is required. The organizers can only passively follow orders from the upper level authorities and simply distribute the money appropriated from the upper level authorities in the desired ethnic regions, or see to it that the development indicators issued by the upper level departments are implemented. Apparently, both sides are in a passive position. Nobody really cares about how many of their efforts would yield actual results.

In fact, of all the projects that are pushed ahead at the same time, some of them are meaningless for the time being; some never have a chance of completion; others are beyond our ability. To rush headlong into action only wastes manpower and materials that are returned with a bunch of fake data. A considerable number of the above-mentioned goals, for instance, are empty. Take per capita income as an example. We have not found the indicators that can accurately measure the ethnic groups in a non-market economy even today. Such a development target is, for the most part, meaningless for ethnic groups without a fully-developed market as currencies are subject to devaluation and prices are subject to fluctuation. A 20% rise in grain price would drive up the per capita income by 20% overnight without any development plans or efforts. What's the meaning to have such a development plan? Another example is the increase in the grain output which is also an unreliable figure. During the era of people's commune, we had accountants in all levels who worked on the statistics, but today, it is impossible for the statisticians, if any, to collect data on grain output by visiting each household. Even some "hard" indicators are not obtainable. The road construction, for instance, seems to be an indicator that can not be misled. However, what we talk about should be the roads in working condition and are in operation, but not symbolic ones. When submitting results, we only emphasize on their symbolic meaning but not their actual economic benefit, let alone how they would survive later. It is just because these plans are made separately by different departments, such an approach of moving forward in equilibrium is crippled by the issue of discordance in the first place. Although subjectively, we want to give a push to the economic development in ethnic regions, such a goal is not attainable in objective term but instead busies the related ethnic people who are at lost, not knowing how to cooperate.

In recent years, we've promoted the idea of a comprehensive treatment of mountain, water, field, forest, road and village, which is a good idea and has played a valuable role in the development of ethnic regions. However, in specific practices, we've followed the old way of doing things and chased various indicators by spending money in different angles, creating a greater symbolic meaning than actual significance. In fact, the comprehensive treatment needs to focus on one thing: how to convince ethnic people to integrate it into their own social activities and continue so that the goal could be achieved naturally after a while. Following the old practices, it would turn out that we spend money and ethnic people follow our orders. The slogan of comprehensive treatment is, as a matter of fact, pushing ethnic people to do what we ask them to do, and the outcome is of course unsatisfactory.

There are successful cases, one of them being the promotion of growing winter vegetables in rice fields in Luodian County. In this case, our people did only one thing which was to prove hands-on to the local Buyi people the feasibility of growing winter vegetables in rice fields. This breakthrough, along with a favorable social market environment and unobstructed commercial channels connecting urban and rural areas, the tradition of doing business in Buyi people, and the fact that it did not disrupt the primary economy in the Buyi region, have created a favorable growth point for growing winter vegetables in this region. Once the technical breakthrough is made, it would soon produce snowballing effect in the Buyi society and spread rapidly. In the meantime, it would drive the Buyi society to make subsequent adjustments. For instance, people would voluntarily build roads to facilitate the transportation of vegetables, and would choose to learn Mandarin to facilitate the sale of vegetables. The neighboring villages that used to have disputes now start to cooperate for their common good. In summary, once a breakthrough is made and the target of main assault is identified, the social development in ethnic regions would be come naturally without us having to attend to everything personally. To locate this point needs more than technical people but concordant efforts between natural and social sciences, as well as joint efforts across administrative departments, scientific and technical people, and related ethnic groups. Meanwhile, each functional department only needs to provide service by attending to their own function.

The production of premium tea in Leishan county is another example. The key to its success is that the operator of this project has focused on distribution and fine processing technique instead of aimlessly putting up all kinds of requests to ethnic groups. Putting efforts on distribution has driven the tea production by local Miao people. Meanwhile, the Miao society has been mobilized to make corresponding adjustments. Consequently, many things that we used to do by ourselves can now be solved successfully through social adjustments in the Miao society. Following this example, to develop the animal husbandry in ethnic groups in northwest Guizhou, we don't need to specify how many cattle each household must feed, or even specify what fine breeds have to be used, nor do we need to make any economic promises, or specify which administrative department has to provide what kind of service. The followings are key: First, to open up distribution channels to ensure that local people can make profit from selling cattle; second, to change the perception of the local people so that they would not feed old cattle. It is feasible if we start from one of the two under the condition that we must take into account the cooperation between the two. If local people can make profit from selling cattle, they would come to the functional departments if they have any questions.

In a nutshell, to move forward in disequilibrium is, with an implicit precondition that ethnic groups are treated as partners in economic development, to identify the stages where cultures of related ethnic groups can be made compatible and integrated, and the growth points for projects while ensuring that the original means of production continue normally. Therefore, to push forward in disequilibrium and to develop in entirety are policy measures that are mutually supplementary, the unity of which is key to produce a force that drives the economic development in ethnic regions.

III The Co-existence of Exchange of Commodities at Equal Prices and Self-Optimization

As we point out in section I of this chapter, the fundamental solution to the development in ethnic regions in Guizhou is to change cross-xiang operations from "one-way" to "two-way" or even "multi-way" operations. Both parties in the "two-way" cross-xiang operations have their own advantages and disadvantages in the social background, level of economic development and natural and living environment. Their starting points vary as well. The principles of entirety and disequilibrium push-forward discussed in previous section must be adhered to mainly by the party in a higher type of economy and with a better developed market, although it has important significance for the party in a lower type of economy and less developed market. To maintain the entirety of the economic system is not only the responsibility of the subjective party. The objective party also needs to selectively cooperate with the subjective party in its operating activities to minimize the shock and maximize the profit. For other projects, it would avoid and boycott but not treat all economic activities from the subjective party in equilibrium. We will continue discussing the basic contents of such a solution from the perspective of the party in a lower type of economy and with a less developed market.

When the party in a lower type of economy becomes the subjective party in the "two-way" operations, it should act the same as the party in a higher type of economy. It must, based on its own characteristics, strive to secure a subjective position in cross-xiang operations and play to the full of its strengths to ensure the stable continuation of the "two-way" cross-xiang operations. To meet this need, the following three inter-related issues must be clarified. First, the basic thinking logic in the selection of projects when a party in a lower type of economy participates in cross-xiang operations. Second, the analysis of pros and cons in the operations and corresponding solutions. Third, what favorable policies can the relevant ethnic societies adopt in macro-control?

Due to the limited energy that the party in a lower level of economy is in control of in cross-xiang operations, its production technology is hard to integrate with the ethnic groups in a higher level of economy, which, intensified by a less developed market, makes it unfeasible for the party to compete with sheer economic capacity and energy in cross-xiang operations. Neither is it possible to seek profit rapidly from price fluctuation. Apparently, when making selections on operating projects, we must try to avoid similar projects. We, on the other hand, need to see that they also have their own strengths. First, these ethnic groups have a higher ratio of self-sufficiency and a higher assurance factor. Subsequently, the products produced in these regions are not prone to sharp price volatility in general. Second, a relatively ample supply of labor with a lower wage level. Third, their social backgrounds are relatively stable and thus are not easily affected by the radical change in economic situations from external world. In the cross-xiang operations, they need a lower investment and thus operating cycle can last longer. These characteristics may be favorable or unfavorable conditions in different situations. Generally speaking, the ethnic groups in a lower type of economy that are the subjective parties in "two-way" cross-xiang operations may be inferior in the "one-way" cross-xiang operations.

When ethnic groups in Guizhou are in a subjective position in "two-way" cross-xiang operations, namely, when their economic characteristics are in a favorable environment, a considerable number of elements are able to participate in the economic activities. Roughly they can be classified into the following types: product, labor, capital, technology, movable production facility etc., whose values can be realized and profits may be generated. The current situations in ethnic groups indicate that in "two-way" cross-xiang operations, not every element is able to participate in commodity exchange, and among those that can participate in the exchange, not every element can generate values and profits. In most cases, it is difficult for ethnic groups in Guizhou to accumulate wealth and vast capital for investment due to under-developed market and the higher level of stability in social life. The values of production facilities in ethnic groups in Guizhou are low due to their low type of economy and a significant part of the facilities are attached to the lands and thus can not be moved freely as the equipment and facility in an industrial society. Therefore, the exchange of equipment and facilities is not feasible in general. The production technology in ethnic groups in Guizhou has been highly adapted to its living environment and is, in normal situations, hard to play its role if transferred to other ethnic regions. As a result, the technology, if participating in the exchange in cross-xiang operations, will not bring value or profit. Therefore, the contents included in the above three types of elements can not be the objects when ethnic groups participate in cross-xiang operations. As to the exchange of technology, there are three exceptions that can generate values when ethnic groups and ethnic Han groups participate in cross-xiang operations.

First, these traditional production techniques of the ethnic groups may be transplanted and may produce higher economic efficiency in some Han regions under exceptional economic backgrounds where living environment and natural background similar to the original ones can be found. The emigration of ethnic Miao people to Jinggangshan region and their reclaiming and cultivation of lands there, as mentioned in earlier chapters, is an example. Of course, rigorous conditions must be met for this to happen and the economic benefits usually are insignificant. Specifically, the transplant of similar production techniques is made possible under the following conditions. First, with the increase of level of industrialization in the Han regions, people from the Han culture tend to abandon and discontinue farming in the regions with lower adaptability. Jinggangshan, as mentioned earlier, is in such a situation. It becomes clear that with the improvement of productivity and the acceleration of urbanization in the Han regions, an increasing number of mountainous areas in the Han region will be abandoned deliberately. Consequently, the immigration from Miao region into these abandoned regions will expand. Second, as the technical export must go hand in hand with the movement of people, whether an economic transfer in this manner is supported by policies will determine the export of similar production technologies. In fact, quite a number of emigrations of ethnic Miao people to the Han regions in recent years have been blocked out of fear by relative authorities of negative political impacts. The above analyses make it clear that, to the ethnic Miao people, such a migration is normal economic activities and thus should not be tied to political impacts and be interfered. The interference in the migration does not have legal grounds, but rather it is necessary to acknowledge the legitimacy of such activities. Third, such migration activities are subject to the restraints of existing land policies such as the system of contracted responsibilities linking remuneration to output, Forest Law, Law of Natural Resources Protection etc. In the above example of ethnic Miao people who migrated to Jinggangshan, although the lands they reclaimed and cultivated were abandoned by the Han people, they had to pay rent to the Han people who had the contracted right to these lands. Despite the irrationality in such a phenomenon, they could not get around the relevant policies in the contract of land. Fourth, these migration activities, when expanded, may trigger disputes across ethnic groups and may restrain these activities. From the perspective of making use of the territorial land resources, they should be protected by laws.

Second, some craftsmanship of ethnic groups can, in exceptional cases, become the contents of export of technology. All ethnic groups in Guizhou have their unique craft techniques that have become part of their traditional culture and are passed on stably for generations. For instance, the embroidery in ethnic Miao group, lacquer-making in ethnic Yi group and wax printing and handcraft weaving in ethnic Buyi and Miao groups, etc. At the time when the level of machinery production remained low, these crafts were not a sharp contrast against similar ones in the Han regions, and thus did not have much economic value in technology exchange. However, at the time when we are transitioning into a socialist market economy that drives up the level of mechanization in the Han regions, these traditional crafts in ethnic regions have increasingly become more contrasted against those in the Han regions, making the export of such crafts from ethnic regions into Han regions a profitable business and would generate considerable economic benefits for these ethnic people in "two-way" cross-xiang operations. The preconditions for the realization of these economic benefits are similar to the export of products that will be covered in the following text.

Third, there are some productions or operational projects in ethnic regions in Guizhou that can potentially be expanded into a regular industry in the Han region. Currently, some of these projects have emerged in ethnic regions in Guizhou to be a regular industry with a considerably high technical level. Under specific circumstances, these production technologies can be turned to the objects of technology export. Examples include the forestry plantation technology in the Dong region mentioned in chapter three and the specialty agricultural and pastural varieties domesticated or bred by ethnic people in Guizhou. To export such technologies requires certain economic background. The export of forestry plantation technology, for instance, depends on intensified policies on ecological protection and the acceleration of urbanization in the Han regions, which would cause a sharp drop in the density of population in mountainous, especially the steep mountainous regions in the Han region, expanding the bases for forestry plantations. Once it becomes a reality, the ethnic Dong people could fetch bigger economic benefits if they can seize the opportunity and turn the forestry plantation technology to the object of export. The export of technologies on specialty agricultural and pastural products must be based on the economy of the Han region in addition to the use of laws as a weapon as we covered in the first section of this chapter. Generally speaking, if a high growth rate sustains and standard of living increases rapidly in the Han region, the demand for specialty agricultural and pastural products would subsequently expand. Under such a circumstance, it is easier for the export of these technologies to bring considerable profits to ethnic groups. It is also related to the expansion of international market. With the expansion in the international market, it becomes key to have an effective protection over technology transfer to ensure that such technologies make profit in cross-xiang operations. Based on the current situation, it is not an easy mission to accomplish. Lack of understanding of relevant laws by the ethnic people, they often sell these rare products as regular ones instead of transfer them as technological fruits. The autonomous governments in these ethnic regions in China, on the other hand, have not realized the importance of playing a protective role for ethnic people. Therefore, the most urgent task for dealing with this situation is to make this function one of the tasks of the ethnic autonomous governments.

The export of labor has seen much progress in recent years. All ethnic groups in Guizhou have considerable quantity of labor force in the Han regions, generating a certain amount of economic benefit for the ethnic groups. We need to realize, however, that the export of labor from ethnic regions has stayed on a lower level due to that fact that the cultures of these ethnic groups have not been integrated into modern scientific knowledge. As a result, the benefit received from such export of labor is quite limited and is restrained by the state of economic growth in ethnic regions. When the Han regions are in a rapid economic growth that causes labor shortage, the export of labor from ethnic regions in Guizhou would be smooth and profitable; otherwise, it would encounter numerous difficulties. No matter what the situations are, as the economic capacity of ethnic groups lags behind that of the Han region by a huge distance, and the degree of social security in ethnic regions is relatively higher and ethnic people demand a lower wage, the labor force of ethnic groups is more competitive than the same labor force in ethnic Han regions. Consequently, even if the economic growth in the Han regions slows down, ethnic regions in Guizhou still remains at a higher ratio of labor export. For this reason, when we plan the "two-way" cross-xiang operations, ethnic groups in Guizhou may put the export of labor as a stable and long-term option.

We need to realize as well that in addition to positive economic benefit, the export of labor also has three latent economic benefits. First, it deepens the ethnic group's understanding of the Han group and enhances the initiative of ethnic groups in cross-xiang operations, which would drive the continuation and development of cross-xiang operations and fetch many indirect benefits for the ethnic groups. Second, it speeds up the integration between the traditional culture of ethnic groups and modern science and technology, which would enhance the economic capacity and rapidly increase the productivity of ethnic groups. Third, the export of labor can also accumulate capital for the development of ethnic groups to a certain extent, which, of course, must not be overestimated as the accumulation of capital is restrained by many external factors. It is not easy to accumulate capital merely from the wages received by the exported labor force. An effective accumulation of capital often depends on the social mechanism of the specific ethnic group and is not accomplished by the labor export alone.

The economic element that is the easiest to exchange in the "two-way" cross-xiang operations involving ethnic groups in Guizhou is products. Therefore, when the ethnic groups in Guizhou participate in cross-xiang operations, the option that is the most important and stable is the sale of products. We will, thus, give a through analysis of the pros and cons in the export of products by ethnic groups in Guizhou as well as corresponding solutions.

A lot of researches have been carried out by the Western economic society on the analysis of the pros and cons in the commodity trade across ethnic groups in different economic types. Certainly, these researches are carried out in the international background with the developed and developing countries as their research targets, which are essentially different from our research on the commodity trade across ethnic groups in China. They, however, have reference values. For this reason, we will, when introducing their viewpoints, make necessary modifications and supplements, and discard the dross and select the essentials so that we can draw our own conclusions. Among the Western economists who did research on this topic, Emanuel, Lewis, and Ronald Findlay were the most acclaimed figures. Below, we will briefly review their theories.

According to Findlay, "in short-term, the international trade balance is determined by the supply of and demand for products exported to the South and North. The GDP growth rate in the countries of the North is determined by the growth rate in labor force adjusted by the technological improvement and productivity, namely 'natural growth rate'. The economic growth rate in the countries in the South, on the other hand, is dependent on the price ratio in the trade between the South and the North, namely the trade terms. In the short term, if the demand for products form the South is greater than their supply, the trade terms for the South will improve and subsequently the national economy in the countries of the South will grow rapidly. To the contrary, the oversupply of export products from the South will drag down the economic growth of the Southern countries."① Findlay perceived that the economic growth of the party that sells primary products depends on trade terms, which is helpful in analyzing the economic trend of each ethnic group in Guizhou. However, the preconditions for such a conclusion do not include all the characteristics of the trade activities conducted by ethnic groups in Guizhou, the most worth-noting ones are the following three. Fist, Findlay overlooked the difference in the varieties of primary products. In fact, it is intolerable when it comes to the trade in primary products in ethnic regions in

① Min Tang, eds., *Topics in the Fronts of Modern Economics*, 202.

Guizhou. Take grains as an example. The varieties of grain produced in ethnic regions in Guizhou are different from those in Han regions. According to the theory of "marginal effect", ethnic groups in Guizhou are able to win the market by making use of the advantages in variety as long as the Han groups have the purchasing ability. Second, he held that the economic development of the party with a developed economy is determined by natural growth rate, which is not an entire reflection of all the facts. In the North-South trade in the world, developed countries may resort to political and military measures in addition to natural growth rate. When China is concerned, such an unreasonableness in trade or the standoff as shown in the North-South trade in the world arena does not exist. However, another situation exists that puts ethnic groups in Guizhou in a disadvantage. The existence of "price scissors" between industrial and agricultural products as a result of the planned economy for a long time in the past have seriously hurt the economic interests of ethnic groups in Guizhou in an implicit and long-lasting manner, which is not discernable on the surface. Third, as most ethnic groups in Guizhou are still in a natural and self-sufficient economy, the output of their products are strictly constrained by the capacity in their consumption, and therefore would not result in product oversupply in normal situations. The favorableness in the trade terms only produce opportunities but would not cause thread to these ethnic groups. To put it more plainly, a vast demand and wider market for the products produced in ethnic regions by the Han regions will encourage ethnic groups to produce more. In case of situations to the contrary, these ethnic people could change the line of production flexibly and thus would not cause disastrous overstocking of products. Given the above and the development in ethnic regions in Guizhou, the following four solutions are critical and necessary measures. First, help ethnic groups enhance their understanding of the Han market, especially of the products for which the Han market has long-lasting and stable demand, through information service and market surveys, and seek to drive the economic development of ethnic groups through these products. Based on the guiding principle of supporting ethnic groups, we would see more prominent results if we can lower taxes on these products to pave the road for direct trade and to remove the intermediary stages for the ethnic groups with the policy force. Second, it may be difficult for us to completely remove the "price scissors" under our current conditions. Although the primary products produced by ethnic groups are different in variety from those in the Han regions, they are characterized with a premium quality and pollution free. The small quantity of these products determines that they are sold mainly to the high-income people in the Han regions and would not affect the livelihood of common people in normal cases. At the time when we can not completely get rid of the "price scissors", the relaxation of the prices of these products will not affect the overall economy of this country, nor cause instability to the livelihood of urban residents. Consequently, it is urgent for us to totally lift the control on the selling price of these products to allow ethnic people the freedom of asking price and exclude them from the list of grains whose prices are under control. Third, according to Findlay, market opportunities have a great impact on such trades. We should encourage trade organizations to be established among ethnic groups to help them seize opportunities and adapt to changes by organizational forces. The government should not control the specific form of organizations given the diversified ethnic societies in Guizhou. If they are organized around extended families, for instance, the administrative departments should not recognize them by the form of laws but instead should acknowledge their legitimacy. Fourth, as mentioned earlier in the book, it has appeared that ethnic people have started migrating into the Han regions, and the immigrants have maintained social and cultural ties with ethnic people in Guizhou. Subsequently, the above four solutions should, in principle, be applied in these ethnic people to enable those who have migrated into the Han regions to have the similar ideal development opportunities, so that they could benefit from them as well as drive the development of their own ethnic group in Guizhou.

We have discussed the basic viewpoints of Lewis in previous chapters and thus only want to emphasize the relevant part. According to Lewis, the trade between nations in the world is unequal mainly attributable to the different productivity between the parties involved in the trade, and therefore, developing countries can attain an equal position only after their productivity is increased. We have two points to make about this viewpoint of his: First, the nature of the trade carried out by ethnic groups in Guizhou is different from the trade between developing and developed countries. As the trade we conduct across different ethnic groups is based on the realization of equality across ethnic groups in China, the unreasonableness in trade resulted from the gap in productivity may be rectified through adjustment by policies. Second, as we have pointed out in previous chapters, when making the same product, each ethnic group is restrained not only by technologies but also by the culture and background in production due to their different cultural characteristics. Hence, the productivity defined by Lewis is meaningful to a certain extent only when making macro qualitative analysis, and does not fully explain the formation of specific products. In other words, it is inadequate if we think of the realization of equality in trade only from the perspective of productivity. When devising trade policies, we should not only focus on the level of productivity when dealing with the phenomena associated with differing productivities, but rather should take into consideration the factor that the specialty products, such as the fragrant pigs produced in Yueliang Mountain ethnic Miao region that we have mentioned earlier, have been created in ethnic regions over a long time in the past. They are no longer pure products but have already contained elements of technical labor by the Miao people in their efforts of breeding and domestication in generations, and thus should be viewed as technical products and be protected by patents as are the case in the products bred by our scientific research organizations. To accomplish this task, we need to assist the scientific research departments in identifying and registering the specialty agricultural and pastural products produced in ethnic regions in Guizhou, separating their value in use from promotion and determining the correspondent patent level. Those that are directly consumed may be sold by the market price while those that are used as breeding stocks should be sold at patented prices. We may retain and contribute some of profits to development funds.

Emanuel separated the trade zones between developed countries and developing countries into unequal exchanges in broad sense and in narrow sense. He further pointed out that the difference in the wages between poor countries and rich countries caused the inequality in exchange. Due to the formation of international price in production subject to the equalization of profit rates, the amount of surplus value received by rich and poor countries before and after the exchange differed. Commodities made in rich countries would end up in a higher price of production as they not only contained higher wages but also a part of the surplus values of poor countries; commodities made poor countries, on the other hand, had a lower price of production as they had to give up a part of surplus values. The transfer of surplus values was made across the two types of countries through international trade. Apparently, such an exchange was unequal, which was caused by the only reason of difference in wages between the two. Subsequently, Emanuel concluded that the economic inequality in the world was a result of unequal exchange when poor countries had to trade the commodities they made with more labor time with those made in rich countries with less labor time. Furthermore, such an unequal exchange would deteriorate when trade terms for poor countries worsened gradually.[①] This viewpoint of Emanuel's offers some direct practical significance in our analysis of trade activities carried out by ethnic groups in Guizhou. Although his theory was based on the international trade and was not completely the same as the situations we address here, the planned economy that dominated our economy for a long time in the past gave rise to huge "price scissors" in the income between industrial and agricultural labors, and caused unreasonableness in the distribution of surplus values in product exchanges, boosting the prices of industrial products higher than their actual values. To the contrary, the ethnic groups who are in agriculture or animal husbandry would always be put in a disadvantageous position if agricultural or pastural products are traded at prevailing prices. To ensure that ethnic groups have the ability of effectively accumulating capital for the expansion of re-production, we should, to some extent, adopt policies of preferential prices, namely to lower the prices of the industrial products sold to ethnic groups within the tolerance of profitability of related producers until the "price scissors" between agricultural and industrial products are removed.

Facing this reality, ethnic groups in Guizhou must also take more stringent measures of trade management for the sake of protecting their own economic interests. Fundamentally, each ethnic group should have the right to apply control over the overall price on the incoming and outgoing commodities by relying on ethnic autonomous governance to ensure a general balance between the total price on the commodities that go out of ethnic regions and that on the commodities that come in from ethnic Han regions, namely the principle of exchanging commodities at equal prices. Lack of such policies, it is impossible for ethnic regions to accumulate enough capital for further development. The biggest barrier in the fulfillment of such a principle is state civil servants and labors who receive salaries as

① Chonggui Fang, eds., *Western Economics Study*.

the majority of these salaries come from tax revenues collected from selling primary products by ethnic groups and they spend most of the salaries on buying the industrial products from the Han regions. Subsequently, ethnic people use the hard-earned money to exchange consumer products at unfavorable prices from the Han regions, making it impossible for the money to play an effective role in the development of local economy. To tackle this problem, the only solution is to downsize administrative organizations and staff to the extent possible.

Without a doubt, ethnic groups in Guizhou are able to accumulate a certain amount of capital that would send them onto the road of self-development instead of relying on relief funds as long as they can balance the values in the overall incoming and outgoing commodities in trade. To achieve this goal, we think that the development of ethnic regions in Guizhou should take three sequential steps. First, the so-called "dual-track" product structure step. Basically, to categorize the products that each ethnic group makes normally into two types. The first type includes those that meet the need of self-consumption and are not required to increase the commodity rate. The second type includes the products that can integrate with the Han culture and are equivalent of export products, which requires a higher commodity rate. The ratio between these two types of products may be adjusted according to market conditions to ensure that ethnic groups in Guizhou live a worry-free life and in the meantime can accumulate the critically needed capital. On selecting the products with a high commodity rate, they should select to the extent possible the products that demand less transportation capacity but warrant higher selling prices, especially the specialty agricultural and pastural products unique to ethnic groups. For the need of establishing such a structure, each ethnic group should give priority to building its own commercial team either through first sending labor force to developed regions and then providing adequate training on them, or through school trainings that use tailor-made training materials. To speed up the establishment of such commercial teams, the country should make corresponding efforts to create favorable conditions for ethnic groups to conduct trading activities in the Han regions, and help them open up direct channels of trade to reduce as much as possible the intermediary interception of profits and ensure that adequate portion of profits are returned to ethnic regions.

The second step is so-called “tri-track”, which is, on the foundation of “dual-track”, to accomplish the goal of integrating the traditional ethnic culture and modern natural science by relying on the accumulated capital and the mastering of external knowledge and information, namely, to add the integration in science and technology to form the “three-track”. Three major obstacles are in the way:

First, the social mechanism formed in the first step through “two-way” cross-xiang operations is in a dispersed state and thus needs a process of capital accumulation for further development. However, there is no social mechanism in place in these ethnic groups for the accumulation of capital. It is apparent that to accomplish the second mission, corresponding social organizations will be subject to a re-structuring, which is doomed to be a difficult process.

The second difficulty has something to do with people’s perception. What is urgently needed for the realization of integration between ethnic culture and modern knowledge is the existence of social demeanor that strengthens the self-esteem, self-confidence and self-empowering of each ethnic group. A social perception must be fostered to love each ethnic group to encourage the members from each ethnic group to work hard toward the integration between the ethnic culture and modern knowledge.

The third difficulty is of technical nature. The integration in knowledge requires unremitting efforts for an extended period of time and the input of vast quantity of manpower and material resources, as well as high-quality people, which demands the cooperation of the society and support by policies. These work contents should be the responsibilities of ethnic autonomous governance based on the existing administrative structure in China.

The completion of the second step precedes the third one, the stage of comprehensive development. This step is mainly symbolized by the fact that ethnic groups are able to take the initiatives to plan and implement own development strategies based on their own reality, including establishing the enterprises based on their own needs and characteristics in resources, plan and construct their own industrial system and improve the social hierarchy based on the cultural traits of their own ethnic groups, making it a social background for the stable operation of ethnic industries. The equality across ethnic groups in both the political and economic status is achieved, enabling ethnic groups to build an overall school educational system that suits each ethnic group, to complete school education on their own and to provide all kinds of human resources for ethnic development.

It is not difficult to tell that the evolvement of the development in the above three steps is an entirety, and a process of self-optimization within each ethnic group. Only when such a process is completed can the corresponding ethnic groups be defined as having stepped in modernization. In summary, the balance in value between incoming and outgoing products and self-optimization by ethnic groups has a relationship of a dialectical unity nature. The lack of the former makes relevant ethnic groups difficult to accumulate necessary capital or break the cage of a natural economy to develop themselves to a higher level. A pure capital accumulation, on the other hand, will certainly not bring social development as the wealth accumulated may be consumed in the natural economy. As a result, to truly develop the relevant ethnic groups, we must help them set a goal for self-optimization and make specific and executable plans for the accomplishment of this goal; otherwise, traditional people can not be turned into modern ones.

The discussion of all the above solutions is under the precondition of a socialist system, without which the country is not in possession of the ability of adjustment and control above specific economic interests and the above solutions would be groundless. In addition, the execution of these solutions must be guaranteed by the socialist system that is beyond specific ethnic interests. No matter how good the policies are, they would inevitably damage the interests of certain ethnic groups or cause the interests lean over another ethnic group within a certain period of time, over some issues or in certain scopes. For instance, the planned economy is more advantageous to the ethnic Han people while the execution of above policies would protect the interests of ethnic groups as much as possible within a legal framework. Without the common belief in socialism across all ethnic groups and if each ethnic group haggles over every ounce, no policies would be able to be executed fully and the common prosperity across all ethnic groups would vanish. The above policies also need the guarantee of a socialist market economy as modernization, including the modernization of each ethnic group, can only be created on the foundation of a market economy. Subsequently, we have proposed the above solutions specifically tailored to the socialist market economy in China, without which these solutions would become meaningless. For this reason, the models in the social and economic development in ethnic regions we have built are different in essence from the "models in the modernization of developing ethnic nations" put forth by economists and anthropologists. They are models of modernization for ethnic groups that are uniquely Chinese and Socialist.

Chapter Ten Case Studies

This article overviews the political, economic and cultural transformation of Shanping village for the past 600 years based on historical records and field surveys in an effort to tell our readers what political and economic changes the ethnic groups as an objective party in cross-xiang operations would undergo and which cultural characteristics are relatively stable that would remain unchanged even after cross-xiang operating activities for a long time, so that we can understand how to organize cross-xiang operations and how to treat the response from the objective parties properly. Our reader will also read from this article that in cross-xiang operations, the way that the objective parties conduct activities are subject to big changes, the result of which may not be advantageous and sometimes may even cause severe disadvantages. The political organizations of the objective parties, on the other hand, often remain relatively stable and would not undergo significant changes in cross-xiang activities that last a long time, and would constrain the further development of cross-xiang operations. The traditional culture of the objective parties, especially the cognitive pattern as part of the traditional culture, is still constraining the economic development of this region even after 600-year cross-xiang operating activities. This demands our serious attention and must be included in our plan of cross-xiang operations as an important content; otherwise, it would severely disrupt and hinder cross-xiang operating activities.

I Brief Introduction to the Subjects of Study

Among all the ethnic groups in China, ethnic Miao is one that has numerous groups and sub-groups. There are more than 8 million Miao people in China (more than 10 million if those who live outside China are included), separated into five major groups and 64 sub-groups. They can be roughly categorized into following groups and sub-groups by location:

A. The eastern group refers to the Miao people who live in the adjacent region across Hunan, Guizhou, Sichuan and Hubei provinces and were jointly referred to as "Hong (red) Miao" in ancient Han literature in the Ming and Qing dynasties. *The Record of Guizhou* by Guo Zizhang (Ming) and *Miaofangbeilan* by Yan Ruyu (Qing) had thorough description of this group.

B. The central group refers to the Miao people who live in the Southeast Guizhou Ethnic Miao and Dong Autonomous Prefecture and the region bordering Hunan and Guangxi provinces and were jointly referred to as “Hei (black) Man” in the Yuan literature and “Hei (black) Miao” in ancient literature of Ming and Qing dynasties. *Yanxijiwen* by Tian Rucheng (Ming) and *Record of Guizhou* by Guo Zizhang (Ming) revealed some materials related to this group, while *Book of Guizhou* by Tian Wen (Qing) and *Pingmiaojilue* by Fang Xian (Qing) had systematic introduction.

C. The northern group refers to ethnic Miao people who live in the region bordering Sichuan, Guizhou and Yunnan, and were nicknamed “Da Hua Miao”by the Han people before the liberation. In the pre-Qing literature, they were referred to as “Mangbu Miao”, “Wusa Miao” and “Dongchuan Miao” by the name of *Tu Si* who were in control. Detailed research on this group may be found in the works of Mr. Yang Hanxian.

D. The western group refers to ethnic Miao people who live in western Guizhou and in Sichuan, Yunnan and Guangxi, as well as some who live in the mountainous region in northern Indo-China Peninsula. They were referred to as “Hua Miao”, “Chuan Miao” and “Shuixi Miao” in the Han literature. *Record of Dading Fu* and *Record of Anshun Fu* of Qing Dynasty had detailed descriptions of this group.

E. The southern group refers to ethnic Miao people who live in central and southern Guizhou who were jointly referred to as “Dong (east) Miao”, “Xi (west) Miao” and “Zijiang Miao” in the Han literature and were named “Bai (white) Miao”, and “Qing (green) Miao” among others in the Qing Dynasty. *Yanxijiwen* by Tian Rucheng (Ming), *Record of Guizhou* by Guo Zizhang (Ming), *Book of Guizhou* by Tian Wen (Qing) and *Record of Guiyang Fu* (Qing) all had systematic descriptions of this group. ①

There are other ethnic Miao people who have not been related to any of the above five groups due to lack of researches on them. For instance, the ethnic Miao people who live in Xuli Hongyan in Wangmo county, and those who name themselves [mhoŋ^{55}tai^{43}] and live in the region bordering Qingzhen, Xiuwen and Guiyang in Guizhou. With regards to Miao people who live outside China, their relationship with the above five groups remains unclear due to inadequate research from domestic and foreign scholars, and

① Torii Ryuzo (Japan), *Survey Report on Ethnic Miao Group*, trans. National Institute for Compilation and Translation (first published in April, 1946), 45.

the reference system and terminology used by foreign researchers have not integrated with ours.

People who belong to different sub-groups speak different languages (dialect, sub-dialect, local dialect) and are difficult to communicate directly with each other. ① They also differ significantly in economic life and a slight difference is seen in customs and traditions, cognitive style, ethics and value. However, they share the same cultural origin and thus have a high homogeneity internally, while the differences are primarily a reflection of the surrounding living environment (including both natural and humanity subsistence background) or a result of introduced disproportion; therefore, these differences do not last long in terms of stability and conformity.

Ethnic Miao people live across a span of hugely different living environments. From the perspective of the natural living environment, they scatter across several extremely different ecological regions, the southernmost of which enters the subtropical mountainous monsoon forests. In the northwest, some Miao people live in the alpine mountainous open forest grasslands. In the east, they live mainly in the subtropical low mountainous thickets, or gently slopped river valleys while in the central and west, they live in medium-altitude thickets or mountain ridge open forest grasslands. In addition, there are some ecological regions of smaller area such as the Karst petrified peak cluster regions in Guizhou and Guangxi provinces, and out-of-wind river valley foehn dry lands in Beipan River, Nanpan River, Zhangjiang River, Dahuan River and Xiaohuan River etc. The culture of relevant Miao groups has adapted to different natural ecological environment differently, which has caused various results.

From the perspective of cultural living environment, the western Miao group is mainly affected by Di Qiang ethnic groups such as ethnic Yi and Hani while the southern Miao group interacts more with Baiyue ethnic groups such as Buyi, Zhuang and Dai people. Ethnic Miao people who live outside China interact closely with ethnic Liao, Siam and Viet (Jing). Ethnic Miao people who live in the north are heavily influenced by ethnic Yi. Ethnic Miao in the south had frequent exchanges with ethnic Yi and Buyi in history. After the 17th century when ethnic Yi retreated from central Guizhou, ethnic Miao people have since been affected by ethnic Buyi group. In central Guizhou, the Miao people interact frequently in the east with ethnic Dong, in

① Fushi Wang, eds., *A Brief History of Miao Dialect* (The Ethnic Publishing House, 1985), 103-106.

the south and west with ethnic Buyi, Shui, Maonan, and Zhuang groups. The eastern Miao group has kept close relationship with Tujia and Dong groups. All sub-groups of Miao have been influenced by the ethnic Han culture in different period of time and to different extent.

All the Miao groups have undergone a few big changes in administrative management. Generally speaking, before the 13th century, nearly all Miao groups had lived in the *Jimi* prefectures and counties where the central government could only govern the ethnic Miao groups through local influences. The records of the Miao lifestyle were rarely seen in the Han literature, or were very fragmented and unsystematic, if any. At the end of the 13th century, the Yuan regime began to successively establish *Tu Si* at different levels, through which the royal court governed the ethnic Miao people indirectly. The establishment of *Tu Si* at different levels was not completed at one time but protracted over a long time. The earliest was Luoluosi followed by Dongchuan, Mangbu and Wusa etc. They represented the central government to rule the northern Miao group. In the period from the 17th to 18th century when Yi *Tu Si* had been revoked successively, their subordinates had not been removed entirely and their rule on the northern Miao group had continued till the eve of the liberation. Yi *Tu Si* such as Shuixi, Pu'an, and Langdai etc., ruled the western Miao sub-group while the Buyi *Tu Si* such as Shaying, Muyi etc., and Zhuang *Tu Si* such as Sicheng and Wangnongchuan etc., were at a lower level. These *Tu Si* were heavily impacted by the change in regime from Ming to Qing dynasty, and subsequently, all the big *Tu Si* were deposed while the power of smaller *Tu Si* were diminished. Regardless of these changes, the Yi *Tu Mu* and small Buyi and Zhuang *Tu Si* had continued their control on the ethnic Miao till the eve of the liberation. The *Tu Si* who ruled the southern Miao group mainly included Shuidong *Tu Si* of the Han group, the eight Zhangguansi as well as Guansi, Kangzuo, Fengning and Duyun *Tu Si* of the Buyi group, and Shuixi, Ninggu and Baiyan of the Yi group. These Tu Si were in a similar situation as those in the western group. The central ethnic Miao group had been special. The kernel area in its territory had long been deemed by the central government as "outlandish" and thus not subject to administrative management until the effort of "replacing local hereditary headmen by officials sent by the central government" in the years of Yongzheng in Qing Dynasty, with the exception of some bordering areas that were indirectly ruled by *Tu Si* of each level. After the reform in the years of Yongzheng, the Han officials and their Miao inferiors co-existed to apply an indirect rule that was in essence a quasi-*Tu Si* system. Although "Xinjiang Liu (six) Ting (a governmental level)" were set up at the time in this region, their power had never reached the inland of the Miao region. Ethnic Tujia *Tu Si* such as Sizhou, Qiuyang and Rongmei had ruled the eastern Miao group, but Sizhou and Sinan Tu Si were deposed much earlier in the years of Yongle in the Ming Dynasty. The Ming regime chose to build "border walls" around the kernel area, similar to the Great Wall, to block the "outlandish" area in La'ershan region where it could not control. It was not until the mid Qing Dynasty when administrative organizations were installed in this region to bring it under the control of the Qing government.

It was customary in both the Ming and Qing dynasties that the government would not measure the lands of the ethnic Miao people under the rule of *Tu Si*, nor would they be put in the national household system, directly levied taxes, or decided on legal disputes. All these matters were handled by the *Tu Si* who were exclusive representatives of and controlled by the central government. Only when the *Tu Si* broke the law, the above powers were partially taken away as a means of punishment and were instead by exercised by local governments. It was not until the *Tu Si* who ruled the ethnic Miao group were eventually deposed and removed when the local governments assumed all the administrative functions and started direct governing. It was also a long process for direct governing to take over indirect governing in the ethnic Miao regions. Due to the numerous and complicated hierarchy within the *Tu Si* system, the dramatically different regions under the control of different *Tu Si*, different customs and practices in ruling their territories, and the reform of *Gai Tu Gui Liu* by the central government that mainly targeted unlawful big *Tu Si,* the removal of the upper-level *Tu Si* was not extended to the lower-level *Tu Si* who continued to exercise their administrative powers. The progress made in the transition from indirect governing to direct governing on the ethnic Miao regions often did not synchronize with that of *Gai Tu Gui Liu.* For instance, the *Tu Si* in Sizhou and Sinan were replaced by officials sent from the central government as early as the 11th year of Yongle in the Ming dynasty, the *Gezhang Zhangguan Si* under their supervision had remained unchanged until the end of the Qing dynasty and the Miao people under its ruling had not been registered by the national household system until the era of Republic of China. Another example is Shuixi *Tu Si*. Although it was replaced by the officials assigned by the central government in early Qing dynasty, and Bina that had originally been put under it was replaced by Zhijin county, the local Anshi *Tu Mu* had continued ruling the local Miao people until the "land reform" that eventually deprived *Tu Mu* of their land ownership and lifted their control on the local Miao people. An opposite example was the Miao people in Guchi Li.[①] As this was a place that situated at the throat of the road leading to Guiyang at the moment, the Ming government registered all the local Miao people in its household system to facilitate corvee while conducting massive construction of garrisons and courier routes in the early Ming dynasty. "Li" was the basic establishment at the time, symbolizing the beginning of a direct ruling on the local Miao people. The Miao tenant peasants of Yunjinzhuang of Songshi who was *Shuidong Tu Si* were registered in the national household system in the years of Tianqi of the Ming dynasty when Shuidong *Tu Si* collapsed. As a result, in the bound copy of the tax collection document of the Qing dynasty, it clearly recorded the number of households and detailed tax amount for the Miao people living in Shitouzhai of Yunjinzhuang. Generally, the Miao people who lived near big cities, along major transportation lines, or under the direct control of big *Tu Si* tended to be removed from an indirect governing and put under a direct governing at an earlier time, and vice versa, with the latest being barely completed at the end of this century.

Although cultural living environments were external causes for the transition in the economic life of ethnic Miao group, their effects should not be underestimated as they not only impacted the process of the transition, but also constrained the way of transition and the origins of the introduced cultural factors. In addition, they also disrupted how adjustments to the transition were made. The diverging and complicated lifestyle across Miao groups was, in large part, caused by different cultural living environments.

It is an extremely difficult task for us to find a village that is representative in the transition of the lifestyle in Miao group and use it as an object of our case study due to the fact that ethnic Miao has numerous and complicated groups and sub-groups that live across huge living environments (both the natural and cultural living environments. The term is used by the

① Wen Tian, *Series of Books on Southern Guizhou*, combined issue thread-bound edition, *Book of Guizhou, IV*.

same definition in the texts to follow). Subsequently, we have to stick to the following three principles when searching and determining the object for our case study. First, it must be a village that belongs to a Miao group that has been heavily studied by our predecessors. Second, it must be a village that has detailed and systematic documentation in literature. Third, it must be close to the central cities and has been subject to significant influence by modern civilization, but in the meantime, has preserved the traditional culture relatively well. After comprehensive comparison, we have chosen Shanping village that is an ethnic Miao township in Gaopo of Huaxi District in Guiyang as the object of our study in the transition in the Miao lifestyle. It has basically met the requirements of the above three principles.

Residents who live in Shanping village belong to a local sub-group of the southern Miao group. They speak general Miao dialect, Huishui sub-dialect and northeast local dialect. This sub-group scatters on the mountain ridge in central Miaoling that is the watershed of two big river systems: Yangtze River and Pear River. In the administrative hierarchy, this territory spans across Guiyang city and four counties of Longli, Guiding, Huishui and Pingtang. Although they report to different administrative authorities, these areas are adjacent to each other to form a large habitat of the Miao people that covers an area of approximately 900 square kilometers. Shanping village is located in the northwest of this region. In the Han literatures of different time, this Miao sub-group was given different names. In the Yuan dynasty, it was called "Ping Fa Miao Man" as was in the *History of Yuan · Biography of Shizu.* In the Ming dynasty, it was called "Dong (east) Miao" as was indicated in the *History of Ming · Biography of Yingzong* and other local annals in Guizhou. In the Qing dynasty, it was called "Bai (white) Miao" as was seen in *Guiyang Fu Annals* (Daoguang) and *Book of Guizhou.* It was occasionally called as "Gaopo Miao" as was seen in (Daoguang) *Guiyang Fu Annals · Tu Si (Qingyantubian).* In the era of Republic of China, some people, such as Wu Zelin, referred to it as "Haiba Miao" and others, such as Luo Rongzong, referred to it as "Bai (white) Miao". Local Han and Buyi people customarily refer to it as "Hongzhan Miao" or "Beipai Miao".[①] These Miao people call themselves as [toŋ^{43} m̥ hoŋ^{24}], east Meng[②]; the local people as Meng Rong,

① Tingshuo Yang, "A Textural Research on the Transition of Haibeiba Miao Names", *Guizhou Ethnic Surveys* (II), (compiled and printed by Guizhou Institute of Nationality Studies, October, 1984), 349.

② Fushi Wang, *Reconstruction of Ancient Miao Pronunciation* (State Research Institute of Asian and African Language and Culture, Tokyo, 1994). The Miao pronunciations in this article were from this namely Miao living in the forests; the Miao group living in the north as [m̥hoŋ^{24}pæ^{31}] Meng Bai, namely Miao living on the mountain top; the Miao group living in the south [mhoŋ24pi13tɕɛŋ13] Meng Bijian, namely Miao living in the cedar forests. All the Miao people from the three groups speak Miao dialect Huishui sub-dialect but with varied local dialects, and can understand each other with some difficulties. After the 18th century, a new title emerged within this group [m̥hoŋ^{24}ɳtaŋ^{31}] Meng Zhang, namely Miao living in the intermontane basins and specifically referring to the Miao residents who were among the first to settle down to cultivate rice fields. The residents of Shanping village belong to Meng Zhang and those who still live in the forests are also referred to as Meng Zhang. Of course, the residents who are called Meng Rong today have settled down and lived on rice field cultivation. The difference in titles only has historical meanings. It is worth noting that the difference between Meng Rong and Meng Zhang is a classification within this group. All other Miao groups that interact with them undistinguishingly call them Meng Rong.

Corresponding to the title of this group, they indeed live in the natural living environment of mountainous thickets. The lowest elevation is 1000 meters and the highest is 1700 meters. The forests are made up of coniferous and broad-leafed forests, with cedar trees mostly in the valleys and pine tress on the mountain slopes, and Fagaceae trees taking the majority of the broad-leafed trees. Pine trees on the grassland background grow sparsely on the mountain ridges above 1500 meters. Compared to the suburbs of Guiyang at the foot of the mountain, the winter here (winter in climate term) is one and half month longer and the summer is one month shorter. The planting of big-season crops is postponed by half a month to 20 days in average. The cedarwood coming out of this region in the past was famous for its dense texture and antiseptic nature, but was in extremely low output of no more than 1 cubic meter per hectare each year due to cold climate and soil depletion. In addition, this region was a major tea producer in the past. "Dong Miao Tea" that was one of the teas of tributes to the Ming royal court was produced by this Miao group.

In addition to ethnic Han group, this Miao group interact the most with the ethnic Buyi people, whom they call "Ye" [ʑɛ^{13}] and who call them "You"

book with a few exceptions that were recorded in the fieldwork by the author.)

[zou^{31}]. Buyi villages are located in the river valleys to the east, west and north of their habitat. There are a few Buyi villages in the Gaopo township where Shanping village is located. They are jointly called "Rao Rao" that is a Miao language similar in sound as the Buyi language meaning at the foot of the mountain. The residents newly moved in from the base of the mountain after the 18th century. In the Ming dynasty, ethnic Yi influence penetrated this region and Shuixi *Tu Si* once built a private residence in Gaopo. Luogui village is recorded in the Han literatures. They had close interaction with Yangren (now confirmed as ethnic Maonan group). Nowadays, there are village names such as Yanghuang village within the region.

Due to its proximity to central cities and major transportation lines, and a settlement that reserves a relatively complete Miao culture, this Miao group attracted attention from domestic and foreign scholars long time ago. Quite a number of distinguished scholars have conducted studies on this Miao group. Torii Ryuzo from Japan was the first one who reported on them to foreign readers in 1905. In the 1940s, ethnologists including Wu Zelin①, Bao Kelan and Luo Rongzong② did specific research on this Miao group. Linguists including Zhang Kun and Wang Fushi carried out research on the language of this group.

This region of ethnic Miao group was viewed as "outlandish" before the Yuan dynasty. The central government had never had any contact with the local Miao people, nor had the people from nearby ethnic groups penetrated into the region. After the unification of China by the Yuan dynasty, the new Songshi *Tu Si* was authorized by the royal court to subdue the local people. In the second year of Taiding of the Yuan dynasty (1325), the mother of the headman of this Miao group answered the call and travelled to Dadu to pay tributes. ③ From then on, the central government began to rule this Miao group through agent. In the early Ming dynasty, the government began to use military forces on the local Miao in an attempt to remove worries in its back before establishing garrisons and courier routes.④ In the aftermath, the government ordered Dapingfa Zhangguan under the Shuidong *Tu Si* to appease the local people and continued to rule by agent. In the years of

① Zelin Wu, "Bull-fighting in the Haiba Miao Regions", *A Collection of Papers in Memory of Wu Zelin* (Hubei Science and Technology Press, June, 1988), 185.

② Rongzong Luo, "The Miao Funerals", *Borderland Research Weekly* no. 38 (Yishi Daily, Chongqing)

③ *The History of the Yuan Dynasty · Taiding* (Zhonghua Book Company, punctuated edition), 654

④ *Veritable Records of the Ming Dynasty • A Compilation of Materials about Guizhou*, 9.

Jingtai and Tianshun, the Miao headsman Ganbazhu took the chance of chaotic situations within the royal court of Ming and rebelled against the Ming dynasty. In the fierce battle in Shimenshan in the third year of Tianshun (1459),① the Ming government mobilized the forces from five garrisons and six *Tu Si* and defeated the Miao rebels, resulting in the death of Ganbazhu and destruction of more than 600 Miao villages by burning.② After the war, the Ming government took the lands of Miao people and granted them to the *Tu Si* as rewards. Shuidong and Jinzhu Tu Si received most of them, followed by Bafan, Dapingfa and Xiaopingfa. The Ming government since began an indirect ruling on this Miao group.

During the period of indirect governing, confrontations between Miao people and *Tu Si* never stopped. Among them, five big ones occurred in the Ming dynasty. In the 13th year of Hongzhi of the Ming dynasty (1500), the memorial stone tablet inscribed by Shuidong Songshi – preface to "Yong Zhen Bian Yi"③ has been kept until today (at present-day Shimen village of Gaopo township). In the 45th year of Jiajing in the Ming dynasty (1065), the Ming troop raided Lali and other villages with the assistance from Longli Zhangguansi and killed the Miao headman Ali.④ In the 25th year of Wanli of the Ming dynasty, the local Miao people feuded with Buyi people who were under the rule of *Tu Si* over Miao's Pigong bullring. The verdict made by Guiyang Fu was inscribed on a stone tablet and has been kept till today (at present-day Banpo of Huishui county). In the years of Tianqi of the Ming dynasty (1621-1627), the Miao people were coerced by Shuidong and Shuixi *Tu Si* to rebel against the Ming government. Subsequently, the Ming troop burned more than 100 Miao villages.⑤ In the 4th year of Chongzhen of the Ming dynasty (1631), the emerging Buyi local force in Qingyantu attacked Gaopo with the support from the Ming court and since became a new small *Tu Si* that ruled the Miao region – Qingyan *Tu Bian*. When recording this event, Jiangtai, which was the old name of Shanping village, was mentioned

① *The History of the Ming Dynasty • Biography of Gui Bai* (Zhonghua Book Company, punctuated edition), 4595.

② *The History of the Ming Dynasty • Biography of Ying Fang* (Zhonghua Book Company, punctuated edition), 4488.

③ For materials from tablet inscriptions in Gaopo township of Guiyang, see *Guiyang Annals Material Studies*, no 3 and no. 7. Same references will not be listed in following texts.

④ *Veritable Records of the Ming Dynasty • A Compilation of Materials about Guizhou*, 827.

⑤ *The History of the Ming Dynasty • Biography of Wang Sanshan* (Zhonghua Book Company, punctuated edition), 6456.

for the first time.①

After the Qing dynasty took over the entire country, given that the big *Tu Si* were deposed and in cooperation with the efforts to replace garrisons with counties, the Qing government encouraged smaller *Tu Si* to divide up and take over the Miao regions. The fight by the Miao people against the oppression by the *Tu Si* was used by the Qing court as excuse to rescind *Tu Si* and subsequently put Miao villages under the direct control of the government, symbolizing the expansion of a direct governing of this Miao group. Five big events occurred in the Qing dynasty. In the 7th year of Yongzheng of the Qing dynasty (1729), the deputy officer Liu Shi in Caishicao included (present-day Yundeng and other places in Gaopo township) more than ten Miao villages under the direct control of Guiyang Fu. ② In the 9th year of Yongzheng (1731), the excessive taxes and levies imposed by Xipai *Tu Bian* of Dapingfa Si had caused the local Miao people to abandon their villages and took flight, forcing the Guiding county government to come out to appease the Miao people and punish Xipai *Tu Bian*. The stone tablet with the inscription of this event has been kept until today (at Zhangji village of Gaopo township). In the 55th year of Qianlong (1790), local Miao people rose against the collection of tea as tributes to the royal court.③ The stone tablet with the inscription of the incident is kept in present-day Yangwang township of Guiding county. In the 10th year of Daoguang (1830), after the Miao residents at Jiadeng village appealed to the government on the heavy taxes imposed on them, the Guiyang government issued the verdict to replace the original payable taxes with the value of a bull head. Unfortunately, this "bull head stone tablet" was destroyed during the "Cultural Revolution". In the years of Xianfeng, the accusation made by the Miao residents from Shanping village on the Qingyan *Tu Bian* for his excessive taxes on the Miao people resulted in the removal of this *Tu Bian* from his office. The stone tablet detailing this event still remains at Shanping village with only the part of year missing. Both events changed the ruling of the Miao villages involved to directly under the government control.

In the era of Republic of China, local warlord government began to

① (Daoguang), *Guiyang Fu Annals* • *Tu Si*, s.v. "Qingyan Tu Bian", in the collection of Guizhou Provincial Library, woodblock prints.

② *Draft History of the Qing Dynasty · Geography*, *Twenty Five Histories* photocopy edition (Shanghai: Chinese Classics Publishing House), 9117 II.

③ Kaizhong Shi, "On the Historical Value of Yangwang Tablet Inscriptions", *Guiyang Cultural Relics*, no. 1 (1986).

completely take over the territories formerly ruled by the *Tu Si* under the name of enclave appropriation and unifying administrative management. With the completion of this measure in 1914, all the regions inhabited by this Miao group were under the direct rule of the government. Four of the inscribed stone tablets in memory of this event are kept in Gaopo township now. However, remaining *Tu Si* influences were not fully eradicated but instead were appointed to be the government officials at the region, township, bao and jia levels. For example, Zhongcao Zheng Zhangguan Xieshi who had ruled all Miao villages in the northwest of Gaopo had remained in office until the liberation when he was suppressed. A complete shift to direct governing had brought two consequences to this Miao group. On the negative side, the government of Republic of China forcefully executed a policy of national assimilation. When Yang Sen was in office, he enforced his two theories – the theory of great harmony and evolution, forcing the Miao people to stop wearing their traditional clothes and speaking Miao dialects in public. On the bright side, the Miao people directly participated in the domestic political battles. In their 25,000 – Li long march, the Red Army passed Miao villages in Gaopo, Shuitang, Shanping, and Pilin, exposing the Miao people who had long been kept in a sealed and inward world to the Communist Party and revolution for the first time in history. During the period of white terror, Xu Jiansheng, one of the leaders in the underground communist party in Guizhou remained in Gaopo for two years under the disguise of a teacher. During the anti-Japanese war period, primary schools in Gaopo and Shanping changed their name to “Protecting Nationals School” as a way of disseminating the truth about anti-Japanese and saving the country. Subsequently, this Miao group had their first generation of teachers and students. Advocated by Luo Changpei and Wu Zelin, “Training School on Qingyan Dialect” was set up to train the cadres for the anti-Japanese efforts for various ethnic groups, which separated the students by their mother tongue and the classes were taught in each mother tongue. Luo Zhongqing and his two fellowmen from Shanping village were able to get in regular schools, and he invited ethnologist Luo Rongzong to pay a visit to Shanping village, followed by Bao Kelan. These visits led to the books specifically about the ethnological fieldwork in Shanping village.

After the liberation, this Miao group, along with all the Miao people in the country, have received care and great support from the Party and the people's government. Gaopo was made a Miao autonomous township as early as 1950s. Since then, some local ethnic cadres have been fostered and first college students have emerged who have equipped the village with their town educational, medical and technical people. Approximately one third of expenditure on assisting ethnic groups in Guiyang city has been spent on Gaopo township. Many Party and State Leaders including President Jiang Zemin have paid visit to Gaopo and Shanping village. Quite a number of agricultural experts and economists have conducted research in Gaopo and Shanping. It is now turned into an ethnic tourist attraction that has received tourists from several countries.

Although Shanping village has fulfilled the principles we have laid out, we can not say that it can represent the transition in the lifestyle of the Miao group for the following three reasons: First, the transition in lifestyle of different Miao groups progressed differently, some faster and some slower than Shanping village. Second, different Miao groups faced different natural living environments and thus have different ways of adjusting to modern lifestyle. Lastly, each Miao group faced different ethnic background and had different origins that cultural elements are introduced from, and thus had different results of digestion and transformation. However, if we observe the transition in the Miao lifestyle from a vertically historical perspective, Shanping village would be very typical. Like all other Miao groups, the transition in the lifestyle of Shanping village started from the same highly homogeneous traditional culture of Miao. The interaction with the developed Han culture characterized with settlement and rice cultivation triggered the first transition in its lifestyle. When the Han society underwent a cultural reconstruction as a result of impact from modernity, the influence from the evolution triggered the second transition in the lifestyle of this Miao group. This is the foundation for us to choose Shanping village as the object of our fieldwork. It is up to our readers and insightful people who care about the development in the Miao regions to determine to what extent and in what ways Shanping village can historically represent the transition in the lifestyle of other Miao groups. To understand the transition in the lifestyle of Miao groups, we must first fully understand the original lifestyle of these people, which proves to be difficult due to the lack of or conflicting historical records in Han language. Therefore, we were forced to find a new pass to look into the ancient lifestyle of Miao, which is to seek breakthrough from the Miao culture itself. Like all other ethnic cultures, the Miao culture is an orderly entirety, the components of which evolved at different rates. For instance, the Miao cognitive pattern evolved extremely slowly and the characteristics in Miao's current cognitive pattern is a reflection of its traditional lifestyle, which makes it possible for us to know Miao's ancient lifestyle with verification by the records in Han literatures. Naturally, our trip to Shanping village started from understanding Miao's cognitive pattern.

II Cognitive Patterns of the Ethnic Miao Group

For the convenience of comparative analysis, we need to divide the evolutionary process of a culture into a few stages. However, culture is an orderly and integrated system that can only evolve gradually in metabolism. No matter how many reconstructions a culture has undergone in history, there would be no clear-cut lines between two reconstructions. Cultural reconstruction merely eliminates and abandons the cultural elements that confront head-on with the new lifestyle and can not be adjusted or transformed, while inheriting the majority of cultural elements that remain. Such an inheritance is not, of course, keeping the cultural elements entirely intact, but instead adjusting, processing and transforming them based on the actual need in the new lifestyle and then incorporating them in the new cultural system to reconstruct a new orderly system that caters to the new lifestyle. Hence, the social life seems to have changed completely after a cultural reconstruction if it is observed from a single side or the representation of life that is regulated by the culture. However, if the observation is made from a macro perspective or from the standpoint of vertical cultural evolution, cultural reconstruction is in fact a clear metabolism process where inheritance and transformation co-exist. Whether a cultural element changes or how to change, if any, depends on the specific needs of the social life and must follow the principle of maintaining the stable and orderly transition in culture.

In the 600-year verifiable history of this Miao group, there were two evident transformations in their lifestyle (since the end of the 13th century until now). After a comprehensive analysis, we find that the local traditional culture was not destroyed. Instead, only the cultural elements that were closely related to the material life and were not compatible with the new lifestyle were replaced while others were transformed to be more ceremonial and symbolic and have retained in the cultural system. As to those that were mainly used in the spiritual life, or were compatible with the new lifestyle although they were also used in material life, these cultural elements rarely changed, or, in case of any change, they were not fundamentally replaced but were subject to some adjustments to certain contents and conditions of operation, and stayed in the cultural system to play their specific social function, the evolution and development of which are hardly detectable by superficial observation. The cognitive pattern of the local Miao group in the village falls into the second category. The cultural elements that make up of their cognitive pattern and the structural relationship across these cultural elements are so stable that once we understand the characteristics of this cognitive pattern, we are able to infer the social lifestyle prevailing at the time when the cognitive pattern became solidified. Due to the lack of Han historical records, it seems extremely important for us to get to know the early-stage lifestyle of Miao through the analysis of their cognitive pattern.

The Miao cognitive pattern is a sub-system of the Miao cultural system. It includes three contents: cognitive framework, cognitive orientation and knowledge classification. Cognitive framework is a set of customs of understanding external world and accumulating knowledge that each member of the Miao group accepts along with the Miao culture. The experience gained only by following these customs can be incorporated smoothly into the Miao cultural system and become the knowledge wealth that belongs to the entire ethnic group. Without relying on these customs as foundation, any individual knowledge or perception is only individual behavior and is hard to be echoed by all the members in the group or produce a rolling effect in perception before it's converted into social norms. Cognitive orientation is another set of customs that guides the Miao group members in their perceptive practices mainly on these issues such as what objects and aspects of these objects to care about, and in what depth and width should they be perceived. Each ethnic group faces complicated and constantly changing external world. Due to the existence of the cognitive orientation sub-system in its culture, each ethnic group always focuses on the things that matter most for their subsistence and development. Ethnic Miao people are no exception. They would not put efforts on the things that do not offer any help in near term. In other words, every ethnic group may try to perceive and understand anything infinitely. However, the perception of each ethnic group is restrained by time and space, and regulated by its respective cognitive orientation. Therefore, when an ethnic group looks insensitive to something, or is even indifferent and turns a blind eye to it, it does not necessarily mean that people from this ethnic group have a defective intelligence, or their ethnic culture is inferior. It is just the mission of cultural anthropologists to detect these differences and help each ethnic group conduct in-depth understanding of its own cognitive orientation so that it can play to the full of the strengths and avoid the weaknesses in cognition, thus attaining the goal of mutual supplement across ethnic groups. Knowledge classification is another set of cognitive customs which include how to classify the gained knowledge, and the representation of each classification of knowledge. The existence of cognitive classification not only directly regulates the storage, accumulation and exchange of the gained knowledge but also relates to how to retrieve and search on prior experiences, and thus regulates the imagination orientation and inference norm of the relevant ethnic group in a deeper level. Apparently, each ethnic group has a unique way of knowledge classification, which in fact is an objective reality but is only perceived from different perspectives by different people. For instance, ethnic Han people give the name of "jade" to some rocks that have different components, properties and appearances, and use them in a similar way, mostly as decoration or ceremonial and ritual objects. The Englishmen name male and female chickens by different names. Similar situations widely exist in ethnic Miao society, but they are deemed as non-scientific and ignorant by the people who observe and judge with unconsciously wearing the polarizing glasses of the evolution theory, and who treat them as soon-to-be-eliminated antiques. They would not realize, of course, that such "non-scientific or ignorant" things also exist in the ethnic groups who view them as the most developed ethnicity.

Since the cognitive framework of the Miao group is a sub-system, it naturally includes a few sets of acquired fixed forms, which are commonly accepted, subject to no verification, as norms by the Miao society. Among all these fixed forms, the ones that were most directly related to the Miao ancient lifestyle are the following three: time setting framework, space setting framework and affinities framework.

The time in the Miao society is set on the foundation of a unique calendar, which used to be called "Miao Jia Zi" but is more appropriate if called "Miao Calendar". It is a kind of phenological calendar that defines months by the appearance of a certain phonological phenomenon. For example, the blooming of birch trees marks the beginning of June; the sprouting of pteridium aquilinum and their coming out of earth trimly symbolizes the beginning of July, while beasts start to grow winter hair harbingers the end of a year as well as the beginning of the first month. We noticed that these are just the phonological symbols of the Miao group we surveyed. Due to the difference in climate, geography and biological varieties, different Miao groups use different phenological symbols and the number in each month varies accordingly. It has come to the attention of many researchers that the same Miao holiday often falls on a different date in different Miao groups, indicating that the Miao culture is a highly homogenous rather than an inconsistent one as they use the same calendar. The variance in the date of a particular holiday is a phenomenon derived from the phenological calendar.

Another characteristic of Miao calendar is that it only has hot and cold seasons in a year instead of four seasons of spring, summer, fall and winter. Both the hot and cold seasons span six months. The change in season not only is a reflection of change in climate but also indicates the difference in the ways and contents in people's social activities. For the same reason that phenological characters in different Miao groups manifest at an earlier or later date across different Miao regions, therefore, the hot or cold season begins at different dates and lasts for different number of days. Generally speaking, the Miao groups in warmer regions start the hot season earlier and end it later and thus have a longer hot season. On the contrary, the Miao groups from colder regions begin the cold season earlier and end it later, thus have a longer cold season. Despite of these variations, the seasons alternate in the same cycle as the solar year because the phenological cyclical change synchronizes with the cycle of the solar year. As a result, there is no leap year in the Miao calendar.

There are 12 months in the Miao calendar. Each month corresponds with one of the twelve zodiac signs. Below is a table that has all the months in the Miao calendar, and their corresponding Gregorian calendar month and Chinese lunar month.

A	**1st month**	**2nd month**	**3rd month**
B	**[plu^{22} ꜗ ha^{43}]**	**[ʑə^{51} ꜗ ha^{43}]**	[Sə^{13} ꜗ ha^{43}]
	◦	◦	◦

C	**Month of Rat**	**Month of Ox**	**Month of Tiger**
D	**Nov. – Dec.**	**Dec.- Jan.**	**Jan. – Feb.**
E	**11th month of lunar year**	**12th month of lunar year**	**1st month of lunar year**

A	**4th month**	**5th month**	**6th month**
B	**[lu^{13} ı ha^{43}]**	[ʑaŋ^{55} ı ha^{43}]	**[na^{24} ı ha^{43}]**
C	**Month of Rabbit**	**Month of Dragon**	**Month of Snake**
D	**Feb. – Mar.**	**Mar. – Apr.**	**Apr. - May**
E	**2nd month of lunar year**	**3rd month of lunar year**	**4th month of lunar year**

A	**7th month**	**8th month**	**9th month**
B	**[min^{31} ı ha^{43}]**	**[ʑaŋ^{55} ı ha^{43}]**	**[lɛ^{24} ı ha^{34}]**
C	**Month of Horse**	**Month of Sheep**	**Month of Monkey**
D	**May – Jun.**	**Jun.- Jul.**	**Jul.- Aug.**
E	**5th month of lunar year**	**6th month of lunar year**	**7th month of lunar year**

A	**10th month**	**11th month**	**12th month**
B	**[qe^{24} ı ha^{43}]**	**[t ı æ^{13}ha^{43}]**	**[mp^{43} ı ha^{43}]**
C	**Month of rooster**	**Month of Dog**	**Month of Pig**
D	**Aug.- Sept.**	**Sept. – Oct.**	**Oct. – Nov.**
E	**8th month of lunar year**	**9th month of lunar year**	**10th month of lunar year**

In the table, Line A is the month in the Miao calendar; Line B is the Miao pronunciation; Line C is the meaning of the Miao calendar; Line D is corresponding month in Gregorian calendar; Line E is corresponding month in Chinese lunar calendar. As the beginning and end of a month is determined by phenological phenomena, the number of days in a month may vary roughly from 26 to 35, unlike the Chinese lunar calendar that has 29 or 30 days in a month.

Days in a month are also labeled by the zodiac signs. As a result, there may be three days in a month that have the same name. To separate, modifiers of [Shɛ^{43}] (early), [ɳtaŋ^{24}] (mid), and [qoŋ^{24}] (late) must be added. For instance, early pig day in the month of snake, mid-pig day in the month of snake, and late pig day in the month of snake, etc. Hence, people celebrate the same holiday in the month of snake three times on three separate days with the same name. For example, this Miao group follows the ritual of *"She Bei Pai"* in the month of snake and it is customary in the area where the Gaopo county government is located ("18 villages above the Ka" in local Miao language) that it needs to be held on the "pig day". Hence, the activities are separated into three days and people would have three holidays in this month. In the area where Shanpin village is located ("18 villages under the Ka" in the Miao language), it is customary that the same holiday be celebrated in the snake day and therefore, people spend three days for the celebration of this holiday.[1] Another example is the "bull-fighting" activities that are supposed to take place in the month of dog. On any dog day of the month of dog, the Miao people from Shanping and other nearby villages would gather in Pigong dog-fighting court in Huishui county to have a grand bull-fighting ceremony, three times in a month that is 12 days apart from each other.

The years in the Miao calendar are also named by the twelve zodiac signs. They cycle every twelve years. Subsequently, the biggest ancestor-worship ceremony is held once every 12 years, called "*Gu She Ji*". The translation of this term varies by people. Some translate it as *"Chi Gu Zang"*;[2] Others translate it as "*Jiang Lue*", or *"Qiao Niu Ji Zu"*. As years, months and days are counted by a cycle of 12, the number 12 has special significance in the life of ethnic Miao people. As we will describe later in the chapter, it almost penetrates in all social organizations, customs, production, or even literature and art, becoming a basic standpoint for ethnic Miao people to perceive and understand the external world. The social concepts directly

[1] Rongzong Luo, "Miao's Entertainment", *Guoshi Quarterly*, no. 14.

[2] Guangzheng Lei, "The Study on the Ethnic Miao's Custom of Worshiping Ancestors through Butchering Cattle and Horse in Guizhou", *Miao Studies* (I) (Guizhou Ethnic Press, July 1989), 195.

derived from such a basic standpoint are even deep-rooted from and mingled with the Miao calendar, which makes it hard to trace back their origins simply by their external appearance. Here, we use the example of how the Miao people describe a man's life as an illustration of this point.

In the Miao culture, a man's lifetime is separated into four stages and a senior period. They are: infant stage [ŋa^{55}lƐ^{24}], juvenile stage [toŋ^{13}laŋ^{31}], **adolescent stage** [toŋ^{13}go^{31}toŋ^{13}ntha^{55} **and adult stage** [qə^{31}mƐ^{55}qə^{31}po^{13}]. For the first two stages, people are not separated into male and female, but in the last two stages, male and female must be separate. The infant stage refers to the first two years after one is born. The duration depends on the birth month because one is deemed as one year old once he/she is born and would turn 3 years old and thus deemed a juvenile at the end of the second year. Only the ones who are born in the beginning of a year have an infancy of a complete two years. Traditionally, as Miao people think that a man's life start from conception and as the old saying goes: "one year in heaven and one year on earth", the infant stage is thus 4 years by the traditional way of calculation. This causes the discrepancy between the age registered with household registration and that one think he/she is. The juvenile stage starts from the end of the infant stage and finishes at the time when one lives through a 12-zodiac cycle, mostly before the adolescence in physiological terms. Children in the juvenile stage do not have sexy impulsion and thus are not separated by gender, which in reality corresponds to human physiogenesis. However, in our fieldwork in Shanping village, we witnessed quite a few cases of juvenile engagement and marriage. Although there is traditional custom in this area, this is a practice against the traditional notion, indicating that the classification of the stages in a man's life was an ancient lifestyle and the prevailing marriage customs are results of subsequent transformation. In ancient time, a person who entered the adolescent stage would go through the puberty rite where males should tattoo their face and hands and females should go through Kak-huak. Although it is not followed anymore, the ancient songs and language materials have reflection of such rites. The adolescent stage also last at least for a full 12-zodiac cycle unless one gives birth to his/her own children. The adult stage starts from the time one has the first child instead of the wedding ceremony, and lasts for two rounds of 12-zodiac signs until one enters the menopause in physiological age, symbolizing that he/she has stepped into the senior period. In the Miao society, old people usually live together with their youngest child.

In the Miao society, the location of the observer is deemed the start point of space. The direction that the observer faces is front and the direction that the observer backs toward is rear. His left hand extends to the left and his right hand extends to the right. Based on where the observer stands, any place above it is up and below it is down. The six major elements to describe location in the Miao language are: front [mplƐ^{24}], rear [qoŋ^{24}], left [tɕaŋ^{31}], right [tƐ^{55}], up [shu^{24}], down [nqa^{31}], while the start point of observation is called [ntaŋ^{24}] center. Apparently, this is a purely subjective orientation system. Therefore, the location determined in this way is not meaningful unless restored to the start point and orientation of the observer. The location of a village determined by its neighboring villagers is in exact symmetry. After long-term interaction with the Han people, the Han concepts of objective direction such as east, south, west and north are introduced in the Miao language.① However, the understanding of these concepts is only limited to where the sun rises and sets, and if one faces or backs the sunlight. In communication, they must be converted into the subjective orientation system of the Miao groups.

The way ethnic Miao people define the spatial range is also a system of subjective determination. The state in which the observer is located is the general basis and start point for determination. As a village is a complete unit in spatial arrangement, the village where the observer is located becomes the most basic spatial sphere, which includes village, farm field, forest, pasture, mountain range, and river etc. Anything within this sphere is deemed "internal" and anything outside this sphere is deemed "external". Based on this sphere, any other village that has a relationship by affinity with this basic village as well as anything that belongs to the village, usually six homogeneous villages that have a relationship by affinity, make up of an upper-level spatial sphere that determines the boundary between internal and external things by the same principle as is in the case of a single village. We should not explain the spatial sphere of this level simply as an extension in space. The basic level spatial sphere is maintained by blood lineage while the spatial sphere of this level is maintained by the relationship in affinity. They have different social nature and function.

① Cunde Wang, *The Han-Miao Dictionary (Eastern Guizhou Dialect)* (Guizhou Ethnic Press, December 1992).

As we did not survey all the villages of this Miao group, we can not tell how many such secondary-level spatial spheres it has. According to the data we collected from Shanping and nearby villages, it is certain that the present-day Gaopo township of Guiyang city is divided into parts that belong to at least three different secondary-level spatial spheres. Shanping village, Jiading, Lali Dongkou and Baisheng of Longli county, and Banpo of Huishui county are in the same secondary-level spatial sphere that is called by the locals as "18 villages under the Ka". The present-day northern Gaopo township, or customarily called "18 villages above the Ka", along with the Miao villages in Qiantao township, are in another secondary-level spatial sphere. Shangwu in the southwest corner of Gaopo township, and the Miao villages such as Guanshan and Jialie in the territory of Huishui belong to another spatial sphere. In addition, Yangwang of Guiding county and nearby Miao villages, the Miao villages around Dailin of Longli county, Xiabaibang and Gangdu in Huishui belong to the spatial spheres of the same level, which are, in parallel with the above spatial spheres, jointly called "36 Jia, 72 Bai." All the Miao people in this sphere are "Meng Rong" who belong to the same group and the spaces they occupy are deemed internal. It is evident that the definition of secondary-level spatial spheres by the Miao people has nothing to do with administrative boundaries. They often span across townships, counties, and prefectures, and as a result, many Miao-related matters tend to concern a few nearby prefectures and counties. They usually are not directly related to distance. Some Miao villages that belong to the same spatial sphere do not border each other or even are tens or hundreds of Li apart. Houlong of Mengguan township in Guiyang city, for instance, is deemed a village of the "18 villages under the Ka".

Spatial spheres of a higher level are defined by oath of alliance or protocol. Oath of alliance is established by jointly worshiping the ancestors of each party by bulls. Each party to the alliance assumes obligations and enjoys rights according to the parts of the bull it receives in the ceremony. In history, the revolt of this Miao group was organized in this manner. Social groups established this way are contemporary and have the nature of crossing the relationship of blood and affinity. They would dismiss once the goal for such alliance is achieved. The alliance is formed by common needs without having to consider the original relationship. For this reason, some revolts in history were joint actions between this Miao group and other Miao groups.

Spatial spheres created by protocol are different, as in protocol, this Miao group is an independent system and often does not have established interactions of protocol with other groups. Spatial spheres created this way are relatively stable. For example, people from up and down the Ka in Gaopo township would invite each other to join the bull-fighting or ancestor worshiping ceremonies where members from both sides view themselves an integrated group. It is said that it had been the practice that villages such as Shanping and Jiading and Yangwang in Guiding and Dailin in Longli would invite each other for such occasions. It was interrupted later out of difficulty to contact each other at time of social unrest. However, it is possible that the practice may resume when all the parties are willing to. It is evident that spatial spheres that are maintained by protocol interactions have a boundary that corresponds to geographic locations, which sometimes is explicit and sometimes implicit.

The spatial sphere of the entire ethnic group is also established by oath of alliance. This Miao group would give a name to any other Miao group that has had a relationship of alliance with it, such as "Miao in cedar trees", and "Miao on the top of the mountain" mentioned earlier. Of course, the counterpart would give this Miao group a specific group name. As a result, the spatial sphere would extend to anywhere that is occupied by other Miao groups who have had contact with them. Anywhere outside the three levels of spatial sphere is unexceptionally deemed external. The Han villages or Buyi villages are all external to the Miao people. While delivering the sacrificial speech in funerals, they would clearly point out the Miao route and guide the souls of their deceased ancestors pass the Buyi and Han areas to the remote areas where all their ancestors had lived together.

Miao's perception of things is symmetric and dichotomic. They think that homogeneous things can always be split in symmetric half. Things that are developing before they can be split in symmetric half are always attached to the original unit to form a dynamic trinitarian unit. Therefore, the composite numbers of multiples of 2 and 3 form the fundamental structural relationship in the world. This set of hierarchical form is demonstrated in language to be the "four-character phrases in the Miao language" as linguists describe it. In fact, such "four-character forms" in language are often compound words that carry uneven weight in meaning, instead of each character carrying real meaning. As we mentioned, this manifests in time to form the year, month, season and days in the Miao calendar that are superposition of the composite numbers of 2 and 3, so does it in social organizations and geographical concepts. For instance, the names of all villages here are given by putting together the names of two villages that have the closest relationship in blood. Shanping village, or [ʑoŋ^{31}tƐ^{55}ʑoŋ^{31}ntæ^{13}] in the Miao language, literarily means Ping village and Chang village, translated phonetically to be "Rong Deng and Rong De". All the villages in this Miao group are formed by two villages. Even the Han and Buyi geographic names are treated the same by the Miao group. Guiyang is called [qƐ^{31}saŋ^{55}qƐ^{31}ʑaŋ^{55}], literarily Big City and Sheep City, Qingyan is called **[**qƐ^{31}lu^{13}qƐ^{31}ʑaŋ^{55}**]**, literarily Rabbit Field and Sheep Field.

A smaller village, Shanmu village, is attached to Shanpin village, which is a new village emerging out of Rongdeng village. It is called **[qo**ŋ^{13}tɕa^{43}**]** in the Miao dialect, meaning "wind hole" and phonetically "Kong Jia". As it does not have a twin village to form a combined village, it can not be an independent unit. When the name of a village represents a region, or a community, it is called "Rongdeng Rongde". When it only represents the location of the village, it is called "Kong Jia". As this name reflects the characteristic of the location, i.e., a hole behind the village that blows cold wind all year round, it can not be an independent unit. Similar situations also exist in the six villages that have affinity relationship with Shanping village. This is the reason why this region is jointly called "18 villages under the Ka", which corresponds with the secondary spatial sphere that is analyzed previously. Broadly speaking, all villages that belong to this secondary-level spatial sphere part of the 18 villages. In addition to the "18 villages above the Ka" that we mention earlier, Guiding Yangwang is also called "18 villages of Yangwang". This notion is extended further to form "36 Jia, 72 Bai" that are the composite numbers of 2 and 3. Such a cognitive pattern has a long history in this Miao group, and can trace back in the Han literature at least as early as the end of the 13th century. All the geographic names mentioned in *History of Yuan · Geography* are duplex village names, such as "Chashan Baina", "Zhongcao Baina", etc. When the headsman of this Miao group paid the first tributary visit to the nation's capital, she brought with her the subordinate units that were the composite numbers of 2 and 3. According to *History of Yuan,* "(in the second month of the second year of Taiding) Ding Hai, the mother of the headsman of Pingfa Miao group brought with her a total of

100,000 households to surrender, and led local headsman in the number of 360 to pay the tribute." [①] These 360 people were apparently the headsmen of basic level villages, and it happened to be the composite number of 2 and 3, indicating that all the basic units were in the composite number of 2 and 3.

Ethnic Miao people apply this set of cognitive pattern in their understanding of society as well as nature. Although Betula luminifera and cherry trees are different plant varieties, they are both the symbolic plants for the month of snake simply because they bloom at the same time. Out of this cognitive pattern, these two plants must be used together but not separately when representing the month of snake. The cognition of celestial bodies follows the same pattern. Miao people believe that sun and moon are a pair of parallel things while stars are derivatives of the two created in ancient time by a hero who shot and shattered the scorching sun and moon to give rise to these fragments called stars. It is apparent that such an explanation seems to have originated from the same place as Shanmu village was derived from Shanping village, which we mentioned earlier. The clue of such a set of cognitive pattern can also be found in morphogenesis, animal reproduction, and human body structure.

The cognitive orientation of the Miao group includes three patterns: prioritized cognitive hierarchy, level of cognitive accuracy and level of cognitive width. Facing a complex and intricate world, the ethnic Miao people would not use their limited cognitive ability in all the matters without prioritization. They must consider the situations and, based on the need of subsistence and development of its ethnic group, prioritize nearby nature and society and rationally apply their cognitive ability, thus giving rise to prioritized cognitive hierarchy. The ethnic Miao people always begin to cognize the world from the matters they interact the most frequently, which, once positioned in the cognitive framework, would become the chief source to extend to the understanding of new things. In the process of extended cognition, when the focus frequency of a certain attribute of a matter drops, it would naturally lead to the decrease of focus on this attribute. Following this line of development, ethnic Miao people have constructed their own level of cognitive accuracy. In the extended cognition, the more distant a matter is from this Miao group, the chance of it being cognized becomes smaller, thus

① *The History of the Yuan Dynasty* (Biography of Emperor Taiding) (Zhonghua Book Company punctuated edition, 2nd print, July 1983), 654.

widening the level of cognitive width and eventually establishing the Miao cognitive orientation.

The characteristics in ethnic Miao's cognitive pattern are obvious and factual. It is hard for us to list them all within a limited space in this book due to the wide influences they have. Some conclusions that we have summarized roughly and listed below, however, are enough to unveil the generality of these characteristics. Ethnic Miao people do not have the concepts such as constellation, star, planet, and ecliptic etc., even in today, but they have a profound understanding of the creatures on earth. Everyone is able to identify hundreds of useful plants and animals, and know very well all the phenological changes. They are able to tell, by the subtle changes on the body of a plant, which kind of insect has caused the harm to the plant. It is as accurate as the insect pest warning issued by entomologists. They also are able to determine the gender and size of a beast by the mark and excrement it leaves behind. Based on this, it is not exaggerating to say that Miao people are expert observers of things on earth but lack the knowledge about heaven. The ethnic Miao people can distinguish the complete metamorphosis from the incomplete metamorphosis of an incest based on its pupation, distinguish a moth from a butterfly by the shape of its antenna, tell apart tens of kinds of trees whose logs can be used as building materials by their texture, and determine that a certain kind of soil is suitable for the growth of what kinds of crops by the composition of phytocoenosium. In fact, they are able to make a qualitative evaluation on the soil acidity and alkalinity, but know little about the organs of insects, and have limited knowledge about rocks with the only exception what kinds of stones can be used as firestone. Based on these phenomena, it is conclusive that Miao people are good at observing external appearance, capturing things in motion, but have insufficient understanding of internal structure. It further confirms the reality in the Miao's cognitive pattern. Basically, the concepts of plain and ocean are not established in the Miao community, and the largest flat place they understand is [ɳtaŋ^{13}], which is in practice phonetically translated as "Zhang". This word is commonly seen in geographic names, which refers to a large plat area that is big enough for thousands of people to dance. They name a cowrie, the shell of a shellfish from the tropical seas that they use as decoration, as "sea". They don't know how to describe the sea, but to the contrary, they know everything about the plants and animals and the meteorological changes in the regions where they live. It is surprising that they know a lot of accurate details about elephants and apes, even about their living habits, but there are no elephants or apes in the regions now. Speculatively, these two kinds of animals might have lived here in large population in ancient time. To be good at understanding things nearby but lack of knowledge in things from a distance is an accurate generalization of the characteristics in the width of their cognitive pattern.

Ethnic Miao people classify the knowledge by its use value, which naturally extends in meaning into types of classification. For instance, edible leafs are named systematically by [mləŋ^{22}] (meaning soft) in Miao language and is a major type of plants. Consequently, taro, morning glory and bamboo shoots are deemed separate plants. The names for trees that are used as building materials all have **[hu^{24}]** as prefix, meaning an individual plant or trunk. Subsequently, gymnosperms such as pine, cedar, cypress are classified as the same type with angiosperms such as birch, chestnut tree, peach tree, pear tree and Chinese toon, while the plants whose fruits are edible are named with **[pi^{13}]** as prefix, meaning fruit; subsequently, not only the fruits that are common to us but also some vines herbaceous plants are classified in this category. For example, some solanaceae and cucurbitaceous plants are called "fruits". Animals are classified by the same methodology. As ancient Miao people fed on honey bee pupae and some kinds of fruit flies, these two kinds of insects were jointly referred to as [moŋ^{31}] in the Miao language.

It is not possible for us to elaborate and list all Miao cognitive patterns here as they are very complex and exquisite, which is demonstrated by a few examples above. With the knowledge in these cognitive patterns in the Miao society, we are able to depict the lifestyle of the Miao people in ancient time.

III From Ancient to Modern Times

This Miao group underwent two verifiable transformations in lifestyle. The first one occurred in the years of Jiaqing and Daoguang in the Qing dynasty, and the second one started in the 1940s and has lasted till today. The first was a transformation from the Swidden cultivation (slash-and-burn cultivation or cultivation by hoes as was previously described) to traditional agriculture. The second was a transformation from the traditional agriculture to modern agriculture. We must point out that, superficially, the two transformations happened when the old means of livelihood was replaced by the new one, but in fact, they contained much wider and deeper contents than the means of livelihood. Anything that is related to the lifestyle was changed to different extents and in different contents. A cultural re-construction is perhaps a more appropriate term to describe the essence of such a transformation. The goal of cultural re-construction is to adjust the culture to be more adapted to the new lifestyle through the selective introduction of new cultural elements that are later incorporated into the overall cultural system after digestion and absorption to eventually give rise to a new cultural structure that is different from the old one, subject to a running-in period in the operation between the old and new cultures. The overall transformation is a process where the new and old cultural elements are organically configured and dynamically re-constructed through operation rather than some simple come-in and get-out.

After the cultural re-construction, the lifestyle has been transformed, making it difficult for regular ethnological surveys to directly restore or take a glimpse into what it used to be like. To probe into the lost lifestyle, two types of materials come in handy in addition to the cognitive patterns that were analyzed in the previous section. One is the ancient literature in Han language and the other is local cultural relics and articles. An accurate reflection of reality requires more than simply putting them together but a comprehensive analysis. The key to the success of such a research methodology is to fully understand the strengths and weaknesses of these three types of materials. The ancient cultural relics are unquestionably authentic but are dead and rigid. They do not have the value of interpretation without referencing the cultural sub-systems that were slow in evolution and development. Ancient literatures, when used for understanding ethnic minority groups, are basically indirect materials but have the dynastic value whose authenticity must be verified with the help of cultural relics and live cultural elements. Cognitive patterns are the live things that we can still see and feel now but are highly abstract whose value of interpretation can not materialize without the verification of direct material evidences, nor can they ascertain the specific time in the transformation of lifestyle without dynastic support by ancient literatures.

The first cultural re-construction was made possible by Yongzheng's (1723-1735) massive measure of *Gai Tu Gui Liu* (to replace local hereditary headsmen with officials appointed and sent from the central government), which impacted and conflicted with the Miao lifestyle primarily in the following three aspects. First, after *Gai Tu Gui Liu*, the northwest part in the Miao distribution area, in the west and north of present-day Gaopo township including Shanping village, was put under Guiyang Fu directly and named "Si Si Li" – *Zhongcao Zheng Zhangguan, Zhongcao Fu Zhangguan, Baina Zheng Zhangguan and Baina Fu Zhangguan.* Although the smaller *Tu Si* were not deposed, they were not allowed to make their own rules but to follow the government laws and regulations. The local Miao people were never subordinates of *Tu Si* but were subjects of the Qing dynasty. *Tu Si* were proxy managers. Subsequently, the Miao people from Shanping village repeatedly came to Guiyang Fu to file accusation of local *Tu Si* for their excessive levying of taxes and extreme cruelty. Secondly, the control on military forces was taken away from *Tu Si*, which was evidenced by the inscriptions on the tombstones of *Tu Si* in generations. Since then, *Tu Si* did not have the power to coerce and force the Miao people into doing anything and the change in the life of Miao people was no longer interfered by *Tu Si*. Third, also the most critical point, the way to levy taxes on and pay taxes by the Miao people was completely changed. Before the change, it was Tu Si who had determined by following customs on the targets to levy taxes and the amount of tax. Now the Miao people followed the national unified tax rules to pay taxes, and thus had the same tax burden as the Han people in the Han regions. Since then, rice, a crop that had not been grown by the Miao people, and silver became the contents of tax payment, which was the direct reason that stimulated the Miao people to begin cultivating rice fields in a massive scale. The radical changes in these three aspects shook the social life in Shanping village and eventually led to a cultural re-construction and subsequent great changes to lifestyle, which were reflected in production and labor, material life, social politics and spiritual life.

Among all types of human economic life, the Swidden cultivation and agricultural cultivation are two completely different types, which differ dramatically not only in production tool, operation of technology, production organization and structure of cultivated lands, but also in the direction of development in the above aspects.[1] Some people call the Swidden cultivation as "primitive agriculture" and think that they would naturally

[1] Feng Liu, "A Rethinking of 'Primitive Agriculture' in the Contemporary Era", *The History of Agriculture in China*, no.1 (1995), 6-16.

evolve into the "traditional agriculture" with the advancement of technology. Such a perception does not look appropriate if the transformation in production in Shanping village is taken into account.

The tools used by the ancient Miao people in Shanping village included long knife, sword, bow and crossbow etc., which, along with other supplementary tools, made up the structure of tool in the dry land Swidden cultivation. This structure underwent a drastic change after the first cultural re-construction and began to be dominated by farm cattle, plough, hoe and sickle. The primary tools that had been used before were diminished to a secondary position, turned into a ritual article, or completely got out of use. In ancient time, the Miao predecessors prepared the cultivated fields by first clearing the weeds and shrubs with long knives and then setting the fields on fire. They took the ears of rice with bush knifes and then bundled them for storage without threshing in the field. They shielded the crops from the damage of animals with their bows and crossbows, and long knives. In Shanping village, we witnessed a real long knife that was a steel knife with 80 cm in length, merely 3.5 cm in width, and an iron ring attached to the handle as decoration. We were told by the owner of the knife that it was a weapon used in the anti-Qing revolt. The obvious horizontal bend on the body of the knife, however, indicated that it was not used on humans but hard wood trunks that measured about 5 cm across. The big decorative ring attached to the handle made it inconvenient in the fight with people, but was there to tie a large piece of cloth or silk that made it easier to find the knife in case when it was dropped in the jungle. The blade tip was worn to a shape of blunt round and had the mark of cut by hard objects, indicating that it was not only used for cutting, but also in carving the land and digging shallow pits. The usage of this kind of long knife was depicted in *Poems about Central Guizhou* by Jiang Jinzhi of the Ming dynasty: "All the mountainous lands were cultivated with fire and everyone went out with knives with them." In addition, the *Book of Guizhou Continued* had designated a piece to "Miao Knife".

After the cultural re-construction, long knives were taken out of usage. As a result, the owner of the knife could not name it in the Miao language but simply called it "combat knife". From the laws in corresponding phonetics in the Miao language, we've found out that the word of this long knife exists in all Miao dialects that refer to exactly the same thing. With the physical relics in Shanping village, it does not make sense that the dialect spoken by this Miao group does not have this word. Based on the ancient Miao phonetics by Professor Wang Fushi, we restored the pronunciation of this long knife in this Miao dialect and found that such word existed in their spoken language pronounced as [ntaŋ^{55}](dang), which was used to refer to the sword carried by Han swordsman. We were encouraged by such a finding. It clearly showed that although some articles that were out of use in the cultural re-construction had become antiques, the corresponding cultural elements in the cultural system would not simply vanish, but instead, would remain in the cultural system, subject to some adjustment and adaptation, in other forms to play some other social functions. The adjustment and adaptation in the cultural re-construction does follow certain rules. The long knives were originally used for dual purposes as agricultural tools and weapons. In the cultural adjustment and adaptation, the function of agricultural tool disappeared but that of weapon was intensified, which was in fact an appropriate method of extension. Following this train of thought, we later found tens of evidences in similar nature, some of which will be explained in detail in the text that follows.

Unlike the long knives, bows, crossbows and picking knives were not completely taken out of usage after the first cultural re-construction, for the reason that in addition to rice, the local Miao people also grew millet, red panicum crus, oat, and wheat where picking knives could also be used. Besides, this region was infested with harmful animals and bows and crossbows could be used to protect crops. The blade of a picking knife was 5 cm in length and 3 cm in width. There were two holds on the back of the knife used to pull through threads that wrap around fingers when in use. Picking knives could only be used to harvest the dry land crops and sticky rice whose grains were not easy to drop and which must be bundled before carrying home. It was also mentioned in the *Poems of Central Guizhou* by Jiang Jinzhi: "The burning marks on the mountain cliffs were clearly visible; The ears of rice smelled good when in the Spring of the next year; The savings of common people are seen from here; It was not like the government that had storage of food." The notes to the poem wrote: "The practice in Guizhou was to store rice but not cereal" (the word "rice" was mistakenly used in this poem. This poem can be used as evidence.) It was due to the limited paddy fields that local Miao people have not totally abandoned growing coarse cereals on the dry lands. This is an issue that has not been eased so far and thus it is an objective fact that picking knives are still being used now.

The bows and crossbows that Miao people used were poisoned. It is a traumatic poisonous plaster that was made by mixing bee venoms and bird heads, and was applied on the heads of arrows to make highly effective weapons when hunting beasts. Although the Qing government explicitly prohibited its use after *Gai Tu Gui Liu*, the poisonous bows and crossbows had been used by Miao people before the liberation. After the 1960s, the destruction of forests and sharp increase in population extinguished wild beasts, pushing the bows and crossbows out of use. Now, they are used only as ritual items in occasions such as funerals, *Qiao Niu Ji Zu,* and *She Bei Pai*. Most bows and crossbows were made from mulberries and were equipped with a crossbow mechanism that was shot by pulling with fingers. The bows measured 60 to 80 cm in length and the arrows were light and short. The bows had great elastic force, enough to shoot the arrows more than 50 meters and able to penetrate the beast skins.

After the first cultural re-construction, the use of technology of ploughing with cattle and harvesting with sickles was widespread. However, both the corresponding concept and technical application were different from the Han and Buyi groups. Unlike the other ethnic groups who treasured farm cattle, the ethnic Miao people raised buffalo and cattle in large number, but only a small part of them were used in cultivation, all the others were used in sacrificial ceremonies. Cattle used for sacrificial ceremonies were raised with extreme care and fed with refined grains and not used for labor work. To the contrary, the cattle used for cultivation were fed with coarse fodder. They don't think that ploughing was the best way of land preparation. After the harvest in the fall, occasions such as ancestor worship, wedding ceremonies or funerals often prevented them from ploughing in time. Although we were worried for them and suggested that they act immediately before the land was hardened which made it difficult for the cattle to plough, they responded with smile in relaxation and told us not to worry as they could always dig by hoes.

From the field survey, we found that the farm cattle trained by the Miao farmers in Shanping village could not make a 360° turn on the spot, but could only turn by a limited angle. Consequently, the furrows in the paddy fields did not run in parallel but were in similar concentric shapes. The often started ploughing from and circling around the raised path through fields, and then moved inward a little bit to make another circle. The process was repeated until the center of the paddy fields. When asked why they ploughed this way, they told us that these paddy fields did not hold water. To plough the edge of the fields and to block the leakage with the mud kept the water in the paddy fields. It sounded that they did it deliberately. They transplanted rice seedlings in the same way, starting from the edge of the fields and left the center for the last. They could not explain why they did that but only said they had never noticed it. Another practice different from the other ethnic groups seemed to be related to this way of operation. When offering compensation, they did not count *jin*, *dou* or percentage, but allocated one or a few lines of output of rice from the edge of the field. According the local Miao, such a practice was clear to both sides and would not give rise to any dispute. Facing such perplexing facts, any rash conclusion would prove to bring more harm than good. We have to admit, however, that although ethnic Miao people have been planting rice for more than one century, the way they use means of production has not be synchronized with the other ethnic groups.

Swidden cultivation and agricultural production are two completely different human economic lifestyles. Both have unique strengths in technology orientation and are difficult to be compatible with each other. After the first cultural re-construction, rice planting was accepted by the Miao people who were willing to develop the rice production but with some objective difficulties. Among the numerous difficulties, the most lethal one was the limitation by the living environment. This region was characterized with high mountains and deep valleys and rugged surface, the fields that could be turned into paddy fields were very limited. It is beyond the ability of the Miao people to expand the paddy fields whether 100 years ago when rice planting was first introduced in this region or today with highly developed technology. As a result, they had to depend on the traditional Swidden cultivation for subsistence even though they liked rice. Consequently, the cultural re-construction did not create a genuine agricultural type of culture but a deformed combination of Swidden cultivation and agricultural production.

Technically, the Swidden cultivation requires that we search, identify and make use of all the plants and animals growing in the region to the maximum extent instead of trying to find ways of increasing the output of a limited number of crops. With the understanding of the cognitive patterns we discussed in previous section, it is not difficult for us to realize that ethnic Miao's cognitive patterns happen to meet the requirements of the Swidden cultivation. The agricultural production is different. It requires that the main technological focus be put on increasing the output of crops and wiping out all the plants and animals that grow naturally but hinder the growth of crops. The incompatibility between the two has made the technical accuracy in the rice planting in the Miao regions lag behind that in the Han or Buyi groups in the intermontane basins not only in the period of more than one century ago but even in today. What is more puzzling is that although local Miao people often come down the mountains to work for the Han and Buyi people in their rice fields and followed the technical instructions from them, when they go back and work on their own fields, they seem to have forgotten what they are told and learn. We have to admit, from these examples, that technological introduction is not only about learning new technologies but, more importantly, is about whether we can find the necessary point for the growth of the learned technologies in the local society and technology. It is not difficult to understand this issue if we expand our vision to observe the dry land cultivation by the local people.

The local Miao people grow no less than tens of different dry land crops including different kinds of bens, wheat, corn, buckwheat, red panicum crus etc. Among them, millet and red panicum crus are the most representative of the Swidden cultivation. They cut all the weeds before they seed in the fall for the purpose of reducing the rate of sprouting in the sandy soil in the next year. They then burn all the weeds and branches that have been chopped in the spring that follows. Millets may be sowed directly on the warm ashes and the dibbling of red panicum crus must wait for the ashes to cool down after a rain. Now they only need to wait patiently for harvesting. Originally, we were worried that the weeds may outgrow the crops in the following year, only found later that our concern was unnecessary. For one reason, local people already mastered the skill of selecting which crops to grow next year. Secondly, many wild plants that grew next year were useful and thus were made use of before they run rampant. For example, ferns had perennial roots and could not be uprooted either by cutting or burning. Ferns that newly sprouted were edible and when growing older, they could be used as fodder.

Their impact on the crops was very limited after being picked a few times. Other dry land crops were often mixed in one plot of land and were harvested whenever a crop was ripe. This was not like agricultural production where a plot of land only grew one or two kinds of crops, which were harvested and stored when they matured at the same time. The technical goal of the Miao people was to ensure that different varieties of plants mature successively so that a continuous supply of food was guaranteed. We have to admit that ethnic Miao people already knew that the Han way of growing rice was able to increase the output by a certain percentage, however, they wound not apply these technologies in their own rice fields before the increase in output was enough to replace all the dry land crops they used to plant. Such a choice was rational and wise, and thus should not be surprising to us.

Agricultural production is an economic type with strong seasonality. Missing a season would mean a drastic reduction of output and the loss of livelihood protection. The Swidden cultivation, on the other hand, was a type where planting and harvesting may take place at the same time. What was most apparent in Shanping village was that their seasons of planting and harvesting lasted longer than those of other ethnic groups. This was not purely a result of late arrival of seasons or lack of water resources, but the result of taking dry lands into account. Dry lands had to be cultivated by planting and harvesting at the same time. While people were busy working on the paddy fields, they had to harvest the wheat and plant corns and beans in the dry lands. From the perspective of agricultural economy, although paddy fields incurred some loss, the output from the dry lands prevented temporary shortage of food. The fields in Shanping village grew quite a number of different varieties of crops. Although the output of each variety was small, they matured at different time in successive order. Consequently, their granaries were not as full as Han groups, but it is less likely to have famine as crops were harvested in every season.

Now let's take a look at organizational transformation. Before the first cultural re-construction, the production organizations in the region made cyclical switch following the seasonal changes in the Miao calendar. In hot seasons, large-season planting and harvesting were carried out by the organizations formed by blood relationship, while in cold seasons, groups formed by affinity began handicraft work and hunting. As Swidden cultivation has nomadic characteristics, these production organizations moved across different areas with the change in season, up to the mountains in hot seasons and down to the intermountane basins in cold seasons. Besides, as land fertility tended to decrease after use for a protracted period of time, the location of the village in hot seasons was subject to constant changes as well. Within a relatively stable region, the village might rotate in cycle among several places but the name was kept unchanged as it was deemed to be linked with the specific patriarchal clan. The name of the village would not change unless the specific patriarchal clan moved to another location. Such a way of nomadic production was also mentioned in the *Poems of Central Guizhou* by Jiang Jinzhi: "The location of Hua Miao moved from place to place and how could we send someone to delivery the declaration of war to the hundreds of the southern barbarians." "Hua Miao" in the poems referred to the Miao group who spoke Guiyang sub-dialect. "Bai Man" (hundreds of southern barbarians) referred to all the ethnic minority groups including this Miao group who were in a Swidden cultivation. Certainly, the nomadic nature in the areas of production and locations of the village appeared strange to the ethnic groups who were in settlement agriculture, and would therefore triggered some misunderstanding and denunciation. It was recorded in the local annals in the early Qing dynasty that "Bai Miao (white Miao) liked to dress in white and were simple-minded and crafty. They moved around and did not settle down in a place, and often left without paying rent when hired by others to farm a land."[①] It is true that they "moved around and did not settle down in a place". They had to move around with their patriarchal clan and therefore could not stick to the lands that they were hired to work on as was the case with the residents who lived in settlement. They did not escape on purpose. With regards to the accusation that they "often left without paying rent", it might have been related to the different ways of calculating the compensation by both parties. It is therefore untrue and derogatory to say that they were "simple-minded and crafty".

The first cultural re-construction did not blow the production organizations significantly for the reason that the smaller *Tu Si* were still in place above them and the local government did not put them in the official household registration system and kept the internal organizations intact, only collecting taxes from the clan chiefs. These chiefs were called *Zhai Lao*

① (Kangxi) *General Annals of Guizhou*, s.v. "Ethnic Miao: White Miao", mimeograph edition in the collection of Guizhou Provincial Library.

(village head) within the ethnic group and "Liang Tou" (literarily grain head) by the government officials. However, a greater change occurred in the way of production activities. Due to the need for planting rice and the increase in the importance of paddy fields in the overall economy, the necessity of the original migration with change in seasons decreased, resulting in the stabilization of the villages. The sites that were village locations for cold seasons subsequently evolved into sites of pure holiday gatherings. The sites for hot seasons had mostly been located near the slash-and-burn lands. After paddy fields were cultivated, the villages were gradually moved down to situate on the hillside above the newly cultivated paddy fields. Shanping village had had a site for hot seasons on the steep hillside to the north of the present-day village where there were only dry lands and many wild flowers, thus was called "Ge Bang" in the Miao language, meaning land of flowers. The large paddy fields at Zhaijiao of Shanping village used to be called [ʑoŋ^{13}mpa^{43} haŋ43], wild boar forest in the Miao language, and was the hunting ground for their ancestors. They were turned into paddy fields in the late period of Qianlong. Originally, as the fields were surrounded with dense forests and steep slopes, buffalos could not get in. Shanping villagers led by Luo Wenkui, *Zhai Lao* in the first generation, built a meandering mountain slab-stone path that eventually let the buffalos in to assist in the rice field cultivation. The stone tablet in memory of this event is kept till today.[①] According to the villagers, Luo Wenkui was the first one in the clan who could speak and read Han language. The name was given to him by his Han tutor in the old-type private school, and, without a doubt, must be the first Han-style name in the entire group. With the help of cattle, the wild boar forests were able to be turned into the paddy fields, which lay the foundation for the current stable site of Shanping village. The little path constructed under the leadership of Luo Wenkui connected two paddy fields in "Sanchagou" and "Zhaijiao" and was the major and only way for Shanping villagers to work in the paddy fields, and was understandably viewed as a treasure by them. It had been in use until 1963 when a highway was constructed to replace it.

The fact that the villages tended to stabilize and paddy fields were cultivated produced one derivative effect: the sites for cold seasons lost

① Longshuo Yang, "Postscript for Long Cun Suo Yao Tablet", *Guiyang Annals Material Studies,* no. 3, (September 1988), 44-47.

economic values, and in the meantime, the slash-and-burn fields that were far from the village settlement were gradually abandoned, resulting in the transformation in the structure of cultivated lands. Our attempt to know the details and the start and end time of such a transformation was frustrated by limited materials. However, below materials have offered some hints to our interest. As mentioned previously, Pigong bull-fighting ground was the site for Shanping and its five affinity villages for cold seasons. Nowadays, the Miao villagers still think that it is their land where each of the five villages has assigned plots. In a bull-fighting event, villagers from each of these villages gathered in the specifically assigned plot, which could be understood as the remainder from the ancient village activities in cold seasons. The bull-fighting ground was now surrounded by Buyi cultivated lands and villages and it enraged the Miao villagers who told us that their possession of this ground had already been decided by the government which, according to them, was evidenced by the inscription on the cliff facing this bull-fighting ground. The contents of the inscription were indeed a reflection what the Miao villagers had said. The verdict was made by Guiyang Fu and Dingfan Fu, present-day Huishui county, in the 5th year of Wanli of the Ming dynasty (1597). ① Both ethnic Miao and Buyi groups were under the control of *Tu Si* at the time. By the laws of the Ming dynasty, the local government might choose not to handle the disputes arising from regions under the control of *Tu Si*. Accordingly, the hearing of this case by the government meant that it was deemed beyond the scope of authority of *Tu Si*. The verdict for the Miao people was also worth noting. It was apparently made based on the historically continuous possession of the land as in the Ming dynasty, lands under *Tu Si* were not registered with the Ministry of Revenue and thus did not have records with the government. The existence of this tablet inscription at least indicated that in the years of Wanli of the Ming dynasty, ethnic Miao people had effectively occupied and used the village sites for cold seasons. The move-in of the Buyi people was a result of its growth in population, and the seizure of their original lands by the Han military and civilian people who emigrated from the Han regions. We want to make one additional point that similar disputes were commonplace in central Guizhou, as were evidenced by similar tablet inscriptions we spotted in Huishui, Longli and Guiding, and

① Huiquan Zhang, "Postscript for Pigong Dog Ground Inscriptions on Precipices", *Guiyang Annals Material Studies,* September (1983), 40-44.

they have lasted until today. In the 1950s and 1960s, the committee of ethnic affairs in Guiyang city re-processed the dispute on Pigong. Other related counties also handled similar disputes. According to *General Annals of Guizhou* (Kangxi), "(Miao) mainly fed on wheat and panicum crus mixed with wild plants as vegetables. Rice was stored and mainly used as tributary foods or to treat guests" indicating that rice planting was not common among Miao people at the moment and had not changed much from what had been described in the tablet in Pigong. As *General Annals of Guizhou* (Kangxi) was completed at the end of the 17th century, it recorded that Miao people last abandoned their production in the cold season after the 18th century. During the years of Qianlong, the repeated military actions caused shortage of official grain supply. To ease the difficulty, the Qing government once demanded that local Miao people turned in rice and grains instead of money as tax payment. In the 11th year of Qianlong (1746), *Tu Si* asked that the old way of revenue collection be restored. As was indicated in the documents submitted to upper level officials for approval, "Some *Tu Si* such as Baina under Guiyang stated that they used to pay tax in silver, but now are asked to turn in rice, which is difficult in transportation."[①] Although it was true that transportation of rice was not easy, it was the Miao farmers but not *Tu Si* who would suffer. The reason that *Tu Si* pleaded on behalf of Miao farmers was, we think, that what remained after paying tax would not be enough for self-consumption due to the limited output of rice. Difficulty in transportation was only a secondary reason. It indicated that the paddy fields in the Miao region were limited in the mid-18th century.

The stone tablet with an inscription about land ownership that is still kept in Shanping village was made in the years of Xianfeng of the Qing dynasty. It was about the Han people who immigrated in the regions around Gaopo and built Huayan Temple, then bought some cultivated lands and fields in Shanping village. The distinction between cultivated lands and fields was made in the inscription and the former outnumbered the latter. Although this tablet did not offer direct evidence for us to estimate the ratio between paddy fields and dry lands, it at least proved that in the mid-19th century, the Shanping villagers had owned quite a number of paddy fields. It is therefore reasonable for us to conclude that the end of the transformation in land

① Zhengdong Zhang, et al., *Veritable Records of the Qing Dynasty • A Compilation of Materials about Guizhou* (Guizhou People's Publishing House, November 1964), 102.

structure was around this time, i.e., the mid-19th century.

While we carried out fieldwork in Shanping, two Zhai Lao, Luo Zeqing (former party secretary of Gaopo township) and Luo Xinjie, took us to the abandoned slash-and-burn fields, which were located far from Shanping on the top of the hills that separated Gebang, Shanping and other villages. What was out of expectation was that we saw few weeds and shrubs, and the trace of man-made terraces was visible. Later we were told that it was the original plan of their ancestors to turn these lands into fixed dry lands so that they would not need to alternate cultivation and fallow, but the results were not satisfactory. In addition, the long distance between their village and these lands added to cause them lose interest in these lands, which were soon abandoned. There were other people in the village who said that the Miao group had been populous who naturally cultivated a large number of lands, which were later abandoned because of decrease in population as a result of killing by the counter-revolutionists. Luo Xinjie was in total disagreement. According to him, they were the ones who knew the best if their ancestors were killed. It was in those prior years when everyone must talk about class struggle that some people made up this explanation. In fact, their ancestors only cultivated lands on the hillsides but not paddy fields. Now, since they started planting rice in the paddy fields, the lands on the hillsides were naturally abandoned. It had nothing to do with population. If they had to find a relationship with population, now was the time that had more people but fewer lands. Although there was truth to what he said, a further analysis revealed that the real problems were more complex then they seemed. The slash-and-burn lands in previous years were located on the bordering areas between the grasslands on the mountain top and the forests in the valley where the soil was not very thin and the forests were not very dense, making it easy to fell trees. When in burn, the flame that went upward wouldn't harm the forests. After the lands were cultivated that made forests in the valley become sparse, soil began to slide downward along the slopes, resulting in the layer of soil in the slash-and-burn lands becoming thinner. The end of alternating between cultivation and fallow further reduced the fertility in the soil, and eventually made it impossible to continue planting crops. The fact that weeds and shrubs are not growing in these lands is a proof. These facts made us realize that, while the incompatibility between the production technologies from the two types of economy and the difference in the development orientation were in place, any improper introduction of technology only produced undesired results.

The great change in the structure of cultivated lands also brought changes to the production of by-products. According to *Records of Guizhou* by Guo Zizhang, the tributes made by *Tu Si* in the Ming dynasty included East Miao tea and horse. The tea named after the Miao group apparently was produced by the Miao people. It was not produced in the tea plantations but was from the tall trees growing in the bushes. Despite the fact that it was a tributary tea, its production method was of no similarity with other teas used as tributes. The bushes shrank in area after the paddy fields were cultivated. The big-season rice transplanting also took away the labor needed for picking tea leaves. Subsequently, the tea production diminished from the Qing dynasty. Nowadays, only a small number of households plant tall-tree teas, which are mostly for self-consumption and not sold on the market. Meanwhile, all clans in this Miao group have developed their own by-line produces. Since the mid Qing dynasty, Shanping village has sold trees in exchange for money. Among Shanping's affinity villages, Jiading depends on the charcoals from green and red chestnut trees as a source of cash, while Lali gets cash from selling fruits and bamboos. Yunding village above the Ka relies on bamboo weaving craft. Dahong Shimen specializes in transportation by horses. In summary, after the cultural re-construction, businesses by clans and households had emerged in this region and had lasted till 1949.

With the completion of cultural re-construction, Shanping village experienced vast changes in material life that affected every aspect in the basic necessities of people's life.

In clothing, the change in clothing style was the most evident. According to *General Annals of Guizhou* (Jiajing of the Ming dynasty), both male and female dressed in *Guan Shou Yi* (a kind of coat made from one piece of fabric without using scissors), skirts and shorts barely stretching beyond their knees. Men did not wear hats, and women twisted the hair into a bun and fastened it with a long hairpin. With the introduction of large quantity of cotton yarns and clothes made of cotton, the original *Guan Shou Yi* became shorter and evolved to be an ornament that people wear outside their clothes today, *Bei Pai* in Miao language. The Miao word of **[$ə^{13}$]** makes this clear. It pronounces as "**ud**" in the southeast Miao dialect and means "upper outer garment". Meanwhile, women's skirts became longer but were only for protocol occasions. They usually wore pants. After Emperor Qianlong accepted the proposal from He Shen and encouraged Miao people to wear Manchurian clothes, many Miao men chose to wear long gowns and braids.[①] We found fragments of single braid, mandarin jackets and long gowns from the decayed human skeletons buried in the cliff burial caves. Until today, some Miao people still think that long gowns are their ethnic garments, which of course is a misunderstanding. Changes to fabric also happened. According to records of the Ming dynasty, Miao people wore clothes made of wax printing fabric and were able to weave "local brocade" but did not mention what kind of fabric it was. We found out in our fieldwork that the rear loincloth that women wore was made of flax fabric and was starched with pig blood. Such a method was similar to that used by the Miao group in southeast Guizhou, suggesting that it was inherited from the ancient time. In addition, as the region did not produce cotton (due to high humidity), we believe that the wax printing fabric in the Ming dynasty was a linen. Under the influence of the ethnic Yi people, they also made clothes from felt. Now, the rocket of wizards is still made of felt. The introduction of cotton fabrics and cotton yarns in the mid Qing dynasty began to make cotton clothes spread gradually. In the meantime, silk began to enter this region. Nowadays, the venerable members in the group who experienced the ceremony of *Qiao Niu Ji Zu* wear long gowns made of red silk similar to the one-piece dress in grandiose occasions, which was the ancient Miao clothing for men before the Ming dynasty and has now ritualized. Ancient Miao people used Hai (sea), a kind of seashell, as ornament and it has lasted till today. There are differences though. The expansion of by-line business since the mid Qing dynasty caused silver to enter the Miao region and turned silver ornaments to be a popular trend. Like all the other Miao groups, they don't value gold ornaments or jade, indicating that they did not indiscriminately accept all the things from the Han culture. It is consistent, however, that Miao women have been experts in embroidery, making threads out of cotton and weaving fabric, which have not been changed significantly by cultural re-construction. The transformation in residence was most evident in the way that Miao people abandoned nomad-style residence and shifted to settlement. Some changes since then, however, should not be overlooked. Although the Miao village evolved from its site in hot seasons, it moved down the

① *Veritable Records of the Qing Dynasty • A Compilation of Materials about Guizhou, 351.*

mountain to the foot of the mountain right above the paddy fields. Meanwhile, the sites for cold seasons became the sites for holiday gathering. Such a displacement was easy to be proved due to the existence of the original sites. Another change was that some Miao people lived in caves while they alternate from sites for hot and cold seasons. The *Zhu Ji* (bamboo chicken) cave on the mountain in front of Shanping village was at an altitude of more than 70 meters from the paddy fields, where necessities for living remained untouched and now became a perfect place for dating. Although Han literatures did not mention directly that this Miao group had an ancient custom of living in caves, they did have explicit description, in *Yan Xi Ji Wen* by Tian Rucheng of the Ming dynasty under the item "*Ke Meng Gu Yang Miao*", of such a custom that existed in the Miao sub-group in Mashan to the west of the village. We noticed in our fieldwork in the Miao sub-group in Manshan that the cave-living relics were similar to Zhu Ji cave. Language materials are the most evident to prove that they had cave-living custom in ancient time. The local Miao people called home as [plæ^{13}], which had another meaning of "cliff cave" and "house". When the Miao people celebrated their New Year festivals in ancient time, they would "worship the cave" and now they celebrate the "cave-jumping festival", which would be further discussed later in this chapter. Now, they live in wooden-framed and tile-roofed houses, but the walls were not sealed entirely. People usually live upstairs and the downstairs are reserved for cooking, dining, dens for domestic animals, and storage. Due to excessive deforestation, the ancient custom of lighting fire in the traditional fireplace is disappearing and only a small number of households in Shanping village still have fireplaces at home.

Under the influence of the Swidden cultivation, the dietary habits of ancient Miao people varied significantly with seasons, basically to eat whichever was ripe. The limited amount of grains, such as millet, oat, buckwheat, tianxing rice or red panicum crus were never staple food but were stored for the time in shortage of other foods. The supply of meat was not in shortage because of hunting and the need for sacrificial ceremonies. Some little animals that were not eaten by other ethnic groups were normal captures and regular foods in the Swidden cultivation. The Miao people liked wild plants and internal organs of animals as food. As the old Han saying went, "Buckwheat and wheat as grains can not stuff people, bones and blood as meat can not stuff people, and bamboo shoots and ferns as vegetables can not stuff people." The favor of Miao people was exactly the opposite where blood and internal organs were deemed the best for sacrificial ceremonies and for showing one's respect for the aged, and wild plants and coarse cereals were a must for each meal. Foods were cooked by putting every material for the meal in a pot and boiling them, seasoned by fermented sour water and smashed plants with additives made from wild plants. The biggest change brought by cultural re-construction was the introduction of foods, which was recorded in detail by the Han literatures. We will not elaborate any more. We came across situations in our fieldwork where staple and non-staple foods were inverted. Rice and corn as staple food were limited in quantity, but bean paste, primarily kidney beans or rice beans, as non-staple food were five times of rice and enough to make one feel stuffed. They also cooked coarse cereals in the way that Han people cooked rice to make coarse cereal rice. The coarse cereals used included barley, buckwheat, corn, and red panicum crus. The coarse cereal rice looked like rice, and tasted different with a unique fragrant flavor. Lastly, some small animals were taken out of the menu but people still kept the tradition of cooking everything in one pot. This was truly reflected in the Han saying that "Miao people are not rational as they put a handful of rice into the pot when stewing a chicken." In holidays or sacrificial ceremonies, Miao people were like their ancient ancestors when they ate big chunks of meat and drank large bowls of wine. Blood and internal organs of animals were still widely favored. While in Shanping, we ate chicken liver, chicken blood, chitterling, and pig stomach and drank excessively for a few times, feeling deeply the hospitality of the local Miao people and later becoming bosom friends.

Before the cultural re-construction, the region had been covered by dense jungles and thickets where roads were barely visible. Local Miao people starched the fabrics they made by animal protein such as blood, skin jelly or egg white to make them water proof and protected them from being torn by thistles and thorns, which was an indirect evidence of the road condition at the time. Today in Shanping village, only the rear loincloth that women wear are made in this fashion, merely an element left from ancient tradition. After the cultural re-construction, for the purpose of shipping wood, charcoal, bamboo weaving items and live stocks such as cattle and pigs, villages began to pave stone-slate paths. In Shanping village, in addition to the little path mentioned earlier, it constructed Gaopo road, and stone-slate roads in Jiading and Pilin. Small roads were only principal lines of transportation before the highways were constructed and made passable. Now, all villages are connected by highways but horses and people still walk on these stone-slate roads.

Apparently, after the cultural re-construction, the lifestyles whose contents were more closely related to materials changed faster. Otherwise, changes were non-significant. Therefore, social and spiritual life did not change much after the first cultural re-construction until the mid-20th century. We will discuss in detail when it comes to the second cultural re-construction.

IV From Modern to Contemporary Times

In the transformation of Miao lifestyle, social lifestyle progressed slowly, but the spiritual lifestyle evolved even more slowly. In Shanping village, the transformation in both parts had not manifested themselves until early 20th century and accelerated after the liberation. Regardless, some of the ancient lifestyles have remained intact.

Xinhai Revolution had an unprecedented impact on this Miao group. From the 3rd year of Republic of China, the local warlord government in Guizhou began to allocate the "enclaves" and work on building a uniform administrative system. As a result, the remaining lower-level *Tu Si* ceased to act as hereditary proxy rulers and lost their power of absolute control over the Miao people although a significant percentage of them were turned into local basic level officials. Legally speaking, the barriers that had prevented Miao people from directly participating in the domestic political life were removed. However, due to the inertia from hundreds or even one thousand years in the past, the Miao people did not realize such a change in the beginning and consequently, the transformation in social and political lifestyle progressed very slowly in the beginning of the 20th century. Essential changes had remained inconspicuous up to the eve before the liberation. The social life in the Miao community basically continued along the route of ancient tradition.

The traditional Miao community was bonded by a blood relationship and constructed on the foundation of male consanguinity. Shanping village had been dominated by the male members who were decedents of the same first ancestor. It was divided into Chang village, Ping village and Shanmu village that all descended from the same first male ancestor. From the perspective of a blood relationship, villages were patriarchal groups. In terms of social relationship, villagers were either brothers or cousins from the father's family who had equal rights and responsibilities. From the living space perspective, the mountain, water, forest and grassland were owned by the village. Everyone in the village had the right to use them. In such a social organization, anyone that was not related in blood could not settle in except through marriage or adoption. The blood relationship is confirmed through father-son family tree. After a Miao child was born, he/she was named by parents or grandparents after a natural object or a tool, after which, he/she would naturally become a member of this patriarchal clan. By local tradition, a son was first called his own given name, followed by the given name of his father, so was his father. Therefore, once a child's name was determined, his seniority in the family tree was determined. Every family had such a family tree and once a person revealed his family tree, people would know which village and patriarchal clan he was from. This was the reason why every Miao member was required to memorize the patriarchal family tree of his clan, without which, his social status would not be guaranteed. No matter how long a person had been away from the village for any reason, his return back to the village would be immediately approved as long as he could recite the father-son family tree.

As male hereditary system was in place in the Miao society, females were also named at birth but would have to follow the naming convention in the patriarchal clan of his husband. During religious ceremonies, for example, females used the name of her husband to replace her own name when accepting the worship of her children and grandchildren. In the event that a female died before she got married, her original name could be kept without linking to her father's name, but instead, "Guo" was added to her original name. In the Miao community, the youngest son in the family inherited from his parents. Male family members must leave home after getting married and lived in a newly built house, thus becoming the representative of an independent "household." He would represent a new family to attend the social activities of his own patriarchal clan. The youngest son would live with and provide for his mother after getting married until her death. However, at time of social activities, he represented an independent "household", the same with his father. "Shu" that had the closest blood relationship and descended from the same ancestor within six generations formed a "family line". Please note that this wording was borrowed by the writer of the book from other cultures. In the Miao language, such a family line was called by the name of their common ancestor with the word "Fang" (house) attached to it. A natural village was a basic patriarchal clan composed of six "family lines". Regular villages such as Shanping village were formed by two or three basic patriarchal clans. The internal structure of the village was best reflected in the *Long Cun Suo Yao Bei Li* erected under the leadership of Luo Wenkui, the ancestor of Shanping village, in the 16th year of Jiaqing of the Qing dynasty.

The purpose for the erection of this tablet was to require that all the members from this patriarchal clan protect and worship the tomb of their ancestors, Ya Zang (cliff burial) cave. It was the Miao tradition that the coffins of all the ancestors in a patriarchal clan were put together in the same cliff burial cave. As Shanping village was a new patriarchal clan coming out of Ping village, ancestors from both villages were buried in the same cliff burial cave. Therefore, the tablet was jointly erected by the two villages by agreement. It listed all the names of the participants. They were all the original names that combined the names of father and son, with their Han pronunciations. The list was divided into Ping village and Shanmu village, and each basic patriarchal clan included six "family lines" with varied number of households. Needless to say, the names on the tablet were all male heads in each household, which we copy here: "It is hereby announced: from today, no one is allowed to cut and sell the trees (in the tombs of our ancestors). Anyone who violates shall be subject to punishment."

Ping village

Rong Lang, Kou You, Wang Kou, Meng Guan, Peng Guan, Lang Tuo, Shou Li, Liu Peng, Shou Peng, Lang Da, Song Nian

Hu Lian, Ba Ye, Meng Ye, Li Ye

Ming Gui, Da Fa, Mu Bang, Ping Jian, Shou Jian, Hu Jian

Meng Yuan, Chu Chou, Zhong Kou, Song Hai, Song Lian, Bao Re, Hu Feng, Ye Song, Wen Song, Gong Qian

Hu Gou, He Gu, Gang Bu, Guo, Gou He, Lian Bai, Wen Song, Wang Ru, Mu Zao, Bao Gu

Gong Liang, Wen Song, Qiong Liang, Mu Ha

Shanmu village

Song Gou, Lang Nian, Ang Guan
Mao Bao, Qiong Hu, Ha Wan
Song Xian, Kou Fu, Gou Hu, Qiong Jian, Hu Yao, Qiong Wang
Nian Qiong, Zhong Yao, Qiong Mu
Guan Meng, Bao Yuan, Yao Yuan, Da Mu
Dou Nian, Wai Dou, Mu Wang

Jointly erected by a total of 67 households from Ping village and Shanmu village.

Inscribed by Luo Wenqui

Respectfully erected by the two villages together on the Shanghuan Day of the eighth month of the 16th year of Jiaqing.

Each line on the tablet was a "family line" and each village had six "family lines". It was not coincident that each basic patriarchal clan included six "family lines" as it was the result of Miao's cognitive framework. We discussed the Miao cognitive framework in section ii and here we make some further clarification. In real social life, each component part of Miao's cognitive framework did not exist in isolation but was organically combined based on actual needs. From the perspective of cognitive hierarchy, Miao people thought that everything in the world existed in symmetry. Therefore, "two" was at the core of all numbers. Before gaining independence, new things would be treated as part of parent body. Consequently, the status before split must be "three", which reflected the status in Shanping village that was made up of three patriarchal clans. The minimum unit in a compound structure must be the product of 2 and 3, i.e., 6. That was why each basic patriarchal clan must consist of six "family lines". The Miao society was built on 2, 3 and 6 in different layers. From the spatial arrangement, each basic patriarchal clan occupied a certain space. Chang village and Ping village, as the core and basic patriarchal clans, were located in parallel on each side of a hill, Ching village being in the east and Ping village in the west. Shanmu village, as a new village split from Ping village, could not be put in parallel with the above two villages, but was built at the foot of a hill opposite to Ping village. Each "family line" within basic patriarchal clans also occupied a specific space. Each of the six "family lines" contained in Chang village and Ping village formed a line along the contour line. In other words, each village had houses across six lines. Of course, the six lines of house might be different in length due to the different number of people each "family line" had. Such a spatial arrangement had lasted till the eve of the liberation. In recent years, the widening gap between rich and poor among Miao households resulted in some wealthy households starting to build larger homes on other locations, which began to break the ancient tradition of Miao group. From the timing arrangement, all villages with an independent status, such as Ping village and Chang village of Shangping village, must occupy a specific location in the cycle of time. To put it more specifically, Chang village corresponded to rabbit in terms of day, month and year, while Ping village corresponded to rooster. Such a correspondence was not an abstract acknowledgement but was down to the norms in actual social activities. Among the many Miao holidays in a year, the ones that were celebrated in the month of rabbit must be led by Chang village and supported by Ping village across the affinity groups of Shanping village. Undoubtedly, the holiday must fall on a rabbit day. Holidays that were celebrated in the month of rooster, on the contrary, must be led by Ping village by the same method in counting time. Some grand holidays in the Miao culture were celebrated once in every twelve years. *Qiao Niu Ji Zu* or "cold funeral", for instance, was sure to be celebrated in the year of rabbit if the ceremony was held in Chang village, and must be in the year of rooster if held by Ping village.

In the patriarchal group of Shanping village, every individual had equal social status and one should win the respect and esteem from the others by hard work, virtue and wisdom. They could achieve this goal in one of the two ways: to do things for the benefit of the village or to win reputation on behalf of one's own patriarchal clan. There were many ways to do things for the benefit of the village. As we mentioned earlier, the road built by the villagers led by Luo Wenkui was an example. Another example was the *Long Cun Suo Yao Bei* that was erected for the purpose of protecting the tombs of their ancestors. The most commonly used method, however, was to accumulate capital to purchase bulls to be sacrificed in *Qiao Niu Ji Zu* ceremonies. The beef was then distributed across members of the same clan. After this ceremony, a title of "Dong Hong" would be added to the name of the contributor. Since then, he would be qualified to appear in public in a formal dress made of red silk and would be respected by everyone. What he said would become authoritative. More importantly, this title would be listed in the name list of the deceased ancestors and be remembered in generations after his death. His descendents would be reminded of his role in the worship ceremonies and it would be passed down through generations. There were also many ways of wining honors for one's own patriarchal clan. Some might apply their skill in communication to mediate disputes among people in the affinity group; Some led the struggle and won the battle against the ruling *Tu Si*; Others found space of activities for their own group and organized the moving of the village. The several revolts mentioned in this chapter were led the figures who have lived in the legends of each patriarchal clan.

In Shanping village, those who had a professional skill or specialty were also respected in the society. *Gui Shi* were invited to direct all religious ceremonies in the patriarchal clan and also acted as teachers in holidays and festivals to educate children from own patriarchal clan to learn religious rituals, and recite the names of deceased ancestors. In the religious ceremonies, *Gui Shi* would be treated with the utmost cordiality and would also receive the best part of the sacrifice. While acting as the teachers in the society, children from his own patriarchal clan must offer wine, meat and sticky rice cakes as gifts to them. Singers who could sing many folk songs were highly respected and would be invited to sing in all holidays and ceremonies, receiving courteous reception as well as physical rewards. Besides, those who played Lusheng (a reed-pipe wind instrument) well and all kinds of craftsmen were also highly esteemed. In the Miao society, however, occupational division was not fully complete and all the above people were farmers who mainly worked on cultivating lands. We got to know a famous singer Luo Chaomei in Ping village who was able to sing more than one hundred folk songs of all kinds, such as "Qiao Niu" song that was sung in sacrificial ceremonies, "Geng Gu" song that told the story about Miao history and lyric "Wei" song. However, he was still a farmer and had to cultivate his own lands. Unfortunately, he could sing much better than farming; consequently, his family was poor and each year, he anticipated the arrival of holidays where he could make some money that could make his life better.

The five villages that are affinity villages in parallel with Shanping village including Guoli, Jiading, Dongkou, Lali, and Rongchu all have the exactly the same internal structure. They all had two or three patriarchal clans and only two of them were basic clans, which were located in parallel. Each had a specific space in the framework of time. For instance, Jiading occupied snake and pig; hence, any holiday that this village spent would be held in the snake ground or pig ground. A holiday that was celebrated in the month of snake, like *She Bei Pai* celebrated across the entire affinity group, was, without a doubt, hosted by Jiading village and the major site of activities would be Jiading village. Guoli village occupied the months and days of pig and dragon; Lali village occupied ox and sheep; Dongkou village occupied pig and horse, and Rongchu occupied tiger and monkey. The 12 zodiac signs were thus evenly spread across the six villages. It is apparent that the affinity group in such a structure was an extension of the patriarchal clan with the difference being that a patriarchal group was formed by external marriage while an affinity group was a social group formed by internal marriages. It shows from the above analyses that both patriarchal groups and affinity groups were substantialization of Miao's cognitive pattern.

Since the beginning of the 20th century, the Miao people from Shanping village began to directly participate in domestic political activities. Some people won fame in the outside world through their own hard-work and efforts, in which they took great pride. However, such fame became conflicting with their cultural tradition when they came back to their patriarchal clan. On the one hand, these people were proud of what they had achieved in the outside world; on the other hand, they were frustrated that such an achievement was not reflected in the change in their status within the clan. As a result, they would need to play a dual role: to achieve and win the honor from outside the clan, and in the meantime to gain the honor one more time within the clan by following the cultural tradition. Luo Guoqing from Chang village received training at "Qingyan Dialect Training Institute" during the Anti-Japanese War and was appointed the local head by the government of Republic of China. He also served as guide and interpreter for ethnologist Bao Kelan and Luo Rongzong. His name appeared in some ethnological works published before the liberation, and thus he was frequently visited. Although people from his clan took great pride in him, they did not elect him to be the village head, nor was he given the honor of wearing the red gown in sacrificial ceremonies simply because he had not *Qiao Niu* (knocked an ox). Amid such a reality, he had to make a concession and bought two oxen in two ancestor worship occasions. It eventually solved the problem. He was later assigned "Dong Hong" and elected to be the village head. His household benefited from the honors from both the internal and external communities and became very prosperous, making it the only landlord in Shanping village at the time of land reform. Luo Guofu from Ping village received middle school education before the liberation, later was sent to the agricultural school in Guizhou to become a veterinarian and then assumed public servant position with the state government. He gave up his government post and returned home in the period of hardship in the 1960s. As a veterinarian, he did many good things for his neighbors in the village, and was highly respected and loved among his neighbors. However, he was still deemed a craftsman and called "animal's medial craftsman" (a directly translation of the Miao language in meaning) in the local Miao community. We met him in the early 1980s when the policy was not flexible and he was not allowed *Qiao Niu Ji Zu*. Therefore, he was unfortunate that he could not be assigned "Dong Hong". Also, no village cadre position was available for him due to his family background of rich peasant and high educational background, for which he felt wronged. Luo Zeqing from Chang village was an activist in the land reform and later became a party member. After he was appointed the party secretary of Gaopo township, people from Shanping village thought that they now had a backer. However, he had to execute the policies of the party before the 1970s. He led people to burn the drums of his patriarchal clan, prohibited *Qiao Niu Ji Zu*, or even playing Lu Sheng, signing and dancing, and set fire to the books in the collection of Shanping middle school. In the 1980s after he retired, Luo Zeqing felt void in spirit and resumed *Qiao Niu Ji Zu* under the traditional influence and was subsequently assigned the first "Dong Hong" after the Cultural Revolution. When we saw him again in the 1990s, he was elected to be the village head, for which he felt content as he would not need to retire from this post. We came across many people like Luo Zeqing in our field surveys who played dual roles, a production team carder outside the village and a Gui Shi, singer or village head within the village. A primary school principal who had served in the military and rendered meritorious service held the Qiao Niu ceremony in 1992 and later became a "Dong Hong". The first thing he showed us when we visited his home was not the awards he received in the army but the color photos of *Qiao Niu Ji Zu*. He beamed with joy when he talked, which is still fresh in our mind. We had not known until we came to the township government that he was a meritorious solider who came back from a battleground. It was difficult for us to merge these two images together although he himself did not seem to realize this. Now, there are many people from Gaopo who work elsewhere. A rough estimation shows that one fifth of the population in Shanping village are working outside the region as worker, teacher, scientists or technicians, in addition to more than 100 school age children who go to school. These people are not willing to come back to the village if they make some achievements outside the village. What they have learned is not useful here, and the honors they've received will not be understood by villagers. This explains why there are quite a number of middle schools or even college students from Shanping village but Shanping middle school is still in extreme shortage of teachers.

With the deepening of the reform and opening-up policy, external world began to impact this region in almost every aspect, and modern new things penetrated the Miao society almost every day. Superficially, the administrative structure at township and village levels in this region was no different from that in the Han regions; Occupational division became more apparent; Modern science and technology spread across ethnic societies; an increasing number of people chose an inter-ethnicity marriage. However, like the teachers in Shanping middle school, these new things had dual natures. Tradition and modernity moved along in parallel without crossing each other. New things did not seem to have found the point for their growth in the traditional society, but had to operate by relying on external forces to float above the Miao traditional society. It was clear that whether we called it a production brigade or administrative village, it was the shell that kept changing and what was at the core was the stable patriarchal group. The country cadres including those from the Miao background were all crystal clear that they were working for the government. They were not sure to what extent the government policies could be implemented. When pushed hard by the upper-level governments, they had no better choice but to force people in their territory to act recklessly. In the spring of 1995, under the pressure from the upper-level government to transplant rice seedlings by pulling a cord to ensure the straightness, they had to assign one cadre to each village to supervise the execution. Whenever they felt unsatisfied, they would force farmers to redo it. The cadres knew very well that they could not keep an eye on every farmer. As a result, they could only force the practice in the conspicuous places, but chose to ignore the remote areas. If the same requirement was made in the year that followed, they would do the same; otherwise, everyone would be at ease. Similar things happened in law dissemination, township enterprise operation, illiteracy elimination, and family planning, etc. As long as they were not pushed by the upper-level government, everything would fall back to the tradition and ran in inertia.

Quite some township enterprises were set up and many of them failed, so were power stations, marble plants, and paper mills. The township government even attracted funds to set up a ferrosilicon plant. These enterprises were intended, in addition to bringing in more economic income, for creating more non-agricultural employment opportunities for local Miao people so that they could abandon the traditional lifestyle and live a modern one. All the good wishes evaporated with the collapse of these enterprises. Despite the continuing occupational division in Shanping village, it was driven by external forces as the village itself could not provide non-agricultural employment opportunities. As we mentioned earlier, one fifth of the Shanping population were employed outside the region, apparently a result of external boost. Guiyang Steel Plant had hired some seasonal workers, many of whom, due to the sluggish economy in recent two years, chose to return to their own villages and used the money they had made while working for the plant to buy new houses or electrical appliances. Although they lived a better life than those who had not left the village, they were not contented as they felt that the wealth they had made did not bring extra respect for them from the villagers. Subsequently, many of them thought about *"Qiao Niu Ji Zu"*.

Some people felt reluctant to go home after losing their jobs at the plant. Hence, they would do anything from small business, picking trash, to even stealing and selling goods and materials. With a hollow soul, these people had only one goal in their mind: make some money and go home. They were clear that they could not stay in big cities forever. Meanwhile, lacking of disciplines by the social norms of their own ethnic group, they would dare do the things others would not. I came across a young man who told me that he made a living by selling fake cigarettes, brand liquors, smuggling used auto tires, and buying mineral products with a forged certificate. He kept asking me not to tell his fellow villagers about his acts for fear that he would be despised by them. His story made us think deeply about how important social constraints were to the social stability, and how dangerous it was to push forward modernity at the expense of destroying the constraining force of tradition.

While youngsters from Shanping village rushed into cities, people from other regions, like administrative officials, scientists and technicians, teachers and journalist, flocked to Gaopo and penetrated into Shanping. They brought science and technology to the Miao people, broadened their vision, aroused their interest in the outside world and ignited their hope of getting rich quickly. However, they, as well as the outsiders, were at loss about what exactly they should do. An old farmer from Chang village hoped to elevate his status through religious help after knowing that freedom of religion was a national policy. He later met a Catholic priest by accident and expressed his wish to bring Gospel from God to the Miao people. Deeply touched by his sincerity (Miao people have been sincere since the ancient time), the priest accepted him into the church, guided him through a free tour of Guiyang city and gave him a one-month training on the religion. His story stirred up Shanping village after he returned home and villagers wouldn't believe what he said. A local party member said, "I have been a Communist Party member for tens of years and I have not been treated on a free tour of Guiyang. He's just joined the church and they paid for him to stay there for one month. This is unbelievable." In fact, the tradition of the Miao group determined that they could not join the Catholic church, but they just could not believe why these churches and priests would do this. Similar things puzzled Shanping villagers. Simply because they were not psychologically prepared and lacked the ability to tell the right from the wrong when things from outside were presented to them, they could not accept the good or resist the bad things resolutely.

In recent years when Shanping region was submerged in the wave of market economy, street venders and all other kinds of people entered Gaopo. Feeling that Miao people were simple-minded and easy to fool, they often tricked and swindled the local Miao people. After sometime, the Miao people became skeptical of outsiders or even formed gangs to deal with them, in the way of stealing or attacking people from outside the region. They did not know, however, that what they did intensified the conflicts and often gave ill-willed people an opportunity. Now, Gaopo was the region in Guiyang region with the worst social order where thefts and murders happened constantly. As some Miao seniors bewailed, they had never had to lock their doors in past generations, and had been able to leave the cattle and horses to graze on the mountain unattended, not worrying about them being stolen. Now they had more money in their pocket but had to live a stressful life. I once consulted the village head about this issue and he said: "we can only control our own people but can not do anything about the outsiders. Our own people would not do bad things within our village. For anything that happens outside the village, we would not be able to know. In the Miao region, all bad things are done by outsiders whom we have no control of. There is only one thing we can do that may put an end to this bad atmosphere: call on all the village heads to form a coalition and jointly crack down on this trend. It proved to be an effective measure in the old time when we successfully revolted against *Tu Si*, but now it is the People's Government which we must follow. If we act without it making the first move, we would be misunderstood as acting against the government and be treated as "anti-revolutionary".

Now, the Miao people here are most interested in technologies, especially chemical fertilizer and hybrid rice, but with reservation. They think that chemical fertilizers are too pricey and would only be willing to use them at a discounted price under government subsidy. Meanwhile, hybrid rice ensures a higher output and therefore they would like to plant hybrid rice, but they also think that hybrid rice is of inferior quality and does not taste good, and therefore each household only uses part of their field for growing hybrid rice, other spaces are still reserved for *Xiao Hong Nian* (small red sticky rice) and *Da Ma Nian* (another kind of rice). However, such a practice caused some conflicts. As *Xiao Hong Nian* and *Da Ma Nian* were both high quality rice, some government workers at the department of grain control refused to take hybrid rice as a fulfillment of agricultural tax, but forced local farmers to turn in *Xiao Hong Nian*. It infuriated the Miao farmers who planted hybrid rice only to pay agricultural taxes, and nearly ended in a collective appealing to the upper-level government by the Miao people. Although the incident eventually quieted down after the intervention of township government and the punishment of responsible government workers from the department of grain control, its negative influence continue to yeast and caused Miao people to begin questioning the government. As one Miao farmer put it, "We had trusted the government and would do what the government wanted us to do even though we were not happy. After this time, we would not do it anymore.

The Miao people had lived in the deep mountains for generations and did not know whether what happened outside our world was good or bad. We've had governments, businesses, and schools that come here to tell us new things, but how can you expect us to follow your instruction without first winning our trust? Nobody wants to be fooled twice."

What he said prompted us to think. It is true that we have imbued a lot on the Miao people in recent years, but most were poorly planned or poorly executed without coordination across different departments on manpower or materials. Our efforts have never been focused on steadfastly gaining their trust, and as a result, a single mistake by one department would disrupt the general plan and cause them to lurch on the way to modernization. Further, the way to modernization by developing ethnicity is often a passive process. Their modernization started before they had time to fully understand what modernization was. Therefore, they were not equipped with the ability to tell the right from the wrong, or the ability to judge if something from the outside world fit the specific situation of the ethnic group. Under such a circumstance, to realize modernization and to play subjective initiative is likely to become an empty talk. What happened in Shanping looks universal and may happen to any ethnic group that is on the way to develop itself. It is our belief that the key for these ethnic groups to gain a proactive status is to integrate their cognitive patterns with modern science and technology. Only by doing so can they make accurate judgment on the things from the outside world and on themselves, and with that can we talk further about adjusting measures to local conditions and enabling them to play a subjective initiative role.

With the transformation in the social lifestyle came the change in spiritual life. Shanping is not far from Guiyang and it is a place where spiritual life such as television and movie is available. President Jiang Zemin gave a transposer station as a gift when he was visiting Shanping, making the information flow in unobstructed by modern media. However, we observed that ethnic Miao people did not exactly copy the things from the outside world, but rather put them in their own spiritual framework to make it easy for a concerted action with the tradition. There were many other similar examples. Here we elaborate briefly on the holidays and beliefs in this region.

Miao traditional holidays were scheduled by the Miao calendar. Activities in hot seasons were of religious nature and they all revolved around the topic of ancestral worship, so were the activities to worship the God of Harvest, bull fight and *Qiao Niu Ji Zu*. With the increasing interactions with the outside world, the Gregorian calendar and Chinese lunar calendar had been introduced into Shanping, and the Spring Festival celebrated by the Han people had begun to influence the Miao people. Now, they were not celebrating the Miao new year holiday anymore. By tradition, the Miao new year holiday fell on the first month in cold seasons, i.e., the month of rat, where the village head hosted the ceremony of offering sacrifices to the cave, killing pigs and distributing the pork among households in the village. In the meantime, they would play Lusheng and dance in the cave, but the patriarchal clans by affinity were not invited. On the days of rabbit and rooster in each month in subsequent cold seasons, villagers would hold the cave-jumping ceremony and young people from all groups of affinity relationship were invited to sing and dance as a dating opportunity. As such activities were hosted by and thus cost dearly for Shanping village, it had no choice but to pick the days where the monetary and material resources it had allowed such activities. Another holiday was *Zuohuayuan* (literarily *sit in the garden*) where young girls from the village gathered inside the fence they built and by the lighted bonfire to do some needlework while waiting for the visit by the young men from the villages of the affinity relations. These young men could go hunting and shared the prey with the girl they fell in love with. However, after the Miao new year holiday, the above three holidays in cold seasons were consolidated into one and was celebrated together in the first month in the lunar calendar. Now, the holiday to offer sacrifices to the cave is celebrated on the new year's eve while *Zuohuayuan* is celebrated on the first and fifteenth day of that month where all women of the Miao community either sit in the garden or go back to their parental home and leave all housework to men, making it a special women's holiday. Cave-jumping starts from the third day and lasts into the eighth day of the first month in the lunar calendar with the practice of arranging the activities by the order of the zodiac signs of each village unchanged: Rongchu, Shanping, Guoli, Jiading, Dongkou and eventually Lali. This example indicates that Miao people are still following their tradition of celebrating holidays, only by adding a shell of a lunar calendar. It is just an example that external factors alone are not capable of destroying the cultural entirety of an ethnic group.

The Miao ethnic people believe in natural religion especially worship their ancestors. They believe that after people die, they would join their ancestors and enjoy a happy life, and that the souls of their ancestors are neither in heaven nor under the ground but are in a remote place far beyond the dense old-growth forest. They think the ancestors that are alive can not travel too far away and they can come back at any time. Therefore, the way they offer sacrifices to the ancestors is like treat them for a dinner. With the popularization of natural science and the widening of their vision, they have come to realize that beyond the forests are cities, factories, and in further distances are seas and oceans. They begin to feel perplexed about where their ancestors have gone. As a result, subtle changes have been brought to the ceremonies of ancestral worship. Instead of calling the names of the deceased ancestors by *Gui Shi*, and then *Da Gua* (cast lots) to prove whether the ancestors who have been called have come back, they are now led by *Gui Shi* to the cliff cave of the patriarchal clan, bringing with them wines and meats, to invite their ancestors in person. Of course, the names of the deceased ancestors are still being called and so is *Zhu Gua*. As a *Gui Shi* once told me, there is no way for them to tell how far away these deceased ancestors live, but we must provide a gathering place for them when they come back. As this cliff burial cave is where their descendents brought them and is close to the village, it is convenient for them and for us to gather and call them back here. Scientifically, what he said is ignorant to some extent, but it had revealed some truthfulness. Religion has unlimited compatibility and it only takes some slight adjustment and adaptation for it to contain new things. It is thus unrealistic for us to think that the development of science would eventually make religions disappear.

We think, after a review of the two cultural re-constructions, that they were typical examples of passive acceptance. Similar transformations in lifestyle have the following four characteristics:

1. Material lifestyle transforms faster than spiritual lifestyle.

2. Lifestyle transformation is not simply to replace the old elements with the new ones, but is a protracted process of gradual digestion, absorption, adjustment and adaptation.

3. An ethnic group should not indiscriminately copy external elements, but should selectively absorb the ones that fit its situation. It is therefore a lesson for the Miao people of Shanping village to have made rice cultivation

as its main line of production when it did not fit its specific conditions.

4. The key to turning passivity into initiative is to integrate science and technology with the traditional culture, especially with the cognitive patterns. It is better late than never to start mending the fences. Our policies should begin from here.

V. The Shanping Lifestyle

No matter how complex large Miao groups are, or how imbalanced the internal development within the Miao groups in the past centuries has been, from the perspective of the essence of lifestyle transformation, the experience in Shanping village is a miniature of the entire Miao society. We can draw a rough picture of the Miao society or even the societies of other ethnic groups similar to Miao after understanding Shanping village. With this perception, we feel regret to admit that the conditions in Shanping are unsatisfactory. It is still an impoverished region and a target of key poverty-relief efforts. It is simply too far behind in the eyes of the Han people from the developed regions in China. What is more puzzling is that we have not found effective measures for these regions. The analysis of Shanping village alone is not enough for us to give a panacea. Any conclusion that is drawn blindly does more harm than good. However, it is necessary to clarify the following issues. By doing so, we at least can deepen our understanding of the lifestyle transformation and help those who care about the livelihood of ethnic minority people get to the essence of these issues.

The contents of the two lifestyle transformations did not change much, both originated and introduced from the Han culture in an attempt to bring its level of development to that of the Han society. As the Han culture was in a constant development, the purpose, requirement and goal in the governance of the Miao region varied from time to time. Consequently, the lifestyle that was introduced into the Miao region in the same time had different focuses and characteristics in contents, but there was no difference when they were accepted passively by the Miao people. It is indeed a good and laudable wish that we hope to introduce, recommend and drive the transformation in their lifestyle and help them realize modernization through our efforts. While we are doing all these, we must keep one fundamental concept in mind: Modernization in the Han society is still a process being explored and nobody can be sure of its success. Therefore, when we copy these measures whose success is still debatable in the Miao societies that have a very different tradition, the chance of their success can only become smaller. Hence, it is perhaps more reliable for us to treat different opinions seriously without rushing to force one model across the entire group.

Although the transformation in the Miao lifestyle looked extremely complex and massive, in essence, it was the manifestation of cultural re-construction. No lifestyle transformation was a simple replacement of the old by the new, but instead was the result of a series of adjustment and adaptation within the culture that gave rise to a new balance. When it comes to the lifestyle, the eventual completion of replacement of the old with the new does not necessarily symbolize that new things are necessarily effective or advanced (to the Miao people of course). However, it surely symbolizes that the cultural adjustment and adaptation in the Miao society has made some progress to have equipped it with the ability to accept and digest these things, or in other words, these new things have found the point for growth in the Miao traditional culture. Although the two cultural re-constructions in Shanping village were caused by repercussion from the outside world, they were not determined by the external world, but rather by the adjustment, development, digestion and absorption in the Miao culture itself. With this in mind, we must not focus on how the outsiders respond but rather how the Miao culture reacts when deciding on the development and advancement of Miao society. We should not take it for granted that new things are necessarily better and more advanced. Whether they offer true value to the Miao people must be determined by the subsequent feeling of the Miao people and should not be determined by anybody else. Such a transformation in the lifestyle will be valuable and pass the test of time if we keep paying attention to the subjective initiative of the Miao people in their lifestyle transformation and mobilize such initiative.

The first cultural re-construction in Shanping village had drawn to an end. As a result, rice cultivation has taken root here and corresponding cultural adjustment and adaptation has been effective, giving rise to a stable lifestyle suitable for the rice cultivation. As the second cultural re-construction is ongoing and it is thus too early to arrive at any conclusions, we can only make our analysis based on the first cultural re-construction. Without a doubt, the acceptance of rice cultivation by Shanping village is not complete, but the Miao people should not be responsible as the full set of agricultural technology introduced from the outside world is not enough to transform the living environment of the Miao group into a place like the middle and lower reaches of the Yangtze River that is suitable for rice cultivation. When the rice cultivation is concerned alone, such a transformation in the lifestyle is undoubtedly very successful, but weaknesses that can not be overcome by manpower arise in the ensuing process of operation. The increase in the rice fields added by the infertility of lands and unfavorable climate combine to drive up the production cost. Consequently, the same amount of input is not rewarded by the same output, and in the meantime, the animals and plants that could be used previously can not be used any more, causing the overall utilization rate of their living environment to decrease. Therefore, from the first day they accepted the rice cultivation, they were doomed to lag economically behind the Han people for a long time in the future although they will get closer in production to the Han group, which can not be alleviated by any favorable policies as this is an issue beyond the power of policies but one of the pertinent structural adjustment and adaptation as well as evolution in the cultural living environment. It will remain a challenging issue for the ethnic Miao people for a long time in the future since their livelihood is tied to the output of rice that is grown in the most unfavorable rice fields.

It is more complex and uncertain when it comes to the tasks in the lifestyle transformation as it is not a unilateral problem but a constant problem. When the Qing government was pushing Miao villages such as Shanping to migrate into the traditional agriculture, although it was under the banner of "treating everyone the same", in essence, it was guided by the thought that one more farmer would produce more tax revenue and labor, and one less farmer who kept migrating from place to place would reduce the administrative burden. It was completely driven by the political self-interests. Yang Sen, who was in power in Guizhou in the era of Republic of China, was even more undisguised when he advocated his two theories: theory of evolution and great harmony. He believed that the Han culture was undoubtedly more advanced and asked that the ethnic minority people to change clothing, language, and customs so that they would become the same as the Han people. It is one thing whether this was doable and another whether such a thought could be eliminated. Today, as everyone knows, all ethnic groups must be treated equally and no one would endorse what Yang

Sen advocated. However, the following two opinions are equally harmful. First, convergence means progress; Second, the introduction of modern advanced technology means development. Both are under the same guiding principle and apparently can not be used as the foundation for the analysis of the transformation in the lifestyle.

We must keep one unshakable fact in mind: The environments provided by the earth for human beings take very different forms and thus the overall level of natural resource utilization would drop naturally if we develop and utilize them with the same culture. Cultural diversification is both an established fact and an intangible asset of all the human beings; therefore, to make convergence the task of lifestyle transformation only destroys the cultural diversification and prompts rivalry over resources. Each time has different science and technology with different connotation. It takes time for science and technology to be digested and absorbed and it is not wise to try to pave the way for the introduction of new technologies by destroying the tradition or at the cost of economic efficiency. To destroy the tradition means to destroy the background for the digestion and absorption stably and steadily. To sacrifice efficiency means the loss of ability to operate the introduced technologies continuously, or of the time necessary for digesting and absorbing these technologies. Therefore, the task in the lifestyle transformation is not to get rid of the tradition, or to get rid of it at a faster speed and to a larger extent. Instead, it should seek to mingle the tradition with modern life and integrate the contents of modern life with the tradition that lasts naturally. Conflicts are unavoidable in the process, but they should not be solved by a life-or-death struggle. Instead, they can be solved by bringing out the best in each other. Lastly, let's talk about the goal of the lifestyle transformation. It is to achieve the integration between the traditional culture and modern technology, enable modern technology to be utilized by ourselves, and to use the technologies we master after integration for the research of problems we face in search for effective measures. To put it in a simple sentence, it is to make the subjective initiative play to its full potential. Unfortunately, not many people have realized this point, and even less people have made it a symbol of progress in the lifestyle transformation. I've been to Shanping more than ten times, and each time I went, I saw changes: power lines erected, TV transposer station established, hybrid rice planted, and cars were sent over to pick me up. They did not surprise me. In a big country as ours, it only takes the movement of fingers of government officials if we want to provide support to the small Gaopo township. The problem is what to do afterwards. A township government official once told me: "We have no right to blame the country. It has given us enough favorable polices and supports, but they don't work. We built factories one after another but they all failed. The power lines we erected were all stolen and the spaces in the school were mostly taken by poorly-performed students from down the mountain instead of the Miao students. If we can not find the way to develop ourselves, we will waste all that is given to us and will always be asking for me." What he said excited me. They eventually realized that no one could build a modernization for them and how important the subjective initiative was. To me, it is a real progress that they finally realized this after the lifestyle transformation that lasted over a century.

To achieve the integration between the traditional culture and modern technology, the core issue is the cognitive pattern of each ethnic group. The key to the success is to make each ethnic group believe that their own cognitive pattern is enough for the deployment of modern science and technology. It is not difficult to make people understand this, but it is more difficult to insist on doing it bit by bit continuously. A century ago, quite a number of people from the West asserted that the traditional culture and lifestyle of the East could not accept the advanced science of the West. Now, the ethnic groups in the West have become competitors of the West. This example showed that it is absolutely possible for the Miao people to be able to do what is necessary for realizing modernization. What is urgent for us to do now is to make them realize this and take actions now.

To achieve this goal, we can take advantage of many favorable conditions. First, we have a superior socialist system that paves the way politically for the development of all ethnic groups and diminishes the disturbances caused by ethnic oppression, discrimination and estrangement to the minimum. Second, our efforts in the past forty some years have produced quite a lot of Miao intellectuals who, although trained in a Han cultural environment, are born in a Miao society and thus have a deeper understanding of the cognitive patterns of the Miao group. They would become pioneers and a vital force in achieving the integration between the Miao cognitive pattern and modern science and technology as long as they have realized the necessity to do so. These favorable conditions and strong support from administrative departments would, in principle, make the integration an achievable task. The real difficulty now lies in the fact that both the Han and Miao scientists and technicians have been educated in a Han educational context so that they would absolutize the role of the Han culture. They would, consciously or unconsciously, tend to think that the promotion of the Han culture is a solution to all the problems without giving consideration to the fact that the issue of integration between traditional and modern culture is one that should not be overlooked in the development of any ethnic group. As a result, such a thing that could have been done has been delayed to now when no one seriously thinks of putting it into action. To deal with this problem, we hereby call for all the people concerned to change a perspective in the field of social science and begin thinking from the angle of ethnic groups, seriously and earnestly discuss the issue of integration between the traditional culture of each ethnic group and modernization, and carry out comprehensive analysis and research in all the relevant disciplines. We are hopeful that a feasible path toward modernization for all ethnic groups can be found in the near future and the modernization of all ethnic groups is surely attainable in the first half of the 21st century as long as we prioritize this research of great significance as a mission of cross-century social science research topic.

(The article was first published in *Principles in Cross-Xiang Operation* in 1995)

Closing Notes

After finishing the book, many readers will surely question: are the contents in the book too wide and the solutions too slow to take effect? They are right. This book indeed concerns the areas that are very wide and puts forth solutions that are not immediately effective. However, we do this for a reason. The topic we are facing is not a simple one and the problems we need to solve are not as urgent as having to put out a fire. "Wide" and "slow" are determined by the nature of the research topic rather than out of personal preference.

In this regard, cultural anthropologists in the West deserve our respect and appreciation. They have correctly pointed out that modernization of an ethnic group is not an issue of merely enhancing the level of material production but a process of complete transformation from cognitive patterns to lifestyle. In other words, it is a process of cultural re-construction but not a problem that can be solved simply by the change of one or two policies or support by providing materials and funds. History can provide some references. No ethnic group in history stepped into modernization leisurely and happily. It took the British nearly three centuries and suffered tremendously to reach its heyday in the Victorian era from the movement of enclosures. China, after one and half centuries of struggle to build a powerful and prosperous nation since the mid-19th century, still remains a developing country. Modernization is never a speedy process, and so is the modernization process for the ethnic groups in China.

Cultural re-construction is a transformation of the entire ethnic culture and thus it must concern all aspects in the social life. The attainment of modernization requires to mobilize all intelligence and wisdom of the people concerned as well as persistent efforts. In its march toward modernization, Japan completely accepted the natural science from the West while in the meantime retained the Confucian tradition introduced from China, even its lifestyle was a complete imitation of the Tang dynasty. Japan was never hesitant in absorbing all favorable cultural elements. It was for this reason that Japan did not start its learning process from scratch and thus its modernization process was not accompanied by widespread and deep social turmoil. Likewise, the development and modernization in the ethnic regions in China would not be achieved without all-round transformation and re-construction or absorption of all useful cultural elements from other cultures. Consequently, "wide" and "slow" are not our intention but inevitable results determined by our goal and the actuality.

The finalization of the book only brought me some slight relief that was soon replaced by greater worries. As an ordinary member in the academic community, we can call for the society to pay attention to some issues and do some things, but we don't have the ability or power to put our thoughts into practice. The most we can do is to manage some pilot programs in one or two small communities under the auspice of the society, which is far from enough to change the situations in ethnic regions in this country. Apparently, it will be a long process for us to reach consensus in the society and seize a good opportunity. In such a process, it is highly unpredictable if we can keep focused on the established targets, and ensure that the future development not subject to surprise repercussions that would disrupt the modernization process in our ethnic regions. This is our first worry.

China is a country that is made up of multiple ethnic groups. The ethnic Han group, as the major ethnic group in China, accounts for more than 90% of the entire population in the country. It is thus totally understandable that the modernization in China must be focused on the Han region while other ethnic regions are supported, to large extent, by our sense of responsibility and emotions. In such a background, it is, objectively speaking, not an easy task to require that the Han regions go all out to offer assistance to the development of ethnic regions without any dissent. In the meantime, ethnic people must establish the notion of relying on themselves and wholeheartedly start researching the problems they face. This is not an easy task either. For this reason, we are not sure what responses our thoughts and recommendations would generate, or to what extent the responses, if any, would turn into actions. Therefore, the modernization process in the ethnic regions would last longer than our readers expect. Can we make it to the end? This is our second worry.

History is a continuous process. What happened in history will continue impacting what happens today whether we like it or not. When it comes to policies, we are not able to isolate the new ones from the old ones, but instead can only make gradual revision and improvement after problems emerge. As a result, all the thoughts we put forth can only be carried out bit by bit. Our train of thoughts works, at most, to make people more active and comprehensive when thinking about these issues. It will not be as easy as allocating some funds or sending a few technicians. Do our government officials and people have such patience? This is our third worry.

Human society is a complex entity where each individual group and region has its own short-term interests and consideration of continuous development. However, within a specific time period, people always tend to prioritize short-term interests over the long-term interests as long as it does not cause chaos. On this issue, we have no reason to blame our administrative officials as their official terms are short and it is thus understandable for them to put short-term interests on the top priority of their work. However, to build modernization in the ethnic regions is a long-term process. Are we able to convince them into integrating the short-term interests with long-term ones? Apparently, it is not achievable by a few individuals. This is our fourth worry.

With these worries, we have a long way to go although we have completed the research and the book has been published successfully. What we can do is only to "keep exploring and keep trying". It remains a question as to how many people we are able to mobilize to do this with us.

We will continue our work that started from this research. It is our plan to apply for the state or provincial level research topic on ethnic development and cultural re-construction to deepen our research. We also plan to organize pilot programs in small communities when conditions permit and launch experiment in small-scale community cultural re-construction. Currently, it is our preliminary consideration to pick Sidazhai of Ziyun county, Longjie of Weining county, Tanxi of Liping county or Liangshan in Sichuan province and Qilianshan mountainous region in Gansu province as our pilot regions. To make it happen, however, depends on the support from all communities in the society, approval from administrative departments and more importantly, cooperation from relevant ethnic people. All these are uncertain factors and therefore, our good wish is waiting for the response from and decision by the society. It is simply for the purpose of obtaining the understanding from the society and all authorities that we expressed our determination on this. We don't care about what difficulties we would encounter when we put them into action but only worry that our understanding would be lost in the joy from short-term gains.

Lastly, during the time when the book was written, researchers from this institute conducted many independent researches around this topic, whose results were very helpful for deepening and verifying the conclusions and in this book. We hereby list these research achievements for readers' reference.

Guizhou Provincial Research Institute of Nationalities: *Strategies on Developing Guizhou - Cultural Factors Affecting the Economic Development in Ethnic Regions*, published in serial form in the 1st, 3rd, and 4th issue of 1995, *Exchange on Party Construction.*

Liu Feng, *A Re-examination of Contemporary Primitive Agriculture*, published in the 1st issue of 1995, *The History of Chinese Agriculture.*

Pan Shengzhi, *The Glory and Worry of "Liuma" Tung Oil in Guizhou*, published in the 1st issue of 1996, *Guizhou Ethnic Research*; *Remainders from an Ethnic Economic Supplementary Structure*, published in the 4th issue of 1995, *Guizhou Social Science.*

Wu Zhiguo, *Economic Development Must Take into Account the Link between Ethnic Culture and Economy*, published in the 5th issue of 1993, *Development.*

Yang Lan, *An Overview of Obstacles for Ethnic Minority Regions to Build a Market Economy*, published in the 5th issue of 1993, *Development.*

The Origins and Essence in the Dilemma of Ethnic Education, Guizhou Provincial philosophy and social science research topic under the leadership of Liu Feng.

Theories and Practices in the Bilingual Teaching, Guizhou Provincial Commission of Education social science research topic under the leadership of Li Jinping.

Epilogue

It had been a long-cherished wish of mine to write a book on modern economics and politics from the perspective of cultural anthropology, but such an opportunity had not unveiled nor had I been able to spare time for such a task for 13 years until 1993 when a rare opportunity fell upon me. In that year, I transferred from Department of Sociology of Guizhou Minzu University to its Ethnological Institute as a researcher, which ensured that I had enough time and energy to finish the book. In the meantime, I was assigned to be fully responsible for the design and execution of the research topic entitled "Analysis of Non-economic Factors Constraining the Social Development of Ethnic Regions in Guizhou" that had been applied for by Director Wu Zhiguo and later approved as the "Eighth Five-year Plan" state social science research topic as Associate Professor Zhao Senlin who was originally responsible for the design and execution was occupied with teaching and did not have time to complete the research work. Before this book is ready for publishing, I would first extend my appreciation to Director Wu Zhiguo for his complete trust and support. I could not have finished the job by the scheduled time without his magnanimity and hands-off attitude, which enabled me to focus on my work at the quiet desk at Guizhou Minzu University. I was given the undisturbed freedom throughout the entire process from the start of fieldwork to the completion of the book with the exception of necessary checking and urging by him. Amid the overwhelming economic tide in China that swept all the teaching and research units, it was nearly impossible for anyone to find a quiet place to conduct research without distractions. A three-year time for focused scientific research was just the desire of me who was an ordinary member in the scientific research community and never hoped to get rich or be promoted.

Special thanks must also be extended to Feng Zuyi, Deputy Director of Guizhou Academy of Social Sciences, for the preface he kindly wrote for me. His spiritual support made me understand correctly the value and meaning of my work, realize the enormous responsibilities on my shoulder and the difficulties I must overcome, and spur me to continue.

Being half blind, I thought more than I could personally do. I could not have achieved today's results without the all-out efforts throughout the entire process from the young colleagues at this institute. Liu Feng, Pan Shengzhi, Yang Lan and Tan Yi from this institute participated in the whole process of social investigation. In addition, Luo Kanglong and 40 students from this institute also offered help in the investigation. Pan Shengzhi transcribed nearly the entire manuscript of the book and Li Jinping proofread and collated the full manuscript for three times. While helping me throughout the book, my colleagues also did researches independently and achieved some results, which strongly supplemented and verified some of the major conclusions in the book. I owed appreciation to Mr. Suo Hongmin who offered his valuable advice on the numbers and math theories in the book. Ms. Chen Min's hard work made the editing and printing of the book a smooth process. I would like to take this opportunity to express my sincere appreciation to all of them.

Author

November 15, 1995

Bibliography

Arthur Lewis, *Dualism in Economy*, trans. Shi Wei, (Beijing College of Economics Press, March 1989).

A Concise Dictionary of Social Sciences (Shanghai Lexicographical Publishing House, May 1987, 8th print).

A Collection of Papers in Memory of Zelin Wu (Hubei Science& Technology Press, September 1988).

Annotations on the Thirteen Classics (II), vol. 12, *Yan Yuan · Zigong Discussing Policies* (Zhonghua Book Company, 2nd print, December 1982).

(Qing·Qianlong) *Annals of Dongchuan Fu Vol 8* s.v. "Hukou" "Fuzhongren", in the collection of the library of Yunnan University

Bozan Jian, *Outline of the Chinese History*, (People's Publishing House, January 1967).

Book of Guizhou· Book of Guizhou Continued· Record of Guizhou · Language of Guizhou (Guizhou People's Publishing House, March 1992).

C.A.Tokarev (USSR), *A History of Foreign Ethnography*, trans. Zhengfang Tang (China Social Sciences Publishing House, December 1983).

Chaolong Li et al. eds., *The Minority Folk-Customs in Guizhou* (Guizhou Education Press, September 1995).

Chunyuan Zhou, Yanyu Wang et al., eds., *The Ancient History of Guizhou* (Guizhou People's Publishing House, December 1982) .

(Song) Chengda Fan, Qiwang Hu, Guangguang Qin, annotation, *Guihaiyuhengzhijiyi Annotation* s.v. "Man Ma"(Sichuan Minzu Publishing House, September 1986).

Commentaries and Notes on the Thirteen Classics (I), Shangshu Zhengyi vol.11, Yuan Ruan ed. (Zhonghua Book Company, October 1980).

Commentaries and Notes on the Thirteen Classics (II).

（US）Carol Ember, *Cultural Anthropology*, trans. Ze Du (Liaoning People's Publishing House, February 1988).

Concise Dictionary of Social Sciences, 2nd ed., s.v. "gold standard system" 654, "silver standard system" 936 (Shanghai Lexicographical Publishing House, December 1984)

Chonggui Fang, eds., *Western Economics Study* (Shanghai People's *Publishing House, December 1991).*

Chonggui Fang, Bocheng Yin, eds., *A History of Economics* (Fudan University Press, August 1989).
Cunde Wang, *The Han-Miao Dictionary (Eastern Guizhou Dialect)* (Guizhou Ethnic Press, December 1992).
Compilation of Materials from Surveys on Ethnic Townships in Guizhou Province (Policy Office, Office of Politics and Laws in Ethnic Affairs Commission of Guizhou Province).
Dongchang He, "Issues on the Rural-oriented Reform in the Education of All Levels and Categories under Middle County Level", *Study of Township Elementary Education Plan* (People's Education Press, 1st edition, March 1989)
Department of Economics, Peking University, comp., *Foreign Economics Review* II (Shanghai People's Publishing House, August 1982).
Dictionary of Organic Chemistry (Science Press, 1987)
Dual-Sector Economy (Beijing College of Economics Press, March 1989).
Draft History of the Qing Dynasty · Geography, Twenty Five Histories photocopy edition (Shanghai: Chinese Classics Publishing House).
Daiju Mou, "On the Methods of Ethnic Minority Economic Investigation and Research in Guizhou", *Guizhou Ethnic Studies*, no. 1, 1984.
Edward Burnett Tylor, *Primitive Culture*, trans. Shusheng Lian (Shanghai Literature and Art Publishing House, August 1992).
*Ethnic Survey in Yueliangshan Region (*Guizhou Ethnic Research Institute, June 1983).
Feng Liu, "A Rethinking of 'Primitive Agriculture' in the Contemporary Era", *The History of Agriculture in China*, no.1 (1995).
Ferdinand de Saussure, *Ecrits de Linguistique generale* (The Commercial Press, November 1980).
Fushi Wang, eds., *A Brief History of Miao Dialect* (The Ethnic Publishing House, 1985).
Foreign Economics Review, compiled by the Department of Economics of Peking University (Shanghai People's Publishing House, February 1982).
General Annals of Guizhou (Jiajing, the Ming Dynasty) , in the collection of the library of Yunnan University.
Guizhou Minzu College Survey Group, "Survey Report on Yaoshan Commune in Libo County", *Ethnic Survey in Yueliangshan Region* (Guizhou Ethnic Groups Research Institute)
General Annals of Guizhou·Longli Wei, handwritten version in the collection of Guizhou Library.
(Qing·Kangxi) *General Annals of Guizhou* "White Miao" under "Miao", mimeo version in the collection of Guizhou Library.

Guangzheng Lei, "The Study on the Ethnic Miao's Custom of Worshiping Ancestors through Butchering Cattle and Horse in Guizhou", *Miao Studies* (I) (Guizhou Ethnic Press, July 1989).

(Daoguang), *Guiyang Fu Annals·Tu Si*, s.v. "Qingyan Tu Bian", in the collection of Guizhou Provincial Library, woodblock prints.

Guizhou Statistical Yearbook – 1987.

Hongmo Yu, "Discussion and Proof of the Tombstone of Chen En, Shuixi Mukui of the Ming Dynasty," *Collection of Manuscripts in Guizhou*, no. 1 (1980).

Huangping Zhou Annals, mimeographed edition, in the collection of Guizhou Provincial Library

Hongmo Yu, "Probe into Jihuo Stone Tablet and Related History," *Guizhou Cultural Relics* , no.2 (1983).

Huiquan Zhang, "Postscript for Pigong Dog Ground Inscriptions on Precipices", *Guiyang Annals Material Studies,* September (1983).

Investigation on the History of Dong Societies (Guizhou Ethnic Press, November 1988).

Jicheng Long, "The Absorption of the Dong Culture by Ethnic Han Immigrants in Border Regions of Hunan, Guizhou and Guangxi," *Journal of South-Central College for Nationalities,* no.4 (1994).

Jizhong Shi et al. eds., *Veritable Records of the Ming Dynasty·A Compilation of Materials about Guizhou* (Guizhou People's Publishing House, 1983).

Jinglong Sun, *The Study of Ethnic Minority Economy In Guizhou* (Guizhou Ethnic Economic Research Institute), 37. *Development Situation of Ethnic Minority Regions in Guizhou and Its Countermeasures*, Guizhou Ethnic Press, 1st edition, September 1991.

(Brazil) Josue de Castro, *The Geography of Hunger* (Sanlian Bookstore, December 1959)

Jianguo Liu, "The Dependence on External Poverty-relief Funds in Under-developed Regions and Analysis of Reasons", *Economy and Society*, no. 3.

Knowledge about South Guizhou·Official Ranks, s.v. "Gu Zhou Tong Zhi," 18 (Guizhou People's Publishing House, December 1992)

Kaizhong Shi, "On the Historical Value of Yangwang Tablet I nscriptions", *Guiyang Cultural Relics*, no. 1 (1986).

Lexicon of Physics (Zhongwai Publishing House, May 1979)

Lewis Henry Morgan, *Ancient Society*, trans. Dongchun Yang et al. (The Commercial Press, August 1977).

(Ming) Lian Song et al., *The History of the Yuan Dynasty V,* s.v. "Barbarian

Officials in Bafan Shunyuan" (Zhonghua Book Company, April 1976).
Liping Fu Annals, in the collection of Guizhou Provincial Library, woodblock print.
Longshuo Yang, "Postscript for Long Cun Suo Yao Tablet", *Guiyang Annals Material Studies,* no. 3, (September 1988).
Malinowski, *A Scientific Theory of Culture,* trans. Xiaotong Fei (China Folk Art Publishing House, February 1987), 14.
Mukui is an official rank in the administration of Tu Si (local hereditary headman) of Shuixi Yi ethnic group in Guizhou, equivalent to the third-rank official in the central government.
Minghua Tan, "On the Development of Ethnic Groups and Its Measurement," *Ethno-National Studies* no. 5 (1992), 7.
Meng Zhang et al., *The Genesis of Mankind* (Sichuan People's Publishing House, June 1987).
Memoir of the Qing Dynasty·A Compilation of Materials about Guizhou (Guizhou People's Publishing House, November 1964) .
(Sweden) Myrdal, *The Challenge of World Poverty: A World Anti-Poverty Program in Outline,* trans. Chaoyang Gu et al. (Beijing College of Economics Press, December 1991).
(UK) Mark Blaug, Paul Sturges eds., *Who's Who in Economics: A Biographical Dictionary of Major Economists* (Economic Science Press, October 1987).
Min Tang, eds., *Topics in the Fronts of Modern Economics (I)* (The Commercial Press, September 1989, Beijing).
Meng Zhang et al. *The Genesis of Mankind* (Sichuan People's Publishing House, June 1987).
"On Sun Yefang's Economic Theory", Reference Room of Institute of Economics of Chinese Academy of Social Sciences, comp. Qingbo Yu "On Planning and the Law of Value" (Economic Science Press, 1984),.
Office for Compilation of Annals of Forestry in the Southeast Guizhou Miao and Dong Autonomous Prefecture, comp., *Annals of Forestry in the Southeast Guizhou Miao and Dong Autonomous Prefecture* (China Forestry Publishing House, 1990).
"Postscript to Cliff Inscriptions in Dog House of Pigong", *Guiyang Annals.* no.3.
Practices and Discussions on Regional Economic Development (The Cadre Training Center for Poverty-stricken Regions, February 1991).
Poverty-relief for the People (State Council Office of Steering Group in the Economic Development in Poverty-stricken Regions), 6.
Qiwang Hu, "Yuanpei Cai and Ethnology", *Ethnological Study* no. 1 , comp.

CUAES (The Ethnic Publishing House, August 1981).
Qianxian He, "Investigations on a Few Issues Regarding the Production and Construction in Southeast Guizhou", *Guizhou Ethnic Studies*, no. 4, 1984.
Qilong Li, *Education and Economic Development in West Germany* (People's Education Press, 2nd edition 1981).
Records of the Grand Historian·Biography of First Emperor of Qin
Renduan Hu, Wenzhou Zhang, eds. *China's Ethnic Statistical Yearbook* (China Statistics Press, January 1993), 206, *Guizhou Economic Development Model* (China Planning Press, August 1989).
Roger M. Keesing, *Cultural Anthropology: A Contemporary Perspective* (Taiwan: Chuliu Publisher).
Raymond Firth, *Human Types,* trans. Xiaotong Fei (The Commercial Press, January 1991, Beijing revised edition).
Roger M. Keesing, *Cultural Anthropology: A Contemporary Perspective*, trans. Gongqi Zhang et al. (Taiwan: Chuliu Publisher).
Rongzong Luo, "Miao's Entertainment", *Guoshi Quarterly*, no. 14.
Rongzong Luo, "The Miao Funerals", *Borderland Research Weekly* no. 38 (Yishi Daily, Chongqing)
Raymond Firth, *Human Types,* trans. Xiaotong Fei (The Commercial Press, 2nd edition, September 1991).
Shengzhi Pan, "Residual of the Supplementary Structure of A Multi-ethnic Economy", *Guizhou Social Studies*, no. 4, 1995.
(Ming) Shixing Wang, Jinglin Lv annotation, *Guangzhiyi* (Zhonghua Book Company, December 1981).
Shineng Chen, Governor, "Speech in the Report Meeting of Administrative Agencies Directly under the Provincial Government on Emancipation of Minds," *Guizhou Daily*, August 1994.
(Jin) Shou Chen, (Liu Song) Songzhi Pei, annotation, *The History of the Three Kindoms· Kindom of Shu·Biography of Zhuge Liang V* (Beijing: Zhonghua Book Company, April 1975， 6th reprint).
Shu Zhang, *Book of Guizhou Continued*
Shengzhi Pan, "The Glory and Hidden Worries of Liuma Tung Oil," *Guizhou Ethnic Studies*, no. 1, 1996.
Sifu Cai, Yansheng Zhang, ed. *An Introduction to Development Economics*, (Beijing College of Economics Press, March 1992).
Shi Yu, "Vigorously Develop Information Resources to Drive the Ethnic Economic Takeoff," *Guizhou Ethnic Studies*, no. 2.
Shaoting Yin, *A Highly Debatable Cultural Ecological System* (Yunnan

People's Publishing House, March 1994).
Selected Works of Xingzhi Tao on Education (Educational Science Publishing House, 1981).
(Qing) Tingyu Zhang et.al., *The History of the Ming Dynasty,* s.v. "Biography of Mu Ying" (Zhonghua Book Company, April 1974).
The History of the Former Han Dynasty·Collected Biographies of Southwestern Barbarians
The History of the Three Kingdoms·Kingdom of Shu (Zhonghua Book Company, punctuation ed.), 919.
The History of the Yuan Dynasty·Table of Kings (Zhonghua Book Company, punctuation ed.).
The History of the Ming Dynasty·Collected Biographies·Xieyuan Zhu (Zhonghua Book Company, punctuation ed.).
The History of the Ming Dynasty· Collected Biographies· Guizhou Tu Si, see materials about Qiyu Chen (Zhonghua Book Company, punctuation ed.).
The History of the Yuan Dynasty · Taiding (Zhonghua Book Company, punctuated edition).
The History of the Ming Dynasty· Biography of Bai Gui (Zhonghua Book Company, punctuated edition) .
The History of the Ming Dynasty·Biography of Fang Ying (Zhonghua Book Company, punctuated edition) .
The History of the Ming Dynasty·Biography of Sanshan Wang (Zhonghua Book Company, punctuated edition).
Tingshuo Yang et al., *Ethnic Culture and the Living Environment*, (Guizhou People's Publishing House, September 1992).
T. Harding et al., *Culture and Evolution*, trans. Jianjun Han et al.(Zhejiang People's Publishing House, September 1987).
Twenty-five Histories vol. 2, *History of the Later Han Dynasty.*
Twenty-five Histories vol. 1, *History of the Former Han Dynasty.*
Twenty-five Histories vol. 1, *Records of the Grand Historian.*
Twenty-five Histories vol. 8, *History of the Song Dynasty (II)·Biography of Southern Barbarians,* 1986 ed. (Shanghai: Chinese Classics Publishing House, Shanghai Bookstore, July 1990 7th reprint).
Twenty-five Histories vol. 8, *Biography of Treacherous Court Officials.*
Twenty-five Histories vol. 10, *The History of the Ming Dynasty·Soldiers (2).*
Twenty-five Histories vol. 3, *History of the Wei Dynasty·Biography of Liao Ethnic Group.*
Theodore W. Shultz, *Economic Growth and Agriculture*, trans. Xibao Guo, Kainian Tong (Beijing College of Economics Press, February 1991).

Torii Ryuzo (Japan), *Survey Report on Ethnic Miao Group*, trans. National Institute for Compilation and Translation (first published in April, 1946).
"The Pollution-free Agriculture is Growing", *Economy and Society*, no. 3, 1991.
The History of the Ming Dynasty, s.v. "Shi Huo Zhi" (Zhonghua Book Company, 2nd edition, March 1984).
The History of Ethnic Groups in China II.
Veritable Records of the Ming Dynasty·A Compilation of Materials about Guizhou (Guizhou People's Publishing House, December 1983).
Victor Barnouw. "Ethnology", *A Collection of Researches in the History of Ethnic Groups in Border Regions in Southwestern China,* no. 4.
(Qing) Wen Tian ed, Shuqin Luo annotation, *Book of Guizhou,* s.v. "Miao Customs" (Guizhou People's Publishing House, March 1992) .
Wen Tian, *Series of Books on Southern Guizhou*, combined issue thread-bound edition, *Book of Guizhou, IV*.
(Ming) Wenzheng Liu, *History of Yunnan*, (Yunnan Education Publishing House, December 1991).
Xun Long, "The Forestry Economy in Dong Societies", *Guizhou Ethnic Studies*, no. 2, 1992.
Xueliang Ma, "On Ethnic Written Languages and Bi-lingual Education", *Guizhou Ethnic Studies*, no. 2, 1986.
Xiguang Yang, eds., *A Probe into Economic Theories in the New Age* (Guangming Daily Publishing House, February 1982).
Xincheng Shu, comp., *Materials on Modern Educational History in China II* (People's Education Press, 1981).
Yougeng Yang, "The Impacts and Roles of Ethnic Han on the Development of Ethnic Minority Forest Region in Qingshui Jiang (I)", *Guizhou Ethnic Studies*, no. 2, 1993.
Yuxiao Long, "What Shackles the Marketization of Ethnic Forestry Economy", *Guizhou Ethnic Studies*, no. 3.
Yougeng Yang, "A Discussion of the Successes and Failures in the Forestry Reform in Jinping and the Reasons", *Guizhou Ethnic Studies*, no. 1, 1989.
Yuan Ruan ed. *Commentaries and Notes on the Thirteen Classics,* (Zhonghua Book Company, October 1980), 319 upper part.
Yuan Zong, "The Cultural Connotation of Place Names in Ethnic Miao Region," *Miao Studies*, no. 3, Li Jinping ed. (Guizhou People's Publishing House, December 1994), 213
Yincai Fu, *Contemporary Western Economics Theories* (Yunnan People's Publishing House, October 1985).

Yingliang Jiang, eds., *The History of Ethnic Groups in China II* (Sichuan Minzu Publishing House October 1990).
Yincai Fu, *Basic Western Economic Theories* (Yunnan People's Publishing House, October 1985).
Zhikun Guo, *Notes on the Thoughts of Xunzi* (Shanghai: Sanlian Bookstore, September 1991)
Zhongnan University of Economics and Law, comp., *Lexicon of Economic Science* (Economic Science Press, December 1987).
(Ming) Zizhang Guo, *Records of Guizhou*, mimeographed edition, in the collection of Guizhou Provincial Library
Zelin Wu, "A Brief Introduction of Boaz and the American Historical School," *Ethnological Study* no. 11 (The Ethnic Publishing House, August 1981).
Zelin Wu, "Bull-fighting in the Haiba Miao Regions", *A Collection of Papers in Memory of Zelin Wu* (Hubei Science and Technology Press, June, 1988).
Zizhang Guo, *Record of Guizhou ·On Tributes and Taxes*, mimeographed edition, in the collection of Guizhou Provincial Library.
Zhonglin Zhou, et al. eds., *Han Fei Index,* s.v. "Shuo Lin Shang" 22, 27 (Zhonghua Book Company, May 1982)
Zhang Wangyuan, "Streamline the Relationship and Expedite the Reform in Collectively-Owned Forest Regions – Investigations on the Forest Regions in Southeast Guizhou Prefecture", *Guizhou Ethnic Studies*, no. 4, 1988.
Zhenghai Cao, Biao Ma, et al., *A Strategic Vision before Take-off* (The Ethnic Publishing House, 1990).
Zhen Zheng (Qing Dynasty), *Zunyi Fu Annals·Farming and Sericulture*, in the collection of Guizhou Provincial Library, woodblock print.
Zeji Ding, "China's Agricultural Issues and Development Strategy", *Issues of Agricultural Economy*, no. 7, 1994.
Zhengdong Zhang, et al., *Veritable Records of the Qing Dynasty·A Compilation of Materials about Guizhou* (Guizhou People's Publishing House, November 1964).
Zhaotao Liang, *Introduction to the Chinese Ethnography* (Yunnan People's Publishing House, 1985).
Zifu Liu, Man Wang, *Where Should We Go* (Guizhou People's Publishing House, October 1990).

This book is the result of a publishing agreement between the author, Prof. Tingshuo Yang and Paths International Ltd (UK)

Title: Principles in Xiangji Operation--Chinese Economic Ethnology
Author: Tingshuo Yang
Translated by Gary Situ
Reviewed by Rui Huang-fu, Hongfei Liu
ISBN: 978-1-84464-546-6
Ebook ISBN: 978-1-84464-547-3

Paths International Ltd

www.pathsinternational.com

Published in the United Kingdom

www.ingramcontent.com/pod-product-compliance
Lightning Source LLC
LaVergne TN
LVHW061749270426
836338LV00011BA/55